MARX'S FATE: The Shape of a Life

MARX'S FATE

The Shape of a Life

BY JERROLD SEIGEL

PRINCETON UNIVERSITY PRESS
PRINCETON, NEW JERSEY

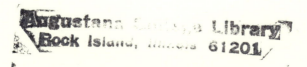

I have often had the fancy that there is some one Myth for every man, which, if we but knew it, would make us understand all he did and thought.

W. B. Yeats

Considering things dialectically means the study of every human matter as a process, as a development, and that standpoint itself implies a critical attitude toward the subject studied.

Lucien Goldmann

In the general relationship which the philosopher establishes between the world and thought, he merely makes objective the relation between his particular consciousness and the real world.

Karl Marx

CONTENTS

ACKNOWLEDGMENTS

I AM grateful to the staffs of the following libraries for smoothing the path of my work: Princeton University Library, New York Public Library, the Reading Room of the British Museum (British Library), and the International Institute for Social History (Amsterdam). The basic research was done during the academic year 1970-71, when I was supported by a Bicentennial Preceptorship from Princeton University. My work at the International Institute for Social History in 1975 was supported by the Princeton University Committee on Research in the Humanities and Social Sciences.

It is not possible to mention all the friends, colleagues, and students who aided my work by discussing parts of it with me or reading portions of earlier versions of the manuscript. I must specifically thank the following, however: Carlo Ginzburg, Martin Jay, Peter Jelavich, Jürgen Kocka, James Obelkevich, Arno Mayer, Theodore Rabb, Carl Schorske. At the Princeton University Press, Jennifer Sparks edited the manscript with sensitivity and care. My wife Jayn, besides clarifying my prose in many passages, has kept me in touch with myself and others in essential ways, teaching me much about humanity and life history.

Chapters, or portions of them, have appeared in *The Journal of Interdisciplinary History*, *History and Theory*, and *The New York Review of Books*. I am grateful to the editors of those journals for permission to reprint this material here.

J. S.

August, 1977

MARX'S FATE: The Shape of a Life

INTRODUCTION

"BUT we know Marx already." Dozens of books and hundreds of articles, many volumes of writings in Marx's original language, and several times as many more in translations, all offer something of him to us. Yet do we know him? Can we reach him through the clatter of conflicting claims to interpret and to possess him? The following pages have been written in the conviction that existing biographies and studies of Marx leave major questions about his life and thought unanswered, and that these are among the features of his story that speak most directly to our condition. Karl Marx was not merely a revolutionary, a theorist of socialism, or a figure in the history of economic or political theory. He was—and remains—an exemplary presence in the development of modern consciousness, whose significance is not exhausted by the truth or falsity of the specific doctrines he propounded. His life exemplifies the link that joins thought to action, and the gap that separates them.

Some of the methods used here to recover this Marxian presence are traditional. They include the close reading of texts to discover multiple levels of meaning in them, and the comparison of Marx's intellectual development with the changing pattern of historical conditions that helped to shape it. But underlying these approaches is one that needs some explicit explanation at the start: psychological biography. One hears a great deal about psychological biography today (often under the more ambitious rubric "psychohistory"); much of the work done in its name has been careless and premature, and too often it has served as a tool to unmask enemies. Something needs to be said, therefore, about the particular mixture of biography and psychology at work here.

In a subtle and insightful introduction to the psychological study of literature, Norman Holland has drawn a portrait of past and present practice that can serve just as well for biography and history:

> Using psychoanalysis as external knowledge can turn it into a rigid scheme of rules and symbols; certainly the earliest applications of psychoanalysis to literature did just that. They converted psychoanalysis into, in Erikson's term, an "originology," which decoded manifest behavior into its source, either events in infancy or illnesses in the adult. Works of art often served primarily as clues to the writer's childhood neuroses or sexual idiosyncrasies, in the esthetic studies by the old masters of psychoanalysis, sometimes even by Freud himself. Today one would recognize that this kind of reading backwards from the adult to

the child or the neurotic tells only half the story. It is at least as important to see the forward move: the way the creative human being transforms the nubs and knots of early life into later achievements which
fulfill the needs of inner and outer reality for the adult. A modern view
would see the human being as playing infinite variations upon a continuing, central identity theme.[1]

In this spirit, the psychological perspective employed below does not
examine Marx's life through a grid of psychological categories external to
his own experience. Instead it attempts to find the organic unity that links
all the aspects of his life together, by focusing on the underlying themes
whose developments and variations constitute the determining elements
of his history.

Although such a sense of how psychology should contribute to biography contrasts with a certain tradition of clinical theory and practice, it is
increasingly to be found in psychoanalytic literature. As one contemporary analyst reminds us, "Analysis is not concerned with the repeatability
of data from case to case, but rather with the inner consistency and pattern
of meaning that obtains within each case." Psychology's aspirations to
give a scientific form to its comprehension of human nature must not lead
it to forget the human qualities of its subject matter: "Meaning is the
central fact of human experience with which psychoanalysis has to deal.
The whole direction of the therapist's effort is toward elaboration of the
full context of meaning in which the whole range of data that he has
gathered about the patient falls into a consistent, coherent, and intelligible pattern."[2]

The unity that psychoanalysis seeks to discover in an individual life has
much in common with literature and drama. Freud testified to the link
between the two in drawing on literature and myth for some of his most
famous metaphors: Oedipus, Electra, Narcissus. Not all lives are best approached through these "universal" symbols, however. Recent studies of
Freud himself suggest that other emblematic figures he invoked reveal
specific conflicts within his life that "Oedipal" imagery bypasses—
Hannibal, for instance. As a distinguished anthropologist reminds us,
"lives contain their own interpretations. One has only to learn how to gain
access to them."[3]

It was just such access that Freud was seeking in dream interpretation.
He learned to understand dreams as unconscious symbolizations of the
dreamer's inner life. Dreams expressed hidden connections between waking acts and unconscious wishes, and between apparently unrelated stages
in the dreamer's history. Because the language of dreams was structured
differently from that of waking life, to comprehend it was analogous to
literary interpretation: "The dream-content seems like a transcript of the

dream-thoughts into another mode or expression, whose characters and syntactic laws it is our business to discover by comparing the original and the translation."[4] Dream interpretation treated dreams rather in the way a good literary critic discovers the core of a poem or drama: by relating individual features and moments in it to the overall poetic or dramatic development. Freud indicated as much when he quoted the poet and dramatist Schiller: "Looked at in isolation, a thought may seem very trivial or very fantastic; but it may be made important by another thought that comes after it, and, in conjunction with other thoughts that may seem equally absurd, it may turn out to form a most effective link."[5] The poetic freedom which found ways to express unconscious fantasies and connections that reason and habit barred from ordinary consciousness became the model for the psychoanalytic discipline that would gain renewed access to those mental contents. By the same method, Freud found meaning by translating other "irrational" acts and expressions into the language of the unconscious: slips of the tongue, failures of memory, patterns of neurotic symptoms.

To be sure, psychoanalysis moved on from these rather literary beginnings to develop a language patterned on natural science, replete with topographical and structural models of the mind, and with quasi-physical descriptions of mental processes: "energy cathexis," "discharge," "displacement," and the like. Even within the psychoanalytic community, there are many people who regret this, observing that psychoanalysis has thereby "landed itself in a morass of reified concepts."[6] It is not necessary to take sides on this issue in order to insist that psychoanalysis did not originate in these conceptual elaborations. Their function was to convert Freud's basic insights into a theory of psychology that could satisfy the scientific expectations and assumptions of his day. The basic work of discovering inner interconnections and patterns in the lives of individuals, of recovering the unconscious levels of life and the presence of past conflicts within present dilemmas, can be undertaken without them. One might even argue that, in going from the interpretations contained in such symbolic expressions as dreams and behavior patterns to the underlying "meaning" they contain, the diagnostic categories clinicians use to classify and order their cases only represent detours. Freud did not need them to make sense of his own dreams in the 1890s, before any of his later terminology had been worked out, and it seems that a growing number of clinicians today find they are not so necessary for effective therapy as an earlier generation assumed.

At the same time, one must be careful not to allow the pendulum to swing too far back toward the "literary" side of psychoanalysis. However profound purely literary insight may be, if the historian turns to psychology, it is in order to see his subjects' lives in clearer and more concrete ways than literary intuition can usually allow. Psychoanalysis makes use of intuition, to be sure, but it must be shaped and disciplined by theory, and expanded and sharpened by immersion in a body of case histories that constitutes the accumulated experience of a long line of practitioners. The biographer who attempts to use psychological techniques must discipline and expand his intuition in similar ways. In the work that follows we shall be drawing particularly on three fundamental principles derived from psychoanalysis as it has developed since Freud's time:

(1) Personality and character are rooted in early experience. The patterns that recur throughout the course of a person's life are shaped first of all in childhood, which in modern Western society means in the parental family. They reflect the manner in which conflicts are expressed and resolved in a given familial context. Post-Freudians (especially those who have expanded the clinical situation to include whole families and not just separate individuals) point out that the shape and "themes" of a family's life may be molded by the family's relationship to the larger society, as well as by the present needs and past experiences of the individual members.[7]

(2) Human development is dialectical. Growth takes place through opposition, and such basically contrary qualities and styles as love and hate, obedience and rebellion, compliance and aggression, not only coexist in the way people relate to the outside world but feed on each other, hide behind each other, absorb and overtake each other. The patterns established within the family, and capable of recurring in the later stages of life, usually have this dialectical character.

(3) Individuals advance from infancy to maturity through a cycle of distinguishable stages. The boundaries between these stages may be fluid, and different individuals move through them at differing rates. Nonetheless, each phase presents a person with the need and opportunity to develop a separate set of qualities and capacities. Each stage also raises the possibility that the particular modes of acting on and relating to the world it brings to the fore may be stunted or distorted if the environment either fails to nurture it or puts too much pressure on its emergence. Freud's own formulation of these stages—oral, anal, and genital phases in infancy and early childhood—emphasized sexual development to the exclusion of other modes, notably social and cognitive ones. But the notion of a life cycle is much older and more broadly based than its Freudian formulation suggests, and it appears in one form or another in many different cultures and historical periods. In our own time Erik Erikson has called attention to it with great sensitivity and insight, placing it in the context of social relations as well as psychic growth. Erikson calls the lasting sense of selfhood a healthy individual evolves as he passes through the stages of the life cycle "identity." Identity means "the accrued confidence that one's ability to maintain inner sameness and continuity (one's ego in the psychological

sense) is matched by the sameness and continuity of one's meaning for others."[8]

In what follows, I have tried to use these principles as the basis for discovering an inner unity in the diverse and manifold aspects of Marx's life. Although I think that some features of Marx's behavior might—like most people's—be described appropriately with clinical categories, I have tried not to use any. Instead, I have sought the coherence of his life history in terms of symbols and patterns suggested by his own thinking or by that of people close to him. His earliest writings, and his correspondence with his parents, sound the themes of his later development more clearly than has been recognized, and place them in relationships that his later and more self-conscious views would veil. Moreover, in the portraits of classical philosophers he included in his doctoral dissertation, Marx provides material for the symbolic interpretation of his own history. Like certain dream images, these figures represented fears rather than positive wishes, symbols of an experience Marx desperately wanted to avoid. Yet, as he well understood, Marx shared certain features with these ancient thinkers—particularly with one of them—and to avoid being like them was not wholly in his personal control. When he wrote about them Marx believed he would escape their fate because society and culture had evolved, eliminating the conditions that had determined it. Later, in a different historical and personal context, and after their features had faded from his consciousness, Marx's inner resemblance to the creatures of his youthful imagination would grow stronger.

Less immediate to Marx than these symbols he himself provided were some literary figures created by others—Schiller, Balzac—but associated with Marx either in his mind or in the views of his friends and family. These symbols help to sharpen and refine our understanding of the psychological themes and patterns that shaped Marx's life.

Making use of these images requires a theoretical perspective Marx himself did not provide; however, we do not need to move outside the context of his life to find such a point of view. Some approaches to the three principles considered on the preceding page were made in his time. Although it is little known, Hegel, who did more to shape Marx's thinking than any other figure, was not only a great philosopher but also a notable psychologist. His writings include a theory of the human life cycle that—especially in its account of adolescence and the crises associated with it—bears remarkable similarities to Erik Erikson's. Moreover, his dialectical logic had psychological aspects and roots, including some in his own experience of psychological crisis and healing. Hegel linked logic to psychology in his famous concept of alienation, and still more clearly in a less well-known but equally central notion of his dialectic—inversion. Both terms were logical and psychological at the same time, suggesting a view of human life that focused on the alternation of conflict and resolution in the progression through stages of development. Although he did not have any pre-Freudian intuition of the importance of early experience in the formation of personality, Hegel's attention to patterns that recurred throughout the whole life history of a subject and linked its original nature to its final destiny implied the existence of modes of opposition and reconciliation present at every stage.

Marx was aware of these aspects of Hegel's thought. Not only did he refer explicitly to Hegel's model of the life cycle, he seems to have had it in his mind at a psychologically critical moment of his own development, his passage to Hegelianism at the age of nineteen in 1837. Hegel's psychological theory even appears to have helped Marx through that crisis. He employed the notion of inversion, as a description of a dilemma at once logical and psychological a few years later, when he wrote about Greek philosophers in his doctoral dissertation, and he remained aware of this twofold aspect of Hegelian inversion at the time he made it a central organizing concept in *Capital*. To consider Marx in the light of these elements of Hegel's psychology is, therefore, not to impose on him a set of categories foreign to his own consciousness.

To seek these inner determinants of Marx's life history is not to argue that they can be understood independently of the external—historical and social—forces that shaped the life of his time. The family context within which his early experience took place was itself shaped by outside social forces (as family life inevitably must be). That some of the developmental patterns of Marx's life were molded by wider cultural factors as well as by narrower psychological ones appears from the similarities that appear between his evolution and the patterns followed by some of his mentors and contemporaries, namely Hegel, Feuerbach, Engels, and Hess. Moreover, the overall configuration of Marx's life was formed as much by the general shape of historical change in the nineteenth century as by his particular manner of experiencing it. The sense of personal identity Marx worked out in the revolutionary 1840s could not survive in the changed environment after 1851 without being reappraised and, in part, reconstructed. The world that emerged from the revolutionary upheavals of 1848 was a crushing betrayal of his youthful expectations about it, and Marx found that he had still to confront for himself certain dilemmas about his role as an intellectual and revolutionary which he had believed historical development was resolving for him.

Understanding his response to this changed situation solves, I think, the much debated problem of "old Marx versus young Marx." Writers have divided between those who point out that Marx's writings of the later 1840s reject the philosophical assumptions of his early Hegelian and Feuerbachian humanism, and those who insist that the *Grundrisse* (1857-58) and *Capital* (mostly written in the 1860s) still breathe the spirit that animated the *Paris Manuscripts* of 1844. Both groups have been right, but not about the same things.[9] The psychological needs of Marx's passage from adolescence to maturity did turn him against his early philosophical humanism in 1845-46. In the changed historical situation of the 1850s and 1860s, however, Marx was forced to return to some of the youthful positions he had thought to abandon before. As a result, the psychological dilemmas he had struggled to resolve in the 1840s returned too. The situation Marx faced in his London years was thus a compound of three things: the historical changes that made the experiences and perspectives of the 1840s questionable guides to theory and practice; the methodological dilemmas created by the need to respond to these changes; the personal and psychological conditions that these historical and intellectual problems both framed and intensified. On this stage was played out the great tragedy of Marx's life: his failure to finish *Capital*.

Because I have tried to set Marx's development within all these contexts, while at the same time working out in some detail the changed view of his intellectual odyssey these perspectives provide, I have not been able to avoid writing a long book. Obviously, much of my own personality and experience have entered into it. My relationship to Marxism is frankly ambivalent; although morally and intellectually drawn to Marx's vision, I remain unable to accept his social theory, or identify with his politics. Writing this book has been an attempt to understand and come to terms with my own position. I think some of the reasons for it resemble the attitudes that underlay Marx's alternation between political commitment and withdrawal, a resemblance that may have caused me to see the recurrence of such a pattern in his life more clearly than others have. Similarly, that Marx's successive philosophical and political stances were (more explicitly than has been perceived before) attempts to avoid the anguish of intellectual isolation is a conclusion that reflects both my attempt to uncover the personal determinants of his thought and my own personal relationship to him. Finally, my conviction that Marx's life is illuminated by an Eriksonian-Hegelian model of development from childhood through adolescence to maturity has been shaped in part by having undergone an evolution that seems to combine consistency and discontinuity in my own life. A desire to be intellectually and psychologically honest makes me say these things explicitly at the start, while diffidence and the conviction that readers are (or should be) less interested in authors than in subjects makes me say them briefly. Personal and highly charged as it is, I suspect that my relationship to Marx shares enough elements with widely held attitudes toward him to make the perspective of this book useful to people who approach him differently. Those who are more exclusively attracted or repelled by Marx will no doubt find reasons to quarrel with my treatment of him. I hope at least that what makes Marx an exemplary figure for me will illuminate some of his features for others.

Part One

BECOMING MARX

CHAPTER ONE

Hegel: Philosophy, Dialectic, and Fate

LOOMING in the background of Marx's life was the giant figure of Hegel. Born in 1770, Hegel followed the events of the French Revolution in his twenties, reached thirty with the arrival of the new century, and lived until 1831, just long enough to witness the revolutionary upheavals that ended the Restoration era. His life thus spanned the first great revolutionary cycle of modern European history. After his years as a student he served as a private tutor during the 1790s, before taking a post at the University of Jena in 1801. He was thirty-seven when he published his first book, *The Phenomenology of the Spirit*. In 1818 he moved to the relatively new and increasingly influential University of Berlin, which was making the Prussian capital the intellectual center of Germany. Hegel's teaching added to the renown of Berlin; his students and followers made a deep impact on German intellectual, religious, and political life. To his *Science of Logic* (1812-16) and *Encyclopaedia of the Philosophical Sciences* (1817), Hegel in Berlin added his treatise on social and political theory, the *Philosophy of Right*, in 1821.

Hegel's world was full of paradoxes. His thinking was so abstract and idiosyncratic that many readers have always found it incomprehensible. Yet so firmly was he oriented toward the content of actual human experience that he has properly been described as "a connoisseur of the real." An enthusiast for the French Revolution in his youth, he became the official philosopher of the increasingly conservative Prussian government; later his disciples would provide some of that regime's most radical critics. The debate about whether Hegel himself was a conservative or a progressive thinker began in his own time, and has never been completely stilled.[1] All these features of his career would be important in shaping Marx's attitude toward him.

The industry of Hegel scholarship is nearly as extended and elaborate as that devoted to Marx himself, and it might be simpler and more convenient to pass over him quickly here. Yet important elements in Hegel's legacy to Marx have been ignored or underplayed. We must examine three of these: his theory of mental health and illness, including his account of the human life cycle, and the personal experience out of which it grew; his discussion of the relation between personality, historical experience, and "fate"; and those features of his notion of dialectic that reveal its inner ties to his psychological speculations and to his own life. These aspects of

Hegel's thought were closely linked to more familiar ones that also need to be recalled when approaching Marx, notably his well-known distinction between "civil society" and the state.

1. Reason and Unreason in Society and the Psyche

Hegel identified philosophy with the need to overcome oppositions. Every area of human life created that need: in religion, the confrontation of God and man; in speculative thought the distinctions between subject and object or "universal" and "particular"; in social life, the competition between individual interests and the general good. Each of these spheres revolved on an axis defined by the same series of underlying dichotomies: division and unity, separation and integration, estrangement and return. Whatever subject he discussed, Hegel found the philosophic answer to human dilemmas in terms of transcendence (*Aufhebung*) and reconciliation (*Versöhnung*). His philosophy sought to preserve the ideal of reason in the face of experiences that seemed to negate it: revolution's failure to reshape the world in reason's image; the parochialism of everyday life.

It was in modern political relations that Hegel believed the modern compound of opposition and reconciliation had attained its most developed and palpable form, in the relations between civil society and the state. In contrast to a long-standing tradition, which used these two terms as synonyms (ancient political theory had equated "the city, or civil society, or the commonwealth"—*civitas sive societas civilis sive res publica*), Hegel presented them as polar opposites. Civil society was the realm of private persons whose only aim was "their own petty selves and particular interests." In society individuals pursued their own personal needs and interests, treating others as means to the fulfillment of private ends. Society was based on private property, and the barriers property created, together with differences in talent and opportunity, led individuals to feel separate and isolated within it, while at the same time creating extremes of wealth and poverty. Life and conduct in the state were oriented in a contrary direction. The state was the embodied principle of a people's collective life and general welfare. Hegel called it "the actuality of the ethical idea." The state worked to overcome the isolation and injustice society bred. It carried the individual, "whose tendency is to become a center of his own, back into the life of the universal substance," infusing him with a concern for the general well-being that private life tended to dissolve. [2]

Hegel presented the opposition between civil society and the state with the clarity befitting a philosophical conception. The sharpness of the contrast served his larger purpose, which here as everywhere in his philosophy was to demonstrate reconciliation. From a broad philosophical perspective the division between the two spheres was only part of their inner essential unity. Civil society led men to the state, because the experience of social interaction helped to reveal beneath men's private needs and individual interests the larger general purposes they all shared, and the common reason that guided their pursuit of them. The appearance that the state ruled in opposition to private rights and interests hid the reality that "it is the end immanent within them, and its strength lies in the unity of its own universal end and aim with the particular interest of individuals." In the *Philosophy of Right*, Hegel analyzed the mediating role of various institutions—guilds, representative assemblies, above all the "universal class" of state servants—which helped to bring individuals out of their separateness and isolation, and into harmony with the state's universal and rational aim.[3]

The relationship between the state and civil society demonstrated one of Hegel's deepest and most characteristic philosophical convictions: that general purposes and abstract ideas (humanity, rationality, justice) only came to have real existence in the world by growing out of conditions that seemed to negate them. "The universal does not prevail or achieve completion except along with particular interests and through the cooperation of particular knowing and willing."[4] Reason and universality only gained real existence by coming to encompass much that seemed irrational and parochial. This was true not only of the external, social world but of the inner, psychic one as well.

Hegel's mature writings on society and politics give only occasional clues to the links he saw between these topics and the problems of human psychology. Yet the ties were close, and they remained more visible in some earlier passages, written when Hegel was closer to his own experience of mental crisis and recovery. Meditating on the debilitating disunity of German public life in the year 1800, he had observed that the grievances of Germany were difficult to redress because the particularism that dominated the country's politics brought with it perils of another sort. "Once man's social instincts are distorted and he is compelled to throw himself into interests peculiarly his own, his nature becomes so deeply perverted that it now spends its strength on variance from others, and in the course of maintaining its separation it sinks into madness, for madness is simply the complete separation of the individual from his kind."[5] This vision of Germany's dilemma adumbrated some of Hegel's more mature political conceptions. It focused on the opposition between a life devoted to private, individual interest—the orientation he would later find represented in civil society—and one shaped by identification with the general good—the attitude he would see embodied, in principle, in the modern state. But the madness Hegel spoke of here was not metaphorical, it was real. The causes that threatened to bring it about were exactly those he would analyze in his developed theory of mental health and illness.

Hegel dealt with psychological topics under the heading of anthropology, which in his time did not refer to the discipline that has grown up in ours, but more generally to the scientific treatment of human nature. Kant had lectured on these topics, and Hegel followed his example.[6] Some of the subjects he treated would belong to anthropology or ethnology today, some to psychology or psychiatry. In his theory—set forth in the *Encyclopaedia of the Philosophical Sciences* and in Hegel's lectures— insanity was described as "a state in which the mind is shut up within itself, has sunk into itself, whose peculiarity consists in its being no longer in *immediate contact* with actuality but in having positively *separated itself* from it." Engrossed in itself, the mind in a state of disease was unable to recognize its relation to the outside world, and suffered from the contradiction between external reality and "the single phase or fixed idea" that ruled within. By contrast, the man of sound mind "is fully and intelligently alive to that reality" outside that constitutes his existence and "which gives concrete filling to his individuality." For the healthy person, the "world which is outside him has its threads in him to such a degree that it is these threads which make him what he really is: he too would become extinct if these externalities were to disappear."[7]

Some of Hegel's analyses of madness seem peculiar to his own style of thought, others share elements with more familiar theories. In the first category is his description of insane ideas as those that regard "an empty abstraction and a mere possibility as something concrete and actual." Hegel perceived this way of becoming abstracted from the concrete world especially in delusions. Such disorders were nothing more than conclusions drawn from "the indeterminate general possibility that since a man, in general, can be a king, I myself, this particular man, am a king." False reasoning of this sort expressed the isolation and abstraction that always constituted one aspect of human life: "I am, in the first instance, a wholly abstract, completely indeterminate 'I' and therefore open to any arbitrary content."[8]

What opening oneself to this content expressed, however, was an uprising of "a feeling with a fixed corporeal embodiment . . . against the whole mass of adjustments forming the concrete consciousness." The mind in this state returned to a condition of "mere *being*," accomplished "a reversion to mere nature," which set free "the self-seeking affections of the heart," the "passions—fancies and hopes" that belonged to an individual's "merely personal" existence. Insanity was a return of the repressed.[9]

Hegel regarded mental disorders as arising from universal aspects of human existence, and he drew from this the ultimate humanistic conclusion: insanity was an inseparable part of human life and a natural stage in human development. Much like Freud, who would find in the human capacity for neurosis the sign of man's unique nature and his distinction from other creatures, Hegel declared that "Man alone has the capacity of grasping himself in this complete *abstraction* of the 'I.' This is why he has, so to speak, the privilege of folly and madness."[10] Before the mind could arrive at the full development that both recognized its separate individuality and integrated it with the world outside, it had to pass through an intermediate stage in which the task of individual differentiation absorbed its whole existence. This state of being "held fast in an isolated particularity" was the insanity to which all men were subject. "This interpretation of insanity as a necessarily occurring form or stage in the development of the soul is naturally not to be understood as if we were asserting that *every* mind, *every* soul must go though this stage of extreme derangement." Like crime, which was a manifestation of the unrestrained human will, insanity was an extreme "which the human mind *in general* has to overcome in the course of its development." In most individuals the possibility of madness only appeared "in the form of limitations, errors, follies," out of which concrete rationality finally emerged.[11]

Hegel explicitly drew the parallel between this development and the evolution of the state out of civil society. Just as "the family and civil society with their well-ordered distinctions already presuppose the existence of the state," so was insanity a rigidly held abstraction that both opposed and presupposed a rational consciousness.[12] Both spheres exemplified Hegel's vision of the way oppositions and divisions in human life were overcome through a process of development that was at once logical and historical, personal and collective. That this vision had important roots in his own personal history becomes clear when we turn to a second aspect of his explicitly psychological theory, his account of the human life cycle.

Hegel divided human life into four stages: childhood, youth, manhood, and old age. The differences between the four moments were "at once physical and mental diversities"; as an individual passed through them his relationship to the life of humanity as a species altered at each phase. In childhood, people were unaware of the "universal" side, and the mind was "wrapped up in itself." Childhood was "the time of natural harmony, of the peace of the individual with himself and with the world." As the child grew into boyhood he entered into the external world, but in a way that still expressed the primitive unity of individual existence. "It is this or that man who forms the ideal which the boy strives to know and to imitate," not any "form of universality." Hegel was far removed from any Freudian sense of the importance of childhood conflicts: "The oppositions which may occur in childhood remain devoid of any serious interest." But he did not romanticize childhood. Its innocence had no value as an ideal, and it quickly gave way to a self-will which "must be broken and destroyed by discipline."[13]

With the onset of puberty, however, things were suddenly different. At this point, "when the life of the genus begins to stir in him and to seek satisfaction," the child reached the stage of youth. (Hegel's language, by the way, always refers to boys and men but he made no distinctions in sexual impulse between them and women. He referred elsewhere to female puberty crises and to women's sexual fantasies.) The physical changes were accompanied by a cognitive advance. The youth models himself not on the individuals who had been his ideal earlier, but on "a universal, independent of such individuality."[14]

Thinking now in abstract terms, but absorbed in his own subjective existence, the youth is filled with "ideals, fancies, hopes, ambitions." Among these are "an ideal of love and friendship" and "an ideal of a universal state of the world. . . . The content of the ideal imbues the youth with the feeling of power to act; he therefore fancies himself called and qualified to transform the world, or at least to put the world back on the right path from which, so it seems to him, it has strayed." This devotion to universal ideals, however, meets opposition in the individual limitations the youth comes to feel at the same time. Those limitations mark "both the world, which, as it exists, fails to meet his ideal requirements, and the position of the individual himself, who is still short of independence and not fully equipped for the part he has to play." As a result, the young man "feels that both his ideal and his own personality are not recognized by the world, and thus the youth, unlike the child, is no longer at peace with the world."[15]

Further growth would eventually resolve these conflicts, by revealing to a person that he can "realize his personal aims, passions, and interests only within the framework of the world of which he is a part." The path to this recognition is strewn with obstacles, however:

> At first, the transition from his ideal life into civil society can appear to the youth as a painful transition into the life of the Philistine. The youth, who hitherto has been occupied only with general objects and has worked only for himself, now that he is growing into manhood and entering into practical life, must be active for others and concern himself with details. Now, much as this belongs to the nature of things, since if something is to be done it is with details that one must deal, the occupation with details can at first be very distressing.

At the transition from youth to manhood, therefore, a person confronts difficulties that interfere with developing a healthy relationship to the outside world. According to Hegel's theory of insanity, such a withdrawal into the self creates a state of mental illness. So did it now. Unable to realize the ideals with which he has come to identify his personality, the person at this stage is likely to become "a hypochondriac."

This hypochondria, however difficult it may be to discern it in many cases, is not easily escaped by anyone. The later the age at which it attacks a man, the more serious are its symptoms. In weak natures it can persist throughout the entire lifetime. In this diseased frame of mind the man will not give up his subjectivity, is unable to overcome his repugnance to the actual world, and by this very fact finds himself in a state of relative incapacity which easily becomes an actual incapacity.[16]

Thus the development of each individual through the stages of the life cycle revealed mental derangement to be a normal stage in human development, just as the consideration of reason and madness did. In both cases a contradiction between the isolated subjectivity of individual life and the objective reality of the external world produced a psychic imbalance. In both cases, too, the ultimate unity of the individual with the world could only be achieved by passing through a stage that allowed individual subjectivity to develop in abstraction. What impelled the individual beyond this intermediate stage was the need for survival, which could only be fulfilled by recognizing his own dependence on the outside world and bringing his person into harmony with it.

Such a harmonization brought the developing individual to the stage of manhood. Maturity rested on "recognizing the objective necessity and reasonableness of the world as he finds it—a world no longer incomplete, but able in the work which it collectively achieves to afford the individual a place and a security for his performance. By his share in this collective work he first really is *somebody*, gaining an effective existence and an objective value." Although such an attitude might seem less noble and altruistic than that of the youth devoted to ideals, Hegel denied that it meant simply accepting the world as it was. "For although the world must be recognized as already complete in its essential nature, yet it is not a dead, absolutely inert world, but, like the life-process, a world which perpetually creates itself anew." A man's work made him part of this "conservation and advancement of the world." Looking back on his work, he would later be able to see the advance to which it contributed. "This knowledge, as also the insight into the rationality of the world, liberates him from mourning over the destruction of his ideals." What was true and realizable in the ideals would have been preserved. All that had really been abandoned were the empty abstractions.

This benign and lofty view, however, could not be expected to reign unopposed in the age of manhood, for the memory of youthful ideals would still sometimes make a person "vexed and morose about the state of the world" and the small hope of improving it. Only in old age did the sense of conflict fully ebb. The comfortable settling into a life of custom and habit brought the lessening of vitality. This, "equally with the dulling of the functions of his physical organism, changes the man into an old man." The last stages brought "freedom from the limited interests and entanglements of the outward present." An old man already knows all that the world has to offer him. His mind "is thus turned only towards the universal and to the past to which he owes the knowledge of this universal." So identified with the outside world has the old man become that he feels his individuality slip away from him. "This lifeless, complete coincidence of the subject's activity with its world, leads back to the childhood in which there is no opposition, in the same way that the reduction of his physical functions . . . leads on to the abstract negation of the living individuality, to death."[17]

2. The Narrows of the Spirit

So sensitive and probing an account of human life was no mere *a priori* construction, however closely it could be made to fit a more abstract and generalized pattern. The experience on which it rested was mostly Hegel's own, although other contemporary accounts of psychological conflict and resolution contributed to it. In the background were the hopes and disappointments called forth by the French Revolution.

Hegel's main recorded experience of psychological difficulty occurred during the 1790s, when he was in his late twenties. Later on, in 1810, he described this period in his life for a friend who was undergoing similar troubles. Hegel tried to reassure him by suggesting first of all that certain kinds of intellectual work exposed people to doubt and depression. "This descent into dark regions where nothing shows itself to be firm, determinate, and secure, where splendors flash everywhere, but next to abysses" led to false starts and an inability to follow a consistent path, robbing a person of the sense of "destiny and direction." But the condition had both a more personal and a more universal side.

> From my own experience I know this mood of the mind, or rather of reason, once it has entered with interest and its intimations into a chaos of appearances and, though inwardly sure of the goal, it has not yet come through, not yet into the clarity and detailed grasp of the whole. I have suffered a few years of this hypochondria, to the point of enervation. Indeed, every human being may well have such a turning point in life, the nocturnal point of the contraction of his nature through whose narrows he is pressed, fortified and assured to feel secure with himself and secure in the usual daily life; and if he has already rendered himself incapable of being satisfied with that, secure in an inner, nobler existence.[18]

Even if there were no contemporary evidence of this moment in Hegel's development, we would suspect it of having occurred in his twenties because of the identity between this account and the moment of transition from youth to manhood described in his *Encyclopaedia*. In fact, a letter to Hegel from his youthful friend Schelling helps to place the few years of Hegel's difficulties around 1796. Schelling took a very different attitude toward Hegel's mental state than Hegel himself did later. "Permit me to tell you one more thing," Schelling wrote. "You seem to be at present in a state of indecision—judging from your last letter to me [which has been lost]—even depression. Phooey! A man of your powers must never allow such indecision to develop in him."[19]

Hegel's youthful development and his mental crisis are documented in his early life and writings. His mother died when he was thirteen. His father, a financial official in the Duchy of Würtemberg, aimed the young man at the Protestant ministry. What Hegel found at the theological seminary in Tübingen, however, helped deflect him to another path. Among his fellow students was a group inspired by Kant and Rousseau, who questioned some of the traditional teachings of Christianity, and who were prepared to welcome the French Revolution. To his father's displeasure, Hegel joined them.[20]

The essays he wrote (but did not publish) at Tübingen and later when he worked as a private tutor in Bern, Switzerland, display a youthful and enthusiastic spirit of radical criticism. Christianity was inhumane, for it "piled up such a heap of reasons for comfort in misfortune . . . that we might be sorry in the end that we cannot lose a father or mother once a week."[21] Moreover, the religious contempt for human life justified the practical disdain for people monarchical governments exemplified in their policies. "Religion and politics have played the same game, " Hegel wrote in a letter to Schelling in 1795. Religion "has taught what despotism desired: contempt for humanity, its inability to achieve anything good or be anything by itself." But men would not remain under this despotic tutelage much longer. "From the Kantian system and its highest perfection I expect a revolution in Germany, which will proceed from principles that are at hand and need only to be generally worked out in order to be applied to all previous knowledge."[22]

The position Hegel took up in his twenties corresponded closely with what he would later describe as the attitude of "youth." Hegel believed in the possibility of immediately realizing an ideal world, which had its source in his own subjective conceptions. In a manuscript from 1796 Hegel declared that "The first idea is naturally the conception *of myself*, as an absolutely free being. Together with the free, self-conscious being a whole world steps forth out of nothing—the only true and thinkable *creation out of nothing*." On the basis of this idea of freedom, Hegel projected a thorough reform of the whole intellectual realm, physics, politics, history, morality, and religion. The result would be "Absolute freedom of all spiritual beings, who carry the intellectual world within themselves and who may seek neither God nor immortality *outside themselves*."[23]

This uncompromising insistence on individual freedom led Hegel to reject the very idea of the state, as being in contradiction to the fundamental postulate of human liberty. Because the state was a mere mechanical conception, there was no place for it in the realm of human thought. "We must get beyond the State!" The world would change once men were infused with the imperatives of rationality and liberty: "With the spread of ideas about how a thing *should* be, the indolence of established people, always taking everything as it is, will vanish."[24]

At the time Hegel put forth these ideas, he was also conscious of his personal isolation. In fact, he valued it for the independence it gave him, and he associated his separation from ordinary life with strongly held feelings of friendship and closeness to nature. This is the theme of the poem "Eleusis" he dedicated to his closest friend, Hölderlin, in August 1796. Writing in the night that freed him from "the never weary care of bustling humanity," Hegel as poet looked forward to his next meeting with his friend, to their warm greeting and "the secret search to find each other out." The climax of the meeting would come in the assurance that the covenant binding the two together was still firm: "To live for free truth only;/ Peace with the *dogma*/ That rules opinions and perception,/ Never, never to conclude."[25] A year later, after he had moved from Bern to Frankfurt, Hegel wrote similarly to a woman friend, recalling the times they had spent together in the Swiss countryside. Just as he had then found reconciliation "in the arms of nature," so now did he "often flee to this faithful mother in order to separate myself again from the men with whom I live here in peace, and under her aegis to preserve myself from their influence and thwart any alliance with them."[26]

Yet these youthful expressions of separation from the ordinary world and rigid opposition between things as they were and as they *"should* be" give only a one-sided impression of Hegel's mind at the time. They rested on an attitude which, even while confirming them, prepared the way for the later transformation of Hegel's early radicalism and isolation into reconciliation with the world. Hegel's feeling of estrangement from his own time rested on a conviction that there had once existed a world in which men had lived in harmony and unity, the world of classical Greece.

That unity and harmony were characteristic of classical art and life had been a conviction of European thinkers since the Renaissance, but this belief had gained a new vitality in Germany at the end of the eighteenth century. The best-known sources of that vitality were in the work of the great German poets Goethe and Schiller, but the idea inspired others of

Hegel's contemporaries, notably his friends Hölderlin and Schelling. Hegel's participation in this admiration for classical ideals has been emphasized recently by Walter Kaufmann.[27] One powerful contemporary expression of it was in Schiller's *Letters on the Aesthetic Education of Man*, which Hegel read with enthusiasm when they began to appear in 1795. Schiller sought a way to give the ideal of free rational morality described in Kant's ethics real existence in the everyday world by means of an art that would join the power of feeling to the purity of thought. His ideal of harmony envisioned both a unity of feeling and thinking and an end to all the fragmentation characteristic of modern life. Not only would the divisions within the arts and sciences be overcome, even the division of labor would give way before the new and unified personalities of the future.

Schiller constructed this ideal on a historical pattern. The original harmony between men and the world that had existed in the Greek city-states had needed to be sundered in order for mankind to progress to a higher level of knowledge and achievement. Particular advances, for instance in philosophy, had required a concentration on them separate from the whole. What beckoned in the future, therefore, was not a mere return to the old Greek harmony, but its reconstitution on a higher level, a developed form of unity that presupposed and profited from postclassical diversity.[28]

Schiller's writing seems to have confirmed Hegel in the belief that modern life had destroyed the unity and harmony of the classical world. In April 1796 he wrote that the Christian man possessed "absolutely no unity" whereas the citizens of the ancient republics had "a unity in their whole sphere of activity."[29] The manuscript noted above, in which Hegel projected a reform of philosophy that would proceed from the conception of the individual as a free and self-conscious being, aimed at restoring this unity. Its basis would be a poetic art that could teach the philosophy of self-conscious freedom through a new mythology. Once poetry made truth accessible to ordinary people, then "the enlightened will join hands with the unenlightened. . . . Then eternal unity will reign among us. . . . Then for the first time can we expect the *equal* cultivation of *all* abilities, both of single individuals and of all individuals. No ability will be suppressed any longer."[30] It was on the basis of this vision of a future restoration of unity that Hegel declared his refusal "to conclude peace" with the existing world.

Hegel's writings of the time reveal extreme swings of mood, from exaltation to fearful anxiety, that recall his later description of youthful hypochondria as a state in which "splendors flash everywhere, but next to abysses." For instance, the exalted vision of a future that would embody harmony and unity contrasted with the comment in one of his manuscripts that the member of an ordinary religious group accepts "the duty, as in the social contract, of subjecting his private will to a majority vote, i.e., to the general will. Fear clutches at the heart if one imagines one's self in such a situation."[31] Hegel's portrait of Jesus at this time resembled his view of himself and his friends. "Jesus, who was concerned till manhood with his own personal development, was free from the contagious sickness of his age and his people; free from the inhibited inertia which expends its one activity on the common needs and conveniences of life; free too from the ambition and other desires whose satisfaction, once craved, would have compelled him to make terms with prejudice and vice." The situation in which such a man had to live was bleak.

In such a period, where a cold, privileged death was offered to the man who thirsted after inner life, who sought a better state in which he could live (he could not live in friendship with the objects around him, he had to be their slave and live in contradiction to the best that was in him, he was treated only as an enemy by them and treated them the same way)—in such a period the Essenes, a John the Baptist and a Jesus created life within themselves, and stood up in a fight against eternal death.[32]

There is no evidence that what Hegel suffered from in this period ever went much beyond the anxieties and difficulties that beset a great many young people in adolescence. For nearly two years, however, he lived a relatively withdrawn and solitary life that contrasts with descriptions of his sociability in student days, and his ambitious intellectual projects came to very little. While he remained in obscurity at Bern and Frankfurt, his younger friend Schelling began a meteoric career—later to fizzle out—which included five published books by the age of twenty-five. It was to Schelling that Hegel wrote sometime before June 1796 in terms that made his friend denounce his depression and indecision. Between the spring of that year and the spring of 1798 Hegel committed very little to paper; when he did attempt to write the results were fragments of three or four pages.[33]

In 1798-99, however, the tempo of Hegel's activity began to pick up. At the same time his relationship to the world appeared to him in a changed light. The nature of this alteration is best revealed in a manuscript composed around the end of 1799 or early in 1800. Although only a fragment, this writing was one of Hegel's personally most revealing and intellectually most fertile attempts to find his way to a satisfying and mature point of view.[34] Hegel began by declaring that the two sides of an ever-growing contradiction were approaching each other. The two sides were two kinds of men: those who lived active lives but found themselves desiring something unknown beyond the limits of their life; and those who had worked out the idea of nature within themselves, but who did not possess a form of real life that corresponded to their vision. "The need of the first to achieve a consciousness of what holds them imprisoned, and their desire to receive the unknown, corresponds to the need of the second to depart from their ideas into life."[35]

Hegel's earlier feeling of separation from men who lived in the everyday world was echoed in this contrast, but it was now altered by a changed sense of what people like himself required. "These men cannot live alone, and *a man is still alone*, even when he has represented his nature to himself, made it his companion, and enjoyed himself in it. He must still find *what he has presented as a living thing*." Those "whom the time has driven into an inner world" have to choose between remaining dead within themselves, or "when nature drives them to life, to transcend the negative quality of the existing world, in order to find themselves in it, in order to be able to live." The need to find his life within the existing world dissolved Hegel's earlier determination to remain separate from it.[36]

Turning to the world did not lessen the distinction between the man of self-consciousness and the man of action. For the former, "His suffering is tied up with the consciousness of limitation, on the basis of which he rejected life as it had been allowed him. He wills his suffering." By contrast, the suffering of worldly men was not willed, because they took the conditions of actual existence and action as absolute and, when these limited their own impulses, sacrificed themselves and others to them willy-nilly. Both were bound by the conditions of life they shared, which neither possessed the power to overcome by force.[37]

What mattered most, however, was that the path to reconciling the contradiction between nature and existing life now appeared open to Hegel. The reconciliation could take place "when *existing* life has lost all its power and its dignity, when it has become a purely negative quality." Not individual will, but historical evolution brought this about. "All the manifestations of our time show that satisfaction can no longer be found in the old life." That life had restricted men to a "servile little world, and also to a self-abnegation and a turning to thoughts of heaven as reconciliation with this limitation." The content of the "servile little world" had been simply "men's property, their things." The satisfactions this world had once afforded had dissolved at the end of the eighteenth century. Both the revolutionary attack on property, and the production of luxury through economic expansion, had shown that men could be the masters, not the servants, of their own activity. One result was an increase in "man's bad conscience for making an absolute of his property, his things, and in his suffering." At the same time, however, the fresh breath of a better life could be felt. Its impulse was nurtured by the great deeds of individual men, by the movements of whole peoples, and by the representation of nature and fate by poets.[38]

These historical movements were creating conditions in the world that harmonized with the oppostion to ordinary existence felt by men of vision and self-consciousness. The attack on "the power of the limited life" was not confined to philosophy, but was now taking place in the real world, "in nature in its actual life as one particular against another." The existing world was proving its identity with nature by developing the means to overcome its own limitations. "The limited life can be attacked by being brought into contradiction with its own truth which lies within it." That truth was "universality," the representation of general well-being and collective interest. The claim to such universality provided existing institutions with their right to rule. In the modern world, however, the powers that were—for instance the fragmented German empire—had forfeited their universal character, and themselves only represented particular interests. Only the thought of universality remained, and it was not compatible with any existing power. Therefore, the powers could be granted their right to exist, but the striving for universality opposed them. It belonged instead to those historical forces that were transforming the world.[39]

Some of the features Hegel discerned within this transformation can be seen in the commentary he wrote on David Hume's *History of England*, probably sometime in 1798 or 1799. Contrasting modern fragmentation with ancient harmony, Hegel now regarded modern social divisions as creating a new form of unity out of themselves. Modern men, divided as they were into diverse social groups, were not "whole men" as the ancients had been. Nor could they make and carry out individual designs in the world, as ancients like Alcibiades and Themistocles had done. Even the activity of great men was now "more a matter of *conduct* in a particular, given circle." This did not mean that no unity joined modern men together. The individuals and groups who made up a modern community each pursued some separate task; unlike the ancients, they were not all inspired by a common idea. Nonetheless, "their power and might is certainly this idea," for their diverse activities issued in a common result. If the historian was wrong to equate this result with the desire of one or another person of power and influence, he was correct in saying that everyone contributed to it. Modern achievements therefore combined "the consciousness of the universal and at the same time opposition, particularity."[40] Hegel's view of modern life now approached his later conception of civil society in relation to the state (although he did not yet use these terms to distinguish them): opposition and particularity did not destroy unity but formed its basis.

Activity in a given sphere, a willingness to concern oneself with "particular against particular" and with the details of which life was made up, a recognition of the rationality and necessity of the existing world—

these were the components of what Hegel would later identify as manhood, the signs that a youth had grown into a man.* On November 2, 1800, he wrote to Schelling deploring the interruption in their friendship, and explaining that in the meantime "the ideal of my youth had to be transformed through contemplation into a system. While I am engaged in it," he added, "I wonder how I may find a way to get back a grip on human life."[41] In 1801 he took his first public teaching post, at the University of Jena, and with Schelling began to edit a philosophical journal. In 1802 his first published essay appeared.

Hegel's old feeling of separation from the world had not been entirely put to rest. He once referred to his hypochondria as lasting into his thirty-sixth year, the year he wrote *The Phenomenology of the Spirit*. Shortly after his marriage at the age of forty, he wrote to his wife that he looked to her "to heal any residue in my mind of unbelief in contentment," and "to reconcile my true inner nature with the way in which I am—too frequently—against what is actual and for what is actual."[42] By the fall of 1800, however, Hegel's worst "incapacity" was behind him. He now entered on his mature life's work.

3. Spirit, History, and Fate

In the years 1798-99, as Hegel was working his way to the position from which he would ask Schelling to help him find a way "to get back a grip on human life," he composed a new essay on religion, which he called "The Spirit of Christianity and its Fate." Here, in an account of biblical Jewish and Christian history, which remained unpublished until 1907, we find the first clear statement of Hegel's mature outlook. His earlier radical hostility to religion and the other products of human history gave way to an attempt to envision them as developing expressions of human life, incomplete and fragmented, but necessary and characteristic.[43]

Hegel depicted the history of the Jews—and later of their Christian descendants—as a reflection of the personal history of their patriarch, Abraham:"his spirit is the unity, the soul, regulating the entire fate of his posterity." Here, for the first time, Hegel made the development of spirit (*Geist*) the central category in the philosophical interpretation of reality. "This spirit appears in a different guise after every one of its battles against

---

*Both Hegel's fragment about the relationship between activity and self-consciousness and his comments on Hume's *History* were influenced by contemporary literary accounts of youth and crisis, as well as by his own experience. The fragment, with its description of two different kinds of men, is in part a commentary on *Hyperion*, a novel of youthful revolt and reconciliation by Hegel's friend Hölderlin, as pointed out by Franz Rosenzweig, *Hegel und der Staat* (Munich and Berlin, 1920), Chap. 6. Hegel seems also to have had in mind Goethe's *The Sorrows of Young Werther* and *Wilhelm Meister*, the stories, respectively, of a failed and a successful transition from youth to maturity.

different forces or after becoming sullied by adopting an alien nature as a result of succumbing to might or seduction." Yet a constant inner character directed a spirit's development in all its phases; the ultimate form in which this character found expression defined the spirit's "fate."[44]

The personal history of Abraham as Hegel conceived it can be summed up in two words: disseverance and isolation. Having left his birthplace with his father, "In the plains of Mesopotamia he tore himself free altogether from his family as well, in order to be a wholly self-subsistent, independent man. . . . The first act which made Abraham the progenitor of a nation is a disseverance which snaps the bonds of communal life and love." His whole life would be ruled by "the spirit of self-maintenance in strict opposition to everything." Abraham's self-conscious isolation echoed the state of mind in which Hegel had found himself two years earlier: Abraham wandered over a large region, "without bringing parts of it any nearer to him by cultivating and improving them. Had he done so he would have become attached to them and might have adopted them as parts of *his* world. . . . The groves which often gave him coolness and shade he soon left again. . . . He struggled against his fate, the fate which would have proffered him a stationary communal life with others." In his spirit the Jews received a law whose principle was the antithesis between their own nation and "the world and all the rest of the human race."[45]

A human being so absorbed in separation from others could have only two possible relationships to the world outside himself: mastery or slavery. "Mastery was the only possible relationship in which Abraham could stand to the infinite world opposed to him; but he was unable himself to make this mastery actual, and it therefore remained ceded to his Ideal." The Jews made their God sovereign of the universe in theory, but in reality they had to submit to enslavement in Egypt. Because they could be "only either mastered or masters," the post-Exodus Jews had no free political existence. In contrast to the independent and self-subsistent Greeks, they evolved no concept of citizenship. A people of masters and slaves could not be citizens. All the subsequent misfortunes of the Jews up to Hegel's own present day "have all of them been simply consequences and elaborations of their original fate. By this fate—an infinite power which they set over against themselves and could never conquer—they have been maltreated and will be continually maltreated until they appease it by the spirit of beauty and so annul it by reconciliation."[46]

Jesus sought to overcome his people's separation from life by a reconciliation in love. Whereas religious life among the Jews had been expressed in commandments and duties, Jesus preached religion as an extension of life, not a set of demands imposed on it from outside. The love he preached was a "feeling for the whole" human community that obeyed the precepts of morality and law out of pure inner harmony with them, not from coercion. If a person who had absorbed Jesus' message harmed another, he did not transgress against an external law, but against his own inner harmony with life. His deed brought its own punishment, and it had to be compensated by an inner resumption of love for the world. By restoring his own lost unity with others he did not submit to any external authority, but returned to his own true self. Hence, there was neither mastery nor slavery in Jesus' teaching: "In contrast with the Jewish reversion to obedience, reconciliation in love is a liberation; in contrast with the re-recognition of lordship, it is the cancellation of lordship."[47]

Just as Hegel had pictured Abraham's isolation in terms that recalled his own earlier state of mind, so did he now present Jesus' reconciliation in a way that matched his own impending return to ordinary human life. Animated by the longing to restore "the lost life," the man separated from it "may still hold himself back from returning . . . ; he may prolong his bad conscience and feeling of grief and stimulate it every moment"—that is to say, in the terms Hegel used about himself, "He wills his suffering." The return must be prepared from the depths of his being. "He avoids being frivolous with life, because he postpones reunion with it, postpones greeting it as a friend again, until his longing for reunion springs from the deepest recesses of his soul."[48] This is what Hegel would later describe, in connection with youthful hypochondria, as being pressed through the narrows of one's own contracted nature, in order to emerge "fortified and assured." It is what Erik Erikson has called "plumbing the depths." The attitude on which Hegel based his return from isolation, and which he would later describe as characteristic of maturity, here appears embodied in religious practice, which Hegel described as "holy and beautiful" because "it is our endeavor to unify the discords necessitated by our development, and our attempt to exhibit the unification in the *ideal* as fully *existent*, as no longer opposed to reality, and thus to express and confirm it in a deed."[49]

Yet Christianity did not bring man to maturity. It was humanity's childhood, not its adulthood. One sensed its essence by recognizing "the holiness of the child's nature." The Christian unity with the existing world was undeveloped and naive. Further spiritual progress required that this primitive harmony give way to separation and particularity. That it would do so was assured by the entanglement of Jesus' teaching in the fate that ruled the Jewish world out of which he came. To overcome the defects of Jewish life, Jesus had to separate himself from it: "He set himself against the whole." Thus, he participated from the start in the attitude of separation bequeathed by Abraham. "Even *his* sublime effort to overcome the whole of the Jewish fate must therefore have failed with his people, and he was bound to become its victim himself."[50]

Jesus' message of unification through love could not bring total reconciliation because it excluded from the start all those spheres of life where it could not find "spirit." The communion of Jesus' disciples was a unification with him in love. Their activities focused on enjoying life in common and on keeping and spreading the faith. Alien to them was "every spirit of cooperation for something other than the dissemination of the faith, every spirit which reveals and enjoys itself in play in other modes and restricted forms of life." This exclusion restricted Christian love to an incomplete development and allowed "the most appalling fanaticism" to issue from it. It still left his followers subject to domination by those human powers in whose purposes it could not join. "Here is the point where Jesus is linked with fate, linked in the most sublime way, but where he suffers under it."[51]

With his eye on the classical Greek city-state, Hegel found this weakness of Christianity particularly exemplified by its relationship to politics. Jesus could find no common purpose with the state, hence he could not bring it into his ideal realm. "His sole relationship with the state was to remain under its jurisdiction," hence his relation to it was one of deliberate subjection. His followers could not actively or positively participate in the "great element in a living union," the "important bond of association" that the state provided.[52]

Hence, the promised unification with the world in love was dissipated by the separation that was the premise of that love. Opposition to the world became a fixed and essential part of Christianity. The organized church would not be able to fulfill "the deepest urge for religion" that Jesus' personal message had inspired, but only turn it into "an endless, unquenchable, and unappeased longing." It was Christianity's "fate that church and state, worship and life, piety and virtue, spiritual and worldly action, can never dissolve into one."[53]

Hegel's notion of fate was an important component of the philosophical attitude through which he was gaining a grip on life as he reached thirty. That attitude viewed reality as a series of parallel but connected circles of spiritual development. Every path of the spirit's itinerary—from disseverance to integration, from childhood to maturity, from mastery and slavery to independent existence, from Judaism to Christianity, from Christianity to philosophy—had the same geography and could be mapped in the same colors. Human nature and history evolved by an eternal return out of division into unity; division presupposed unity and led back to it, only to begin the cycle again. Every object in the human world was part of the developing journey of spirit, and one had only to recognize the features that marked it as the product of a particular stage in order to discover its harmonious relation to the whole. Hegel had not given up his earlier ideal of harmony and unity, but that ideal no longer found obstacles in those parts of the world that did not display the wholeness of nature and reason.

Instead of driving him into isolation, the ideal of harmony and unity now tied Hegel firmly to the world.

4. Dialectic, Method, and Madness

In a passage in the *Philosophy of Right* aimed against those in his time who made religious feeling the foundation of both truth and political obedience, Hegel wrote: "The genuine truth is the prodigious transfer of the inner into the outer, the building of reason into the real world, and this has been the task of the world in the whole course of its history." The staggering sweep and uncompromising monism of Hegel's vision are nowhere more purely concentrated than in this sentence.[54] Hegel insisted that "everything is latent in the mind of man"; what comes from without provides only "an impulse towards the development of spirit. All that has value to man, the external, the self-existent, is contained in man himself and has to develop from himself." The rational understanding of how spirit unfolded through continually confronting the external world was the task of spirit that had become conscious of itself. This task belonged to philosophy.[55]

This view of the nature of human life and philosophy lay behind Hegel's decision to introduce his philosophical system with a book called *The Phenomenology of the Spirit*. The title, forbidding in itself, means a general account of the development of spirit, "a science of the experience through which consciousness passes."[56] Convinced that every form of human life embodied the same inner force and could be understood in the same underlying terms, Hegel took "experience" here in its widest sense. Simply to list all the topics discussed in *The Phenomenology* would require pages. A multitude of moments in individual life and human history pass in review, all presented as facets of the growth of human perception and self-consciousness. The reader is led from sense perception to abstract thinking, from thought to life, from life to struggle, from struggle to subjection, from subjection to revolt, from revolt to philosophy, from ancient philosophy to its dissolution; from religion to science to nature to the development of modern culture and history, and finally to the culmination of the development of modern self-consciousness in contemporary forms of art, religion, and philosophy. At the end, Hegel said that what he had done was "simply to gather together the particular moments, each of which in principle exhibits the life of spirit in its entirety," and to show the way in which its "content was disclosed in these moments." The result was "a slow succession of spiritual shapes, a gallery of pictures, each of which is endowed with the entire wealth of spirit."[57] The richness of life was visible at each stage, but their succession was also a necessary aspect of spiritual development. "The truth is the whole," because every concrete form of life, "just where it believes it is working out its own self-preservation and its own private interest, is, in point of fact, doing the very opposite, is doing what brings about its own dissolution and makes itself a moment in the whole."[58]

Hegel described both the method and the content of his philosophy as "dialectic." The term dialectic had a history as old as ancient Greek philosophy, and in using it Hegel probably meant to underline the continuity of his thought with the tradition of Western philosophy (just as in using "spirit" he declared his tie to traditional religious speculation). The content he gave to the notion of dialectic transcended the term's earlier meanings, however. Hegel's dialectic sought to match the logic of thought to the logic of life.

He analyzed the form and substance of this dialectic in his *Lectures on the History of Philosophy*. Every embodiment of spirit developed from a state in which its essential nature was only implicit (*an sich*) to one in which this nature became explicit, that is actually present as an object and a content of consciousness (*für sich*). Before any innate quality of a subject could acquire actual existence for that subject, the quality had to be objectified, to come to exist outside the subject. Only in this way could the subject take actual possession of its own quality, by an act of self-recognition that made the quality an explicit property of the subject. "All knowing, learning, science, even all action has in view nothing more than to draw out of itself what is implicit, potential, and to make itself objective."[59] Like the plant impelled by the inner force of nature to objectify the form inherent in it and thus to progress from seed to flower, all being was driven to develop its implicit nature by the force of the contradiction between its actual and its potential existence.

Two terms recur over and over in Hegel's account of the dialectic of spirit: alienation and inversion. The first, alienation, has been appropriated by so many writers and with so many different purposes since Hegel's time that its original meaning is difficult to recover from beneath the debris of common usage. The second, inversion, was in its way just as important to Hegel and his followers as the first, but its importance and meaning have been obscured by the exclusive concentration of modern cultural criticism on alienation.

Alienation (*Entfremdung*) is one of a group of words with closely related meanings in Hegel's writings, the others being objectification (*Entäusserung*) and separation or disseverance (*Entzweiung*). All are part of the general process of development through which what is potential and implicit comes to be actual and explicit. They describe the process whereby spirit "duplicates" itself "in order to be able to find itself, in order to be able to come back to itself."[60]

Objectification was a constant feature of development; alienation was also a recurring part of that process but, as Hegel used the term, it referred to a situation that arose only after the first objectification of spirit had already taken place. Only the spirit that had already produced a substantial world by objectification was subject to alienation; or, in more ordinary language, only the person who found an external world in existence independent of his present will and consciousness could feel his own existence as foreign to him. Such a spirit (or person) was subject to alienation when it found itself unable to recognize its own nature in the substantial world outside, when it could not recognize the world as its own product.

Hegel also used the term alienation to describe the spirit's reaction to this situation: it yielded up—alienated—some part of itself, will or consciousness, in order to reestablish harmony and unity with the substantial world outside. In the "process by which the moments are thus made actual and give each other life, the alienation will be found to alienate itself, and the whole thereby will take all its contents back into its concept." In this way a subject's identity was realized and preserved as its own activity altered the conditions—and hence the actual character—of its existence. Alienation was the moment of a subject's conscious division against itself, out of which its higher, developed unity could arise.[61]

The second term that was central to Hegel's exposition of dialectical development was inversion. The ideas clustered around it were to be one of Hegel's most powerful and pervasive legacies to Marx. The famous metaphor of setting the dialectic—which Hegel had stood on its head—on its feet was to be only the most obvious and superficial instance. The adjective *verkehrte* (meaning inverted, reversed, or sometimes perverse), the verbs *verkehren* (to turn over), *umkehren* (to turn around, turn into, or return), the adjective or adverb *umgekehrt* (reverse, inverse, or *vice versa*), and the noun *Verkehrung* (inversion or reversal), all recur often in Hegel's writings; the notions they express were central to his thought. All the most characteristic expressions of Hegel's intellectual vision can be described as inversions or reversals: the discovery of unity in diversity, the transformation of negation into affirmation, the transition from fixed existence into the fluidity of opposites. One of the most celebrated chapters in *The Phenomenology*, Hegel's discussion of the dialectic of lordship and bondage, describes the inversion of the original relationship between a master and a slave.[62]

In Hegel's view, philosophical Reason (*Vernunft*) differed from the mere Understanding (*Verstand*) of common sense precisely in its ability to perceive these inversions or reversals within the world of actual existence. To common sense, which regarded the world as made up of discrete and separate beings with fixed boundaries and oppositions, the world of philosophy was itself topsy-turvy. "Philosophy . . . is philosophy only by being altogether opposed to the understanding, and thus even more to healthy common sense, which means the geographical and temporary limitations of a group of men. Compared with this, the world of philosophy is an inverted [*verkehrte*] world."[63]

This notion of philosophy as the inversion of ordinary common sense, implicit in much of Hegel's writing, appears explicitly at critical moments in both the *Phenomenology* and the *Science of Logic*. The inverted world was a definite stage in the itinerary of consciousness, reached at the moment when mind failed in its attempt to comprehend the world through the discovery of an inner reality opposed to the phenomena revealed by sense experience. Traditional philosophy, and much of science, attempted to interpret the world of experience as the reflection of a supersensible world said to lie "behind" it, whose laws governed events in the world of phenomena. In particular, Kant had posited a division of reality into a world of appearances and a world of "things-in-themselves." The latter realm of pure existence controlled the sphere of appearances but, since human knowledge began with sense impressions, men could not have real knowledge of the supersensible world (although they might sometimes attain to intimations about it). In Kant's view, to speculate about the ultimate reality that could not be perceived by the senses led in the end to contradictory conclusions: matter was made up of indivisible atoms, or it was infinitely divisible; space was the really existing framework of physical events, or it merely expressed the relative position of objects; the world was contained within material limits, or it was infinite.

To Hegel, these Kantian "antinomies" demonstrated that abstract speculation about inner reality led this kind of thinking (like common sense, it was Understanding as opposed to Reason) to the experience of discovering not one supersensible world, but two. "The first supersensible world, the changeless kingdom of laws . . . has turned round into its opposite. . . . This second supersensible world is in this way the inverted world (*verkehrte Welt*), and . . . the inverted form of the first."[64] Up to this point the mind had regarded the supersensible world as the realm of essential reality. When that reality suffered alteration through inversion, a new realization dawned. The supersensible world did not provide an escape from the ever-changing world of mere appearance into a world of stability and certainty; the purely conceptual world turned out to be made up of contradiction, change, and motion too. This revelation prepared the transition from merely conscious understanding to self-conscious reason. "We have to think pure flux, opposition within opposition itself, or Contradiction." Only now, as the thinking mind became aware of its own inescapable immersion in the changing world of appearances, could it really grasp and comprehend actual existence. "It is to itself conscious of being inverted, i.e., it is the inverted form of itself; it is that world itself and its opposite in a single unity." Conscious of the inversion taking place within itself, reason became aware of its own participation in the continual development through inversion that constituted the process of reality. "All moments of the sphere of appearance are thereby taken up into the inner realm."[65]

The experience of inversion was, therefore, the moment of thought's arrival at consciousness of its real relationship to the world. In the *Phenomenology*, the discussion of the inverted world occurred at the point of transition from "consciousness" to "self-consciousness." In the *Science of Logic*, it marked the passage from explanation based on the laws of phenomena to what Hegel called the "essential relationship."[66] Out of the realization that the attempt to understand the existing world in terms of a supersensible world said to lie behind it led to the positing of an inverted reality arose the realization that concepts could only be adequate to reality if they were themselves present in the actual world, not separate from it. Mind could comprehend the world only if it was itself present in the world; real knowledge of the outside world was, at the same time, self-consciousness.

Inversion was an essential experience in the development of spirit, revealing reason's inner tie to the external appearances that seemed to contradict it. That inversion showed how mind was linked to its opposite should prepare us for the otherwise surprising turn Hegel gave to the history of spirit at this point: inversion demonstrated the closeness of reason to madness. In the *Encyclopaedia* Hegel would make madness a necessary stage in the development of reason; in the *Phenomenology* he made the same point in a less straightforward but equally explicit way. At the time Hegel was working on his book, Goethe published a German translation of Diderot's *Rameau's Nephew*, a book its author had never made public, and that had therefore remained generally unknown before. Hegel was deeply struck by Diderot's picture of Rameau (the nephew's name as well as his uncle's), a highly original but distracted and eccentric character who lived on the social and intellectual margins of the French Enlightenment. Diderot had described him as "a compound of elevation and abjectness, of good sense and lunacy."[67] Self-absorbed and uncompromising, Rameau refused to live by accepted standards, and his barbed, witty conversation exposed the hollow foundations on which ordinary morality rested. His discourse left common-sense values and expectations in a topsy-turvy shambles.

The passage in which Hegel described Rameau would later be one of Marx's favorites; in 1869 he sent Engels a copy of *Rameau's Nephew*, and took the trouble to copy out for his friend the following section of Hegel's commentary:

The honest soul takes each discrete element of experience [*Moment*] to be a permanent and essential aspect of existence, and is in the uncultivated and thoughtless condition of not knowing that by this very procedure it does the reverse [*das Verkehrte*]. The disintegrated soul, however [the character of Rameau in Diderot's dialogue] is the consciousness corresponding or belonging to inversion, of absolute inversion. What rules in him is the principle of conceptual thinking, which brings together thoughts that lie far apart for the honest soul, and his discourse is therefore rich with spirit.

The content uttered by spirit and uttered about itself is, then, the inversion and perversion [*Verkehrung*] of all conceptions and realities, a universal deception of itself and of others. The shamelessness manifested in stating this deceit is just on that account the greatest truth. . . . The placid soul that in simple honesty of heart takes the melody of the good and true to consist in harmony of sound and uniformity of tones, i.e. in a single note, regards this style of expression as a "fantastic mixture of wisdom and folly."[68]

Hegel spoke here specifically of the "madness" (*Verrücktheit*) of Rameau's character. The inversion that the mind experienced at the moment of its passage from understanding to genuine reason was linked to the appearance of perversity and frenzy the man of self-conscious spirit—absorbed in the continual dissolution of the objects whose bounds were fixed in ordinary perception—presented to the world.

The link inversion established between reason and madness reminds us of an aspect of the term alienation usually ignored in discussions of Hegel's use of it. One of the meanings of alienation in the language of Hegel's day was insanity. The most common term for mental derangement in French then was *alienation mentale*, and when Goethe translated Rameau's work he rendered this as *Entfremdung des Geistes* (alienation of the spirit). This usage of alienation, with its explicit reference to madness, was one of the immediate sources for Hegel's notion of "self-alienated spirit."[69] Moreover, Hegel noted this usage of alienation in his discussion of mental illness in the *Encyclopaedia*. There he described insanity as a spiritual state that exactly fitted the pattern of alienation in the more general, philosophical sense. Speaking of the "animal magnetism" that made Mesmer so famous at the time, Hegel explained that this hypnotic state was an illness: "The essence of disease must be held to consist in the isolation of a particular system of the organism from the general physiological life, and in virtue of this *alienation* of the particular system from the general life, the animal exhibits its own finitude, its impotence and dependence on an *alien* power."[70]

Hegel's recognition that the state of insanity expressed part of the intellectual potential on which reason drew in arriving at its full development has not been given the place it deserves in his thought. It is related to his view that truth emerged from a state of mind that was at once philosophic calm and Dionysian frenzy: "The truth is thus the bacchanalian revel, where not a member is sober; and because every member no sooner becomes detached than it *eo ipso* collapses straightaway, the revel is just as much a state of unbroken calm."[71] It also conveys the quality of Hegel's own personality, with which his view of the nature of philosophy was so closely linked. The adjectives he applied to Rameau, "distraught" and "disintegrated" apply to Hegel himself, even long after the crisis of his twenties had been resolved. True, Hegel was a fairly dependable husband and father, and an established figure in his time. Nevertheless, his conversation sometimes approached the outrageous sallies of Diderot's Rameau. Heinrich Heine recalled that one evening after dinner Hegel responded to Heine's enthusiasm about the beauteous heavens with the startling retort: "The stars, hum! hum! the stars are only a gleaming leprosy in the sky." What, Heine threw back, is there no place where the virtuous are rewarded after death? "But he, staring at me with his pale eyes, said cuttingly: So you want to get a tip for having nursed your sick mother and for not having poisoned your dear brother? Saying that, he looked around anxiously, but he immediately seemed reassured when he saw that it was only Heinrich Beer, who had approached to invite him to play whist." A more harmonious person, Walter Kaufmann has observed, "would hardly have looked upon harmony as such a high and significant goal."[72]

Hegel's awareness that the alienation by which the human spirit progressed shared a certain ground with mental derangement resembles what some more recent theorists have noticed about originality. Openness to novelty, to new experience, is dangerous for that portion of personal integration that rests on a particular way of structuring experience. Creative people must sometimes face up to the peril of "coming apart." They may display "a looseness of self," a "repeated slipping in and out of personal integration" that seems sometimes to reflect an underlying security and sometimes a weakened sense of self. "The extremes of creativity and novelty lead to madness" because they may bring on an "inability to form structures that could be the basis for a perception of reality at all."[73]

Hegel's dialectical method was an expression of his unstinting conviction that the extremes of division and wholeness were the truth underlying the moderate and seemingly more stable experiences of everyday life. "Division is a necessary agent of life, which takes shape through eternally opposing; and the most vital wholeness is only possible through recovery out of the most complete division." The only genuine unity was inseparable from "the process of breaking asunder."[74] With that conclusion in mind, we can begin our search for the unity in Marx's life.

CHAPTER TWO

Starting Out: Vocation, Rebellion, and Realism

MARX'S mature vision of the world would focus on society, not psychology. History was the history of social groups, and individual existence only revealed its real significance in the light of class relationships. To employ—as Hegel had—categories that derived from inner, subjective experience, offered the mind no purchase on the real social world.

Yet Marx was, as Hegel said of Jesus (thinking also of himself), "concerned till manhood with his own personal development." In growing to maturity he had to face the problems of youth much as Hegel had described them, and Hegel's awareness of those dilemmas was one thing that drew Marx to Hegel in the first place. Marx's earliest writing under Hegelian auspices, his doctoral dissertation, did not address the topics of social and political theory that would later occupy his mind; it analyzed the character of philosophical thinkers in isolation from the world. Like Hegel, Marx saw such isolation as linked to a condition of inversion that could border on madness. To overcome it, he looked to the special harmony between Hegelian philosophy and modern life.

Recognizing these concerns will help us to understand what drew Marx to Hegel and what led him away. The path along which he became first a follower of Hegel and then a pursuer of him led onward to Marx's own mature identity. That is the path we must follow now, beginning with the points that determined its original orientation, Marx's city and his family.[1]

1. The Lessons of Trier

The Rhineland town of Trier is one of those small European cities whose history has taught it to view its particular and local experience in the light of wider historical currents. The center of an important region of wine production, Trier took on both military and commercial importance from its strategic location astride the plain on the eastern bank of the Moselle river. The town became an important provincial capital under the Romans, and a center of ecclesiastical administration in the Middle Ages. As the seat of one of the three archbishops among the seven electors of the Holy Roman Empire, it was the capital of an independent electorate until the end of the eighteenth century, when it was incorporated in the expanded territory of revolutionary France. In 1815 it was ceded to Prussia as part of the Rhineland Province created by the Treaty of Vienna.[2]

Trier claimed to be the oldest German city. Inscribed on a house near the main square, not far from where Karl Marx grew up, a false but expressive medieval motto proclaimed (as it still does): "Trier stood for 1,300 years before Rome existed." Between 1815 and 1848 Trier's burghers expressed a similar resistance to the pretensions of foreign imperial power in their attitude toward Prussia. Hostility to Prussian control helped keep alive the enthusiasm for the French Revolution felt by many leading citizens, including the mayor and the head of the local Gymnasium. In the 1840s a local paper, the *Trierische Zeitung* (*Trier Gazette*), was the main organ of radical republicanism and utopian socialism in Germany. The town joined the revolutionary movement with enthusiasm in 1848, and in the elections in May of that year became the only Rhineland district to send an entire delegation of left-wing republicans to the Frankfurt Assembly.[3]

The years when Karl Marx attended the classical Gymnasium from 1831 to 1834 were politically the most active of the post-Restoration period in the city. Throughout Germany the French revolution of 1830 was reflected in increased popular agitation for reform, followed by government repression. Trier shared in that pattern. The news of the outbreak in Paris stirred hopes that French arms would free the city, and an anonymous pamphlet appeared in the town denouncing the "Prussian yoke." In 1832 a town delegation attended the national German festival at Hambach, where liberal and patriotic speakers were heard; the next year a poem circulated in Trier pictured German princes trembling before "the voice of the German people."[4]

The agitation in Trier reached its peak in January 1834. On January 13 the local Casino Society, a middle-class social and cultural organization, held a banquet to honor Trier's representatives at the Rhineland Diet. The main speech was given by a lawyer who had been on the banquet's organizing committee, Heinrich Marx. His oldest son Karl was then just short of seventeen. The elder Marx was careful to direct a full measure of praise to the king of Prussia for establishing representative institutions, but he made it clear that he did not share the official conception of them. He referred to the provincial assemblies, which had first met in 1823 (despite an earlier promise, no central Prussian assembly was established), as "the first institution of popular representation." The word Marx used in German, *Volksvertretung* (literally representation of the people) was not welcome to the Prussian government, because it implied the equal representation of all citizens. The official term, *Ständeversammlung* (assembly of estates), presupposed separate (and unequal) aristocratic and popular delegations. Heinrich Marx used that word too, but he spoke of the assembly of estates as the first form of a representation that would become more popular. He also praised the town's representatives—who shared his views—as having "fought for truth and right with word and deed and sacrifice and courage." Twelve days later another banquet was held, following which some of those present remained to sing French revolutionary songs. The French flag was displayed and a certain Herr Brixius reportedly exclaimed: "Had it not been for the French revolution of July [1830] we would all have to eat grass like cows." Heinrich Marx was present on that occasion too, although he may have left after participating in some of the singing.[5]

The Prussian government took none of this lightly. One minister complained that Trier had shown the danger of public banquets at which the "madness" of regarding deputies as representatives of the people instead of estates was encouraged. Brixius was accused of high treason. (He was acquitted.) In the following year the government forced the progressively minded head of the Gymnasium to accept a much more conservative co-director, and soon began a series of manoeuvers that would lead the liberal mayor, Haw, to leave his post during 1839.[6]

The Gymnasium director deserves special mention. He was Johann Hugo Wyttenbach, under whose aegis a school once known primarily as a training ground for priests acquired a reputation as a hotbed of radicalism. A lifelong admirer of Kant and Rousseau, Wyttenbach was a republican who saw the Enlightenment revolution in philosophy as a parallel to the French Revolution in politics, and thought that "the dawn of freedom" broke with the storming of the Bastille in 1789. Drawing on Kant and on the tradition of Christian morality, he emphasized the duty of each man to dedicate his life to others. "Whatever our station in life may be, our duty to humanity never ends," he wrote. Among Wyttenbach's admirers in Trier were both Heinrich Marx and the young Karl.[7]

Alongside the political agitation taking place in Trier between 1815 and 1848, and probably responsible for some of its radical edge, was a marked sense of social crisis. The economic conditions of the Restoration era were poor. Trier, like other Rhineland cities (notably Barmen, where Frederick Engels was growing up in the same years) had derived considerable economic advantage from access to French markets and protection from English competition during the Napoleonic period. After 1815 the loss of duty-free commerce with France and the influx of cheap British textiles dealt severe blows to both the commercial and manufacturing sectors of the Rhineland economy. The agricultural sector, still the largest in the Moselle region, was even more badly damaged. After annexation to Prussia, the traditionally poor Moselle farmers at first saw their economic prospects improved by the opening of the large Prussian market to their wines. In the late 1820s, however, Prussia entered into a series of customs treaties with other German states, which allowed much cheaper wines to come onto the Prussian market duty free. Prices collapsed; by 1828 wine was selling for around a third of what it had brought in 1818, and by 1830 it was down to a tenth. In 1831 an observer could complain that "The Moselle wine business is ruined." The cry arose that "grapes and misery flourish on the Moselle."[8]

In Trier itself poverty was also increasing. During the French period a local woolen industry had grown up to supply the army; this now collapsed. Only the river port continued to flourish, and it did not provide employment for more than a couple of hundred workers. Meanwhile food prices were rising. Reports of hunger and poverty marked the whole three-decade period from the teens to the 1840s. Conditions became especially critical in years when harvests were bad all over Europe, such as 1817, the late 1820s, and the mid-1840s, but these particular moments only accented the chronic underlying economic weakness and made it more visible. Like some other regions of Europe, Trier and the Rhineland would not really recover from the post-Napoleonic economic difficulties until after 1848.[9]

Various measures were undertaken to aid the poor. Among these were soup kitchens, public works projects, loan societies, and a public food depot to sell bread at reduced prices. This last project was supported by eighty-four people who bought shares, including Heinrich Marx, who purchased two of them. Only sixteen wealthy citizens took more than two.[10]

As early as 1825 a local official acquainted with French socialist writings, Ludwig Gall, addressed the problem of alleviating poverty. In a pamphlet, "What Could Help?" he declared that in a world in which— with few exceptions—men thought only of themselves, every interest was represented except one: "Only *humanity* finds no representatives, and one looks in vain for proposals that can help out of their difficulties those people who, left only with their nearly worthless ability to work [*Arbeitsfleiss*], are totally alienated from every purely human joy by their struggle against daily cares and their constant feeling of the most pressing dependency." Gall gave a full and fearful picture of the poverty he had witnessed in and around Trier, and appealed for help from those who were better off. His ideas were later taken up in the radical newspaper the *Trierische Zeitung*. Through Gall and others, both Fourier and St. Simon were made known in Trier in the 1830s; according to one of Marx's daughters, Marx's future father-in-law Ludwig von Westphalen was among those with an interest in St. Simon.[11]

Heinrich Marx's role in Trier's political life was hardly a major one, but he was a recognizable figure. He identified clearly with the progressive impulse of the time, and shared the liberal coloration of his city. Various circumstances of his life help to account for this. That he had probably studied in France may have increased his sympathy for liberal politics; in addition, he was a self-made man, with a natural sympathy for the revolutionary slogan of "careers open to talent." Little is know about his early life, but his letters to his son pointed to his difficulties in completing his legal studies, and to the fact that his family gave him little or no help. [12]

What tied Heinrich Marx most closely to the liberal currents of his age was his Jewishness. Both he and his wife came from notable Jewish families with distinguished genealogies. Both had many rabbis among their forebears; on Heinrich Marx's side these included the rabbis of Trier itself, dating back to the seventeenth century; his elder brother Samuel was chief rabbi of Trier until his death in 1827. Perhaps because he was a younger son, Heinrich himself does not seem to have been aimed at the rabbinate; the question of what career he would follow thus depended on what paths were available to Jews. The one he chose, law, would not have been open to him in a number of German states, including Prussia, where a ruling of 1812 granted Jews many civic rights but specifically excluded them from certain public professions, including those connected with the courts. As long as Trier remained under French rule, his occupation was not endangered by his origins. A French law of 1791 annulled all special laws concerning Jews and recognized them as French citizens with all the usual rights and duties. Once Trier came under Prussian control, however, he had to face the personal consequences of living under a regime that did not treat all men equally as citizens but differently according to their "estate."[13]

Heinrich Marx dealt with this situation in the only way that would allow him to remain both in Trier and in his profession: he became a Christian, probably sometime in 1817 or shortly after. That he did this with reluctance, not sharing the view of Heinrich Heine—who may have been his wife's distant cousin—that "Baptism is the ticket of admission to European culture," is indicated by several circumstances. One is that in April 1816 a Rhineland official sought an exemption that would have allowed Heinrich Marx to retain both his religion and his livelihood. Less than a year earlier, moreover, Marx himself had sought to convince the Prussian government not to impose a separate status on Jews.[14]

His intervention was not prompted by the decree of 1812, under which his own occupation would be threatened, but by a threat to some of his coreligionists. In 1808 Napoleon had issued an edict reducing the civic rights Jews had obtained by the law of 1791, and limiting their freedom of movement. Regarding Jews in general as given to usury, the decree restricted their ability to make and retrieve loans, and forbade them to contradict Christian testimony in civil suits. The decree had never been fully applied in Trier during the French period. In the German Confederation after Napoleon's defeat the edict was given its full force, however; no exceptions were to be allowed under it. This was the ruling against which Heinrich Marx protested.

His memorandum reveals much about him. He spoke as a man of the

Enlightenment, praising the eighteenth century for the tolerance it had brought, and describing contrasting religious dogmas as all "based on the same morality." At the same time, he was a forthright defender of the Jews. Despite the attempts by men like those responsible for the 1808 decree to make the Jews appear less than human, "we were and are still men. . . . And anyone who is not completely corrupted after such a long oppression bears the unmistakable stamp of noble humanity; in his breast lie indestructible seeds of virtue, and his spirit is animated by a spark of divinity." To be sure, contemporary Jews had their faults, but some of these were attributable to the conditions imposed on them, and others were shared by non-Jews. "I will not go into the question of how far the reproach of usury against many of my coreligionists is justified, nor seek out the possible causes of this in the nature of their previous political circumstances. . . . Admitted that it be true, why does one not punish them to the full extent of the law? But surely there would first have to be strong laws against usury, which—I would say in passing—would also be a very salutary restraint for many of the uncircumcised."[15]

Although he did not elaborate the reasons behind Jewish misdeeds beyond mentioning the group's political circumstances, Heinrich Marx did try to explain the origin of the Napoleonic decree that discriminated against them. In the furious days of the French Revolution, he suggested, many a French politician who wanted to make his way up "without mind and heart," had to forge his power "in the coffer of some Alsatian Jew." "But a metal which is to substitute for mind and heart is a costly treasure and cannot be too dearly bought. At least the Jew, who was not permitted to possess any other treasure, thought so. But when the demagogue attained his ambitious goal he forgot his auxiliary; and remembering only the humiliation he had suffered, he hatched his revenge."[16] These words (like his speech in 1834) reveal that Marx's father possessed a certain literary flair, as well as a willingness to speak out on public issues. They also show that he had absorbed the eighteenth-century view that men were formed by their circumstances, and that he understood both money's power and its ability to substitute for human qualities. But his appeal on behalf of the Jews was to no avail. Not only was the Napoleonic decree of 1808 applied against them, the Prussian edict of 1812, on the basis of which he himself had to undergo baptism, was also enforced. Heinrich Marx's life exhibited a dedication to the liberal principles of the Enlightenment, but it also demonstrated that the world was not really governed in accord with them.

These lessons would not be lost on his son. Karl Marx learned much from Trier. We shall see that his first public political utterances addressed exactly the political and social issues that agitated his native town while he was growing up. He would not speak out on them until he had been out of Trier for several years, however, most of which he spent as a student of law and philosophy. What he wrote in his student years was focused mostly on personal rather than political issues. On these too, his father's experiences left their mark.

2. Vocation

Karl Marx's earliest preserved writings are the series of three essays he wrote in 1835 as graduation exercises for the classical Gymnasium in Trier. He was seventeen then, one of the youngest members of a class whose average age was around twenty. One of the essays, on Roman history, suggests he already held some political convictions. Marx answered the question "Does the Reign of Augustus Deserve to be Counted among the Happier Periods of the Roman Empire?" affirmatively, on these grounds: "When people have grown soft and the simplicity of morals has disappeared, but the state has grown greater, a ruler is more capable than a free republic of giving freedom to the people." Presumably the implication was that as a general rule a republican government was preferable to a monarchy, a view that would probably have squared with Wyttenbach's, and which Marx certainly held by 1842.[17]

Marx's second essay, on religion, seems farthest removed from the man he would become, since it is an explanation and justification of Christian—and specifically Protestant—belief. It was as a Protestant that Marx had been reared since his baptism at the age of six. If his essay betrays no particular religious passion, still it shows that Marx was able to take the intellectual content of Christianity seriously. Some of his comments emphasized the connections between religion and the brotherhood of men. What seems most significant about his remarks, though, is that they showed a familiarity with ideas that constituted the Christian roots of Hegelian philosophy. Marx—who probably had little or no knowledge of Hegel in 1835—gave voice to these when he wrote that, through the union of the believer with Christ, "we feel all our iniquity but at the same time rejoice over our redemption, we can for the first time love God, who previously appeared to us as an offended ruler but now appears as a forgiving father, as a kindly teacher."[18] A similar sense that the full consciousness of sin was the ground of salvation, that men found themselves precisely where they felt most lost, and that God revealed his mercy when men most feared his justice, lay behind some of Hegel's descriptions of recovery from alienation, and behind his own view of himself as a Lutheran.

It was in Marx's third graduation essay, "Reflections of a Youth on the Choice of a Vocation," that he revealed most about the directions his life was already taking. In contemplating his future, Marx indicated how it would grow out of his past, and gave a sensitive self-portrait that is all the more valuable for not sifting his personal concerns through the screen of his own later, intensely self-conscious views about the nature of human experience.[19]

Some of what Marx wrote here was commonplace, and a few of his statements seem traceable to Wyttenbach, who sometimes spoke about the essay's topic and also assigned it. Marx avowed that the youth about to choose a profession should be guided by "the welfare of humanity, our own perfection," and that it was wrong to believe that these two interests were opposed. "Man's nature is so ordered that he can achieve his fulfillment only when he works for the perfection and welfare of his fellows."[20] Some of the other members of his class expressed similar sentiments. Yet only Marx would construct his mature identity around the rejection of any society that did not make this ideal a reality, and devote his entire life to a future in which "the free development of each is the condition for the free development of all."[21] For that reason it is important to examine the feelings and visions that arose in Marx's mind as he developed his theme.

Despite its assertion of harmony between individual and social welfare, Marx's essay linked devotion to the progress of humanity with a series of anxieties about his own future. If choosing a vocation provided a young man with an important opportunity, it also faced him with a powerful threat. "This choice is a great privilege over other creatures but at the same time an act which can destroy a man's entire life, defeat all his plans, and make him unhappy." A person deluded into making the wrong choice would find that "what we ardently pressed to our breast soon repels us, and we see our whole existence destroyed." Ambition may inspire an unsuitable choice: "Soon we shall see our wishes unfulfilled and our ideas unsatisfied. We shall have a grievance against the Deity and curse humanity."[22]

In addition to the dangers arising from the possibility of choosing wrongly, a youth was faced with personal limitations restricting his choice. The first was social: "We cannot always choose the place to which we believe we are called. Our social relations, to some extent, have already begun to form before we are in a position to determine them." This is the sentence most often quoted from the 1835 essay, for it seems to point forward toward Marx's later social theory. Because it does, however, readers easily overlook the fact that in the young Marx's mind a different "material factor" assumed much greater importance: the human body. Following the single sentence on social relations, Marx wrestled for half a page with his physical constitution. Even while recognizing the power of bodily limitations to shape a person's life, he admitted a reluctance to accept their control.

Even our physical nature often threateningly opposes us, and no one dare mock its rights!
To be sure, we can lift ourselves above it, but then we fall all the

faster. We then venture to construct a building on rotten foundations, and our entire life is an unfortunate struggle between the intellectual and the physical principle. When one cannot calm the elements fighting in himself, how can he stand up against life's tempestuous urge, how is he to act calmly? . . .

Although we cannot work for long, and seldom joyfully, with a physical nature inappropriate to our position, the thought of sacrificing our welfare to duty, of acting with weakness, yet with strength, always arises.[23]

Confronted with the limits imposed on life by bodily existence, Marx saw himself tempted—and threatened—by an impulse to "mock its rights," to revolt against physical restrictions in the name of a more ideal life. Years later he would echo the formula he used to describe this, "acting with weakness, yet with strength," in a description of proletarian revolution. "Why," Marx would declare on the eve of 1848, "social reforms are never carried by the weakness of the strong, but always by the strength of the weak."[24] Moreover, Marx's youthful temptation to try out the strength of his own weakness called up in his mind an image of "struggle between the intellectual and the physical principle." Thus, two themes that would be at the center of Marx's later vocation appeared closely linked in this early discussion of it: rebellion, and the conflict between "ideal" and "material" determinations of human life. At seventeen, Marx saw "the intellectual and the physical principle" as "elements fighting in himself," not as alternative bases for philosophical views of the world. We shall see, however, that in his doctoral dissertation six years later Marx would relate a person's manner of resolving this struggle to the philosophical position he occupied, and to the overall pattern of his life.

Choosing a vocation led Marx to reflect on one final problem: the special dangers confronting those whose calling was the life of thought. In discussing them, Marx seems to have been attempting to answer the question of his own vocation. Yet he never made that explicit, circling around the question warily before coming to rest.

The vocations which do not take hold of life but deal, rather, with abstract truths are the most dangerous for the youth whose principles are not yet solid, whose conviction is not yet firm and unshakeable, though at the same time they seem to be the most lofty ones if they have taken root deep in the breast and if we can sacrifice life and all endeavors for the ideas which rule within them.

They can make him happy who is called to them; but they destroy him who takes them overhurriedly, without reflection, obeying the moment.[25]

Why were the intellectual vocations the most dangerous? Was it only that a commitment once made to a position was difficult to review? Marx would make that point, but much more forcefully, seven years later in the newspaper article in which he first gave attention to communist theories: "*Ideas*, won by our intelligence, embodied in our outlook, and forged in our conscience, are chains from which we cannot tear ourselves away without breaking our hearts; they are demons we can overcome only by submitting to them."[26] Probably he meant to say something similar in the cooler language of 1835. Tied up with this peril was the same theme of self-sacrifice that Marx sounded with regard to his physical nature. Intellectual vocations were attractive because they offered the chance to "sacrifice life and all endeavors for the ideas which rule within them." Did this mean that such careers gave special license to the temptation to lift oneself above physical limitations, and thereby called forth the "unfortunate struggle between the intellectual and the physical principle?" Marx's words gave no clear answer to that question, but his life would offer many opportunities for reflecting on it.

Marx's essay on choosing a vocation points forward to his mature life, but before we can follow it there, we must let it lead us in the opposite direction, back into his childhood. Marx himself signaled the need to look there when he wrote that "where our reason deserts us" in the search for a place in life, "our heart calls upon our parents, who have already traveled life's path, who have tested the severity of fate."[27] We already know something of what Marx would find there, or rather, of what he had been finding as he grew into adolescence.

Karl Marx was born within a year of his father's forced conversion to Christianity. Whether or not this change in the family colored his life then, he had occasion to be affected by it later. Marx's mother, pleading concern for her own parents, did not immediately follow her husband into Protestantism; she was not baptized until 1825. None of the Marx children were baptized until August 1824, when Karl, with his younger brother and five sisters, entered the Evangelical church.[28] How did Marx respond to his own experience of baptism—into a religion still resisted by his mother—at the age of six and a half? What was he told about it? No answers to these questions exist. Sooner of later, however, he came to know that his father's calling had been the handle by which a hostile world had grasped and bent Heinrich's personal identity. Karl Marx spent his earliest years in a family whose religious division was a witness to the way society's power over men's livelihoods could play tricks on their self-conceptions, forcing them to deny their convictions.

We do not know how Heinrich Marx explained all this to his son, but we do know that he feared the effects anti-Semitic treatment of Jewish fathers might have on their children. In his protest against the Napoleonic decree of 1808, he had dealt with the claim that the edict aimed at the moral improvement of Jews, through encouraging them to give up moneylending. If that was its purpose, Heinrich asserted, the measure was badly misconceived. It could have no effect on grown-up men, fathers of families, since they were too old to learn new trades. Did it envision the reform of the young?

> But in order to win the young, one begins by depriving their fathers of their livelihood; that could only inflame the spirit of revenge in the hearts of the children. And since to serve this purpose one completely violates the fundamental laws of the state, and does not even think it necessary to preserve the usual formalities, the young must naturally become distrustful of their rights of citizenship, and choose to find security in the same old grind, because someone in a state of degradation at least evokes sympathy.[29]

Heinrich Marx was not a moneylender, hence his words did not apply directly to himself. However, two years later, when the threat to the livelihood of other Jews became a threat to his own, the consequences of his government's treatment of Jewish fathers became a question for his own son. Karl Marx would have a score to settle for his father. He would not respond quite in the way his father envisioned, but revenge and distrust toward governments were feelings not far from those he would later display. Heinrich's experience formed a backdrop for the drama of his son's choice of a calling, and it helps us to understand why he painted the decision in such anxious colors.

This is not the only aspect of Marx's feelings at seventeen that reflects his parental environment. There were more personal dimensions to Marx's relations with his family, and we can learn something about them from the surviving letters his parents wrote to him. Although all the letters come from the period after Marx left home to become a university student in 1835, the messages they contain seem to flow out of a long-established stream of parental admonition. In fact, what Marx's parents were saying to him in their letters had already taken root in his personality by 1835, and their failure to recognize this was itself a significant part of their relationship to him. There is less evidence about his mother than his more literary and intellectual father, but let us begin with her.

Henriette Marx was not entirely at home in the world she had to inhabit. Born in Holland, she found the adjustment to German and Christian Trier more difficult than her husband. Her command of the German language was never complete; at least her letters reveal very personal notions of spelling and a general lack of punctuation. Her conversion to Christianity exhibited more resistance than Heinrich's. She held back from baptism when he submitted to it, on the grounds that her parents were living, but in fact they were still alive when she finally gave in during 1825.[30] Her family regarded her life as a continual sacrifice to the welfare .of her children. In the twenty-three and a half years of her marriage she bore nine offspring, of whom three died in infancy. Those figures were not unusual for the time; nonetheless, they outline the difficulties of Henriette Marx's life.

Her letters to her son reveal her continual attention to the two basic needs of material well-being, money and physical health. Her first question to her son at the University of Bonn was about how he arranged his "little household," and "whether economy really plays the main role, which is an absolute necessity for both big and small households." Related to this was the matter of hygiene: "I will allow myself to remark, dear Karl, that you must never regard cleanliness and order as secondary things, for health and happiness are dependent upon them. Make it a point to have your rooms scrubbed often, establish a regular time for it. And scrub yourself once a week with soap and a sponge." She wanted to be informed about the little details of his life: "What about coffee—do you make it yourself, or what?" The report that he had been ill evoked her anxiety and a series of detailed instructions.

> Dear dear Karl! Your being unwell has afflicted us greatly, but I hope and wish that you are restored again. And although I am very anxious in regard to the health of my dear children, yet I am convinced that you can reach a ripe age if you take care of yourself reasonably. But for that purpose you must avoid everything that can bring on illness. You should not get too warm, nor drink much wine or coffee, nor eat anything sharp, with a lot of pepper or other spices. You should not smoke tobacco or stay up too late, and you should get up early. Protect yourself from the cold, too, and don't dance until you are fully restored. It may seem amusing to you dear Karl that I play the doctor so. But you do not know how it affects parents when their children are not well, and how many sad hours it has already caused us. Parents care only that their children are well in body and in morals, and are unconcerned about the rest.

Henriette Marx was a practical, down-to-earth woman, absorbed in the task of caring for her family. In a letter of this period Marx called her an "angel-mother."[31]

Yet that description was not his last word about his mother (later she was just "the old lady"), and it cannot be ours either. Little as we know about her relations to her family, there is reason to believe that the quality of Henriette Marx's mothering was rather intrusive and manipulative. She warned her son that his failure to follow her advice would bring him danger and her suffering. The concreteness of her demands left little to his own devising: she told him how and how often to wash himself, and exactly what not to eat, drink, and do. This style of nurture was reflected in her son, first of all in his attitude toward bodily health.

Marx was no stranger to illness as a youth. He was exempted from Prussian military service on grounds that suggest he may have suffered in his teens from tuberculosis or pleurisy, the disease that claimed his father in 1838, probably cut short the life of two of his siblings, and to which he himself finally succumbed in 1883. But his state of health did not keep him from any ordinary activities, and he obtained the medical exemption from military service at his own initiative.[32] Part of his worry about the physical nature that "threateningly opposed" him at seventeen may have been rooted in his actual experience of illness, but it also mirrored his mother's manifest and pointed fears. Even many years later, some of Marx's most characteristic behavior consisted in doing exactly the things his mother warned him against: he smoked too much, seasoned his foods highly, and worked through the night, all to the damage of his health. This neglect of bodily needs was what Marx in 1835 called "acting with weakness, yet with strength," and if we place it against his mother's detailed instructions, we see the element of revolt—against parental control as well as physical necessity—contained in it.

After his father's death in 1838 most of Marx's relations with his mother revolved around money. Heinrich had been extremely generous with money during Marx's time as a student in Bonn and Berlin (although sometimes complaining about the aristocratic scale of his son's expenditures), and Henriette, who controlled most of her husband's estate, continued to send him cash. Yet a strain of suspicion and hostility colored her support. In 1840 she wrote to him that "You will never make the moral sacrifices for your family that we have all made for you." By the beginning of 1843 Marx was writing to Arnold Ruge that "As I wrote you once before, I have fallen out with my family, and as long as my mother lives I have no right to my inheritance." In fact, he received a sizable advance on his share of the family estate in 1848 to float the *Neue Rheinische Zeitung*, but for about a decade afterward he and his mother seem to have had little to do with each other, and she gave him no aid during his leanest years in the early 1850s. Relations were reestablished in 1861, when Marx visited her in Germany and she offered to pay some of his debts. At her death two years later he received a sum large enough to support his family for over a year.* Marx probably exaggerated her stinginess, but all in all their rela-

---

*Henriette received half her husband's estate on his death (together with the return of her own dowry); the other half was to be divided one-quarter to the mother and three-quarters to the children, but the mother got the usufruct of another one-quarter while she lived as well. The amount due each of the then living children was 361 Rhenish thaler, to which another 120 thaler would be added on Henriette's death (plus a share of whatever other value her estate contained). In fact, however, Marx received payments from his mother between 1838 and 1840 amounting to 1,111 thaler. This was a substantial sum, equal to the one-third down payment Heinrich had applied to the large house he bought in 1819. It is not clear how much of the money was supposed to represent Marx's inheritance from his father, and how much constituted a continuation of the family's support of a promising member who as yet had no regular income. Marx's student expenses before his father died sometimes amounted to over 500 thaler per year, a level of expenditure which

tions were never easy or mutually trustful. A few days before his fiftieth birthday he recalled her jibe at him: "If only Karl had made some capital instead of writing a book about it."[33]

During the 1840s Marx would write angrily about parents who attempted to control their children's lives too tightly, and whose petty tyranny led to crises "analogous to those of revolutions" within families: "The most cowardly people, those least capable of standing up against others, become inexorable as soon as they are able to enforce absolute paternal authority. The misuse of the same is like a crude substitute for the various forms of subordination to which they must submit willy-nilly in civil society."[34] As we shall see in a moment, Marx would not have been likely to see his father in these terms, for his problems with Heinrich were different. Henriette did mix her nurture with demands for submission to control, and when the control failed, so might the love that accompanied it. The intrusive and overbearing quality of her relations with her son was hidden, perhaps even from herself, by the importance of maternal care in an age when, as her experience showed, the survival of children was still a precarious thing. At the same time, her desire to be central and dominating within her family may well have been a substitute for the weakness she felt outside it. Giving in to baptism in 1825 does not seem to have made her feel more comfortable in German Christian Trier. After Marx became engaged to Jenny von Westphalen in 1836, Heinrich had developed good relations with her family, who were socially above the Marxes. By 1840 Henriette was complaining that since her husband's death the von Westphalens had refused to pay her any attention.[35]

Whether its source was in his mother or not, the young Marx seems to have felt hemmed in by outside control. Not only his later comment about authority within the family but what we know about his relations with his sisters also indicates that he experienced life within a mold of domination and subjection, which shaped his perception of others. The only description of Marx as a child that has come down to us is his daughter Eleanor's account of what "I have heard my aunts say, that as a little boy he was a terrible tyrant to his sisters, whom he would 'drive' down the Markusberg at Trier full speed, as his horses, and worse, would insist on their eating the 'cakes' he made with dirty dough and dirtier hands. But

---

his father supported while loudly complaining about it. In 1841 Marx renounced any further claim to the 361 thaler in recognition of the payments his mother had already made to him, but it does not seem that this arrangement satisfied him. It may have been connected with the argument he referred to in the letter to Ruge cited in the text. The sum Marx received in 1848 was equal to slightly over 5,000 Dutch guilders. When his mother died in 1863 this sum was listed as an advance against his inheritance from her, but the earlier 1,111 thaler was declared a gift and not counted against him. Heinz Monz, *Karl Marx* (Trier, 1973), 284-91; Werner Blumenberg, "Ein Unbekanntes Kapitel aus Marx' Leben," *International Review of Social History* 1 (1956), 54-111.

they stood the 'driving' and ate the 'cakes' without a murmur, for the sake of the stories Karl would tell them as a reward for their virtue."[36]

The sources of the story are far removed from the events it purports to describe, and one must be careful not to make too much of it. Little boys often tyrannize their sisters. Yet this picture of Marx as a young boy has a special quality, suggesting that even if its details may have been exaggerated, the personal relationships it pointed to were real. Not only does it call to mind later descriptions of Marx dictating to or tyrannizing others, pushing them in directions they did not wish to go, and making them swallow ideas and opinions which felt and tasted much less savory to them than Marx's personal vision promised; it juxtaposes this image of Marx with the counterpart it would contain in his later life: Marx the intellectual seer, the story and history teller whose imaginative power allowed him to convince himself and others that his own position did not depend on willfulness or violence, but on vision.

To deal with the aggressiveness and desire for domination Marx sometimes displayed in his personal relations requires sensitive treatment because it touches on knotty and hotly disputed questions about the relations between socialism, freedom, and authoritarianism. The notion of "aggression" calls up negative images and feelings in most of us, and much conventional psychological discussion of it regards aggressive drives as abnormal, arising from frustration (at best) or from pathological strivings. More recently, however, analysts of aggression have come to recognize it as a positive and necessary part of life. The origin of aggression lies in the need for power—not power over others, but the power to be oneself and assert the independence of one's individual existence. Its sources in infancy are the young child's first movements outward from the self toward others. Indeed, the word's Latin root simply means a movement outward toward another person. "At origin," D.W. Winnicott suggests, "aggression is almost synonymous with activity." Hence, Rollo May is able to regard the opposite of aggression as "not loving peace or consideration or friendship, but isolation, the state of no contact at all." The point is that these early infantile movements are intrusions into other people's territory—in ordinary circumstances that of the child's parents—and the way adults respond to their offspring's first attempts to assert his or her own selfhood will determine where on the range between cooperative matter-of-factness and obstinate defiance the style of self-assertion any individual learns will fall.[37]

The infant must find his strength through weakness: "In origin the infant shows his power and aggressiveness always in conjunction with its opposite, i.e., with his need to be dependent and to be nourished." The young child's cry "Let me do it" is, to use Marx's language, a form of "acting with weakness, yet with strength." If that cry is heeded, the infant's need for independence will not become an issue in his life. If the cry meets recurrent resistance, then the needs it expresses can only be met by a more determined and desperate form of self-assertion. Those people who display a style of personal interaction that is aggressive in a hostile and manipulative sense are those who have experienced powerlessness in an oppressive and threatening way. In them, the need to "act with weakness, yet with strength" cannot be met by acting in harmony with other people's wills, but only in defiance of them.[38]

These remarks seem to fit both what we know about Henriette Marx's style of mothering and the mode of personal relationship that characterized her son in many stages of his life, but we must offer them with caution. In fact, we do not know how regularly she sought to control and dominate him in the way her letters to Marx at Bonn suggest. Nor would all of Marx's later relations with others fit the pattern of domination and subjection projected in the story of his youthful treatment of his sisters. Nonetheless, Marx was perceived as aggressive and domineering often enough in his later life to justify our looking closely at this early evidence. The likelihood that Marx's need to assert himself in aggressive and defiant ways was rooted in an experience of oppressive control and powerlessness in childhood is especially worth considering, since it suggests that the same early experiences that helped form this aspect of his personality may also have prepared his later sympathy for others who experienced oppression and powerlessness, and whose activity in their own behalf he labeled "the strength of the weak." It is notable that in his later role as a father Marx precisely inverted the story of his relations with his sisters, turning himself into the "horse," which his daughters were encouraged to ride and drive, either by sitting on his shoulders or by harnessing him to chairs. He was, as one of them said, "a splendid horse."[39] In this way the symbol for his childhood attempts to dominate others became an emblem of his mature sympathy for those who were weak enough to be dominated.

In contrast to his feelings about his mother, Marx always expressed warmth and respect toward his father. According to one of his daughters, he carried a picture of Heinrich with him in later life. Perhaps the elder Marx's public commitments help to explain that. Heinrich was a man of education and culture. He left a sizable library at his death (mostly composed of legal books, however), and his letters to his son sometimes touched on intellectual matters. He seems to have identified himself philosophically with Kant. In one letter he called to mind a passage he admired in Kant's *Anthropology*; in his remarks to the king of Prussia against the Napoleonic edict on the Jews he praised Kant for "giving boundaries to the philosophers." Although he wrote nothing to his son that can be called specifically either Jewish or Christian, he several times emphasized that a belief in God—the belief of "Newton, Locke and

Liebniz"—was a necessary aid for moral living. He respected practicality, morality, and devotion to duty. In his own view he was a straightforward and prosaic man.[40]

The letters he wrote to Karl Marx contained a more elaborate and complex set of messages than his wife's. In them praise alternated with condemnation, encouragement with doubt, and acceptance with rejection. He had a huge emotional investment in his son's future, and admitted that he hoped to see Karl become the man that he, Heinrich, might have been, had he begun life in circumstances as promising as Karl's. His son, therefore, possessed the disquieting power to fulfill or destroy the father's dreams. "Perhaps it is at once wrong and imprudent for one man to build his best hopes on any other, and thereby to undermine his calm, but even strong men are sometimes weak fathers," he confessed. Yet he did not expect to be disappointed. He recognized that his son possessed unusual talent, and he took over his wife's view that Karl was a "child of fortune." There were no limits to what his future might hold: "God willing, you have still a long time to live for the welfare of yourself and your family, and—if my presentiments do not err—for the welfare of humanity."[41]

On one point Heinrich Marx insisted above all else: Karl's success had to be based on moral goodness. "You know that as highly as I value your intellectual talents, they would be totally without interest to me, without a good heart."[42] It was this insistence that injected a strong note of doubt and ambivalence into his relationship with his son. While often reassuring Karl that he believed in his moral qualities, he seemed to take every opportunity to question them. The first letter he sent to Bonn contained an apparently justified reproach, for Karl had been out of Trier more than three weeks before sending any report home. Heinrich, however, did not upbraid him only for lack of consideration. "This confirms me too much in the opinion I carry with me despite all your good qualities, that egoism prevails in your heart." It is unfortunate that we do not possess Marx's reply to his father's first letter, for Heinrich's second one suggests that Karl had been upset by his father's criticism. "Certainly I entertain no doubts about your good will," Heinrich reassured him, "your energy, or in connection with your resolve to do something excellent. . . . That you will remain morally good I don't really doubt at all. However, a pure faith in God is a great aid to morality . . ."[43]

Later, after Karl had moved from the University of Bonn to Berlin in 1836, the pattern was repeated. This time we do not know exactly what Karl had done to provoke his father's initial reproaches, but he clearly took offense at them, for Heinrich insisted in return that his son was being too sensitive, and that the father had no *animus calumniandi*. Yet it is hard to be sure where the elder Marx's feelings really lay. "If I did not have a high opinion of your good heart, I would altogether pursue you less, and suffer less at your errors. . . . But you yourself admit that you have previously given me some cause to entertain some doubts about your self-denial. And in consideration of that you might have been somewhat less sensitive toward your father."[44]

Just how intense and consuming Heinrich's visions and doubts about his son could become only became clear after Karl became engaged to Jenny von Westphalen during the summer of 1836. Jenny's family was socially above the Marxes. Her father Ludwig was descended from a family of state servants and bureaucrats ennobled during the eighteenth century, which had intermarried with the Scottish nobility. He was a Prussian official in Trier, but he held liberal opinions and belonged, like Heinrich Marx, to the Casino Society. Little is really known about the relations between the two families, but it seems that only the betrothal of Karl and Jenny created close connections between them. That the von Westphalens were far from certain to approve of the engagement is indicated by the fact that it was kept from them until sometime in 1837.[45]

It was in the period before Karl and Jenny dared tell the von Westphalens of their betrothal that Heinrich Marx's complex feelings about his son received their most lyrical expression: "Sometimes my heart revels in thoughts of you and of your future. And yet, at other times, I cannot rid myself of sad ideas that raise a presentiment of fear, when like lightning the thought closes in: does your heart correspond to your head, to your talents?" Was Karl touched by really human feeling, or was he ruled by an evil demon? What had brought Heinrich to his worry this time was nothing Karl had said or done, but an observation Heinrich had made of Jenny. Sometimes she seemed to him to display—against her will—a fear, a presentiment, which the elder Marx could not explain, but which he could not get out of his mind. What caused this worry in Jenny? "Unfortunately my experience does not allow me to be easily led astray"—it was Karl. His son's future advancement and the flattering hope that he might someday be famous and wealthy were fantasies that had struck deep roots in the father's heart. But these feelings were the products of his own weakness: "pride, vanity, egoism, etc. etc. etc." Realizing such visions would not make Heinrich happy. Only (how many times had he repeated the theme before?) "if your heart remains pure and beats in a purely human way, and no demonic spirit is capable of estranging your heart from finer feelings" would he be preserved from seeing "the finest aim of my life in ruins."[46]

What Heinrich Marx made clear in this letter was that his tortuous relationship to his son reflected not only fears about Karl's moral failings but also about his own. Did he somehow hope that the perfect purity he dreamed for in his son's life would make up for a lost quality of wholeness in his? Other fathers have pinned such heavy hopes on their sons. Erik Erikson, writing of Gandhi's childhood, pointed to the likelihood "that a highly uncommon man . . . already senses in himself early in childhood some kind of originality that seems to point beyond competition with the personal father." This may make him seem "older in single-mindedness than his conformist parents, who in turn may treat him somehow as their potential redeemer. Thus he grows up almost with an obligation, beset with guilt, to surpass and create at all cost."[47]

Marx was treated in just this way by his father, and he certainly felt the obligation Erikson describes. If he was "beset with guilt," his feelings reflected Heinrich's, whose fears about his own egoism fed a moral attitude in which sacrifice was the first principle.

> The first of all human virtues and powers is the will to sacrifice oneself, to neglect ones "I" when duty, when love require it—and not in brilliant moments of romance or heroism, the act of fancy or romantic feeling. Even the greatest egoist is capable of those, for exactly then the *I* shines most brightly. No, it is those daily and hourly returning sacrifices that spring from the pure heart of the good man, the loving father, the tender mother, the loving husband, the thankful child, which lend to life its only charm and beautify it in spite of all adversities.[48]

In the face of this model of denial, one is tempted to respond to Heinrich Marx's worries about his son's egoism with a phrase Marx would use in *Capital*: *de te fabula narratur* ("the story is about you"). That is only partially to the point, however; what counts for us is the power Heinrich's ethic of sacrifice was already assuming in his son's life.

Not only was sacrifice a major theme of the essay on choosing a vocation, it was already a visible part of Marx's behavior. In his actions it took exactly the form he had written about in 1835: trying to rise above his physical limitations, and thus "sacrificing our welfare to duty" in a way that produced illness and a struggle between "the intellectual and the bodily principle." Marx's parents, however, did not regard this behavior as the fruit of the ethic they had sought to implant in him, and warned him continually against what seemed to them a pointless penchant for illness.

In his second letter to Karl at Bonn, in November 1836, Heinrich Marx advised his son not to neglect his body while he fed his mind, for the body was the mind's constant companion, and it "conditions the functioning of the whole machine." And he added a caution, which he would repeat a few months later: "A sickly scholar is the unhappiest being on earth. Don't study more than your health can stand." The warning was prophetic: by the end of the year Marx had become ill in a way which, "Unless the description of your condition was somewhat poetical—as I hope it was—is well adapted to cause us disquiet." Heinrich added that he hoped the sad experience would show Karl the need to be more attentive to his health, "after a good conscience a man's highest good." A year later, after Karl moved to Berlin, his father again entreated him: "The only thing I ask of you is not to overdo your studying, but conserve your bodily strength and your so badly tried vision." (In later life, Marx would sometimes have to break off work for a period to recover from eye inflammation brought on by working through the night in poor light.) And a month after that: "It is high time that you did away with the tension that drives your mind and body apart."[49]

Heinrich's comments suggest that he regarded Karl's pattern of overwork and sickness as visible even before he left Trier. Perhaps what Marx wrote in his graduation essay about attempting to rise above bodily limitations reflects earlier conversations between them. But in Karl's mind, "acting with weakness, yet with strength" was associated with the ideal his father so insistently sponsored: self-sacrificing devotion to humanity. Why did Heinrich Marx fail to see that his son's behavior embodied the very quality of sacrifice he demanded? What blocked his vision at this point was that his picture of sacrifice was framed by conformity with the everyday means of making one's way in the world. He insisted that Karl give attention to the needs of advancement in some career (although he was willing to let his son decide exactly what that career would be) and pestered him to make contacts with people who might be helpful to him later on. He demanded that Karl look into the specific requirements of age and experience for an academic post, and he expressed pleasure when his son showed some willingness and talent for doing these things. Karl's "rigorous principles" against any improper self-advancement reminded him of his own youthful scruples, but he placed them firmly beneath practical necessity.[50]

To Heinrich, then, any behavior that interfered with his vision of Karl's future smacked of egoism, not self-sacrifice. It demonstrated that Karl was placing his own desires and impulses above his parents' expectations. Thus, Karl's unconcern about his health signified rebellion, not obedience. All the elder Marxes' hopes would be dashed if their son let himself sink into chronic illness through too much studying.

The younger Marx's conduct bespoke a different sense of the relationship between egoism and self-sacrifice. Self-sacrifice did not mean submitting his personal desires to his parents' practical counsels but merging his being with some universal goal. From his point of view, the ordinary bourgeois careerism his father sought to foster in him must have appeared—as indeed it was—difficult to reconcile with the ethic of service to humanity. Obeying his father on one level required rebelling against him on another. Thus, a complex and powerful dialectic of egoism and sacrifice entered his life as his growing sense of his own individuality interacted with his family's hopes and values. Making sense of this confused inheritance would be one of his lifelong tasks.

Closely associated with that task would be Marx's attempt to determine the place of intellect in human life. In this region, too, his father helped prepare the ground. The elder Marx was something of an intellectual. He was well read, seemed to enjoy writing, spoke out in public, moved in cultured circles, and held views on a wide variety of general topics. He referred to Kant with admiration and gave evidence of having actually read him. He knew something about Hegelianism too; as we shall see, he disapproved of it. Like a good *Aufklärer* he placed a high value on freedom of thought. His devotion to intellectual freedom emerges from a letter discussing the choice of a subject for a long poem Karl hoped to write. Heinrich suggested the defeat of Napoleon. Apart from being a topic that recommended itself to Prussian patriotism, he thought it could not fail to arouse enthusiasm because Napoleon had threatened to place humanity "and especially the mind" in chains. "Whoever has studied his history and seen what he understood under the foolish expression Ideology can celebrate his defeat and Prussia's victory with a good conscience."[51]

Ideology: the term would later have a central place in Marx's world view. He was aware of it long before he and Engels wrote *The German Ideology* in 1845-46. The word had been coined late in the eighteenth century, by a group of French thinkers who called themselves *"idéologues,"* and who sought to establish a science of the human mind. In their usage ideology did not mean any of the things it has come to signify in our language, but (in the words of Destutt de Tracy) "a precise and concrete description of our intellectual faculties, of their principal phenomena, and their most noteworthy determinants." Continuing the eighteenth-century tradition of environmental determinism that stemmed from Locke and Condillac, the *idéologues* sought to construct a science of intellectual life based on both physiology and social experience. But Napoleon gave the term a different meaning. From being supporters of Bonaparte, the *idéologues* became some of his sharpest critics, and in responding to them he turned their belief in the dependence of thought on real life to his own uses. Speaking to the French Council of State in 1812, Napoleon characterized "ideology" as "shadowy metaphysics" that sought to base politics on "first causes," rather than on "the human heart and the lessons of history." Because its supporters attributed to the people "a sovereignty they were incapable of exercising," ideology was the source of vain abstractions that made an ordered social and political life impossible.[52]

In the early nineteenth century Napoleon's recoinage of the term was widely known. Walter Scott explained that by ideology Napoleon had meant "every species of theory of which, resting in no respect upon the basis of self-interest, could, he thought, prevail with none save hot-brained boys and crazed enthusiasts." Friends of liberty were angry at the French emperor for his attitude. Ralph Waldo Emerson complained that "the advocates of liberty and of progress are 'ideologists' in his mouth."[53] Like other progressives of his age, Heinrich Marx was repelled by Napoleon's belief that only those ideas that expressed some practical interest mattered; mind was not bounded by interest. Although in his remarks on the Napoleonic decree of 1808 he had praised Kant for giving "boundaries to the philosophers," Heinrich understood that Kant had meant to restrict speculative thinking in order to shore up two other sources of general ideas, morality and religion.

We do not know whether Karl Marx first learned the word ideology from his father, but that is not important. He was certainly the witness to a set of contradictions inherent in Heinrich's use of it, contradictions that paralleled the questions of egoism and sacrifice. At the same time that he protested Napoleon's general reduction of creative thinking to practical interest, Heinrich encouraged his son to treat his poetic endeavor as a means to advance his personal self-interest. He was proud of Karl's youthful poetry (although he confessed he was too prosaic to understand much of it), but he saw it principally as a tool for speeding up his professional advancement by making a name as a writer. The desirability of making a reputation without delay increased, he felt, after Karl's engagement to Jenny von Westphalen created the need to show himself worthy of an aristocratic young woman and her family. Heinrich had no trouble making his ambition for his son morally presentable, but he firmly subordinated the poetry to its practical purpose: "One who takes on higher duties must be consistent with them, and in the eyes of the poet himself the cunning, the prudence will be made holy by the high and fine fulfillment of duty."[54]

Here, as in his views on egoism and sacrifice, Heinrich Marx's practical advice compromised his theoretical position: in general he valued thought for its freedom from self-interest, but in Karl's case he schemed to make poetry serve a practical need. Part of Marx's later development would suggest a struggle to make sense of these messages. As a Hegelian journalist in 1842-43 Marx would identify himself with reason as the promoter of the general welfare against all forms of selfish interest; around this idealistic conception he began a successful journalistic career. Later, however, when Marx declared all thought to be the reflection of social interests, he would remove himself from the ladder of private ambitions and recognized occupations toward which his father had pointed him.

In all these ways the direction Marx's life was taking in his days as a Gymnasium and university student was shaped by his family. His parents' behavior toward him embodied some of the ambivalence and contradiction he later discovered in bourgeois society, while at the same time providing the mold for much of his own formation. His reception of their nurture was also ambivalent and contradictory, mixing obedience and rebellion; absorbing their values into his life, but in a fashion that expressed his developing sense of independence. His vocation was not yet chosen, but he already displayed some of the elements that would compose it.

3. Conversion

Exactly why Marx transferred from the University of Bonn, which was relatively close to Trier, to faraway Berlin is unknown. The Marx family approved of the move, but the story told in old biographies that Heinrich wanted to separate Karl from Jenny is false. The engagement made Heinrich a bit nervous, but it nurtured his hopes for his son's future, and did not jar with his plans. Marx himself was more that a little distracted by thoughts of Jenny, whom—now as later—he loved with a deep romantic passion, for which, as he said, poetry could be the only expression. But his father kept reminding him of his practical goals, and tried to keep his mind on the realities of his situation.[55]

At first Marx seemed to follow the lines his father was setting down for him. He made contacts both men expected would be useful to him, much to Heinrich's pleasure. In February 1837 the elder Marx praised his son for showing evidence of overcoming "the little weaknesses which, by the way, disquieted me" and for giving attention to assuring his future.[56] It was in this period that Karl Marx took up an intellectual position Heinrich welcomed and probably inspired: opposition to Hegel. The connection of Marx's early anti-Hegelianism with his father is not usually noticed, but the evidence for the link is clear enough. Heinrich Marx had a fondness for Kant; not only did he praise and cite him, his whole ethic of duty and self-sacrifice was colored by Kantian philosophy. This was one thread that tied him to Karl's teacher, Wyttenbach. When, in the fall of 1837, Karl confessed that he had become a Hegelian, Heinrich was incensed, condemning Hegel's followers as "the modern demons."[57] What he meant by that phrase is not perfectly clear; however, David Friedrich Strauss's book, *The Life of Jesus*, which made visible the split between left and right Hegelians when it appeared in 1835, identified Hegelianism with the radical criticism of religion, and Heinrich, as we know, was worried about Karl's preserving his faith in God.

Heinrich rejected the Hegelians on another count, and it is this that ties his son's early anti-Hegelianism most clearly to his own. In his view, Hegel's followers "screw their words up so tightly that they cannot hear themselves; because their torrent of words conveys no thoughts, or confused ones, they baptize it as a birth of genius."[58] Heinrich's condemnation, spewed out in the midst of a stream of deeply felt reproaches against his erring son, bears the stamp of genuine conviction. It is remarkable, therefore, that Karl Marx had elaborated exactly this image of Hegel a few months earlier, in a series of epigrams contained in a book of poems dedicated to his father on Heinrich's birthday. One of them read:

Words I teach in a demoniacally confused to-do,
And everyone may then think what he chooses.

At least he will never more be restricted by limiting fetters,
For as out of a roaring flood pouring from a projecting rock,
The poet invents the words and thoughts of his beloved,
And perceives what he thinks and thinks what he feels,
So everyone can sip the refreshing nectar of wisdom;
After all, I am telling you everything because I have told you
  nothing.[59]

If not actually inspired by Heinrich, this image of Hegel was certainly welcome to him.

If these features of Karl Marx's first months in Berlin reflected loyalty to his father, however, the personal evolution he described in his only preserved letter to Heinrich could only appear to his father as a betrayal. Written in the night between November 10 and 11, 1837, Marx's letter recounted the events of the past year and showed how they led him to Hegel.[60] The journey took a form of which Heinrich was bound not to approve. Whereas the elder Marx had advised his son to establish connections with influential men and not to overdo his studying, Karl "broke all existing ties, reluctantly made very few visits, and sought to immerse myself in science and art." Whereas Heinrich warned Karl to preserve his health and keep his practical goal firmly in mind, the young man followed a different course. "During the first semester I was awake many a night, engaged in these multifarious occupations. I went through many struggles and experienced much stimulation from within and without. Yet, in the end, I found that my mind had not been greatly enriched while I had neglected nature, art, and the world, and had alienated my friends. My body apparently reacted. A physician advised a stay in the country." In place of the idealism with which he had arrived in Berlin, "nourished with Kant and Fichte," Marx described himself as born "into the clutches of the enemy," Hegel. Even if—for reasons that will appear in a moment—we cannot share Heinrich Marx's view that Karl's course amounted to a betrayal of the father, it certainly meant an estrangement from him. Marx recognized his experience as one of those "moments in life which mark the close of a period like boundary posts and at the same time definitely point in a new direction."[61]

Marx felt—and tried to make his father see—that his Hegelianism was true to his family's expectations. For him, the move to Hegel meant a turn toward realism. In one of his earlier epigrams he had derided Hegel for not seeking the ideal outside of ordinary life, as Kant and Fichte had done, but instead finding the materials of his philosophy "in the street."[62] Marx was referring to the contrast between Kant's ideal of duty, which could only be discovered by reason and which could not be justified within the world of experience, and Hegel's presentation of ethics and reason as growing out of real experience and becoming manifest in actual life. In his

Kantian phase he had written poetry that he now described as made up of "onslaughts against the present, broad and shapeless expressions of unnatural feeling, built out of moon rock, the complete opposition of what is and what ought to be."[63] What he meant can be seen from portions of one of his verses, "Feelings":

> I am caught in endless strife
> Endless ferment, endless dream;
> I cannot conform to life,
> Will not travel with the stream.
>
>   . . .
>
> Worlds I would destroy for ever
> Since I can create no world,
> Since my call they notice never,
> Coursing dumb in magic whirl.[64]

Marx attributed this state of mind first of all to the freshness of his passion for Jenny, and to the fact that since the von Westphalen family was still in the dark, she could not write to him. Yet it was not only his "position" that called forth these feelings but also his "whole previous development."[65]

The contrast between this mood of isolation and destruction and the standpoint Marx thought Hegel offered him was one he could reasonably have expected Heinrich to appreciate. He turned to Hegel to calm the conflict he had felt between ideal and reality. His purpose was "seeking the Idea in the real itself. If formerly the gods had dwelt above the world, they had now become its center." Marx's attempts to work out a philosophy of law on a Kantian basis had led him to pure abstraction, arbitrary organization, and ultimate emptiness. Hegel, on the other hand, offered an approach to "the concrete expression of the living world of thought," in which categories were not imposed from outside, but grew out of actual experience. Once he had arrived at a Hegelian position, Marx felt himself free to turn to "positive studies."[66] Was not all this what his parents were demanding of him? "I take the actual state of things as it is," Heinrich had written in an earlier letter. His point of view was that of "real life, as it actually is," he repeated in his reply to Karl's confession of November 10. Henriette, too, tried to make her son see that "the higher and better is achieved through the lower."[67]

Arriving at his new position cost Marx a great deal of pain. To begin with he suffered a physical illness whose exact nature is not known, but which Marx saw he had brought on himself, both by neglect and overwork, and—as he said in his letter—from "grief . . . futility . . . [and] vexation."[68] His Berlin sickness recalled his earlier bout at Bonn. Even more clearly than the earlier episode, it was a surrender to that temptation to revolt against physical necessity, to act "with weakness, yet with strength," to which he had confessed in his 1835 essay.

Marx's suffering was not only physical. His various projects—law, philosophy, poetry—all came to nothing. He had written a philosophy of law that extended (he reported) to nearly three hundred pages before convincing himself of its emptiness. Feeling the need for a philosophical orientation after this failure, he had attempted to write a "new basic metaphysical system," but "Upon its completion I was again constrained to recognize its futility and that of all my previous endeavors." In poetry, too, he experienced a moment when "the realm of true poetry flashed open before me like a distant faery palace, and all my creations collapsed into nothing." Finding himself drawn into the camp of the Hegelians whom he had earlier detested, he felt himself carried "into the clutches of the enemy." Thus, his crisis reached its deepest point at the moment of its resolution: "Because of my vexation, I was for several days quite unable to think. Like a lunatic I ran around in the garden. . . . I even went out hunting with my host and then returned hotfoot to Berlin, wishing to embrace every loafer at the street corners."[69]

It was a sense of having lost his moorings that brought Marx to Hegel. Having read fragments of Hegel earlier and found his "grotesque, craggy melody unpleasing," Marx plunged in again, "but with the definite intention of discovering our mental nature to be just as determined, concrete, and firmly established as our physical." By the time he wrote to his father he believed that intention fulfilled, for he compared his position to those moments when world history eases "itself back into an armchair to comprehend itself and penetrate intellectually its own act, the act of the mind." He could write about his experience because "every transformation is to some extent a swan song, to some extent the overture to a great new poem." Although he knew Heinrich would not be pleased at what he had to tell him, he expected clemency and sympathy. "How could much that is objectionable and blameworthy better find compensation and pardon than by becoming the manifestation of an essentially necessary condition?"[70] Marx looked to Hegel for moral and psychological reassurance, even—given his state of mind and health—a kind of therapy.

Hegel himself had experienced the psychological strains of adolescence, and from his experience he had constructed a theory of the human life cycle. Did Marx know that theory in 1837? It is certain that he knew it later, for he corrected some of Max Stirner's borrowings from it in 1845. It may not be correct to take literally Marx's claim in the letter to his father that he already knew Hegel "from beginning to end." Yet it would not be unreasonable to suppose that Marx meant by this phrase that he had read the only comprehensive summary of Hegel's whole philosophy, the *Encyclopaedia of the Philosophical Sciences*. It was there that the life cycle theory appeared in its most explicit form.[71]

Whether Marx knew the theory or not, the description of his development he gave his father corresponded closely to it. In the terms of Hegel's life cycle, the position Marx believed he had attained in 1837 was "manhood." It was based on "seeking the Idea in the real itself." It succeeded an earlier stage in which "everything real grew vague," when Marx had written "I cannot conform to life,/ Will not travel with the stream," and when he had given himself over to "onslaughts against the present." In between had come a period of physical and mental sickness, and an inability to do productive work. Becoming a Hegelian did not solve all Marx's problems, for he seems to have been taken ill a second time after his return from the country, and his mood was one in which "all tones were muted and a fit of irony possessed me as was natural after so many negations." However, he was able to pursue "positive studies," and before finishing his letter to his father he returned to the discussion of how to further his career.[72]

Marx's Hegelianism became part of his attempt to prepare a future livelihood. Although some members of the Hegelian left would later lose their jobs or be hounded out of Prussia, to become a Hegelian in 1837 was by no means to place oneself outside respectable society. As a Hegelian, Marx had every expectation of attaining a university post. Some of the friends he now made among Hegel's philosophical followers in the Berlin Doctor's Club—notably Bruno Bauer and Adolf Rutenberg—had already begun to get a foot on the academic ladder. In the next few years Marx himself would complete and publish a dissertation on classical philosophy, and later—when the changed official attitude toward Hegel closed off a university career—become the editor of a newspaper backed by eminently respectable Cologne businessmen.

Nor did Marx break with his father in 1837. Although Heinrich was hurt and outraged by his son's behavior and his conversion, he later accepted Karl's assurance that (as Heinrich repeated it) "your philosophy satisfactorily agrees and harmonizes with your conscience." Once again he assured his son of his faith in his "high morality."[73] It was the last repetition of the old pattern, for Heinrich Marx died soon afterward, in May 1838. Despite the growing tensions between the two, only death broke off relations between them.

With Marx's conversion to Hegel, a chapter in his life ended. The next years would show, however, that—contrary to his view at the time—what he had attained at nineteen was not manhood but only a critical moment in his adolescence. The discovery of his mature place in the world, his own manner of becoming "really *somebody*"—as Hegel put it—still lay in the future. Nonetheless, the themes of Marx's early development would continue to sound in his later life. He would still feel the need to preserve himself from the isolation that the thinker's revolt against the limitations of ordinary existence entailed when, some years later, he would try to link his philosophy to reality through a different kind of rebellion.

CHAPTER THREE

The Young Hegelian

MARX'S encounter with Hegel colored his whole life, but the period in which he was a declared disciple, "chained to the current world philosophy" (as he wrote to his father), lasted some six years. This period, between his Berlin conversion to Hegelianism and his departure from the *Rheinische Zeitung* early in 1843, covered the end of Marx's teens and his early twenties. It was a time of impressive achievement. Before reaching twenty-five Marx had published a learned and original doctoral dissertation, and successfully edited a widely read newspaper in Cologne. He had begun to make a name for himself in Germany, both as a philosopher and as a journalist. His progress along this path came to a sudden stop, however, following the Prussian government's repression of the *Rheinische Zeitung*, and his marriage to Jenny von Westphalen in 1843. By the end of that year he had left Germany for France and begun to discover a new perspective on the world and his place in it.

The subjects of Marx's writings in this period were philosophy and politics. He dealt with these topics in ways that foreshadowed his later, more famous, writings, but the positions he took contrasted with his later views. As a Hegelian, he was a philosophical idealist and a political liberal, albeit one with clear radical overtones. Underlying his explicit philosophical and political commitments, however, were a set of implicit concerns that were still visible at this stage, although they would recede from view as time went on. More clearly now than later, Marx's politics and his views of the contemporary world were colored by a meditation on the shape his own life would take.

1. Philosophy, Isolation, and Inversion

Of all Marx's early writings, his doctoral thesis sheds the most light on both his early orientation and his later development; yet of all his works it is among the least known. Devoted to the history of classical philosophy, the dissertation Marx wrote in Berlin (but submitted to the University of Jena, because degrees were easier to obtain there) was called *The Difference between the Democritean and Epicurean Philosophy of Nature*.[1] In that form, however, it was to be (Marx declared) "only the preliminary to a larger essay, in which I will present in detail the cycle of Epicurean, Stoic and Sceptical philosophy, in relation to all Greek Speculation." Marx regarded these later Greek schools as "the key to the true history of Greek philosophy," and devoted himself to them because "the gigantic thinker," Hegel, while he had perceived the overall character of late Greek thought, had failed to recognize "in these systems the great importance that they have for the history of Greek philosophy and for the Greek mind in general." Marx admitted that the three later systems did not embody Greek philosophy in its full strength and vigor, "but the death of a hero resembles the setting of the sun, not the bursting of a frog which has blown itself up." The death of Greek thought reflected its life. "Here we observe, as it were, the *curriculum vitae* of a philosophy focused to the subjective point, just as one can conclude a hero's life story from the way he died."[2] The theme Marx sounded was one of Hegel's favorites: fate is character.

Marx developed this theme by focusing on the personal character of individual Greek philosophers, who represented what he called "the subjective form, the spiritual carrier of philosophical systems, which we have until now almost entirely ignored in considering only their metaphysical pronouncements."[3] He explained this concentration on individuals in an essay he wrote as part of his projected larger history of Greek thought, but which he did not include in his published dissertation. Here he sketched the overall history of Greek speculation through an account of the *sophos*, the wise man or sage. The essay showed that the special position held by individual men of wisdom in Greek culture was a sign that Greek philosophy faced a tragic destiny which, thanks to Hegel, modern thinkers could avoid.[4]

The fact that all the Greek schools made use of the *sophos* in explaining the notion of philosophical wisdom proved that Greek thinking was bound up with the experience of individual wise men, beginning with the seven ancient sages, and best represented by Socrates. In Greece wisdom had belonged exclusively to the inner world of particular individuals, not the outer world of actual existence. "The Greek philosopher is a demiurge, his world is other than the one that flourishes in the natural sun of substantial existence."[5]

Greek thinking had not always displayed this separation of thought from life; its earliest forms embodied a primitive unity of man and nature. Philosophy was the spirit of collective life. As the Greek states developed, however, their early social and political harmony dissolved. Reason or mind (*nous*) no longer appeared as the expression of actual social life, but as "the reason proper to the philosopher." By the time of the sophists and Socrates, the original Greek equation of rationality with collective life "is inverted. Now it is ideality itself, in its immediate form as a *subjective spirit* that becomes the principle of philosophy." As philosophical reason withdrew from the world of actual existence, everyday life appeared to degenerate into "a mass of accidentally limited forms of existence and institutions," whose inner unity and identity had been usurped by the "subjective spirits" of the sophists. Actuality was now judged by a philosophical vision of the way things "ought" to be.[6]

In Socrates this split between reason and existence reached full expression. Its symbol was the "demon" Socrates said accompanied him through his life, the inner voice to which his outer actions had to submit. The demon represented the ideals of reason, independent of actual life, and Socrates' personal existence was devoted to serving it. As a man of flesh and blood, however, Socrates could not survive the split between the ideal reality he carried within him and the material world in which he had to live. He was "divided within himself and condemned," and his death stood for the wider fate of Greek thought, revealing "the relationship of Greek philosophy to Greek life and thereby its inner contraction into itself."[7]

Marx contrasted Greek philosophy's withdrawal into a realm where reason and life could not meet with the modern, post-Hegelian situation. Modern philosophy was not condemned as Greek thought had been. "How foolish it was in recent times to compare the relationship of Hegelian philosophy to life with that of Greek philosophy and thereby to deduce a warrant for its condemnation appears at once. The specific malady of Greek philosophy is exactly that it stands in an external relationship to the merely substantial spirit. In our time both sides are spirit and both want to be recognized as such." Hegelian philosophy could discover the ideal component of existence within actual life because it had discovered how reason emerged from the struggles of the real world. Therefore, it would not withdraw from life in the name of thought. Founded as it was precisely on a rejection of the subjectivism that had been the root malady of Greek speculation, modern philosophy would be preserved from the self-destructive isolation that had been the fate of the Greeks.[8]

Marx's account of the origin and nature of Greek philosophy as represented by the figure of the *sophos* followed Hegel in outline, but Marx colored the images with a more somber palette. Hegel had presented Socrates as a man whose entire existence was determined by an independent ideal of reason, and had seen that Socrates was condemned by the contradiction between this ideal and Greek reality. He had emphasized also that Socrates' personality, wholly shaped by "one inward principle," resembled a perfect classical work of art in its harmony and unity.[9] Marx did not focus on Hegel's vision of the unity and harmony of classical civilization; what he noticed and elaborated was the isolation suffered by ancient thinkers.

Marx saw in the Greek philosophers the symptoms of a condition he believed he had overcome. His own pre-Hegelian idealism, as he told his father in 1837, had led him to "onslaughts against the present," based on "a complete opposition of what is and what ought to be." Like the Greeks, he had rejected ordinary reality and its limits in the name of mind. The result of this inner division had been illness, not serious enough to threaten his life, but in its way painful enough. Hegel had shown Marx the way out of these straits in 1837; the power Marx now attributed to Hegel, to preserve modern philosophy from the fate of ancient thinkers, projected his own experience onto a wider historical stage.

In his published dissertation, Marx sought to describe the dilemma of ancient philosophy as it was revealed by the contrast between Democritus and Epicurus as philosophers of nature. This was a less ambitious project than his planned history of the post-Aristotelian Greek schools; it dealt with only one late Greek thinker, Epicurus, and contrasted him (except for occasional hints) with a pre-Socratic thinker, Democritus. Nonetheless, Marx was able to draw broad lessons even from this narrower subject.

The basic difference was that Democritus was a complete materialist in his natural philosophy, whereas Epicurus analyzed nature as a compound of ideal and material existence. Discovering this contrast was the chief technical originality of Marx's treatise. An authoritative tradition of commentary from Cicero to Pierre Bayle had described Epicurean physics as a simple copy of Democritus' atomic theory, distinguished only by some arbitrary and inconsistent modifications of it. Marx presented Epicurus instead as an original and important thinker whose differences from Democritus reflected a more profound understanding of the meaning of atomic theory.

True, Epicurus had derived the basic theory of matter from Democritus. He followed the earlier thinker in attributing two motions to the atoms, an original one of falling in a straight line, and a second that arose through the repulsion of each atom for every other. Epicurus had added a third form of atomic motion, the "swerve," or declination from a straight line, which he regarded as essential. Until Marx, Epicurus had been universally derided for introducing this swerve of the atoms, since he offered no causal explanation for it. In Marx's view, however, it was precisely the declination of the atoms that made Epicurus' theory superior to that of Democritus, and allowed him to present the concept of the atom as the foundation of existence.

In order to posit the atom as the underlying reality of nature, the primary form of being, it had to be conceived as "a pure form, the negation of all relativity, of all relation to another mode of being." If its original motion was thought to consist only in falling, then the atom's existence would be determined by the straight line it followed, it would be "nothing but a moving point, a point without autonomy," which "renounces its individuality." If its motion were only a straight line, then "its existence is purely material."[10] That Epicurus had offered no causal explanation for the extra movement only demonstrated his deeper understanding of what atomic theory was about. "To ask about the cause of this determination is consequently to ask about the cause which makes this atom a principal element—a question which is clearly senseless in the eyes of those for whom the atom is the cause of everything but is itself without cause."[11]

Epicurus' ability to comprehend both "the material side" and "the ideal side" of existence in a single description of reality gave him a link to Hegel that the materialist Democritus could not claim.[12] Yet Epicurus' overall philosophical standpoint was not Hegel's, for he had necessarily shared the conceptual limitations of his time. Greek philosophy had not been able to find rationality in "the whole," the concrete unity of individual and collective existence. As "the first form of self-consciousness," Greek speculation could not get beyond the immediate individual in his separate existence, the "abstractly individual thing."[13] As a result, Epicurus' philosophy of nature fell into contradiction with itself as soon as it attempted to go beyond individual existence (i.e., the existence of the atoms) and comprehend "the general" that lay outside. This point was reached in Epicurus' attempt to describe the existence of the stars and planets.

Rejecting the view of all other Greek thinkers, Epicurus had denied that the heavenly bodies were indestructible, and he refused to accept any regular, scientific account of their motions. This seemed difficult to understand, since his atomic theory was offered as an explanation of natural phenomena, and the celestial motions were the obvious place to test it. The planets and meteors were a kind of visible show of atoms in motion: "the heavenly bodies are atoms become real." For Epicurus to regard the whole display of planetary motions as transitory and inexplicable was certainly contradictory, for "he alleged that he created the atoms so that immortal foundations would lie at the basis of nature." Yet not only did he deny any underlying regularity in the heavens, he even insisted that one could not know more about them than the senses revealed. He claimed that the sun was no larger than it seemed. "He fights not only against astrology but against astronomy itself, against eternal law and reason in explaining the heavenly system."[14]

The reason for this, Marx believed, lay in the basic principle of Epicurean—and all classical Greek—speculation: the autonomy of the abstract, individual self-consciousness. Epicurus could express the existence of this form of consciousness with perfect consistency only by objectifying its inner contradictions. This meant he had to deny that any other form of existence was either rational or necessary. In refusing to admit any necessity outside the individual, he swept away the traditional Greek conception of heavenly powers ruled by eternal laws. Thus, "his greatest contradiction"—the denial of the rationality of nature as manifested in astronomy—was also his "most thorough consistency" and "the deepest wisdom of his system." At this point in his system, "the individual self-consciousness steps out of its husk, announces itself as the true principal element and contends against nature which has become autonomous."[15]

In his essay on the history of the *sophos* Marx had found the character of the Greek sage expressed "most consistently in the atomic philosophy of Epicurus."[16] One reason he thought so should be clear now. In Epicurus, Greek philosophy died a hero's death. He carried Greek subjectivity to its highest point, making abstract individuality into the principle of nature itself, and basing a whole system of natural philosophy on it. His was the only genuinely philosophical approach to nature possible in his age, because it consistently employed the only concept available to the Greeks, that of simple, abstract individuality. His contradictions only made explicit the necessary limitations of all Greek thought. Because of his thoroughgoing rationality, Epicurus became the defender of philosophy against the whole existing world. He was "the greatest Greek representative of the Enlightenment." Through his efforts religion was "cast down and trampled underfoot, whilst we by the victory are exalted high as heaven."[17]

Like Epicurus, Democritus also fell into contradictions that vitiated his attempts to explain natural phenomena, but in his case they arose at the beginning rather than the end of his philosophical project. Ancient views about him suggested his inconsistency. In one passage Aristotle reported that Democritus had been a philosophical sceptic, who held "that either there is no truth or we cannot discover it." In another place Aristotle described him as a believer in the truth of sense perceptions, for whom "the phenomenon is the true." These contradictions were manifest in his views about nature. Democritus claimed that the atom was the principal element of existence, yet he denied that any phenomenon of nature made the atoms perceptible in the visible world. For him, the world of sense impressions was a realm of mere opinion and illusion. As a materialist, however, Democritus had to regard the world of ordinary experience as the only world, "the sensible appearance is the only true object." His contradictory view of the material world as at once real and illusory made it impossible for him to achieve—as Epicurus would—a philosophical account of nature consistent with his own first principles.

> Democritus, for whom the principal element does not enter appearance and remains without reality and existence, is on the other hand faced with the world of sensible perception as a real and concrete world. This world is, to be sure, subjective illusion, but just because of this, it is torn free from the principal element, left in its autonomous reality; at the same time it is the unique, real object, and as such has value and importance.

Faced with his inability to make sense of the natural world in purely philosophical terms, Democritus was led to look beyond philosophy. "Democritus is consequently driven to empirical observation. Dissatisfied with philosophy, he throws himself into the arms of positive knowledge." Democritus fled from philosophy to the empirical study of nature.[18]

Marx approved the devotion to real knowledge demonstrated by this turn to natural science, but from a philosophical point of view it constituted a weakness. It reflected Democritus' inability to comprehend the true essence of nature, which Epicurus would discover in the atoms' individual autonomy and ideality. Able to see only the material side, Democritus missed the element within nature that resisted control by purely material forces. As a result, he had no philosophical basis for resisting that control himself. He could not support the struggle for autonomy and independence waged by individual men in the present, but saw those qualities as attainable only in some "beyond," in an other-worldly future. Whereas Epicurus had pulled religion down in order to raise humanity up, with Democritus "the door is opened wide to superstitious and servile mysticism."[19]

These contrasts between the philosophical views of the two Greek writers were intensified by Marx's portraits of the character and personality of each. Marx found the personal situation of each thinker expressed in the content of his system. "In the general relationship which the philosopher establishes between the world and thought," he declared, a philosopher "merely makes objective the relation between his particular consciousness and the real world."[20] Democritus and Epicurus represented the two poles of that relation to reality in classical Greece.

The two thinkers shared the general inability of Greek speculation to comprehend the individual and the external world as part of a unified whole. Neither possessed the qualities necessary to understand both spheres; the virtues that would all be present in a complete philosophical personality were divided between them. Epicurus was able to work out his philosophy of nature on the basis of individual self-consciousness because he preserved an undiluted scorn for positive science. Only in the materialist Democritus could Marx discover enthusiasm and seriousness in the search for natural causes. Marx admired his declaration: "I would rather discover a new etiology than acquire the dignity of the Persian crown!" Epicurus was manifestly "not at all interested in investigating the real causes of objects." He wanted to determine only "what is abstractly possible, what can be conceived. . . . Whether this possibility is also real is a matter of indifference, because we are not here interested in the object as object."

Epicurus sought edification, not science. "He is merely interested in soothing the explaining subject," not in acquiring "knowledge of nature in and of itself." His life was a model of withdrawal and passivity. Whereas the search for knowledge drove Democritus into all parts of the world, "Epicurus leaves his garden in Athens scarcely two or three times to travel to Ionia, not to give himself to studies, but to visit friends." At the approach of his death he "takes a warm bath and calls for pure wine, and recommends to his friends that they remain faithful to philosophy." It was a fitting end to a static and withdrawn life.[21]

By contrast, the contradictions present in Democritus' system from the start bred in him a passion for erudition, which made his life an endless wandering through all the disciplines of science and half the countries of the known world. He became competent in every art, traveled to Egypt and Persia, perhaps even to India and Ethiopia. But the thirst he sought to quench always arose again. "On the one hand it is the lust for knowledge that leaves him no peace, but it is at the same time the dissatisfaction with the true, i.e., philosophical knowledge, that drives him afar. The knowledge which he considers true is contentless; the knowledge that gives it content is without truth." Democritus was torn between an inner bond to philosophy and an equally deep repulsion for it; he both depended on the power of his mind to penetrate the secret of existence and distrusted what it found there. The truth of philosophy clashed with the content of empirical science. The result was tragedy in the classic sense: "It could be a fable, but it is a true fable because this anecdote of the ancients describes the contradiction in his being: Democritus is supposed to have blinded himself so that the sensible light in the eye would not darken sharpness of intellect. This is the same man who, according to Cicero, traveled through the whole world. But he did not find what he was seeking."[22]

The world of ancient philosophy, as Marx depicted it, was a world of stunted human development that implied—and in some cases even engendered—self-destruction. The Hegelian category Marx employed to describe these features was not alienation but inversion. Summarizing Epicurus' and Democritus' position "in all that regards the relationship of thought and reality in general," Marx found that the two men "oppose one another step by step." At each pass, their opposition inverted its own previous form. Democritus was sceptical of philosophy's ability to comprehend the world, Epicurus dogmatic about it; the first considered the world of appearances to be a world of subjective illusion, the second regarded it as objective appearance. From here the perverseness of their relationship unfolded. Democritus,

> who considers the sensible world subjective illusion devotes himself to empirical science and to positive cognition and displays the restlessness of experimenting, universal learning, observing the wide world. The other, who considers the phenomenal world real, scorns empiricism;

embodied in him are the calm of thought which finds its satisfaction in itself and the self-sufficiency that draws its knowledge *ex principio interno*. But the contrast goes even further. The sceptic and empiricist who holds nature to be subjective illusion [Democritus], considers it from the point of view of necessity and endeavors to explain and to understand the real existence of things. On the other hand the philosopher and dogmatist who considers the appearance real, sees only chance everywhere, and his manner of explanation tends rather to destroy all the objective reality of nature. There seems to be a certain inversion in these contrasts.[23]

One translator of Marx's dissertation has rendered the word inversion (*Verkehrtheit*) in this passage as "perversity," and it is clear that Marx was drawing on both senses. As a description of the relationship between the two thinkers, the inversions reflected the limitations of Greek thought, and the consequent inability of any individual thinker to achieve intellectual wholeness. The perversity that became explicit in Marx's portrait of Democritus was a psychological counterpart to this intellectual condition. Putting out his eyes in order to see better, Democritus expressed what Heinrich Marx had called "the tension that drives mind and body apart." His behavior exemplified what the younger Marx had described as "acting with weakness, yet with strength."

In various ways Marx identified himself with each of the characters in his philosophical drama. Certainly he admired Epicurus for his devotion to philosophy and his enlightened criticism of religion; exactly when Marx cast off the religious faith he seemed to possess in one of his graduation essays is not known, but it was undoubtedly gone by the time of his dissertation. On the other hand, it was Democritus who displayed seriousness, involvement in the world outside, and a determination to discover the true causes of things rather than just to "soothe the explaining subject." Elements of both figures contributed to the image of philosophy Marx put forward in his preface. Philosophy was "absolutely free and master of the universe." This meant that, like Epicurus, it made no secret of its opposition to religion. "The profession of Prometheus: 'In simple words, I hate the pack of gods,' is its own profession. . . . It allows no rivals." But the Promethean image tied philosophy also to Marx's portrait of Democritus, for it projected a vision of philosophy not "blissful" and self-satisfied, but fated to struggle against the world. Like Prometheus, Marx's philosophy refused to exchange "my state of evil fortune for your servitude/ Better to be the servant of this rock/ Than to be faithful boy to Father Zeus." Prometheus was "the most eminent saint and martyr in the philosophic calendar"; like him and like Democritus, philosophy might have to sacrifice itself to the truth it served.[24]

One characteristic shared by Epicurus and Democritus suggests that

Marx's refusal "to be faithful boy to Father Zeus" was also a resistance to the demands long made on him by father Marx. Both philosophers agreed with Marx in the refusal to subordinate mind to the demands of physical well-being. The specific resemblance between Democritus' blinding himself and what Heinrich Marx called his son's "badly tried vision" is largely fortuitous and should not be overplayed. Like Democritus, however, Marx acted out his devotion to truth over bodily health and, like Epicurus, Marx expressly upheld it. In one of the preparatory essays for his dissertation, Marx sided with Epicurus on this point against Plutarch. Epicurus had been "in general right, that the wise man regards illness as a thing without existence. . . . If he is sick that is a vanishing state with no duration. . . . If he is well, he honors this as his proper state, acting like a well man."[25] The same attitude appeared also in Marx's dedication of his dissertation to his future father-in-law, Ludwig von Westphalen. Praising him for his "sun-bright idealism," Marx concluded: "I need not pray for physical well-being for you. The spirit is the great physician versed in magic, to whom you have trusted yourself."[26]

Marx's dissertation, then, shows how the themes of his original conversion to Hegel in 1837 continued to color his vision of the meaning of Hegelian philosophy in his time. Hegel preserved modern thinkers from the fate suffered by their ancient counterparts by overcoming the separation from actual life that had infected philosophy at its origin. Modern philosophy was not condemned to withdraw into an isolated world of abstract self-consciousness, or suffer the personal truncations of Epicurus and Democritus. Marx even seemed confident, despite his own earlier experiences, that a philosophical indifference to physical health would go unpunished in those who entrusted themselves to the modern philosophical spirit.

That Ludwig von Westphalen died in the following year may have helped erode Marx's confidence in that aspect of spiritual power; in any case, Marx would soon enough lose his belief in Hegel's ability to shield modern thinkers from the intellectual and psychological condition that plagued the ancients. Once he did, Marx's portraits of Greek thinkers would take on a different relation to his own situation. By 1846 Marx would come to regard himself as free of philosophical idealism, and concentrate, like Democritus, on the "material side." Like Democritus, Marx would be led to abandon philosophy (to "leave it aside," he would later say) and "throw himself into the arms of positive knowledge." Also like him, however, he would retain an inner bond to philosophy and be faced with the need to resolve a tension between "truth" and "content." In "value," the Marx of the later 1850s and after would discover a truth underlying the illusory appearances of ordinary life, on the basis of which he would seek to comprehend existence. But, like Democritus, Marx would thereby posit a "principal element" that "does not enter appearance," and he would come to regard (in *Capital*) "the world of sensible perception as a real and concrete world" that was at one and the same time "subjective illusion" and "the unique real object." Seeking to comprehend a world that was at once and in its same features reality and illusion, Marx would face the very dilemma from which Democritus had been unable to escape. The figure of Democritus would become a symbol of his fate. The path to that destiny was long, however, and led through stages and turnings that could not be glimpsed in 1841.

2. Companions

Marx was not alone in his attempt to bring Hegel's legacy to bear on the problems of his time. In the early 1840s he appeared to be simply one of a number of post-Hegelian thinkers and writers loosely grouped together as Young Hegelians. The hopes and concerns shared by these people are fairly well represented by Marx's own Hegelian criticism. Yet some brief general view of the post-Hegelian movement will help to place Marx's development in context and to suggest how much Marx shared with his friends and associates, and what set him apart from them.[27]

The major theme of Hegelian writers in the early 1840s was "the realization of philosophy." Although the meaning of this slogan varied in different writers, the idea that philosophy should animate the world of real existence was shared by both left (or Young) Hegelians and right (or Old) ones. If Hegel's thought marked the end of an era, it had also to be the sign of a new beginning. Carl Ludwig Michelet, a leader of the Old Hegelians, described philosophy as "not only the owl of Minerva, but the cockcrow which announces the dawn of a new-breaking day"—a metaphor that Marx would also employ, following not Michelet but Heinrich Heine—and said that the need of the present was "to carry science into life." True theory was "implicit practice" (*an sich Praxis*), the philosophical consciousness strove "to permeate reality in a practical manner."[28]

These were very general aspirations, however, and conservative followers of Hegel voiced them with a different intent from that of Marx and his friends. Briefly, the difference was that the old Hegelians sought to realize philosophy by a process of reconciliation; for the other party the way to make knowledge practical was through negation or criticism. Carl Ludwig Michelet saw Hegelian philosophy as an expression of the truth of Christianity, and understood the realization of philosophy as bringing modern life into harmony with the truth of religion. Marx's friend Bruno Bauer (at least after he himself passed from the right to the left of the movement) saw the mission of modern philosophy as the destruction of religion. Christianity had been a necessary and progressive stage in human development, since it marked man's arrival at consciousness of the universality of his power; but in Christianity man had denied himself by attributing his own powers to an alien and illusory divine being. These contradictions within Christianity "are contradictions against man himself, but it lies in the nature and vocation of man that in his historical development he enter into contradiction with himself and bring this contradiction to a culmination before he can attain harmony with himself." In the aftermath of Hegelian philosophy, man's denial of his own nature had reached this high point. By negating this negation, philosophical criticism would now lead man through the smoke of battle to a new age. "The catastrophe will be frightful, it must be a great one, and I would almost go so far as to say that it will be greater and more monstrous than that with which Christianity entered the world."[29]

We have met the idea that consciousness can realize itself by making war on the world before. It is "Youth," Hegel's own picture of the relationship between adolescent self-involvement and the outside world. The Young Hegelians were young not only in chronological fact but in Hegel's very terms. In them, as Marx observed, philosophy was "turned against the world." Yet it is important to remember that these young men were Hegelians too: the foundation of their thinking was a view of the world that equated philosophy not with youth but with the mature recognition that consciousness was an inseparable part of real existence. Following Hegel, they found human rationality realized in actual existence, not in religion, to be sure—which, as men who had mostly begun as students of theology, they were busily engaged in shaking off—but as Hegel himself suggested, in the state. To Bauer, religion was by its very nature a denial of humanity; the state, however, even when it failed to live up to its ideal concept, had still to be recognized and retained as the locus of liberation. After the Prussian state, under Frederick William IV, moved toward a closer alliance with religion that Bauer called (perhaps following Marx) "Byzantine," he still remained loyal to it. "If the state rejects us, yet we do not reject the state, but hold fast to the principle of the state as the highest there is. The final analysis will show that we have chosen the better part."[30]

The left Hegelians thus suffered from an internal contradiction: they sought to be young and Hegelian at the same time, to turn philosophy against a world they recognized as itself the product of "Spirit." Marx would later find their radicalism woefully incomplete, and in fact many of those who had been radical Hegelians in their youth became supporters of Bismarck once they had reached a certain age. Young Hegelianism had other weaknesses as well. It consisted of several small groups, scattered at various German centers and tied together only by a few short-lived organs of publicity. Only the succession of periodicals edited by Arnold Ruge from 1841 to 1843 and Marx's own *Rheinische Zeitung* gave any semblance of unity to the movement. The Prussian censorship—although relaxed briefly at the end of 1841—made life difficult both for Ruge's journals and for the Cologne paper, finally putting an end to both early in 1843.[31]

Moreover, the brief appearance of a unified movement created by these publications hid from view the fact that all the major contributors to them were also young in the sense that their ideas were in the process of rapid evolution. Bauer, Feuerbach, Ruge, and Marx all believed they had left behind by 1846 the positions they had occupied in 1841 and, even where the changes took place along parallel paths, the rapid intellectual motion made agreements and alliances slippery and weak. By the end of 1844 the movement had dissolved into its component parts, with all its representatives loudly declaring their independence from the others.

In what way did Marx's intellectual development reflect the influence of these Young Hegelians? Certainly his outlook was colored by the Young Hegelian atmosphere. When he joined the Hegelian Doctor's Club in 1837 he was younger than the other members. His closest friends, Rutenberg and Köppen, were both ten years older than he. Bruno Bauer was nine and Ruge sixteen years older than Marx. Marx absorbed a general orientation from his older friends; in addition, some of his particular interests—notably late classical philosophy—were probably suggested by them.

Beyond these very general observations, however, little can be demonstrated of the Young Hegelian influence on Marx. At the time of Marx's conversion to Hegel there was little Young Hegelian literature beyond David Friedrich Strauss's *Life of Jesus* and the Berlin lectures of Eduard Gans. Bruno Bauer, who would later be the most prominent Berlin Hegelian to be in close touch with Marx, did not even move from the right to the left section of the party until after 1839—by which time Marx's studies for his dissertation were already begun. In his dissertation, Marx acknowledged the influence of his friend Friedrich Köppen, but Köppen himself did not regard Marx's thinking as derivative from his own. In June 1841 Köppen wrote to Marx that only after Marx's departure from Berlin (Marx returned to the Rhineland after obtaining his degree) had Köppen begun to think independently: until then his ideas had all come out of Marx's house in the Schützenstrasse. Moreover, Köppen thought Bruno Bauer had taken over some of Marx's ideas too, about the "Byzantine" character of the king of Prussia's "Christian state." "You see," Köppen concluded, "you are an arsenal of thoughts, a workhouse, or to speak the Berlin language, an ox's head of ideas."[32] Marx was precocious and independent minded; in Trier he had already learned something of the contemporary intellectual and political scene. His Hegelianism was as much an independent response to his own development as a reflection of the promptings of others.

Two features of Young Hegelianism in Berlin especially set Marx apart from it. In the first place, most members of the group saw religion as the main target of their criticism. Marx shared this interest to a degree; his dissertation stressed Epicurus' opposition to Greek religion as one of his noteworthy features. Yet the specific project of attacking Christianity could not enroll much of Marx's effort. He never wrote either about the Gospels or about the contemporary church; once he proposed to write about Christian art, but before abandoning the project he broadened its subject to religious art in general.[33] Christian belief had never been enough of a reality in his life to make the abandonment of it a matter of much moment to him. He sloughed off the Christianity of his school days with hardly a trace.

Second, while Marx shared with his fellow left Hegelians a deeply felt antipathy to existing society, his public language and behavior were more restrained and considered than theirs. Bauer, as we saw above, spoke of an approaching "dreadful catastrophe"; elsewhere he appealed to "the deed," as did Moses Hess in some of his early writings.[34] Marx had invoked visions of violent upheaval in his poetry of 1836-37, but those images were formed before he discovered himself to be a Hegelian. In public his "onslaughts against the present" took a different form. When, during 1842, a group of Hegelians in Berlin began calling themselves "the free," and dramatizing their own personal libertinism as a source of wider liberation, Marx refused to have any truck with them. Such antics, he wrote in the *Rheinische Zeitung*, had to be "loudly and decisively disavowed in a time that requires earnest, manly and upright characters to struggle for its exalted purposes."[35] Only later on would Marx's compound of youthful antipathy and manly earnestness openly reveal its revolutionary core.

3. The Moor

If Frederick Engels' later recollection was accurate, it was during Marx's years as a student that he received a nickname that remained with him for the rest of his life. The name was "Moor." In the years he lived in London, Marx was regularly called Moor within his family (the other members had nicknames too, as did Engels, who was called General when he was with them). According to Engels, Marx was also called Moor by the staff of the *Neue Rheinische Zeitung*, the newspaper he edited during the revolutionary days of 1848-49.[36] It does not seem that the name was used by his later political associates; at least Marx was not called Moor by his collaborators in the First International. Nonetheless, it always remained the preferred name for Marx among those with whom he was most intimate.

Where did the name come from? The reason given for it by Engels and by others who have offered explanations was that it reflected Marx's dark complexion, but that cannot have been the whole story. Anyone who knew Marx at all knew that he was no Moor, and that his swarthy cast had a different non-European source: his Jewishness. Throughout his life Marx was identified as a Jew: by the head of the Cologne Jewish community who in 1843 got Marx to sign a petition on behalf of the Jews there; by Arnold Ruge with whom he worked in the following year; by various political enemies who used anti-Semitism as a weapon against him; and by his daughter Eleanor, who told her London colleagues in the Labor movement: "I am a Jewess." To call Marx Moor was, to begin with, a veiled reminder of his Jewish origins.[37]

But why specifically Moor? There were not many living models of what North Africans were like in Berlin during the 1830s. If the nickname did in fact arise in a circle of students, however, there is a good likelihood that the reference was meant to be literary. In literature there were a number of notable Moors, some of whose features may have lurked behind Marx's appellation. The most obvious one to English readers, Shakespeare's Othello, would have been well known to Marx's friends in Berlin, since Shakespeare was immensely popular in Germany during the eighteenth and nineteenth centuries. Marx himself was steeped in Shakespeare and passionately devoted to him. We shall see later on that during his years in Berlin Marx sometimes displayed one of Othello's best-known characteristics: amorous jealousy. Many years later, writing to his wife about his love for her, Marx compared himself to the Moor of Venice.[38]

There were models closer to home, however, in the plays of Schiller. Marx had certainly read Schiller in school; both Wyttenbach and Heinrich Marx were great admirers of his work. Marx wrote some verse dramas during 1837 that contained certain echoes of Schiller, as did the project he had in mind at one point to devote himself to dramatic criticism. There were two Moors in Schiller's plays. The one in *Fiesco, or The Genoese Conspiracy* was not a flattering model. He was immoral, confused by difficult choices, and wantonly destructive; Schiller had him done away with at the end of the drama. However, he also had seemingly superhuman energy, and an almost magical ability to ferret out secrets. These were qualities the left Hegelians associated with their own philosophical criticism.

However, it is the second of Schiller's Moors whose character deserves most consideration in connection with Marx's nickname. This one appeared in one of Schiller's most famous plays, *The Robbers*, and he was one of Schiller's best-known characters. He was not a real African or an actual Moor at all; only his name was Moor (spelled *Moor* in German, as it is in English, not *Mohr* as the word and Marx's nickname were spelled in German). But he had another name in common with Marx: Karl. Karl Moor (or Karl von Moor, to be precise) was one of Schiller's great romantic heroes. Condemned to a life of violence by a brother's treachery, he became the leader of a robber band, yet remained devoted to a higher standard of justice than the one that ruled ordinary life. His motives were not those of his followers, as one of them explained:

> He does not commit murder as we do for the sake of plunder; and as to money, as soon as he had plenty of it at command, he did not seem to care a straw for it; and his third of the booty, which belongs to him of right, he gives away to orphans, or supports promising young men with it at college. But should he happen to get a country squire into his clutches who grinds down his peasants like cattle, or some gold-laced villain, who warps the law to his own purposes, and hoodwinks the eyes of justice with his gold, or any chap of that kidney; then my boy, he is in his element, and rages like a very devil, as if every fibre in his body were a fury.[39]

Aware that his actions in freeing one of his companions had caused the death of innocent bystanders and that some of his band enjoyed the bloodshed, he resolved to abandon robbery; later, at the end of his road, he refused the easy exit offered by suicide so that "a poor creature, a day-laborer, with eleven living children," could turn him in and claim the price on his head.

Several features of Schiller's Karl Moor matched ones Marx's friends of the time saw in him. His qualities of leadership were recognized by Friedrich Köppen, who regarded Marx as the source of many Young Hegelian ideas. Later on, Engels described the editorial structure of the *Neue Rheinische Zeitung* as "simply the dictatorship of Marx," and went on to explain how Marx's "clear vision and sure policy" had to rule if the enterprise was to work.[40] Schiller's characters regarded their leader similarly: "Without Moor we are a body without a soul." It seems significant, therefore, that a friend who had known Marx in the days of the *Neue Rheinische Zeitung* referred to him in 1850—in an altogether friendly fashion—as "the robber captain" (*der Räuberhauptmann*).[41] This reference constituted one clear link between Marx and the Moor of *The Robbers*. (Marx's father had earlier pictured his Berlin student son in parallel, if less complimentary terms as "a wild ringleader of wild young fellows.")[42]

Schiller's Karl Moor had another trait in common with Marx: he was inwardly angry, and disdainful of the world around him. His first words in the drama were: "I am disgusted with this age of puny scribblers." He compared the men of his time to "rats crawling about the club of Hercules." Condemning the present "weak, effeminate age, fit for nothing but to ponder over the deeds of former times," he nurtured a revolutionary vision: "Set me at the head of an army of fellows like myself, and out of

Germany shall spring a republic compared to which Rome and Sparta will be but as nunneries."[43]

These characteristics closely resembled ones that Marx's friends saw in him as a student. When in 1842 Frederick Engels—who as yet knew Marx only by reputation—described the members of the Hegelian left in a poem, he pictured Marx as "a remarkable monster" (*ein markhaft Ungetüm*), who:

> Blusters full of rage, and as if desiring to pull
> The broad canopy of heaven down to earth,
> Stretches his arms high up into the sky.
> His angry fists clenched, he rages against rest
> As if ten thousand devils had him by the hair.[44]

In one of his prefatory essays for his dissertation, Marx described the philosophers of his time much as Karl Moor viewed his contemporaries. The "subordinate, trifling" thinkers of the present "hide behind a philosophical giant of the past" but, in their small-mindedness, mistake the part of the great philosopher's body they comprehend for the whole: "Thus originate hair, toe, and excrement philosophers." A few years later he would declare "*War* on German conditions," as Schiller's hero had, proclaiming the essential pathos of philosophical criticism to be "*indignation*, its essential task, *denunciation*."[45]

Throughout his life Marx would make his indignation felt by means of denunciations directed against those who failed to display his own clarity and commitment. Practically all his major writings began as critiques of other writers: Hegel, Ruge, the Bauer brothers, Stirner, Proudhon, the representatives of both classical and "vulgar" political economy. Marx was seldom able to state his own position in a matter-of-fact way. To denounce or repudiate others was his way of setting forth and establishing his own views. This personal style reflected the revolutionary passion of Marx's revolt against existing society, but it was characteristic of Marx well before his discovery of the proletariat. Earlier we suggested that some of the sources of this aggressive mode of interaction can probably be found in Marx's early life, shaped as it was by his mother's attempt to make up for the isolation and weakness she felt outside her family by establishing rigid control over her children. Marx's father, too, had experienced a powerlessness to preserve his own identity against Prussian strength, which probably helped the young Marx to equate personal independence with defiance and opposition to others. These qualities all seem recognized in the nickname Moor.

One further aspect of Schiller's Karl Moor makes it worth considering the possibility that the young Marx was associated with him. Karl Moor's character and his fate specifically charted the difficulties that barred the passage from adolescence to manhood in the Germany of Schiller and his readers. The young Moor was unable to make the transition to manhood for which his stage in the life cycle called; his outlawry and the rest of his history followed from a frustrated need for reconciliation.

At the opening of Schiller's play, Karl Moor has been seeking to reconcile himself with his father—whom he deeply loves—after provoking his anger by the antisocial behavior he displayed as a student. His earlier pranks had led to a near revolution when, in revenge for the maiming of his pet dog, he bought up all the meat in Leipzig, causing the town officials to threaten action against him. "But we students turned out lustily, seventeen hundred of us, with you at our head, and butchers and tailors and haberdashers at our backs, besides publicans, barbers, and rabble of all sorts, swearing that the town should be sacked if a single hair of a student's head was injured." To his companions' regret, Moor repented of this past, and desired to end the rebellion in which he had been caught up. "I have already, last week, written to my father to implore his forgiveness, and have not concealed the least circumstance from him; and where there is sincerity there is compassion and help."[46] If no direct connection tied this admirer of Prometheus and believer in his father's mercy and sympathy to the young Marx, some inner likeness joined them together.

What prevented the reconciliation both Karl Moor and his father desired was the jealous scheming of his younger brother, Franz, who succeeded in making the elder Moor believe that Karl had not truly repented, and in convincing Karl that his father would not forgive him. The latter's reaction was to "let manly resignation give place to raging fire."[47] The "normal" Hegelian return from adolescent isolation to social integration being blocked, Karl Moor turned instead to a perpetuation of the mutual warfare between youth and the world. As a drama of adolescent rebellion, guilt, and fear, *The Robbers*—published when Schiller himself was only twenty-two—is a remarkably perceptive analysis of the dilemma of youth in an age of disruption and disorientation—the same conflict Goethe captured in *The Sorrows of Young Werther*. Although Schiller recognized the share adolescent rebellion had in creating this dilemma, the play made society primarily at fault for blocking the reconciliation. Karl's younger brother Franz acted from the same motives of greed and selfishness against which Karl's life became a continuing and ultimately self-destructive struggle: the moral was that society's vices prevent if from enjoying its best members' virtues.

Marx himself certainly knew the figure of Karl Moor. Heine included the following lines in a poem Marx quoted in 1852: "Schinderhannes [another outlaw], Karl Moor—these I took as models." Marx did not quote Heine in reference to himself, but with regard to a Prussian official

he was trying to discredit.[48] By then he probably would not have welcomed the association of Schiller's character with himself. Would he have
done so earlier? Whatever the answer to that question Marx's path after he
left the University of Berlin would bear a striking similarity to his
namesake's: official society rejected him before he rejected it. Marx became an outlaw only after failing in an attempt to serve his convictions in
a legitimate and respectable career. The story of that failure is contained
in Marx's editorship of the liberal Cologne newapaper, the *Rheinische
Zeitung* (*Rhenish Gazette*).

4. Philosophy and Journalism

Marx's association with the *Rheinische Zeitung* lasted for less than a year,
from the spring of 1842 until the beginning of 1843, and he served as the
paper's editor only for the last five months of that period. Yet this brief
season was important in his life, for it gave him his first opportunity to
write about the political questions of the day, including the questions of
poverty and socialism. Marx was a highly successful editor, nearly dou-
bling the paper's circulation before the Prussian government forced it to
close down.[49]

The paper represented much the same current of Rhineland progres-
sivism that had been visible during Marx's boyhood in Trier, and of which
his own father had been a representative. Its criticism of the Prussian regime was not always moderate, but it claimed loyalty to the state's true,
underlying principles, just as Heinrich Marx had done in his speech of
January 1834. Among its backers were respectable Cologne citizens with
some similarities to Heinrich Marx, including several prominent Jews. As
its successful editor and one of its most notable writers, Karl Marx now
became known to important sections of the German public, much as
Heinrich had hoped he would even earlier. Marx was by no means the
communist he would later become during his days as editor; the government's rejection of his attempt to reform political life from within was one
thing that helped move him in a more radical direction.

Even before Marx obtained his degree he seems to have contemplated
becoming a political writer, for his friend Bruno Bauer—who hoped Marx
would join him as a teacher at the University of Bonn—warned him
against it in March 1841. "It would be foolishness if you dedicated yourself to a political career," Bauer cautioned. "Theory is now the strongest
practice, and we cannot at all predict in how important a sense it will
become practical." Marx's journalism would reveal that on a certain level
he agreed with Bauer, but by the end of his stay in Berlin he already believed that the calling of modern philosophy lay in the arena of public,
political life. In August 1842 he wrote to one of the *Rheinische Zeitung*'s

backers that "True theory must be clarified and developed in connection with concrete circumstances and existing relationships."[50]

Marx wrote on a variety of topics for the Cologne paper: freedom of the press, legal theory, the Prussian representative estates, peasants who illegally gathered wood from privately owned forests, the crisis of the Moselle wine producers, communist theories in Germany, divorce. In each of the social and political contexts he analyzed, Marx underlined the connection between Hegelian critical philosophy and the public issues of the day. In a world dominated by private interest, Marx contended, only the independent spirit of philosophy could educate public life to a higher human level.

Philosophical criticism was essential to politics because only philosophy was able to perceive an inner, essential rationality behind the welter of confused phenomena present in ordinary experience. Just as a viewpoint that showed a painting as a mere mass of lines and colors had to be abandoned for a better one, "so must a standpoint which shows the world and human conditions only in their most external appearances be left behind." In order to know and judge the actual world, one had to "measure the existence of things with the yardstick of the essence of the inner idea." For instance, in deciding whether a free press or a censored press was to be preferred, the two alternatives were not to be measured by their possible results or be tested by experience, but judged by "the right of their ideas." The question was "not about their consequences, but about their basis, not about their individual application, but about their general right."[51]

As a means for transcending the confusing lessons of experience, philosophy served a function Marx would later assign to revolution: educating the educator. When a speaker in the Rhineland Diet opposed freedom of the press on the grounds of human imperfection, offering the censor as the educator of imperfect humanity, Marx replied that, to be sure, everything that develops is imperfect, simply by the fact of being incomplete. "What is incomplete requires eduation. Is not education also human, and therefore incomplete? Does not education also need education?"[52] Three years later, in his "Theses on Feuerbach," Marx would declare again that "the educator must himself be educated," and he would assign the pedagogical role to "revolutionary practice." In 1842, however, it was philosophical criticism that had to take experience in hand, leading it beyond its own narrow limits.

As in his dissertation, Marx proceeded from the conviction that Hegelian philosophy provided a set of intellectual tools that could gain a firm purchase on the world of actual existence. Unlike the ancient philosophers, who identified reason with the abstract individual, separated from society, modern philosophy derived its concept from "the idea of the whole." Although in the actual world "no ethical *existence* corresponds to its *essence*, or at least does not *have* to correspond to it," still, "when a particular existent no longer fully corresponds to its essential determination," the natural result was "dissolution and death." Hence: "World history decides when a state is so much at odds with the idea of the state that it no longer deserves to continue." Because only philosophy had access to the essential ideas that ruled experience, only philosophical criticism knew the underlying tendencies the world of experience concealed behind appearances.[53]

Marx derived the notion that reality was animated at its center by an inner idea from Hegel, and at times he followed Hegel in analyzing actual life as the embodiment of abstract principles. For instance, the character of modern private property reflected the operation of the faculty of Understanding (*Verstand*) as distinct from Reason (*Vernunft*) in modern social relations. In the Middle Ages, the sharp and unambiguous forms of modern property ownership had not existed. Forests and fields had been the property of landlords, but peasant communities possessed certain customary rights over them—gleaning and wood gathering—which the lords could not legally take away. Modern agrarian reforms had abolished the old collective rights and vested property ownership unconditionally in individuals. As a result, the poor peasants who continued their traditional practice of gathering fallen tree-trunks and branches were not exercising a customary right but committing a crime. In Marx's view, the organ that had done away with the medieval ambiguities was "Understanding, and Understanding is not only one-sided, but its essential business is to make the world one-sided."[54]

The principle of Understanding played an important role in history, "for only one-sidedness forms and draws the particular out of the inorganic slime of the whole." No individual thing could come into existence without being isolated by Understanding. Hence, Understanding brought forth diversity, "for the world would not be many-sided without its many one-sided things."[55] Yet, for all its importance in the everyday world, Understanding had to yield to the higher principle of Reason. Understanding had forgotten that "even looked at purely in terms of private law, a double private law was at hand here, a private law of the possessor and a private law of the non-possessor." Unable to distinguish between instances where the principle of abstract, undifferentiated property rights was beneficent and those where it was harmful, Understanding turned poor peasants whose survival depended on the traditional forest rights into criminals. At this point, therefore, Reason had to supercede Understanding, by establishing the principle that the state must protect all its citizens.[56]

As this example shows, Marx used these abstractions, as Hegel also had, to provide an acutely realistic picture of the actual world. Like

Hegel, too, Marx saw that world as composed largely of private and egoistic interests, all trying to extend their control and power. In seeking to have wood gathering by peasants punished as theft, the forest owners were attempting to transform the state authority into their servant, "so that everything sinks down to an expedient of the forest owner, and his interest appears as the determining soul of the whole mechanism. All the organs of the state become ears, eyes, arms, legs, within which the interest of the forest owner hears, spys, values, grasps and runs."[57]

Marx's consciousness of private interest's importance and power included a recognition that thought itself sometimes expressed the needs and desires of a social group. In the *Rheinische Zeitung* Marx did not hesitate to treat some thought as ideology. In contrast to his later position, however, Marx at this point regarded only some types of thinking as determined by particular social interests. Philosophical criticism was still not bound by these limits.

In his very first article, Marx presented the speakers who debated freedom of the press in the Rhineland Diet as voicing the thoughts of their "estate," their social group. "The debates bring us a polemic of the princely estate against the free press, a polemic of the knightly estate against the free press, a polemic of the urban estate, so that not the *individual* but the *estate* polemicizes."[58] The speaker who represented the knights expressed the social conditions of their existence. "When the knightly speaker mistakes personal privileges, individual freedoms in opposition to those of the people and the government, for general rights," he gave voice to "the exclusive spirit of his *estate*." Because the consciousness of the modern knights sought to comprehend "inner, essential, general determinations" by means of "external, accidental, particular curiosities," to see freedom as "tied up with particular human individuals" without being "bound to the essence of man, to reason in general, and thus common to all individuals, they necessarily take refuge in *the marvelous* and *the mystical*." Because their actual position in the world did not correspond to their ideas about themselves, their move from practice to theory was a departure for the beyond, a flight to religion. But their religion had a particular polemical and bitter quality, and more or less consciously served as "the sacred cloak for quite worldly—but at the same time quite fantastic—desires."[59]

When he came to the representative of the towns, Marx did not present the speaker's ideas as reflections of the social conditions of the urban estate, but rather as typical of its consciousness and world view. This speaker had himself expressed a suspicion that contemporary demands for "a constitution and the freedom of the press were not for the welfare of the people, but for the satisfaction of the ambition of certain individuals and the domination of factions." Marx clearly took much pleasure in unmasking this argument.

> It is well known that a certain psychology explains great matters from small causes, and in the correct presentiment that everything man struggles for is a matter of his interest, proceeds to the incorrect opinion that there are only "small" interests, only the interests of stereotyped egoism. It is further known that this kind of psychology and anthropology is especially found in *cities*, where it still passes for the sign of a sly head to see through the world and to see, sitting behind the cloud-cover of ideas and facts, jealous tiny little intriguing mannequins who wind up the whole thing with little threads. Except that it is similarly known that if one peers too deeply into the glass, he bumps into *his own head*, and the anthropology and worldly knowledge of these clever people is chiefly a mystified bumping into their own heads.[60]

Unlike the representative of the knights, the townsman was not led into fantasy and mysticism, but too deeply into the well of practicality. His error had been to push the practical sense learned in everyday city life into a region where its presuppositions did not hold. The wider world was not made in the businessman's image. What the two speakers had in common was that each mistook his limited, partial perspective for the wider standpoint of the whole.

In Marx's view, this latter perspective was available, and the philosophical critic could attain to it. Discussing a proposal to have the intellectual professions represented in the Rhineland Diet, Marx argued that although one form of intelligence merely served particular interests, there was another, higher form. "*Useful* intelligence, that fights for hearth and home, is distinguished from *free* intelligence, that knows how to fight for what is right in spite of its hearth and home. There is one form of intelligence that serves a particular goal, a particular matter, and there is another intelligence, that rules every matter, and only serves itself." The genuine free intelligence did not judge general issues according to some particular interest, "but it will determine this particular matter in line with the general concern."[61]

While Marx treated some thinking as ideological, therefore, and criticized his opponents' ideas as masks for their interests, he still remained far from reducing all thinking to ideology. In fact, his attitude toward that term still resembled his father's, and recalled what Heinrich Marx had once said about it. Marx was careful to make clear that he himself was not given to empty abstractions. "Let us take the world as it is, let us not be ideologues," he declared in one article. In his dissertation, too, Marx had written: "Our life does not need ideologies and empty hypotheses, but that we live without confusion." In his debate with the forest proprietors, however, he made clear that he rejected Napoleon's views about the ideological nature of philosophy. When one representative condemned any state protection of the peasants' customary rights as a restriction of "the free will of private persons," Marx seized on the idea of free will for his reply. It was "just as joyful as it was an unexpected piece of news, that man possesses a free will, and that it is not to be restricted in any manner." But such ideas were surprising in the mouths of the landlords. "How shall we understand this sudden rebellious appearance of ideology, for in relation to ideas we have only followers of Napoleon before us?" They employed the general notion of free will only as a cloak for their particular interests; while they were followers of Napoleon, Marx was not.[62]

Opposed in Marx's mind to all such upholders of private interest were two organs of universal good: the press and the state. Marx's characterization of the nature and power of the free press stood at the very center of his philosophical and political point of view:

> The free press is the eye of the popular spirit, opened everywhere, the embodied trust of a people in itself, the vocal tie, that binds the particular individual to the state and the world; it is civilization embodied, which transforms material struggles into spiritual struggles, and idealizes their crude, substantial form. It is the relentless confession of a people before itself, and it is known that the power of confession is liberating. It is the spiritual mirror in which a people perceives itself, and self-perception is the first condition of wisdom. . . . It is the ideal world, which ever rising out of the real one, flows back as an ever richer spirit, animating it anew.[63]

Here, as elsewhere, Marx's standpoint recognized that material conditions lay behind political struggles, but pictured the critical intellect as able to rise above their limits. Thought reflected reality, but in a magic mirror that gave the beholder power over the self-image he saw there. Ideas were the product of ordinary life, but they possessed the power to transcend and enliven material existence.

Marx's view of the state—the essential state, not the existing Prussian regime—exactly paralleled this image of the press. However powerful the material forces of property and self-interest might be, the state that corresponded to its concept recognized them only as principles, "spiritual powers," and dealt with them as such. "Only in their public resurrection, their political rebirth do natural powers have the right to vote in the state." The state was not mired in material life: "The state interlaces the whole of nature with its spiritual nerves, and at every point it must appear that not matter but form, not nature without the state but the nature of the state, not the *unfree object*, but the *free man* rules."⁶⁴ By judging each sphere of social life according to the principle that ruled within it, the state gave each part its proper place within the whole.

Because the state had the same role of animating and transcending the material world that Marx also attributed to the press, the two had a natural affinity for each other. The press carried the material struggles of competing interests into the public arena, where they could be judged in the context of the general interest—not in "the clouded language of private opinion," but in "the clarifying words of public rationality."⁶⁵ In order for the state to order life in line with general principles, it needed the press.

In Marx's journalism, therefore, the struggle for freedom and rationality in political life was inseparable from the struggle for intellectual liberty. The latter struggle was important from a public point of view, but Marx did not hide the degree to which it was also his private, personal battle. Writing and criticism were his vocation, and his life was bound up with them in a profound and special way. Even those speakers in the Rhineland Diet who argued in favor of a free press had not sufficiently understood the question. The reason was that "they have *no real relationship* to their protegé. They have never known the freedom of the press as a *need*. To them it is a matter of the head, in which the heart has no part."⁶⁶

When, for instance, one speaker defended the freedom of the press on the ground that journalism had as much right as any other trade to freedom, Marx protested. To be sure, it was good to have the question brought down to "the solid ground of reality," not given up to the common German fancy for "the music of the blue sky," which was partly responsible for the fact that "freedom until now has remained a fantasy and a sentimentality" in Germany. But the press was not a trade like others. If the writer had to earn a living in order to write, still he did not write for the purpose of earning a living. "The writer in no way regards his works as *means*. They are ends in themselves. So little are they means for the writer himself and for others, that when necessary he sacrifices *his* existence for *their* existence." The writer followed a variation of the precept "Obey God rather than men," subordinating his own needs and wishes to duty. Hence "*The first freedom of the press consists in not being a trade.* To the writer who reduces it to a material means is due, as a punishment for this inner unfreedom, the outward unfreedom of censorship; or rather, his existence is already his punishment."⁶⁷

In this passionate portrait of his calling, Marx sounded the themes that had accompanied his choice of a vocation in 1835: duty, self-sacrifice, service to humanity. On one level it was Heinrich Marx's ethic his son still voiced, but Marx refused those compromises with worldly necessity that his father—more tolerant of self-contradiction—had sought to impose on him. Where Marx's determination to give full and consistent expression to these values would lead was not yet clear in his journalism. Yet, with hindsight, it is impossible not to notice that the most anxious tones Marx sounded in his newspaper were called forth by the need to discuss a theory of society that sought the total annihilation of self-interest and the triumph of the general good, but was regarded as beyond the pale of existing society: communism. Here, too, Marx subscribed to the primacy of ideas over material forces, but in a way that saw in the power of thought a threat of enslavement rather than a promise of liberation.

When the *Rheinische Zeitung* printed some reports on German and French communist movements, it was attacked by a more conservative paper, the *Augsburg Allgemeine Zeitung* for spreading dangerous notions. In defending his paper's policy, Marx characterized the desire to exclude reports about communist activities as a simple flight from reality. Commenting on a report that had equated the position of the contemporary middle class with that of the nobility in 1789, Marx wrote: "It is a fact that the class possessing nothing today *demands* to share in the wealth of the middle class—a fact clearly evident in the streets of Manchester, Paris, Lyons, without the talk in Strasbourg and the silence in Augsburg. Does the Augsburger really believe that indignation and silence refute the facts of the time?" What the conservative press found intolerable, Marx suggested, was accurate reporting of real communist activity by a progressive paper in Germany, where communist ideas were not being spread by liberals, "but rather by your *reactionary* friends."[68]

Marx's own interest had already been aroused by communist theories. His paper, he said, could not "even concede *theoretical reality* to communistic ideas in their present form," much less "wish or consider possible their *practical realization*." However, "writings such as those by Leroux, Considérant, and above all Proudhon's penetrating work" were a serious concern of the time, and the *Rheinische Zeitung* would submit them to "thorough criticism":

> We are firmly convinced that it is not the *practical effort* but rather the *theoretical explication* of communistic ideas which is the real *danger*. Dangerous practical *attempts*, even *those on a large scale*, can be answered with *cannon*, but *ideas* won by our intelligence, embodied in our outlook, and forged in our conscience, are chains from which we cannot tear ourselves away without breaking our hearts; they are demons we can overcome only by submitting to them.

Marx went on to say that his opponents knew nothing "of the *troubled conscience* evoked by a rebellion of man's subjective wishes against his objective *understanding*, *because it possesses neither* understanding *nor conscience*."[69] Was Marx already finding that his conscience led him closer to communism than his understanding liked? Conversion to communism appeared in these lines as a looming presence on his intellectual horizon, but one he would approach against his will.

Once before, in his original conversion to Hegelianism, Marx had found that the contents of his mind led him "like a false-hearted siren into the clutches of the enemy." Now, on the brink of passing beyond Hegel, the experience seemed about to be repeated. In 1835 he had written that the vocations concerned with abstract truths were "the most dangerous for the youth whose principles are not yet solid, whose conviction is not yet firm and unshakeable." Was the danger that the young man did not yet know where truth would lead? Marx's experience as a journalist was one stage in revealing what the consequences of a commitment to abstract truths—combined with a determination to "take the world as it is"—would be for the youth he was.

5. Beyond Hegel

What had Marx's intentions as a journalist been? Did he really believe that the Prussian state could be brought closer to its "concept" through philosophical criticism? As early as March 1842 he had expressed disgust with the Prussian constitution in a letter to his friend Arnold Ruge. He was then embarked on a critique of Hegel's political theory, he told Ruge, in which "The core is an attack on the *constitutional monarchy* as a thoroughly self-contradictory and self-cancelling hybrid." Earlier, in October 1841, one of the *Rheinische Zeitung*'s backers, Georg Jung, had described Marx as a "desperate revolutionary." Marx was certainly aware of the possibility of revolution in 1842, for he expressed sympathy with the Belgian revolution of 1830. Even while denying a conservative writer's allegation that the Belgian uprising was due to the activities of an unrestrained press, Marx agreed that the press had participated in it. "The revolution of a people is *total*," he declared, "that is, each sphere revolts in its own way—why not also the press as press?"[70]

Yet it should be remembered that the Belgian revolution had not been a radical upheaval, and that it had ended with the establishment of a constitutional monarchy, precisely the form of government Marx had to live under in Prussia. Georg Jung may have meant less than he seemed to say, for he placed Marx in the not very revolutionary company of Bruno Bauer and Ludwig Feuerbach. Marx himself in August 1842 warned against policies that might separate the paper from "the great number of liberal-minded, practical men who have taken on the difficult role of fighting step by step for freedom, within constitutional limits."[71]

Marx himself helps us to reconcile these contradictory indications, in a letter of 1843. He noted then that the first two years of the Prussian King

Frederick William IV's reign had made people believe for a moment that "the old fossilized servants' and slaves' state" of Prussia was being revitalized. The new king had begun his regime in 1841 by removing some of the old restrictions on speaking and writing—his liberalization of the censorship made the *Rheinische Zeitung* possible—so that "For a moment the old order of things seemed to be turned upside down. Indeed, things began to assume human forms."[72] This state of affairs did not last, however. The censorship was tightened again at the end of 1842: a liberal Leipzig paper was suppressed and Marx's own publication placed under the scrutiny of two censors instead of one. It would seem, therefore, that Marx thought the reform of the Prussian state possible only for a brief time, in the late summer and fall of 1842. By the end of that year he appears to have concluded that Prussia was hopelessly at odds with its "concept"—and perhaps that any modern state necessarily had to be.

Marx intimated as much in a series of articles he contributed to the paper in January 1843. The articles marked his last attempt to work within the framework of reformist Hegelian politics that had characterized the *Rheinische Zeitung*; at the same time they revealed that he had already moved beyond it. The articles, called "A Justification of the Anonymous Correspondent from the Moselle," were a defense of an earlier anonymous reportage his paper had carried on the critical situation of the Moselle wine producers. The earlier reports had stated that the inhabitants of the Moselle region had "enthusiastically hailed the greater freedom of the press effected by the Royal Cabinet order of December 24, 1841, because of their especially oppressed situation." In addition, the report asserted that the state officials had treated the Moselle population's complaints as "insolent screaming." These articles had provoked criticism from the governor (*Oberpräsident*) of the Rhineland Province; Marx's "Justification" was a response to him.[73]

Marx sought to justify his paper's articles in an unusual way. He did not offer any empirical testimony to the enthusiasm of the Moselle people for the free press, nor for the official treatment of the complaints as insolent screaming. Instead he argued that both were the direct consequences of a "necessary relationship." Too often, he observed, political conditions were explained on the basis of the desires of the people involved, instead of from *"the objective nature of the relationships."* This was an inadequate standpoint: "There are *relationships*, however, which determine the actions of private persons as well as those of individual authorities, and which are as independent as the movements in breathing. Taking this objective standpoint from the outset, one will not presuppose an exclusively good or bad will on either side. Rather, one will observe relationships in which only persons appear to act at first."[74] Whatever actually existed reflected both the conditions that made its existence necessary, and the external circumstances that brought it about. These notions recall Marx's earlier view that real existence had to be measured by the inner idea that animated it, since empirical experience was ruled by the life of the concept. Now, however, this principle revealed the defects of the Prussian regime.

What kept the state from fulfilling its ideal function was the administrative bureaucracy. Marx now ascribed to the state officials who dealt with everyday affairs the same inability to transcend private interest that he had earlier found among the various estates. The state official necessarily viewed things from a peculiar standpoint, which distorted even the clearest reality: "The particular official confronting the wine grower *not purposefully* but *necessarily* sees circumstances as better or different than they are. He believes that the question of whether his region is healthy is the question of whether *he* administers it well."[75] Hence, if a province found itself in a state of real emergency, as the Moselle wine growers did, the bureaucracy could only respond by denying the depth of the need, and by looking around for ways to make administration easier. With the best will in the world, the state officials could not break through the necessity that grew out of the "essential relationship" constraining them. That unavoidable constraint was "the bureaucratic relationship."[76]

Given this bureaucratic barrier, the higher standpoint and spiritual freedom of the writer were more than ever necessary. The free writer provided a "third element, which is political without being official," and which was *"civil [bürgerlich]* without being immediately involved in private interests and their needs." The writer had "the head of a citizen and the heart of a member of nonofficial society." Speaking not in the voice of bureaucratic officialdom, but in "the passionate language of the relationships themselves," the press bore the need of the people "to the steps of the throne, to a power before whom the distinction between administration and administered disappears and where there are only equally close and equally distant *citizens*."[77]

Marx preserved the façade of loyalty to Prussia with his reference to "the steps of the throne" (Heinrich Marx, in his speech of January 1834, had also hoped that the truth would "arrive at the steps of the throne"), but his analysis left little scope for associating the Prussian regime with those "spiritual nerves" he had earlier ascribed to the state. When he learned on January 25, 1843, that the *Rheinische Zeitung* was to be shut down, he was not disappointed. Writing to Ruge, he declared that his piece on the Moselle situation, with its criticisms of important state officials, had been one cause of the paper's demise. Marx did not regret this, for the suppression of the paper was an advance for political consciousness in Germany. It was also a release for Marx personally: "The government has set me free again." Years later he recalled that at this moment he eagerly seized the opportunity to "withdraw from the public stage into the study."[78]

Once there, Marx began to move away from a notion of criticism that sought to reform the state by confronting it with its concept, and toward new conceptions of the relation between philosophy and modern political life. Having given up the attempt to base political freedom on the concept of the modern state as the embodied spirit of collective human interest, he would no longer be a Hegelian. Although Marx would not fully reach that point until after he took up residence in Paris at the end of 1843, the demise of the *Rheinische Zeitung* already saw him far advanced along that path. By reducing the bureaucracy, which Hegel had regarded as the "universal class" mediating between the state and civil society, to a prisoner of the bureaucrats' own private interest, Marx had already weakened Hegel's notion beyond repair.

Marx would continue to base his political point of view on a third element, which was "*civil* without being immediately involved in private interests and their needs," but in the future this would be neither the state nor the press, but the revolutionary proletariat. As for Hegel, Marx would come to see his thinking no longer as based on the concept of "the whole," but simply on the individual subjectivity of the philosopher. In fact, by 1844 Hegel would take on in Marx's eyes the features of an earlier idealist thinker: Epicurus. He would exhibit philosophic withdrawal, a failure to comprehend "the object as object," and an interest not in determining causal relationships in nature, but only in "soothing the explaining subject."

At this point it would become clear that Marx's youthful Hegelian reformism had played a role in his life remarkably similar to the one played in Hegel's by Kantian radicalism. Both had been based on an *a priori* construction not yet tested by any actual experience; both attributed a reality to the world created by philosophy that each man's later experience would reveal to be false. Marx had been misled by Hegel into believing that his own Hegelianism brought him to manhood. In reality, like Hegel's Kantianism, it was a form of adolescent idealism. Like Hegel, Marx would find his own form of maturity only in abandoning the youthful philosophy that was turned against the world, and turning instead against the philosophy of his youth. But, for the Moor, this reversal of his previous standpoint would not bring about a Christian reconciliation with the present. The question remaining was what form the inversion of this reconciliation would take.

CHAPTER FOUR

Philosophy Inverted, I: Materialism, the Proletariat, and the Jewish Question

1. From Mind to Matter

MARXISM has been often—and correctly—described as a materialist theory of history and society, born from the womb of idealist philosophy. Marx and his fellow Young Hegelians were not alone in their attempt to make German idealism give birth to a more practical and realistic off-spring. As early as 1834 a French observer noted that German thinkers, after their thirty-year adventure of idealism, felt a deep need for more solid ground: "They cry that they are hungry and thirsty for the real world, and don't know what to do to get a hold on it quickly enough."[1]

One of the Germans to whom this description applied was then living in Paris, as he still would be nine years later when Marx arrived and met him there. He was the well-known writer and poet, Heinrich Heine. Like Marx, Heine was a baptized Jew; in fact the two may have been distant relations, although there is no evidence that they were aware of the connection.[2] As a student in Berlin during the 1820s, Heine had been deeply impressed by Hegel, whom he saw—together with Kant and Fichte—as preparing a revolution in Germany. Heine himself tried to contribute to this revolution by his biting social satire, and by a series of writings that emphasized humanity's need and ability to achieve happiness in the present.

Among Heine's major themes was "the rehabilitation of matter" from the degradation it had suffered at the hands of Christianity. "The immediate aim of all our modern institutions is the rehabilitation of matter," he wrote, "its restoration to former dignity, its moral recognition, its religious sanctification, its reconciliation with the spirit." Heine was no full-fledged materialist, but he believed that to rehabilitate matter was to restore humanity to health, to establish harmony between body and soul. This was a theme he shared with the St. Simonians, who influenced him while he was living in Paris. Like them, he believed that a great revolution would put an end to Christian spiritualism, introducing a new era of universal history.[3] German classical philosophy had "served to develop revolutionary forces that only await their time to break forth and to fill the world with terror and with admiration." That the revolution in Germany had so far been in the realm of thought only guaranteed that it would be more mighty once it broke through to reality. "The thought precedes the deed as the lightning the thunder. . . . There will be played in Germany a drama compared to which the French Revolution will seem but an innocent idyll."[4]

Marx read Heine either as a student in Berlin or earlier, and had him on his mind when he wrote to his father about his conversion to Hegel, since he quoted him in passing in that letter.[5] Heine's caustic view of middle-class society probably appealed to him, and Marx was living in the post-Hegelian atmosphere Heine described. Yet, despite his distinction both as a poet and as a philosophical popularizer, Heine was no philosopher himself, and his notion of the rehabilitation of matter seems to have had little direct influence on Marx's passage to materialism. The philosophical writer whose confrontation with Hegel shaped Marx's development more directly was Ludwig Feuerbach.

Feuerbach was (apart from Marx) the most intellectually distinguished follower and critic of Hegel in the early 1840s; his ideas were widely taken up, appearing, for instance, in the essays of Richard Wagner. His influence on Marx was strong in part because the two were evolving in similar directions. Fourteen years older than Marx, Feuerbach came from a German pietist background. Like Marx's, his father was a Kantian, and he was similarly incensed at his son's conversion to Hegel. Feuerbach, who heard Hegel lecture and corresponded with him, regarded Hegel as a second father.[6] Yet much of his own intellectual evolution was a process of freeing himself from Hegel. The direction of his development was toward an ever more determined materialism, in the light of which both Hegel's and his own earlier attempts to transcend the idealist-materialist dichotomy all took their place as forms of idealism. Around 1846 he arrived at a position whose stark materialism definitively separated him from his Hegelian youth, and in 1850 let slip the much quoted epigram "You are what you eat" (*man ist was er isst*).[7]

Feuerbach resembled other post-Hegelian thinkers—for instance, Bauer—in that his major concern was with religion and the human meaning of religious experience. His most famous work, *The Essence of Christianity* (1841), addressed precisely this problem. Marx considered him insufficiently aware of politics, even at the moment when he most admired him, but this did not prevent Marx from believing that Feuerbach had accomplished a theoretical revolution. It was not *The Essence of Christianity* that embodied this upheaval, however, but two shorter articles published in 1843: "Preliminary Theses for a Reform of Philosophy," and "Principles of the Philosophy of the Future." In these writings Feuerbach turned from religion to speculative thought in general, and specifically to Hegel.

A number of features of Feuerbach's thinking were particularly congenial to Marx, especially after the failure of the *Rheinische Zeitung* at the beginning of 1843. The first was Feuerbach's insistence that human thought was not (as Hegel had believed) a reflection of Spirit and its objectifications, but rather a mirror of real human existence. Feuerbach developed this notion first in regard to religion, in *The Essence of Christianity*. Religious descriptions of God, Feuerbach explained there, were only veiled accounts of man's own essential qualities. Religion was a "mystified" knowledge of man, its secret was "anthropology." Religion alienated humanity's essential qualities by projecting them into a foreign, other-worldly realm of divine existence. In religion, "Man first of all sees his nature as if *out of* himself, before he finds it in himself. His own nature is in the first instance contemplated by him as that of another being." The other being, God, was therefore imaginary, but the qualities attributed to him—his "predicates"—were not. Love, justice, and mercy were indeed divine, but they were qualities of humanity. "What was formerly contemplated and worshipped as God is now perceived as something *human*. . . . Man is seen to have adored his own nature."[8] Once the real nature of religion was understood, then the knowledge of humanity it contained could be revealed. "The work of the self-conscious reason in relation to religion is simply to destroy an illusion. . . . And we need only . . . invert the religious relations—regard that as an end which religion supposes to be a means—exalt that as primary which in religion is subordinate . . . —at once we have destroyed the illusion and the unclouded light of truth streams in upon us."[9]

In 1843 Feuerbach applied the same analysis to Hegelian philosophy. Hegel's account of Spirit simply described human nature in an inverted form. Feuerbach proposed to treat philosophy just as he had treated religion earlier: "The method of reformatory Criticism of *speculative philosophy in general* is no different from that already applied in the *philosophy of religion*. We need only make the *predicate* in every case the *subject* and thus as *subject* into the *object* and *principle*—in this way only *invert* speculative philosophy and we have the unconcealed, pure, bright truth." Speculative thinking consisted in positing the essence of something—nature, man, thought—as an independent being outside itself, thereby creating the inverted appearance that actual existence depended on a higher reality. The qualities and powers Hegel attributed to Spirit were the real qualities and powers of mankind. "Everything lies hidden within Hegelian philosophy, but always together with its negation, its opposite."[10]

The central methodological device Feuerbach employed to find the truth behind Hegel's abstractions was "inversion." It is seldom recognized that Feuerbach learned this procedure from Hegel himself. As we have seen, however, the notion of inversion had been central to Hegel's own enterprise. Many Hegelians of the 1840s recognized this and made explicit use of the idea of inversion. We have already seen the idea at work in the early Marx; Bauer, Hess, and Engels all employed it too. What was distinctive about Feuerbach's use of it was that in his hands the application of Hegel's rather abstract notion of inversion to Hegel's own philosophy became a call to turn philosophy into the study of the empirical world. "The path of speculative philosophy up to now, from the abstract to the concrete, from the ideal to the real has been an inverted one. Along this way one never arrives at true objective reality but only at the realization of his own abstractions." To arrive at reality, one had to begin with reality. "Philosophy is the knowledge of *what exists*. To think and know things and essences *as they are* is the highest law and the highest task of philosophy."[11]

Realism and empiricism were, therefore, primary terms in Feuerbach's vocabulary. The only way to perceive reality was actively, through the senses. "The real in *its reality*, or *as the real* is the real as an *object* of sense." Thus, sense experience was man's immediate and primary relation to the world. Ideas, too, had their origins in the real world, when men, who were essentially social beings, shared their experiences with others: "Ideas arise only from communication, from the conversation of man with man." Thought also had its roots in feeling: "Before you think a quality, you *feel* the quality. *Passion* goes before thought."[12]

To reform philosophy thus meant turning it away from what was intellectual and abstract toward what was passionate, sensual, and concrete. "The philosopher must take as the text of philosophy that in man which does *not* philosophize, what is rather *against* philosophy, *opposed* to abstract thought, and which Hegel therefore relegated to the notes. Only thus does philosophy become a *universal, unopposed, irrefutable, irresistible* power. Philosophy must *begin not with itself, but with its antithesis, with non-philosophy*. This unphilosophical, absolutely *antischolastic* essence opposed to thought within us is the principle of sensualism."[13]

Yet all these declarations meant something less than may appear. Feuerbach did not approach the empirical world directly and immediately, but by a detour, namely through the criticism of religion or of Hegelian theory. The reason for this was that Feuerbach's vision of human existence presupposed a human "essence" (*Wesen*), which attained to full existence only in the generality of mankind or humanity, in the human species. What gave humanity its special character was that man was a "species-being" (*Gattungswesen*), a being whose true individual existence required membership in mankind as a whole. It was precisely this consciousness of human universality that religion (in its highest form, Christianity) and speculative philosophy at once expressed and concealed, and which critical philosophy would reveal through its inversion of religious and philosophical speculation. In a world where religion still veiled the truth of human existence, the genuine species-essence of man could be an object of sense only to eyes that had been prepared by philosophical criticism to see it. Feuerbach called for a return to life here and now, but it was a return that could be made only by those who had already taken a trip into the speculative beyond.[14]

In line with these presuppositions, Feuerbach's position turned out to envision less a subordination of mind to matter than a parallel or union of the two. Philosophical thinking was not to be done away with altogether. "Direct observation [*Anschauung*] yields only the essence that is *immediately identical* with existence, thought yields the essence that exists through the intermediary of *differentiation, of separation*." Truth could not proceed from the heart alone, but required the head too. Man was at once a being of material existence and spiritual power. "Hans Sachs was indeed a shoemaker and a poet at the same time. But his shoes were the work of his hands, his poems the work of his head. The product is like its cause."[15]

Although Feuerbach sometimes used the term "materialism" to describe his position in 1843, it was a materialism that could not be distinguished from other conceptions. "In this essay the differences between materialism, empiricism, realism and humanism are of course a matter of indifference." Feuerbach preferred not to designate his philosophy with any special name; it was simply "man thinking." His philosophy was humanism.[16]

Feuerbach's writings of 1843 (like Heine's in another sphere) show both the power of the impulse to advance from idealism to materialism that was abroad in the post-Hegelian atmosphere and the distances that those making the journey had to cover. Only later would he in his own eyes "fully 'shake off' the philosopher and cause the philosopher to give way to the man." At that point Feuerbach himself would refer to his earlier position as "still haunted by the abstract Rational Being, the being of philosophy, as distinct from the actual, sensual being of nature and humanity."[17] This further evolution would move Feuerbach away from his emphasis on the human species, and closer to a concentration on individual, sentient human beings.

For Marx, too, Feuerbach's humanism would be only a stage—necessary and powerful, but not lasting—in the progress toward a different position. While it lasted, however, Feuerbach's influence on Marx was both deep and invigorating. Coming just when the failure of the *Rheinische Zeitung* faced Marx with the need to reconsider his own attempt to "realize" philosophy, Feuerbach's essays touched chords in Marx's mind. Marx had been well prepared for Feuerbach's use of inversion, having employed it himself in his dissertation. In the *Rheinische Zeitung*, too, Marx had directed this form of criticism against his opponents. "If one exactly reverses [*umkehrt*] the author's assertion," he wrote, "one gets the truth. The writer has turned history on its head."[18] Feuerbach even used the same image as Marx to express his horror of those thinkers who did not trust their senses. "I differ *toto caelo* from those philosophers who pluck out their eyes that they may see better," he asserted, evoking the story about Democritus that Marx had found to the point earlier.[19]

Marx's writings that reveal the immediate stamp of Feuerbach's critical inversion of Hegel include his *Critique of Hegel's 'Philosophy of Right'* undertaken in 1843, his essays for the *Deutsch-Französische Jahrbücher* (German-French Annals), which he edited with Arnold Ruge in 1844, the famous *Paris Manuscripts* written in the spring and summer of that year, and *The Holy Family*, Marx's first collaboration with Frederick Engels, published in 1845. One reason Feuerbach's injunction to find in Hegelian philosophy the basis for a more realistic view of the world found such a ready echo in Marx was that it harmonized with the set of messages he had long been receiving from within his family. Those messages were now taken up and amplified by the person who was rapidly becoming the new center of his emotional life.

2. Jenny

In the early months of 1843 Marx was casting about for a project to replace the *Rheinische Zeitung*. By March he had agreed to join Arnold Ruge as coeditor of a new journal. The venture was to be housed in Paris, where it would seek to establish contact between the left Hegelians and French radical politics. Marx saw the prospect of leaving the narrow confines of Germany for the broad and free atmosphere of France as deeply liberating.[20]

He did not propose to go alone, however. On March 13 he wrote to Ruge: "As soon as we have completed the contract, I want to go to Kreuznach and get married. . . . I can assure you without any romanticizing, that I am head over heels and altogether seriously in love. I have been engaged for over seven years, and my fiancée has on my account fought the hardest of struggles, which have ruined her health." Both Jenny's pietistic and aristocratic relatives and Marx's own family had made these campaigns necessary, he explained, and the "useless and exhausting" battles had gone on for years.[21]

Little is known about the conflicts to which Marx referred in this letter. Many years later Marx denied a report that the von Westphalen family had objected to the marriage because of his Jewish origins, but it is hard to be sure that this did not contribute to the resistance. Marx indicated that politics played a role, a number of Jenny's relatives being conservative upholders of the Prussian status quo. Whatever the reason, Henriette Marx complained in a letter of May 1840 that the von Westphalen family was ignoring her, and she may have looked on the match with some displeasure as a result.[22]

Nor does much evidence survive about the relations between Marx and Jenny in the years of their long engagement. Probably they saw each other a few times a year—more often after Marx left Berlin at the beginning of 1841—communicating by letter in the intervals, but only scattered relics of the correspondence—all on Jenny's side—remain. Her letters are all spirited, tender, loving, and devoted, but they give evidence of the suffering Marx mentioned to Ruge. They also indicate that Jenny continued to display the anxiety about her future that had troubled Marx's father in 1837.

Jenny saw her worries as arising first of all from the limited possibilities life offered to women. Without protesting, or wishing for any other role, she noted that "A girl, of course, cannot give a man anything but love and herself and her person, just as she is, quite undivided and for ever. . . . The girl must find her complete satisfaction in the man's love, she must forget everything in love." But Jenny was not just any girl; she was "such a peculiar one as I am."

> Oh, Karl, what makes me miserable is that what would fill any other girl with inexpressible delight—your beautiful, touching, passionate love, the indescribably beautiful things you say about it, the inspiring creations of your imagination—all this only causes me anxiety and often reduces me to despair. The more I were to surrender myself to happiness, the more frightful would my fate be if your ardent love were to cease and you became cold and withdrawn.

Her fears arose both from within and from without. She had an "inclination to sad thoughts," but it was fed by Karl's distrustfulness. They quarreled when someone told Marx he had a rival, and the fact that Jenny had not written for a time caused him to credit the story. Even after the rift was made up, Jenny remained "shattered by your doubt of my love and faithfulness." Twice in two pages she complained: "You have no regard for me, you do not trust me." Karl had expressed his doubts "so dryly in writing," "so coldly and wisely and reasonably." This made her worries that Karl might grow cold and withdrawn seem justified.[23]

These comments reveal that Jenny's image of Marx shared some features with the one his father saw. Like Heinrich, Jenny was troubled by the contrast between the passionate poetical form in which Marx conceived his relations to the world—in this case, to her—and the dry, uninvolved quality sometimes reflected in his actions. Because the second side of his character led her to fear the permanence of his love, Jenny would not let herself become absorbed by his vision of it. Instead, "I often remind you of external matters, of life and reality, instead of clinging wholly, as you can do so well, to the world of love, to absorption in it and to a higher, dearer, spiritual unity with you, and in it forgetting everything else, finding solace and happiness in that alone."[24] Jenny was taking over Marx's parents' role of bringing him back to the real world.

Yet in the days of their engagement Jenny had sometimes to rely on poetic imagination to express her sense of their relationship, just as Marx did. When she gave her fantasies free rein, the images that emerged combined mutual dependency and sacrifice in a bright yet dark vision.

> So, sweetheart, since your last letter I have tortured myself with the fear that for my sake you could become embroiled in a quarrel and then in a duel. Day and night I saw you wounded, bleeding and ill, and, Karl, to tell you the whole truth, I was not altogether unhappy in this thought: for I vividly imagined that you had lost your right hand, and Karl, I was in a state of rapture, of bliss, because of that. You see, sweetheart, I thought that in that case I could really become quite indispensable to you, you would then always keep me with you and love me. I also thought that then I could write down all your dear, heavenly ideas and be really useful to you.[25]

Were this a book about Jenny we might try to disentangle the hostile and loving feelings her vision embodied. A disabled Marx could not engage in those lofty flights that both so fascinated and worried her; but what else her happy fantasy of a mangled and helpless lover might have meant in her own psychic history we shall not try to say.

Yet we must recognize the vivid prophecy Jenny's vision contained about what her later life with Marx would be like. Even without maiming himself, Marx would depend on Jenny in just the way she fantasized. He would often suffer illness, brought on by struggles against the world he would take on partly for the sake of his family, partly in the interest of his "higher" ideals and his theoretical work. Sick or well, he would need her to carry on his correspondence, to make clean copies of his manuscripts, to care for the practical details of life. His weakness and impracticality would lead her to refer to him in their London years as "my big baby."[26]

It must be added, however, that—now as later—Marx was not the only one to suffer illness. Each of her surviving letters before her marriage testified to Jenny's ill health. In the earliest one she asked Marx "not to be so much concerned about my health. I often imagine it to be worse than it is. I *really do feel better now than for a long time past.*" That was in 1839 or 1840; in the summer of 1841 she was confined to bed again, and in 1843 complained about fatigue and loss of appetite.[27] Marx recognized that one of the causes of Jenny's maladies lay in the struggles she had to go through on his behalf and, just as those struggles would not cease, so would Jenny's health always continue to be a problem. Years of exile, hardship, and worry would leave her nerves shattered and her physical constitution permanently weakened.

Marx chose the life he led. Did Jenny choose it too? Certainly she had little sense of where marriage with Karl would lead her when she became engaged to him. On August 10, 1841, she wrote to him: "Ah, dear, dear sweetheart, now you get yourself involved in politics too. That is indeed the most risky thing of all. Dear little Karl, just remember always that here at home you have a sweetheart who is hoping and suffering and is wholly dependent on your fate."[28] All the same, she followed Marx into politics, and she seems to have had radical instincts that made his successive positions appealing to her. In 1843 she read Feuerbach, with understanding and admiration according to Marx, and by 1844 she could write of the coming revolution with the same straightforward seriousness her husband displayed.[29] Her intelligence and steadfastness would be exhibited many times in later life. She would need both.

3. Hegel Inverted

Karl and Jenny Marx were married on June 12, 1843. After a honeymoon trip to the Falls of the Rhine they settled down for a time in Kreuznach, a spa not far from Trier where Jenny's mother had been living since shortly after Ludwig von Westphalen's death. There Marx continued his work on a project that had been on his mind for over a year, a critique of Hegel's *Philosophy of Right*. Marx had always been a reluctant Hegelian, converted against his will, critical of his philosophic master even while recognizing his dependence on him. Now, helped on by Feuerbach, he began to separate himself from Hegel, and to give a new shape to his intellectual position, just as he had recently established a new stage in his personal life. In his relations with Jenny, however, it was she who (like his parents) tried to bring the philosopher back from a "higher, spiritual" view of the world with reminders about ordinary life and reality; in addressing Hegel it was Marx who spoke against idealism in the name of actual existence.

Marx's critique of Hegel's political philosophy was directed explicitly against Hegel's defense of constitutional monarchy, in place of which Marx upheld a radical form of democracy. Hegel's attempt to depict existing states as able to harmonize private interests with the general interest, and establish the principle of rationality in the world of ordinary experience, was a mere fantasy. Marx reduced each of the political organs Hegel presented as rising above private interest to an inescapable reflection of it: the monarch, the system of representative estates, and the "universal class" of state servants and bureaucrats. Only democracy—the full participation of all people as citizens in the people's collective political life—could transcend the egoism of civil society and give real existence to the collective life Hegel sought to find in the state.[30]

The democracy Marx envisioned was of a very radical kind. It included "the extension and greatest possible universalization of voting," in order to permeate everyday life with a political consciousness that could dissolve the concentration on private, individual interests described by Hegel as the essence of "civil society." True democracy would end the divorce between society and the state that Hegel had found at the center of modern social and political life. In calling for the dissolution of civil society as a separate pole of modern existence, Marx was consciously looking forward to the abolition of private property: property was the basis of civil society. Hence, his notion of democracy pointed forward to his later and more explicit communism (as several writers have pointed out); in addition, his vision of the dissolution of the political state as an entity separate from society foreshadowed his later notion that, in communist society, the state would disappear too.[31]

Just as this political theory was still a stage distant from his later communism, however, so was its philosophical underpinning still separate from his later materialism. What framed Marx's general orientation was Feuerbach's method of discovering the truth about existence by criticizing Hegel. Like Feuerbach, Marx believed that Hegel's writings contained true descriptions of reality, but presented them in an inverted and mystified form. In Hegel, Marx declared: "Empirical actuality is thus understood as it is. It is also pronounced rational." But since Hegel presented all the features of the real world as determinations of the Idea or of Spirit, he made the facts of existence appear to be reflections of speculative abstractions, with the result that the real relations among the elements of existence were inverted. "The conditioning factor is presented as the conditioned, the determining is presented as the determined, and the producing is presented as the product of its product."[32] Hence, as Feuerbach had recognized, the truth Hegel's writings both contained and veiled could be extracted from them by the method of inversion. Hegel had accomplished a "reversal of subject and predicate," an "inversion of subject into object"; hence "It is evident that the true method is turned upside down." This was true specifically of the relationship between the state and the components of society. "Family and civil society are the presuppositions of the state; they are the really active things; but in speculative philosophy it is reversed."[33]

Like Feuerbach, Marx did not identify his point of view here as a specifically materialist one, but only as true to empirical reality and free from speculative abstractions. He explicitly rejected "abstract materialism," as identical with "abstract spiritualism," describing both materialism and spiritualism as extremes that were present in Hegel's state, and would be abolished once politics had been absorbed back into society. "The Corporations are the materialism of the bureaucracy, and the bureaucracy is the spiritualism of the Corporations. . . . The spiritualism vanishes with its opposite materialism." Marx described the elements he identified as the determinants of social and political life—family and civil society—not only as material forces, but as "actual spiritual existences of will."[34]

Continuing the criticism of bureaucracy he had begun in the *Rheinische Zeitung*, Marx denied that the state servants deserved to be called a "universal class." Hegel was right to search for a source of universality within society, but wrong to think he had found it in the bureaucrats. What mattered was "the capability of the universal class to be really universal, i.e., to be the class [*Stand*] of every citizen. But Hegel proceeds from the postulate of the pseudo-universal, the illusory universal class, universality fixed in the form of a particular class." For Marx only the citizens as a whole, all men as citizens, could constitute a universal class.[35]

What Marx now thought about the place of classes in society appears from his remarks on the character of the modern German *Mittelstand*. Marx was acutely aware—as Hegel had also been—that modern social relations differed from earlier ones because the old political estates had been transformed into "merely social distinctions" through the separation of civil society and the state. This change had occurred first under the absolute monarchies of the eighteenth century, and been completed by the French Revolution. But the resulting social groupings, which Marx here still labeled as *Stände* (estates or orders) and not as *Klassen*, the term he would use a few months after, were not the clearly established determinants of modern life about which he would speak later. On the contrary, the modern *Stand* was "a division of the masses whose development is unstable and whose very structure is arbitrary and in no sense an organization." Membership in these orders did not reflect the communal character of life as in former times; "rather, it is partly chance, partly labor, etc., of the individual which determines whether he remains in his class [*Stand*] or not, a class which is, further, only an external determination of the individual."[36]

Part of what Marx had in mind when he spoke of the accidental and capricious nature of these groupings was that membership in an official estate did not always reflect an individual's actual position or activity in society. "He stands in no actual relation to his substantial activity, to his actual class." Thus "one businessman belongs to a class [*Stand*] different than that of another businessman, i.e., he belongs to another social position." Although this criticism showed Marx to be conscious of the difference between official estates and "real" classes, he still did not see the latter as defining the nature of modern society. The underlying principle and pervasive fact of contemporary social life was not class membership but individual isolation. "Present civil society is the accomplished principle of individualism: individual existence is the final end, while activity, labor, content, etc., are merely means." Modern men were unconnected atoms, each one isolated in his "pure, bare individuality." The principle of the modern state was "abstract personality," the single individual unrelated to communal life. In Hegel's state this principle of abstract personality received full and untrammeled expression.[37]

No longer, then, did Marx see Hegel as superior to ancient thinkers because they had begun from abstract individuality and he from the idea of "the whole." On the contrary, it was in his own earlier image of the Greek philosophers—whose only concept was abstract individuality—that Marx now cast Hegel. Moreover, for Hegel, as for the Greek *sophos*, "the medium here is the absolute will and the world of the philosopher; the particular end is the end of the philosophizing subject, namely, constructing the hereditary monarch out of the pure Idea." Like Socrates, Hegel "is not allowed to measure the idea by what exists; he must measure what exists by the idea." What had been true for the Greeks was now true for Hegel: "Real knowledge appears to be devoid of content just as real life appears to be dead, for this imaginary knowledge and life pass for what is real and essential." Marx still occupied the same position in regard to idealism he had in 1837 or 1841; but now it was Hegel who represented this idealism and Feuerbach who offered a way to integrate the rational ideal with actual life.[38]

4. Proletarians and Others

Marx would pursue this integration very differently from the way Feuerbach had: by identifying his cause with that of the European working class. It was in the late fall of 1843 that Marx first called up the vision of proletarian revolution that would remain the center of his world view for the rest of his life. Before we examine that vision we must say a word about the reality that lay behind it.

Worry and anxiety about the position of workers in European society had grown in the post-Napoleonic period; by the 1840s there existed a widespread sense of social crisis. The ills of the early nineteenth-century working class are most often attributed to industrialization, and there is no doubt that the new techniques of mechanized manufacturing were beginning to make their appearance. On the continent, however, in contrast to England, the progress of mechanized industry was hesitant and sporadic. Continental manufacturers were in a situation less favorable to large-scale innovation than their counterparts across the Channel. Markets were smaller and less well integrated than in England, and wages were lower, making investments in expensive labor-saving machinery less attractive. The rapid rise in population that had begun in the second half of the eighteenth century brought an expansion in the pool of available labor, increasing competition for jobs and allowing manufacturers to respond to English competition by pushing wages down instead of introducing more productive techniques. Workers increasingly experienced poverty, dislocation, and rootlessness (especially in the case of rural workers who sought jobs in the rapidly growing towns and cities); they made known their discontent in uprisings like those of the Lyon silk workers in 1831 and 1834, and of the Silesian linen weavers in 1844.[39]

To describe the visible and troubling polarization of society, a new "language of class" grew up both in England and on the continent, expressing the demise of the older social order with its reassuringly stable hierarchy of organically integrated and legally regulated status groups. Social observers made increasing use of a term that had seldom been thought to describe European workers as a whole: proletariat. The people for whom this term was used were for the most part not factory hands. Employed in traditional crafts still organized in the old ways, they nonetheless faced impoverishment and the loss of their traditional social status in the new conditions. The St. Simonians saw them as subject to "exploitation," and the German conservative Franz von Baader referred to their "inflammability and revolutionability." In 1842 the term received widespread public notice in Germany through the account of French working-class life and radical social theory given by another conservative writer, Lorenz von Stein.[40]

Marx first invoked the possibility of proletarian revolution in an essay intended as the Introduction to the *Critique of Hegel's 'Philosophy of Right'* we have just discussed. He began the Introduction at Kreuznach, and finished it in Paris during December 1843, or January 1844. ("To Paris, the old high school of philosophy—*absit omen!*—and the new capital of the new world," he had written to Ruge on the eve of his departure.) Published in the *Deutsch-Französische Jahrbücher* early in the new year, it was the only portion of Marx's critique of Hegel's political philosophy to appear during his lifetime. In it Marx extended the Feuerbachian principle of finding the truth by inverting Hegel's view of the world. How he did this suggests that there were close links between his view of revolution and the question of his philosophical identity.[41]

In his Introduction Marx presented the critique of Hegel as an extension of the criticism of religion begun by the Hegelian left. The premise of that criticism had been that religion arose because man's real being was not allowed actual existence in the present. "Man is *the world of men*, the state, society. This state and this society produce religion, which is an *inverted consciousness of the world* because they are an *inverted world*. . . . It is the *fantastic realization* of the human essence inasmuch as the *human essence* possesses no true reality." Now that this truth about religion had been revealed, the task of philosophy "is to unmask human self-alienation in its *unholy forms* now that it has been unmasked in its *holy form*."[42]

Marx addressed himself to Hegel's interpretation of German conditions rather than to the German situation itself because the latter was "below the level of history, beneath all criticism." Only German philosophy stood on the level of real existence elsewhere; hence it was from Hegel that the criticism of German life had to begin. In describing the course that criticism had taken so far, Marx returned to a theme he had sounded in some preparatory notes for his dissertation, the division of critics into two parties: a positive one that "turned against philosophy," and a theoretical one that "turned against the world." The first party committed the error of starting in the wrong place: "You demand starting from *actual germs of life* but forget that the actual life-germ of the German nation has so far sprouted only inside its *cranium*. In short: *you cannot transcend philosophy without actualizing it*." The theoretical party had committed "the same error but with the factors *reversed*." It failed to recognize "that *previous philosophy* itself belongs to this world and is its *complement*, although an ideal one." Hence, the defect of the critical party was that "It believed that it could actualize philosophy without transcending it."[43]

The way out of this dilemma was the discovery of an actual, existing force in German society whose real situation embodied the negation of existing conditions that philosophical criticism also expressed. "Theory is actualized in a people only insofar as it actualizes their needs." Where could this force be sought?

> In the formation of a class with *radical chains*, a class in civil society that is not of civil society, a class that is the dissolution of all classes, a sphere of society having a universal character because of its universal suffering and claiming no *particular* right because no *particular wrong* but *unqualified wrong* is perpetrated on it. . . . This dissolution of society as a particular class is the *proletariat*.

The proletariat would be philosophy's negative counterpart and partner because it shared on a practical level the philosopher's negation of existing society in the theoretical sphere. Like the philosophical critic, the worker had no personal, private interest to pursue and could only find human fulfillment through the realization of humanity's universal character. "As philosophy finds its *material* weapons in the proletariat, the proletariat finds its *intellectual* weapons in philosophy."[44]

What Marx found historically significant about the proletariat was not simply its position in society but the parallel between its situation and philosophy's. So close was the connection between the two that Marx described the proletariat here in terms he had earlier applied to the free press. In the *Rheinische Zeitung* it had been the press that was *"civil [bürgerlich]* without being immediately involved in private interests and their needs." It was the writer whose productive life took place outside the existing structure of trades, and who sacrificed his personal existence to his work.[45] It is likely, moreover, that these links between the proletariat and the philosophical critic were not merely *post factum*: the connection probably was one reason Marx turned to the proletariat in the first place. What makes this likely is the fact that Marx was not the only writer to discover an inner link between the life situations of workers and German critical philosophers in these years. At least two others, both Marx's friends at the time, also did so.

Of the two, less weight attaches to the observations of Bruno Bauer. Bauer described the parallel between philosophy and the proletariat as a reason for Marx's passage to communism. But his analysis only appeared in 1847 in a *Complete History of the Party Struggles in Germany during the Years 1842-46*. Bauer's book was a justification of his own position and much of it revolved around an attack on the writers associated with the *Rheinische Zeitung*. The major target of his hostility, however, was not Marx but the man who had been the paper's Berlin correspondent, Karl Heinzen, a romantic whose brand of communism Marx also found it necessary to reject by 1847. Bauer even praised Marx's "Defense of the Anonymous Correspondent from the Moselle."[46]

Bauer argued that the confidence the *Rheinische Zeitung* placed in the Prussian state, and in the paper's own ability to influence the state's actions, was bound to lead to disillusionment. When the journal was suppressed, its writers were deprived of the belief that criticism could create a political community in which "man is given the opportunity to develop according to his true nature, and which alone can give him the opportunity to feel himself a man." In that situation, the writers were prepared to receive the news that " 'out there,' in France, existed a great class of men, who, like them had reaped only despair as the fruit of their labors and as their portion of history." The intellectual radicals' spiritual needs matched the workers' bodily needs, the political needs of the first met the "general historical need" of the second. Both were characterized by "separation from worldly interest" and disillusionment with the actual world. The radical writers joined themselves to the proletariat because they discovered the principle of its existence to be the same as their own.[47]

Written three years after Marx had joined the proletariat to critical philosophy, Bauer's words tell us only that the connection between the espousal of proletarian communism and Marx's earlier position was understood by one of his contemporaries. More interesting was Arnold Ruge's identification of radical writers and proletarians, since it was published early in 1843, before Marx had made that identification himself and at a time when Marx was beginning to work with Ruge. Ruge's comments appeared in an essay called "The Press and Freedom," published in *Anekdota Philosophica*, a collection of essays Marx knew well, for he contributed to it himself, and he found in it Ludwig Feuerbach's "Preliminary Theses for the Reform of Philosophy."[48]

Ruge defended the free press as the only instrument through which human reason could develop within the actual world. The existing German censorship flew in the face of reason; therefore it would soon be overcome. If it seemed powerful for the moment, the reason lay in the apparent character of its opponents, the critical journalists whose work it had seized or destroyed—Ruge mentioned no names, but in 1843 Marx himself was one of these. It seemed, Ruge observed, "as if the more recent among the writers who have come into conflict with the censorship are only a few proletarian individuals, propertyless, malevolent fomentors of discontent and blinded idealists," who would never gain the sympathy of the mass of quiet and loyal breadwinners. So far the writers had in fact failed to win the sympathy of the people, even when arbitrary police action had deprived them of their work—their property—and their reputation without a proper hearing.[49]

What would destroy this false appearance of the proletarian character of the writers would be a historical revolution that would infuse the whole of civic life with the ideal interest of politics, ending the subjection of men to the power of the police. "With the concept of the *free citizen* there will also be born the concept of the *free writer*; then will the appearance that the free writers were so free only because they were civil proletarians cease."[50]

Whether Ruge's identification of the radical German journalists as seeming proletarians was one source of Marx's turn to the workers as allies of critical philosophy or not, it does indicate that Marx was neither the only one nor the first of the left Hegelians to perceive the connection. The identification of middle-class radical intellectuals with the proletariat had also been anticipated by one of the followers of St. Simon: Enfantin had declared that "The bourgeois and the learned have deserted me. We are proletarians."[51]

To be sure, neither Ruge nor Enfantin reached Marx's vision of proletarian revolution; but in 1843 Marx himself had not quite reached his later understanding of it either. Marx's invocation of proletarian upheaval in his Introduction to the critique of Hegel was not yet founded on his later notion of class conflict. True, important parts of his later schema were present. Although he did not yet abandon *Stand*, Marx now employed the term *Klasse*, using the two interchangeably.[52] Social conflict in Germany did not produce the clarity of domination it yielded in France, however.

In Germany "Society is forever splitting into the most varied races opposing one another with petty antipathies, bad consciences, and brutal mediocrity." Hence, no class could claim to represent the whole of society. "Every class lacks not only the consistency, penetration, courage, and ruthlessness which could stamp it as the negative representative of society," but also "that breadth of soul" and revolutionary boldness that could allow it to stand for and lead the people as a whole. No class could defeat any other because "every section of civil society goes through a defeat before it celebrates victory, develops its own obstacles before it overcomes those facing it, . . . and each class is involved in a struggle against the class beneath it as soon as it begins to struggle with the class above it."[53]

Because no coherent social group had yet been able to dominate German politics, the revolution of the German proletariat would be directed not against a ruling bourgeoisie but against despotism and the general degradation of German life. In France, where the bourgeoisie had freed itself in the name of general liberation and established itself at the head of society, emancipation proceeded by stages, and "partial emancipation is the basis of universal emancipation." In Germany, the reverse: "universal emancipation is the *conditio sine qua non* of any partial emancipation." Thus, Marx conceived the role of the proletariat not according to stages of social and political development but in a national and human context: "Once the lightning of thought has deeply struck this unsophisticated soil of the people, the *Germans* will emancipate themselves to become *men*."[54]

Nor was the proletariat Marx invoked in this essay quite the same as the one he would address in the *Communist Manifesto*. By the end of the 1840s Marx would identify the proletariat with the growing class of factory workers. In 1843, however, he still used the term in the way earlier writers such as Franz von Baader or the St. Simonians had used it, to refer more generally to those workers who had lost the stable place in society traditionally assigned to European labor, who were "in civil society" but not "of civil society." The reference to workers he would include in the *1844 Manuscripts* a few months later spoke specifically of "communist artisans."[55] Although Marx spoke of the proletariat beginning to appear in Germany as "a result of the rising *industrial* movement," he did not yet regard the growth of proletarian organization and consciousness as dependent on the advance of mechanized industry. This is clear from the comments on the Silesian weavers' revolt of 1844 that Marx published in the Paris German newspaper *Vorwärts* in June of that year. Marx recognized that industrial development in Germany was very far behind that of England or France; nonetheless, he pictured the Silesian weavers—handloom weavers in a "putting out" system, not factory hands—as in advance of English and French workers. The theoretical superiority of the Silesian weavers over all French and English labor movements was demonstrated, Marx believed, by the fact that the *Weavers' Song* did not mention "hearth, factory and district," but directly opposed private property. Because of this, "The Silesian uprising *begins* precisely where the French and English labor revolts *end*, with the consciousness of the nature of the proletariat." This theoretical precocity of German workers was explained not by economic and social factors, but on the grounds that the backwardness of Germany made philosophy more necessary for them—as for Germans in general—than for the English or French.[56]

What defined Marx's approach to the proletariat in 1843-44, therefore, was less economic analysis or social observation than the inner link he perceived between their situation and that of critical philosophy as parallel negations of existing society. If the workers Marx observed in Paris impressed him as the practical means for the coming liberation of humanity, the reason was not that they were modern factory workers but rather that Marx's theory of proletarian revolution did not yet distinguish clearly between artisans and proletarians. Marx came to the view that workers in the nineteenth century were revolutionary before he came to see their development as equivalent with the growth of the factory system. Both that perspective and the materialist view that freed the coming revolution from dependence on "the lightning of thought" were still in the future.

5. The Jewish Question

Before leaving Kreuznach for Paris at the end of October 1843, Marx wrote another article, which was published in the *Deutsch-Französische Jahrbücher* early in the next year. Its title was "On the Jewish Question." In a strictly chronological ordering, we should have considered this essay before the Introduction to Marx's critique of Hegel. Its significance for Marx's development is more clearly revealed by reversing the order, however, so that the links emerge between Marx's view of Jews and his conception of the proletariat. In Marx's progress toward the ultimate materialism of his mature writings, his relationship to Jews and Jewishness had an important role to play.

That role has been difficult to grasp, however, because Marx's essay has been read through the smoke of a polemic fed by all the ideological fires of the twentieth century, the question "Was Marx an anti-Semite?" The question is not easy to answer. Everyone acknowledges that anti-Semitism played no role in Marx's most influential writings, neither in the rhetorical declamations of the *Communist Manifesto* nor in the deeply theoretical analyses of *Capital*. He never pictured Jews as inferior to any other, "higher" or "more developed" race or people. He never denied his own Jewish origins, several of his close friends were Jews, and he argued in favor of giving Jews full civic rights. At the same time, it is also clear that, both in the essay "On the Jewish Question" and in some of his letters and journalism, Marx spoke disparagingly of the Jews as a group, and of individuals who displayed what he thought were Jewish characteristics. Undeniably, he sometimes felt hostility toward the Jews. If, on balance, it is not possible to describe Marx's relationship to Jewishness—his own or others—in the simple terms of anti-Semitism, it is essential to recognize that Marx felt a deep ambivalence toward Jews and Judaism.[57]

Much of the evidence usually cited for Marx's anti-Semitism comes from his later comments—mostly in letters to Engels—about Ferdinand Lassalle. Lassalle helped Marx, both financially and in his relations with German publishers. Yet, from about 1856, Marx's private view of Lassalle grew hostile, and he and Engels began to cover him with anti-Semitic epithets. He was "Itzig," "Ephraim Gescheidt," a "true Jew." Did this mean that Marx rejected Lassalle out of anti-Semitic prejudice? The evidence does not bear this interpretation. Marx began as a defender of Lassalle; the *Neue Rheinische Zeitung* supported him during the revolution of 1848.[58] In 1853 Marx said of him simply: "Despite the many 'buts,' he is hard and energetic."[59] Eventually the "buts" won out. Lassalle was not an easy colleague. He devoted much of his energy to the defense of his mistress, a German countess, and made his affair with her public knowledge. He was a dandy, who dramatized his self-importance with aristocratic airs. It was also true that Lassalle was an effective speaker and organizer in a way that Marx was not, and it is certainly possible that jealousy played a part in Marx's growing hostility toward him. The turning point in Marx's relationship with Lassalle came when a representative of a workers' group in Düsseldorf—named Levy, it should be noted—visited Marx to accuse Lassalle of exploiting the workers' organization for his own ends, particularly his defense of the countess von Hatzfeldt. Marx wrote to Engels that he had submitted Levy to a sharp examination, and had been convinced that he was right: a man whose real importance equaled Lassalle's pretensions would not have sacrificed ten years of his life to the "bagatelle" of his love affair. "The *whole thing* has made a *definitive* impression on me and Freiligrath," Marx told Engels, "however much I was taken by Lassalle and however mistrustful I am of workers' gossip."[60] Many contrasts of personal character contributed to Marx's final hostility toward Lassalle, but the relationship cannot be explained on the basis of anti-Semitic prejudice. In 1867 Marx described another German political figure, Wilhelm Marr, as "in his personal manner Lassalle translated into a Christian— naturally worth a lot less."[61]

Certainly, Marx's language in regard to Lassalle was hostile and ugly. When he really lost patience with him, however, it grew still uglier: not merely a Jew, Lassalle became a "nigger," worse, a "German-Jewish nigger": his physical characteristics and his actions all betrayed this hybrid origin.[62] Was Marx, therefore, anti-Negro as well as anti-Semitic? Yes, in a way. But Marx also spoke of the French mulatto Paul Lafargue as a "nigger," and he used this language at exactly the moment he was accepting Lafargue as the fiancé of his daughter Laura. Lafargue was "our Nigger," or "our little Nigger" (*unser Negrillo*). Moreover, it was to Paul and Laura Lafargue that Marx commented on the racial theories of Gobineau, which were beginning to grow more influential in late nineteenth-century European politics: "For such people it is always a source of satisfaction to have someone to estimate according to their opinions and to despise." Gobineau, Marx observed, had been forced to recognize the important contributions of black people to civilization in spite of himself.[63] Again, Marx's own feelings were complex and ambivalent, and unexamined prejudices were at work in them. However, if his language makes us squirm, his actions do not justify putting him in the camp of the racists.

Toward Jews and Jewishness Marx always retained many positive ties. Among his closest friends were the Jews Heinrich Heine and Ludwig Kugelmann; for a time he was close to Moses Hess, and he helped the former Cologne communist Abraham Jacoby emigrate to America (where he became an influential physician). Moreover, Marx was recognized as a Jew. His dark complexion and his physical appearance, recognized in the nickname Moor, were often described as Jewish. Arnold Ruge thought of Marx as a Jew at the time the two worked together on the *Deutsch-Französische Jahrbücher*. The first public anti-Semitic attack on Marx himself, by Eduard von Müller-Tellering, appeared in 1850.[64] In regard to the Cologne communist trial of 1851—in which the Prussian government sought to demonstrate the existence of a conspiracy organized around Marx—he wrote: "The Jew-hunt naturally increases the enthusiasm and interest." A few years later Marx told wryly of a "warning" issued about him by a German-American paper, explaining his "abstruseness" from the Old Testament and his influence from the German habit of following "the clever writers of the Old Testament nation." To his uncle Lion Philips— himself an atheist whom Marx proudly described as maintaining his anti-religious convictions to the end—Marx once wrote of Benjamin Disraeli as "our racial colleague." Marx disliked Disraeli, but not because of his origins. "He is the best proof of how great talent without conviction creates rascals."[65]

It is clear, moreover, that in the early 1840s Marx was a supporter of civic rights for Jews, and that this support formed the background for "On the Jewish Question." The *Rheinische Zeitung* had a number of Jewish backers, and it published articles in favor of Jewish rights. In the spring of 1842, before Marx became its editor, the paper opposed a proposed Prussian law that would have organized Jews into separate "corporations" to assure that they would have no authority over Christians. In three articles written by Moses Hess (who at that time was by no means at peace with his own Jewish origins), the paper argued that the state should treat all its citizens equally: in modern states where the Jews were treated like other citizens, namely France and North America, the supposed "national" characteristics of the Jews vanished.[66]

In his own first contribution to the Cologne paper, Marx took a similar position. "Once a state includes a number of confessions with equal rights," he observed, "it cannot be a religious state without violating particular confessions; it cannot be a church which condemns members of another confession as heretics, makes every piece of bread depend on faith, and makes dogma the link between particular individuals and civil life in the state."[67] When Bruno Bauer attacked the upholders of Jewish civic rights in the essay on the Jewish question that provoked Marx's reply, one of his targets was Marx's *Rheinische Zeitung*. Defending the position of Carl Hermes, who had favored the Christian state and opposed Jewish rights in the rival *Kölnische Zeitung*, Bauer rejected the argument on behalf of the Jews offered by Ludwig Philipson in Marx's paper.[68] In August 1842 Marx himself collected the same Hermes's articles against the Jews with a view to answering them. Just before Marx left Cologne to live at Kreuznach, he agreed to a request from the leader of the Jewish community there that he present a petition to the Rhineland Diet in favor of Jewish rights. By that time Bauer's views had appeared, and Marx wrote to Ruge: "However detestable the Jewish religion is to me, Bauer's conception is too abstract."[69]

Bauer, like Marx, wrote about religion under the influence of Feuerbach. He addressed himself to the question of civic rights for Jews from an atheistic position, which condemned Christianity as well as Judaism and looked forward to the liberation of mankind from all religious delusions. But he viewed Christianity as representing a higher stage in human history than Judaism and therefore attributed to the Christian state certain rights over the Jews. Jews brought oppression on themselves by defining their existence in opposition to the rest of mankind, and by declaring their subjection to a law that derived from an outside, alien power (God) instead of from their own essential being. Because Jews refused to give up "their peculiar essence" they were not entitled to the rights of man. Nor, for the same reason, were they entitled to the rights of citizens in a Christian state: as a separate group they could be subjects with special privileges, but not citizens.[70]

In his related essay on "The Ability of Present-Day Jews and Christians to become Free," Bauer asserted that the only path to liberation for Jews lay in becoming Christians. Not that Christians themselves were free men: on the contrary, their loss of humanity was absolute. However, because Christianity comprehended the power of humanity as unlimited—

identified man with God—even while it projected that power into the alien and inverted heavenly beyond, the dissolution of Christianity would yield full human freedom. For the Christian, emancipation required only the destruction of his existing religious consciousness. For the Jew, however, the same liberation required the initial step of proceeding to a Christian consciousness. Only from a Christian standpoint could the criticism of religion unveil the essential humanity within all men.[71]

Marx made his reply to Bauer an occasion for discussing many questions that occupied him at the time, in particular the relation between the state and civil society, which he thought Bauer had confused. Because Bauer overvalued political liberty in itself, he posed the wrong question when he asked whether Jews deserved political rights within existing states. "Bauer asks the Jews: Have you the right to demand *political emancipation* from your standpoint? We ask on the contrary: Has the standpoint of political emancipation the right to demand from the Jews the abolition of Judaism and from man the abolition of religion?" Political emancipation was not the same thing as "human emancipation," for even in the most highly developed modern states the equalization of political rights still left men chained to the delusions of religion and divided from each other by the barriers of private property. Even in a democracy (such as the United States), "Religion remains the ideal, unsecular consciousness of its members because it is the ideal form of the *stage of human development* attained in the democratic state." In America people were expected to profess "religion in general, any kind of religion." There was, therefore, no contradiction between men having civic rights and preserving any particular religious consciousness. In its full development the state "acknowledges itself as a state and ignores the religion of its members."[72] Hence Jews should be granted full civic and political rights.

The same sharp distinction between the "imaginary universality" of political life and the real world of particular interests that controlled it underlay Marx's assertion that, contrary to what Bauer believed, modern Jews ought also to be accorded the "rights of man." Since these rights of man proclaimed by the great eighteenth-century revolutions were distinguished from the "rights of the citizen," what could they be but the rights of men in their private lives as members of civil society, the rights of men to pursue their individual, egoistic interests? "None of the so-called rights of man goes beyond the egoistic man, the man withdrawn into himself, his private interest and his private choice, and separated from the community as a member of civil society." Bauer's denial that Jews should have these rights thus made no sense: Jews were private individuals as much as anyone else. Rather than assert the rights of existing society against the Jews, therefore, Marx defended the Jews against existing society. Not Judaism but "political emancipation" had limitations that needed to be overcome. "If you Jews want to be politically emancipated without emancipating yourselves humanly, the incompleteness and contradiction lies not only in you but in the *essence* and *category* of political emancipation. If you are engrossed in this category, you share a general bias." The general illusions of the present needed to be abolished, not the particular illusions of Judaism.[73]

In the whole of this first part of Marx's essay, answering Bauer's pamphlet *The Jewish Question*, there is not a single sentence that can be called anti-Semitic. All the offending phrases occur in the second part of his article, where Marx responded to Bauer's related essay on "The Ability of Contemporary Jews and Christians to become Free." Here he declared the secret of the Jew to be "self-interest" and his worldly god to be money, and described society as producing the Jew "out of its own entrails."[74] What was the context of these remarks? The subject of this part of Marx's essay was not the Jewish character, but the question posed by Bauer's contrast of Judaism and Christianity: "Which of the two is *more capable of emancipation?* . . . Which emancipates more, the negation of Judaism or the negation of Christianity?" Bauer's answer had been clear: Christianity. Marx's response was equally clear: Jewishness.

Marx arrived at his answer by rephrasing the question in his own terms: "We will try to break with the theological formulation of the issue. The question concerning the Jew's capacity for emancipation becomes for us the question: What specific *social* element is to be overcome in order to abolish Judaism? For the modern Jew's capacity for emancipation is the relation of Judaism to the emancipation of the modern world." Thus, the declaration that the basis of Judaism was self-interest and its god money prepared Marx's answer to Bauer's question: "Very well! Emancipation from *bargaining* and *money*, and thus from practical and real Judaism would be the self-emancipation of our era. . . . When the Jew recognizes this practical nature of his as futile and strives to eliminate it, he works away from his previous development toward general *human emancipation* and opposes the *supreme practical* expression of human self-alienation." Precisely because Judaism was based on self-interest, because its real life was the life of bargaining and money, Jewishness rather than Christianity provided the Archimedean point from which to effect the emancipation of modern society. The connection between Jewishness and money making Marx presupposed here was widely assumed in early nineteenth-century Germany. One meaning of *Judentum* was simply commerce. Marx incorporated vulgar and hostile views about Jews current in Germany into his treatise; clearly he shared them on one level, but he also transformed them into the foundation for his claim that Jewishness offered a more genuine basis for liberation than Christianity.[75]

The first implications of this assertion were personal. If Bauer was a former religious Christian who had freed himself by denying Christianity, Marx was in origin a secularized Jew who regarded himself as liberated from "practical Judaism," self-interest. Marx's claim against Bauer was that his own personal standpoint—granting all its defects—rather than Bauer's, provided the point of entry for true human liberation. Here we find Marx asserting for the first time that a purely materialist standpoint—what he called "practical need" or "egoism" and not just "practice" in a Feuerbachian sense—was the source of true liberation and that this recognition defined his own personal position. In the perspective Marx took up here, materialism was Jewish, and its implications were positive.

Moreover, the image of the Jews Marx presented in "On the Jewish Question" presented surprising similarities with the group he discussed in his Introduction to the *Critique* of Hegel, published at the same time: the proletariat. Of course the two were vastly different. The proletariat was propertyless, the Jews propertied; the proletariat did not claim any "particular right," it "does not partially oppose the consequences but totally opposes the premises of the German political system." Nonetheless, the proletariat shared with the Jews the important characteristic of being a group whose life took place wholly in the realm of material need. The proletariat was the only class that could emancipate the Germans because it was forced to action "by its *immediate* condition, by *material* necessity, by its *very chains*." Judaism, too, since it was "the religion of practical need," by its very nature "could not find fulfillment in theory but only in *practice*, simply because practice is its truth." The proletariat was "a passive element," its existence a consequence of modern social development. Judaism also "remains passive, never willfully extending itself but only *finding* itself extended with the continuous development of social conditions." The proletariat's existence was an announcement "heralding the dissolution of the existing order of things." The Jews were "a general and *contemporary anti-social* element" whose development to a high point meant that society had reached "a point at which it must necessarily dissolve itself."[76]

Marx wrote the essay "On the Jewish Question" before he penned his description of the proletariat. The similarities in the two portraits suggest that—consciously or unconsciously—Marx's image of the Jews was a stage on his path to conceiving the proletariat as he did. It was one link between his immediate personal identity and the group with whom he was increasingly coming to identify his own future, just as the features the proletariat shared with his earlier picture of the free press were another. Moreover, Marx's controversy with Bauer over Jewish rights did not end with the *Deutsch-Französische Jahrbücher*, but continued in *The Holy Family*. There, as we shall see, the inner ties between Judaism, materialism, and communism would become still more visible and pronounced.[77]

For the moment, Marx's position was not yet materialist in his later sense. Although he referred to emancipation "from bargaining and money" as the liberation required in the present time, he still admitted the existence of historically significant spiritual forces. The presuppositions of the state were either "material elements such as private property or spiritual elements such as education and religion," and the main conflict in Marx's mind was not one between various material interests, but "the conflict between *general* and *private interest*." Even civil society itself was made up of "on the one hand *individuals* and on the other the *material* and *spiritual elements*" that defined individual situations. Marx's view of history did not yet focus on stages of economic and social development, but on stages in the history of "man." In the present, "Actual man is recognized only in the form of an *egoistic* individual, *authentic* man, only in the form of *abstract citizen*."[78]

Despite some of his declarations, therefore, Marx was not yet focusing so clearly and determinedly on material, "Jewish" forms of existence as he later would. When he did he would be ready to go beyond Feuerbach's form of realism and empiricism, just as he had gone beyond Hegel's. Before that evolution was accomplished, however, Marx would employ a Feuerbachian perspective—and the contributions of some friends—to set down one of his most famous and intriguing series of reflections, the *Economic and Philosophic Manuscripts of 1844*.

CHAPTER FIVE

Philosophy Inverted, II:
Alienation and Society

1. *Verkehr* and *Verkehrung*: Commerce and the Inverted World

IN THE autobiographical preface he wrote for *A Contribution to the Critique of Political Economy* in 1859, Marx explained that the critical review of Hegel's political philosophy he undertook in 1843 led him to conclude that law and the state "are to be grasped neither from themselves nor from the so-called general development of the human mind, but rather have their roots in the material conditions of life." Hegel and his predecessors had summed up these conditions under the name "civil society," whose anatomy, Marx added, "is to be sought in political economy." Yet Marx's critique of Hegel did not lead him immediately to economics. As a Feuerbachian critic of Hegel his concerns were political before they were social and economic. His analysis of the contradiction between the modern state's announced principles and its real presuppositions contrasted the illusion of universality with the truth of egoistic individualism; it did not focus on production relations or on the economic basis of social groups or classes. In the 1859 preface he even recalled that his first discussions of "so-called material interests" in the *Rheinische Zeitung* articles on the forest laws had caused him embarrassment.[1]

Two of Marx's fellow left Hegelians had been less hesitant about confronting economic life, however, and preceded Marx in writing about it late in 1843, using terms that reflected Feuerbach's critique of Hegel. Marx already knew both these writers, and both would remain associated with him throughout his life, albeit each in a different way. The first was Frederick Engels, whose unique friendship with Marx has become a legend, and with whom we shall deal briefly at this point because we must give him more sustained attention later. The second was Moses Hess, whose brief period of closeness to both Marx and Engels is often obscured by the distance at which they kept him afterward. Although he lacked Marx's intellectual precision and clarity, Hess did anticipate some of Marx's ideas and interests, and Marx admitted as much in 1844. Before examining Marx's first comments on economics in the *Paris Manuscripts*, we must see what he learned from Engels and Hess.

Like Marx, Engels was a Prussian Rhinelander, born in Barmen (now part of the conurbation called Wuppertal) in 1820. Brought up in a strongly pietist atmosphere of stern moralism and biblical literalism, Engels moved first to a more rationalistic form of religion and then to a rejection of all religious belief. Reading Hegel and Feuerbach were important stages on the journey. Feuerbach's criticism of religion had a personal import for Engels it lacked for Marx. Although he knew Feuerbach's essays of 1843, Engels always thought of him primarily as the author of *The Essence of Christianity*.[2]

Having decided early to follow a career in business rather than in government, Engels did not matriculate at a university. He came to Berlin in 1842, however, by taking advantage of the Prussian military regulation allowing middle-class youths to choose their service if they volunteered instead of waiting to be drafted. Spending his obligatory year as an artillery man in the Prussian capital, he heard lectures, and fell in with the group of Hegelian radicals Marx had left behind there just as Marx was falling out with them. Because of Engels' association with "the free," as the Berliners were calling themselves, Marx regarded Engels with suspicion when the two met in Cologne in November 1842. During 1843 Engels contributed to the *Rheinische Zeitung* and other German radical papers from England, where he went to work in a branch of his family's business. Meanwhile he gathered material for the book on the condition of English workers he would publish in 1845. At the end of 1843 he sent an essay for Marx and Ruge's *Deutsch-Französische Jahrbücher*, which Marx greeted with enthusiasm and which brought a new phase in the relations between the two men. It was called "Outlines of a Critique of Political Economy."[3]

Engels' essay was marked by a moral passion that betrayed his pietist orgins and a radical vision that transcended them. The qualities he saw in modern commerce and the economic theories that interpreted it were immorality, hypocrisy, and the mystification of life. Modern political economy, beginning with Adam Smith, pretended to pursue the interests of consumers against the intrigues of manufacturers but, like Luther, it claimed to base itself on man himself only to deliver him over to an alien power. In fact it bore the "hypocrisy, inconsistency and immorality" of old-fashioned commerce into the modern world, where humanity's oppression by the economic system was growing more clear every day. The factory system was the final outcome of this history of inhumanity, undermining even "the last vestige of common interests, the community of possessions constituted by the family." The subject of Engels' essay was not machine industry, however, but the more basic, underlying economic regime of private interest and free trade.[4]

The abstraction and mystification of the economists began with their basic category, value. Modern economic theorists agreed in positing "a *double* value—abstract or real, and exchange value," the latter being equivalent to price. However, they divided over the nature of "real" value. The English school of McCulloch and Ricardo asserted that real value was determined by the costs of production, while the French writer Say measured value by an object's utility. Both were equally abstract and one-sided. To claim that real value rested on production costs was to forget that those costs themselves were set by supply and demand, by competition. The Ricardians' image of economic life depicted "a man without a body, a thought without a brain to produce thoughts." Moreover, a product had to have some use or it would not be sold. Not only competition but utility, which the English writers affected to remove from the determination of value, cropped up in the real creation of it. "Abstract value and its determination by the costs of production are, after all, only abstractions, nonentities."[5]

The same one-sidedness marked Say's analysis. Only competition decided the utility of an object in the regime of private interests. Once competition entered in then so did production costs, "for no one will sell for less than what he has himself invested." In both cases "the one side of the opposition passes over involuntarily into the other."

Engels' solution was to bring the two opposing theories together, so that "Value is the relation of production costs to utility," as demonstrated through competition. But Engels insisted that the value determined in this way was exchange value, not "real value." If the economist were honest he would admit that value was simply price. It was a correct and "fundamental law of private property, that *price* is determined by the reciprocal action of production costs and competition." The economist spoke of real value because "he has still to keep up some sort of pretense that price is somehow bound up with value, lest the immorality of trade become too obvious."

To this moral condemnation Engels added a philosophical one. The economists had begun with the purely empirical truth that price was determined reciprocally by production costs and competition. Then, assuming the equilibrium state in which supply and demand balanced each other, they had abstracted "real value" from the price obtained in those conditions. In this way the real quantity, price, was made to depend on the illusory abstraction, value. "Thus everything in economics stands on its head. . . . As is well-known, this inversion is the essence of abstraction; on which see Feuerbach."[6]

Engels thus described modern economic theory as the mystification of basically correct empirical observations. It was characterized by a "passion for generalization," and it displayed the philosophical inversion that was the mark of all abstract thinking. These features added up to a portrait with striking resemblances to Marx's contemporary image of Hegel. The similarities are one reason why Marx was immediately struck by Engels' essay, and they prepared the ground for Marx's declaration a few months later that "Hegel's standpoint is that of modern political economy." Engels helped Marx to envision the combined criticism of political economy on the one hand and of Hegel on the other that would be the program of the *1844 Manuscripts*.

If Engels helped to shape Marx's critique of political economy in 1844, Moses Hess anticipated the general approach to human history Marx would take then. Marx and Engels would later reject Hess as a "confusionarius," a judgment Marx anticipated as early as 1842, but in the early 1840s he and Engels both worked closely with him. Hess had been involved in the founding of the *Rheinische Zeitung*, and although plans to make him the editor misfired, he wrote many articles for it. It was Hess who converted Engels to communism during 1842, while Engels was making the same visit to Cologne that occasioned his first meeting with Marx. As Hess recounted the story, "We spoke about questions of the day. And he, a year one revolutionary [i.e., a supporter of the principles of 1789] departed from me as the most enthusiastic communist." Engels spent a lot of time with Hess after he returned to Germany in 1844, and edited a magazine with him during the next year. In Brussels during 1845-46 Hess lived near Marx and Engels, and for a time it seemed he might collaborate with them on *The German Ideology*.[7]

The ups and downs of Hess's relations with Marx and Engels can be understood if we remember that he was enough older than they—six and eight years respectively—to have preceded them on some paths, and that although his later development clashed with theirs, temporarily he had important things in common with both. He, too, was a Rhinelander and, like Marx, a Jew. That his upbringing was explicitly Jewish and observant separated him from Marx, but his struggles to free himself from his early religious loyalties gave him something in common with Engels. Moreover, his personal attitude toward Jewish belief in the 1830s and 1840s was ambivalent and at times even hostile. Like Marx, he saw Judaism as linked to commerce and money. Combined as it was with his support for Jewish civic rights, this position resembled Marx's at the same time. Only in 1862 did Hess emerge as an early proponent of Zionism, in his book *Rome and Jerusalem*. That Hess's negative attitude toward Judaism in his earlier life could hide the kernel of his later Zionism may help us to understand how Marx's apparently anti-Semitic statements of the same period could hide a partly unconscious residue of positive identification. The trajectory of his life contrasted with Marx's, but for a time their paths intersected.[8]

By the time he and Marx met in 1841, Hess had already published two books. The first, *The Sacred History of Humanity*, appeared as early as 1837, the second, *The European Triarchy*, in 1841. Both projected a vision of future society based on equality and resting on the greatly expanded productive capacity of modern industry. The first saw the new era as the product of German theory and French politics, to which the second added English practical and productive life—hence the triarchy. Hess was an autodidact, and the variety and diversity of his sources reflected the eclectic and somewhat chaotic openness of his mind. He drew on the Bible, Spinoza, Hegel, Schelling, the St. Simonians.

In 1841 Hess met Marx; the impact was immediate. "Prepare to meet the greatest—perhaps the only genuine—philosopher now alive," Hess enthused to his friend Berthold Auerbach. Marx was "Rousseau, Voltaire, Holbach, Lessing, Heine, and Hegel fused into a single person—fused, I say, not juxtaposed." Previously Hess himself had been a mere bungler in philosophy, he said. "But patience! Now I shall learn something."[9] Marx probably changed Hess's attitude toward Hegel; having criticized Hegel in *The European Triarchy* for not seeking to know the future, Hess praised him in an essay published a month after meeting Marx. "Hegel had enough to strive and fight for, in order to make Spirit adequate to itself," Hess now wrote; "the further task of moulding life adequate to Spirit he had to leave to others."[10] Like Marx, however, Hess read Feuerbach in 1842 and 1843; as a result both his vocabulary and his attitude toward Hegel changed. Some of the results would appear in the essay he sent to the *Deutsch-Französische Jahrbücher* at the end of 1843. Called "On the Essence of Money" (*Über das Geldwesen*) the piece combined what Hess had learned from Hegel, Marx, and Feuerbach with the vision of equality and human fulfillment he had projected in his own earlier writings.[11]

Hess analyzed the nature of money in the framework of an outline of human history based on the Hegelian and Feuerbachian notions of alienation and inversion. Unlike Marx in the critique of Hegel, however, Hess applied these ideas not to the opposition between the state and civil society but to social and economic development. Within that schema, money appeared as the expression of human nature in its alienated and inverted state. Moreover, in depicting the inverted world (*verkehrte Welt*) as the consequence of commerce (*Verkehr*), Hess allowed the linguistic link between the two terms to emerge for the first time. Hess did not stress the connection by punning on it, but simply allowed it to appear as if the *verkehrte Welt* were the natural and necessary result of *Verkehr*.

Human life, Hess began, was based on the exchange of productive activity; out of this exchange real human nature developed. The pun that made the real (*wirkliche*) nature of man arise from his activity (*wirken*) was one Hess did play on, just as Marx and Engels would in *The German Ideology*: "The mutual *exchange* of individual life-activity, *commerce*, the mutual *excitation* of individual powers, this common activity [*Zusammenwirken*] is

the *real* [*wirkliche*] essence of individuals, their *real* [*wirkliches*] wealth."
The common activity first gave actual existence (*Zusammenwirken . . . ver-
wirklicht*) to the productive power of each of the individuals; accordingly it
was the real essence or nature of each one. [12]

Human nature developed through history, beginning from the point
when the earth was prepared to receive human life, and proceeding to the
full development of man in the perfected state of "organized humanity."
The troubles and difficulties of history so far all arose from the fact that
man's individual existence still opposed his social nature. As long as individuality prevailed over social life, men lived in a world of robbery, murder, and slavery. "The individual raised to the *end*, the species lowered to
the *means*: that is the general *inversion* [*Umkehrung*] of human and natural
life." The natural relationship was one that exalted the species over the
individual: love was stronger than egoism. "The inverted world view
rules, on the contrary, in conditions of egoism, because this condition itself belongs to an *inverted* [*verkehrten*] world." This inverted world had its
most highly developed expression in commerce, and its most concrete
embodiment was money. [13]

In money, the species life of man was given an illusory existence outside
individuals instead of within them, and the collective wealth of humanity
was reduced to a mere means for individual aggrandizement. "What God
is for its *theoretical* life, money is for the inverted world's *practical* life: the
alienated wealth [*entäusserte Vermögen*] of men, their life-activity that has
been sold off." However much men emancipated themselves theoretically
from their inverted consciousness in religion, "as long as we are not free of
the *inverted world* as it exists *in practice*," society would be no better than a
pack of wolves. "Money is the product of mutually estranged men, the
alienated man." [14]

Now, however, this inhuman form of social relations was approaching
its end. While men had lived divided from each other they had needed a
means of exchange (*Verkehrsmittel*), an outside agency of interaction, because they were not internally united. Once they established immediate
and human interchange with each other then the external and inhuman
means, money, would not be needed. It would not be abolished by command, Hess declared, but because human needs had ceased to require it.
Exchange between isolated individuals was no longer historically necessary; the new world of organized humanity was waiting to take its place.
All spheres of life would thereby be transformed: when commercial speculation disappeared, so would philosophical and religious speculation; the
politics that presupposed civil society would cease with the religion that
corresponded to it. [15]

Reading Engels and Hess helped Marx shift his focus from Hegel's conception of the state to modern economic life. Both essays would contrib-

ute to the reflections he set down in Paris during the spring and summer
of 1844, the famous *Economic and Philosophic Manuscripts*.

2. Political Economy and Human History

The *Economic and Philosophic Manuscripts of 1844*, also called the *Paris
Manuscripts* or simply the *1844 Manuscripts*, were unknown to Marx's contemporaries, and remained unpublished until after the First World War.
In the debates about the nature and significance of Marxism that have followed the Russian Revolution, the rise of fascism, and the Cold War,
these writings have been made to play a central role. Around them has
developed the debate about the "young" as opposed to the "old" Marx,
and the relative place of humanism and positive science in his thought.
No study of Marx can altogether avoid this debate, but to clarify it requires altering the terms in which it has usually been cast. The relation
between the various parts of Marx's life and thought is a real and important issue. However, the young Marx was not only the writer of 1844, he
was the student of 1837 and the doctoral candidate of 1841 too. Against
that earlier background the *1844 Manuscripts* take their place in the whole
pattern of Marx's life.[16]

   In his preface Marx related the book he hoped his manuscripts would
become to his previous development by telling whom he stood with and
against in the intellectual world of his day. He praised Hess's essays on
socialism published a year earlier in *Twenty-One Sheets from Switzerland*, a
collection of radical writings, and Engels' "Outlines of a Critique of Political Economy." Most of his enthusiasm went to Feuerbach, however, with
whom "positive, humanistic and naturalistic criticism begins." Feuerbach's writings would exercise a deep and enduring effect, for they were
the only ones since Hegel's *Phenomenology* and *Science of Logic* "to contain a
real theoretical revolution." Marx declared his intention to go on from
them to "the settling of accounts with *Hegelian dialectic* and Hegelian philosophy as a whole," a task that set him apart from the *"critical theologians
of our day"* (Bruno Bauer and his friends) who had been Marx's associates
earlier. Freeing himself from Hegel and the Berlin group in whose company Marx had entered the Hegelian fold, Marx now had Hess, Engels,
and Feuerbach for companions.[17]

   To understand the position in which this placed him, we shall here look
briefly at Marx's ideas about economic theory and especially the notion of
value in 1844, then try to situate the *Paris Manuscripts* in relation to the
philosophical identity Marx was reexamining and the communist identity
he had not yet quite assumed during his months in Paris. To accomplish
this we must examine the import of Marx's famous theory of alienated
labor and the way he tried to settle accounts with Hegel.

Marx's discussion of labor and value followed Engels' Feuerbachian "Outlines," rejecting modern economic theory as the abstraction and mystification of real human relationships. His views appear most clearly in a set of notes not usually grouped with the *Paris Manuscripts*, but written at the same time, in the form of annotated excerpts from James Mill's *Elements of Political Economy* (which Marx read in the French edition). There Marx said that the elder Mill, "like the school of Ricardo in general," erred in his approach to prices and costs of production. These writers spoke about values and prices in terms of an "*abstract law*, without the variation or the constant cancellation of this law—through which it first comes into being." To Marx the variation of everyday phenomena from the law was as important as the law itself. "If it is a *constant* law, that for example the costs of production determine the price [in the manuscript Marx wrote "value" above "price"} in the last instance—or rather according to the sporadic chance happenstance correspondence of demand and supply—then it is just as *constant* a *law*, that this relationship never corresponds, therefore that value and costs of production stand in no necessary relationship."[18]

Since supply and demand only corresponded at scattered moments, it made little sense to speak of a law that presupposed their equalization; such an abstraction simply left concrete reality out of account. "This *real* movement, from which that law is only an abstract, accidental and one-sided moment, is made into an accidental circumstance by modern political economy, into something unessential. Why? Because if they wanted to express that movement abstractly, with the kind of sharp and exact formulations to which they reduce political economy, the basic formula would have to say: 'In political economy law is determined by its opposite, lawlessness. The true law of political economy is *chance*, from whose movement we, the men of science, arbitrarily fix certain moments as the law.' " Marx made the same point more briefly in the *Paris Manuscripts* themselves. "Whilst according to the political economists labor is the sole constant price of things, there is nothing more uncertain than the price of labor, nothing exposed to greater fluctuations."[19] Such an approach to economic theory contrasted sharply with the position Marx would take up in the *Grundrisse* and *Capital*. In those later works the notion of a value determined by labor time and totally distinct from price would be Marx's central analytical category; here he rejected it.

Although he condemned the economists for the abstractness of their value theory in 1844, Marx still employed a terminology that would later appear to him even more vague and metaphysical: his analysis of economic relations sought to uncover the history of "man," of humanity in general. To be sure, Marx wrote about the economic conflict between workers and employers in terms that approached his later concentration on more concrete and specific social relationships. He exposed the increasing vulnerability and dehumanization of workers and the growing polarization of classes brought about by the development of private property, and he looked forward to the revolution these conditions were preparing. The question that framed his discussion of wages, however, was "What in the evolution of mankind is the meaning of this reduction of the greater part of mankind to abstract labor?" At the end of his discussion of rent he declared that landed property had to collapse "just as industry both in the form of monopoly and in that of competition had to ruin itself so as to learn to believe in man." In his comments on Hegel he wrote that "History is the true natural history of man."[20]

Marx believed that the shape of this history could be perceived if social development were examined through the category of "alienated labor." Economic theory in its existing form was powerless to comprehend human development in a philosophical way. "Political economy starts with the fact of private property, but it does not explain it to us." Taking the relations between labor, land, capital, wages, and profit: "As to how far these external and apparently accidental circumstances are but the expression of a necessary course of development, political economy teaches us nothing."[21] The purpose of Marx's analysis of alienated labor was to remedy this situation: not simply to discover and analyze modern productive life in terms of alienation, but to uncover the underlying and necessary shape of human evolution.

Marx began with alienated labor as "an economic fact *of the present*. The worker becomes all the poorer the more wealth he produces, the more his production increases in power and size." Marx did not mean to suggest, however, that private property was the cause of alienated labor. Quite the contrary, he concluded, private property was "the product, the result, the necessary consequence, of *alienated labor*, of the external relation of the worker to nature and to himself." True, Marx discovered alienated labor in a situation where private property already prevailed. "But on analysis of this concept it becomes clear that though private property appears to be the source, the cause of alienated labor, it is rather its consequence just as the gods are *originally* not the cause but the effect of man's intellectual confusion. Later this relationship becomes reciprocal."[22]

It was to demonstrate how private property derived from alienated labor that Marx gave his well-known fourfold analysis of it. First, alienated labor estranged man from his own product. This occurred because "The worker puts his life into the object; but now his life no longer belongs to him but to the object. . . . The greater this product, the less is he himself." Second, the worker was estranged from the very activity of his work. "How could the worker come to face the product of his activity as a stranger, were it not that in the very act of production he was estranging himself from himself?" The root of this estrangement lay in the fact that labor itself was "not the satisfaction of a need," but "merely a *means* to satisfy needs external to it." Hence labor separated man from his own inner needs. Third, alienated labor divided men from the life of the human species. Because men characteristically appropriated nature for their needs in a free and conscious (as opposed to a merely instinctual) fashion, human labor distinguished man from all other species and marked him as a free and conscious being. By creating a world of specifically human objects, "man . . . treats the species as his own essential being." But under alienated labor individuals appropriated nature for their own particular purposes; the labor of each separate individual therefore changed "*the life of the species* into a means of individual life." (Here, as elsewhere, Marx echoed Hess.) The final form of alienation was "the *estrangement of man* from *man*." Each person viewed every other as a potential recipient of the objects that embodied his labor, hence each viewed all the others as foreign beings opposed to his own existence. "The *alien* being, to whom labor and the product of labor belongs, in whose service labor is done and for whose benefit the product of labor is provided, can only be *man* himself." Hence, the product of labor became private property.[23]

Marx therefore concluded that private property "results by analysis from the concept of *alienated labor*, i.e., of *alienated man*, of estranged labor, of estranged life, of *estranged* man." On this philosophical basis the whole conceptual structure of modern economics could then be erected: "Just as we have derived the concept of *private property* from the concept of *estranged*, *alienated labor* by *analysis*, so we can develop every *category* of political economy with the help of these two elements." These categories represented the fundamental phenomena of economic life: trade, competition, capital, money.[24]

In this way Marx would be able to account for many features of modern development. But he had not yet quite explained how it all came about, for he had not said how labor came to be alienated in the first place. "How, we now ask, does *man* come to *alienate*, to estrange, *his labor*? How is this estrangement rooted in the nature of human development?" That the process was "rooted in the nature of human development" was already a partial answer to the question, Marx averred: "We have already gone a long way to the solution of this problem by *transforming* the question of the *origin of private property* into the question of the relation of *alienated labor* to the course of humanity's development. For when one speaks of *private property*, one thinks of dealing with something external to man. When one speaks of labor, one is directly dealing with man himself. This new formulation of the question already contains its solution."[25]

That Marx thought so simplified things for him but not for us, since he broke his discussion off, unfinished, before making his answer more clear.

What Marx implied, however, was that something in the way men performed their labor—even before private property arose—led to its alienation. If the labor process itself was not the source of alienation, something very closely tied up with it was.[26] Marx suggested what he believed that element to be in another part of his manuscript, where he discussed the relationship between the division of labor and exchange. There he described the belief that *"labor is the essence of private property"* as "an assertion which the political economist cannot prove and which we wish to prove for him." This was the same proof Marx had pursued in his discussion of alienated labor. Of the factors to be considered in this context Marx mentioned only one: "the *propensity to exchange*—the basis of which is found in egoism." A page earlier he had noted, similarly, "The motive of those who engage in exchange is not *humanity* but *egoism*."[27] It seems more than likely, therefore, that Marx's answer to the question of how men came to alienate their labor was that, at an early stage in human evolution, before the establishment of a genuine human community was possible, human development could only be advanced by means of selfish individuals who sought to improve their situation by exchanging their products with others. This primitive egoism engendered trade, brought men to regard the purpose of their labor as "the mere increase of wealth," estranged man from the activity and products of his work, from his species life, and from other men, and thereby brought forth private property. From this point, as Marx said elsewhere, everything in modern economics followed.

The theory of alienation as Marx employed it in 1844 was, therefore, a theory of the relationship between human nature and human history. The products men created by alienating their labor were the expressions of their essential nature; once the reality of alienation was understood, human needs and qualities could be perceived and examined through the history of industry. "The history of *industry* and the established *objective* existence of industry are the *open book* of *man's essential powers*, the exposure to the senses of human psychology." Mankind both developed and revealed its inner nature and potentiality through the development of productive relations. Humanity's innate capabilities gained concrete existence and became visible in the real world through the progress of the division of labor. Out of the differentation of productive tasks sprang "the great *diversity of human talents*" modern conditions disclosed. Under alienation, however, division of labor also led to "the impoverishment of individual activity, and its loss of character." Because the division of labor was a natural result of private property, these two effects defined the necessary but limited role private property had to play in human history: "Precisely in the fact that *division of labor* and *exchange* are embodiments of private property lies the twofold proof, on the one hand that *human* life required *private property* for its realization, and on the other hand that it now requires the supersession of private property." Thus, the perspective of alienation revealed not only where humanity had come from, but where it was going.[28]

The image of essential human powers exposed "to the senses" through the "open book" of industry foreshadows Marx's later declaration in the *Communist Manifesto* that, under developed modern conditions, "man is at last compelled to face with sober senses his real conditions of life, and his relations with his kind."[29] The two stages in Marx's thinking must not be confused, however. In 1844 the immediate perception of human nature through the senses—and without any help from philosophy—was still reserved for the future. Solely under socialism could it be said that the senses would become "directly in their practice theoreticians," because then alone would the human species receive objective and visible embodiment in a genuine community. In the present, only those who could understand human nature and history through the philosophical category of alienation were able to read the story of human development in the book of industrial advancement. Ordinary eyes were able to perceive human nature only in an alienated and inverted form. What caused men to experience human qualities and capacities in this topsy-turvy way was the power of money. Through money the lame became swift, the ugly beautiful, the stupid talented. Money was, therefore, "the visible divinity—the transformation of all human and natural properties into their contraries, the universal confounding and inversion [*Verkehrung*] of all things." Money was the general inverting power, turning every quality into its opposite, "the inverted world."[30] This inversion made a philosophical perspective all the more essential in order to comprehend society and history.

Because they lacked this perspective, none of the existing movements to abolish private property in favor of communism or socialism were able to grasp their own historical significance. Some (like the school of Etienne Cabet) had no awareness of the role played by alienated labor in history or of the need to transcend it. They did not conceive the abolition of private property as the appropriation of human nature for man. The community their schemes envisaged was "only a community of *labor* and of equality of wages," and the capitalist still remained in the form of the community as a whole, which paid wages to individual workers. Other socialist theorists (like Proudhon) looked forward to the abolition of the state, and announced their program as "the reintegration or return of man to himself." However, because they did not grasp "the positive essence of private property"—its role in human history—"and just as little the *human* nature of need," they failed to comprehend the essential character of future society.[31]

Only when communism was conceived "as the *positive* transcendence of *private property* as *human self-estrangement*, and therefore as the real *appropria-tion of the human* essence by and for man" would it be equal to "fully devel-oped naturalism" and "humanism." In this form "Communism is the rid-dle of history solved, and it knows itself to be this solution." Although Marx subscribed to communism in 1844 more clearly than he had done before, his real loyalties were still to a philosophical vision of which com-munism was only an approximation. *"Communism* is the necessary pattern and the dynamic principle of the immediate future, but communism as such is not the goal of human development—which goal is the structure of human society."[32] Ending private property meant "the advent of prac-tical humanism," and communism was the mediation through which his-tory would arrive at its humanistic goal. "Only through the supersession of this mediation—which is itself, however, a necessary premise—does positively self-deriving humanism, *positive humanism*, come into being." Marx looked forward to *"actual* communist action to abolish actual private property," but his vision did not stop there. "We must regard it as a real advance to have gained beforehand a consciousness of the limited character as well as of the goal of this historical movement—and a consciousness which reaches out beyond it."[33]

In the *1844 Manuscripts* Marx was not yet the communist he would later become. His identification with communist thought and action was limited by his conviction that both needed to be interpreted from a philo-sophical perspective that transcended them. This perspective, within which the notion of alienated labor was a principal element, provided an overview of human evolution based as much on inherent qualities and in-nate needs of human nature as on property relations. Alienation preceded private property and prepared the way for it; the theory of alienation was proof of philosophy's superiority to political economy. Marx still iden-tified himself with the role of philosophical critic he had assumed all along. What was clearer to him now was how he had to distinguish his philosophical manner from Hegel's.

3. Settling up with Hegel

The "settling of accounts with Hegelian *dialectic* and Hegelian philosophy as a whole" Marx proposed to accomplish in 1844 had a wider scope than the critique of Hegel's political philosophy he had undertaken a year ear-lier. It aimed at exposing the abstract and unrealistic orientation that underlay all Hegel's thinking, even his revolutionary *Phenomenology of the Spirit*. Such a project resembled the later attempt to "settle accounts with our erstwhile philosophical conscience" he and Engels would make in *The German Ideology*. It also recalls Marx's reorientation of 1837, in which he rejected his pre-Hegelian idealism "nourished with Kant and Fichte" in favor of "seeking the Idea in the real itself." Then it was Hegel who rescued Marx from "the conflict between what is and what ought to be, a conflict peculiar to idealism," and allowed him to turn to "positive studies." Now, in 1844, it was Feuerbach who "justifies starting out from the positive facts which we know by the senses."[34]

In 1837 Marx had conceded to his earlier position at least the virtue of "a certain warmth of sentiment and a struggle for movement." Now Hegel's positive achievement was similarly "the dialectic of negativity as the moving and generating principle." Hegel understood that man created himself through a process composed of objectification, alienation, and recovery. In describing that process Hegel grasped "the essence of labor" and conceived real, objective man "as the outcome of man's *own* labor." Hegel's standpoint was limited, however, just in the way modern political economy was defective. He saw only the positive side of labor, because the only labor he knew was "abstractly mental labor." Because of this, Hegel's philosophy never arrived at a true transcendence of alienation but only succeeded in confirming and reestablishing it.[35]

The root of this failure could be discovered at the beginning of Hegel's system, in the *Phenomenology*. There Hegel conceived the essence of man to be self-consciousness. To Marx this meant that Hegel regarded man "as a non-objective, spiritual being." That is to say, Hegel did not seek to liberate man from an inhuman and estranged form of existence, but from objectivity as such, from the whole realm of actual existence insofar as it did not correspond to self-consciousness.[36]

Marx insisted that man had his life in the world of real objects. As a "living, natural being," man expressed his essential powers by establishing "a *real*, objective world." This was not in itself the cause of human alienation. A real, natural, objective being did not depart from his essence by creating a world of objects but only by creating a particular kind of world, one whose structure and content alienated him from his genuine life. For Hegel, "it is *objectivity* which is to be annulled, because it is not the *determinate* character of the object, but rather its *objective* character that is offensive and constitutes estrangement for self-consciousness."[37]

Because he did not grasp alienation as arising out of a particular form of human life but equally out of all objective existence, Hegel offered criticism no purchase on the sources of real human alienation. Hegelian self-consciousness could know itself in all objects, because it posited all objects as products or expressions of its own activity: "That which appears to it as an object is only itself." Hence the self-conscious man, confronted with a world of alienation, "passes it off as his true mode of being—reestablishes it, and pretends to be *at home in his other-being as such*." He recognizes religion as a form of alienation, "yet finds confirmation of himself in *religion as religion*." Man thrives on what opposes him: "Reason is at home in reason as unreason.'' Because the world of alienation was not conceived as a real, existing world but only as an abstraction, "The supersession of the alienation is therefore likewise nothing but an abstract, empty supersession of that empty abstraction."[38]

This critique of Hegel's understanding of alienation and human existence owed much to Feuerbach, but the general picture of Hegel Marx now gave drew also on a model found in his own earlier writings: the sketch of the Greek *sophoi* Marx penned in his dissertation. Then, Marx had contrasted Hegel with the Greek thinkers: their thought arose out of separation from real life, his from unification with it. Now, however (as in Marx's analysis of *The Philosophy of Right*), it was Hegel's consciousness that confronted the world of real objects as an alien and hostile one. In the *Phenomenology* "it is precisely abstract thought from which these objects are estranged and which they confront with their presumption of reality." Hegel had set his particular existence as a thinker in opposition to the world. "The *philosopher* sets up himself (that is, one who is himself an abstract form of estranged man) as the *measuring rod* of the estranged world." As Socrates had carried within himself the opposition between substantial existence and abstract reason, so now was Hegel's estrangement from the world "the opposition, within thought itself, between abstract thinking and sensuous reality or real sensuousness." As this inner character of Greek philosophy had been objectified in the contrast between abstract idealism and abstract materialism that Marx described in his dissertation, so with Hegel "there is already latent in the *Phenomenology* as a germ, a potentiality, a secret, the uncritical positivism and the equally uncritical idealism of Hegel's later works—that philosophic dissolution and restoration of the existing empirical world."[39]

When Marx described Hegel's philosophy of nature, his approach to the world outside individual consciousness, it was in the old costume of Epicurus that Hegel now stepped forth. With Hegel, "abstraction resolves to forsake abstraction and to have a look at nature free of abstraction." But just as Epicurus in the end merely gave objective form to his abstract thinking, so for Hegel, too, "It goes without saying that the abstract thinker who has committed himself to the direct observation of nature observes nature abstractly." Nature already existed in the thinker's mind as an image of his own activity, and "what he has really let emerge from himself is only this *abstract nature*, only nature as a *thought-entity*— but now with the significance that it is the other-being of thought . . . nature distinguished from abstract thought." Hegel's views of nature matched Epicurus' astronomy: "the whole of nature merely repeats the logical abstractions in a sensuous external form." Like Epicurus, who had been interested not in the object as such but only in "soothing the explaining subject," Hegel taught man to take pleasure even in the most inhumane and irrational aspects of life. As Epicurus had refused to allow any independent necessity to the natural world itself, so with Hegel, "*Nature as nature*—that is to say, in so far as it is still sensuously distinguished from that secret sense hidden within it—nature isolated, distinguished from these abstractions, is *nothing*—a nothing *proving itself to be nothing*—is *devoid of sense*, or has only the sense of being an externality which has to be annulled."[40]

The position Marx now took up differed from Hegel's in a way that paralleled Marx's earlier contrast between Hegelian philosophy and the Greeks. Like the Greek thinkers, a being that embodied the self-consciousness Hegel posited, a being that neither was an object nor had any real objects as part of its existence, would be isolated in its uniqueness: "it would exist solitary and alone." By contrast, "atheism and communism are no flight, no abstraction, no loss of the objective world created by man."[41] With Hegel the mind was equated with the abstract philosophical consciousness; but in communist society "activity and mind, both in their content and in their *mode of existence*, are social: *social* activity and *social* mind." Under these conditions the subjectivity and isolation of the thinker would come to an end. "Social activity and social mind exist by no means *only* in the form of some *directly* communal activity and directly *communal* mind. . . . But also when I am active *scientifically*, etc.,—when I am engaged in activity I can seldom perform in direct community with others—then I am *social*, because I am active as a *man*." No longer would the philosopher's commitment to "the general" set him in opposition to the particular interests that composed the world of actual existence. "My *general* consciousness is only the *theoretical* shape of that which the *living* shape is the *real* community, the social fabric." When real existence would match the philosophical vision of it, then: "Thinking and being are thus no doubt *distinct*, but at the same time they are in *unity* with each other."[42]

In this future, the distinction between philosophers and ordinary men would dissolve. When private property was annulled by its "positive transcendence, . . . i.e., the *perceptible* appropriation for and by man of the human essence and of human life, of objective man, of human achievements," ordinary men would be able to perceive man with their senses in the same way that philosophers already perceived man with their reason. When "seeing, hearing, smelling, tasting, feeling, thinking, observing, experiencing, wanting, acting, loving" have all been given the opportunity to take in a fully human reality, then "The senses have therefore become directly in their practice *theoreticians*." Once man's powers became objects of perception in the everyday world, then "man is affirmed in the objective world not only in the act of thinking, but with *all* his senses." This was what Marx meant by "the complete *emancipation* of all human senses and qualities": the elevation of ordinary experience and ordinary perception to the level of a philosophic vision of humanity.[43] In this way a demand Marx had put forth in 1843 would be met: "It is not enough that thought should seek its actualization, actuality must itself strive toward thought."[44]

Settling accounts with Hegel in 1844 still left Marx with large debts to him. Not only did Marx's portrait of Hegel himself draw on the iconography of his earlier, Hegelian depictions of Greek philosophers, the whole struggle to separate himself from Hegel was in the service of the same project that had drawn him to Hegel in the first place: ending the opposition between philosophy and ordinary reality. In Marx's perspective of 1844, humanistic communism took over from Hegelian philosophy the task of bringing the theoretical consciousness into harmony with everyday experience. Because Marx in 1844 still remained so tied up with the philosophical perspective of his earlier youth, he would need to make another attempt to free himself from his "erstwhile philosophical conscience" a year later, before leaving that youth behind. That attempt, *The German Ideology*, would not take shape in "the old high school of philosophy," Paris, but in the much more pedestrian and materialistic environment of Brussels.

4. Not Finishing

Marx left the *Paris Manuscripts* unfinished; several of the chapters contain long and undigested excerpts from economists, and a number break off in the middle of arguments or ideas. This was not the only one of Marx's youthful works to remain incomplete. The project that preceded it, Marx's critique of Hegel, never advanced from the section on the state to the section on society, and only the Introduction was published in Marx's time. In 1841 Marx had announced his dissertation as "only the preliminary to a larger essay," which would treat the history of later Greek philosophy as a whole. That work, too, Marx abandoned. Even without the various projects he began earlier in Berlin as a student, Marx's early literary production was a string of fragments.

The string was longer than Marx's biographers have usually been aware. One can see how it grew in the letters Marx exchanged with several friends and associates during 1841-42. Nearly a year before the appearance of his dissertation in the truncated form that won him his degree in 1841, Marx sent Bruno Bauer a letter to be delivered to a Bonn publisher named Marcus. The letter is lost, but its apparent purpose was to secure Marcus as Marx's publisher. If Bauer's reaction is at all to be trusted, however, Marx's approach was not calculated to win Marcus over. Bauer described the letter as "so bad that I could not possibly deliver it. I suppose you can write to your washerwoman more or less in that way, but not to a publisher whom you are just trying to obtain." Bauer offered his help, but he thought Marx needed to take a more realistic attitude. "You must first write to me what you should have written to Marcus long ago: whether the book exists, whether it is finished, how many printer's sheets it will take up, and how much of an honorarium you want."[45] Bauer's questions to Marx were harsh, but they would recur in Marx's later life. Soon after Bauer posed them, Marx's project for a general work on later Greek philosophy simply dropped out of sight. One reason for this may have been that Bauer's dismissal from the University of Bonn in October 1841 (ostensibly for proposing a political toast at a banquet) effectively meant the collapse of Marx's immediate prospects for an academic career. In any case, Marx turned to other interests.

Late in 1841 Bauer published an anonymous pamphlet purporting to be an exposure of Hegel's fundamental atheism but really containing an attack on Christianity, *The Trumpet of the Last Judgement over Hegel the Atheist and Antichrist*. Marx planned to write a second part to Bauer's work, on the subject of Christian art. When Bauer sent his manuscript to the publisher, however, Marx's part was not yet ready. On February 10, 1842, Marx wrote to Arnold Ruge that he would be sending off the manuscript in "a few days," explaining that he had been ill. Nearly a month later, however, on March 5, the work was still not finished. Now, the reason was that Ludwig von Westphalen had died on March 3, and Marx had been unable to work properly during the period von Westphalen lay ill. At the same time, however, Marx now reported plans for a new work, his criticism of Hegel's political theory. Two weeks later Marx spoke about his work again; he had had to revise the essay on Christian art completely, turning it into a general discussion of "religion and art, with special reference to Christian art." He was, therefore, not yet finished with either work.[46]

Marx now expected to publish both the critique of Hegel and the essay on art in a book of philosophical writings on current affairs that Ruge was editing. On April 27 he wrote to Ruge: "You must not become impatient if my contributions take a few days yet—but *only a few* days. Perhaps Bauer will explain to you orally how greatly all manner of external confusion has made work almost impossible for me this month." Despite all that, Marx said, he was nearly finished, and he would now be sending Ruge four separate essays: "1. 'On Religious Art'; 2. 'On the Romantics'; 3. 'The Philosophical Manifesto of the Historical School of Law'; 4. 'The Positive Philosophers.' " Of these, Marx said, the essay on religious art had grown under his hand almost to be a book by itself, "and I have fallen into all kinds of inquiries that will still take rather a long time."[47]

Despite Marx's belief that he would be sending Ruge some manuscripts within a few days, Ruge wrote two months later that he had had no word from Marx since April. On July 9 Marx apologized again, blaming "unpleasant external matters"—including a quarrel with his mother over financial affairs—for his failure to finish. In a few days Marx would be going to Bonn, and he promised "to touch nothing until I have finished the contributions for the *Anekdota*." On October 21, however, Ruge wrote to Marx that he had finally had to send the material for the book to the printer, and that Marx should send his contributions directly there.[48]

Marx's notebooks of this period show that he made notes and excerpts relating to all the topics he mentioned in this correspondence, but only one of these essays, the one on the historical school of law, was finished at this time. Marx returned to another, the critique of Hegel, a year later. Marx did write other things in these months. For Ruge's *Anekdota* he finally supplied a criticism of a Prussian circular relating to the interpretation of the laws on censorship.[49] In addition, he began his contributions to the *Rheinische Zeitung* in the spring of 1842. Now, as later in his life, Marx was far from being an unproductive writer. Yet his control over the products of his pen was not strong. An essay would seem to be within a few days of completion, only to grow under his hand to proportions he had not willed; its claim on Marx's energy would be disputed by other works and by various forms of outside hindrance, until finally it dropped out of view.

Daily journalism, with its limited dimensions and clear deadlines, did not pose the same problems for Marx, and there is no indication that he had any difficulty finishing his articles for the *Rheinische Zeitung*. The pattern emerged again in Paris, however, and the incomplete state of the *Economic and Philosophic Manuscripts* is not the only sign of it. The description Arnold Ruge gave of Marx in a letter of May 15, 1844, presents a similar picture of him. Admittedly Ruge had come to regard Marx less favorably by the spring of 1844 than he had when he first suggested that the two work together; both political and personal considerations were leading to a break between them. Yet Ruge's picture of Marx in Paris fits the other evidence, and corresponds so closely with what we know of his mode of living and working at other times that there is little reason to suspect it. Marx was a special sort, Ruge said, well suited to learning and writing, but not to journalism—despite his success on the *Rheinische Zeitung*. "He reads very much; he works with uncommon intensity, and has a critical talent, that sometimes degenerates into arrogant dialectics; but he finishes nothing, he breaks everything off and always plunges himself again into an endless sea of books. By his learned disposition he belongs completely to the German world, and by his revolutionary manner of thinking he is excluded from it." Moreover, he was often irritable and impetuous, "most of all when he works himself sick and does not go to bed for three, even four nights in a row." Ruge seemed not to know about Marx's work on the *Paris Manuscripts*, but he mentioned some other projects. "Marx wants to write a history of the Convention [i.e., the legislative body during the most radical period of the French Revolution] and has gathered the material for it and worked out some very fruitful points of view. He has put aside the critique of Hegel's philosophy of law."[50]

Ruge was not the only person to be concerned about Marx's finishing his work in Paris. Jenny, who had returned to Germany in June with the Marxes' month-old daughter in the hope of improving the child's health, expressed her concern about it during the summer. "Oh, Karl," she wrote, "whatever you do, do it quickly. . . . Please, dear heart, let the pen run over the paper for once, even if it should fall and stumble sometimes." The quality of Marx's thoughts would make up for any defects in his style, she thought. Let the ideas be clothed lightly, like French soldiers, not tightly turned out like Prussians.[51]

Jenny was probably not referring to the *Paris Manuscripts* either, but to the book that became *The Holy Family*, published under Marx and Engels' joint names early in 1845. This work would seem to be the exception to Marx's inability to finish his projects during the Paris period. Even though it appeared in print, however, the shape it took revealed some of the same qualities in Marx's mode of work that kept him from completing his other writings. When he and Engels met in Paris at the end of the summer they had agreed to issue a joint pamphlet against the "critical criticism" of the Bauer brothers and their friends. Engels departed from Paris, leaving a brief essay behind and expecting Marx to contribute something on the same scale. What emerged in print, however, was a work of over 200 pages. Engels was taken aback, and wrote to Marx that, although the content was excellent, "the sovereign disdain with which we treat the *Allgemeine Literatur-Zeitung* forms a sad contrast to the twenty-two printer's sheets we dedicate to it."[52] The growth of *The Holy Family* resembled the expansion of Marx's essay on Christian—or religious—art in 1842. The result was an unwieldy compilation that few people would or could read.

Moreover, Engels already understood that getting finished was a special problem for Marx, and early in 1845 he began to send out the stream of advice and encouragement to "get it done" that would continue throughout most of Marx's life. While still in Paris Marx concluded the first of his series of contracts with publishers for a book on economics, a "Critique of Politics and Political Economy." Engels, who may have known that Marx had drafted sections of such a work in 1844, was both enthusiastic and concerned about the project. Just such a "big work" was needed now, to settle important theoretical questions. "See that you get done soon with your book on political economy, even if you should still be dissatisfied with much. It does not matter. Minds have ripened and we must strike while the iron is hot." There was no time to develop the theory in a German manner. "Therefore get the thing ready *before* April. Do what I did [with *The Condition of the Working Class in England*]. Set a time limit, at the end of which you absolutely *will be finished*, and see that the book is printed at once."[53]

What kept Marx from following Engels' advice? Of course, he may not have thought the need quite so pressing as his friend did. Yet he certainly intended his books to be printed, and in the preface to the *1844 Manuscripts* he said his decision not to go ahead with his critique of Hegel's political philosophy had been made "while preparing it for publication." Moreover, his comments on that abandoned book suggest where some of his hesitations lay. He explained that dealing with a diversity of subjects in a single work of that sort would have led to an overly aphoristic style, and "would have given the *impression* of arbitrary systematism."[54] Arbitrary systematism was a specter Marx had tried to exorcise before, and would again. It was the overly schematic quality of his own 300-page work on the philosophy of law that led him to abandon it in 1837; indeed, it was to escape from an "unscientific form of mathematical dogmatism—where the subject wanders about the topic, argues hither and thither, while the topic itself is never formulated as something rich in content, something alive," that Marx had turned to Hegel in the first place.[55] Now, abandoning Hegel, Marx was seeking to escape such abstractions again by following the path opened up by Feuerbach. Yet his first attempt to criticize Hegel led to the impression that he was still under the sway of some arbitrary schema. By early in 1845 Marx would conclude that the same disease still infected Feuerbach himself, and criticize—as arbitrary and abstract—some of the positions Feuerbach had inspired Marx to take.

At all these moments—and later on too—the dangers of abstraction had to be overcome by "positive" or empirical studies. Hegel seemed to offer Marx a point of entry to empirical reality in 1837, as Feuerbach appeared to now. In the preface to the *1844 Manuscripts* Marx thought it "hardly necessary" to assure his readers that "my results have been attained by means of a wholly empirical analysis." Nonetheless, Marx felt a constantly recurring need to nourish his dedication to empiricism by devouring piles of books on some subject or area of knowledge. To demonstrate his turn to positive studies in 1837 Marx told his father he had read—with copious note taking—Savigny, Anselm Feuerbach, Grolmann, Cramer, Weinning-Ingenheim, Mühlenbruch, and Lautenbach. In addition, he "read through and made extracts from almost all the first part of Gratian, *Concordia discordantium canonum*, as well as its appendix, and Lancelotti's *Institutiones*. Then I translated part of Aristotle's *Rhetoric*, read *De dignitate et augmentis scientiarum* of the famous Bacon of Verulam, occupied myself intensively with Reimarus, whose work on the mechanical instincts of animals I followed through with delight.''[56] To Marx this reading signified not arcane erudition, but immersion in the details of empirical, positive knowledge. Much the same driven dedication is suggested by Ruge's description of Marx in 1844, plunging over and over again into an endless sea of books. In Paris, too, as in Berlin, Marx worked through the night—three or four nights in a row according to Ruge—until he made himself physically ill.

The dialectic of abstraction and empiricism is a part of every writer's experience, but it was particularly powerful and intense in Marx's intellectual personality. Its presence was, moreover, partly conscious and partly unconscious. Consciously, Marx was always moving toward the empirical, positive pole; yet his life was a continual rediscovery of his own persisting abstraction. Marx recognized the abstract element in his intellectual make-up, but he always identified it with a past he was overcoming; empiricism stood for the present he was creating.

The reasons underlying this were partly cultural. No national intellectual tradition, at least in the West, displays such a powerful mixture of philosophical abstraction and empirical erudition as does the German. In Hegel and Feuerbach, as well as in Marx, the lines of force emanating from both poles met and conflicted. Partly, too, the reasons were historical. Marx's search for a realistic viewpoint was part of the larger nineteenth-century drive to replace idealism with ''reality,'' in which the two perspectives were sometimes confused with each other.[57] In Marx's case, however, one is able to see that the dilemma also had a psychological component. For Heinrich Marx's son, devotion to the contents of his own mind signified self-involvement, egoism, and rebellion; attention to actual conditions in the real world meant duty and obedience. Marx was always in flight from his own mental constructions, always seeking to assure himself and others that their apparent abstractness actually demonstrated a commitment to real, empirical knowledge. But proving this required forms of life and behavior that were driven and self-destructive, and which made the very act of working on his books a barrier to the completion of them. The outlines of this pattern are visible in the months Marx spent in Paris. The pattern would take final form in the years Marx lived in London, still trying to finish the book on political economy Engels had urged him to complete in 1845. By then its title would be *Capital*.

5. Beyond Feuerbach

The Holy Family is among the least read of Marx's works. Its lengthy and involved dissections of minor figures in Bruno Bauer's wing of the Hegelian left hardly seem worth the trouble today—as they did not to Engels even in 1845. Yet many of the ideas that underlay the *1844 Manuscripts* appeared there, albeit in fragmentary and undeveloped form. Moreover, although *The Holy Family* still takes the same Feuerbachian point of view displayed in Marx's other Paris writings (and Engels' works of the same time), there are signposts in the book that point beyond it.

That the book's orientation was Feuerbachian, Marx admitted even years later, when he read it again and told Engels that the two need not be ashamed of it, "although the cult of Feuerbach strikes me as very amusing."[58] In the book itself Marx praised Feuerbach for having brought criticism "to the direct perception of *actual man*" and for having identified idealist philosophy as "speculative and mystical empiricism." Speculative philosophy had developed the appearance of giving up abstraction, but in reality had not abandoned it at all. In Hegel, real empirical knowledge was sometimes presented in the course of developing some purely speculative construction, so that the reader might be led to take the speculative content for a real one. But in the "critical critics" of Bauer's school, there was never any real content. With them, "the inversion of reality by philosophy" reached its most complete and comical form.[59]

As he had in the *1844 Manuscripts*, Marx discovered a similar inversion of actual conditions in political economy. The economists began by describing the relationship between wages and capital as a friendly and cooperative one: "Subsequently it turns out that they stand in the most hostile, *inverted* relationship." Value was supposed to be determined rationally by production costs and utility: "Subsequently it turns out that the determination of value is entirely fortuitous and need have no connection either with the costs of production or with social utility." Wages seemed to be set by a free contract; later they turned out to be determined by the coercion of the capitalist and the force of circumstances.[60]

Although much of *The Holy Family* was addressed to other topics, Marx clearly presented his vision of the proletariat as the motor of future emancipation, and related its role to its alienation. "The propertied class and the class of the proletariat represent the same human self-alienation. But the former feels comfortable and confirmed in this self-alienation, knowing that this alienation is *its own power* and possessing in it the *semblance* of a human existence. The latter feels itself ruined in this alienation." Marx's view of the proletariat drew not only on Feuerbach, but also on Hegel. Adapting the description of the "rabble" of paupers Hegel depicted as characteristic of poor workers under modern conditions in the *Philosophy of Right*, Marx described the proletariat as, "to use Hegel's words, . . . *abased* and *indignant* at its abasement." This combination of abasement and indignation prepared the revolution. Because "man is lost" in the proletariat, but is at the same time aware of his loss, and driven to revolt by urgent and compelling need, the proletariat could and would emancipate itself. In transcending the conditions of its life it would also abolish *"all the inhuman conditions of present society which are summed up in its own situation."*[61]

Marx noted that "a large part of the English and French proletariat is already *conscious* of its historic task and is continuously working to develop that consciousness into complete clarity."[62] Yet he still looked to criticism by theorists who stood outside the proletariat as the agency of that clarification. The limits he set to the workers' independent consciousness can be seen in his comments on Proudhon. Rejecting Edgar Bauer's characterization of Proudhon as writing in the interest of the proletariat, Marx insisted that he "does not only write in the interest of the proletarians; he himself is a proletarian, a worker. His work is a scientific manifesto of the French proletariat." This did not bring his perspective into line with Marx's own. His formula of "equal possession" was "the expression within political economy—hence the still estranged expression" of essential human qualities and relationships. A few pages later Marx described Proudhon's position as "the criticism of political economy from the standpoint of political economy" and explained that such a perspective "recognizes all the essential determinations of human activity, but only in an estranged, alienated form." Proudhon's proletarian point of view saw social relations from within the condition of alienation; hence he could not penetrate beyond it.[63] What Marx had called "the lightning of thought" still seemed required to illuminate—perhaps also to energize—the working class. Referring to the criticism of contemporary society emanating from Fourier, Owen, and others, he asserted that "the great mass . . . responded immediately in practice to this communist criticism."[64]

Nonetheless, there were indications in *The Holy Family* that Marx was moving beyond the position he occupied under Feuerbach's influence. Alongside his devotion to Feuerbachian real humanism Marx now revealed a greater interest in materialism as such. In opposition to the critical critics, he traced the history of materialist thinking in British and French philosophy, and concluded that "French materialism flows directly into *socialism* and *communism*." On the Lockean premise that "man forms all his knowledge, perception etc. from the world of sense and experience in the world of sense," it followed that "the empirical world must be so arranged that he experiences and gets used to what is truly human in it, that he experiences himself as man. . . . If man is formed by circumstances, then his circumstances must be made human." Marx found the doctrines of Enlightenment materialism behind the socialist visions of Fourier, Owen, Cabet, and "the more scientific French communists," who developed materialism into real humanism as "the logical basis of communism."[65]

Marx also moved closer to outright materialism in his discussions of a matter that had drawn him close to it once before, the Jewish question.

He dealt with the position of Jews again in *The Holy Family* because Bruno Bauer had written several articles responding to the Jewish critics of his pamphlet *The Jewish Question*—including Marx—in his periodical *Die Allgemeine Literatur-Zeitung*. In these replies, Bauer had characterized all his Jewish opponents as representatives of "the mass," to which he opposed himself as standing for "spirit" and "criticism." All real progress depended on spirit, whereas the mass only stood in the way.[66] When he spoke of the mass Bauer did not have in mind only Jews, nor did Marx when he took over Bauer's terms and turned them against him. For Bauer the mass stood for all his opponents; for Marx it included Jews, ordinary people, and the proletariat. It is not usually noticed, however, that Marx chose Bauer's reply to his Jewish critics as the basis for his own discussion of spirit and mass, and that when he proceeded to "accompany absolute criticism in its campaigns against the *mass*," it was to the defense of Bauer's Jewish critics that Marx turned.

Marx did not regard these writers—Gustav Philippson, Samuel Hirsch and others—as very distinguished opponents for a man of Bauer's stature; nonetheless, "absolute criticism" could not defeat them. Many of Marx's observations repeated what he had said in his own essay "On the Jewish Question." In particular, he reaffirmed the distinction between merely political emancipation and human emancipation, which Bauer still failed to comprehend, and insisted that the modern state—precisely because it left men free as private individuals—could not demand a religious test as a condition for citizenship. In addition, he paused to underline his agreement with Hirsch that Bauer had been wrong to deny the Jews a positive role in modern history. To insist on their contribution was altogether correct, Marx declared.[67]

Moreover, in the course of identifying himself with the "massy" Jews, Marx now moved closer to the communism of the masses than he had before. In the *Paris Manuscripts* Marx had cited Bauer's "antithesis of the critical Christ and Mankind, the rabble," as evidence for the need to settle accounts with the whole Hegelian enterprise. Now, in *The Holy Family*, Marx's reaction to Bauer's view of the Jews pushed him still further from philosophy, and toward a form of communism that did not rest on it. Marx characterized Bauer's position as follows: "To the massy, material Jews is to be preached the *Christian* doctrine of *spiritual freedom*, *of freedom in theory*, that *spiritualistic* freedom that *imagines* itself to be free even in chains, that is blissful in '*the idea*' and that is only embarrassed by all massy existence." Bauer equated the progress of the Jews toward freedom with the advance of their theoretical understanding. "From this statement [Marx replied] one can measure at once the critical cleavage that divides *massy*, profane communism and socialism from *absolute* socialism. The first principle of profane socialism rejects emancipation *in mere theory* as an illusion, and desires for *real* freedom, besides the idealistic *'will,'* very palpable, material conditions."[68] There was little that was specifically new for Marx in these words. But by contrast with the careful distinctions between various forms of communism he made in the *Paris Manuscripts*, and the rejection of any "crude" form, Marx here put no barrier between himself and "massy, profane communism and socialism." Like this communism, the Jews with whom Marx sided were massy and material too.

Marx's discussion of the Jewish question in *The Holy Family* prefigures the more straightforwardly materialist position that would replace Marx's Feuerbachian humanism during 1845. After all, in Feuerbachian terms Bauer had been right: Christianity was a more advanced form of religious consciousness than materialistic Judaism, and the overcoming of alienation required precisely the negation of Christianity. The negation of Judaism promised no such universal consequences because Jewish consciousness did not focus on the species. There are indications in Marx's later writings that one of the impulses leading him away from Feuerbach was an underlying feeling that Feuerbach's perspective was a "Christian" one. In *The German Ideology* Marx would oppose "the Christian fantasy about property—which is truly nothing but the property of Christian fantasy" to "the transformation of the real property relations and production relations." When, early in 1845, in the first of the "Theses on Feuerbach," he criticized the Feuerbachian view that "regards only the theoretical attitude as the truly human attitude, while practice is understood and fixed only in its dirty Jewish form of appearance," his target was not Jewishness, but the opposite of it which failed to comprehend the world of ordinary material life in its full scope and richness. As Marx would observe in *The German Ideology*, Feuerbach reduced real material life to "the flatly obvious," subordinating it to a higher reality. The "Jewish" point of view that focused wholeheartedly on the material world would by then be Marx's own.[69]

By the end of 1844 Marx was abandoning the identification of himself with the Christian-Germanic world of post-Hegelian philosophy on which he had been attempting to build his vocation since falling under the spell of Hegel in 1837. In a different, more uncompromisingly materialist— "Jewish"—framework he would finally find his own way of becoming "really somebody."

CHAPTER SIX

Real History: Materialism, Philosophy, and the Path to Maturity

1. *Le Doux Commerce*

EVEN in their own time people predicted that the friendship between Marx and Engels would grow to be a legend, a kind of modern Damon and Pythias; so it has. Like many friendships, it was not symmetrical. Engels acknowledged that his part was "second fiddle," and there is very little to suggest that he resented not being first.[1] Yet Frederick Engels was a man of extraordinary talent and achievement, and without his presence, Marx's life would have had to follow some different course, especially in the years after 1850. Moreover, Engels' own development reveals much about the sources and nature of what has come to be called, perhaps a bit one-sidedly, Marxism.

While he was in Berlin, serving out his one-year service in the Prussian army, Engels received a letter from Arnold Ruge, addressing him as "Dr. Engels." In his reply Engels paused to point out that "Incidentally I am not a doctor [of philosophy] and can never become one. I am only a businessman and a royal Prussian Artillerist."[2] Tinged as it was with irony, Engels' self-description contained some abiding truths about his life. The son of a businessman and manufacturer, he worked in the management of firms either controlled by or connected with his family until he was able to retire and live on investments in 1869, the only break after his youthful military service coming in the period 1846-50. His income was for a long time the chief material support of Marx and his family; in fact his financial aid to Marx began almost immediately after the two met, when he gave Marx the honorarium he earned for *The Condition of the Working Class in England* and organized a subscription to support him when Marx was expelled from Paris early in 1845. Although he once considered—like Marx—a legal and administrative career, his only attendance at a university occurred during the year of his military service. From that service he retained an interest in and knowledge of military affairs that was reflected in much later writing. He also kept up with and wrote on a subject that other nineteenth-century Germans pursued in connection with either industry or military affairs: natural science.

It may seem out of character that one of the founders of modern revolutionary socialism was not only born into manufacturing but continued to be active in it. The contrast was noticed at the time, and Engels was sensitive to the accusation that he himself was exploiting workers while claiming to work for their liberation.[3] Quite apart from the old truth that necessity makes strange bedfellows, Engels' career points up some important features in the history of the nineteenth-century European middle class, out of which so many revolutionary leaders came.

The city of Barmen had a long history as a manufacturing center, and when Engels was born there in 1820 it was still under the control of the old-fashioned burgher class that had long dominated it. Stolid, determined, active, close-knit, and staunchly Calvinist, this social group traced its origins—like that of the textile industry it managed and lived on—back to the sixteenth century, and in some respects beyond. Next to religion and business, the burghers of Barmen were devoted to duty and civic patriotism. Their lives were oriented toward public responsibility just as much as toward private interest; indeed, they belonged to a world in which the division between private and public life Hegel found at the center of modern "civil society" had not yet taken place. Toward their workers—mostly skilled artisans whose residence in the city in some cases covered as many generations as their employers'—they could be demanding and distant, but their overall orientation was one of patriarchal concern.[4]

The character of this class can be illustrated by one of its members, Johann Wilhelm Fischer, who during the period of hard times that followed the defeat of Napoleon in 1816-18 ignored his business to devote his entire attention to relief of the poor in the city. Fischer helped manage the Barmen *Kornverein*, an agency to provide food at lower than market prices (similar to a project in which Heinrich Marx bought shares at Trier). His only rewards, as he later recounted, were a letter of thanks from the king, recognition from his fellow citizens, and the satisfaction of having helped the city in a time of need. Among the other leaders of the *Kornverein* was Frederick Engels' grandfather, Johann Caspar Engels, a man known also for the help he gave his own workers, and for the schools he established to educate their children.[5]

To be sure, there was much self-interest behind this devotion to duty. Nonetheless, the orientation and style of life it reflects contrast with that of the industrial middle class that would take the old patricians' place during the century of machine industry. Moreover, the contrast was felt in the period of Engels' youth. The first representative of Barmen in the Rhineland Diet was a foe of the industrial revolution. With an eye on the social consequences of the new inventions in England, he spoke out against the introduction of cotton-spinning machines. A similar hostility to the new techniques and their representatives can be found elsewhere in the traditional and established European middle class.

The new techniques came to Barmen, and their effects—combined with those of population growth, competition, and cyclical crisis—were visible in the city by the end of the 1830s, when Engels himself described them in a series of newspaper articles. Those who fostered the changes profited economically, but for years they were kept at arm's length by the old burgher patricians. The most prestigious social club, the Concordia Society, was closed to them, and the new manufacturers joined organizations that conferred less honor and status. Only as the century neared its end, and spurred on by the economic crises of 1873 and the 1890s, did the separation between the old burgher patricians and the new captains of industry disappear. By the First World War marriages, economic cooperation, and politics had all combined to create a reunified middle class.

The new group contrasted in striking ways with the old one. It was much more completely absorbed in business activity than the earlier patricians had been; the conditions of modern industry required closer and more continuing attention, in order to keep track of distant situations and react quickly to cabled information. Partly as a result of this, but partly as a consequence of extended suffrage and the rise of working-class political parties, the new group no longer ran the city in the way the older one had. The sense of unity between private interest and public responsibility displayed by J. W. Fischer had evaporated. The symbol of this evolution also confirmed it: the new middle class moved out of town. Whereas the chief families of the old order had always lived in the center of the city, at the end of the nineteenth century the well-off were moving into a new "Villa Quarter" outside.

Many features of Engels' development recall his membership in Barmen's old, preindustrial, patrician middle class. One of them is the way he chose, and followed, his occupation. He gave up his original notion of a path that would lead through legal study to administration in 1837, choosing then to enter business instead. One version suggests that Engels' father vetoed his university studies, another that Frederick himself did not relish entering the Prussian bureaucracy. Probably, as Steven Marcus has suggested, the wills of father and son coalesced. But the choice did not mean what it may seem to. When he left Gymnasium, the school's director (a family friend) described his decision not to go to university as determined by his having chosen business as his "external career." The implication was that Engels would follow some other, "internal" occupation at the same time, and both his proclivities then and his activities in the following years suggested that this would be writing. By the age of seventeen Engels was already deeply involved in literature and poetry.[6] That Ferdinand Freiligrath, the radical poet, was working for a business firm in Barmen at the time may have given Engels a model for the kind of life he had in mind, but the presuppositions underlying his choice also lay closer to home. For the old patricians of Barmen, business was an occupation that left time for other pursuits, notably those that expressed a devotion to public life and duty. Engels both preserved and transformed this pattern. Throughout his life he was able to support himself by business, while regarding his real, inner, vocation as literary and political. That Freiligrath remained Marx and Engels' friend and (barring some disagreements) political associate in London while managing the branch of a Swiss bank, suggests that the old model remained alive in others as well.

Moreover, Engels was not the only scion of an old Barmen family to be attracted to communism in the 1840s. In those years the city saw the emergence of a Popular Party based on working-class support and middle-class leadership, and a number of younger members of old notable families joined the cause. Their radicalism reflected the contrast between the old patrician order and the conditions of nineteenth-century life. In the early months of 1845 Engels, together with Moses Hess, participated in a series of meetings organized for the discussion of social issues in general and communism in particular. At the last of these—before they were ended by the government—held in Barmen's sister city of Elberfeld (today the two form the single unit of Wuppertal), Engels reported that every patrician family of the town had a representative at the communist table. Even allowing for exaggeration, Engels' report suggests how his own evolution was linked to the social history of his class and town.[7]

To be sure, Engels' advance to communism was not welcomed in his own family. His parents' expectations for their son had been very different, focusing on the moral and religious content of their own staunch pietism. In his teens, young Frederick gave evidence of fulfilling their hopes, displaying genuine religious commitment and enthusiasm. From the start, however, the family atmosphere had included another side, represented by his lighthearted, fun-loving, and rather literary mother. Perhaps her indulgence of her son's penchant for poetry and romance accounts in part for the "carelessness" Engels' father mentioned when he discovered a "dirty book"—a thirteenth-century chivalric tale—in the boy's desk. The view Engels' father took of him as a student recalls the picture Heinrich Marx formed of his son. His talents were impressive, but his personality made the elder Engels uneasy. "Let the dear God take the boy under his protection," he wrote to the boy's mother, "so that his disposition is not spoiled. So far he is developing a disquieting lack of thoughtfulness and character, in spite of his other gratifying qualities."[8]

It was not selfishness that the Engels family feared would spoil their son, for one of the stories handed down about his childhood told how—following a family example—he had given his pennies to the poor. But they feared lest he not develop the high degree of seriousness and moral uprightness they expected of him. In fact, qualities that seemed to contradict those—love of fun and sexual freedom—cropped up later on in

Engels' life. As it turned out, his family need not have worried. He was a model of solid responsibility (one function of his friendship with Marx was that it allowed him to display this), and his moral passion was deep and strong. If its targets were not ones his father would have chosen, its underlying values had clear roots in the old patriarchal and patrician middle class.

The other part of the identity Engels described in his letter to Ruge was that of royal Prussian Artillerist. The adjectives would drop away later on, but some features of the military man would remain. Whereas Marx was dark and intense, Engels was blond and outgoing. He loved horses and fox hunting ("the greatest physical pleasure I know," he once told Marx),[9] and impressed some who saw him as having the bearing of an army officer. Quite a ladies' man in his youth, he fell in love with an Irish working-class girl, Mary Burns, on his first visit to England, and lived with her for many years without marrying her. There is some evidence that Marx (and even more Jenny) had difficulty freeing himself of the uneasiness about Engels' libertinism that had made him reject his later friend as a representative of the Berlin "free" when they first met in 1842.

In addition to the vigor and energy of the soldier, Engels sometimes betrayed a tendency to see himself as dependent on older and stronger men, a trait in his character that is worth noticing, whether it is connected with his military side or not. During his early period as a writer his model was Ludwig Börne, the novelist who was a leader of the literary movement called Young Germany (not to be confused with the Mazzinian nationalist organization), and who had been one of the first German writers to make political criticism a central element in his literary activity. In a poem of this period, Engels wrote that "It is the oak Börne on whose branches I have climbed," along with the other songbirds of freedom, "and I would rather be a sparrow among them than a nightingale, were I obliged to be in a cage and serve a prince with my song." Even the musical metaphor presaged his later role as second fiddle. Nor was Marx the only man with whom Engels later saw himself in a similar relationship. Writing of three fellow members of the London Communist League whom he met at the age of twenty-three, Engels later said: "I shall never forget the deep impression that these three real men made upon me, who was then only wanting to become a man."[10]

His own manfulness remained somehow problematic to him. In a letter to his mother about a young friend of the Engels family he befriended in Manchester, he lamented that: "We Barmeners all seem to come very late out of our youth."[11] Such a sentiment from a man whose liteary precocity had him creating a stir with his newspaper articles before he was twenty is surprising. Those articles, "Letters from the Wuppertal," whose descriptions of working-class life foreshadowed his later reports on English conditions, in fact appeared first anonymously and then under a pseudonym, Frederick Oswald. Only after leaving Berlin did Engels begin to write under his own name. Even then, after casting off his youthful diffidence long enough to emerge in his own name as the author of articles about British affairs and *The Condition of the Working Class in England*, he would soon retreat—partially but definitively—behind the shadow of Marx.

That it took a very sturdy bushel to hide even part of Engels' light is clear to anyone who takes the trouble to read his book on English affairs. *The Condition of the Working Class in England* is a masterly achievement, its range and power truly extraordinary in a man who was not yet twenty-five. Its purpose was nothing less than to educate his overly theoretical countrymen about the conditions of the real world. Whereas even German communists had arrived at their position "by way of the Feuerbachian dissolution of Hegelian speculation," Engels offered a real, empirically based, historical and social analysis. He did not speak merely of workers in general, but described the differing kinds and the position of each, combining his own minute personal observations with official and unofficial statistics on working-class incomes, expenses, housing, mortality, and sanitary conditions. He based his account not on categories that derived from the writings of economic theorists, as Marx still did in 1844, but on the invention and spread of machine industry.[12]

Once or twice Engels appeared to display a degree of uncertainty as to whether the conditions he described were the consequence of private property itself or of the factory system. In one passage he attributed the rise of the proletariat to the competition that increased the wages of weavers "so inducing the weaving peasants to abandon their farms." His more constant position was that "The history of the proletariat in England begins . . . with the invention of the steam engine and of machinery for working cotton."[13] This uncertainty points toward a more widespread and continuing confusion about whether the conditions Marxism presupposed were—and are—those of capitalism in general or only those of a particular phase in the history of industrialization. Despite that—or because of it—Engels offered a view of social development from which Marx had much to learn.

Engels' image of modern society underlined the dependence of productive industry on the division of labor, and the oppressive experience of isolation that resulted from it. The fundamental principle of contemporary life was narrow self-seeking, and it led to "the unfeeling isolation of each in his private interest." The result was the complete "dissolution of mankind into monads of which each one has a separate principle and a separate purpose, the world of atoms." Competition brought forth a battle of life and death, fought "not between the different classes of society only, but also between the individual members of these classes. . . . The workers are in constant competition among themselves as the members of the bourgeoisie among themselves. The power-loom weaver is in competition with the hand-loom weaver, the unemployed or ill-paid weaver with him who has work or is better paid." It was the war of all against all.[14]

This image of a society of monads or atoms was only the backdrop for Engels' depiction of the shape he saw in the foreground of modern development. This was the formation of two great classes, the bourgeoisie and the proletariat. The preindustrial worker "was no proletarian, he had a stake in the country, he was permanently settled, and stood one step higher in society than the English workman of today." By contrast, nineteenth-century industry was creating (note the Hegelian echoes) "a class which bears all the disadvantages of the social order without enjoying its advantages, one to which the social system appears in purely hostile aspects." Modern conditions were turning (here the echoes of Hegel ceased) "the toiling lower middle-class into the toiling proletariat," reducing the former gradations of the population "to the two opposing elements, workers and capitalists." Earlier, a worker had possessed the prospect of rising into the lower middle class by "establishing himself somewhere as master artificer, perhaps employing journeymen and apprentices"; now that possibility had collapsed, and "for the first time, therefore, the proletariat was in a position to undertake an independent movement." The English workers were "a race apart." Society was divided into "two radically dissimilar nations, as unlike as difference of race could make them."[15] Gathered together in the great cities but separated from the bourgeoisie, "The workers begin to feel as a class, as a whole: they begin to perceive that, though feeble as individuals, they form a power united." Through the growth of working-class political movements, Owenite socialism, and especially working-class Chartism, "all the workers employed in manufacture are won for one form or the other of resistance to capital and bourgeoisie; and all are united upon this point, that they, as working-men . . . form a separate class, with separate interests and principles."[16]

Like Marx, Engels examined the sources of this growing class feeling, but he explained it differently. Linking German workers to German philosophy, Marx had depicted the future proletarian consciousness as a response to the lightning of thought. The consciousness of German workers was more advanced than that of French or English ones, he believed, because the poverty of German reality called forth a richness of understanding: "Only in socialism can a philosophical people find its suitable practice."[17] In Engels' view the intellectual clarification of the working class originated not in philosophy but in industrial development. "The degree of intelligence of the various workers is in direct proportion to their relation to manufacture." It was, therefore, in mechanized factories that one found "the most intelligent and energetic of all the English workers."[18] As for the preindustrial workers, "intellectually, they were dead."

> In the patriarchal relation that hypocritically concealed the slavery of the worker, the latter must have remained an intellectual zero, totally ignorant of his own interest, a mere private individual. Only when estranged from his employer, when convinced that the sole bond between employer and employee is the bond of pecuniary profit, when the sentimental bond between them, which stood not the slightest test, had wholly fallen away, then only did the worker begin to recognize his own interests and develop independently; then only did he cease to be the slave of the bourgeoisie in his thoughts, feelings, and the expression of his will.

The intellectual enlightenment of the English workers had progressed so far that Engels found among them readers of "Helvetius, Holbach, Diderot, etc.," as well as practically the only English group with real knowledge of David Friedrich Strauss, Proudhon, Bentham, and Godwin.[19]

The view of social development Engels offered in his book was a firm step closer to the account of history he and Marx would provide in *The German Ideology* than were Marx's own writings of 1844. The long passage on working-class consciousness just quoted would find clear echoes in the *Communist Manifesto*.[20] If historical materialism was primarily a framework for understanding human history, and for placing individuals in contact with the direction of historical change, then it is difficult to understand why Engels should have attributed the chief place in its development to Marx. Yet there was an important difference between Engels' book and later Marxism. Engels had not drawn the philosophical consequences from his realistic and empirical approach to history that Marx would draw. Despite his insistent realism, Engels in 1844, like Marx at the same date, was still a Feuerbachian.

Years later Engels would recall the deep impact Feuerbach's thinking had made on the whole world of post-Hegelian German criticism. Upon the appearance of *The Essence of Christianity*, he reported, "we all became at once Feuerbachians."[21] By then he was aware that *The Condition of the Working Class in England* still showed the impact Feuerbach had made on him. Writing a new preface for his early book in 1892, Engels explained that since socialism did not yet exist as a "science" in 1844, his work "exhibits everywhere the traces of the descent of modern socialism from one of its ancestors, German philosophy. Thus great stress is laid on the dictum that communism is not a mere party doctrine of the working class, but a theory compassing the emancipation of society at large. . . . This is true enough in the abstract, but absolutely useless, and sometimes worse, in practice."[22]

It was particularly in his descriptions of workers that Engels' language of 1844 retained the vocabulary of Feuerbach's humanism. The condition of modern workers was not merely turning them against the bourgeoisie, he observed, but "forcing them to think and demand a position worthy of men." Workers struck even against their own immediate interest "because they feel bound to proclaim that they, as human beings, shall not be made to bow to social circumstances, but social conditions ought to yield to them as human beings." In addressing the English working men at the end of his book, Engels declared (in contrast to his earlier, class-based descriptions) that "I found you to be more than mere *Englishmen*, members of a single, isolated nation, I found you to be *Men*, members of the great and universal family of mankind, who know their interest and that of all the human race to be the same." Thus, Engels hailed them as "Human Beings in the most emphatical meaning of the word." In a contemporary letter to Marx about German workers who were being driven to crime by their situation, Engels said that if the Germans developed according to the same laws as English workers, "they will soon see that this way of protesting against the social order as *individuals*, and violently, is useless, and protest as *men*, in their general capacity, through communism."[23]

Before either Marx or Engels could set forth historical materialism as a comprehensive and consistent view of human experience, they would have to discard the Feuerbachian distillate that still colored their language and tinted their view. They would take that final step in confrontation with a very different perspective on individual and social history.

2. Stirner: The Cycle of a Private Life

On November 19, 1844, while still at work on his account of English workers, Engels wrote to Marx about a book he had been reading, Max Stirner's *The Unique Person and His Property* (or, as the title has been oddly translated, *The Ego and His Own*). Engels was critical of the book, whose theme of self-conscious egoism appeared to him as "merely the essence of present-day society and of current men brought into consciousness." Nonetheless, he thought the book too important to be put aside; rather it had to be exploited as "the complete expression of the existing madness," and it offered the opportunity *"even as we invert it*, to build on it."[24]

Stirner was right, Engels thought, that men acted for a cause only when it was in their own egoistic interest and not simply the expression of some abstract interest. To put it another way, Stirner was correct to criticize Feuerbach, whose notion of "man" was "crowned with the theological halo of abstraction." Feuerbach had arrived at his concept of man by reflecting on the concept of God, whereas the correct way was "the reverse. . . . We must start out from the 'I,' from the empirical corporeal individual . . . and raise ourselves from there to 'man.' " Feuerbach himself had sometimes said similar things; yet Stirner's book was important as a warning against the tendency to return to speculation that was still alive in the post-Hegelian atmosphere (and which Engels thought especially pronounced in Moses Hess).[25]

Engels' first reaction to Stirner presaged the important role Stirner's book would play in moving Engels and Marx away from their admiration for Feuerbach. But the limits of Engels' appreciation of Stirner are indicated in his suggestion that his perspective offered a better way of working out the concept of man. In *The German Ideology* it would become clear that the confrontation with Stirner moved Marx and Engels not to revise that notion, but to discard it as an element in historical analysis. A look into Stirner's book will help to make clear why it could play that role.

Max Stirner was the pseudonym of Johann Caspar Schmidt, a member of the Berlin circle of left Hegelians. Thirteen years older than Marx, he had heard Hegel lecture at Berlin in the 1820s. His life was filled with illness and insecurity, and included a period of caring for his mother, who was suffering from some form of mental illness. Taking a job as a Gymnasium teacher in Berlin, Schmidt contributed to the *Rheinische Zeitung*, and became one of "the free" during 1842.[26]

Stirner understood the Feuerbachian technique of inverting Hegel perfectly well. He argued, however, that the product of this inversion was not "the pure, bright truth," but merely another abstraction. Inverting Hegel or speculative theology, one eliminated the abstraction "God," only to replace it with other abstractions like "love." The product was not the man of real human existence, but some quality declared to be his "essence." The inner man thus stood ranged against the outer: " 'Our essence' is brought into opposition to *us*—we are split into an essential and an unessential self." What Feuerbach called sense-experience was by no means the experience of individual men, but an abstraction to which he arbitrarily gave the name "sensuousness." Feuerbach was, therefore, an abstract philosopher like all the rest.[27]

Stirner proposed to replace abstract philosophical speculation with a program of radical individualism. In moving from philosophy to real life he employed a perspective that had played a role in Hegel's own philosophy: the human life cycle. Stirner's theory of the life cycle had only three stages, childhood, youth, and manhood. (Hegel's fourth condition, old age, Stirner claimed he would have time enough to discuss when he arrived at it.) Life history was a drama of identity: "From the moment when he catches sight of the light of the world a man seeks to find out *himself* and get hold of *himself* out of its confusion, in which he, with everything else, is tossed about in motley mixture." Childhood was passed in a series of conflicts with authorities whom the child struggled unsuccessfully to defeat. These combats made the child subject to the "lordship" of the outside world. In his struggle the child learned to try to get to the "bottom" of things and to look "behind" them. (The anatomical aspects of this fascination with the bottom and the behind were implicit but undeveloped in Stirner's discussion.) Only as childhood ended did a person begin to discover that what stood behind the rod was courage, shrewdness, obduracy, and that these were qualities he possessed himself. "And what is our trickery, shrewdness, courage, obduracy? What else but—mind!" (Stirner's language here played on the German sense of *Geist* as conscious determination as well as intellect.) "*Mind* is the name of the *first* self-discovery, the first undeification of the divine," and this discovery marked the arrival of the child at the stage of youth.[28]

Youth was the time of intellect, of involvement in abstract ideas. The youth "does not try to get hold of things (e.g. to get into his head the *data* of history) but of the *thoughts* that lie hidden in things, and so, e.g., the *spirit* of history." Youths were thus commanded by their thoughts much as children had been subjected to their parents. Plunging into the world of abstract thinking, they pursued logic for its own sake. "To bring to light *the pure thought* or to be of its party, is the delight of youth; and all the shapes of light in the world of thought, like truth, freedom, humanity, Man, etc., illumine and inspire the youthful soul."[29]

This self-discovery was at the same time a self-loss, however, for the only way the youth could regard mind or spirit as the ruler of the world was to invent a great Spirit who ruled the world from a point outside it—God. Before this "complete Spirit" the individual had to prostrate himself. In order to arise he had to rediscover himself, not in the element of mind but through its opposite, corporeality. The return to real, physical, and bodily existence was manhood. The man "takes pleasure in himself as a living flesh and blood person," and recognizes that he has a particular, egoistic interest in the world. "The man is distinguished from the youth by the fact that he takes the world as it is, instead of everywhere fancying it amiss and wanting to improve it, model it after his ideal. In him the view that one must deal with the world according to his *interest*, not according to his *ideals* becomes confirmed."[30]

This self-centeredness allowed a second self-discovery: "As I find myself back of things and that as mind, so I must later find *myself* also back of *thoughts*—to wit, as their creator and *owner*." Whereas, during youth, abstractions had assumed a reality that subjected the individual to them, now the man recognized that the only true corporeal reality was his own being, and that thought was subject to it. "And now I take the world as what it is to me, as *mine*, as my property; I refer all to myself."[31]

Stirner's theory of the life cycle (or of the first three stages of it) was often crudely formed and awkwardly expressed; at times it seems merely a baroque parody of Hegel. Nonetheless, it contained a clearer sense of the relationship of childhood conflicts to later development than Hegel had possessed, and some of its descriptions of youth—following Hegel's—resemble modern psychological accounts of adolescent cognitive development.

Much more than Hegel's, however, Stirner's theory was also—like some other attempts to account for human experience in psychological terms—a revolt of the private man against all outside and public claims on his energy and loyalty. It was this revolt that Stirner clothed in the terminology of egoism and the unique individual. The whole book was prefaced with a rejection of all so-called higher causes, whether they were called God, the nation, or mankind. "I am . . . the creative nothing, the nothing out of which I myself as creator create everything," Stirner proclaimed. All claims from outside the individual were attempts to annihilate the self: "As the unholy man renounces *himself* before Mammon, so the holy man renounces *himself* before God."[32]

Among the claims Stirner rejected on this basis were those of politics. Every political party was the representative of a principle and therefore of an "essence" opposed to real human life. Liberals asked men to deny themselves in the name of liberty, Feuerbachians in the name of humanity, and communists in the name of free labor. Each group accepted individuals only to the extent that they conformed to some abstract definition of man. Communism was an advance over bourgeois liberalism in that the principle of labor was less abstract than that of competition. "But at the same time the laborer, in his consciousness that the essential thing in him is 'the laborer,' holds himself aloof from egoism and subjects himself to the supremacy of a society of laborers." Only the recognition that society had no existence apart from the individuals who made it up, and that therefore "we have no social duties, but solely interests for the pursuance of which society must serve us," could truly liberate man.[33]

This account of liberation from external abstractions was presented as the story of Stirner's own life, but he offered it as a mirror in which others could contemplate their development. Each individual would find it easier to remember and comprehend the stages in his own life history, the transformations of his views and principles, "when he has before his eyes the unrolling of another's life."[34] Moreover, Stirner believed that his mirror would reflect not only the life history of other individuals but the collective development of humanity. Phylogeny had the same shape as ontogeny; the whole human race had developed through childhood and youth toward the dawning manhood of the present.

Stirner's historical scheme was abstract, idealistic, and rather poorly informed, as Marx would demonstrate with devastating thoroughness. The triad, childhood—youth—manhood, was transformed first into

Negro—Mongol—Caucasian, then into Ancients—Moderns—Egoists, all on the basis of a rather superficial account of anthropology and history. Despite this, some of Stirner's views retain interest today. He pictured history, much as Freud later would, as a series of revolts against "fathers" by their children and, perhaps more clearly than Freud, he saw that the causes in the name of which the rebels rose up were ones that had been prepared by the fathers themselves.

In its own time Stirner's book was immediately criticized for its many weaknesses, but his approach fascinated and affected his readers. Engels, as we saw, was impressed with the need to build on it. Arnold Ruge thought it represented the last form post-Hegelian speculation could take, and therefore gave proof that German thought was about to move into the realm of action. Moses Hess took a similar view. In a book called *The Last Philosophers* he argued that the most recent German thinkers had taken speculation about the antithesis between individual and collective life as far as it could go. All such theoretical attempts to reconcile the individual and the species, "the son and the father," necessarily misfired, Hess averred; only the practical unification of individuals in a real human community—through socialism—could put an end to the dilemma.[35] It was in this atmosphere that Marx, too, read Stirner.

3. Youth Transcended

Although Marx was acquainted with Stirner's book soon after it appeared in the fall of 1844, he seems to have decided to write about it only a year later, after Stirner and Bauer together attacked *The Holy Family* in a German quarterly. By then Marx was living in Brussels, where he had migrated after being expelled from Paris at the beginning of February 1845. Engels joined him there in March, and in the summer the two friends visited England, in order to observe conditions and have access to recent English economic and socialist literature.

The work they undertook together in the fall and winter of 1845 was directed against Bauer as well as Stirner, but the section devoted to Bauer was brief and insignificant compared to the massive assault (nearly 400 pages in the English edition) on Stirner. Beginning early in 1846 Marx and Engels added two shorter parts to their work, a general exposition of their position directed particularly against Feuerbach, and a final "Critique of German Socialism According to its Various Prophets." The whole rather unwieldy collection received the title *The German Ideology*.[36] Marx later described the book as the product of his and Engels' desire "to work out in common the opposition of our view to the ideological view of German philosophy, in fact to settle accounts with our erstwhile philosophical conscience."[37] Criticizing Stirner's book provided the occasion to complete the settling of accounts with Hegelian speculation projected earlier, in the *1844 Manuscripts*.

The German Ideology was a joint effort of Marx and Engels, and on many particular points it is not possible to separate the contributions each made. Nonetheless, the distinct orientations and personalities of the two friends suggest some basic differences in what each one brought to it. Many of the historical formulations would follow the lines Engels had indicated in *The Condition of the Working Class in England*. Engels' views of the relationship between "atomic" individualism and class formation would reappear, as would his ideas about the effect of social and economic change on consciousness. But much else had to come from Marx. Detailed criticism of other writers on such a mammoth scale was not in Engels' style, as his reaction to *The Holy Family* revealed. Not only had he been annoyed by the bulk Marx had allowed that critique to take, he added that "most of the criticism of speculation and of the abstract essence will remain incomprehensible to the larger public and will not be generally interesting." A similar criticism might be leveled at *The German Ideology*. Even in his first letter to Marx about Stirner's book, Engels had expressed his weariness with theoretical arguments and his desire to exchange them for real action. The need to achieve a consistent theoretical position was one Marx felt more deeply and personally than Engels.[38]

One way in which *The German Ideology* sought to fulfill this need was through a criticism of Stirner's life cycle theory. Rejecting Stirner's invitation for others to find their development mirrored in his progression from childhood to manhood, Marx sought to reduce Stirner's picture of adolescence in general to a portrait of "the young 'Stirner,' the studious Berlin youth busy with Hegel's logic and gazing admiringly at the great Michelet." Only of such a youth, Marx claimed, was it "rightly said, page 17: 'to bring to light *pure thought*, to devote oneself to it—in this is the *joy of youth*, and all the bright images of the world of thought—truth, freedom, mankind, Man, etc.—illumine and inspire the youthful soul." Yet many features in Stirner's portrait of youth fit Marx as a student too, reading through the night and contemptuous of external things. When Marx altered Stirner's account of how the youth replaced natural, parental authority with rational, abstract authorities, in order to emphasize that thanks to this transfer "the good youth reconciles obedience and fear of one's parents with his speculating conscience, and everything remains as before," it was his own conversion to Hegel that he recalled. And when Marx singled out Stirner's reference to the maxim "One should obey God rather than men" to describe the young man's powerful sense of conscience, the trail did not dead-end at Stirner but led straight to himself.

This was the very maxim Marx had used to describe the writer's attitude toward his craft—his refusal to make it a self-serving trade—in the *Rheinische Zeitung*.[39]

Marx did not deny that the transition from youth to manhood was a definite and important occurrence in an individual's life. What he contested was Stirner's conception of what took place at that moment. According to Stirner, the man who recognized that his youthful conceptions of "the Emperor, the Fatherland, the State, etc." were fantasies, actually destroyed *"all these powers* by getting out of his head his false opinion of them."* What really happened was the opposite: "Now that he no longer looks at the world through the spectacles of his fantasy, he has to think of the practical interrelations of the world, to get to know them and guide himself by them. By destroying the *fantastic* corporeality which the world had for him, he finds its real corporeality outside his fantasy." Stirner's account should have read, "I take the world as it is *independently of myself*, in the form in which it *belongs to itself*. . . . I relate myself to everything and only to that extent do I relate everything to myself." To Marx—as to Hegel, it should be recalled—the youth became a man by learning to discover himself in the world, not vice versa. Stirner's was a maturity of withdrawal, a renunciation of all that limited the independence of the private individual. Marx's was a maturity of social involvement, basing individual life on historical development. To this conception of life history dependent on world history Engels contributed, as well as Hegel. Engels, too, was concerned about his personal arrival at manhood, but in his book on English conditions he had criticized the Owenite socialists in similar terms: "They acknowledge only a psychological development, a development of man in the abstract, out of all relation to the Past, whereas the whole world rests upon that Past, the individual man included."[40]

Against the theory of the life cycle as Stirner presented it, Marx and Engels put forward four criticisms, three of which have been echoed by later critics of similar theories. (I shall comment parenthetically on each of them here.) First, Stirner ignored "the physical and social changes taking place in the individuals, which produce an altered consciousness." (This was not a stricture that could be established against Hegel's life cycle theory, nor, in our own time, would it be correct to offer either part of it against Erik Erikson.) Second, unconcerned about these concrete conditions of life, Stirner "consistently abstracts from historical epochs, nationalities, classes, etc., or, which is *the same thing*, he inflates the prevailing consciousness of the class nearest to him in his immediate environment into the normal consciousness of 'human life.' " The life history of "a young English factory worker or young Yankee, not to mention the young Kirghiz-Kazaks," would not fit the mold. (This stricture could be turned with nearly equal effectiveness against Hegel, and with some justification against modern psychological theories as well, although the latter have tried to counter it by introducing comparative data from non-European experience. The point is relatively unimportant here, since Western life cycle theories are being employed only with reference to the society and the social class that generated them.)

Third, Stirner took a purely subjective point of view, which equated the truth about youths and men with the illusions they had about themselves. (Psychological approaches often focus more on subjective consciousness than sociological ones do, but to equate this difference with the distinction between illusion and truth was a simplification whose dangers Marx himself would have to confront later on. Whether maturity is merely a subjective matter is a question we shall return to below.) Finally, Stirner had truncated and distorted the view of life history Hegel gave in the third part of his *Encyclopaedia*. "Whereas Hegel, for example, takes so much account of the empirical world that he portrays the German burgher as the slave of the world around him, Stirner has to make him the master of this world, which he is not even in imagination." What had been a theory of man as a social being in Hegel's hands Stirner distorted into a justification for anarchistic individualism.[41] (This was perfectly true of Stirner, as we have already noted. Hegel would not have agreed that he regarded men in civil society as "slaves," but we may recall that, in psychological terms, he had said of the healthy person that the contents of the outside world "make him what he is: he too would become extinct if these externalities were to disappear."[42] The difference Marx acknowledged between Hegel and Stirner reminds us that Hegel did not posit the primacy of individual experience over social life. His life cycle theory—like Erik Erikson's—was based on the recognition that individuals *must* live in a world created by forces outside themselves.)

Despite the distinction he made between Stirner and Hegel, the thrust of Marx's criticism was to emphasize the social basis of life so strongly as to deny the psychological perspective any independent place in accounting for human experience. It was in his confrontation with Stirner that Marx's thinking became explicitly counterpsychological, rejecting the sort of attention to individual consciousness he himself had given in his doctoral dissertation. Doing so led him to deny—falsely, I have argued—the presence in his own life of some of the developmental issues Stirner had pointed to; moreover, other persistent themes in Marx's life can be discovered below the surface of his confrontation with Stirner. These included, first, the relationship between egoism and self-sacrifice, and second, the problem of vocation—particularly the philosophical vocation—and personal fulfillment.

In advancing the principle of egoism, Stirner attacked two different champions of self-sacrifice whose attitudes and relations mattered greatly to Marx: middle-class moralists and communists. Both in ordinary *bourgeois*, and in communists and socialists like Cabet and Buchez (a radical St. Simonian), Stirner found a hostility to selfishness and a glorification of sacrifice that negated egoism. Despite their ostensible political contrast, both groups displayed the same slavish willingness to subordinate human nature to self-denying abstractions.

Marx had earlier identified himself with the principle of self-sacrifice, as had his father. His graduation essay on choosing a vocation envisioned a career in which personal ambition would be fulfilled in the name of sacrifice. In the *Rheinische Zeitung*, too, he had declared the freedom and special quality of the writer to consist in his separation from personal, worldly interest, and his willingness to sacrifice himself to his craft. Marx's identification of himself with self-sacrifice brought his personal orientation into harmony with a central theme of radical and communist social criticism, for the opposition to individualistic egoism had been a constant element in the tradition that ran from Rousseau through Babeuf and Buonarrotti to the French communists.[43] Aware of this aspect of communist theory, Stirner had criticized it as a remnant of the same philosophical abstraction by which Feuerbach tried to subordinate the individual to "love" or "man." Engels, who found this criticism troubling when he first read Stirner's book, proposed to reply that "the human heart is unselfish and sacrificing right at the start, in its very egoism."[44]

The response of *The German Ideology* was different. Marx explained the opposition between egoism and sacrifice not as resulting from any universal characteristic of human nature, but on the basis of social relations, and he presented the impulse toward self-sacrifice as a means of self-assertion rather than the other way around. The contradiction derived from the basic conditions of social life, in which individuals had to find fulfillment through collective existence. The "general interests" to which individuals claimed to sacrifice themselves were personal interests that had developed "into class interests, into common interests which acquire independent existence in relation to the individual persons, and in their independence assume the form of *general* interests." This occurred, moreover, only "within the frameworks of definite *modes of production*," which were independent not only of separate individuals but of all together, and which stood above them. "Individuals have always started out from themselves, and could not do otherwise"; therefore, both egoism and sacrifice "are aspects of the personal development of individuals; both are only expressions of *one and the same* personal development of people and are therefore only in *seeming* contradiction to each other." It was in this context that one could understand how "the personal behavior of the individual is bound to undergo substantiation, alienation, and at the same time exists as a power independent of him."[45]

Communists, therefore, did not preach self-sacrifice, or any other form of morality, but explained the real conditions out of which moral demands arose. "They are very well aware that egoism, just as much as self-sacrifice, *is* in definite circumstances a necessary form of the self-assertion of individuals." They understood that the two sides, "private" and "general" interest were constantly produced by each other, "so that this contradiction is in practice always being destroyed and reproduced." With the disappearance of the form of society that created oppositions between individuals and the whole, "this contradiction together with its unity also disappears."[46]

Hence, Stirner's assertion that modern bourgeois were not real egoists because they subscribed to a morality of sacrifice missed the real basis of bourgeois morality. An actual bourgeois would reply with reason that "Things are just the reverse." The members of the bourgeoisie were the real egoists, they "bring practical egoism to perfection precisely by denying the phraseology of egoism." That denial allowed them to pretend that their individual and class interests were the interests of their fellow men.[47]

The personal sources of Marx's discussion of egoism and sacrifice are revealed in this portrait of bourgeois egoists, for it is difficult to imagine a purer denial of self-interest combined with a clearer devotion to practical advancement than the one displayed by Heinrich Marx. Marx's image of the practical egoist was a slap at his father. Yet, curiously, it was a justification of him too. In opposition to Stirner, Marx insisted that the ethic propounded by Heinrich Marx did not deny the real conditions of his life but precisely corresponded to them. Heinrich's consciousness, with all its contradictions, was the correct translation of his social being. If those contradictions were to be eliminated, no mere philosophical reform of consciousness was adequate to the task. One could not cure what ailed Heinrich by preaching a different form of morality, but only by transforming the whole structure of society. In the meantime, the communists who saw that both egoism and self-sacrifice were necessary forms of individual consciousness were making the only consistent sense possible out of Heinrich's inner contradictions.

That Heinrich Marx's type of consciousness did not need to be revised to correspond to modern life brings us to a second theme in Marx's personal evolution that contributed to *The German Ideology*, the question of vocation. In Marx's previous writings, his task in life had been precisely the philosophical "reform of consciousness" that he now declared the modern bourgeoisie did not require. That philosophy could and should correct the consciousness of ordinary men had been Marx's position in the *Rheinische Zeitung* and in a series of letters to Ruge published in the *Deutsch-Französische Jahrbücher*.[48] In the *1844 Manuscripts* he still regarded his philosophical perspective as affording a consciousness that "reaches out beyond" the limited historical movement of ordinary, practical communism.[49] In *The German Ideology* this view of philosophy was firmly set aside.

It was an old philosophical trick to pretend that, if people changed their consciousness, it was the philosopher's demand to alter it that brought the change about. "This entire separation of consciousness from the individuals who are its basis and from their actual conditions, this notion that the egoist of present-day bourgeois society does not possess the consciousness corresponding to his egoism, is merely an old philosophical fad." The general belief that criticism could reform consciousness was the characteristic of Young Hegelian philosophy that Marx singled out for attack in the preface to the book. The belief that philosophical criticism could liberate men "from the chimeras, the ideas, dogmas, imaginary beings" that oppressed them was the "innocent and childlike" fancy that historical materialism would unmask.[50]

Some months before he began his reply to Stirner, Marx had denied the distinction between philosophical consciousness and ordinary awareness in one of the "Theses on Feuerbach" Engels later found in a notebook Marx kept in Brussels. Even from a materialist point of view (like that of the French *philosophes*) the notion that some members of society could clear the heads of others collapsed in contradiction: "The materialist doctrine concerning the changing of circumstances and upbringing forgets that circumstances are changed by men and that it is essential to educate the educator himself. This doctrine must, therefore, divide society into two parts, one of which is superior to society."[51] Once before, in the *Rheinische Zeitung*, Marx had asked the question, "Does not education also need education?" Then, too, the answer had been that it did, but the role was assigned precisely to philosophy, from which Marx now recalled it in order to assign it to the revolutionary "changing of circumstances."

Marx now declared that the whole question of what vocation a man chose did not depend on subjective desire but on objective circumstances. If an individual gave himself over to the satisfaction of a single passion, "e.g., that of writing books," "if therefore the satisfaction of the individual appears as the one-sided satisfaction of a single passion," the reason was not to be sought in his consciousness, but in "the empirical development and manifestation of life of the individual, which in turn depends on conditions in the world." And if that person were "a parochial Berlin school-master or author," with his limited horizons and provincial life style, "when he experiences the need to think, it is inevitable that his thought becomes just as abstract as this individual and his life itself, and that it confronts him, who is quite incapable of resistance, in the form of a fixed power."[52]

Here, as in his portrait of youth, it was Stirner that Marx declared himself to be describing. Yet the liberation from a single activity, particularly from a form of philosophy tied to fixed abstractions, was one he had long sought for himself. The way in which Marx now pursued it appears best from the section of *The German Ideology* directed not against Stirner but against Feuerbach, where Marx's general view received more concise and systematic expression. Here Marx declared that communist society would put an end to the one-sided fixation of human activity by abolishing the division of labor. The division of labor implied "the contradiction between the interest of the separate individual or the individual family and the communal interest of all individuals," and it therefore provided "the first example of how, as long as man remains in natural society, that is, as long as a cleavage exists between the particular and the common interest . . . man's own deed becomes an alien power opposed to him, which enslaves him instead of being controlled by him."

> For as soon as the distribution of labor comes into being, each man has a particular, exclusive sphere of activity, which is forced upon him, and from which he cannot escape. He is a hunter, a fisherman, a shepherd, or a critical critic, and must remain so if he does not want to lose his means of livelihood; while in communist society, where nobody has one exclusive sphere of activity but each can become accomplished in any branch he wishes, society regulates the general production and thus makes it possible for me to do one thing today and another tomorrow, to hunt in the morning, fish in the afternoon, rear cattle in the evening, criticize after dinner, just as I have a mind, without ever becoming hunter, fisherman, shepherd or critic. This fixation of social activity, this consolidation of what we ourselves produce into an objective power above us, growing out of our control, thwarting our expectations, bringing to naught our calculations, is one of the chief factors in historical development up till now.[53]

I have given this passage at length even though it is a well-known one, because much of the unexamined background for Marx's redefinition of his vocation in *The German Ideology* can be perceived through it. To begin with, what Marx presented as the source of enslavement was not any determinate set of working conditions, but the situation that assigned to each individual "a particular, exclusive sphere of activity"; slavery was not found only in working for the interest of another person, but in the very need to have a defined occupation in a world where each person had a bounded sphere of activity. So radical and unrelieved a view of the way division of labor imprisoned the human personality went beyond the critique handed down from Schiller, and even beyond what Engels had said in *The Condition of the Working Class in England*, where the division of labor forced men to sacrifice "the best qualities of their human nature."

More than the words of any other writer, what Marx was echoing here was his own comment on choosing a vocation written eleven years earlier. In 1835, however, only an ill-advised choice of vocation was "an act which can destroy man's entire life, defeat all his plans, and make him unhappy."[54] Now there was no occupation in existing society that did not turn a person's activity into an alien and uncontrolled power "thwarting our expectations, bringing to naught our calculations." Moreover, the Marx who in 1835 had chosen precisely the vocation he regarded as most dangerous, the life of mind, had found that it involved him in some of the very experience he now described. Marx's products had grown out of his control, beginning in 1837 with the 300-page philosophy of law he had destroyed in Berlin and the philosophical dialogue that had born him "like a false-hearted siren into the clutches of the enemy." His expectations for his own work had been continually thwarted, leaving his writings unfinished. Whatever relief the abolition of the division of labor might bring to others, Marx's account of its promised benefits occupied an important place—consciously or unconsciously—in his own personal ledger.

Moreover, beneath the surface of Marx's description of life free from the division of labor there lurked a particular set of psychological motifs, which his accent on the theme of social determination did not quite succeed in blotting out. The image of a man who would "hunt in the morning, fish in the afternoon, rear cattle in the evening, criticize after dinner," had a specific source. It came from Charles Fourier's account of the day a rich man would spend in the utopian community of Harmony. Mondor, as Fourier named his imaginary communitarian, would include in his summer schedule a session with the hunters at 5:30 a.m., one with the fishermen at 7:00 a.m., one with the sheep-raisers late in the afternoon, before his last meal, and attend to "art, concert, dance, theatre" after he had eaten.[55] Thus, Marx's vision of life in a society free of the division of labor echoed Fourier's theory of community. But Fourier's reasons for doing away with the division of labor, although tied up with a critique of the social and economic evils of existing society, derived equally from his reflections on human psychology and the nature of human passions.

Fourier's theory of personality and the passions was too complex for us to do it justice here. Tied to a quasimystical numerology and weighted down by astronomical correspondences, it counted 4 "movements" governing nature and history, 810 temperaments or characters in human beings, and 12 (sometimes more) distinct passions ruling human behavior. Leaving those details aside, however (as Marx certainly did, even while taking Mondor's day seriously), there remain elements in Fourier's theory with a greater claim on our attention. Fourier proposed to "compare passion with mania, which is a diminutive form of passion," and he added:

"All repressed passion produces its counterpassion which is as malevolent as the natural passion would be beneficial. The mechanism is the same for manias." To illustrate the effects of repression Fourier told the story of Madame Stroganoff, whose sadistic cruelty arose from the frustration of her unconscious lesbianism. She tortured the very girl who aroused her desires, "subverting her true feeling, and persecuting its object, with whom she should have found pleasure." As in Madame Stroganoff, so in all the great evildoers of history, "This predilection for atrocity is again but the counter-effect of the suffocation of certain passions."[56]

It was to assure the free expression of basic human passions that Fourier planned the life of Harmony. The passions he made special provision for were the ones whose existence he thought he had discovered himself, and which he called the "cabalist," the "butterfly," and the "composite" passions. The cabalistic passion was the desire for competition and intrigue, and in Harmony its positive function would be to "stir up discords or competitive rivalries between groups." The butterfly passion was the one that "impels men and women to flit from pleasure to pleasure," and made any prolonged activity boring and painful. The composite was the desire for "simultaneous enjoyment of sensual and spiritual pleasures," and its satisfaction produced exaltation and romantic enthusiasm. By providing satisfactions for all these passions the life of Harmony—with its abolition of the ordinary division of labor—opened the doors to a degree of fulfillment and happiness that ordinary, civilized life could never offer. "Perfect health is only to be attained by this continual alternation of occupations, which, exercising successively every part of the body and every faculty of the mind, maintains both in activity and equilibrium."[57]

Marx was neither unconcerned about the satisfaction of passion nor unaware of the effects of frustrating it. In one of his letters to Ruge in 1843, Marx found potentially revolutionary energy in the shame Germans felt about their political situation because "Shame is a type of anger, introverted anger."[58] In *The German Ideology* Marx discussed the fixation and distortion of human desires, in response to Stirner's presentation of compulsions and fixed ideas as remnants of earlier phases in the life cycle. Rejecting Stirner's approach to a developmental view, Marx insisted that "Whether a desire becomes fixed or not, i.e., whether it obtains exclusive power over us," depended on material circumstances, "on the actual conditions, and the possibility of development they give each individual." Marx underlined the importance of basic physical needs, observing that "No one can do anything without at the same time doing it for the sake of one or other of his needs and for the sake of the organ of this need," but he understood this differently from Stirner: "If the conditions of the world prevent him from satisfying his stomach, then his stomach becomes the master over him, the desire to eat becomes a fixed desire, and the thought of eating becomes a fixed idea—which at the same time gives him an example of the influence of world conditions in fixing his desires and ideas."[59]

The example of hunger was an effective weapon against Stirner, but the fixed desires and ideas that concerned Marx more immediately were different. It was the one-sided fixation on thought separate from life exemplified in the German idealism of his own youth that Marx wanted to dissolve, and whose isolation and abstractness he sought to transcend. A different form of life would produce a different quality of thought. "In the case of an individual, for example, whose life embraces a wide circle of varied activities and practical relations to the world, and who, therefore, lives a many-sided life, thought has the same character of universality as every other manifestation of his life."[60] In this connection Marx had written about unfulfilled passion that had been distorted into a kind of mania once before, giving a portrait that shared important features with Fourier's picture of Madame Stroganoff. This was the sketch of the philosopher Democritus he included in his doctoral dissertation.

Democritus had tortured himself rather than others, blinding himself "so that the sensible light in the eye would not darken sharpness of intellect." His affliction had been rooted in the conditions of his time: unlike the fortunate post-Hegelian generation (as Marx believed in 1841) the Greeks did not have access to the concept of "the whole," and could only employ the notion of the abstract individual, thereby cutting themselves off from philosophically grasping the concrete, substantial world of actual existence. Democritus had responded to this situation in a particular way, however (one that contrasted with his counterpart, Epicurus), reflecting his ambivalent passion for philosophy. "On the one hand it is the lust for knowledge that leaves him no peace, but it is at the same time the dissatisfaction with the true, i.e., philosophical knowledge that drives him afar." This tension was the root of his inner contradictions, his ceaseless wanderings, and his ultimate self-destructiveness.

Aware of both the historical and the psychological aspects of this Democritean condition, Marx had earlier sought therapy for both in Hegel and Feuerbach. Modern philosophy had seemed to offer a purchase on the real world, a remedy for the social isolation of ancient thinkers and an innoculation against its psychological consequences. Marx was still seeking to preserve himself from that condition in 1846: the picture of men—especially men of thought—isolated and estranged by the division of labor Marx presented in *The German Ideology* was an enlargement from the same negative image of abstract thinkers isolated from the world that had inspired Marx's conversion to Hegel in 1837 and his doctoral dissertation of 1841. Hence, the abolition of the division of labor, which Marx made the central feature of communist society, was a direct substitute for the solution to the dilemma of intellectual isolation he had once found in Hegelian—and then in Feuerbachian—philosophy.

But whereas Marx the Hegelian had distinguished himself from his image of Democritus by declaring philosophy to be "master of the universe," he now moved closer to the Democritean condition of being a philosophical rebel against philosophy, seeking in the real world for answers to the enigma to which Hegel had once provided the solution. In 1846 this alteration did not lead Marx to share the condition he had attributed to Democritus. Democritus had been continually disappointed in his attempt to find phenomena in the real world that corresponded to the expectations philosophy had bred in him; in the revolutionary atmosphere of the later 1840s, Marx was able to believe that society was about to transform itself along the lines of his original philosophic vision. Only later, as these expectations were disappointed, would his compound of entanglement and dissatisfaction with philosophy pose the threats to him it had created for the Democritus of his dissertation. Before we can begin to follow Marx into that later situation, we must look more deeply at his self-proclaimed abandonment of philosophy in *The German Ideology*, at its effects on his views of history, revolution, and ideology, and at some additional personal sources for this intellectual reorientation.

4. The World Right-Side-Up

The approach to history Marx and Engels presented systematically in the chapter of *The German Ideology* called "Feuerbach" was on the one hand a theory of social development and revolution, and on the other an account of the origin of consciousness and ideology. Its basis, they insisted, was not philosophical vision but empirical observation. Because the premises from which it began were "real individuals, their activity and the material conditions under which they live," this starting point was not arbitrary, and could be "verified in a purely empirical way." No special intellectual perspective was necessary to perceive the conditions that shaped and determined men's lives in the modern world. The growth of productive forces brought about "the actual empirical existence of men in their *world-historical* instead of local, being." The "transformation of history into world history" was not a matter of theory, but "a quite material, empirically verifiable act, an act the proof of which every individual furnishes as he comes and goes, eats, drinks, and clothes himself."[61]

The tasks Marx had previously assigned to philosophical criticism were now taken over by history, and especially by revolution. Forms and products of consciousness could not be dissolved by criticism—men already had the consciousness that corresponded to their existence—but only by practical changes in social relations. "Not criticism but revolution is the driving force of history, also of religion, of philosophy and all other types of theory." This dissolution of consciousness began first as competition made industrial production the dominant power in people's lives, and thereby "destroyed as far as possible ideology, religion, morality, etc., and where it could not do this, made them into a palpable lie." But it was actual revolution that would complete the destruction of previous forms of consciousness, for in it "the proletariat rids itself of everything that still clings to it from its previous position in society." Revolution was necessary not only to overthrow a ruling class "but also because the class *overthrowing* it can only in a revolution succeed in ridding itself of all the muck of ages and become fitted to found society anew."[62]

In this situation Marx no longer needed philosophy, and he declared his independence from it: "When reality is depicted, philosophy as an independent branch of knowledge loses its medium of existence. At the best its place can only be taken by a summing up of the most general results, abstractions which arise from the observation of the historical development of men." Even more specifically, the traditional problems of philosophy were resolved into questions of "empirical fact" once things were conceived in their real existence. For instance, the question of man's relation to nature could only be discussed in regard to the different modes of appropriating nature men devised as industry developed. The path to such a purely empirical perspective had been indicated, Marx and Engels declared, in Marx's essays in the *Deutsch-Französische Jahrbücher*. However, since the language there was still philosophical, German readers had thought Marx's view simply a further extension of speculative theory. (Stirner had interpreted Marx in just that way.) Therefore, "One has to 'leave philosophy aside,' one has to leap out of it and devote oneself like an ordinary man to the study of actuality, for which there exists also an enormous amount of literary material, unknown of course to the philosophers."[63]

Marx made the relationship between contemporary history and the traditional tasks of theory still clearer a year later, in his polemic against Proudhon, *The Poverty of Philosophy*. In the early stages of socialism, when "the productive forces are not yet sufficiently developed in the bosom of the bourgeoisie itself to enable us to catch a glimpse of the material conditions necessary for the emancipation of the proletariat," the theorists of working-class liberation had to engage in speculation, to "improvise systems and go in search of regenerating science." Later, however, this search for a special scientific knowledge became unnecessary. "In the measure that history moves forward, and with it the struggle of the proletariat assumes clearer outlines, they no longer need to seek science in their minds; they have only to take note of what is happening before their eyes and to become its mouthpiece."[64]

In *The German Ideology* this view of history was put forth in a chapter directed against Feuerbach, and one of its purposes was to make a clean break between Marx and Engels and their earlier Feuerbachian viewpoint. Feuerbach was still praised—but only in a passage later crossed out in the manuscript—as "the only one who has at least made some progress." But his direction did not lead to Marx's goal. Because Feuerbach's view rested on a conception of "man" rather than on the perception of "real, historical men," he necessarily came up against facts of experience that disturbed the harmony between human nature and existence he presupposed. "To remove this disturbance, he must take refuge in a double perception, a profane one which only perceives the 'flatly obvious' and a higher, philosophical, one which perceives the 'true essence' of things." He could only cope with the real "sensuous"—empirical—world "by looking at it with the 'eyes,' i.e., through the 'spectacles' of the philosopher."[65]

One particularly revealing example of what Marx meant was provided by Feuerbach's view of poverty.

> When, for example, he sees instead of healthy men a crowd of scrofulous, overworked and consumptive starvelings, he is compelled to take refuge in the "higher perception" and in the ideal "compensation in the species," and thus to relapse into idealism at the very point where the communist materialist sees the necessity, and at the same time the condition, of a transformation both of industry and of the social structure.

This comment on Feuerbach was a witness to Marx's own evolution, for in the *Paris Manuscripts* Marx had taken a similar attitude toward poverty himself.

> It will be seen [Marx wrote] how in place of the *wealth* and *poverty* of political economy comes the *rich human being* and the rich *human* need. . . . Not only *wealth*, but likewise the *poverty* of man—under the assumption of socialism—receives in equal measure a *human* and therefore social significance. Poverty is the passive bond which causes the human being to experience the greatest wealth—the *other* human being.

Now Marx abandoned the philosophical spectacles that had allowed him to perceive this higher reality in the world of real human existence.[66]

His new way of seeing discovered the contradictions driving human society toward revolution and communism, not in the conflict between existence and essence, but wholly within the sphere of actual material life. In *The Holy Family* Marx had still written that revolution would occur "because man is lost in the proletariat but at the same time has won a theoretical awareness of that loss." In *The German Ideology* there was no more talk of the loss of "man." The impetus to revolution was now seen in the fact that industry and commerce had "rendered the great mass of humanity 'property-less,' and produced, at the same time, the contradiction of an existing world of wealth and culture, both of which conditions presuppose a great increase in productive power, a high degree of development."[67]

This reorientation led Marx to abandon also the view of historical development Feuerbach had inspired him to work out in Paris, the view that regarded history as the successive alienation and recovery of the human essence. Philosophers had interpreted history as alienation by conceiving "individuals who are no longer subjected to the division of labor . . . under the name of 'Man.' " They sought to understand history as the evolution of "man" rather than as the development of historically determined individuals.

> The whole process was seen as a process of the self-alienation of "Man," essentially because the average individual of the later stage was always foisted on the earlier stage and the consciousness of a later period on the individuals of an earlier. [Self-Alienation.] Through this inversion, which from the beginning has been an abstraction of the actual conditions, it was possible to transform all history into an evolutionary process of consciousness.[68]

Marx still spoke of men as under the control of alien forces and of estrangement ("a term," Marx observed, "which will be comprehensible to the philosophers") as an experience. But it was not man's own nature in an alienated form that held him in subjection, it was the world market. Marx echoed his earlier views, too, when he wrote of "the transformation, through the division of labor, of personal powers (relationships) into material powers." What had to be abolished in order to end this situation was not alienation, however, but the division of labor.[69] History was not the alienation and recovery of the human essence, because there was no essence—separate from real, empirical individuals and their relationships—to be alienated.

The whole question of alienation in Marx's writings after 1844 is a complicated and cloudy one, and a rounded view of it can only be achieved later on, from the perspective of the *Grundrisse* and *Capital*. In those works the philosophical anthropology represented by the use Marx had made of alienation in 1844 would reappear. Its recurrence then would testify to the place Hegel's model of dialectical progression always continued to occupy as an underlying pattern for Marx's perception of history: the world men created as a means to assure their existence faced them as a power they could not control. But in order for that implicit conception to lead Marx back to the language of alienation he was putting aside in 1845-46, events would first have to cause Marx ro reexamine his conviction that modern conditions made it possible to comprehend the world in a purely empirical way, without the aid of philosophy. How that occurred we shall try to grasp later. For now, we should note that what replaced alienation theory as the keystone of Marx's historical vision in *The German Ideology* was a category that could claim to be altogether social in its origins and content, but which in fact had—as we have just seen—deep personal significance for Marx: the division of labor.

The view of human nature and its history Marx now gave made the division of labor the measuring rod of social and individual development. Men differed from animals in that they produced the means of their subsistence and hence the bases of "their actual material life." The productive activity in which any given group engaged was "a definite form of expressing their life." It was thus the fundamental basis of their existence: "As individuals express their life, so they are." But since the form of production any group pursued depended "first of all on the nature of the actual means of subsistence they find in existence and have to reproduce," Marx was able to state the primary thesis of historical materialism: "The nature of individuals thus depends on the material conditions determining their production."[70]

These conditions were set by the division of labor. Production presupposed the commerce of individuals with each other, and the form of this commerce depended on the extent to which a given society "has developed its productive forces, the division of labor and internal intercourse." The internal structure of any nation rested on the development of production within it, and this "is shown most manifestly by the degree to which the division of labor has been carried." Not the originally individual process of producing objects into which labor was objectified—as in 1844—but the inescapably social phenomenon of collective organization of productive tasks was the constant phenomenon which, correctly observed, made history comprehensible.[71]

This altered perspective, moreover, had important practical consequences. When Marx had first called forth the vision of proletarian revolution in the *Deutsch-Französische Jahrbücher* of 1844, he had projected the image of the proletariat against a very special background. The possibility of proletarian revolution, he explained, arose out of conditions in Germany. "Radical revolution, *universal human* emancipation is not a utopian dream for Germany. What is utopian is the partial, the *merely* political revolution, the revolution which would leave the pillars of the house standing." In France such a partial revolution had occurred, because in France the middle class had been able to present itself as the representative of all excluded and oppressed segments of civil society against the aristocracy. This was not possible in Germany, where no class possessed "the consistency, penetration, courage and ruthlessness which could stamp it as the negative representative of society." On this basis there was clearly no room for supposing that the German proletariat would work for any cause other than its own; it could not ally with any other social group. Its partner was not another social class, but philosophy, whose ideal negation of German conditions matched the proletariat's actual negation.[72]

In 1846, however, Marx's notion of how the proletariat's action would relate to that of other groups took a sharp turn. In his meetings with other German communists he now argued—as he would publicly in the *Communist Manifesto* at the end of 1847—that the final triumph of the proletariat required the immediate victory of the German bourgeoisie, and that the proper policy for the revolutionary proletarian party in the present was cooperation with the "bourgeois democrats." As Wilhelm Weitling reported the view Marx expressed on this question at a gathering of German communists at the end of March 1846: "There can be no immediate prospect of the realization of communism: the bourgeoisie must first come to the helm."[73]

The grounds for this changed view were explained in *The German Ideology*. The development of the proletariat depended on the advance of production and the worldwide hegemony of bourgeois industrial relations. Unless this development were complete in the most populous and powerful countries before the communist revolution took place, then communism would exist as a mere "local event," and "each extension of intercourse would abolish local communism." In the *Communist Manifesto* Marx declared that the communists followed policies in each national context that reflected the particular conditions of action that obtained there: "In Germany they fight with the bourgeoisie whenever it acts in a revolutionary way, against the absolute monarchy, the feudal squirearchy, and the petty bourgeoisie." Philosophy, of course, no longer had any role to play.[74]

The world Marx confronted in *The German Ideology* contrasted in one more way with the one he had depicted in his Paris writings: it was not "inverted." In the *Deutsch-Französische Jahrbücher* Marx had declared that "the inverted world is the actual one"; in the *Economic and Philosophic Manuscripts of 1844* the role of money had been to invert the reality of human powers and turn them into their opposites. But just as there was now no human essence to be alienated, so there was none to be inverted. Money received more than a dozen mentions, including one extended discussion in *The German Ideology*, but at no point was there any suggestion that its effect was to turn the world upside down. On the contrary, instead of distorting reality, money now revealed a truth, namely that "the relations of production and intercourse as a whole assume an independent existence."[75]

The notion of inversion itself remained, indeed it grew more prominent than it had been in 1844; but instead of describing something that actually occurred in the real world, it referred to something that happened in speculative minds: only thinkers were inverted now. We saw a moment ago that Marx described the theory that based history on alienation as an inversion, the product of philosophic spectacles. The same spectacles were worn by Stirner, who repeatedly displayed inversion. In his views, "reality is again turned upside-down"; from his belief in the importance of ideas derived "his manner of turning everything upside-down."[76]

In fact inversion now became the identifying mark of thought that attempted to deny its own dependence on the real conditions of life, the kind of thinking Marx now called ideology. At an early stage in human history, consciousness had been "directly interwoven with the material activity and the material intercourse of men, the language of real life." Hence it was the "direct efflux" of actual behavior. Later, the relation between thought and reality changed. "If in all ideology men and their circumstances appear upside-down as in a *camera obscura*, this phenomenon arises just as much from their historical life-process as the inversion of objects on the retina does from their physical life-process."[77]

Here, too, the central explanatory device was the division of labor. Marx described its effects most clearly in a note written at the end of the manuscript book containing the first part of *The German Ideology*: "The influence of the division of labor on science" was its first heading. After a few brief jottings Marx moved to the question *"Why the ideologists turn everything upside-down."* The explanation for this inversion was "ideological subdivision within a class. 1. *The occupation assumes an independent existence owing to division of labor*; everyone believes his craft to be the true one. The very nature of their craft causes them to succumb the more easily to illusions regarding the connection between their craft and reality." In other words, the man whose life was devoted to religion, law, or politics viewed his own activity as the determining form of human life, and the concepts describing his own manner of entering into and explaining human relationships as "the real active driving force." Thus, men came to see their lives as ruled not by real, material relationships but by "Idea of justice. Idea of State." Not only philosophers but priests, lawyers, and politicians saw the world in this inverted way; all were ideologists.[78]

Marx's conception of ideology in 1846 echoed some of his own earlier comments on the relation of thought to society. In one respect it resembled the portrait he had drawn of Greek thinkers in his doctoral dissertation. The similarity emerges especially clearly in the third part of *The German Ideology*, where Marx applied his critique to the German "true socialists" (Karl Grün and others) who sought to interpret socialist society as an ideal realm of unconditional freedom, no longer subject to material limitations. Marx found in these thinkers a perverted view of the relationship between thought and life, which derived from their belief that thinking was not subject to the conditions of ordinary existence. Such a position exactly matched the one Marx had attributed to the Greek *sophoi*, with their project of measuring life by the standards of thought. At the basis of true socialism Marx saw the old philosophical opposition between reason and substantial life. "The [true] socialist opposes to present-day society, which is 'based upon external compulsion,' the ideal of true society, which is based upon the 'consciousness of man's *inward* nature, i.e., upon reason.' It is based, that is, upon the consciousness of consciousness, upon the thought of thought. The true socialist does not differ from the philosophers, even in his choice of terms."[79] Like Greek philosophy, German speculation was the work of a special class of thinkers, cut off from real life and withdrawn into themselves. This accounted for the inversion Marx discovered in the consciousness of both groups.

In his earlier, Hegelian approach to the relation between thought and reality, Marx had already been aware of a second central characteristic of ideology: its reflection of particular social interests. The account he gave of debates in the Rhineland Diet for the *Rheinische Zeitung* revealed how individual speakers mirrored the social position of their estate. In these debates "not the *individual* but the *estate*" had spoken, and the ideals they claimed to serve had been merely "the sacred cloak for quite worldly—but at the same time quite fantastic—desires." So now the "bleating" of the German ideologists "merely imitates in a philosophic form the conceptions of the German middle class."[80]

Even the prescription Marx offered to rescue thought from these limitations recalled his earlier one. It was the integration of thought with the totality of human development. In its Hegelian version this had meant that modern philosophy achieved a "more ideal and profound view" because it did not proceed, like earlier thinkers, from the concept of the abstract individual, but rather from the idea of the whole. Unlike the Greek thinkers, therefore, it was not condemned to internal contradiction, and unlike the representatives of the German estates it was not useful intelligence in the service of particular interests, but free intelligence in the service of reason itself. No kind of thinking was free in this sense in *The German Ideology* but, by uniting itself with the actual process of history, communist theory escaped the inversions to which ideology was always subject, and even overcame the limitations of class interest. The communists spoke for the proletarians, but also for a historical process that would abolish class rule altogether, and hence do away with the necessity "to represent a particular interest as general or the 'general interest' as ruling."[81]

All these basic materials of Marx's theory of ideology had been available to him before. What brought them together in a new way was his identification of thought with the "passive" instead of the "active" side of human

life. On this point Marx effected a complete inversion of his earlier view.
As a Hegelian and Feuerbachian philosopher Marx had consistently identified activity with thought; passivity was the predicate of the material
world on which spirit acted. Thus in the Introduction to his *Critique of
Hegel's 'Philosophy of Right'*, published in the *Deutsch-Französische
Jahrbücher*, Marx wrote that: "Revolutions require a *passive* element, a
material basis." On this element philosophy had to act; when Marx used
the famous metaphor of the "lightning of thought" striking the "uncultivated soil" of the people, he projected a clear image of where revolutionary
action was initiated and where it found a response. In the contemporary
essay "On The Jewish Question," Marx equated the "merely material"
world of civil society with passivity: "The *egoistic* man is the *passive* and
given result of the dissolved society . . . a *natural* object." In the same
place he indicated, more generally, that "practical need, whose rationale
is self-interest, remains passive, never willfully extending itself but only
finding itself extended with the continuous development of social conditions." These statements reflect similar ones of Feuerbach, who had also
equated "activity" with philosophy and the "German" principle, to match
the "passivity" of material life and "France."[82]

In Marx's earlier writings, too, we find him picturing the world of
Spirit as active in relation to everyday material life, in his images of the
free press "plunging" into the ordinary world "to give it life," and of the
Hegelian state extending its "spiritual nerves" throughout society. Marx's
inversion of Hegel in his critique of the *Philosophy of Right* at times gives
the appearance that he had reversed the identification of active with
spiritual forces in 1843, but a closer reading shows that he had not. To be
sure, he insisted that: "Family and civil society are the presuppositions of
the state; they are the really active things." But he conceived the family
and civil society then not as merely material forms of existence, but as
"actual spiritual existences of will." It was as such that they were the
active force.[83]

Marx may have begun to alter this perspective in *The Holy Family*, for
he wrote disapprovingly there of Bruno Bauer's depiction of "the Mass" as
the "passive, spiritless, unhistorical, *material* element of history," against
which criticism ranged itself as "the active element." The earliest clear
and definite reversal of his earlier terminology came later, however, in the
first of the "Theses on Feuerbach." Because materialism had not previously conceived the natural world as the world of "sensuous human activity," it was left to idealism to attempt to comprehend and develop "the
active side" of human life. Feuerbach himself, while attempting to achieve
a materialist perspective, had identified real human activity with "the
theoretical attitude." It was for this reason that Feuerbach did not "grasp
the significance of 'revolutionary,' of 'practical-critical' activity." In *The*

German Ideology Marx added that it was because Feuerbach did not see that "the world surrounding him is not something directly given and the same from all eternity but the product of industry and . . . the result of the activity of a whole succession of generations" that he had to oppose perception of the "flatly obvious" to perception of the "true essence" of things. The same perspective that discovered transforming activity in the material world itself made the philosophic notion of inner essence both unreal and unnecessary.[84]

The German Ideology was, in one regard, a set of variations on the theme that material life was the active segment of human existence and thought its mere passive reflection: "The phantoms formed in the human brain are also, necessarily, sublimates of their material life process. . . . Life is not determined by consciousness but consciousness by life." Marx saw his own earlier view reflected in the fact that the ideologists of the ruling class who made "the perfecting of the illusions of the class about itself their chief source of livelihood" seemed to be active, "while the others' attitude to those ideas and illusions is more passive and receptive." The truth was actually the reverse: the practical men were "in reality the active members of this class and have less time to make up illusions and ideas about themselves."[85]

Marx's new attitude toward the relationship between thought and life brought him into harmony with one particularly significant member of the active bourgeoisie: his father. Among the consequences of the division of labor for thinkers Marx detailed in *The German Ideology* were some Heinrich had suggested to him. Marx's idea that each occupational group—jurists, politicians, philosophers—distorted the world in a way that reflected the experience and the assumptions of their jobs was not original. Among the earlier writers who had described such a process was Schiller. In his *Letters on the Aesthetic Education of Man* Schiller complained that the spirit of business, accustomed to "judging all experience whatsoever by one particular fragment of experience," tried "to make the rules of its own occupation apply indiscriminately to all others." In a similar vein, Fichte wrote that the division of society into parts or estates meant that individuals educated themselves only for the station they had chosen in life. From that arose a partiality and one-sidedness that Fichte chose to call "pedantry," and which consisted in regarding "the formation proper to one's particular station as universal human culture."[86]

Heinrich Marx, who may have come across this notion in Fichte, and who almost certainly read Schiller's *Letters*, repeated this idea to his son. It formed part of his warning against Karl's indulging his intellectual interests too far. Human development, "ennoblement," as Heinrich termed it, required the cultivation of man's physical, moral, intellectual and political capacities. "Limited to a single sphere, the most upright striving produces not merely no good result, but caricatures; cultivated alone the physical part yields simpletons, the moral part exalted fanatics, the political part intriguers, the intellectual part learned boors."[87] This had not been Marx's view when in 1841 he wrote of philosophy in its Promethean independence as "master of the universe." But by 1846 Marx had concluded, in agreement with his father, that "the real intellectual wealth of the individual is the wealth of his real connections," that the division of labor makes a man "one-sided, cripples and determines him," that "if the circumstances in which the individual lives allow him only the one-sided development of a single quality at the expense of all the rest . . . then this individual achieves only a one-sided, crippled development."[88]

Marx moved closer to his father in a second, closely related way, too. His adolescent perspective had viewed the world not only through the spectacles of philosophy but also through those of poetry. It was poetry that occupied Marx during much of his first year in Berlin, and still in the days of the *Rheinische Zeitung* he had associated his own vocation as a writer with the calling of the poet. With *The German Ideology*, however, Marx began to identify his outlook as a specifically "prosaic" one. For Stirner, Marx asserted, the world remained highly unprosaic despite his own claims to the contrary. The true meaning of Stirner's inverted observations was that "the world has lost its divine character . . . it is freed from my fantasies . . . it has become prosaic, consequently its relation to me is prosaic and it disposes of me in the prosaic way it likes."[89] Later, during the revolution of 1848, Marx emphasized that his view of events corresponded to their prosaic truth: the June days with their bloody massacres revealed the "prosaic" reality behind the poetry expressed the previous February; the "prosaic North wind" of counterrevolution had dispelled the romantic fantasies of the Germans.[90] Marx's identification of himself as prosaic brought him into harmony with his father, for Heinrich Marx had regarded himself as a preeminently prosaic man, a quality he thought distinguished him from his adolescent son. Speaking of Karl's reply to his reproaches for the conduct to which the son had confessed in the letter of November 10, 1837, Heinrich said he feared "that poetic vein. I will answer prosaically, out of real life as it is," he exclaimed, "even if I run the risk of appearing to my lord son as too prosaic."[91]

These various echoes of Heinrich are one sign that Marx's intellectual reorientation of 1845-46 marked his arrival at maturity in a psychological sense, the end of his adolescence. In psychological theory the task of adolescence is "object-relinquishment and object-finding," replacing one set of people, institutions, and beliefs as the framework of individuality and identity with another. To effect these changes is often a stormy task, involving disengagement from parental values through negation and rebellion against them. Whereas the conflicts between children and parents are concrete and direct in early childhood, in adolescence they take place on the more abstract level of values, world views and life styles, on the characteristically youthful plane of theory. Hegel noted that the youth no longer identifies himself with his individual parents, but with a generalized "Universal."[92]

The transition from adolescence to maturity usually brings a waning of this earlier rebellion, a "delayed obedience" that makes the individual's redefined identity both preserve and transform—in Hegel's language, transcend—his family origins. The end of adolescence sees a relaxation of the intensified concentration on self-development often visible in the late teens and early twenties. Psychoanalysts speak here of the waning of adolescent narcissism—a displacement of the individual's own inner life from the center of the world. Jean Piaget also describes a process of "de-centering" at this stage, in which the assumption of a specific occupation "leads thinking away from the dangers of formalism back to reality." These modern formulations recall Hegel's description of manhood as accepting the need to locate one's personal identity in a defined and limited sphere of existence, replacing the youth's attempt to attribute universal significance to the self. This new configuration provides the opportunity to overcome some specific features of the earlier struggle against parental values and identity elements, relating a person's inner conflicts to his conscious aims and purposes in a new way. As Peter Blos concludes: "Infantile conflicts are not removed at the close of adolescence, but they are rendered specific, they become ego-syntonic, i.e., they become integrated within the realm of the ego as life-tasks. They become centered within the adult self-representations." The result is a new mental formation that "perpetuates familiar, antecedent trends within the adult personality," while orienting the individual toward significant external objects in a new way.[93]

Marx's redefinition of his personal identity in 1845-46 fits this pattern in a number of respects. His sense of himself and of his task in life deepened, altering his self-image in ways that allowed him to make peace with the shade of his father on several specific points where they had clashed before. The world of post-Hegelian philosophy Marx now abandoned had been the emblem of separation from his family and its values. Marx's invocation of the prosaic reality of everyday life and his rejection of philosophy as a separate vocation contained explicit echoes of Heinrich's injunctions. Marx's abandonment of abstraction and idealism was no longer mediated by his adolescent identification with philosophy, but cast directly in the terms his father had urged on him. Moreover, behind his picture of the division of labor, with its consequences of frustration, unhappiness, and the crippling of individual development, there lurked not only his own difficulties in finding a vocation within existing society but also his father's discovery as a Jew that state power would make its control over occupations into a handle, distorting individual lives to suit its hostile and alien will. Replacing idealist philosophy with materialism, Marx embraced a point of view he had earlier associated both with Jews and with ordinary practical men, raising it a "higher" level.[94]

Marx now knew "where I'm going and who's going with me." Writing *The German Ideology* cemented the friendship between Marx and Engels. Until then it had still seemed possible that Moses Hess would form a third member of their team. He had been involved in a project to publish communist literature with Engels during 1845; he lived near them in Brussels for a time, and it even seemed that he might contribute to *The German Ideology*. From early in 1846, however, Marx and Engels' correspondence reveals the growing distance at which they held Hess. Hess was too deeply colored by the philosophical enthusiasms of their own youth; the partnership would have no third member.[95]

Now, too, Marx began to enter into and work with the actual communist organizations his earlier philosophical perspective had allowed him to observe with approval but not join during his stay in Paris. In the same months that the last parts of *The German Ideology* were written, Marx and Engels turned to the formation of communist correspondence committees, placing themselves in contact with Ewerbeck and Proudhon in Paris, and the radical Chartist leader George Julian Harney in London. Out of these contacts would grow their association with the Communist League of German artisan exiles in London, for which, late in 1847, they would write the *Communist Manifesto*.

When Marx sketched his autobiography in 1859, it was *The German Ideology* he pointed to as the first written expression of his mature point of view. The fact that he and Engels had been unable to publish it was unimportant; the two friends "abandoned the manuscript to the gnawing criticism of the mice all the more willingly as we had achieved our main purpose—self-clarification."[96] *The German Ideology* thus witnessed Marx's transition to maturity, to the personal and intellectual identity that he—and history—would continue to recognize as his own. This did not mean, however, that the conflicts he had faced in his earlier life had all been resolved.

5. Personal Style: Weakness and Strength

Now, as before, making new personal ties was inseparable from breaking old ones. From his student days to the time of *Capital* Marx's characteristic mode of defining himself was by opposition, excluding others from the personal space he occupied. Politically Marx was often able to cooperate with people whose views differed from his, but his life was punctuated by moments of polemical separation and distancing, marking out his own position by eliminating former or potential colleagues from it.

The time of *The German Ideology* was such a moment. At the end of March 1846, Marx attended a meeting of communist publicists in Brussels. Arguing for the first time in public his view that before communist revolution could take place society had to pass through a phase of bourgeois rule, Marx announced his intention to fight against both "artisan" and "philosophical" communism. The Communist party had to be subjected to a "sifting out," and this purification was the most important task facing communists at the moment. It would take place through criticism of those who were no longer useful, and by attempts to separate them from the sources of funds that allowed them to publish their views. According to Wilhelm Weitling, who attended the meeting, and who represented one of the currents Marx opposed, Marx was very excited and vehement on this occasion. The meeting ended in an uproar with Marx and others shouting and running around the room.[97]

On one level Marx's hostile behavior toward Weitling and others who described themselves as communists can be understood as a normal and ordinary response to the situation in which he found himself. Anthony Storr observes that "Whenever identity is threatened by too close an identification with others there will be an increase of aggression leading to differentiation."[98] Yet Marx's style of separating himself from others also had in it something specific to his own personality. It was at this time that the Russian liberal critic P. W. Annenkov came to know Marx, and formed an image of him that has often been cited.

> With a thick black mane on his head, hands covered with hair, his coat buttoned up crooked, he had the bearing of a man who had the right and the power to command respect, however strange his appearance and doctrines might seem. His movements were angular, yet sharp and self-assured. His manners were in opposition to all regular social forms. Yet they were proud, with a trace of contempt, and his piercing voice that rang like metal, harmonized remarkably with his radical judgments on men and things. He spoke only in imperatives that tolerated no opposition, and which were sharpened by the tone that characterized everything he said, and which affected me almost painfully.

He seemed to feel a mission to dominate the minds of others. To Annenkov he appeared as "the incarnation of a democratic dictator, as one imagines him in moments of fantasy."[99]

That Annenkov's sketch described Marx's usual style of relating to his political associates is confirmed by much other testimony. The portrait has some similarities to the one Engels gave of Marx in 1842, and also calls to mind Engels' later description of the editorial structure of the *Neue Rheinische Zeitung* as "the dictatorship of Marx."[100] Naturally, these characteristics were more often evoked by those who admired him less. Carl Schurz, the liberal German who later became a well-known figure in United States politics, found "offensive, unbearable arrogance" in Marx's behavior. If Marx disagreed with someone, Schurz recounted, he directed his sarcasm at the ignorance of his opponent or questioned his motives. "I well remember the cutting, contemptuous, I am tempted to say spitting way in which he uttered the word 'bourgeois'; and he denounced as 'bourgeois,' as clear examples of profound spiritual and moral debasement, all who dared to disagree with his views."[101] Even people who came to like and respect Marx agreed that he made this impression at first. The British socialist H. M. Hyndman, who retained his warm feelings for Marx even after the break in their personal relations, wrote that "The longer I knew Marx the more my admiration and regard for him increased, and the more I could appreciate the human side of his character." Yet Hyndman recognized that "at first the aggressive, intolerant, and intellectually dominant side of him preponderated; only later did the sympathy and good nature which underlay his rugged exterior become apparent."[102]

Earlier we considered the possible sources of Marx's aggressive style of personal interaction in his mother's intrusive and dominating mode of nurture, and we noted that Marx's formula, "acting with weakness, yet with strength," comes very close to describing aggression in the terms of recent psychological theory. In separating himself from communists of a more philosophical variety, Marx was seeking to purge the sources of his own earlier weakness. Soon after the Brussels meeting at which he spoke of the need for sifting out the useful communists from the others, Marx wrote a polemic against Hermann Kriege, editor of a German-language newspaper in New York, and a representative of the "true socialism" Marx and Engels attacked in *The German Ideology*. Kriege propounded a form of agrarian communism based on Feuerbachian notions, in which the principles of self-sacrifice and devotion to mankind were central. At one point he ventured to declare that anyone who refused to support the "party of humanity" could be "treated as an enemy of mankind." To Marx, this claim presaged a return to the persecution of heretics by a new religion, which "like every other one, hates and pursues its enemies to the death." By contrast, Marx's party merely fought against its enemies, it did not seek to punish them as heretics. Yet the claim to moderation in this formulation was counteracted a page later as Marx warmed up to his attack on the "self-contempt" contained in Kriege's willingness to sacrifice individual interests to those of mankind. This was a doctrine for monks, not for energetic men in a time of struggle. "All that is lacking is that these brave monks castrate their 'worthless selves' and thereby sufficiently demonstrate their faith in the ability of 'humanity' to produce itself."[103]

This was precisely the sort of sarcastic sally that Annenkov, Schurz, and others found so offensive in Marx. Yet the blow was aimed not only against Kriege but also against Marx's own earlier Feuerbachian humanism, with its equation of "real" human wealth and actual poverty, the "wealth of needs." Distancing himself so violently from Kriege was a part of that separation from his earlier philosophical conscience Marx was attempting to guarantee after 1845. In *The German Ideology* Marx described philosophy and the study of actuality as having "the same relationship to one another as onanism and sexual love."[104] In Marx's mind the philosophy he was struggling to put behind him carried overtones of sexual immaturity and impotence. In later years he would list his favorite virtue in men as "strength."[105] But so determined and aggressive a cultivation of strength always remained colored by a recurring fear of weakness.

That Marx distanced himself from his own earlier standpoint in such emotionally charged language leads us to ask whether he experienced the period of *The German Ideology* as a time of personal crisis. Conventional treatments of Marx's life offer no evidence that he did. Yet Marx's arrival at historical materialism may have been more troubled that it is usually made to appear. Once before Marx had been subject to a crisis, the moment of his conversion to Hegel at the age of nineteen. His "vexation" had then made him depressed and physically ill; at one point, as we saw earlier, "like a lunatic I ran around in the garden."[106] Later on Marx even indicated that he regarded periods of psychological difficulty as natural in lives like his own. Writing to his uncle Lion Philips about the *Weltschmerz* being suffered by his young cousin Jacques in 1861, Marx explained that such depression was "a sickness that is easily explained by the fact that, unlike the great majority of men, he is critical of himself and he still has not worked out a solid political standpoint that satisfies himself."[107]

Moreover, it is almost never remembered by Marx's biographers that at the time he and Engels were writing *The German Ideology*, Marx published an essay on suicide. The essay appeared in a periodical edited by Moses Hess (and with which Engels was also associated), called the *Gesellschaftsspiegel* (*Mirror of Society*) early in 1846. Reprinted by the editors of the first project to publish Marx and Engels' complete works (the *Gesamtausgabe*) beginning in the 1920s, Marx's essay has been omitted—without explanation—from the much more comprehensive *Werke* published in East Gemany since the end of the Second World War. Perhaps that may account in part for the apparent ignorance demonstrated by writers on Marx and Marxism in regard to it. An additional reason for the obscurity within which the essay has remained is that it was—ostensibly at least—not an original product of Marx's pen, but a translation from a book by a French police archivist, Jacques Peuchet, and for that reason bore the title "Peuchet on Suicide."[108] Yet even if the fact that Marx took the trouble to translate Peuchet's pages on such a subject were not worthy enough of notice in itself, a comparison of Marx's translation with Peuchet's original reveals that Marx made a number of changes in the text, some of them possessing considerable interest.*

Jacques Peuchet, who served as archivist of the Paris police during the Restoration, and who died with that regime in 1830, had begun his career in the last years of the prerevolutionary French Enlightenment. Living on the boundary between the literary Enlightenment and the recurring attempts at administrative reform, he was employed in government administration both in the last years of the old regime and during the first year of the Revolution. But as politics turned more radical he withdrew from public affairs, spending the revolutionary decade partly in retirement and partly as a royalist journalist. He returned to public life under Bonaparte and the restored Bourbons.[109]

His views combined the late eighteenth-century passion for reform with the conservative conviction that public disorders had their source in the vices of private life. Following Rousseau, he called modern society a realm of animality and a desert. Solutions were to be found in the better organization of public administration—especially "police" in the broad sense of order and restraint—and in changed moral attitudes. Suicide, for example, could not be controlled if society persisted in assigning to any person who took his or her life the main guilt for the act. In most cases suicides were provoked either by others or by society's inability to provide a livelihood to its members. Peuchet was well aware that economic causes were at the root of many suicides. He noted that their number grew in times of economic hardship, and he spoke of the need to reorder the general system of agriculture and industry so as to increase wealth. These proposals may have been inspired by St. Simon, whom he is reported to have known.[110] But his own major concern was with people's private moral lives and the way in which the eternal vices of jealousy, cruelty, ambition, and the desire to control others made existence unbearable for many. His pages on suicide contain stories of private ruin provoked by uncontrolled passion and the conflict between individual needs and social demands that have some of the quality of Marx's favorite French writer, Balzac.

Peuchet's discussion of suicide appeared as a chapter in a history of the

---

*Since this chapter was written, an English version of the essay has appeared in Karl Marx and Frederick Engels, *Collected Works* (New York, London and Moscow, 1975) IV, 597-612. The editors point out some of Marx's alterations to Peuchet, but not all, neglecting to mention what seems to me the most significant addition. See below.

Paris police, which Marx probably read during 1844, when he planned to write about the French Revolution (Peuchet's chapter on suicide forms part of his section on the Revolution). In introducing Peuchet's pages in 1846 Marx offered them as an example of how modern French social criticism revealed the contradictions and monstrosities present in every aspect of modern life. Marx compared Peuchet in this respect to Fourier, but noted that criticism of these conditions was by no means confined to socialists. Such criticism showed how wrong the philanthropic bourgeois were to believe that charity would solve modern social evils, "as if only the worker degenerates under contemporary social conditions, and for the rest the existing world is the best one."[111]

Yet Marx did not allow Peuchet to present the case for this view entirely in his own way. That Marx shortened Peuchet's account by leaving out two of the most complicated narratives of suicides and made a variety of minor changes in language and style made little difference. What made slightly more was Marx's virtual elimination of Peuchet's religious concerns and his replacement of them with his own social analysis. When Peuchet wrote that "In order to comprehend the human heart one has to begin by having the charity and pity of Christ," Marx simply left the sentence out. When Peuchet wrote that "in eras of unbelief" the tendency of many poor but honest people to prefer suicide to criminality disappeared, so that "hostility makes itself seen, and the poor man frankly takes his chances with robbery and murder," Marx made the shift from suicide to crime depend on the degree to which "our commercial era progresses." When Peuchet said with regard to the general analysis of the causes of suicide that "Without dwelling on theories, I will try to present the facts," Marx transformed modesty into revolutionary conviction, making Peuchet say: "I found, that apart from a total reform of the comtemporary social order, all other measures would be in vain."[112]

Marx also eliminated Peuchet's heavy emphasis on the effects of individual psychological differences. Peuchet had noted that some suicides were provoked by apparently minor incidents, but that the diversity of temperaments and sensibilities was such that "an occurrence which causes only an imperceptible feeling in some people can give birth to a violent pain for others. Happiness or unhappiness have as many manners of existing and showing themselves as there are differences among individuals and minds." And a page later he suggested that the causes of suicide were imperfectly known because too little study had been given to the mental convulsions caused by terrible moments in life, and to the "poisonous germs that long-lasting sadness can develop within the character." Marx eliminated both these sentences from his translation.[113]

Yet Marx did not tone down Peuchet's strong insistence on the importance of family experience in determining the quality of people's lives. He placed in italics one of Peuchet's most striking observations on this score. *"The revolution has not overthrown all the tyrants; the evils with which arbitrary governments were reproached continue within families. Here they cause crises that are analagous to those of revolutions."* A page later Marx inserted an observation of his own along the same lines, but which Peuchet had not offered: "The most cowardly people, those least capable of standing up against others, become inexorable, as soon as they are able to enforce absolute paternal authority. The misuse of the same is like a crude substitute for the various forms of subordination and dependency to which they must submit willy nilly in civil society."[114] As suggested earlier, it seems unlikely that Marx would have included his own father among those who misused paternal authority in this way, but entirely possible that he had his mother in mind.

The translation of Peuchet was not Marx's only reference to suicide in the mid-1840s. In 1844 Marx had published a criticism of his erstwhile colleague Arnold Ruge, called "Critical notes on 'The King of Prussia and Social Reform,' " an attack on one of Ruge's essays. Explaining that the state could not abolish poverty because to do so was to eliminate existing society, and therefore to destroy the state itself, Marx commented that "No *living person*, however, believes that the defect of his specific existence is rooted in the principle or essence of his life, but rather in circumstances *outside* his life. *Suicide* is unnatural." In "Peuchet on Suicide," this is exactly what Marx denied. In existing society, as Peuchet's mirror showed, suicide was perfectly natural. Peuchet had quoted Madame de Stael's assertion that suicide was an unnatural act, but he replied that so common an occurrence could hardly be against nature. "What is against nature does not occur. On the contrary, it lies *in the nature of our society* to bring forth many suicides, while the Tartars do not do away with themselves."[115]

The Marx who in 1844 had asserted that no one regarded the "defect of his specific existence" as inseparable from "the principle or essence of his life" was the Marx who was still trying to remake and preserve the philosophic identity he had assumed as a student in Berlin. This was the Marx who in 1843 had written that "It is not enough that thought should seek its actualization; actuality must itself strive toward thought." By 1846, however, Marx was rejecting the separate life of thought on the grounds that the inversion of reality perpetrated by professional thinkers—ideologists—derived from the very existence of thinkers as a separate group created by the division of labor. The defect of Marx's earlier existence as a philosophical critic was indeed rooted in the principle or essence of his life, and it was this circumstance that made the ritual annihilation of left Hegelian philosophy in *The German Ideology* both natural and necessary.

Let it be clearly stated that Marx's translation of Peuchet offers not the slightest bit of evidence that he ever considered suicide himself. Although he was no stranger to depression in later life, and would sometimes again (at least in the depths of a London winter) find suicide natural and understandable, he never sought the ultimate escape. Yet his essay on suicide, with its slap at weak individuals who become tyrannical within families, and its underscored description of crises in individual lives "analagous to those of revolutions," does suggest that Marx had his mind on the experience of inner crisis in this period, even as he focused so intently on external conditions in his social theory. His interest in the topic of suicide points up the degree to which his reorientation required the ritual elimination of an earlier self.

Moreover, there was one persisting feature of Marx's life that both tied him to the sources of his earlier weakness, and showed how he could turn the aggressive feelings he often expressed toward others on himself—his illness. It was in regard to his penchant to "mock the rights" of his body that Marx had used the phrase "acting with weakness, yet with strength," in 1835. Marx's arrival at a materialist standpoint did not put an end to the pattern of overwork and illness that had been visible in Bonn, Berlin, and Paris. In Brussels, too, Marx worked into the small hours of the night (keeping Engels awake with him), and we know that during at least part of his stay there he was ill. Engels later dated the beginning of Marx's chronic illness in 1845 (we shall see later on how closely Engels linked Marx's poor health to his mode of living and working), and Marx afterwards remembered having almost daily attacks of vomiting in Brussels. Moses Hess heard that Marx was suffering there from spasms in the chest, and thought the trouble had been caused by "repeated agitation" over the failure to get *The German Ideology* published. Marx himself excused the delay in sending his work on political economy to the publisher Leske on grounds of "my very weakened state of health," and he spoke of the need to take sea baths to aid his recovery.[116]

Years later, in connection with his inability to finish and publish another book, Marx would turn his anger against himself in a verbal way, calling the work on economics he could not complete "shit" and "crap." Then it would appear still more clearly that Marx's style of aggressive repudiation of other people flowed from the same current of feeling that, directed differently, fueled his self-induced illnesses. Like the "repudiative and anal patterns" Erik Erikson has examined in Luther, Marx's hostile and aggressive style served as a substitute for self-repudiation.[117] Marx never escaped from the need to reject his earlier self: despite *The German Ideology*'s settling of accounts, many elements of the philosophical identity he continually sought to cast off still clung to him.

6. The Hegelian Residue

However clearly settled Marx's account with his earlier philosophical conscience seemed to be in 1846, it was not to remain permanently closed.
Marx's debts to Hegel would never really disappear from his writings, and
Marx would still be struggling to pay them off in *Capital*. In part, as we
shall see, the reappearance of Hegel in Marx's later method of analyzing
economics and society would be a regression to his earlier views, imposed
by history's failure to follow the lines projected in *The German Ideology* and
Marx's other writings of the late 1840s. But Hegel would reappear on the
surface of Marx's consciousness only because residues of his way of thinking had remained underneath all along.

Marx admitted that his disdain for the Young Hegelians with whom he
had associated earlier was more muted in regard to Hegel himself, despite
Hegel's own speculative excesses. In *The Holy Family* he had given Hegel
credit for real empirical knowledge, which Bauer and his friends did not
possess, and he continued to do so in *The German Ideology*. Moreover,
Hegel's writings contained a number of specific notions about modern history that were still central to Marx's historical theory in 1846. In the *Philosophy of Right* Hegel had written about an essential "universal and objective element in work," which "subdivides production and brings about
the division of labor." The process that grew out of this, Hegel observed,
"makes necessary everywhere the dependence of men on one another and
their reciprocal relation in the satisfaction of their other needs. Further,
the abstraction of one man's production from another's makes work more
and more mechanical, until finally man is able to step aside and install
machines in his place." Hegel pointed out that "when needs and means
become abstract in quality, abstraction is also a character of the reciprocal
relation of individuals to one another," and he specifically considered the
implications of this for intellectual life. Theoretical and practical education arose from work and reflected "the multiplicity of objects and situations" in the real productive world. In the *Phenomenology* Hegel had
exposed the ideological pretensions of "various classes and stations," discovering in them (at some moments in history at least) "a spirit which
keeps for its own behoof what suits itself best, in spite of its words about
the universal best, and tends to make this clap-trap about what is universally best a substitute for action bringing it about."[118]

Like Marx, Hegel had regarded the existence of some form of "universal
individual" as the precondition for ending the abstraction and isolation of
modern society, hence opening the way to a fully developed human life.
The notion of "empirically universal individuals," which appears several
times in *The German Ideology*, recalls Hegel's idea of "individuality *qua*

universal objective being," the form of individual existence that nourishes itself—like Diderot's Rameau—on the very social universe that stands opposed to it. In Marx's view, it was the proletariat that first made it possible for individuals to have such a universal existence. The proletariat signified "world historical existence of individuals, i.e., existence of individuals which is directly linked up with world history." Earlier communities had all been illusory: men did not belong to them unconditionally, as individuals, but only to the degree that their lives fit the conditions of membership in the class dominating them. By contrast, membership in "the community of revolutionary proletarians" required no special conditions, but only existence as a human being; hence, for this community "it is as individuals that the individuals participate in it." It was in opposition to all the imaginary universalities offered by Hegel— state, monarchy, and bureaucracy—that Marx presented the proletariat as the only human grouping in which community membership and individual needs could build on each other. But the notion that human history both prepared and required such a unity was Hegel's.[119]

In *The German Ideology* Marx no longer spoke of his method as inverting Hegel (as he had, under Feuerbach's influence in 1843) but instead as materialism and the direct study of empirical reality. Nonetheless, it is clear that Hegel's vision of human development, turned upside down, but with many of the underlying patterns retained in an altered form, still colored Marx's perceptions. Like Hegel, Marx reached his mature point of view by declaring his intention to take the world as it was rather than as philosophy desired or imagined it to be. Like Hegel, too, his acceptance of actual existence rested on a conviction that the world in the present was transforming itself along lines that precisely fulfilled the philosophical vision with which he had begun. The incandescent intensity of Marx's belief was fed by the revolutionary fuse that sizzled toward the explosion of 1848. Once the smoke had cleared, however, Marx would discover that even revolution did not make history into the substitute for philosophy which, in the excitement of the 1840s, it seemingly promised to become. Events would show that Marx's sense of what was real in history made him more deeply and permanently dependent on philosophy than, at twenty-eight, he believed.

Part Two

INVOLVEMENT AND ISOLATION

CHAPTER SEVEN

Revolution and Revelation

1. The Only Revolution

THE revolutionary movements that began in the winter and early spring of 1848 announced the only major social and political upheaval the European continent as a whole was to experience in the nineteenth century. To Marx the outbreak and rapid spread of revolution represented the fulfillment of a personal prophecy, and a chance to immerse himself in a struggle in which the whole destiny of humanity was at stake. Now his faith in the power of revolution both to reveal and to realize the meaning of human history would find its test.[1]

Italy was the scene of the first events, but it was in Paris that the revolution of 1848 took on real European stature. There, street fighting at the end of February led to the abdication of the Orleanist King Louis-Philippe and the establishment of a provisional republican government. Radical groups of workers and socialists pressed for democratization and thorough reform. In the next few weeks the news from Paris helped to provoke rioting and demands for political change in a number of German areas, culminating in the Berlin and Vienna uprisings of mid-March. Fearing for their thrones, the kings of Prussia and Austria both promised constitutions, and the Hapsburg court fled Vienna. By mid-May a national assembly was meeting at Frankfurt to try to give Germany both a liberal constitution and political unity.

Yet before the end of the year the hopeful visions of the revolutionary spring were ebbing away. In France the elected assembly that replaced the provisional government turned out to share neither its republicanism nor its openness to social reform. By abolishing the National Workshops that had at least given work to the unemployed in Paris, the new regime provoked the bloody social war known as the June Days. Thousands of workers perished in three days of barricade fighting. When, in the following December, the new post of president of the republic was won by Louis Bonaparte, an adventurer full of dreams and plans but with little sympathy for republican politics, the likelihood that France would follow any of the paths projected in February diminished still further. In Austria the Hapsburgs took advantage of a similar conflict between the provisional authorities that had appeared in March and the assembly elected to replace them to return to Vienna, and then to organize the military repression of the city by General Windischgrätz at the end of October. Encouraged by that example, the Prussian king also replaced the liberal ministry that had emerged from the spring uprising with a more conservative government, and discovered that the real power of the Hohenzollern monarchy was still intact.

During the first half of 1849 the Austrian government succeeded in suppressing the most important revolutionary authorities that had emerged in Italy. The Prussian king refused the German crown offered him by the visibly powerless Frankfurt Assembly. An attempt at insurrection by republican leaders in Paris failed to produce any real threat when it was called for in June, and by the end of the second postrevolutionary summer the scattered remnants of concessions made elsewhere had practically disappeared. The German authorities solidified their renewed control while making minor or sham concessions during 1850. Only in France did the situation remain uncertain and fluid through 1851, as Louis Bonaparte struggled with various factions in the Assembly over who would rule after his four-year term of office was to expire in 1852. But the question was settled in a manner few had predicted, by Bonaparte's *coup d'état* of December 2, 1851. Bonaparte proceeded to proclaim the Second French Empire, and himself as Napoleon III, in 1852.

The revolution provided momentary flashes of utopian cooperative feeling, which some took as a foretaste of future social harmony. It also allowed both middle- and working-class groups to establish short-lived institutions—assemblies, corporative organizations—that embodied their separate visions of how to reorganize political life.[2] Of all the expectations the revolution as a whole aroused, however, only those of general political upheaval and violent social conflict were really fulfilled. Old governments departed the scene everywhere, but either returned, as in Germany and Italy, or were finally replaced by regimes no one had foreseen and few could comprehend, as in the France of Napoleon III.

Nowhere did middle-class liberals achieve lasting power (the great victory of European liberalism during the 1840s, the repeal of the British Corn Laws in 1846, occurred without revolution and provided a model that continental liberals admired but were unable to reproduce). Their temporary or merely presumptive attempts to govern (for instance in the German National Assembly at Frankfurt) only demonstrated how far removed liberal programs were from the experiences and hopes of the peasants and artisans who constituted the majority of the population.

The needs and demands of manual workers provided much of the energy that kept the revolutionary situation alive. The latent conflict between workers and the middle classes came to the surface with unprecedented violence in the Parisian June Days with their pitched battles and bloody massacres, and in smaller but similar episodes such as the one that took place in Vienna during August of 1848. Workers were themselves divided, some supporting the restoration of guild power in Germany and some opposing it, some (recruited into the Garde Mobile) even joining with the forces of order against "anarchy" in the Paris days of June. By the time Louis Bonaparte established his personal rule at the end of 1851, those who had seen in the revolution a coherent power to bring society a stage further along the path toward political freedom or social cooperation all emerged disappointed and even shaken by the experience. Chief among these was Marx.

2. Society Revealed—and Reveiled

The theory of historical materialism as Marx worked it out in *The German Ideology* depended on the conviction that the nature of society, and hence the real meaning of history, was being revealed on the surface of events in the nineteenth century. Revolution was at once the motor of history and the revelation of the forces that made the motor run. Awareness of these truths allowed Marx both to separate himself from the philosophy of his youth and to unite himself with the powerful historical currents from which ideologists, with their philosophical fantasies, remained cut off.

Although both *The German Ideology* and *The Poverty of Philosophy* (Marx's polemic against Proudhon) contained a prophecy of revolution, Marx's real treatise on its coming was the *Communist Manifesto*. Written together with Engels toward the end of 1847, the *Manifesto* appeared in February 1848, only a few weeks before the overthrow of the French king announced the start of the European upheavals. Conceived as political propaganda and as a popular call to action, the pamphlet was also—like every product of Marx's pen—a serious statement of theoretical principles. It included a commentary on previous socialist literature, which borrowed from *The German Ideology*. The *Manifesto* presented the communist movement as the product of human society's whole previous development, which it therefore sketched out in broad and general yet carefully chosen terms.

Central to the historical vision the *Communist Manifesto* offered was the theme of revelation: modern life revealed basic features of history and society that had previously remained mysterious or hidden. "A specter is haunting Europe—the specter of Communism," the text began, and the task of the *Manifesto* was to reveal the truth behind this ghostly presence. "It is high time that Communists should openly, in the face of the whole world, publish their views, their aims, their tendencies, and meet this nursery tale of the Specter of Communism with a manifest of the party itself."[3] In these words Marx announced a historic turning for the European socialist movement, away from older forms of organization based on secret societies, and toward the open and recognized parties that would emerge during the nineteenth century. His words also echoed themes in his own earlier history. In the *Rheinische Zeitung* of 1842, he had sought to exchange "the clouded language of private opinion" for "the clarifying words of public rationality." This desire now found fulfillment in the open and public appearance of communism on the historical stage, and in the revelation of history's underlying shape which communism's presence brought about.[4]

What cleared the air now was not rationality but history. When Marx declared in his most-often quoted pronouncement that "The history of all hitherto existing society is the history of class struggles," he added in the next sentence that this was a "now hidden, now open fight." The struggle was growing ever clearer in the modern world. The distinctive feature of "our epoch, the epoch of the bourgeoisie," was that "it has simplified the class antagonisms. Society as a whole is more and more splitting up into two great hostile camps, into two great classes directly facing each other: Bourgeoisie and Proletariat." Such a face-to-face struggle contrasted with the situation of earlier ages, when society had consisted of a larger number of less directly opposed classes, and "in almost all of these classes, again, subordinate gradations."[5]

This simplification of class antagonisms had been brought about by the ascendant bourgeoisie, who had literally conquered the world, established the world market and "pushed into the background every class handed down from the Middle Ages." In pursuing this course, the bourgeoisie had dissolved the fog that once kept men from clearly perceiving the world around them. "The bourgeoisie, wherever it has got the upper hand, has put an end to all feudal, patriarchal, idyllic relations. It has pitilessly torn asunder the motley feudal ties that bound man to his 'natural superiors,' and has left remaining no other nexus between man and man than naked self-interest, than callous 'cash payment.' " Religion, chivalry, sentiment, freedom—all had been reduced to their simplest basis, money and trade: "In one word, for exploitation, veiled by religious and political illusions, it has substituted naked, shameless, direct, brutal exploitation." The bourgeoisie's work of stripping all aspects of human life to naked economic truth went further. It "has stripped of its halo every occupation hitherto honored and looked up to with reverent awe," by making physicians, lawyers, priests, poets, and scientists its "paid wage-labourers." The bourgeoisie had disclosed the truth about the vigor of the Middle Ages—that it was complemented by indolence—and "it has been the first to show what man's activity can bring about."[6]

Marx explained this revelationary vocation of the bourgeoisie on the basis of its revolutionary character. "The bourgeoisie cannot exist without constantly revolutionizing the instruments of production and thereby the relations of production, and with them the whole relations of society." This need, which distinguished the modern industrial bourgeoisie from all previous classes, made the age of the bourgeoisie an era of unceasing change in which no human relationship had a chance to cover itself with a veil of tradition or sentiment: "All fixed, fast-frozen relations, with their train of ancient and venerable prejudices and opinions, are swept away, all new-formed ones become antiquated before they can ossify. All that is solid melts into air, all that is holy is profaned, and man is at last compelled to face with sober senses, his real conditions of life, and his relations with his kind."[7]

The increasing visibility of these real conditions in modern society also explained the emergence of communist theory. "In times when the class struggle nears the decisive hour, the process of dissolution going on within the ruling class, in fact within the whole range of old society, assumes such a violent, glaring character, that a small section of the ruling class cuts itself adrift, and joins the revolutionary class, the class that holds the future in its hands." Although Marx spoke of "a portion of the bourgeois ideologists, who have raised themselves to the level of comprehending theoretically the historical movement as a whole," he made their understanding dependent on changes that were visible to ordinary men as well. "The theoretical conclusions of the Communists are in no way based on ideas or principles that have been invented, or discovered, by this or that would-be universal reformer. They merely express, in general terms, actual relations springing from an existing class struggle, from a historical movement going on under our very eyes."[8]

The outbreak of revolution in Paris found Marx still in Brussels, but it did not allow him to stay there. Within a few days of each other, a member of the French provisional government invited him to return to Paris, and the Belgian authorities arrested him and transported him with his family to the French border. A month later he was in Germany, preparing to publish a revolutionary newspaper, the *Neue Rheinische Zeitung*. The paper, based like its namesake of 1842-43 in Cologne, appeared for slightly over a year, until Marx was expelled from Prussia in May 1849. During that time he poured most of his effort into journalism, although he also participated actively in local revolutionary politics.[9]

Despite the defeats suffered by the revolutionary forces in this period, Marx retained his belief in the revolution's ultimate success. Recognizing that the party of the workers was still in its infancy in Germany, he and Engels were careful not to exaggerate the progressive forces' power; when the setbacks came, the *Neue Rheinische Zeitung* was not surprised by them. Nonetheless, Marx's confidence in the revolution was sustained by his sense that the defeats of the revolutionary party served to clarify the real conditions of action at the time. Perhaps the most striking expression

Marx gave to this belief was in his response to the Paris June Days of 1848, the most violent and awesome conflict of the entire revolutionary years. In Marx's view, the June Days destroyed the "delusions and illusions of the February revolution" by separating society into the two antagonistic classes that composed it.

> The last official remnant of the February Revolution, the Executive Commission, has melted away, like an apparition, before the seriousness of events. The fireworks of Lamartine have turned into the war rockets of Cavaignac. *Fraternité*, the fraternity of antagonistic classes of which one exploits the other, this *fraternité*, proclaimed in February, written in capital letters on the brow of Paris, on every prison, on every barracks—its true, unadulterated its prosaic expression is civil war, civil war in its most fearful form, the war of labor and capital. . . . The February Revolution was the beautiful revolution, the revolution of universal sympathy, because the antagonisms, which had flared up in it against the monarchy, slumbered peacefully side by side, still undeveloped, because the social struggle which formed its background had won only a joyous existence, an existence of phrases, of words. The June revolution is the ugly revolution, the repulsive revolution, because things have taken the place of phrases, because the republic uncovered the head of the monster itself, by striking off the crown that shielded and concealed it.[10]

Thus, the "monster" of the class struggle, so horrible to bourgeois eyes, became visible once the revolution allowed the true forces in opposition to emerge from behind the traditional political and sentimental veils— monarchy, brotherhood—that had hidden them. In revolution the naked truth of history became visible. Summing up the experience of 1848 at the close of the year, Marx therefore wrote: "The main fruit of the revolutionary movement of 1848 is not that which the people have won, but that which they have lost—*the loss of their illusions.*" The great events of the revolution were "giant milestones" in "the disenchantment and sobriafication of the European popular understanding." In Germany, in particular, "the prosaic North wind of Prussian counterrevolution" wilted the "flowers of popular fantasy." And two months later, comparing the situation at the beginning of 1849 with that of the opening of the previous year: "What progress! In Italy no more Pius the Ninth, as in France no Lamartine. The fantastic period of the European revolution, the period of confused enthusiasms [*Schwärmerei*], of goodwill and flowers of rhetoric, has worthily been concluded with cannon shots, wholesale slaughters and deportations."[11] Just as the revolutionizing of the means of production by the bourgeoisie had, in the *Communist Manifesto*, brought men face to face with the true conditions of their everyday social existence, so now the political revolution of 1848 destroyed popular illusions about the real nature of political life. All through 1848 and 1849, therefore, Marx continued to regard the defeats of the revolutionary forces as the preparation of its rapidly approaching triumph. Even after Marx was forced to leave Germany in the spring of 1849, his confidence remained.

Marx went first to France, but when the French government (no longer the one that had invited him to French soil a year earlier) sought to confine him to Brittany, he fled to London, where he would reside in exile for the rest of his life. His first project there was to attempt, together with Engels, to keep the *Neue Rheinische Zeitung* alive as a monthly review. For this journal Marx wrote, late in 1849 and early in 1850, an account of the French events of 1848, which later received the title *The Class Struggles in France*. Three installments of Marx's history appeared in the first three months of 1850. A final section saw the light in the fall of the same year.

Even more clearly than a year earlier, Marx now organized his conception of the revolution around the notions of the destruction of illusions and the revelation of the truth behind events. When, in 1830, the banker Laffitte had remarked that under Louis Philippe the bankers would rule, he "had betrayed the secret of the revolution" of 1830. 1848 cleared up more important mysteries. That the state was not independent of society, but the servant of the ruling class, became manifest to all once the monarchy was replaced by the republic of February, based on universal suffrage. "Instead of a few small fractions of the bourgeoisie, whole classes of French society were suddenly hurled into the circle of political power, forced to leave the boxes, the stalls and the gallery and to act in person upon the revolutionary stage! With the constitutional monarchy the semblance of a state power independently confronting bourgeois society also vanished, as well as the whole series of subordinate struggles which this semblance of power called forth!" When the provisional government set up a commission in the Luxembourg palace to deal with the problem of labor, the commission could only operate within the limitations imposed by the economic development of France at the time, and by the early stage in the revolution during which it was set up. Nonetheless: "To the Luxembourg commission, this creation of the Paris workers, remains the merit of having disclosed from the European tribune the secret of the revolution of the nineteenth century: the emancipation of the proletariat."[12]

It was, however, the operation of universal suffrage that had the most revelatory part to play in 1848 in France. Universal suffrage made the romantic conception of a united and harmonious "people" give way before the reality of class division: "Universal suffrage did not possess the magic power which republicans of the old school had ascribed to it. They saw in the whole of France, at least in the majority of Frenchmen, *citoyens* with the same interests, the same understanding, etc. This was their cult of the people. Instead of their imaginary people, the elections brought the real people to the light of day, *i.e.*, representatives of the different classes into which it falls." To Marx, therefore, the universal suffrage demanded by bourgeois democrats was an important lever in unveiling the truth of politics and society to those who participated in the revolutionary events.

If universal suffrage was not the miraculous magic wand for which the republican duffers had taken it, it possessed the incomparably higher merit of unchaining the class struggle, of letting the various middle sections of petty-bourgeois society rapidly live through their illusions and disappointments, of tossing all the fractions of the exploiting class at one throw to the head of the state, and thus tearing from them their treacherous mask, whereas the monarchy with its property qualification only let definite fractions of the bourgeoisie compromise themselves, and let the others lie hidden behind the scenes and surrounded them with the halo of a common opposition.

Universal suffrage unmasked the political actors and the modern state itself.[13]

The revolution had still more to teach its participants, especially at the point where the class struggle was clearest: the days of June. We need not quote Marx's main description of the revelatory mission of the June barricades, for he himself simply reproduced the passage from the *Neue Rheinische Zeitung* cited above. Before June the republic might still appear to be the republic of all the people, but in the struggle that broke out then: "The veil that shrouded the republic was torn to pieces."[14] The sacrifice of the lives of the Paris workers was therefore repaid: "By making its burial place the birthplace of the bourgeois republic the proletariat compelled the latter to come out forthwith in its pure form as the state whose admitted object is to perpetuate the rule of capital, the slavery of labor."[15]

Even after the struggle between proletariat and bourgeoisie no longer occupied the center of the stage, the progress of the revolution meant the replacement of phrases with the real truth behind events. The appointment of the banker and financier Fould as finance minister marked the open entry of the economic leaders of the bourgeoisie on the political stage. "The bourgeois republic everywhere pushed into the forefront what the different monarchies, Legitimist as well as Orleanist, kept concealed in the background. It made earthly what they had made heavenly. In place of the names of the saints, it put the bourgeois proper names of the ruling class interests."[16]

These formulas carried the conviction about the revelatory power of nineteenth-century conditions Marx had developed in the 1840s forward into the experience of revolution itself. They justified his expectation that all the defeats of the revolutionary party were merely temporary, and that the process begun in February 1848 would lead more or less directly to the proletariat's triumph. Yet the belief that the social and political struggles of the revolutionary period were unveiling the truth of class conflict to those who participated in them was not based on empirical evidence: what would validate all these assertions would be the proletariat's actual victory. Marx's confidence that the revolution was the great solvent of illusions, therefore, could not survive the realization that the actual outcome of the revolutionary events was to be very different from the one he had anticipated. During the summer of 1850 Marx acknowledged that the revolution's progress had been stalled, and had to await the return of economic crisis before it could start up again. At that time, however, he still expected the forward movement to renew itself within a few months. It was Bonaparte's *coup d'état* of December 2, 1851, that caused Marx to view the chain of events begun in 1848 in a different light.

What his new perspective entailed appeared in *The Eighteenth Brumaire of Louis Bonaparte*, written between mid-December 1851 and March 1852. To be sure, Marx did not expect Bonaparte's power to last very long, much less to continue until 1870. The Bonapartist pretender could not survive any serious military conflict: "When the imperial mantle finally falls on the shoulders of Louis Bonaparte, the bronze statue of Napoleon will crash from the top of the Vendôme Column."[17] Nonetheless, Bonaparte's *coup* had caused the republic Marx had described as the open and unveiled form of bourgeois rule to disappear from view. What replaced it was a form of government that claimed to be independent of mere class interests, and to represent the welfare of society as a whole. Certainly, this could be regarded as a mere appearance, beneath which a very different relationship between society and politics was concealed. But that is just the point: *The Eighteenth Brumaire* described a relationship between underlying reality and surface experience that overturned the one Marx had believed to exist in the late 1840s. Appearance had ceased to be the increasingly direct translation of reality, and become a veil, masking the real conditions of social life.

In *The Eighteenth Brumaire* the metaphors of revelation so triumphantly employed in *The Class Struggles* gave way to veils and masks. The power of the past generated fantasies in the minds of men trying to free themselves from it: "The tradition of all the dead generations weighs like a nightmare on the brain of the living." For this reason, men in a "period of revolutionary crisis . . . anxiously conjure up the spirits of the past to their service and borrow from them names, battle cries and costumes, in order to present the new scene of world history in this time-honored disguise and this borrowed language." The masquerade had begun with the Revolution of 1789: "In the classically austere traditions of the Roman republic its gladiators found the ideals and the art forms, the self-deceptions that they needed in order to conceal from themselves the bourgeois limitations of the content of their struggles and to keep their enthusiasm on the high plane of the great historical tragedy." In 1848 the power of illusion was raised to a higher degree; now "only the ghost of the old revolution walked about, from Marrast, the *républicain en gants jaunes*, who disguised himself as the old Bailly, down to the adventurer, who hides his commonplace repulsive features under the iron death mask of Napoleon."[18]

If *The Class Struggles* had been the history of a nation's increasingly clear revelation of its own inner character, *The Eighteenth Brumaire* presented the image of a country unable to free itself from delusion. "The nation feels like that mad Englishman in Bedlam who fancies that he lives in the times of the ancient Pharaohs and daily bemoans the hard labor that he must perform in the Ethiopian mines as a gold digger, immured in this subterranean prison, a dimly burning lamp fastened to his head." The revolution had not revealed the underlying truth about society, but re-created the illusion of the state independent of society. "On December 2 the February revolution is conjured away by a cardsharper's trick, and what seems overthrown is no longer the monarchy, but the liberal concessions that were wrung from it by centuries of struggle. Instead of *society* having conquered a new content for itself, it seems that the *state* only returned to its oldest form, the shamelessly simple domination of the sabre and the cowl." The therapy of revolution left the social patient just as deluded as before.[19]

In a purely literary manner, Marx continued to employ some metaphors of revelation in *The Eighteenth Brumaire*. Thus, the whole content of the constitutional republic "has vanished like a phantasmagoria before the spell of a man whom even his enemies do not make out to be a magician." Or again, "Present-day France was contained in a finished state within the parliamentary republic. It only required a bayonet thrust for the bubble to burst and the monster to spring forth before our eyes."[20] What was revealed when these illusions vanished, however, was not what Marx had expected to become visible in the late 1840s. Instead of the truth of class struggle as the key to history, what the revolution brought to light was only the confusing spectacle of a state independent of society, and the stage show of a modern and developed country ruled not by a class but by a buffoon and an adventurer.

That beneath the illusions there remained the reality of class struggle was a truth Marx had now to reveal himself, for events had not done it. With regard to the whole period from May 1849 to December 2, 1851, Marx wrote that "If any section of history has been painted gray on gray, it is this. Men and events appear as inverted Schlemihls, as shadows that have lost their bodies." Only when one put on Marx's special critical spectacles did the illusion depart: "If one looks at the situation and the parties more closely, however, this superficial appearance, which veils the *class struggle* and the peculiar physiognomy of this period, disappears."[21]

This reversal of Marx's earlier point of view appeared not only in general but specifically with regard to the mechanism that had worked most forcefully to reveal class divisions in *The Class Struggles*: universal suffrage. In *The Eighteenth Brumaire*, at the same point in the narrative where Marx had earlier discussed the revelatory power of universal suffrage—the meeting of the National Assembly in May 1848—we find no unveiling of the class struggle, but only the appearance of "the mass of the nation, the peasants and petty bourgeois," as supporters of "the old powers of society." Instead of the earlier view of the revolutionary assemblies as projections of the true image of the nation, political revelations of the social reality of national life, Marx now regarded the same assemblies as fomentors of illusion. They represented "that peculiar malady which since 1848 has raged all over the Continent, *parliamentary cretinism*, which holds those infected by it fast in an imaginary world and robs them of all sense, all memory, all understanding of the rude external world."[22]

The account of revolution Marx gave in *The Eighteenth Brumaire of Louis Bonaparte* thus contrasted with the conviction he had displayed from *The German Ideology* to *The Class Struggles in France*, that the nature of society and its relationship to politics were becoming increasingly visible on the surface of events in the nineteenth century. This was not the only one of Marx's earlier historical conceptions that the outcome of the revolution of 1848 seemed to call into question. Linked closely together with it was Marx's theory of class struggle.

3. Class Formation and Class Dissolution

In a well-known letter to his friend and colleague Joseph Weydemeyer, in March 1852, Marx tried to lessen the degree to which he was already being made responsible for the whole notion of class conflict as a determining element in modern history.

> As to myself, no credit is due to me for discovering the existence of classes in modern society or the struggle between them. Long before me bourgeois historians had described the historical development of this class struggle and bourgeois economists the economic anatomy of the classes. What I did that was new was to prove: 1) that the *existence of classes* is only bound up with *particular historical phases in the development of production*, 2) that the class struggle necessarily leads to the *dictatorship of the proletariat*, 3) that this dictatorship itself only constitutes the transition to the *abolition of all classes* and to a *classless society*.[23]

That others had spoken of classes and class conflict before Marx was certainly true; as we noted above, the language of class was widely diffused in Europe in the 1830s and 1840s.[24] As an example of the views of "bourgeois historians" Marx mentioned here, let us listen for a moment to the well-known British writer Thomas Babington Macaulay. During the debates on the English Reform Bill of 1832, Macaulay argued in favor of the Bill's passage in the following terms:

> All history is full of revolutions, produced by causes similar to those which are now operating in England. A portion of the community which had been of no account expands and becomes strong. It demands a place in the system, suited, not to its former weakness, but to its present power. If this is granted, all is well. If this is refused, then comes the struggle between the young energy of one class and the ancient privileges of another. Such was the struggle between the plebians and the patricians of Rome. Such was the struggle of the Italian allies for admission to the full rights of Roman citizens. Such was the struggle of our North American colonies against the mother country. Such was the struggle which the Third Estate of France maintained against the aristocracy of birth. Such was the struggle which the Roman Catholics of Ireland maintained against the aristocracy of creed. Such is the struggle which the free people of colour in Jamaica are now maintaining against the aristocracy of skin. Such, finally, is the struggle which the middle classes in England are maintaining against an aristocracy of mere locality.[25]

Macaulay's words reveal how easily the notion of class conflict could be applied to social and political struggle in the nineteenth century, but also how broad and imprecise the idea of class usually was. A modern historian might find elements of class conflict in each of the examples Macaulay offered, but it sounds odd to hear, for instance, the North American colonists as a whole described as a different class from those who remained resident in England. To Macaulay, a class was, as he said, simply "a portion of the community."

French historians in the early nineteenth century, seeking to describe the origins of the French Revolution or to justify one or another of its parties, used the term class somewhat more precisely. Writers like Thierry and Guizot saw the conflict between the third estate and its opponents stretching far back into the Middle Ages, beginning with the appearance of the urban communes in the twelfth century. With this in mind, Guizot wrote that "Modern Europe was born from the struggle of the various classes of society."[26] Taking the recognition of class conflict still further, and giving it a consciously socialist coloration, the St. Simonians in 1829 declared that, in all past societies, "the distinctions that were established between classes or castes were at the same time the political expressions of the different degrees of man's exploitation by man." At present only one form of exploitation remained: the "class of proletarians" was exploited by the owners of property. A revolution was therefore required to end human exploitation once and for all.[27]

In working out their own views about classes and class struggle, Marx and Engels were able to draw on this considerable body of earlier writing. Neither the fact of class struggle, the nature of the classes involved, nor even the prospect of a future order free of conflict and exploitation, were novel ideas when the two friends began to employ them. But, as Marx pointed out in his letter to Weydemeyer, his use of class analysis tied the existence of classes more closely to concrete historical circumstances than earlier writers had done. He did not simply assume the existence of classes at all stages in history, but described how they came to exist, and how classes as a whole were related to the individuals and subgroups that constituted them. His focus was not simply on the opposition between one class and another, but on the historical process through which classes were formed. Far from being abstract or *a priori*, as is sometimes claimed, Marx's theory of class struggle was firmly oriented toward the empirical study of historical events. However, it was also based on the conviction that under modern conditions class relations—like society as a whole—were developing in a definite and irreversible direction.

Marx spoke about classes and class struggle both in *The German Ideology* and in the *Communist Manifesto*. In both writings he presented classes as the product of a historical development that unified individuals and groups whose conscious interests and viewpoints did not always coincide, and who may have had no direct connection with one another to begin with. That these people shared the same underlying conditions of life was not enough to bring them firmly together. Their unification as a class also required an experience of conflict, particularly of revolutionary conflict. Such struggle allowed the forces favoring class formation to overpower the tensions working to dissolve classes into their original component parts.

Thus, in *The German Ideology* Marx described the development of the European bourgeoisie against the dual background of the townsmen's shared economic and social circumstances on the one hand, and their internal competition on the other: "In the Middle Ages the citizens of each town were compelled to unite against the landed nobility to save their skins. . . . Out of the many local corporations of burghers there arose only gradually the burgher *class*. The conditions of life of the individual burghers became, on account of their contradiction to the existing relationships and of the mode of labor determined by these, conditions which were common to them all and independent of each individual." Splits within the class retained importance, however, and at times overpowered the factors making for unity. Only when the bourgeoisie had to struggle against a common enemy was its unity made clear in the face of its existing divisions: "The separate individuals form a class only insofar as they have to carry on a common battle against another class; otherwise they are on hostile terms with each other as competitors."[28] As we shall see in a moment, the French bourgeoisie in the nineteenth century constituted a similar union of hostile and conflicting elements.

In the *Communist Manifesto*, Marx presented the formation of the proletarian class in parallel terms. There, Marx described the fruit of the workers' battles against capital as lying "not in the immediate result, but in the ever-expanding union of the workers." This unification progressed at a speed far surpassing the slow progress of the bourgeoisie, just as the speed of a modern railroad train outstripped that of a horse and cart. Nonetheless, it was subject to the same counterpressures as the formation of the bourgeoisie had been, for the interests of individual workers conflicted before they harmonized with each other. Hence Marx described the immediate aim of the Communist Party as the "formation of the workers into a class." Such class unity came about through political struggle, and was essentially the equivalent of political organization: "This organization of the proletariat into a class, and consequently into a political party, is continually being upset again by the competition between the workers themselves. But it ever rises up again, stronger, firmer, mightier."[29]

It was precisely this dynamic process of class formation—with its progressive unveiling of classes as the real actors on the stage of history—that Marx saw taking place in *The Class Struggles in France*. At the beginning of the events of 1848 it was not apparent that the upper bourgeoisie formed a single, unified class in France. The main body of the bourgeoisie seemed instead to consist of two mutually hostile and competing groups. "The bourgeois class was divided into two big factions, which, alternately, had maintained a monopoly of power: the big landed proprietors under the restored monarchy, and the finance aristocracy and the industrial bourgeoisie under the July monarchy." In addition to these two groups, Legitimists and Orleanists, the constituents of the bourgeoisie included republican-minded journalists centered around a Paris newspaper, but "The bourgeois republicans of the *National* did not represent any large fraction of their class resting on economic foundations." The real source and power of bourgeois republicanism—of the determination of the bourgeoisie to retain a republican government—was the need of the two opposed groups of bourgeois monarchists to share political control in order to suppress the proletariat. In the revolutionary years, this union of the two bourgeois factions first appeared under the guise of "the party of order." Formed "directly after the June days," the party of order would soon "disclose the secret of its existence, the coalition of Orleanists and Legitimists into one party."[30]

To the bourgeois factions themselves, the unity they achieved during the revolution was both unexpected and undesired. The individuals in each faction had grown up into political life with the consciousness of being followers of one or the other royal house that claimed the French throne. Nonetheless, the circumstances of the revolution drove them together.

> Forced by antagonism to the revolutionary proletariat and the transition classes thronging more and more round this as the center, to summon their united strength and to conserve the organization of this united strength, each faction of the party of order, as against the desires for restoration and overweening presumptions of the other, had to assert their joint rule, i.e., the republican form of bourgeois rule.

If ever the party representing the working class disappeared entirely from the political stage, the unity of the bourgeois factions would dissolve: "It must have broken up into its original component parts from the moment when not even the appearance of an opposition held it together any longer." However much such a dissolution would have pleased some individuals within the two factions, they were not able to end their cooperation without also destroying the conditions of their economic and social existence. "Condemned by history to help overthrow the monarchy they loved, they were destined by her to conserve the republic they hated." Only by uniting could they resist the proletarian challenge. Hence, each found itself defending the republic—the joint form of bourgeois rule— against the desires of the other to restore the monarchical regime representing its segment of the bourgeois class.[31]

Thus, *The Class Struggles* bore out what Marx had said about class formation in the *Communist Manifesto*: the formation of a class was also the formation of a political party, and the whole process depended on the competition of one class with another. This consolidation of the bourgeoisie into a class was, moreover, matched by the consolidation of the proletariat.

The proletariat had certainly appeared as a class during the June uprising, Marx believed, but that defeat temporarily removed it from the stage of events. During the months that followed, "the proletariat, forced by the terrible material defeat of June to raise itself up again through intellectual victories and not yet enabled through the development of the remaining classes to seize the revolutionary dictatorship, had to throw itself into the arms of the doctrinaires of its emancipation, the founders of socialist sects." At this point the party of the bourgeois democrats, called "the Mountain" after a radical group in the Great Revolution during the 1790s, and led by Ledru-Rollin, "represented the truth of the revolution."[32]

By the summer of 1849, however, the proletariat began to recover its independent existence, and to reassert its revolutionary leadership, especially after the Mountain suffered a defeat in the failed uprising called for June 13 of that year. "June 13 had struck off the heads of the different semirevolutionary parties; the masses that remained won their own head." As the republic came to be increasingly recognized as a means of bourgeois domination, the proletariat grew increasingly aware of the real requirements for its emancipation. The result was that "the proletariat rallies more and more round revolutionary socialism, round communism." Although Marx noted that in France this form of socialism bore the name of Blanqui, he regarded it as the equivalent, in French circumstances, to his own position: "This socialism is the declaration of the permanence of the revolution, the class dictatorship of the revolution, the class dictatorship of the proletariat as the inevitable transit point to the abolition of class differences generally."[33] Thus, the revolution worked on the proletariat just as it had on the bourgeoisie, unifying it as a class, and giving expression to this unity through a political party.

There was a third force in the French political equation, President of the Republic Louis-Napoleon Bonaparte. Where did he fit in? Bonaparte had been elected on December 10, 1849, by the votes of millions of French peasants, but to Marx in *The Class Struggles* it was inconceivable that he might turn out to be anything more than a tool of the ruling bourgeoisie. His first minister—on the advice of "the chiefs of the royalist bourgeois factions"—had been Odilon Barrot, that "incarnation of bourgeois liberalism." And when Bonaparte revealed his real intentions toward the peasants by taxing their salt, "the Napoleon of the peasant insurrection dissolved like an apparition, and nothing remained but the great unknown of royalist bourgeois intrigue."[34]

Although he seemed to clash with the party of order at various moments in the year that followed, his relations with the National Assembly early in 1850 "prove the unity of the two powers of the constitutional republic [i.e., the legislative power of the party of order and the executive power of Bonaparte] so far as it is a question of repression of anarchy, i.e., of all the classes that rise against the bourgeois dictatorship." Every attempt to reform the existing regime was met by the ruling bourgeoisie with the accusation of socialism, for any change in the existing political arrangements meant the danger of replacing the bourgeois dictatorship with proletarian revolution. "The different factions of the majority are again united among themselves and with Bonaparte; they are again the saviors of order; he is again their neutral man."[35]

Despite its unity, the bourgeoisie was powerfully threatened. The *raison d'être* of the united party of order was repression, and "its power of repression has diminished tenfold, while the resistance has increased an hundredfold." Finding its position impossible to maintain in existing conditions, the bourgeois party acted with desperation: on March 10, 1850, the Assembly abolished universal suffrage. "By repudiating universal sufferage, with which it had hitherto draped itself and from which it sucked its omnipotence, the bourgeoisie openly confesses, 'Our dictatorship has hitherto existed by the will of the people; it must now be consolidated against the will of the people.' " This was the signal for the proletariat to act. Leading all the regime's opponents in the struggle the suffrage question would touch off, the workers would act as a united class, imposing the dictatorship that would transform modern society and end class rule.[36]

Thus, in March 1850 Marx was able to describe actual events in France as the fulfillment of his expectations. The country was divided into two hostile camps, one representing and led by the bourgeoisie, the other clustered around the proletariat. But the history he was writing was still happening as he wrote it, and the looked-for revolution did not come. In the months following publication of the third part of *The Class Struggles*, Marx and Engels' *Neue Rheinische Zeitung Revue* was not able to appear, and Marx did not return to his account of French affairs until the fall of 1850. At that time he had a reason to advance for the delay of the revolution: the return of prosperity. The revolutionary events of 1848 had been called forth by the depression and crisis of the late 1840s; but after 1848 economic conditions had begun to be favorable again. While prosperity remained, revolution would be delayed.[37]

Marx was thus forced by events to abandon his earlier timetable for the revolution, but he did not yet abandon any of his earlier analysis of it. The theme of the last part of *The Class Struggles in France* was simply postponement. The party of order, the political union of the two competing bourgeois factions, continued to exist on the same terms. "The comedy of the *républicains malgré eux* . . . the ever renewed threat of the party of order to split into its single component parts, and the ever repeated reunion of its factions . . . this whole unedifying comedy of errors never developed more classically than during the last six months."[38] The issue confronting the French parties was what would happen in May 1852, when Louis Bonaparte's term of office as president was scheduled to expire. According to the constitution under which he had been elected, he could not succeed himself. His enemies therefore believed that his power would be ended on the second Sunday in May. His supporters, however, agitated for a revision of the constitution, to allow Bonaparte another term. Marx believed that the latter would win out, because the existing political arrangements in France were the only ones that allowed bourgeois rule to continue: the bourgeoisie had either to extend the term of the president or face the consequences of renewed political agitation in France. A new election was "utterly inadmissible for the ruling class," because the open political struggles that would accompany it threatened "chaos, anarchy, civil war." Therefore, the question had to be dealt with by postponing it. "The only possible solution in the bourgeois sense is the postponement of the solution. It can only save the constitutional republic by a violation of the constitution, by the prolongation of the power of the president."[39]

At the same time, however, Marx saw Bonaparte's rule as possible only in partnership with the bourgeois party of order. The prospect that Bonaparte might act successfully against the politically organized bourgeoisie could be excluded. "Bonaparte, already humbled by lack of money, will, despite all preliminary protestations, accept this prolongation of power as simply delegated to him from the hands of the National Assembly. Thus the solution is postponed; the status quo continued."[40] In his letters of 1851, Marx continued to regard Bonaparte as the most likely candidate for the presidency of the French republic after May 1852, but he did not envision the possibility that Bonaparte would establish his own power against the party of order and overcome the National Assembly. Marx believed that the rule of the bourgeoisie was rule by the bourgeoisie. In *The German Ideology* he had written against Max Stirner: "Saint Max believes that an absolute monarch, or someone else, *could* defend the bourgeois just as successfully as they defend themselves. . . . Let Saint Max name any country where, with developed conditions of trade and industry, in the face of strong competition, the bourgeois entrust their defence to an 'absolute monarch.' " After Bonaparte's *coup d'état* of December 2, Marx confessed himself "quite bewildered."[41]

Marx did not allow his bewilderment to last very long, for by March 1852 he had completed his second account of the 1848 revolution in France, *The Eighteenth Brumaire*. Placing events under the strong light of his own critical scrutiny, Marx had no trouble—as we saw a moment ago—recognizing the shape of class struggle now veiled by the "superficial appearance" of what had taken place. But the history of classes Marx wrote from the perspective of Bonaparte's victory contrasted with the one he had presented from a viewpoint that saw bourgeois or proletarian class rule as the only possibilities. The conviction that revolution created unified classes out of otherwise separate groups now appeared in reverse: Instead of the formation of proletariat and bourgeoisie each into a class "and consequently into a political party," Marx now found that the experience of revolution dissolved each class into its constituent parts. This process of dissolution—like the earlier one of formation—was clearer with regard to the already developed bourgeoisie than it was for the only emerging proletariat, but the contrast with what Marx had written earlier was evident in both cases.

In *The Class Struggles* Marx had recognized the need that the proletariat recover from the defeat of June in order to constitute itself as a class and a political party, and he declared that this evolution had indeed taken place in 1849 and 1850. In *The Eighteenth Brumaire*, however, Marx described the proletariat as not recovering from the June defeat during the rest of the revolutionary years. The dissolution of its unity which followed June therefore characterized it during the whole of the period Marx described. Throwing itself into *"doctrinaire experiments, exchange banks and workers' associations"* that fragmented it, the proletariat could no longer appear as the revolutionary lever to transform the whole of society. Losing its class unity, the proletariat disappeared from the political stage, because it sought "to achieve its salvation behind society's back, in private fashion, within its own limited conditions of existence."[42]

With regard to the bourgeoisie Marx had to tell a longer and more complicated story. Just as in his earlier account, Marx presented the party of order as the political expression of the united bourgeoisie. The two bourgeois monarchical factions "do their real business as the *party of Order*, that is, under a *social*, not a *political* title; as representatives of the bourgeois world order, not as knights of errant princesses; as the bourgeois class against other classes, not as royalists against the republicans." In *The Class Struggles*, however, the conflict of the bourgeois class with the proletariat served precisely to recreate this unity whenever competition among the factions weakened it; in *The Eighteenth Brumaire* the reverse was true. Only the struggle against Bonaparte—in the earlier essay a representative of the bourgeoisie itself—united them: "Every time the royalists in coalition come in conflict with the pretender that confronts them, with Bonaparte, every time they believe their parliamentary omnipotence endangered by the executive power . . . they come forward as *republicans* and not as *royalists*." On the other hand, when the bourgeois factions had to "confront the subjugated classes and contend against them without mediation, without the concealment afforded by the crown" then "a feeling of weakness" caused them "to recoil from the pure conditions of their own class rule" and return to their traditional monarchical character.[43]

Whereas in *The Class Struggles* the question of the revision of the constitution in order to allow Bonaparte a second term as president had cemented the bourgeois party against the threat of anarchy, here it "was bound to inflame openly the conflict of interests which split the party of Order into hostile factions. The party of Order was a combination of heterogeneous social substances. The question of revision generated a political temperature at which the product again decomposed into its original constituents." Moreover, the political unity—the class unity—of the bourgeoisie was destined to break down further: "Each of the two great factions, in its turn, underwent decomposition anew," into subfactions recalling earlier struggles: "The parliamentary party was not only dissolved into its two great factions, each of these factions was not only split up within itself, but the party of Order in parliament had fallen out with the party of Order *outside* parliament." Finally, the bourgeoisie turned against its own press, "its speaking and writing section," so that its existence as a class was completely shattered.[44]

What Marx now argued was perfectly consistent in itself: the bourgeoisie gave up its political rule in order to preserve its social power—"in order to save its purse it must forfeit the crown."[45] This was a full reversal of what he had believed until 1851, namely, that to assure its power over society the bourgeoisie would have to take command of the state machine. Now, instead of that public manifestation of bourgeois control, Marx was talking of a hidden connection between bourgeois power and political life. Like the proletariat, Marx might have said, the bourgeoisie was seeking its salvation behind society's back.

Here the two topics we have been examining in this chapter—class formation and the correspondence of appearance and reality—merge into one. Marx's earlier conviction that class struggle was becoming visible on the surface of society depended on the belief that modern conditions—especially revolutionary conditions—were polarizing society around the two great classes, the bourgeoisie and the proletariat. Class struggle both was and appeared to be the motor of history. Now, however, Marx had to contend instead that class conflict was the essential underlying historical reality despite all appearance to the contrary. Since history did not reveal this itself through revolution, the communist critic had to shoulder the task of pointing it out.

This is precisely what we find Marx doing in *The Eighteenth Brumaire*. The revolution created a great illusion: "Only under the second Bonaparte does the state seem to have made itself completely independent. As against civil society, the state machine has consolidated its position so thoroughly that the chief of the Society of December 10 suffices for its head, an adventurer blown in from abroad, raised on the shield by a drunken soldiery." To this illusion Marx had ready a reply: "And yet the state power is not suspended in mid air. Bonaparte represents a class, and the most numerous class of French society at that, the *small-holding peasants*."[46] To a reader of Marx's earlier works, this would have been a secret indeed. To be sure, Marx had pointed out, as everyone in Europe knew, that Bonaparte had originally been elected by the votes of the French peasantry. But in *The Class Struggles* Marx depicted Napoleon as having turned against the peasants by taxing them, in order to unite himself with the only basis of real power in contemporary France, the bourgeoisie. In describing how the French peasantry was led to rally around the revolutionary proletariat, Marx in 1850 had declared the peasants' estrangement from Bonaparte: "From the moment when Montalembert elevated taxation to a god, the peasant became godless, atheist, and threw himself into the arms of the devil, socialism. The religion of order had lost him; the Jesuits had lost him; Bonaparte had lost him."[47] To make Bonaparte the representative of the peasants in *The Eighteenth Brumaire* was a desperate attempt to "save the appearances." The class struggle in the nineteenth century as Marx had conceived it in *The German Ideology* and the *Communist Manifesto* was a struggle between proletariat and bourgeoisie. It had no place for a modern state resting on peasants. We shall see that in the revived revolutionary atmosphere of the Paris Commune during 1871, Marx himself would revise this judgment, denying that Bonaparte's apparent dependence on the peasantry was real.

At the end of *The Eighteenth Brumaire* even the revolution itself had disappeared from view. Whereas the *Communist Manifesto* had traced "the more or less veiled civil war, raging within existing society, up to the point where that war breaks out into open revolution," in 1852 Marx found the revolution itself banished to an invisible—did he remember that it was also imaginary?—place: "It is still journeying through purgatory." In another famous metaphor, he compared it to an animal working beneath the soil to undermine the ground on which contemporary European society had its existence. When it had done its work, "Europe will leap from its seat and exultantly exclaim: Well grubbed, old mole!"[48]

The shape of Marx's earlier vision remained. He still looked for things hidden in the dark wings and underground passages of social existence— "private illusion," the communist "specter," class struggle, revolution itself—to emerge into the clear light and open stage of public view. However, all these clarifying revelations, so confidently greeted in the present of the later 1840s, now seemed relegated to the future in 1852. "Society now seems to have fallen back behind its point of departure; it has in truth first to create for itself the revolutionary point of departure, the situation, the relations, the conditions under which alone modern revolution becomes serious."[49] Society as Marx depicted it in *The Eighteenth Brumaire* had suffered a regression that brought it close to madness. It was confined "like that mad Englishman in Bedlam," in a "subterranean prison."

It was not society alone that had to work itself free of a past it seemed to have overcome before. Marx, too, had fallen back on some of his earlier points of departure.

4. The Return of the Past

The sharp contrast in perspective between Marx's two histories of the 1848 revolution in France, *The Class Struggles* and *The Eighteenth Brumaire*, raises the question of how he was able to produce the second version so quickly (between December 1851 and March 1852) and yet make the ar-

gument so vigorous and coherent. Part of the answer surely lies in his extraordinary powers of analysis and inventiveness, but in this case the task
was lessened somewhat by the availability of an explanatory model Marx
had used earlier. Marx had analyzed the social basis of a despotic political
regime before, namely in the picture of Germany he gave in the *Deutsch-
Französische Jahrbücher*. There, in the Introduction to his projected critique
of Hegel's political philosophy, Marx had set forth the characteristics that
distinguished German conditions from the more advanced situation of
France.

> Not only do German kings ascend their thrones *mal à propos*, but every
> section of civil society goes through a defeat before it celebrates victory,
> develops its own obstacles before it overcomes those facing it, asserts its
> narrow-minded nature before it can assert its generosity, so that even
> the opportunity of playing a great role has always passed before it ac-
> tually existed and each class is involved in a struggle against the class
> beneath as soon as it begins to struggle with the class above it. . . . The
> middle class hardly dares to conceive the idea of emancipation from its
> own perspective. The development of social conditions and the progress
> of political theory show that perspective to be already antiquated or at
> least problematic.[50]

In this way Marx had explained the contrast between France, where the
bourgeoisie had come to dominate society and politics by emancipating
itself from feudalism and despotism, and Germany, where such partial
emancipation was impossible. In Germany despotic rule and universal
human emancipation were the only conceivable alternatives.

In 1846 Marx abandoned this view even for Germany. The premises of
historical materialism required that the bourgeoisie come to power there,
as well as in France, before the conditions of proletarian rule could be
established. For this reason Marx's paper during 1848-49, the *Neue
Rheinische Zeitung*, had come forward as the "organ of democracy," ad-
vocating an alliance between the proletarian forces and bourgeois democrats. The democratic republic Marx worked for would, he recognized, be
controlled at first by middle-class groups, but within it the proletariat
could develop in strength and unity, in order to prepare its later victory.

The alteration in Marx's perspective that followed Bonaparte's *coup
d'état* reversed the movement he had accomplished between 1843 and
1846: instead of generalizing the French model and applying it to Germany he now projected the German pattern onto France. The inability of
any social class to achieve unity of purpose and action meant that the
bourgeoisie had failed to achieve its own partial emancipation there too.
As a result, society as a whole was subjected to a retrograde and baroque
despotism. The revolutionary drama had not unfolded according to the

logic of historical progress and advancement, but in the spirit of a more primitive and backward dialectic.

Marx's experience from 1848 to 1851 followed a pattern of disappointment many of his later followers would rediscover for themselves. Like him, twentieth-century Marxist revolutionaries would invest revolutionary expectations developed in "backward" countries with a significance that required the fulfillment of potentialities assumed to be present in more advanced societies. When the revolutionary moment passed, leaving those potentialities unfulfilled, they, too, would have to recognize that neither gradual nor sudden change freed human society so fully from the weight of its past as they had hoped and believed. These lessons would be learned in both Russia and the West during the 1920s and 1930s, and in the Third World after 1945.

There was one feature of his earlier "German" model of revolution that Marx did not explicitly recall now. When he had analyzed the weakness of class formations in Germany in 1843, Marx had pictured the proletariat as acting not in alliance with any other major social group but in combination with philosophy. It had not been middle-class revolution but "the lightning of thought" that would bring the workers to the political stage. From the time of *The German Ideology* Marx had ceased picturing the proletariat as the partner of philosophy, and he no longer described the theoreticians of the working class as philosophers. Did the failure of the revolution to create class unity and to consummate the marriage of appearance and reality mean that Marx would be forced back into his older philosophical role?

The answer to that question was not yet positive, for in the early years of the 1850s Marx continued to expect the early return of conditions that would both reveal and solidify class struggles. Yet, after half a decade of continued disappointments, he would find (as we shall see later on) that a return to philosophy—Hegelian philosophy—was indeed necessary in order for historical materialism to account for the conditions of the time. *The Eighteenth Brumaire* gave certain intimations of this. One was the Shakespearean metaphor of the revolution as a mole. Marx had used the figure of the mole in an earlier writing, one of the preliminary essays for his doctoral dissertation. There he had described the task of the historian of philosophy as being to discover the true significance of a philosophical system beneath the surface appearance it had presented to contemporaries, and even to its author. The historian had to separate "the ever-progressing mole of real philosophical knowledge" from the "verbal, exoteric, and variously behaving phenomenological consciousness of the subject, which is the vessel and energy of the former's development." In this context, the inner progress of consciousness was quite separate from its external embodiment, and the philosophical critic had to search out the mole, to distinguish the truth beneath the surface from the appearance that hid it.[51]

Philosophical criticism was not the only one of Marx's abandoned identities that now reemerged. On December 27, 1851, while he was working on *The Eighteenth Brumaire*, Marx wrote to his friend, the poet Ferdinand Freiligrath, asking him to compose a poem for Weydemeyer's new American journal, for which Marx's essay was also written. "Under present circumstances," Marx explained, "I consider it really more possible to write in verse than in prose."[52] No doubt Freiligrath considered the comment a bit of wry humor, but there is reason to suspect it was more than that. The distinction between poetry and prose had a special significance for Marx, exemplified in his accounts of the 1848 revolution. We have quoted his description of class war as the "true, unadulterated, prosaic" expression of the poetry of brotherhood proclaimed in February 1848, as well as his reference to the early stages of the revolution, with their illusions, as the period of "flowers of rhetoric," and his declaration that the "flowers of popular fantasy" had been chilled by "the prosaic North wind of counterrevolution."[53] The passage from poetry to prose had a place in Marx's personal history too; like his devotion to philosophy, Marx's early identification with poetry testified to his ambivalence toward a more realistic standpoint. To say in December 1851 that the present could better be described in poetry than in prose was, therefore, not only to recognize that the earlier illusions had returned, but to approach the question of whether Marx's own development from poetry to prosaic realism—from philosophy to an ordinary perception of the real world—might have to be reexamined.

The fact that Napoleon III remained firmly in control of French affairs made Marx's dilemma more acute. In January 1853, after an incident in which Bonaparte had succeeded in representing himself as a democrat, Marx wrote to Engels: "This burlesque figure appears to be called on for the complete inversion and ridiculizing [*zur völligen Verkehrung und Ridikulisierung*] of all the traditional positions and parties."[54] No longer right-side-up as in the later 1840s, the postrevolutionary world was once again inverted. And Marx, who had believed that historical materialism overcame the isolation of ideology in 1845 (as he had thought Hegelian philosophy cured the isolation of thinkers once before) found himself again isolated from events in a topsy-turvy world.

CHAPTER EIGHT

Exile and Politics

1. A New Era

MARX was not alone in finding that Louis Bonaparte's *coup d'état* of December 2, 1851, marked an unexpected turning point in his history. One contemporary who experienced a similar disappointment and need for reorientation was a man not often linked to Marx, Richard Wagner. Like Marx, Wagner had begun his career in the afterglow of Hegel, and had for a time oriented himself around the twin guideposts of Feuerbachian humanism and the approach of revolution. Although without much practical understanding of politics, he greeted 1848 with enthusiasm, and for a time took an active part. Even after being forced to flee Germany for Switzerland, he did not abandon hope, believing that the French presidential election scheduled for 1852 would bring the revolutionary flame back to life. As he later recalled:

> I always pointed . . . to this hopeful and fateful year, my opinion being that we should calmly wait for the expected upheaval, so that when no one else should know what to do, we could make a start. I cannot measure how deeply this hope had taken root in me; I soon, however, was forced to recognize that the confident pride of my assumptions and affirmations was largely due to the greatly increased excitement of my nerves. The news of the *coup d'état* of the 2nd December in Paris seemed to me absolutely incredible: I was certain the world was coming to an end. When the news was confirmed, and it became clear that events no one had thought possible had happened and seemed likely to endure, I turned away from the investigation of this enigmatic world, as one turns from a mystery the fathoming of which no longer seems to be worth while.[1]

Marx, of course, made no such radical break with his determination to comprehend the real world. As we shall see, however, disillusionment and withdrawal would be powerful themes in his life during the early 1850s, just as they were in Wagner's.

Rather like the seventies of the twentieth century, the fifties of the nineteenth were harsh to expectations formed in the revolutionary air of the preceding decade. Then as now no single event alone accounted for the change; it was the manifestation of a far-reaching transformation of social life. Once the upheavals of 1848 had been suppressed, European commercial and industrial society entered on the high Victorian era of relative social peace and unprecedented material progress. The symbol of the age's aspirations and successes was the great London exhibition of 1851, celebrating the productive ingenuity of the emerging industrial world. Like the *coup* of December, the Crystal Palace Exhibition gained lasting power as a symbol because it was sustained by developments taking place on other levels.[2]

It was in the 1850s that the new industrial civilization really began to transform French and German economic and social life, instead of distorting the traditional patterns of production and employment, as it had mostly done before. Although England still led her continental rivals in all the significant productive sectors, for the first time the other nations now posted figures that were on the British scale. Population pressure in the countryside continued to feed a steady stream of immigrants to the burgeoning cities, which now grew even faster than they had in the years before 1848. However, whereas the newcomers in the first half of the century had sought jobs in the traditional handicraft industries, helping to force wage levels down, those of the period after 1850 increasingly found employment in better-paying economic sectors that were expanding through the effects of railroad construction and investment in machine industry. Factory employment itself meant a gain in income and stability for many workers who had earlier clung to the countryside and suffered the problems and uncertainties of the putting-out system.

The transformation remained far from complete, and some places—notably Paris—continued to be dominated by traditional industries organized in the old way. Yet there seems little doubt that, in strictly economic terms at least, the situation of European workers was getting better. British historians still argue fiercely about whether the working-class standard of living was improving or worsening before 1850, but no one denies it was advancing after that date. Real wages are difficult to calculate, yet it seems fairly safe to say that on the continent they had fluctuated strongly and tended to fall somewhat in the decades after 1815, whereas they began to rise around 1855 and continued to increase—albeit at a fluctuating rate—for the rest of the century. Moreover, sometime around 1870 or shortly after, the predominant attitude of European workers toward wages reached a new point. In preindustrial society, wages had been protected by custom, and most workers regarded a fair wage as one that met customary standards and expectations. The conditions of the early nineteenth century had weakened the hold of custom on wage levels, as capitalists pressed by competition and encouraged by an abundant labor supply pushed the pay level down. Controversies arising from employers' refusal to pay customary wages had sometimes sparked workers' revolts, as at Lyons in 1831. The uncertainties and hostilities (as well as some of the injustices) this situation bred began to diminish in the later nineteenth century as workers, especially organized ones like English trade-union members, came to accept new criteria for determining wage levels: market conditions and productivity. In this way workers learned what E. H. Hobsbawm has called "the rules of the game," and began to improve their lot by skillful and determined play. It would be very wrong to suppose that workers were liberated from all the conditions that had oppressed and exploited them earlier. Many still lived in wretched conditions, and working-class living standards probably grew more slowly than the wealth of society as a whole, so that the gap between working and middle classes did not close. But whereas the quarter-century after 1825 had seemed a period of decline for most workers, the quarter-century after 1850 appeared to many as a time of improvement.[3]

English historians have called the decades that witnessed these developments "the age of equipoise," in which society achieved a balance and calm that neither the 1840s nor the 1880s allowed. The political and social tensions of the immediately preceding period were muted. In England, Chartism, which had seen a final revival in 1848, entered a decline from which it never recovered, and on the continent the radical temper that had raised both fears and expectations in the prerevolutionary period also receded. Especially in England and France, political life came to be dominated by coalitions of groups that had been hostile to each other before: Whigs and Tories, Orleanists and republicans. The party conflicts to which observers and participants had grown accustomed during the 1840s largely disappeared. For two decades, more or less—the period of the Second Empire in France, the years before the Reform Bill of 1867 in England—political tempers cooled and Europe experienced a period not unlike one that in a later century was to make people speak of "the end of ideology." In the nineteenth as in the twentieth century, ideology soon enough returned to haunt those who had exulted in the report of its death; but for a time things appeared mysterious and moribund to those others who identified the vitality of society with the clarity of its social and political contrasts. Marx was not happy to spend most of the second half of his life in such a time.

2. Political Illusion and Secret Diplomacy

Marx's first sustained writings while in England were *The Class Struggles in France* and *The Eighteenth Brumaire of Louis Bonaparte*, whose contrasting images of revelation and mystification, class formation and class dissolution we have just examined. The differences between the two accounts were patent enough, but the bitter lessons of the second did not immediately lead Marx to abandon the faith in history's clarifying and simplifying power he had proclaimed in the first. If France suffered beneath the monstrous delusion that history had reversed directions and receded behind its original starting point, there was reason to believe that Britain would not share the same fate. Here was a truly modern country with the most advanced industry and the most unified and conscious working class in Europe. In 1852 Marx began to report on English affairs for the *New York Daily Tribune*. The view of English life he projected in his first articles gave off the same bright and revolutionary colors with which Marx had painted the world before.[4]

Reporting on the parliamentary election of the summer of 1852, Marx took the opportunity to comment on the nature of the dominant British parties, the Whigs and Tories: "Up to 1846 the Tories passed as the guardians of the traditions of Old England." But the struggle over repeal of the protectionist duties on cereal grains (the Corn Laws) in that year showed their true character. It "proved that they were enthusiasts for nothing but the rent of land, and at the same time disclosed the secret of their attachment to the political and religious institutions of Old England." These institutions guaranteed the continuing dominance of large landed property. Hence, "the year 1846 brought to light in its nakedness the *substantial class interest* which forms the *real base* of the Tory party. The year 1846 tore down the traditionally venerable lion's hide, under which Tory class interest had hitherto hidden itself. . . . Tory was the sacred name, Protectionist is the profane one."[5]

As for the Whigs, they were simply "the *aristocratic representatives* of the bourgeoisie, of the industrial and commercial middle class." Whig aristocrats lived from politics rather than from rents, hence they could support measures their Tory cousins had to fight. The Whigs' interests and principles were not their own, but those the bourgeoisie had imposed on them over the course of history, from 1688 until the present: "The Whigs as little carried out the Reform Bill of 1831 [Marx meant 1832] as they carried the Free Trade Bill of 1846. Both Reform movements, the political as well as the commercial, were movements of the Bourgeoisie." It followed, therefore, that as the middle class developed its independent strength and grew able to defend its own interests, its dependence upon aristocratic protectors and advocates would dissolve. The Whigs were "a distastefully heterogeneous mixture," they would not be suffered for long: "The mass of the English people have a sound aesthetical common sense. They have an instinctive hatred against everything motley and ambiguous, against bats and Russellites." Hence, the Whiggish confusion of aristocratic and middle-class identity would evaporate once the middle class developed its own political party, whose nucleus was already visible in the Free Traders.[6]

As that nucleus grew, England would move toward revolution. The middle class might try to keep its own advance at a slow pace in order to retard the collision with the already visible working-class challenge to its power, but this tactic would not succeed: "They cannot avoid fulfilling their own mission, battering to pieces Old England, the England of the Past; and the very moment when they will have conquered exclusive political dominion, when political dominion and economic supremacy will be united in the same hands, when, therefore, the struggle against capital will no longer be distinct from the struggle against the existing government—from that very moment will date the *social revolution of England*." Revolution would take a different form in England than elsewhere, because English conditions were so far in advance of the rest of Europe. The English revolution was already present in the Chartist demand for universal suffrage.

> Universal Suffrage is the equivalent for [sic] political power for the working class of England, where the proletariat forms the large majority of the population, where, in a long, though underground civil war, it has gained a clear consciousness of its position as a class, and where even the rural districts know no longer any peasants, but only landlords, industrial capitalists (farmers) and hired laborers. The carrying of Universal Suffrage in England would, therefore, be a far more socialistic measure than anything which has been honored with that name on the Continent.

Much as he had earlier done for France in *The Class Struggles*, Marx depicted England nearing the point of final conflict evoked in the *Communist Manifesto*. The result of the whole process would be *"the political supremacy of the working class."*[7]

Yet it was not long before Marx found it necessary to retouch the hard-etched lines of this portrait and soften the view of English developments it gave. As early as October 1852 he reported the lowering of the political temperature that accompanied continuing prosperity. The mass of the people, "fully employed and more or less well off," did not constitute "at present a very malleable material for political agitation." The middle class, having "thrown itself into the mighty process of industrial production," had "no time to agitate, to revolt, not even to get up a proper show of indignation." In November Marx explained how this situation put its stamp on the new political groupings that emerged "as the hitherto predominating parties dissolve themselves, and as their distinctive marks are effaced." In place of the increased clarity of political alignment he had predicted only a few months earlier, Marx now found a series of "miserable compromises and backslidings," in which all political centers agreed to follow a common policy of "going backward." Chartists retreated to mere democracy, democrats became less demanding electoral reformers. Political opposition transformed itself into agreement: "The political flaccidity and indifference consequent upon a period of material prosperity," added to "the knowledge acquired by some popular leaders that the people are too indolent to create, for the moment, a movement of their own—all these circumstances produce the phenomenon that parties attempt to make themselves acceptable to each other, and that the different factions of the opposition out of Parliament attempt a union by making each other concessions, from the most advanced downwards."[8]

Marx had now to revise his views of the relations between the middle class and British politics. In 1854 he reversed his earlier judgment that the bourgeoisie would be forced willy-nilly to destroy the political dominance of the aristocracy—now it seemed to him that only the workers could bring such a change about. "The feudalism of England will not perish beneath the scarcely perceptible dissolving processes of the middle class; the honor of such a victory is reserved for the working classes."[9] In 1855, writing about Lord John Russell, Marx also retreated from his description of the Reform Bill of 1832 as a measure that served middle class, rather than Whig party interests. Once the Bill came into effect, "The middle classes themselves discovered that Lord Althorp, the soul of the Reform cabinet, had not used a rhetorical figure when telling his Tory adversaries that 'the Reform Bill was the most aristocratic act ever offered to the nation.' " The county voters in the countryside still predominated over the towns, and the counties were the tools of the aristocracy. Some of the reform provisions even disfranchised town voters: "The new arrangements were, on the whole, calculated not for increasing middle-class influence, but for the exclusion of Tory and the promotion of Whig patronage."[10]

Marx's optimism about the transformation of the archaic and arcane British party system into a rational and modern struggle between one declaredly aristocratic and one clearly middle-class party sometimes returned, as in 1858. In June of that year he reported the consummation of the process that was producing "absorption of the Whig faction into the Tory faction, and their common metamorphosis into the party of the aristocracy, as opposed to the new middle-class party, acting under its own chiefs, under its own banners, with its own watchwords."[11] The crystallization of new parties did not take place then, however, and in 1861 Marx had to admit that the old system of compromise he had decried earlier still survived. The master of that system was Palmerston, and in writing about him Marx had to admit that "since the French *coup d'état*, when the Government by faction was in England superseded by the Government by the coalition of factions," Palmerston had faced no real challenge to his control over foreign policy from any rationally organized and clearly presented class interest.[12]

Marx's unfulfilled prophecy of clarification in British politics was closely tied up with his other disappointed prediction for the 1850s: the return of economic crisis. When, in 1855, Marx believed he saw the return of crisis on the scale of the 1840s coming in "a few months more," he asserted that it would bring both struggle and revelation in its train. "The conflict between the industrial proletariat and the bourgeoisie will be resumed at the moment when the conflict between the bourgeoisie and the aristocracy reaches its peak. Then the mask will fall which has up till now hidden the true features of Great Britain's political face from countries abroad."[13]

This was not the first time Marx had been disappointed. He had not expected to wait long for the crisis to appear when, in the last chapter of *The Class Struggles in France*, he made the recurrence of economic decline the condition for the resumption of revolutionary activity. But by 1852 he and Engels both found their certainties about the approach of the crisis giving way to tinges of doubt. Early in February Marx told Engels that he could no longer make sense of what was happening to commerce. "At one moment the crisis seems to stand at the gates," at the next business had picked up again. Engels attributed the continuation of prosperity "longer than was to be expected earlier" to the effects of freer trade and the opening of new colonial markets, but said that conditions in India and America "do not let one expect that the thing will go on much longer."[14] On April 20 Engels unhappily admitted that the prosperous conditions showed signs of continuing for a long time, but concluded optimistically: "In the end however, it is most certain that within six months more or less the old rule will hold." In August he predicted the crisis for the following October or November, while admitting that "California and Australia are two cases that were not foreseen in the *Manifesto*: the creation of great new markets out of nothing."[15] For some months after January 1853 the two friends talked less about a coming crisis, although they continued to expect it. In September Marx pointed out the signs of approaching economic collapse in the *New York Daily Tribune*, and predicted a commercial downfall like that of 1847 for the following spring. In October he suggested Engels write an article for the *Tribune* explaining how this would lead to "doing away with the Bonaparte regime."[16]

During 1854 Marx's confidence in the approach of crisis seems to have reached a low point, for he appears not to have mentioned it. But in January 1855 he thought he saw it coming again, and his expectation remained in March, when he wrote in the *Tribune* that "the mask will fall" once the critical economic situation made itself felt in the political realm. After that, his confidence waned again and remained at a low point until the fall of 1856, when he predicted an outbreak for the following year. This time, in 1857, the crisis finally came.

The economic crisis that began in the autumn of 1857 brought serious difficulties both to the United States, where it began, and to the European industrial countries. Some of its effects were felt well into 1859 in Britain and France, and probably as late as 1860 in Germany. Moreover, the decade that followed it saw a slower pace of industrial expansion than in the fifties, and a general atmosphere that was less confident than before.[17] Marx and Engels exulted at the outbreak. Engels called it "beautiful" and Marx said he had not felt so "cosy" since 1849. Yes, Engels wrote back, "In 1848 we said: 'now our time is coming,' and it came in a certain sense; this time however it is coming completely, now it is a matter of life and death."[18] Yet, unlike the critical years of the late 1840s, the economic disruptions a decade later brought no serious political upheavals. Only the economic part of Marx's prophecy now seemed justified; the political consequences expected to follow—the falling of the mask—never came.

During the years when Marx waited unsuccessfully for the economic crisis he hoped would bring the reality of British politics to light, he devoted considerable energy to exposing the masks that kept the false political appearances intact: the power of illusion became a main theme of Marx's political commentary. The "sound aesthetical common sense" of the British people was deceived by the theatrical talent of two leading politicians, Russell and Palmerston. Russell excited Marx's contempt; his whole career was a mere semblance, a "sham." The illusion that enveloped him also infected those on the political stage with whom he interacted:

> The pettiness of his views on all things spread to others like a contagion and contributed more to confuse the judgment of his hearers than the most ingenious perversion could have done. His real talent consists in his capacity to reduce everything that he touches to his own Lilliputian dimensions, to shrink the external world to an infinitesimal size and to transform it into a vulgar microcosm of his own invention. His instinct to belittle the magnificent is excelled only by the skill with which he can make the petty appear grand.

His whole life had been lived on "false pretenses," but they were pretenses that successfully veiled from others the reality Marx perceived.[19]

It was Palmerston, however, whose despicable but consummate deceptions bulked largest in Marx's mind. The first description of Palmerston's character Marx penned, in October 1853, began with poetical allusions:

> Ruggiero is again and again fascinated by the false charms of Alcine, which he knows to disguise an old witch—sans teeth, sans eyes, sans taste, sans everything, and the knight-errant cannot withstand falling in love with her anew whom he knows to have transmuted all her former adorers into asses and other beasts. The English public is another Ruggiero, and Palmerston is another Alcine.

Palmerston was, Marx went on, "if not a good statesman of all work . . . at least a good actor of all work." He had great talents of memory, experience, tact, presence, versatility, and knowledge of parliamentary life, but like Russell his success demonstrated above all the power of illusion in British politics. He aimed not at the substance but at "the mere appearance of success." He exulted in "show conflicts, show battles, show enemies."[20]

When Marx first began to write about Palmerston's career he evoked only the general quality of mystery and disguise that clung to him. Soon, however, Marx became convinced that one particular secret lay behind the lord's political theatrics: Palmerston was a Russian agent. In October 1853 Marx had not been sure of this, and wrote only that "Accused by the one party of being in the pay of Russia, he is suspected by the other of Carbonarism."[21] But on November 2 he told Engels: "Curious as it may seem to you, through closely following the footprints of the noble Viscount over a twenty-year period, I have come to the same conclusion as the monomaniac Urquhart, that Palmerston has been sold out to Russia for several decades." The following spring he made the point less apologetically to Lassalle: "For me no conclusion is more solid than this, that Palmerston . . . is a *Russian agent*." Marx's conviction was the result of "a very conscientious and careful" study of his whole career, using official inquiries and parliamentary debates. "The work was in no way amusing, and it stole away a lot of time besides, but it paid off in so far as it contains the key to the secret diplomatic history of the last thirty years."[22] Marx never quite made the same assertion openly in print, picturing Palmerston only as the enemy of freedom everywhere. But on no other contemporary politician did Marx pour out so much anger and hostility.

Marx's conclusion about Palmerston put him in the rather bizarre company of David Urquhart, a radical Tory journalist and politician who had served for a time in the British embassy in Constantinople. Urquhart shared Marx's hostility to Russia, but from quite a different direction. Marx saw in Russia the bastion of European reaction; to Urquhart she was the enemy of the nation he most admired: the Turks. It was he who first asserted that Palmerston was in the pay of the Russians.

No evidence to support this idea has emerged in the century and a quarter since, and modern students of Victorian politics simply do not take it seriously.[23] What sort of man Urquhart was emerges from Marx's account of a meeting with him in February 1854. He was, Marx told Engels, a "complete monomaniac," who believed firmly that he would become prime minister of England, called by his countrymen to save them. "During conversation, particularly when he is contradicted, he falls into fits, which made all the more comic an impression on me, since I know all his phrases and citations by heart. This even made the 'fits' appear somewhat suspect to me, and rather like a theatrical exhibition." He believed that Russia ruled the world through "a specific excess of brain," and that to cope with her one had to have the brains of an Urquhart, share his ideas, have been in the East, and have assimilated some Turkish spirit.[24]

Marx did not say so, but some striking similarities linked his portrait of Urquhart with one of his favorite literary characters: the central figure of Diderot's *Rameau's Nephew*. Like Diderot's Rameau, Urquhart had a spirit and wit that dissolved the solid convictions of common sense, and his estrangement from the ordinary world brought him to the borderland between theater and madness. In Marx's eyes he possessed the mixture of perversity and vision Hegel had called inversion. Marx's acceptance of Urquhart's view of Palmerston brought him close to Hegel's idea in the *Phenomenology* that the truth of an inverted and alienated world was best conveyed by an inverted and alienated person. It is hard to imagine Marx in the company of an Urquhart during the late 1840s; only after 1851 did the association make sense.

Marx's link with Urquhart provided the context for a further venture into secret diplomatic history, one that recalled Hegel in a different way. This was Marx's *The Secret Diplomatic History of the Eighteenth Century*, published first in two Urquhartite newspapers during 1856.[25] The work was not long, but it was the product of a considerable amount of research in eighteenth-century pamphlets and letters in the British Museum. Marx wrote to Engels about it with some pride in February 1856—his work on the subject may have begun several months earlier—saying that he had made some "historical discoveries."[26] What Marx thought he had discovered was certainly interesting, but what strikes the reader of his account is the total absence from it of any analysis that might identify its author as the originator of historical materialism. The historical thinking Marx employed here was of quite a different kind from either *The Class Struggles* or *The Eighteenth Brumaire*.

Marx's purpose was to explain the favoritism British policy had shown toward Russia at the time of the Northern Wars of the early eighteenth century. The reasons for the policy emerged from pamphlets and letters Marx had discovered in the British Museum, and which he published verbatim in his work. The documents showed what Marx called the abject servility and cynical submission that English statesmen in the eighteenth century displayed toward Russia. What was the explanation for their attitude? Were economic reasons at the base of it? Some politicians had thought so at the time, just as similar policies were being justified in similar ways in the nineteenth century. Marx insisted that these explanations were false. The scope of English trade with Russia had been greatly exaggerated, and after comparing the figures Marx concluded that "England suffered positive loss by her new commercial relations with Russia under

Peter I and Catherine I." To be sure, a small group of British merchants had profited from the commerce, but the interests of this section of the *haute bourgeoisie* merely provided the oligarchy with *"mercantile pretexts*, however futile, for their measures of foreign policy." The same pattern had recurred in Marx's own century: "We will, *en passant*, show, by a few modern instances, what desperate shifts those foreigners have been driven to, who feel themselves obliged to interpret Palmerston's acts by what they imagine to be English commercial policy."[27]

The real answer, Marx went on, lay in the nature of Russian power and in the character of her relations with other countries. The strength of Russia's continuing influence in European affairs had continually surprised the West and, after all her achievements, her power was still often "treated like a matter of faith rather than a matter of fact." With respect to Russia some were "spiritualists" and some "materialists." The latter considered "her power as a palpable fact"; the former regarded it "as the mere vision of the guilt-striken consciences of the European peoples." This division arose, Marx went on to show, because of the peculiar mold in which Russia's political personality had been formed, a shape Marx summarized in the phrase "the slave as master."[28]

The pattern of relationships determining this quality of Russian history went deeply into the Russian past. Subdued by the Mongols, the princes of Muscovy learned to employ their conquerors' power against them: They corrupted the Mongols by bribes and subterfuges, using the money their masters allowed them to collect to buy off those masters themselves. Ivan III (the Great) accomplished the liberation of Muscovy from the Tartars, but through their power rather than his own: at the decisive moment the Tartars were beaten by dissident groups within their own ranks, not by Ivan, who refused to stand up and fight. "He caught one Tartar with another Tartar," and then exploited the false halo of the conqueror that clung to him to make "a magnificent entry among the European powers."[29]

Ivan III could play both slave and master; what he could not allow was the independence that rejected both roles, and found its political expression in republics. He destroyed the republic of Novgorod by allying first with the patricians and then with the plebeians, and his policy echoed throughout later Russian history. "It is still worthy of notice what exquisite pains were always taken by Muscovy as well as by modern Russia to execute republics. Novgorod and its colonies lead the dance; the republic of the Cossacks follows; Poland closes it. To understand the Russian mastication of Poland, one must study the execution of Novgorod, lasting from 1178 till 1528."[30]

Thus, the basic pattern of the slave as master recurred again and again: "A simple substitution of names and dates will prove to evidence that be-

228 Exile and Politics

tween the policy of Ivan III, and that of modern Russia, there exists not similarity but sameness." After Peter the Great oriented Russian policy toward the West rather than the East, England was bribed and deceived to play the same role of lending her power to the expansion of Russia that the Mongols had played under Ivan. In the seventeenth century England was the greatest sea power, and if Russia was able to expand into the Baltic, she must have done so with English connivance. "England must have had her hand in this great change, . . . she must have proved the main prop or the main impediment of the plans of Peter the Great. . . . Real history will show that the Khans of the Golden Horde were no more instrumental in realizing the plans of Ivan III and his predecessors than the rulers of England were in realizing the plans of Peter I and his successors."[31]

The implication was that the pattern still held in the age of Marx and Palmerston. Russian power still relied on shadow, not substance, and on the bribed cooperation of the real arbiter of European affairs, Great Britain. It was an inspired historical vision, but a remarkably un-Marxian one. Not the open and palpable relations of production and exchange but the secret and invisible ties of personal corruption shaped the history of diplomacy. Not the succession of historical epochs determined by changes in the forms of economic organization, but the recurrence of a once-established and inalterable pattern of dependence molded the political character of a major European nation.

The result was a historical perspective that emphasized not economy and society but psychology. Russian power was, in fact, "the mere vision of the guilt-stricken consciousness of the European peoples," and Marx turned out to be a "spiritualist" rather than a materialist in regard to it. Moreover, the historical method he applied to Russian history directly recalled his Hegelian origins. In the *Phenomenology* Hegel had analyzed the dialectic of mastery and slavery, and Marx's account of Russian history adapted some elements of Hegel's view. But in a curious way, Marx's commentary on Russia more closely resembled an unpublished writing of Hegel, which Marx did not know except through its echoes in other works, "The Spirit of Christianity and its Fate." Just as Hegel there had presented the whole later history of Judaism and Christianity as a continual recurrence of Abraham's original relationship to the world he inhabited, so did Marx find the history of Russia patterned on the relations of the two Ivans to the Tartars. "The whole policy of Muscovy, from its first entrance into the historical arena, is resumed in the history of these two individuals,"[32] and that policy would be repeated both in the eighteenth century and the nineteenth. Moreover, the mixture of mastery and slavery Marx found in the Russian character was the same that Hegel had found in Abraham and the Jews; both peoples exhibited the same alienation from the more balanced life of an independent republic.

Only one of the central themes of Hegel's portrait of Abraham was missing from Marx's account of the political destiny of Russia: isolation. Abraham and his people owed their fate to the original isolation from the surrounding world in which the patriarch had maintained himself; that he and his posterity could relate to the rest of the world only by subjecting it to themselves or themselves to it derived from his original refusal to live in harmony with external reality. Marx, who had found that the Hegelian theme of isolation and its consequences spoke to his condition at critical turning points in his life before, did not sound it in *The Secret Diplomatic History of the Eighteenth Century*. However, if he did not offer isolation as a significant theme in the history of Russia, he knew perfectly well that it was one in his own political life.

3. The Politics of Isolation

Like Marx, a number of other members of the Communist League had emigrated to London in 1849. There they attempted to keep their own organization in being, and to establish contact with Englishmen sympathetic to the revolutionary cause, as well as with other continental groups. Marx joined the efforts to raise money for penniless exiles, and reentered the Communist League, which he had abandoned during the livelier days of 1848, when secret organizations had seemed unnecessary.[33] In January 1850 he attempted to foster the creation of small nuclei of communist activity in Germany, loyal to the principles of the *Communist Manifesto*, but prepared to carry out agitation and propaganda in secret as long as necessary. In March the same year he and Engels wrote a circular instructing the German communists on strategy for the approaching renewal of revolutionary activity. Believing that the imminent upheaval would see the victory of the middle-class democrats and the beginning of a fight to the finish between them and the communists, Marx and Engels sketched out what Marx later called "a war plan against the Democrats."[34] It called for arming of the proletarian forces with all kinds of weapons, and warned against continuing the earlier cooperation with democratic groups in the more advanced situation to come. The policy of the petty-bourgeois democrats was to bring the revolution to a conclusion as quickly as possible, so as to limit it to the achievement of their own restricted program. By contrast, "it is our interest and our task to make the revolution permanent," that is, to keep up the revolutionary pressure until the possessing classes had been defeated, state power had come into proletarian hands, and the internationally organized working class had gained control over "at least the decisive productive forces."[35]

During the summer of 1850, however, the continuation of economic prosperity and political calm led Marx and Engels to conclude—as we noted earlier in a different context—that the revolutionary movement had died down temporarily, and that it could not be revived until economic crisis breathed new life into the masses. This conviction set them apart from less patient members of the Communist League who still thought a return of the struggle possible at any time, and who, in Marx's eyes, were too eager to join government coalitions that less radical groups would still be able to dominate. This more adventurous faction, led by August Willich and Karl Schapper, had strong backing in the League, especially among the artisan exiles. In September, following an attempt by Marx to counter the Willich-Schapper group's influence by having the Central Committee of the League transferred from London to Cologne, the organization split in two. All through the following years the hostility between the rival factions was bitter and open, issuing in shouting matches, fistfights, and on one occasion in a duel. Reports of the Willich-Schapper organization's doings fill many of Marx's letters to Engels (who had left London for Manchester in November 1850).[36]

At first Marx and Engels managed to keep some of the leaders of the English Chartists—which the two friends recognized as the only English political movement capable of representing the proletariat—loyal to them. In November 1850 George Julian Harney's *Red Republican* published the first English translation of the *Communist Manifesto*. By early in 1851, however, the two authors of the *Manifesto* found their English political friends one by one deserting them in favor of the Willich-Schapper group. When Harney refused any longer to take sides with Marx and Engels against their rivals, the two had to recognize that they had been left quite by themselves.

In a letter to Engels of February 11, 1851, Marx reflected on the situation. Quite apart from Harney's defection, he declared, "the public, authentic isolation in which we two—you and I—find ourselves now, pleases me very much. It corresponds fully to our position and to our principles. The system of mutual concessions, of half-measures born for decorum's sake, and the duty publicly to accept one's measure of ridiculousness in the party with all these asses—that has now ended." Engels echoed and amplified Marx's words in the following days. The emigration would turn everyone who did not separate himself from it and take up an independent position against it into an ass and a fool. "Now we finally have again—for the first time in a long time—the opportunity to show that we need no popularity, no support from any party of any country, and that our position is totally independent of such silliness. . . . Have we not acted for so many years as if Joe Blow were our party, when we had no party at all, and when the people whom we counted as belonging to our party, at least officially—did not even understand the starting points of our position?" How could people like Engels and Marx be part of a party? "What should we, who spit on popularity and who grow confused about ourselves when we begin to become popular, do with a party, i.e., a band of asses who swear on us because they think us like them?" Such independence, Engels believed, was certainly worth a little loneliness. When the next revolution came, the two friends would be stronger for it.[37]

The sense of isolation continued in the months that followed, coloring the two men's relations with workers as well as with middle-class revolutionary leaders. In May 1851 Engels recollected that even in 1848 he and Marx had had to "conquer" their position of influence over the Cologne workers, and added that "the democratic, red, or even communist mob will never *love* us." A year later, in July 1852, Marx referred to Cologne workers in still more unfriendly terms, calling them the derisive name *Straubinger*, and adding: "Bad business, that world history is to be made with such people."[38]

Throughout the 1850s Marx and Engels remained more or less cut off from active politics. They abstained from membership in any political organizations, and in 1860 Marx informed his somewhat estranged friend, the radical poet Ferdinand Freiligrath, that he had refused a request to aid in reorganizing the Communist League in 1857, on the grounds "that I have had no ties with *any* organization since 1852, that I stand by my firm conviction that my theoretical works help the working class more than joining associations, whose time is past on the continent." This was still Marx's position in 1860. He had been accused of inactivity, and doctrinaire indifference, but did not contest the charge. "If you are a *poet*, I am a *critic*, and I truly had my fill of the 1849-52 kind of experiences."[39]

Brave, rueful, and insistent by turns, Marx's declarations of his isolation provide a clue to his state of mind in the 1850s, but they need to be placed in a larger context. In the politically more congenial days of the late 1840s Marx had reacted to the self-proclaimed isolation of a Belgian political journalist, Adolphe Bartels, in the following terms:

> M. Adolphe Bartels claims that public life is finished for him. In actual fact, he has returned to private life, and in order not to leave it, every time some political event comes to his attention, he limits himself to making protests and to proclaiming loudly that he believes he belongs to himself, that the movement takes place without him, M. Bartels, and against his will, M. A. Bartels, and that he has the right to refuse it his supreme sanction. One perceives that this is a way of taking part in public life like any other, and that by means of all these declarations, proclamations, protestations, the public man hides beneath the humble appearances of the private man. In this way the misunderstood and unrecognized genius reveals himself.[40]

So were Marx's own declarations of isolation sometimes—as Marx would surely have agreed—"a way of taking part in public life." He had not given up his public and political persona just because he had broken his ties with organized political groups. The pleasure Marx claimed to take in isolation was, like Bartels', also in part compensation for his own sense of being misunderstood and unrecognized.

When Marx wrote about Bartels, however, it was against the background of his conviction that although isolation was a common experience of thinkers, especially German ones, it was a condition that he himself had overcome. In fact, overcoming it had been a recurring project in his early life. In his doctoral dissertation, he had envisaged Hegelian philosophy as a remedy for the isolation from which he himself had suffered, because it replaced the subjective basis of previous philosophy with the objective notion of "the whole." Later, after Marx lost his faith in Hegel's power, he set forth a parallel role for historical materialism, in overcoming the separation from the real world into which even Feuerbach's attempt to achieve a philosophical realism necessarily fell. Just as each of these two moments was animated by the conviction that his earlier isolation had been overcome, so each was followed by a renewed experience of it.

That this was a recurring pattern in his personal history was something Marx partly acknowledged, and partly did not. In the autobiographical preface he wrote for *A Contribution to the Critique of Political Economy* in 1859, Marx recalled that, when the *Rheinische Zeitung* was about to be suppressed by the Prussian censor in 1843, he had eagerly seized the opportunity "to withdraw from the public stage into the study." The pleasure he claimed to take in his renewed isolation during the 1850s flowed from the same current of feelings as that earlier eagerness. Yet Marx did not refer to it in 1859 and, although he admitted his need for "a solution of the doubts which assailed me" at the time of his withdrawal from the *Rheinische Zeitung*, the autobiographical preface gave scarcely a hint of the worries and uncertainties that confronted Marx after 1851.[41] Privately, however, in his letters to Engels, Marx gave vent to his doubts.

In February 1863, following the Polish uprising, Marx announced to Engels: "So much is certain, the era of revolutions is now fairly opened again in Europe." The general situation was good. Yet his hopes were no longer those of 1848. "The pleasant delusions and the almost childish enthusiasm with which we greeted the revolution before February, 1848, are for the devil." The intervening years had carried off too many of the old comrades, and no replacements for them had come into view. "In addition we now know what a role stupidity plays in revolutions, and how they are exploited by scoundrels."[42] Two months later, in April, Marx reread Engels' book of 1844, *The Condition of the Working Class in England*, and found that he looked on its prophecies with grim nostalgia.

Rereading your book has made me regretfully aware of our increasing age. How freshly and passionately, with what bold anticipations and no learned and scientific doubts, the thing is still dealt with here! And the very illusion that the result will leap into the daylight of history tomorrow or the day after gives the whole thing a warmth and vivacious humor compared with which the later "gray in gray" makes a damned unpleasant contrast.[43]

For Marx, as for Hegel, the "gray in gray" testified not just to age but to the broken unity of experience and consciousness, the gulf between (as Hegel put it) "inward strivings and external reality." Marx's need was again—as we shall see when we come to his economic theory—for philosophy.

A twentieth-century evocation of the alternation between involvement and isolation in revolutionary politics—penned by a writer closely allied with Marxism at the time he wrote—reminds us of the dimensions with which Hegel had invested the problem. At the end of his novel of revolutionary striving and failure, *Man's Fate*, André Malraux offers a meditation on revolution and human destiny that recalls both Hegel's image of the self-conscious person who "wills his suffering" and Hegel's consciousness of the threat of madness that isolation brings. Old Gisors, the philosophical father of the defeated and now dead revolutionary leader, Kyo, concludes: "At bottom, the mind conceives man only in the eternal, and the consciousness of life can be nothing but anguish." The conflict between universal consciousness and individual existence, Gisors added, revealed that an element of insanity formed part of every human personality. "Every man is a madman . . . but what is a human destiny if not a life of effort to unite this madman and the universe." The effort, continually made, continually failed, for all men remained "separated from the universe whose heart beating somewhere up there in the shimmering light seized them and threw them back upon solitude."[44]

These themes of isolation, anguish, and absurdity that have flowered in twentieth-century existentialist philosophy have some of their main roots in Hegel, coming down through Kierkegaard, who had been Hegel's student. Marxism, which seemed devoted wholly to a different problematic in the late nineteenth century, has come back into contact with these existential dilemmas in the twentieth, thus reestablishing a connection between politics and personal experience that had been central in Hegel but is usually not noticed in Marx. Yet the problem of isolation and its consequences was part of Marx's personal and political history, just as it had been for Hegel and would be again for some of Marx's followers.

The consequence of isolation was not madness for Marx; nor had it been for Hegel; nor is it for most of us. Yet, in the 1850s, Marx's self-deceptive obsession with the notion that Palmerston was a Russian agent and the link it created between him and the "monomaniacal" eccentric Urquhart, reminds us that there were seeds of madness in him as in all human beings. Solitude and isolation, however much pleasure Marx might take in them, threatened—as he knew or had once known—to make those seeds grow. Isolation created the need for involvement.

Analyzing the consequences of isolation in "The Spirit of Christianity and its Fate," Hegel had noted that when a man whose inner character fitted him for isolation from the external world finally came into close touch with life outside himself, he would be limited to one of two relationships with objective reality: mastery or slavery, domination over things outside himself, or domination by them. This was the dichotomy Marx employed in his account of Russian history. To see what weight it carried in Marx's life we must look at what happened when the isolation of the 1850s ended, and he returned to active political life.

4. The Politics of Involvement

Marx's separation from organized political action ended in the fall of 1864, with the founding of the International Workingmen's Association (the First International) in London. The new organization arose out of currents that had grown up in British—and to a lesser extent French—workers' movements since the late 1850s; in part it was the delayed reaction to the economic crisis of 1857 Marx had looked for earlier, but in a form that differed markedly from the political currents of the late 1840s. Contributing to its foundation were strikes and demands for a shorter working day by London building trade workers beginning in 1859, contacts between British and French workers partly sponsored by Napoleon III, the cotton shortage engendered by the American Civil War, and the political issues of Negro emancipation, working-class suffrage, Polish liberation, and Italian unification. On September 28, 1864, a "monster meeting" to demonstrate international workers' solidarity was held in St. Martin's Hall, London, and with it the First International was born.[45]

The effective life of the new organization was eight years, although groups within it either tried to keep it alive or claimed to represent its continued existence for some time afterwards. It drew membership from all the major Western European countries (plus Russian exiles) and the United States. The Association held a series of international congresses, five in all; between times its affairs were directed by a General Council located in London, and by conferences—which were smaller and restricted versions of the Congresses—held on two occasions. Although it achieved a certain public recognition earlier, the First International gained its greatest notoriety with the revolutionary upheaval of the Paris Commune from March to May 1871. The International had little to do with the revolt that established the Commune, although some of its members were participants. The two came to be closely linked in the public mind, however, especially after Marx's pamphlet in defense of the Commune, *The Civil War in France*, appeared as an official communication of the General Council. By that time, however, the organization was being plagued by growing splits within the membership—we shall look into them in a moment—and, following the transfer of the General Council to New York at the Hague Congress of 1872, the First International was allowed to sink toward a quiet death.[46]

Marx played no part in the events leading to the International's foundation, but at the last minute he was asked to recommend a German worker to speak at the meeting in St. Martin's Hall (he sent an old member of the Communist League, Eccarius), and he himself agreed to sit "as a mute figure on the platform." He knew little in detail about most of the major participants, but because he recognized that the meeting brought together representatives of genuine and potentially powerful workers' groupings, he accepted membership in the Provisional General Council. Yet he moved slowly to make his influence felt, missing the Council's second meeting (he was ill), at which the International's program and principles were to be discussed, and attending the next only after an urgent appeal from Eccarius warned him that the draft program then being drawn up was sentimental and unsuitable. It was to replace that draft that Marx made his first major effort on behalf of the International, the Inaugural Address of the Working-Men's International Association.[47]

The Inaugural Address tells a good deal about Marx's attitude toward the International, and his relationship to it. He wrote to Engels that the difficulty in writing it had been "to frame the thing so that our view should appear in a form acceptable from the present standpoint of the workers' movement." The English leaders were moderates who saw their participation in the IWA as fully compatible with working alongside middle-class suffrage reformers. "It will take time before the reawakened movement allows the old boldness of speech. It will be necessary to be *fortiter in re, suaviter in modo*." Marx could not put forward his own views directly, but had to interpret the activity of others in a way that harmonized with their own consciousness, while still preserving his more developed and generalized understanding.[48]

In the Inaugural Address Marx did this by concentrating on the condition and achievements of the working classes since the 1840s. He recounted the failure of workers' living standards to keep pace with the economic progress of society as a whole since 1850. Without explicitly denying that any improvement had taken place, he insisted that "on the present false base, every fresh development of the productive powers of labor must tend to deepen social contrasts and point social antagonisms." Although workers had been able to do little to improve this situation since the defeats of 1848, Marx pointed to the British Ten Hours Bill (of

1847) and the growth of the cooperative movement as signs of progress. He gave these advances strong support, calling the ten-hour day "the first time that in broad daylight the political economy of the middle class succumbed to the political economy of the working class," and declaring that the value of cooperative experiments "cannot be overrated." Yet such reformist measures were not sufficient, for "the lords of land and the lords of capital" would fight against the emancipation of labor; hence "To conquer political power has therefore become the great duty of the working classes." Marx ended with an echo of the *Communist Manifesto* that not all his readers would recognize: "Proletarians of all countries, Unite!"[49]

The Inaugural Address is sometimes taken as a sign that Marx's politics had grown more reformist during the 1850s.[50] But to read it in that way (apart from neglecting what he told Engels about it) is to forget what his political strategy had been before. Since the late 1840s, when Marx began to work actively in political organizations, he had always recognized that existing working-class movements, however undeveloped from his own perspective, were the necessary expressions of real conditions; hence they had to be accepted on their own terms. Only through common experience and struggle could they come together in a movement that represented the generalized interest of the proletariat as a whole. It is true that socialists with orientations fundamentally different from Marx's, notably Proudhon, saw in his attempts to internationalize the workers' movement a veiled attempt to impose his own doctrines. Proudhon was correct to the extent that Marx expected the workers' movement to develop toward his own perspectives. But that evolution required an experience of unifying organization and action: it could not take place immediately or by fiat. Thus, in the *Communist Manifesto* Marx defined the role of the communists differently in different countries, according to the diversity of social and political conditions that shaped the situation in each. "In what relation do the communists stand in relation to the proletarians as a whole?" The answer was that "The communists do not form a separate party opposed to other working-class parties. They have no interests separate and apart from those of the proletariat as a whole. They do not set up any sectarian principles of their own, by which to shape and mould the proletarian movement." In each national context the communists would join the struggle on its own terms, while at the same time working to "point out and bring to the front the common interests of the entire proletariat, independently of all nationality." Likewise: "In the various stages of development which the struggle of the working class against the bourgeoisie has to pass through, they always and everywhere represent the interests of the movement as a whole."[51]

These were still Marx's expectations in the time of the International. In March 1869 he wrote to Engels:

Since the stage of development of the different workers' sections in the same country, and of the working class in the different countries is necessarily very different, the real movement necessarily expresses itself in very different theoretical forms. The community of action, which the International Workers' Association calls to life, the exchange of ideas through the different organs of the sections in all countries, finally the direct debates in the general Congresses will gradually create a common theoretical program for the international workers' movement.

Earlier, in 1866, Marx told Kugelmann that in the program he wrote for the London delegates to the Geneva Congress of the International, "I limited it intentionally to such points as would allow the immediate understanding and cooperation of the workers, and would provide immediate nurture and impetus for the needs of the class struggle and the organization of the workers into a class." (In the *Communist Manifesto*, too, Marx had defined the party's immediate aim as forming the proletariat into a class.) In 1868 Marx characterized the difference between his own general point of view and Lassalle's "sectarian" one as arising first from Lassalle's failure to consider that conditions in France and England were different from those in Germany and that, more basically, Lassalle, "instead of looking among the genuine elements of the class movement for the real basis of his agitation, . . . wanted to prescribe the course to be followed by this movement according to a doctrinaire recipe." Such sects had eventually to be merged in the wider movement, where whatever had general validity in their programs would serve to enrich the larger struggle. Explaining what he thought the General Council provided for the British labor movement that English workers did not possess by themselves, Marx listed revolutionary enthusiasm and "the spirit of generalization."[52]

The policy of mixing the particular character of each national movement with the spirit of generalization worked very well for Marx in the first years of the International's existence. The historians of the International in Britain attribute much of the appeal it made there to the fact that it recognized existing struggles in their own terms, and made no attempt to preach unfamiliar doctrines.[53] Within the General Council Marx came to exercise recognized leadership, and his moderation and tact especially won the English working-class leaders to him. Without Marx's presence on the General Council, the International might well have foundered on the inability of the British members to understand and deal with the rivalries between French Republicans and Proudhonians, as some of the English leaders were aware. When French Proudhonians attempted to establish the principle that only workers—and not middle-class intellectuals—should be eligible to be delegates to the Association's Congresses, the English carpenter and union leader W. R. Cremer, who had been one of the founders, insisted that the movement owed much to people who were not manual workers. "Among those members I will mention one only, Citizen Marx, who has devoted all his life to the triumph of the working classes."[54]

Marx understood the extent of his influence, and in September 1867 he wrote to Engels about the public attention the organization was beginning to attract, adding: "And in the next revolution, which is perhaps nearer than it appears, *we* (you and I) will have this powerful engine *in our hand*. Compare this with the results of Mazzini's, etc. operations since 30 years!" It had all been done without money, and in spite of the intrigues of Proudhonians and Mazzinians, the jealousy of the English, and inadequacies of the German sects. "We can be very content!"[55]

Nonetheless, as the hostility Marx showed to some of his fellow Internationalists in that letter indicated, the union between particular national groups or currents and the general aims Marx saw within the organization as a whole was not easy to maintain. The power of particular circumstances and traditions was not lessened by the attempt to merge them with the common aims of workers everywhere. When the next revolution did break out—the uprising of the Paris Commune in 1871—it seemed at first to strengthen the International, but quickly weakened it instead by underlining the divergences between various national factions and parties. The events of 1871-72 dissolved "the general" into a welter of contrasting and competing groups. They also forced Marx into positions he would not have chosen, bringing him to withdraw from the International and effectively to put an end to it.

To understand how this came about we must look for a moment at the situation of the International in individual countries, beginning with Germany. It was in his own native land that Marx expected strongest support for his views for, unlike the English, the German workers possessed "heads for generalizing" that would not suffer sectarian leadership for long.[56] In fact, however, the retreat from involvement with the International by the German workers' organizations after 1871 was one of the major factors that undermined Marx's position within it.

During the 1860s the working-class movement in Germany began to acquire the organizational strength and grass-roots support that would make it the leader of European socialism in the following decades. The seeds of its growth, however, were also the source of its later divisions. Two quite separate movements sprang up, and the history of the International in Germany was largely the story of the competition between them. The division was at once geographical and political, expressing the diversity of radical political traditions in long-fragmented Germany.[57]

One group, the General Union of German Workers (Allgemeine Deutsche Arbeiterverein or ADAV), founded in 1863, was centered in

Prussia, where its leader was Ferdinand Lassalle, with whom Marx had a long but deeply troubled and ambivalent friendship. Lassalle was an old Hegelian who retained enough of Hegel's idealization of the state to make cooperation between the workers' movement and the Prussian government a central element in his program. That Bismarck's policy before 1866 set him at odds with middle-class liberals provided an added basis of attraction. Lassalle's politics were unconditionally antibourgeois, and during 1863 he actually held several meetings with Bismarck to discuss possible cooperation between the two. (Bismarck concluded that Lassalle had too little to offer, and broke the meetings off.)

The second organization was called the Social Democratic Workers' Party (or Eisenach Party after the foundation meeting it held in that city in 1869), but its roots were in an earlier grouping called the League of German Workers' Clubs (Verband Deutscher Arbeitervereine). The leading personalities in this group were Wilhelm Liebknecht, a 48-er whom Marx had come to know well in London, but who returned to Germany in 1862, and August Bebel, a self-educated carpenter whom Liebknecht tried to instruct in Marx's ideas as he understood them. Neither the Eisenach Party nor the earlier League was really a Marxist organization, however. Both grew primarily out of the native radical traditions of Saxony and southwestern Germany, in which cooperation between middle-class and artisan groups was much more marked than in Berlin, and the resulting orientation more often suggested radical democracy than socialism. One passion that united the otherwise loosely connected groups that formed the League of German Workers' Clubs was opposition to the growth of Prussian power in Germany. Liebknecht and Bebel were firm anti-Prussianists, and this stance, combined with the many links their organization maintained with middle-class radicals, placed them at the opposite pole of radical politics from the Lassalleans.

During the first years after the founding of the International in 1864, neither of the German groups showed much interest in working closely with it. The Lassalleans were momentarily disorganized following their leader's death in a duel in 1864 and, although Marx tried briefly to work with the group's new head, J. B. von Schweitzer, contrasting orientations and mutual suspicion soon brought the relationship to a close. On the other side Liebknecht showed little interest in the International, being too deeply involved in resistance to the growth of Prussian power. Only around 1868 did this situation change. By then Bismarck had moved closer to the German middle class (following his great triumph over Austria in 1866-67), leaving the Lassalleans more isolated. In addition, the prestige of the International was growing: its activity in support of strikes made its value increasingly apparent to workers; the first volume of *Capital*, published in 1867, brought Marx's name to the attention of Germans;

and a campaign of propaganda in favor of the International conducted by Johann Philip Becker brought the organization to the notice of many who would not otherwise have heard of it.[58]

In this context Schweitzer turned to Marx in an attempt to make up for some of the outside support he had lost through Bismarck's rapprochement with the liberals. Liebknecht, fearing that the prestige of the International would pull increasing numbers of workers into the Lassallean camp, moved to have the League of German Workers' Clubs declare in favor of the International too. At its foundation conference at Eisenach in 1869, the Social Democratic Workers' Party declared itself to be a branch of the International. In the meantime a factional dispute within the Lassallean group led those people within it who opposed any deviation from Lassalle's original principles to break away from the Internationalists, leaving Liebknecht and Bebel's party as the major representative of the International in Germany.

Harmony between the Eisenachers and the General Council in London was never complete, but from 1869 until 1871 Liebknecht provided Marx with significant support, sending sympathetic delegates to the International Congresses. That Marx was able to keep the upper hand against the Proudhonians and Bakuninists who contested his influence during these years owed much to the International's strength in Germany. But this situation ended when events took a critical turn in 1870-71. Bebel and Liebknecht refused to support Bismarck in the Franco-Prussian war and, once the uprising of the Paris Commune had taken place, their position on the war added fuel to conservative and liberal attacks on the Eisenachers as the German tools of an anarchistic, terroristic, and foreign-dominated group. The link with the International had turned from an advantage for the German party into a serious threat to its political position. In the 1871 elections, all but one of the socialist deputies to the Diet of the German Confederation lost their seats. Themselves imprisoned for a time, Bebel and Liebknecht began to realize that their party was the only grouping within the International with a real and effective national organization. Identification with an international workers' movement, which might support radical ventures like the Commune and frighten away the solid base of support being built up for an organized workers' party within Germany, was a dangerous luxury the Germans could not afford. Liebknecht sent delegates to the Hague Congress of 1872 to help Marx against the Bakuninists, but the time when Marx could look to Germany as a major support within the organization seemed very nearly at an end.

The erosion of support for the International in Germany corresponded in time with other tremors that undermined the organization's foundation. The most visible of these was the personal struggle between Marx and Bakunin that culminated at the Hague Congress in 1872. Bakunin's challenge to Marx would not have toppled the whole structure, however, if his presence had not served to amplify and deepen divisions within the membership, which the outbreak of the Commune also served to intensify.

A physically enormous and personally charming man, Bakunin was a romantic and impractical but deeply committed and effective mountain of revolutionary enthusiasm. He shared with Marx the reputation of long dedication to the overthrow of existing society, to which was added the nimbus of several years confinement in Czarist prisons. Formed as he was in an East European context, Bakunin gave less weight to economic transformation than Marx. He placed greater faith in particular measures of social improvement—notably the abolition of the right to inherit property—than did Marx, with his emphasis on the basic determinants of social organization. His scenario of revolution also gave a larger role to peasants and artisans than did Marx's emphasis on the proletariat. His most important doctrinal contrast with Marx, however, was his sharply focused opposition to political organization and authority as such, and his denial that the communist abolition of private property would dissolve the state's despotic power by itself. Ending enslavement and exploitation required an uncompromising rejection of the very principle of political authority, in favor of local communal autonomy and social libertarianism. His aim was revolution and only revolution, and neither social reforms nor the establishment of a working-class political party were acceptable intermediate aims for him. In contrast to what he called state communism, Bakunin was a collectivist and an anarchist.[59]

Despite the differences between them, Bakunin respected Marx for his theoretical brilliance, and the two hit it off well when they met for the first time in sixteen years during the fall of 1864 in London. At one point the Russian even declared himself to be Marx's disciple, and after the first volume of *Capital* appeared in 1867 Bakunin thought for a time of translating it. But as he began to spread his own views and set up organizations in Italy and Switzerland in the later 1860s, Bakunin's collisions with Marx began. Toward the end of 1868 Bakunin, with some of his disciples, founded an International Alliance of Social Democracy with a program calling for "the equalization of classes" and the abolition of inheritance. Branches were set up in Switzerland, Italy, Southern France, and Spain. In spite of Bakunin's antiauthoritarian principles the new body had a central organization, which assured his own personal leadership. Hence when Bakunin requested that the organization as a whole become part of the International in 1869, Marx—not unreasonably—feared that to admit it would create "a state within a state." The proposal would have left Bakunin's groups with an international structure of their own, unlike any of the other sections of the IWA, whose ties derived from the General Council and the Congresses. A compromise was worked out, which allowed the members of Bakunin's association to join the International as individuals, and in theory the Alliance of Social Democracy was dissolved; in fact much of its separate identity remained.

Bakunin's agitation had its most disruptive effect on the International in the country where socialism was probably spreading most rapidly around 1870: Italy. Dissatisfaction with the Piedmontese monarchy's success in unifying the country without providing democratic institutions helped to channel some of the enthusiasm that had previously nurtured the cause of national unification into more radical directions. The chief symbol of this dissatisfaction with the *Risorgimento* was Giuseppe Mazzini. When Mazzini condemned the Paris Commune in 1871, Italians who saw in the French uprising a continuation of the same libertarian insurrectionism his Action Party had once represented moved to identify themselves with more radical leadership. It was to Bakunin that most of them finally turned.

Bakunin's early Italian contacts were made before he himself felt the need to clarify his differences with Marx, and at first few people in Italy seem to have been aware that any important contrast between them existed. Even in 1871, when the Paris Commune drew attention to the International, and Bakunin defended it against Mazzini's attacks, it was not clear that Bakunin represented a different position within the International from Marx's. The upsurge in the International's prestige in Italy pleased Marx and Engels before it began to trouble them. Engels, who was the organization's secretary for Italy, increased and intensified his contacts there, and hoped to find support for the General Council in the new Italian sections.

This hope dissolved, however, as leading Italian radicals came to be drawn into the affairs of the Association, and began to understand what the Londoners stood for and what Bakunin represented. Especially in the South, a native tradition of antiauthoritarian insurrectionism, linked to the name of Carlo Pisacane, a former Mazzinian who had died in an attempt to set off the revolutionary bonfire in 1857, prepared the ground for Bakunin's ideas. Both Engels' main contacts in Naples, Carmelo Palladino and Carlo Cafiero, were drawn to Bakunin's rejection of authority and his political abstentionism. Palladino decided against the General Council before the end of 1871, and in the summer of 1872 Cafiero, too, was converted to Bakunin's side in the dispute. Thus, by the time the Congress of the IWA met at the Hague in the fall of that year, Marx and Engels had recognized that the General Council could not command support against Bakunin in Italy.[60]

In England, too, the Association's earlier unity was breaking down. Until the fall of 1871 the General Council in London had been the only body to coordinate the activities of the various English branches of the IWA, but some English leaders, notably John Hales, had long sought to establish a British Federal Council that would give more independence to the British membership. In September 1871 the General Council agreed to this proposal, and the British Federal Council was set up in the following month. Why Marx, who had long resisted such a step, now went along with it, remains unclear. Some indications suggest he expected the new body to support the General Council against Bakunin; but it is also possible that he had already come to regard the days of the International as numbered, and allowed the British sections to create a separate organization in order to preserve them from foreign influences that were not his own. Optimism and pessimism succeeded each other quickly in Marx's mind at this time. In any case, the British Federal Council became a center of intrigues among rival English leaders, and a platform from which the special nostrums—Marx would have said sectarianism—of current British leaders were proclaimed: land, credit, and currency reform. Hales himself was quite content to let the long-term social goals of the International recede quietly into the background. Moreover, although he had as little in common with the Bakuninists as any prominent Internationalist, during 1872 Hales adopted their slogan of opposition to the "centralizing and despotic power" of Marx and the General Council. It was not anarchist doctrine that made that slogan so powerful within the International in 1871-72, but the centrifugal forces that were breaking down the organization into its component parts.[61]

That this fragmentation was indeed the chief reason for the First International's collapse has not always been recognized; in particular, some observers have blamed the campaign of defamation and repression launched by conservative governments following the Commune. That campaign certainly weakened the labor movement in France and Germany for a time, but during 1871 and 1872 the International was expanding in spite of it. Engels recognized that growth, not contraction, was what tore the International apart. In 1874 he observed that the various groups had been able to unite in the first place only because the theoretical position of each had been very unclear in 1864. "The first great success was bound to explode this naive conjunction of all factions. This success was the Commune. . . . When, thanks to the Commune, the International had become a moral force in Europe, the row at once began. Every trend wanted to exploit the success for itself. Disintegration, which was inevitable, set in." Most modern students of the International's history now subscribe to Engels' view.[62]

In this way Marx's belief that the specific forms taken by the workers' movement in the various European countries could be joined together through the spirit of generalization—that practice could be united with theory—received a severe practical test from 1864 to 1872, just as his conviction that the underlying shape of historical development was becoming visible on the surface of society had been tested between 1848 and 1851. Exactly what sort of dilemmas this created for Marx himself, and for his manner of participating in politics, can be seen if we turn now to the the positions he took—and was made to take—on the two crucial and intertwined issues of these years: the Commune, and the organizational structure of the International.

Although Marx's first reactions to the possibility of a revolutionary outbreak in Paris during 1871 were cautious and even sceptical, he was soon caught up in the excitement of the moment, abandoning most of his earlier doubts and hesitations. Highly pleased at the prospect that the defeat of France by Prussia would finally put an end to the regime of Napoleon III, he recognized that Bonaparte's fall might spark a Parisian uprising. "If a revolution breaks out in Paris, the question will be whether it will have the means and leaders to put up a serious resistance to the Prussians," he told Engels. "One can't hide the fact that the twenty-year Bonapartist farce has brought enormous demoralization. One is hardly justified in counting on revolutionary heroism. What do you think about it?" Ten days later he said he had not slept for four nights running because of rheumatism "and all the time I fantasize about Paris, etc."[63] But he concluded that the situation called for restraint, not revolutionary action. When he drafted an address on behalf of the General Council to the membership of the International at the beginning of September 1870, he pictured the task of French workers as assuring the permanence of the Republic that had been proclaimed to replace the Second Empire. With the Germans at the gates of Paris, "The French workmen must perform their duties as citizens; but, at the same time, they must not allow themselves to be deluded by the national *souvenirs* or 1792, as the French peasants allowed themselves to be deluded by the national *souvenirs* of the First Empire. They have not to recapitulate the past, but to build up the future."[64] At the same time Marx told Engels that a representative of the General Council was going to Paris to advise the French against "making stupidities in the name of the *International*. 'They' want to bring down the provisional government, establish a commune of Paris, name Pyat French ambassador to London, etc." Reporting on French affairs to a Belgian socialist, Marx declared that "It is our duty not to deceive ourselves by illusions," and added: "The misfortune of the French, workers included, consists in *great memories*." Events might finally have to make an end of "this reactionary cult of the past."[65]

Marx had not lost his enthusiasm for revolution: the basis of his moderation during August and September of 1870 was tactical. It was the weakness of the French workers' position that should have imposed calm and patience on them: the "national *souvenirs* of 1792" were memories of military glory, the illusions they fostered were visions of French armed victories.[66] Once the Commune was finally proclaimed in mid-March 1871, Marx saw his own earlier caution as superseded by events. Within three days of the Commune's proclamation Marx sent a letter to the London *Times*, denying reports of his opposition to the French actions that had found their way into the press. On April 12 he wrote to Kugelmann praising the heroism of the Parisians. "They rise, beneath Prussian bayonets, as if there had never been a war between France and Germany and the enemy were not still at the gates of Paris! History has no like example of their greatness! If they are defeated only their 'good nature' will be to blame."[67]

A few days later he added—quite in the spirit of his earlier determination to join each struggle of the working classes, regardless of the form in which it might be expressed—that one could not judge the significance of revolutionary events merely according to the likelihood of their success. "World history would indeed be very easy to make if the struggle were taken up only on condition of infallibly favorable chances." Accidents that speeded up or delayed the process always played a part. "The decisively unfavorable 'accident' this time is by no means to be sought in the general conditions of French society, but in the presence of the Prussians in France and their position right before Paris."[68] In the draft of what would become "The Civil War in France" that Marx began at the same time, he presented social evolution and political revolution as inseparable partners in historical development, very much in the way he had always regarded them since 1845. The working classes, he explained, knew that their emancipation could "only be the progressive work of time," that it required "a long process of development," and that the work would "be again and again relented and impeded by the resistance of vested interests and class antagonisms." However, the workers knew "at the same time that great strides may be [made] at once through the Communal form of political organization and that the time has come to begin that movement for themselves and mankind."[69]

Marx's enthusiasm even led him at times to lose sight of the hopelessness of the Communards' position. In the first outline of "The Civil War in France" he wrote that if the Commune had only been established in November 1870—a time when Marx had still regarded the idea of it as a dangerous illusion—it would have been imitated all over France, "altogether changed the character of the war," and "electrified the producing masses in the old and the new world."[70] In May he wrote to two of the leaders in Paris that the Commune was wasting too much time in trivialities and quarrels, and that other influences were present besides the workers. Nonetheless: "None of this would matter if you were able to make up for lost time." And in June Marx exclaimed in a letter, "If only the Commune had listened to my warnings! I advised its members to fortify the northern side of the heights of Montmartre, the Prussian side, and they still had time to do this."[71]

The excitement of the Commune brought Marx to reconsider some of the views of revolution he had expressed in the pessimistic *Eighteenth Brumaire*, allowing him to revive some of the more optimistic perspectives of *The Class Struggles*. Whereas in 1852 Marx had depicted the bourgeois party of order as dissolving in the face of working-class challenges to it, he now described it as dividing into its component factions only later, "as soon as its rule seems secured (guaranteed) by the destruction of the material revolutionary forces."[72] Thus, Marx revived his old notion that social conflict exalted explicit class formations above all other social and political groupings: only social peace interrupted society's polarization in class terms. Whereas in 1852 Marx had fulfilled the needs of his theory by making Napoleon's regime rest on a class that had no major role to play in the larger historical drama, the peasants, the renewal of conflict allowed him to return to the main lines of the plot. The Empire only "professed to rest upon the peasantry. . . . In reality, it was the only form of government possible at a time when the bourgeoisie had already lost, and the working class had not yet acquired, the faculty of ruling the nation." By contrast, the Commune appeared as "the political form at last discovered under which to work out the emancipation of labor."[73]

The spectacle of Paris in revolution also reopened the question of whether modern conditions revealed or veiled the underlying reality of social life. In one of his early drafts he contrasted Paris, "full of heroic reality," with the government at Versailles, "a world of antiquated shams and accumulated lies." The Commune's existence brought the reality into view: it "presupposed the nonexistence of monarchy, which, in Europe at least, is the normal incumbrance and indispensable cloak of class rule." Moreover, the apologies for existing society provoked by the revolt tried to defend "Wages Slavery . . . as if capitalist society was still in its purest state of virgin innocence, with its antagonisms still undeveloped, with its delusions still unexploded, with its prostitute realities not yet laid bare."[74] These comments recalled the old link between revolution and revelation; if Marx did not develop the theme with the clarity and confidence with which he had treated it in the *Communist Manifesto* and *The Class Struggles*, we will find the reasons for that when we come to his economic theory.

Whatever inner doubts he may have retained, the Paris Commune allowed Marx the exhilaration of politics conducted on terms that did not require the sorts of compromises he had been making in the International since 1864. He no longer needed to speak *suaviter in modo* in order to be *fortiter in re*. At a meeting in the fall of 1871 he declared that the Commune had shown the way toward the abolition of capitalism, and that the path led through a "proletarian dictature."[75] Revolution, however much it responded to the particular situation that called it forth, raised the general questions at issue between classes in an explicit way. Yet, the Commune had a number of particular characteristics and features that made Marx's relationship to it more problematic than these enthusiastic comments suggest.

A basic uncertainty about the Commune was whether it was really socialist in spirit. To call it—as Marx did—the political form for effecting the emancipation of labor seemed to imply that it was. Yet ten years later Marx admitted flatly in a letter that "the majority of the Commune was in no wise socialist, nor could it be."[76] This was not a recognition that dawned on Marx only later, for in one of his drafts he wrote of the Commune's social measures that "there is nothing socialist in them except their tendency." Even in the final version of his pamphlet Marx admitted that the explicit social changes envisioned by the Commune were limited, arguing that "The great social measure of the Commune was its own working existence."[77] But the way Marx was read is well illustrated by what Engels wrote to Bernstein in 1884: "That in *The Civil War* the *unconscious* tendencies of the Commune were put down to its credit as more or less conscious plans was justified and necessary under the circumstances."[78]

Some of those plans and tendencies were closer to anarchism than to socialism as Marx understood it. The Commune's leadership reflected the continuing strength within the French left of ideas represented by Blanqui and Proudhon, with their respective lack of emphasis on economic development and political organization in the manner conceived by Marx. The Communards thought more in terms of communal independence or revolutionary activity itself than about the social organization of productive forces. In his account of the Commune's intentions, Marx did not hide its strong antiauthoritarian and antistatist emphasis, which had emerged more clearly in its pronouncements than had socialism as such. The Commune's existence in Paris implied that "the old centralized government would in the provinces, too, have to give way to the self-government of the producers." Local autonomy would be established as the basis of a new form of national unity, represented "by the destruction of the State power which claimed to be the embodiment of that unity independent of, and superior to, the nation itself, from which it was but a parasitic excrescence." The Commune sought to regenerate France by restoring "to the social body all the forces hitherto absorbed by the State parasite feeding upon, and clogging the free movement of, society."[79]

To be sure, Marx made clear his conviction that only the emancipation of the working class could genuinely liberate society from the state's despotism, and that state domination was in reality class domination. Nonetheless, he caught the special spirit of French radicalism better than he expressed his own general point of view when he wrote in one of the drafts: "It was a Revolution against the *State* itself, of this supernaturalist abortion of society, a resumption by the people for the people of their own social life." That Marx recognized the possibilities for misinterpretation this created appeared a few pages later, when he praised the political form of the Commune while still reserving a place for the independent development of social forces outside it. "The Commune is not the social movement of the working class and, therefore, of a general regeneration of mankind, but the organized means of action." Marx did not want his account of the Paris insurgence to justify those who believed that mere revolutionary action could effect the regeneration of mankind. Emancipation had to be prepared by the social movement of the working class.[80] Yet, given the reality of what had taken place, the barrier Marx tried to construct against the opposite interpretation was not an easy one to maintain.

Marx had taken the Paris Commune as he had taken each separate form of working-class protest and aspiration during the period of the International. It was a genuine and necessary expression of the French working-class struggle, which had both to be accepted on its own terms and leavened with the spirit of generalization that arose from an understanding of the common needs and aims of workers everywhere. But the effect of Marx's pamphlet had been to lend the prestige of "the general" to a particular view of revolution, one that emphasized revolutionary spontaneity and antiauthoritarianism to the exclusion of the long-term political activity and organization Marx himself believed the victory of socialism required. This was precisely the view being championed at the same time against Marx by Bakunin and others within the International who believed that Marx's control over the organization was too tight.

How easily Marx's praise of the Commune might be turned against the theoretical and personal position he was seeking to defend in the International can be seen from a letter Bakunin sent to one of his adherents in 1872:

> Since 1868, the time of my entry into the International, I have called for a crusade against the principle of authority itself and preached the abolition of states, including in the same malediction that so-called revolutionary dictatorship which the Jacobins of the International, the disciples of Marx, recommend to us as a provisional means—absolutely necessary, they claim—for the consolidation and organization of the people's victory. I have always thought and I think that such a dictatorship, an unexpected resurrection of the state, can have no other effect than to kill the vitality and the truly popular force of the revolution.[81]

The distance between such a view of revolution, and the view Marx himself gave of the Commune did not seem great to some members of the International. Engels tried to counteract just such an interpretation of the Commune in January 1872, when he wrote to an officer of a Turin workers' association that "phrases like 'authority' and centralization" were much misused. "I know of nothing more authoritarian than a revolution," Engels insisted, and went on: "It was the want of centralization and authority that cost the Paris Commune its life. . . . And when people speak to me of authority and centralization as of two things deserving condemnation in all possible circumstances, then in my view those who speak that way either don't know what a revolution is, or are revolutionaries only in word."[82]

Marx had long been aware that his leadership of the International provoked attacks on his "personal dictatorship," and in August 1868 he had seriously considered letting the management of the organization pass to somebody else. Now that the Germans were joining the Association in force, thus reducing the relative weight of the Proudhonists, "it is my plan to move the *General Council* to Geneva for the next year, and have us here function only as British Council. It seems to me a prudent step, if the proposal comes from us. At the same time it will show the asses in Paris etc. that we are in no way anxious for this pleasant dictatorship." Engels took the proposal quite seriously, but warned Marx against it. It reminded him of the transfer of the Communist League's Central Committee to Cologne in 1852, which had effectively put an end to the League. It might put the International's affairs in hands that could not take care of them, and left open the possibility that other cities—less friendly to Marx's views—might be suggested.[83] The idea was dropped, but it showed that Marx had no desire to keep a tight grip on the reins as long as the road seemed fairly smooth.

From the Basel Congress of 1869, however, when Bakunin and his adherents began to offer their own views of the International's program and organization, Marx started to take a less relaxed attitude. In Marx's eyes it was Bakunin who was trying to establish a dictatorship. But the result was a campaign to strengthen the control of the General Council—in London, to be sure—over the local sections. The strategy culminated in a private conference of the International—held in place of the regular Congress that had not met since Basel—at London in the fall of 1871. Here the principle was proclaimed—more clearly than in the Inaugural Address—that the emancipation of labor required the formation of a specifically working-class political party. In addition, the General Council was to be recognized as a central executive committee that could function as a governing body.[84]

In the context of the antiauthoritarian excitement engendered by the Commune, this attempt to create discipline in the International made

Marx extremely vulnerable to attacks by those who shared Bakunin's point of view. In response to the London Conference, they held a meeting at Sonvillier, in the Swiss Jura, and issued a circular declaring: "We accuse the members of the General Council of trying to introduce the principle of authority into the International so as to bring about the triumph of their personal point of view." Authority, as experience showed a thousand times, always corrupted "those in whose hands it is placed."[85] That these charges expressed the dominant mood within the International by the end of 1871 is shown by the progress Bakunin's views continued to make in Italy and elsewhere, and by Marx's decision to assure that the General Council not fall into anarchist hands by packing it off to New York in the fall of 1872.

We can now see how events had dealt with Marx's faith that social development, cooperation, discussion, and the experience of common struggle would bring the diverse segments of the workers' movement to unity around a common theoretical program. Instead of being able to stand on central ground common to all the groups in the International, by late in 1871 Marx found himself trying to occupy both flanks in a formation whose center was hard to find. He was led to foster both a greater degree of revolutionary spontaneity and a tighter and more disciplined form of working-class political organization than he actually favored. His defense of the revolutionary spontaneity of the Commune made the International a dangerous ally for those of its members in Germany who feared identification with anarchistic violence as a threat to their political organization. At the same time, his attempt to hold a tighter rein on the International itself convinced many members that his leadership was stifling the free expression of the movement in all its forms.

The pattern of Marx's dilemma would reappear in the later history of socialist movements. George Lichtheim has analyzed the history of Marxism in modern France as a series of attempts to forge unity between persisting traditions of social reformism on the one hand, and anarchist radicalism (in its modern form, Syndicalism) on the other. As long as historical conditions seem to allow the unification of these diverse sections of the working class through common action and discussion, then authoritarian coercion has not been a necessary part of Marxist politics. It is at moments when the combination of diverse elements begins to come unstuck that authoritarian tendencies emerge, drawing on elements of revolutionary Jacobinism.[86] In much the same way did the specter of an unwished-for personal authority haunt Marx as the International fell apart into sections emphasizing successful organization on the one hand and revolutionary spontaneity on the other.

In Marx's own case, it must be added, the need to exercise personal authority arose alongside its apparent opposite: the desire to withdraw from political life. The proposal to transfer the General Council to Geneva in 1868 would have meant Marx's withdrawal from the International's leading position. Despite the arguments Engels offered against such a move then, Marx renewed his proposal that the General Council be taken out of London—this time to Brussels—as late as June 1870, after the Bakuninist challenge had become serious. Echoing what he had told Engels in 1868, Marx advanced the view that "We must not let it crop up as a privilege that the Council sits in London."[87] The motion was defeated, and in any case Marx probably intended it mainly as a tactical move against those who used the charge of dictatorship against him. But it expressed the same willingness to have the burden taken off his shoulders that he had voiced in 1868, a desire that was fulfilled after 1872.

These proposals all recall the pattern that alternated Marx's periods of participation in active political life with periods of withdrawal into the study, which had been played out in 1843, and again after 1851. Marx felt the desire to abandon active involvement with the International almost from the beginning of his work for it: the time it took interfered with finishing *Capital*. At the end of July 1865 Marx told the members of the General Council that he was going on a journey, and would not be able to attend any meetings. This deception was necessary, he explained to Engels, "in order to have at least fourteen days wholly free and undisturbed for pushing on with the work." Four weeks later he reported that the people in the International had found out he had not been away after all, and summoned him to a meeting. The ruse had been in vain, for "The four weeks during which I disappeared were totally spoilt" by illness. At the end of the same year he confessed to Engels that the International and its affairs "weigh like an incubus on me, and I would be happy to be able to shake it off." (Marx's feelings about his book were no happier in that year: on August 5 he complained that it "weighs on me like a nightmare.")[88]

In 1866 Marx made progress on the book in spite of the time he gave to the International, and in the next year Volume One of *Capital* was published. His desire to withdraw receded from view for some time, although the proposals to transfer the General Council out of London in 1868 and 1870 probably reflect its survival. Marx made his decision to end his work for the General Council once and for all in the spring of 1872. The Hague Congress would mark "the end of my slavery," he told a Belgian socialist. "Afterwards I shall become a free man," taking on no more administrative functions. To his Russian friend Danielson he wrote on the same day that "I can no longer afford—for some time at least—to combine two sorts of business of so very different a character."[89]

Thus, within months of the London Conference at which Marx had sought to increase the authority of the General Council and at the very time that he was growing more authoritarian in the eyes of many members of the International, he was also planning his withdrawal. The line from authoritarian control to withdrawal traced one of the coordinates of Marx's political activity. The line from political organization and social reformism to revolutionary spontaneity marked the other. Ideally, Marx's political position existed at the intersection of these two coordinates. Taking that point as center, a circle could be traced that drew all forms of working-class and socialist political activity into a unified whole, through the force of historical development and without the necessity of authoritarian coercion. Yet only history could draw such a magic circle, and if events proved recalcitrant, Marx could be pushed out to occupy the extreme points on the lines instead of the center where they intersected. In 1872 his ability to participate in politics collapsed at the extremes of authoritarianism and withdrawal, organization and spontaneity.

Various students of Marx have sought to identify his political theory and practice exclusively with one or another of these alternatives. Out of these attempts have come images of a Marx too impractical to have an impact on day-to-day politics, and a Marx totally devoted to political *praxis*; a Marx who opened the way for Leninist authoritarianism and a Marx committed to social-democratic reformism.[90] Particular aspects of either Marx's thought or his life may lend support to each of these pictures of him, but all are one-sided. Marx's project was not to choose among these alternatives but to transcend them, and the drama in his political activity was the confrontation between the animating spirit of generalization that was to dissolve these fixed oppositions and the heavy weight of the material circumstances that kept them in being. The real question about Marx's politics is not whether he was an authoritarian or a democrat (he was, at particular moments, both), but how his vision of overcoming the dichotomy between coercion and resignation fared in the real empirical world of politics. That his interpreters have claimed his support for both social-democratic and Leninist visions of politics is a sign that the alternatives Marx sought to avoid and encompass have remained the poles of political orientation for his followers, but that like him, they have not succeeded in transcending them.

CHAPTER NINE

Misery and Philosophy: Marx in his Family

1. The Long Dark Night of Exile

MARX lived just over half his life in London, some thirty-four years. Whereas his participation in politics alternated with periods of abstention from public activity, Marx's private life as husband and father underwent no similar interruptions. That life was one of recurring suffering, privation, and sorrow. The story has often been told; yet in order to understand Marx's political and intellectual activity within the larger context of his life we must see how they were related to his personal and family history.

The years of Marx's London life fall into three periods. During most of the first, which lasted until the fall of 1856, Marx lived in two—at times three—rooms in a crowded and impoverished section of Soho, having moved there (after being evicted from a larger house in Chelsea) in 1851. The family then consisted of Marx himself, his wife, their servant Helene Demuth (called Lenchen), and between two and four children. Three Marx children—out of the six born alive—died between 1850 and 1856. In September of that year the second period of the family's London life began, with their move to a more comfortable house near Hampstead Heath, the first of a series of houses the Marxes would inhabit in North London. The number of the children was always three in this period: the surviving daughters Jenny (born in Paris in 1844), Laura (born in Brussels in 1846), and Eleanor (born in Soho in 1856). Lenchen remained, and from 1857 to 1862 she was joined by her sister Marianne, so that the Marxes then had two servants. Certainly the family was better off and lived in a different style after 1856. Yet the financial troubles that had plagued them in Soho did not really abate until the beginning of 1869. In that year Engels, who had worked in the cotton factory his family owned (in partnership with Gottfried Ermen) in Manchester since November of 1850, sold the interest he had accumulated in the business, and began to provide Marx with a regular—and in those days substantial—income of £350 per year. From 1869 to Marx's death in 1883 one can date the third period of the family's London life, the period of relative financial security.

The years in Soho were the worst. Evicted and persecuted, perpetually short of money, hounded by creditors, plagued by illness, attacked and defamed (not always falsely) by former comrades, shattered by the death of their children, the Marx family experienced what Jenny would later call

"years of great hardship, continual acute privations . . . and real misery."
Marx himself usually felt the burden of these troubles less than his wife,
but already in March 1851 he described himself to Engels as "riddled with
petites misères," and as standing "up to the crown of my head in petty-
bourgeois crap." In the winter of 1852 Marx told Engels he was unable to
go out because his coat was in the pawn shop, and unable to eat meat
because the butcher would not give him credit. At the beginning of 1853
he wrote that "the crud has reached its climax," and that he could not
even buy postage stamps. In June 1854 Marx wrote that he was sitting
"over my ears in crud," and that he had nearly failed to convince the doctor to visit Jenny during a sickness because a bill for £26 (more than a
year's rental on the Soho flat) remained unpaid.[1]

A series of deaths moved the family out of Soho. The first and saddest
took Marx's only son, Edgar (named for Jenny's brother, who had stood
fairly close to the Marxes politically), called Musch, in April of 1855. Although he was the third of the children to die, he was the family's favorite
and, unlike the other two, who had both succumbed at the age of one
year, he was nine when the end came. A week after the death Marx wrote
to Engels: "I have already gone through all kinds of crud, but now for the
first time I know what real unhappiness is. I feel broken down. Happily,
since the day of the funeral I have had such terrible headaches that thinking, hearing and seeing have left me." In July he was still "deeply shaken
in my heart and head." Jenny was, if anything, more intensely affected.
Marx described her as "sicker than ever before from mental agitation,"
even before the death occurred, and "completely downbroken" in the following summer. She believed (as she wrote ten years later) that "Had we
been able to give up our small unhealthy apartment and take the child to
the seaside we might perhaps have saved him." Whether or not she was
right to think so, the memory of death now clung so strongly to the flat in
Dean Street that the Marxes were determined to leave it at the first
chance.[2]

The chance came in 1856; in May Jenny received a small inheritance
from an uncle, and the following July her mother died while Jenny was
visiting her. The inheritance provided the family with enough money to
pay their debts, and rent and furnish a house. In September Marx found
one on Grafton Terrace, in one of the sections of London then being
opened up to middle-class housing development. The move took place at
the start of the next month.

The house in Grafton Terrace was not large but, as Jenny put it later, it
"seemed to be a kind of palace compared with the places where we had
lived before." "When we slept in our own beds for the first time, sat on
our own chairs and even had a parlor with second-hand furniture of a
rococo style—or rather, bric-à-brac, then we really thought that we were

living in a magic castle. . . ." Marx described it to Engels as "very pretty for the price," which was kept low by the fact that the district was still new and the surrounding streets were somewhat unfinished. The move seemed to presage an end to the troubles of life in Soho.[3]

But Marx's financial troubles would not go away. In January 1857, not four months after the move, Marx wrote Engels that he was "completely stranded," unable to make ends meet, "without prospects and with growing family expenses. I absolutely don't know what to do, and I am actually in a more desperate situation than five years ago. I believed that I had absorbed the quintessence of the crap. *Mais non.* The worst is that this crisis is not temporary. I don't see how I'm going to work myself out of it." The following March he apologized for not writing to Engels (who had sent money to help out) because "the total situation of the house is in such a crisis that my head is buzzing too much to write." A year later things had come to such a pass that Marx did not believe he would be able to pay his debts even if he drastically altered his life style, took his children out of school, and moved to a "purely proletarian" dwelling. The family faced "the specter of an unavoidable final catastrophe."[4]

In the fall of 1859 Marx found himself facing another crisis, which he again described as "worse than ever before, because I see no way to make shift." Big bills were piled on little ones, and the family was threatened with having their gas and water turned off. In October Marx reported that unless he could "make some kind of coup" his situation would become "*completely* untenable." In January 1860 he was being sued by tradesmen over the payment of bills. Throughout that year Marx had to struggle to pay a series of accumulated debts. In January 1861 he could not meet his expenses, and "I really don't know what to do, although I saw this crisis coming for a long time." Short of money in the summer of that year, Marx wrote Engels in October that he thought he felt "firm ground under my feet again." But by November he was gloomy once more, and the family was "oppressed by miserable vexations." In June 1862 Marx told Engels that "My wife tells me every day that she wishes she and the children were in their graves, and I really can't blame her, for the humiliations, tortures, and horrors, that have to be gotten through in this situation are in fact indescribable." In January 1863 things reached a critical point again, the children were without clothes or shoes and "all hell is loose." This time Marx seemed determined to end the stream of tortures. He would arrange for his two elder daughters to take places as governesses, let Lenchen find another post, and go with Jenny and little Eleanor (Tussy) to live in a City Model Lodging House, a working-class tenement.[5]

Suddenly, the clouds cleared. Before the end of the month Engels had sent £100, which allowed Marx to pay off most of his debts. Another old friend, Ernst Dronke, provided Marx with cash and a large, interest-free loan. Then, in December 1863, Marx's mother died. His share of the in-heritance was sizable, nearly £600. Moreover, the following May Marx received another inheritance, this time from his old friend Wilhelm Wolff (Lupus, as he was called, to distinguish him from Frederick Wolff, "the red Wolff"), amounting to £825. The total, in nineteenth-century values, was a substantial sum of money, enough to support the Marx family for three of four years on the level they lived during the 1860s. The family moved into a larger, "friendly, sunlit house with bright and airy rooms," and in October Jenny gave a ball there, followed by several small parties.[6]

Yet, by the summer of 1865, the vision of financial solidity had again fallen to pieces. "For two months I've been living purely out of the pawn-house," Marx told Engels, and the storm signals were piling up and growing more threatening. So much of the inherited money had gone to pay off old debts and set up the new house, that Marx had been able to live on it for only slightly more than a year. Engels quickly sent £50, but by mid-August Marx was again unable to pay his butcher bill and his rent. Throughout 1866 and 1867 Engels regularly sent Marx money in sums that were often £10 and sometimes £50. In October Marx asked Engels to be his security for a loan of £100. It was in April 1868, facing his fiftieth birthday, that Marx despondently told Engels of the jibe his mother had made about him: "If only Karl had made some capital, instead of writing a book about it."[7]

Then, in November 1868, Engels suddenly asked Marx what the total of his debts then amounted to, and whether, once they were paid off, the family could meet its regular expenses—not counting medical bills and other emergencies—on £350 per year. At that time Marx calculated that he owned £210 (the sum turned out to be larger, since Jenny hid some debts from him and later unsuccessfully tried to pay them out of the regular income Engels sent), and that he could live on the £350, although the family's expenses had run higher than that in the past years.[8] By February 1869 Engels had begun to send the money in quarterly installments. Soon after, the history of Marx's recurring financial crises ended; exactly what Engels provided beyond the regular £350 cannot be determined; the fact that Engels moved to London in 1870 meant that the regular corre-spondence between the two friends—hence our information about Marx's financial difficulties—ended too.

2. The Structure of a Domestic Economy

Underlying the history of Marx's financial troubles was the structure of his domestic economy. That structure was built up not only of income and expenditures, but of expectations, attitudes, and the relationship Marx felt to exist between himself and the world of work and consumption.

Marx had three sources of income during his years in London: his work as a journalist and writer, contributions from friends, especially Engels, and inheritance. (At one point he also claimed to have made some money on the stock market, but it seems unlikely that he really did.) The actual amount he had available to live on in any given year seldom equaled the total of these three sources, however, because Marx was constantly borrowing money against his future income (and until 1863 against his family inheritance too), so that his available cash would be inflated by loans, or diminished by the need to pay interest.

The largest source of income from work was *The New York Daily Tribune*, for which Marx was a regular correspondent from 1851 to 1862. Marx had met the paper's editor, Charles Dana, during 1848; then, as later, Dana was deeply impressed with Marx's talents and his grasp of the contemporary European situation. During most of this period Marx received £2 per published article, but the number of pieces printed slipped from a high of eighty in 1853 and 1854 down to twenty-odd in 1856, when the economic situation forced the paper to cut back on its foreign correspondents. Desperate, Marx threatened to look for another paper and, beginning in 1857, Dana agreed to pay Marx for one article per week whether published or not. However, at the end of 1859 this number was reduced by half, and in 1862 the American Civil War caused the New York paper to give all its space to domestic news. Marx's yearly income from the *Tribune* therefore sometimes reached as much as £160, but the average was more like £100, and in some years it was considerably less.[9]

Marx supplemented this by sending articles to two German papers, the *Neue Oder Zeitung*, a radical paper published in Breslau for which Marx wrote in 1855, and the Viennese *Presse*, which employed Marx in 1861-62. The German papers paid less well than the *Tribune*, and it is unlikely that Marx's total income from both these papers exceeded £100.[10] Between 1857 and 1860 Marx also wrote articles for the *New American Cyclopaedia*, a venture in which Dana also had a hand, and to which he asked Marx to contribute.

Although Marx's correspondence makes clear that he expected to earn money from his books as well as his journalism, and even to achieve financial security once his work on economics appeared, these expectations were never fulfilled. Marx did get £25 in 1852 for the satirical biographies of exiled political figures that became *The Great Men of the Emigration*, but it was not published then; the money came from the Hungarian exile Bangya who had commissioned it, and who later turned out to be a police spy. Marx's pamphlet on Lord Palmerston sold very well, but because he had made no clear agreement with the publisher Marx got no income from it. The *Revelations on the Cologne Communist Trial* of 1852, printed in England with the intention that it would be smuggled into Germany and sold, fell into the hands of the police and never reached the German market. A similar fate lay in store for *Herr Vogt* in 1860, with the added misfortune that this time Marx was successfully sued by the London printer to recover the production expenses. Marx received a small honorarium for *A Contribution to the Critique of Political Economy* in 1859, and again for the first volume of *Capital* in 1867, but it was not enough to affect his financial situation very much, and the English translation of *Capital*, from which he expected to make substantially more, only saw the light after Marx's death, in 1886.

Twice Marx made gestures toward developing some income from business rather than writing. In the fall of 1862 he informed Engels that it was possible ("although all kinds of things still stand in the way") he would go to work in a railway bureau at the start of the following year. But before the new year began Marx let Kugelmann know the plan had fallen through ("Shall I call it good luck or bad?"): his poor handwriting prevented his getting the job. Ten years later Marx participated briefly in a company formed to produce and market a new kind of copying machine, which had been invented by a friend of his son-in-law, Paul Lafargue. But the enterprise soon broke up in a quarrel over who held the rights to the patent.[11]

Given the very limited income Marx's various attempts to earn money produced, contributions from his friends (and above all from Engels) became a major source of income for him. Engels' help to Marx did not consist only of cash. A significant proportion of the newspaper articles that appeared over Marx's name, and for which Marx always received and kept the proceeds, were actually written by his friend. In August 1851, when Dana offered Marx the chance to contribute to the *Tribune*, Marx was deeply wrapped up in his work on political economy, which he then expected to complete in a short time. He therefore asked Engels to write for Dana. Although busy with other matters himself, Engels obligingly produced a series of sixteen articles on the revolution of 1848 in Germany, later collected under the title *Revolution and Counter-Revolution in Germany*. Since the articles appeared over Marx's signature, he was long believed to be the author, and even recent editions mistakenly present them as his work. Although Marx himself began to write *Tribune* articles in 1852, for the whole of that year he was still unable to write in English, and all the articles—copied out in legible form by Jenny—were sent to Manchester for Engels to translate. "Don't make them so long!" Engels implored on one occasion.[12]

Even after Marx became the real author of most of the reports, Engels continued to write pieces when Marx felt unable to do so. For months at a time he would do one article per week, so that Marx could send two to New York. Of the total of nearly 500 articles printed in the *Tribune*, fully one-fourth were actually written by Engels. Engels also wrote for the *New American Cyclopaedia*, producing many more of the entries Marx supplied than Marx himself did, fifty-one out of sixty-seven.[13]

In purely monetary terms these contributions were less important for Marx's budget than the cash Engels sent him. When Engels went to Manchester in the fall of 1850 his father was uncertain how the young revolutionary would represent the family's interests, and placed him in a position that limited both his income and his control over funds. But in the spring of 1852 the elder Engels visited Manchester and found his son's conduct of the business quite reassuring. As a result Engels' income and his freedom of action were increased. Then, in 1860, Engels was made a partner in the firm, which brought an even more significant improvement in his position.[14]

Each step upward in Engels' business career meant he had more money available to help Marx and, although business conditions sometimes reduced his income sharply, his help was unfailing. The money came regularly, in money orders or bills cut in two with each half sent in a separate envelope, £2 or less at a time in the early years, often £5 or more later on. In addition to these regular contributions, Engels sent much larger amounts in emergencies. Twice, in 1860 and again in 1863, Engels sent £100 at a time. Even without these large emergency sums Engels' contributions to Marx's budget must have come to around £100 per year in the darkest Soho days, rising to more than twice that in the early 1860s. In the five years before he began to provide Marx with £350 per year on a regular basis in 1869, Engels sent Marx no less then £1,862.[15]

Other friends contributed too. Among them were old revolutionary colleagues like Ferdinand Freiligrath, Ernst Dronke, Georg Weerth, and Ferdinand Lassalle, as well as members of Marx's own and Jenny's family. David McLellan has calculated that in 1851 Marx received at least £150 in gifts, and since this is only the total mentioned in surviving correspondence, the actual amount was no doubt more.[16] Friends and relatives often lent money, too; for instance, Lassalle loaned Marx £60 in 1862.

Although less than the amount received as gifts from friends, the total the Marx family derived from inheritance was probably larger than what Marx earned from writing. Jenny's inheritance was only a couple of hundred pounds, but to that must be added the goods she brought to the marriage, including the valuable silver service which the family pawned and redeemed several times during the London years. (The silver came from Jenny's Scottish ancestors and bore an aristocratic crest. Once when Marx, shabbily dressed and speaking little English, brought it to a broker, he was suspected of stealing it, and jailed for a day.) Marx's own inheritance, from his mother and from Wilhelm Wolff, was nearly £1,500, in addition to the money—6,000 German Taler—he had spent on the *Neue Rheinische Zeitung* during 1848-49. Although the inheritances could not put an end to the Marxes' recurring financial crises, each one produced a change in their immediate circumstances. Jenny's allowed them to move out of Soho in 1856, and Marx's led to the family's taking a larger house in 1864. (Later, after the two elder girls married, the Marxes moved again, to a smaller house on the same street.)[17]

What the various information about Marx's income allows us to see is that, in spite of being continually short of money and many times on the brink of financial collapse, the Marx family's domestic economy was always predicated on the maintenance of a middle-class life style. Marx's situation was painful, but it can only be called poverty relative to his expectations. Even a skilled worker in the middle of the nineteenth century could expect to earn little more than £50 per year; a clerk in a business or bank joined the lower middle class on £60 to £75. Marx's friend Ferdinand Freiligrath, who was the manager of a Swiss bank in London earned between £200 and £300 per year, on which he and his family lived comfortably enough to be a financial resource for Marx. From around 1860 the Marx family budget was over £300 per year, and it approached that figure in some earlier years too. When Marx told Engels late in 1868 that he could live on £350 per year, he admitted that his family had spent more in the previous year. A few months earlier he told Kugelmann that it cost him £400-500 per year to live in London.[18]

Where did the money go? Rent, property taxes, food, doctor bills, and school bills were among Marx's biggest recurring expenses. That the Marx family had a servant (and for a time two) tells something about their middle-class expectations, but keeping Lenchen Demuth and her sister Marianne did not cost the Marx family very much beyond room and board—perhaps as little as £10 to £15 per year. Education was a bigger expense, since the three daughters had private lessons in music and drama as well as their regular schooling, and sending them to private school meant dressing them well, too. In the same category of expenses was the piano, bought on time payments in 1859. Marx regarded these outlays as costly but necessary.

> I live too dearly for my circumstances in any case, and this year in addition [Marx wrote in July 1865] we have lived better than before. But it is the only way that the children—quite apart from how much they have suffered, and for which they were compensated, at least for a short time—can enter into relations and circumstances that can assure them a future.[19]

If on the one hand Marx felt the need to spend for his family's future, he was also weighed down by its past. Not only was he constantly having to pay interest to lenders and pawnbrokers but, as he told Engels in 1868, being systematically in debt to tradesmen meant that "everything is bought at much too high price." That the family had to overpay for many items was probably true throughout their period in London, even before their move out of Soho and into "respectability" brought their expenses to a higher level than before.[20]

There was another way in which being constantly in debt created additional expense: it added to the doctor bills. Just as anxiety and worry had driven Jenny Marx to her sickbed in the days before her marriage, so did they now. It was she who had to face the anger of unpaid merchants and tradesmen day by day. In 1851 Marx described her as ill "more from commercial [*bürgerlich*] than physical causes"; in 1854 she took to her bed "partly out of physical illness, partly out of anger because the good Dr. Freund has bombarded us again with bills." In 1858 the doctor prescribed a period of rest for Jenny at the seaside, but Marx was convinced that even had he been able to send her, the remedy would be of no use "as long as the daily pressure and the specter of an unavoidable final catastrophe pursues her." Medical expenses were often a significant part of Marx's budget; the bills mounted up until Marx owed £26 in 1854, and in 1858 he again had piled up a medical debt of £17. Moreover, beginning in 1858 the family did begin to use the often-prescribed but relatively costly nineteenth-century remedy of several weeks by the seaside as a means of restoring its sick members—at first Jenny, but later Karl too—to health.[21]

During the years in Soho Marx attempted to meet the "crap" with unconcern, but when his indifference faltered he grew angry and depressed. In August 1851 he wrote to Weydemeyer that he let his various external troubles disturb him "not one minute in my work." In September 1852 he wrote to Engels that "I wade through the shit with great indifference, even when I'm stuck in it and hear of nothing else." In July 1853, unable to find money even for "the most necessary things," Marx described himself as "by now used to the crap and to the situations it brings with it." Yet beneath this unconcern a current of deeper worry was already present, especially when the financial problems were compounded by sickness or death. Ten days after the loss of his daughter Franziska, Marx admitted that "Although I'm a hard character, this time the shit affected me considerably." And in early March 1854 he confessed to Engels that a spring and summer of "the same chronic pressure" was a disgusting prospect; the income from the *Tribune* by itself would not even cover his past debts, and "I become wild from time to time, that the shit never ends." By June he was seriously depressed: "I assure you that through these last *petites misères* I have become a very dull dog." In July 1856 he reported that his beard had been whitened by "black care," and that no cosmetic could restore its color.[22]

Yet, confined in a darkness that bred despair, Marx many times thought he saw the way out. In March 1853, only a day after he heard of the failed attempt to smuggle 2,000 copies of *Revelations on the Cologne Communist Trial* from Switzerland into Germany, Marx was made optimistic by Charles Dana's willingness to let him draw his pay from the *Tribune* articles by writing bank drafts on New York instead of waiting for the money to be sent. "Since then I have sent seven more articles to the *Tribune*. Tomorrow I will send another. I would work myself free now, if I didn't have the blasted *dette consolidée* on my back. Even that would have been significantly diminished, if the miserable Swiss had not thrown me into the abyss again." Eighteen months later, after a period of unrelenting crisis, he wrote to Engels of a plan for consolidating his debts and reorganizing his finances.

> I have reduced my total debt to less than £50, which is around £30 less than at the beginning of the year. You see that great financial artistry has been applied. If a negotiation that I have entered into with Lassalle succeeds, and he lends me £30, and you the rest, then I will finally stand in the clear again, and change my whole domestic set-up, whereas I now have to pay 25% to the pawn shop alone and in general can never get things in order because of the arrears.

It would be interesting to know what Marx's "financial artistry" involved, since he admitted at the same time that he had had to resort to "extraordinary means" just to keep the household afloat during the past months. Many details of Marx's finances remain obscure.[23]

Out of Soho, the prospects for reaching firm ground grew still clearer in Marx's mind. In January 1859 he wrote to Engels about his *Contribution to the Critique of Political Economy* that "If the thing sells in Berlin, it is possible that I will get out of all the crap. It is high time." The following April a different solution seemed more than merely possible. Writing for the Vienna *Presse* would "shortly double my income and make an end to the inveterate crap." Although the happy announcement was accompanied by a request for money, "I hope that this time the business is definitively at an end, and the impositions on you will come to a decisive stop." Both these hopes were disappointed, but when, in February 1860, Marx decided to sue the *Augsburg Allgemeine Zeitung* for printing Karl Vogt's accusations against him he expected that the publicity of the case would prepare the market for his book on economics. He would finish the work "in six weeks, and *after* the suit it will *sell*." *Capital* was not to be ready then, or soon after, but when the first volume was finally at the printer in the spring of 1867 Marx told Engels: "I confidently hope and believe that I will be well enough set up in a year's time so that I can fundamentally reform my economic situation and finally stand on my own feet again."[24]

These recurring and in the event always unrealistic hopes reveal that beneath all the complaints, Marx retained an underlying confidence in the improvement of his personal situation that recalls his belief in the coming betterment of society as a whole. His optimism survived numerous clashes with reality. When his family arrived in London Marx took a flat in Chelsea at a rental of nearly £6 per month, or £72 per year, more than three times the £22 he would struggle to pay in Dean Street, and exactly twice the cost of the house on Grafton Terrace. When he moved out of Soho on the strength of Jenny's inheritance in the fall of 1856, he clearly expected that the worst of his financial problems were behind him, and the surprise he expressed in 1857 on finding things basically unaltered reveals the height and the fragility of his hopes. Yet the very same things recurred when Marx received his own inheritance from his mother in 1863: the new house, the available cash sunk in setting it up, and the rapid and disappointing discovery that behind the new façade nothing had changed.

Given all the pain, embarassment, and unhappiness that Marx's life brought him, were there any positive advantages that tied him to it? In particular, why did Marx continue to work in journalism, even after events demonstrated that he could not make ends meet with it? Marx's "real" work during the London years was his book on economics, and one might expect that living as he did somehow helped him to keep at it. This was not the case. During most of the time Marx lived on Dean Street he did not work on political economy. Although he began his London residence with an intense bout of reading in economic literature, this activity ended during the first months of 1852, and it did not become Marx's central concern again until sometime in 1856. Marx used his time in the British Museum to expose the career of Lord Palmerston, to study Spanish and Spanish history, and to reveal *The Secret Diplomatic History of the Eighteenth Century*, but not to work out his views on economic theory. (We shall look into some of the reasons for this later on.)

Moreover, Marx did not regard newspaper writing as positively connected to his theoretical work. In September 1853 he wrote to his friend Adolf Cluss that he now expected the next economic crisis to come before he was able to finish his book on economics, adding that his newspaper work had kept him from it. "The perpetual journalistic scribbling wearies me. It takes away and wastes much of my time, and in the end amounts to nothing. However independent you try to be, you are bound to the newspaper and its readers, especially if you receive cash payment, as I do. Purely scientific works are a totally different thing."[25] Although Marx occasionally was able to make a connection between his theory and journalism, for instance during the worldwide economic crisis of 1857, what he told Cluss represented his usual attitude. Nor did he have much sympathy for the politics of the *Tribune*, despite its progressive image, or—even less—for the German papers to which he contributed.

It cannot be argued that working at journalism and living as he did left Marx more time free than some other kind of employment might have done. He found newspaper writing extremely time consuming. Even in the periods when Marx was not working on economics at all, he was often unable to send the *Tribune* two articles unless Engels supplied one. Later, when the New York paper reduced the contract to one article per week Marx complained that the new arrangement saved him no time. "In fact I am now forced to condense the material for two articles into one," he wrote to Engels, "thus I give double work for half the price." To the time that the work itself took there was added the hours Marx regularly spent running around London trying to satisfy his creditors and discover new sources of loans. Often his letters picture him losing whole mornings or afternoons in this way.[26]

Were there no alternatives? Marx was an extremely talented and clever man with a great deal of energy. He was not averse to money earned in bourgeois society—where else did the revenues of the *Tribune* come from, not to mention the Manchester cotton firm of Ermen and Engels? The author of the *Communist Manifesto* was not shunned as a dangerous revolutionary in London, for little was known about him until 1871, when the Paris Commune, and Marx's defense of it, made him a visible enemy of established society. So respectable did he appear that in 1868 he was made an honorary constable. He was, in other words, not unemployable. His plan—however serious it actually was—to work in a railway agency in 1862 recognized this.[27]

Other radical political exiles lived quite different lives, not only better off financially, but able to devote as much or more time than Marx could to independent pursuits. Engels is the obvious example, less for the level of his income (often over £1,000 per year), which Marx might not have been able to match, than for the time his work left over for literary and political activity. But Engels was not alone. In London lived Ferdinand Freiligrath, the radical poet who was—with some interruptions—Marx's friend and financial helper through most of the London years. Freiligrath had been working in Barmen as a clerk at the time Engels decided that accepting business as his "external" career might leave him the time he needed for a separate intellectual calling. Both men retained something of that older European figure, the business man who was also active in public and intellectual life.[28]

Certainly, Marx valued his independence from the ordinary pursuits of business, and not only for the time that his freedom might have been expected to provide him. His sense of himself was at stake. As he wrote to Weydemeyer in 1859, "I must pursue my goal through thick and thin, and not allow bourgeois society to transform me into a money-making machine." Yet here, too, as in Marx's hopes that he could free himself from his situation, the reality was very different from the ideal image. As he explained to Lassalle in 1862, "During the last year I have had to do the most vile mechanical stuff in order not to starve to death, and often for months at a time I could not write a line on the 'thing.' " Far from remaining independent of outside pressures through his refusal to change his mode of life, Marx's determination gave external conditions more power to shape his life and thwart his plans than the daily business of making a living exercised over Freiligrath or Engels. Apologizing once to Lassalle for the way his financial situation forced him to behave in regard to a loan Lassalle had made him, he wrote: "I admit to you, without beating around the bush, that as a man sitting on a volcano, I allowed circumstances to control me in a manner not fitting for a rational animal." Marx found himself on the same volcano over and over again, and the situation made him continually prey to the circumstances whose control he sought to escape.[29]

Why then did Marx live as he did? The desire for independence and the conditions of exile account for some features of his life in London but, as the example of other radicals suggests, not by any means for all of them. More intimately personal forces were also at work. Like his thought, Marx's life was stretched between the opposite poles of an idealism that claimed freedom from domination by merely material forces, and a materialism that affirmed the ubiquity of their control. Marx's life style asserted his ability to rise above the ordinary world of moneymaking, but his experience was one of continual submission to its power. Both extremes were necessary to him. When Marx was asked to play the popular Victorian parlor game called "Confessions," in which participants wrote down their responses to a series of personal questions, he listed his idea of happiness as "to struggle," and his idea of misery as "to submit."[30] These were appropriate enough answers for a revolutionary, but they were also descriptions of a dialectic that ruled Marx's own life. (Engels, asked the same questions, listed Château Margaux 1848 and having to go to the dentist.) Happiness and unhappiness were inseparable for Marx: the need continually to submit made the unending struggle both possible and necessary. Marx never seriously tried to change his style of life in London because, within, its mixture of struggle and submission was the life he chose.

Closely tied to the polarity of struggle and submission that oriented Marx's life in London was another, the opposition of "egoism" and "self-sacrifice." This dialectic, so strongly present in his relations with his father, and visible later in *The German Ideology*, also described much of Marx's relationship to work, family, and friends. Marx's friends and family saw his life in terms of sacrifice; as Jenny wrote to Kugelmann in 1868: "If the workers had any notion of the sacrifice that was necessary to complete this book, written solely for them and in their interest, they might perhaps show a bit more interest." Marx himself wrote in 1867 that "I have sacrificed my health, my happiness, and my family" to the completion of his book. The sacrifices were real, but they were after all made on the altar of Marx's own work, for the personal goal which, as he told Weydemeyer, he would pursue "through thick and thin." Although what Jenny said about the sacrifice being in the interest of others was true on one level, on another Marx sacrificed himself—and his family—to his own fulfillment.[31]

One moment that reveals how deeply tangled together egoism and self-sacrifice were in Marx's life was the crisis he faced during January 1863. At one and the same time, Marx's friendship with Engels and the continuation of his life style were suddenly called into question. Late in the evening of January 6, Mary Burns, the Irish girl whom Engels had known since the 1840s, and with whom he had lived devotedly but without the official sanction of marriage for many years, died suddenly and without any warning. The news reached Marx at a moment of impending financial breakdown. Marx wrote to Engels the day he heard: "The report of Mary's death has in equal measure surprised and dismayed me. She was very good-humored, witty, and devoted to you." Then followed a long paragraph on Marx's own financial troubles ("All hell is loose.") Marx returned to the subject of Mary's death before ending the letter, wishing his mother had died instead of Mary, observing in a postscript that it was "extraordinarily hard" for Engels, since he had had a carefree home with Mary, where he could go whenever he liked (as a well-known figure in the Manchester business world, Engels also maintained an "official" residence, and did not live in Mary's house all the time)—and how was he going to arrange things now?[32]

Behind Marx's flat and colorless response to Engels' sadness lay a history of coolness between the Marx family and Engels' unconventional household. Marx himself sometimes sent greetings to Mary Burns in his letters, but Jenny never mentioned her. She was never invited to visit the Marx's house when Engels came to London. The surviving correspondence contains no unflattering references to Mary Burns or to Engels' relationship with her, but such passages may have existed among the letters Marx's daughters destroyed after his death to save Engels embarassment.[33] Like the bohemianism that had associated Engels with the Berlin "Free" in the early 1840s, the *liaison* with Mary Burns was a source of tension between him and Marx.

Engels' knowledge of the Marxes' attitude toward Mary may have prepared him somewhat for the meagerness of the comfort Marx sent him at her death. Nonetheless, he was hurt. "All my friends, philistine acquaint-ances included, showed me more sympathy and friendship than I could expect on this occasion—which was bound to affect me closely. You found the moment appropriate to show off the primacy of your cool disposition. So be it!" Yet Engels did not hold back from offering advice about the critical state of Marx's finances. He promised to send money as soon as he could, and offered to sign a note for Marx too. It might not be enough, but it was all he could do.[34]

Marx saw that things could not be left as they were. After waiting ten days to let things cool down, he sent Engels a detailed apology. He had not written as he did out of "heartlessness." On the morning he received the news of Mary's death he had been "just as shattered as at the death of one closest to me." But he had not been able to write until the evening, after a day of pressure "from the most desperate circumstances," including threats from creditors, a lack of coal and food, and the illness of little Jenny. Marx did not stop with his apology. He went on to say that he had not been displeased with the news that Engels could not bail him out of his financial crisis. He had wanted his wife to see the "*non possumus*" be-cause the situation in which the family had hitherto lived, "roasting on a little fire that consumed my heart and head," had to end. His wife now agreed with the proposal Marx had long ago made to alter their life. He would hold off his creditors by threatening to declare bankruptcy, let the landlord take the furniture, place his older daughters as governesses, find Lenchen another situation, and go with Jenny and the youngest of the children to live in a working-class housing project.[35]

Engels accepted Marx's apology. He also gave voice to some of the feel-ings Mary's death had called up in him: "With her I felt I buried the last bit of my youth." At least Marx's explanation of his earlier letter meant that Engels had not also lost "his oldest and best friend." Then he turned to Marx's affairs. On receiving Marx's letter he had sought to borrow money for him, but without success. He tried to sell yarn bought on speculation, but could not find a taker. He could not get his hands on any cash. "And yet I cannot let you carry out the plan that you described to me." He had therefore endorsed to Marx a note for £100 which one of his firm's clients would pay at the end of February. Marx could sell it in Lon-don (for something less than its face value, but nonetheless quite a large amount), and Engels would not have to account for the sum for several months. It was "a very hazardous stroke," but it had to be risked. Marx was saved.[36]

There is no way to uncover Marx's motives in this affair; he may not have known what they were himself. However, several things are clear. The first is that Marx did not need to be asked twice to take what Engels sent and use it to go on living as he had before. The resolve to take up a new life style and cease roasting on the "little fire" dissolved with the money. Second, whether Marx desired it or not, his "decision" to break up his household had forced Engels' hand. The same threat of bankruptcy he proposed to use against his creditors had worked to make Engels rescue him, and at great danger to himself. Moreover, there is one circumstance that suggests Marx may have been manipulating Engels. In the apology letter of January 24 he claimed that his wife had agreed with his plan to reduce the household; but in response to Engels' help he said that Jenny "naturally had no notion of what I wrote, but with a bit of reflection she could have figured out that something similar had to come out of it."[37]

The themes of egoism and self-sacrifice are so deeply woven together in this episode that one can hardly see where one takes over from the other. Marx acknowledged in his first letter of the series that his conduct was "hideously egoistical," but he added that "In my own house I play the taciturn Stoic [suffering in silence] in order to counterpoise the outbreaks from the other side," that is, from Jenny. "To work under such circumstances becomes simply impossible," and it had been nearly so all along, roasting on the fire that "consumed my heart and head." Yet Marx's very threat to put the sacrificial fire out forced Engels to supply the fuel to keep it going, and Marx would feel its heat many more times in the years to come.

The crisis in Marx's relationship with Engels revealed that its structure shared elements with other important relations in Marx's life, notably his relationship to his father. Between Heinrich and Karl the crises had come more frequently; yet their basis had usually been behavior by the younger Marx which in his terms evidenced sacrifice to a higher goal, but which in relation to the other man signified coldness and egoism. Behind those earlier crises and their resolution was the deep emotional investment Heinrich had made in his son's future, and the father's determination not to let Karl destroy himself through his impractical and dangerous behavior. Engels had taken Heinrich Marx's place, not only as the provider of Karl's sustenance but as the practical businessman whose knowledge of how to survive in the everyday world saved Marx for "higher" goals whose achievement would justify the sacrifice that the more earthbound provider of material support made. In this psychological gymnastics each member of the team depended equally on the other, and support from "above" was just as necessary to prevent a collapse as sustenance from "below." Hence, the crisis in the two friends' relationship ended with Marx returning to the life he had been leading, supported by Engels' deepened commitment to maintain him in it.

Beneath the patterns of work, income, and expenditure that made Marx's domestic economy a source of suffering and of recurring crises stood the deeper dialectic of his personality, which matched struggle against submission and egoism against self-sacrifice. Marx was not the only person caught up in this web.

3. A Family Interior

In spite of the unending parade of financial troubles the Marx family had to witness, there is considerable evidence that relations between the members were often warm, sympathetic, and supportive. Writing to Weydemeyer about the family's early troubles in London, Jenny concluded that, as for Karl, "Never, not even in the most frightful moments, did he lose his confidence in the future or even his cheery humor, and he was satisfied when he saw me cheerful and our loving children cuddling close to their dear mother."[38] Jenny's picture was not uninterested, of course, and it was penned in 1850, before the experiences of the London years had become chronic. Yet other witnesses testify that the good-humor and warmth of the Marx family survived the onset of their troubles.

One of these was Wilhelm Liebknecht, who had also fled to London after 1848, and who lived there until he returned to Germany in 1862. In the 1860s Marx and Engels grew impatient and hostile toward Liebknecht, whose politics derived as much from south-west German democratic radicalism as from revolutionary socialism. But while in England he had been among their friends, visiting the Marx family often. His portrait of the family, drawing friends and visitors into the circle of warmth and good feeling it generated, is a convincing one, even though he pointedly concentrated on the Sunday outings to Hampstead Heath rather than on the weekday struggle with "emigration misery." The company would set out for its weekly picnic around 11 a.m., in order to complete the hour and a half walk to Hampstead in time for lunch. The meal was substantial: "a joint of roast veal was the main course, consecrated by tradition," carried by Lenchen Demuth in an outsize hamper, together with "tea and sugar and occasionally some fruit." Food was followed either by quiet activities like talk, newspaper reading, or rest, or more vigorous ones like races, sports, or donkey rides. The walk home was accompanied by songs and stories. So happy were those Sundays that everyone who participated looked forward to them all week long, and Liebknecht declared that "Were I to live to be a thousand I should never forget them."[39]

One source of the happy feelings to which Liebknecht testified was Marx's love of children. In Liebknecht's view, Marx's feeling for children was a key to his character. "Marx had an extraordinary love for children. He was not only a most loving father who could be a child for hours with his children, he felt drawn like a magnet toward other children."

Liebknecht's description was confirmed by Marx's youngest daughter, Eleanor, who believed that "never did children have a more delightful playfellow." Down on all fours, Marx would pull his children around on chairs tied to his body, or carry them over long distances on his shoulders.

> Once, I remember, a small schoolboy of about ten, quite unceremoniously stopping the dreaded "chief of the International" in Maitland Park and asking him to "swop knives." After a little necessary explanation that "swop" was schoolboy for "exchange," the two knives were produced and compared. The boy's had only one blade; the man's had two, but these were undeniably blunt. After much discussion, a bargain was struck, and the knives exchanged, the terrible "chief of the International" adding a penny in consideration of the bluntness of his blades.

Even a Prussain spy who reported on Marx in 1852 declared that "As father and husband, Marx, in spite of his wild and restless character, is the gentlest and mildest of men."[40]

Reading the family's correspondence, as well as descriptions by both members and outsiders, one has the impression of a closely knit unit within which each person's individuality was recognized and respected. Each of the children—like Marx himself—had a nickname which served as a reminder of some earlier characteristic or enthusiasm. The eldest daughter, Jenny, was called Qui Qui, Emperor of China, because of a fascination with the orient, and when the youngest, Eleanor, showed a similar turn of mind, she became Quo Quo, Successor to the Emperor of China. She was also called Gnome Alberich after one of her favorite mythological heroes. Laura, the middle daughter, was Hottentot or Kakadou. In these names Marx and Jenny employed their qualities of imagination, curiosity, and humor to bestow special recognition on their children, defining a place and an identity for each that recognized some particular quality or interest. Within the family both literary and political concerns were shared, the former practically from the time the children could read, and the latter as early as they could be made intelligible. Enthusiasms for Walter Scott, Balzac, and Shakespeare were transferred from parents to children; in the late 1860s the girls were staunch partisans of the Irish, and a few years later active supporters of the Paris Commune and benefactors of its refugees.

These images of Marx's family testify to the presence of affection, directness, and warmth in the relations between its members. Yet, other realities were present at the same time. The family's financial troubles brought personal tensions in their train. One reason Marx could not preserve the indifference to his difficulties he at first vaunted to Engels and others was that his wife was much less resistant than he. When he first found that the situation interfered with his work, the reason was as much the disturbances within the family as the pressures from outside it.

> I would have been finished in the library long ago. But the interruptions and disturbances are too great, and at home, where everything is always in a state of siege, and streams of tears bother me and make me furious for whole nights at a time, I naturally can't do much. I am sorry about my wife. The main pressure falls on her, and at bottom she is right. Industry needs to be more productive than marriage. In spite of all that, you remember that I am by nature not very tolerant and even a bit hard, so that from time to time I lose my composure.[41]

Jenny, more exposed to the everyday horror of butchers and bakers demanding to be paid cash that did not exist, and unable to retire into the British Museum library or to plead the necessity of work, was also much more vulnerable than Marx, and—as in the days of their engagement—less sanguine too. The troubles were more immediate and real for her than for him. In 1852, when Marx was in Manchester working on "The Great Men of the Exile" with Engels, Jenny wrote a deeply depressed letter about the reality of life in London. "I sit here and go to pieces. Karl, it is now at its worst pitch. . . . I sit here and almost weep my eyes out and can find no help. My head is disintegrating." Marx replied that he was glad she had told him her troubles. "When you, poor little devil, have to go through the bitter reality, it is no less than just that I live through the torture at least ideally."[42] The last word, *ideal*, is difficult to convey simply, but for Marx, ever conscious of the contrast between reality and the ideal transformations of it effected in their own interest by those who stood outside, it captured the difference between Jenny's direct experience of the trouble and Marx's, mediated not only temporarily by distance but permanently by indifference, disdain, and determined involvement in other concerns.

Although a deeply emotional person who hid her feelings less well than her husband, Jenny Marx was also capable of being hardheaded and practical. The image of herself as more realistic than Karl, which she had projected before their marriage, continued to be reflected in her relations with him in London. She often wrote to friends asking for money, sometimes without her husband's knowledge when his attempts to come up with cash in emergencies failed. More than once she thought Marx too soft and undemanding in regard to financial questions. Already in 1850 she wrote to Weydemeyer with regard to the failure of the *Neue Rheinische Zeitung Revue* in that year, that her husband could have asked his friends "to show more energy in business and more support for his *Revue*. . . . That little was his due. I do not think that would have been unfair to anybody. That is what grieves me. But my husband is of a different opinion." In January 1863, when Marx had his near falling-out with Engels, he wrote that one thing leading him to write about his own troubles on the day he heard of Mary Burns' death was Jenny's insistence that Marx had not made the extent of the family's crisis clear to his friend. According to Liebknecht, she sometimes called him "my big baby."[43]

Jenny's realism kept her from sharing some of Marx's illusions about his ability to get out of the financial swamp. When his negotiations about becoming a writer for the Vienna *Presse* led Marx (and Engels) to hope that his income could be increased radically by the new post, Jenny did not hesitate to throw cold water on their enthusiasm.

> I hope you are coming to a fixed "point of fact" with Friedländer [the editor of the *Presse*]; there is never very much to be made from a German paper, and I don't understand how you could ask to do more than *one* article [per week] for the *enormous* sum of £1 ½, especially since they have a correspondent for ordinary business, and don't need more than a bit of embellishment. The most to be made from the *Presse* as an average maximum will be £2, don't deceive yourself about it. Engels may well say "You can make £10 a week there," and such self-deceptions are momentarily very pleasant, but they work out badly in reality.

This was the Jenny who, in 1840, had often found it necessary to remind Karl about the real practical details of life when he became absorbed in visions of "higher" things. Now, however, the reality was more painful, and in speaking about it Jenny's tone grew harsher, as here, or more desperate, as in 1852.[44]

Jenny's pessimism was justified, of course, but it was just as much a part of her constitution as Marx's recurring optimism was of his. One can trace it through the moments of her life, constant in times of happiness and of pain. Earlier we cited her exclamation of 1839: "Oh, Karl, what makes me miserable is that what would fill any other girl with inexpressible delight—your beautiful, touching, passionate love, the indescribably beautiful things you say about it, the inspiring creations of your imagination—all this only causes me anxiety and often reduces me to despair." Life gave her little reason to doubt the message of her fears, and by the 1860s they had become more generalized. In 1863 she wrote to a friend: "Perhaps the enduring sorrows and sad experiences of the last years have darkened my mind and eye so that I see everything rather blackly, and only paint gray in gray." At the end of 1866, when the manuscript for Volume One of *Capital* was finally preparing to go to the printer, and her daughter Laura was becoming engaged to Paul Lafargue, she wrote to Engels that finishing the book "rolled a giant weight off my heart. Weights and sorrows enough remain, however, especially when young girls fall in love and get engaged, and with Frenchmen yet, and medical students! I wish I could see everything *couleur de rose*, like the others, but the many enduring sorrows have made me anxious, and I often see black in the future, where a happier nature sees everything rosy. That's between us." In 1868 she told Kugelmann that she had lost much of her confidence and vital energy; in 1872 she wrote to Liebknecht that the daily cares of a woman's life "slowly but surely gnaw one's vital energy away. I speak out of more than thirty years' experience, and I can truly say that I have not let my courage sink lightly. Now I have grown too old [she was fifty-eight] to hope for much more, and the last unhappy events have completely shattered me."[45]

Marx, who had known Jenny's anxiety throughout his life, also knew her courage and resiliency. In 1852, responding to Jenny's mood of despair, he reminded her: "I know in addition how infinitely elastic you are, and how the least favorable thing revives you again." But even as she bounced back time and again, the accumulated pressure took its toll. The pattern, already visible before her marriage, which made her respond to outside pressures and anxieties with physical illness, recurred and intensified as the London years wore on. Already in 1843 Marx had told Arnold Ruge that the struggles Jenny went through on his behalf had ruined her health. As we saw earlier, Marx several times attributed her London illnesses to other than physical causes too, writing in 1858 that no remedy would be effective "as long as the daily pressure and the specter of an unavoidable final catastrophe pursues her." In November 1868, as Engels made his offer to supply Marx with a regular income of £350 per year, Marx confessed that things had become so difficult at home that he was not unhappy to have the oldest daughter, Jenny, take work as a tutor with an English family. "For some years my wife—understandably in the circumstances, but no more pleasant for that reason—has totally lost her 'temper' [Marx used the English word, clearly meaning her mental balance] and tortures the children to death with her wailing and irritation and bad humor, although no children could bear it all in a more jolly way."[46]

Marx's attempts to wade through the economic problems with stoical indifference began to have a different function as it became clear that the exterior troubles brought interior ones with them: he tried to remain quiet to keep Jenny calm. In 1863 he told Engels that he played "the taciturn Stoic in order to counterpoise the outbreaks from the other side," that is from Jenny, whose "eccentric excitement" he partially blamed for his own "egoistic" behavior. Four years later, as Marx looked forward to what he thought would be the final year of work on *Capital* from the refuge in Germany where he had carried the manuscript of the first volume, he told Engels that he greatly feared the return to London, not only for the pressure of his creditors, but also for "the family wailing, the inner collisions."[47]

These unpleasant realities were kept hidden from the outside world, of course. In fact, the need to keep things covered up, to preserve appearances, came to be a major project of the Marx family. To Jenny, the great attraction of London as a place to live was the privacy it allowed. The family might have been able to live more cheaply in Germany, but London had the advantage that "it is so collossal, that one vanishes into nothing. Here the individual is worth nothing, and for that very reason one ceases to be important to oneself and to others—one can retire into himself and his snail's shell, nobody takes any notice." Yet this privacy was far from absolute, and at the time Jenny wrote about it her own snail's shell was constructed out of a tissue of appearances. In the sketch of her life she wrote in 1865, Jenny dated the beginning of the family's involvement with respectability from the move out of Soho.

> The road to "respectability" lay open with our ownership of a house. *La vie de bohème* came to an end, and where previously we had fought the battle of poverty in exile freely and openly, now we had the *appearance* of respectability, and held up our heads again. . . . I first came to know the real oppression of exile during this first phase of our truly bourgeois life as Philistines. . . . Everything conspired to bring about a bourgeois existence, and to enmesh us in it. We could no longer live like bohemians when everyone was a Philistine.[48]

Marx, too, saw the style of life the family adopted after 1856 as bound up with the bourgeois need to maintain appearances. Such keeping up was itself a source of expense, but necessary in order to preserve the family's credit. As he told Engels in 1858: "The 'show of respectability' that we have kept up until now was the only way to prevent a collapse." In 1863 he described the "false appearances" as "equally damaging for me and the children"—at a moment when it seemed the time had come to give the illusions up. Yet they remained, especially when visitors appeared in the Marx household. Lassalle's arrival in the early summer of 1862 sent Jenny to the pawn house with "everything that isn't tied or nailed down," in order "to keep up a certain exterior." When Paul Lafargue became engaged to Laura Marx in the fall of 1866 Marx found his financial troubles all the more dangerous because "the real state of things must be anxiously hidden from him."[49]

It was true, as Jenny said, that the need to keep up appearances grew in some ways when the family moved out of Soho, but it did not begin then. Liebknecht's description of the Sunday outings from Dean Street indicate that the determination to preserve a surface of well-being animated the family even then. "We had grounds enough for melancholy, but we were charmed against it by our grim humor. . . . Whoever started to complain was immediately most forcibly reminded of his duties to society." Marx sometimes admitted that he felt a need to keep up appearances even in the worst of times. When the communist poet Georg Weerth—an old and trusted comrade from the *Neue Rheinische Zeitung*—visited Marx in Soho in 1852, Marx wrote to Engels that the visit gave him little joy even though he liked Weerth very much. "It is painful, when one sits up to the neck in crap to have such a fine Gentlemen opposite, from whom the most shameful parts must be hidden." Except for Jenny's illness, Marx did not think Weerth had glimpsed "too deeply into my cards."[50]

In the Soho period it was nothing so simple as economic difficulties that Marx had to hide from the world outside his family. There was a much more embarrassing and dangerous skeleton in the closet. The fact was well hidden, and remained so—except to a few discrete eyes—until very recently, but it is now generally recognized that the baby to whom Lenchen Demuth, the family's faithful and lifelong servant, gave birth in June 1851, was Marx's son. Called Henry Frederick (the names of Marx's father and Engels), the infant was taken out of the house and raised by foster parents, although Lenchen maintained contact with him. The Marx children knew that Freddy existed, but they were made to believe that Engels rather than Marx was his father. When Engels was near death in 1895, however, and had not mentioned Frederick Demuth in his will, he let his friend and housekeeper Louise Freyberger (Karl Kautsky's ex-wife) know the truth lest he be thought to have disowned his own son. Louise Freyberger told Eleanor Marx who, unbelieving, made Engels tell her too.[51]

Although no evidence illuminates Frederick Demuth's upbringing, we do know that he became a machinist, and lived in London until his death in 1929. He was active in Labour Party politics in Hackney. He seems not to have had many contacts with the Marx family, but there were some. Contrary to what is usually said about Marx's correspondence containing no reference to him, his name appears at least once in the printed letters. In February 1877, when Marx and Engels were concerned about the spread of anarchist ideas in Switzerland and Italy, Engels wrote to Marx that it was time for "Herr Demuth" to subscribe to one of the Bakuninist papers "as decided," so that Bakunin's followers' doings could be kept more closely in view. Hence, not only were Marx and Engels in contact with Marx's illegitimate son, he had some tie with them in political matters.[52]

Much mystery clouds the story of his birth. Nothing is known of Marx's intimate relations with his housekeeper. Jenny, of course, learned the truth ("In the early summer of 1851," she wrote in her brief self-portrait, "there occurred an event which I shall not touch upon further, although it brought about a great increase in our private and public sorrows"), and it does not seem likely that Marx's relations with Lenchen went on after the baby appeared. Whether they had an effect on Lenchen's place within the family cannot be determined either. Jenny seems never to have shown anything but affection and gratitude toward Lenchen, and all the outsiders who observed her in the family saw only devotion in her attitude toward the Marxes. Was that devotion fed by an amorous attachment to Marx? If so, it was of an unusual sort. Liebknecht, who probably did not know about the child, described her place in the family as based on a remarkably independent sense of her position. "Marx could not impose on her. She knew him with all his whims and weaknesses and she could twist him around her little finger. Even when he was irritated and stormed and thundered so that nobody else would go near him, Lenchen would go into the lion's den. If he growled at her, Lenchen would give him such a piece of her mind that the lion became as mild as a lamb." To be sure, these words can hardly be read quite in the way Liebknecht intended, given what we now know about Marx and Lenchen. But far from clearing up the mystery of their relations, they only cloud them further.[53]

Frederick Demuth was born on June 21, 1851. If he was a full-term baby then he was conceived late in September of 1850, but it is quite possible that the conception took place as early as late August, or as late as October or November. The August possibility is worth considering because in that month Jenny Marx was out of London, trying unsuccessfully to borrow money from Marx's relatives in Holland. Given the fact that the whole family was then living in two rooms on Dean Street (at number 64, not the flat they occupied a few months later in number 28), the conception may well have occurred with Jenny away. The November date has a certain significance too, because early in that month Frederick Engels moved from London to Manchester. His presence in London until then would have helped give credence to the story that he, not Marx, was the father.

That story seems to have had its origin at the time Lenchen's condition became noticeable. On March 31, 1851, at the end of a letter filled with details about financial troubles, Marx wrote to his friend: "But finally, to give the situation a tragi-comic peak, there is a *mystère* in addition, which I will reveal to you in very few words. But just now I'm being disturbed and have to go to help my sick wife. The other thing, therefore, in which you also play a role, next time."[54] Marx did not come back to the mystery when he next wrote Engels two days later, but said he would tell him about it in person when he visited Manchester at the end of April. The caution makes it fairly clear that the mystery was Frederick Demuth. The reference to Engels' role must have been related to his later part as presumptive father. Did Marx therefore cast his friend in that role without consulting him? To do so would have presumed very far on their friendship, although it should be noticed that a few months later, when Marx was invited to write for the *New York Daily Tribune*, he did not hesitate to assume that Engels would begin the job for him. Moreover, Marx may have felt a strong need to try to hide the truth from Jenny, who had herself given birth (to Franziska, the daughter who died a year later) on March 28. Another possibility is that Lenchen made up the story about Engels' paternity; she, too, may have thought to shield Jenny from the truth at a time when excitement might have been dangerous for her. It should be added, of course, that the evidence is not really ironclad that Engels was not the father after all (later he sometimes sent money to Lenchen, which she may have used for the child's care), although it is nearly impossible to doubt his deathbed testimony.[55]

Hence, the whole matter of Marx's illegitimate son remains wrapped up in mystery and speculation, and only one thing appears with complete clarity, beyond the fact that the child existed: Marx's overwhelming need to keep the secret. We do not know how much of his time and effort drawing the veil required—finding the foster parents, arranging time for Lenchen to visit—or whether one of the hidden expenses in the family budget was contributing to the boy's support. It seems, however, that the birth itself came to light, and that reports were abroad identifying Marx as the father. In August, six weeks after the birth, Marx complained to Weydemeyer that his enemies on the democratic left were spreading around "the most unspeakable infamies" against him. "Naturally I would laugh at the crap, I don't let it disturb me for a moment in my work. But you will understand that my wife, who is ill and who sits from morning to night in the most unpleasant domestic distress, and whose nervous system is affected, is not refreshed by it, when stupid scandalmongers bring her every day the vapors of the pestilential democratic latrine." Some of the rumors to which Marx referred touched less intimate subjects than Frederick Demuth. Marx was accused of financial skulduggery in connection with the *Neue Rheinische Zeitung*, of trying to live off other exiles in London, as well as of more purely political misdeeds such as attempting to achieve a personal dictatorship and rule the workers by decree. Against these other accusations public denials could be made, and in 1853 three of Marx's friends who had gone to live in the United States, Weydemeyer, Adolf Cluss, and Abraham Jacoby, issued a circular defending Marx and explaining the financial sacrifices he had made in 1848. But the rumor of the illegitimate son was, as Marx said, "unspeakable," and could not be mentioned.[56]

Whatever else the existence of Lenchen Demuth's child meant in Marx's life then—and we can assume that it lay behind some of the inner tensions that grew up within the family—it meant an intensification of the need to keep up appearances. In fact it places the family's acknowledged attempts to do that in a new light. The need to maintain respectability on the financial level could be admitted, talked about; the other secret could not. Marx's friends could know something about his financial situation, and knowing what they did they could assume that the outer, economic problems were the cause of whatever inner, emotional tensions and anxieties the family displayed. Hence, the very problems which the economic "show of respectability" was designed to cover up—and the veil was never very effective—became in turn a shield against the knowledge that a more intimate and inadmissable anxiety both drew the household together and threatened to break it apart.

Such a situation may have been especially painful for Marx because his self-image was of a man completely free of pretension, false airs, and self-dramatization. In his answer to the parlor game of "Confessions," he listed his favorite virtue as "simplicity." What he meant is indicated by a letter he wrote to his daughter Jenny two weeks after his wife died. The letters of condolence he had received were, he said "animated with a truthfulness and inspired with a profound sensibility such as are not often to be met with in letters of this kind, which for the most part are purely conventional. I account for this by the fact that everything about her was natural, sincere, and unconstrained; that nothing was artificial. That is why the impressions formed of her by these others are so vivid and luminous."[57]

Although he wrote these words about his wife, Marx saw himself in the same terms. He hesitated for days before he could bring himself to print "The Author reserves to himself the right of translation" on *A Contribution to the Critique of Political Economy*, because he was made uncomfortable by the pretension the formula implied. What Marx called then "my antipathy for all humbug and vanity or pretension" appeared in many of his personal relationships, and fed his growing dislike for those among the 1848 exiles whom he regarded as inflated by feelings of self-importance, and whom he satirized as "the great men." Liebknecht observed that Marx "detested men who acted a part," and reported that Marx was fond of telling about Louis Blanc's visit to the flat in Dean Street. Blanc, believing he was alone in front of a small mirror, "struck an attitude . . . contemplated himself with delight and frisked like a March hare and tried to look imposing. Mrs. Marx, who also witnessed the comic scene, had to bite her lips not to laugh." Whether the details were true or not, the story illustrates Marx's aversion for false appearances and his need to believe himself free of them.[58]

It is not too much to say, then, that every level of Marx's private life was penetrated and infused with a tension between his antipathy to false appearances and his inescapable entanglements with the need to preserve them. The power of this motif in Marx's personal existence links that part of his life to recurring themes in his conception of society, and may have helped to give those themes a heightened importance in his writing. One can trace a line from his desire in the *Rheinische Zeitung* to exchange "the clouded language of private opinion" for "the clarifying words of public rationality," through his description of critical philosophy's work in 1843 as "a confession, nothing else," to the *Communist Manifesto*'s public exposition of the truth behind the "specter" of communism, and Marx's general conviction during the late 1840s that history was bringing appearance and reality into line. With Marx's return to the isolation of private life in the 1850s these images came to be inverted, beginning with the masks and illusions of *The Eighteenth Brumaire of Louis Bonaparte*, written in the first year of Frederick Demuth's life. Marx always believed that he knew where truth left off and false appearance began, and one of the major goals of *Capital* would be to explain how the surface relations of production and exchange veiled the economic and social realities on which capitalism rested. As we shall see, however, the ability of "appearance" to overpower "reality" would be one source of the difficulties Marx faced in his economic theory, just as their tangled relations complicated his personal life.

4. The Children

The "emotional warp" of a family, the frame and mold for human growth it provides, can often be seen reflected in its children.[59] Seven children were born to Karl and Jenny Marx, but one died at birth. Two others, Franziska and Guido, died after slightly more than a year, and one, Edgar, at nine. Most of what the children have to tell about the family comes from the three girls who lived into adulthood, Jenny, Laura, and Eleanor. To be sure, their later lives were shaped by many factors outside the Marx family, which we cannot examine here. Nonetheless, what the family imparted to them and how they mirrored its interior in their own lives is part of Marx's story as well as their own.

As might be expected, the three girls were talented, energetic, and charming. They amused their parents and won over their friends. The same was true of their brother, Edgar, until his death. All seem to have grown up in an atmosphere of relative freedom; toys were reported to be scattered throughout the flat in Dean Street, and at least the youngest, Eleanor, had free entry to Marx's study, even when he was working. As the girls grew up they did well in school, winning prizes and showing special talents for languages and literature. They learned music and singing, and two (Jenny and Eleanor) developed a deep interest in theater. Later they took on some of the family's correspondence, and wrote spirited and colorful letters. All three gave every evidence of being staunchly devoted to their parents, especially their father. All became involved in aspects of socialist politics, if only by marrying men who were active in public life, and one (Eleanor) became an important figure in the British labor movement.

At the same time, they had to make their way through the privations,

worries, and disappointments that their parents' life contained. Sometimes they were able to do this with the same qualities of good humor and
fortitude that Marx and Jenny tried to display. In 1853 Jenny told Engels
how Musch (age seven) had met the baker to whom the family owed
money while playing in the street outside the house. Asked "Is Mr. Marx
at home?" the boy replied "No, he a'nt upstairs," took three loaves of
bread under his arm and "quick as an arrow ran away to tell Moor about
it." There was, of course, anxiety as well as spirit in such behavior, and
the same was true of the children's experiences of political hopes dashed.
"Little" Jenny (then in her mid-twenties) wrote to Kugelmann during the
Franco-Prussian War: "We have not yet recovered from our surprise and
indignation at the turn affairs have taken. It is not easy to reconcile oneself
to the thought that instead of fighting for the destruction of the Empire,
the French people are sacrificing themselves for its aggrandizement, that
instead of hanging Bonaparte they are prepared to enrol themselves under
his banner. Who could have dreamt of such things a few months ago when
the revolution in Paris seemed a fact." In the next year the fact of revolution in Paris would return in the shape of the Commune, only to be bru-
tally repressed, endangering members of the Marx family (Laura was by
then married to Paul Lafargue and living in France) and bringing the
problems and sufferings of the refugees into the Marxes' house.[60]

Marx and Jenny both believed that the conditions of their life were
damaging to the children. Jenny associated Guido's poor health with the
fact that she breast-fed him, and "The poor little angel drank in so much
worry and hushed-up anxiety that he was always poorly and suffered hor-
ribly day and night." In 1859 Marx hoped Engels would find time to
spend a few days with the Marx family because the continual experience of
seeing their parents hounded for unpaid debts made it necessary for the
girls to see a *Mensch* in the house—an upright and respected person. "The
poor children have been tortured too soon by the domestic shit." A few
years later Marx blamed little Jenny's ill health on the family's troubles.
She was by then old enough (seventeen) "to feel the whole pressure and
dirtiness of our situation, and that, I believe, is the main cause of her
physical sickness." In 1863 Marx's wife told a friend that she, too,
thought their daughter Jenny's troubles arose from her having taken "our
situation too much to heart." By 1868, as we saw above, Marx was happy
to have his eldest daughter out of the house, because the children were
being "tortured to death," not from outside the family, but from inside,
by his wife's "wailing and irritation" and the loss of her mental balance.[61]

Although Marx regarded the regime of false appearances as damaging
to the children's development, he also described the family's life style as
necessary in order to provide "relations and circumstances that can assure"
the girls' future. Yet the future the girls found had more roots in the fami-

ly's political identity than in its connections with respectable English society. Two of the three married Frenchmen, important in socialist politics, and the third cast her lot with an English writer who at least thought
of himself as a socialist and a follower of Marx. Marx liked both the
Frenchmen, Paul Lafargue and Charles Longuet (we should not make too
much of the fact that one shared Marx's first name) and coupled them together as "my very good friends" in June 1866, before either was seriously
attached to any of his daughters. But he was never quite happy with their
politics, characterizing both as Proudhonians in 1866, and as "the last
Bakuninist" and "the last Proudhonian" respectively a number of years
later. It was in regard to what he saw as Lafargue's overly abstract and *a
priori* use of Marxian ideas that Marx once declared "I am not a Marxist."
Following that episode, however, he thought Lafargue's writings improved.[62]

That marriage to men who shared his commitment to socialism was not
calculated to still Marx's anxiety about his daughters' futures is shown by
his behavior at the time Laura became seriously involved with Lafargue.
Marx wrote Lafargue a long letter, demanding first of all that he pay his
court to Laura in a restrained fashion, appropriate to London, and not in a
way that suggested (at least to Marx) Lafargue's semitropical origins (he
had been born in Cuba). Marx's main concern was that Lafargue not think
he could marry Laura before he had some prospect of supporting her. "As
far as it is in my power," he declared, "I intend to save my daughter from
the rocks on which her mother's life has been wrecked." Inasmuch as
Lafargue declared himself to be a realist, he ought not to expect that Marx
would treat the future of his daughter "like an idealist" or let Lafargue
"make poetry" to her disadvantage. Marx's fears were stilled when it
turned out that Lafargue's family was well-off and willing to give the
couple enough money to cushion their start in life.[63]

Both the two elder daughters' later lives contain bits of material that
might inspire psychological speculation, but our information about them
is so slight that no persuasive inferences can be made. Jenny died at
thirty-nine in 1883, the same year as Marx, from some sort of abdominal
condition which may have been cancer. There is no way to know whether
her illness was linked to the maladies she suffered earlier, most of which
were connected with the chest and lungs, and diagnosed sometimes as
pleuritis, sometimes as asthma. Her sister Eleanor later wrote that Jenny
had been "glad to die," but nothing really makes clear what she meant.
Her brother-in-law Lafargue (who was a trained physician) blamed the
timing of the crisis that hastened her end on her negligence: "instead of
caring for herself she continued to neglect her health completely," a trait
that Engels had observed in her earlier. In 1880, three years before her
death, when Jenny heard from her old friend Liebknecht that his return to

Germany in 1862 had brought him much unhappiness, but that it had been his fate to go back there, she wrote to her husband: "To which I said amen. There is a prophecy (or rather a fate) that guides our life, however we may plan it!" What she thought her fate to be, and whether she found it, we cannot say.[64]

Laura had her share of suffering, losing all her three children in the first four years of marriage. Moreover, she, like her younger sister Eleanor, ended her life by suicide. But she was by then (in 1911) sixty-five, and had spent many busy and at least in some respects happy years with her husband in France, where Paul Lafargue became an important figure in the Parti Ouvrier, and for a time a socialist member of the Chamber of Deputies. It seems that she and Lafargue made a calm and considered decision not to expose themselves to the uncertainties of old age. One night they returned home from the theater and ended their lives together.

There is little evidence about her inner life. The one existing source that might be expected to provide some, her letters to Engels, show a spirited and clear-headed woman involved both in politics and her everyday domestic concerns. She seemed, like her mother, to accept the role of wife without question. "As I am in the habit of keeping in the background," she told Engels once, "I am very apt to be overlooked and forgotten." Perhaps that view of herself reflected the experience of being a middle child. She was the only one of the three girls who did not consider making a career as an actress.[65]

It was Eleanor (Tussy) who lived the saddest life. She and Marx seem to have agreed that of the three children, her character was most like his. "Our natures were so exactly alike!" she wrote to a friend. "Father was talking of my eldest sister and of me, and said: 'Jenny is most like me, but Tussy . . . *is* me.' "[66] Like her two sisters, she had a romantic attachment with a Frenchman, the historian of the Paris Commune, Prosper Lissagaray, whose book she later translated into English. But she did not marry him, in part because Marx thought him personally untrustworthy and for a time refused to let Eleanor see him. Although engaged to him for a number of years, she broke the tie about a year before Marx died.

Eleanor was both intellectually and politically the most active of the three daughters, but she was also the most noticeably affected by psychic stress. Already in 1874, when she was nineteen, Marx described her as "seriously, dangerously, ill," with one of "these female complaints, in which the hysterical element plays a part." At that time she went with Marx to take a cure at Carlsbad, where both father and daughter lived "strictly according to the rules." In 1881 Marx described her to Engels as in a state of utter nervous exhaustion, without appetite and unable to sleep. Her doctor found no organic cause for her illness, and attributed it to her "dangerously overwrought nervous system." Early in the next year

Marx reported that she was "under a mental pressure that completely ruins her health. Neither travel nor change of climate nor physicians can do anything in this case." Several immediate circumstances contributed to her condition at that time: the strain of ending her engagement to Lissagaray; the recent death of her mother, who she believed had died thinking (because of her engagement) "that I had been hard and cruel, never guessing that to save her and father sorrow I had sacrificed the best, freshest years of my life"; and the illness of her father. Yet her earlier and later depressions suggest that she was also burdened by longer-standing troubles.[67]

Marx believed that only one therapy could help Tussy during her crisis in 1881-82, and it was one she herself demanded: the chance to work at becoming a professional actress. She saw a theatrical career as a path to an independent life, telling Jenny Longuet that "The chance . . . of independence is very sweet." Her sister expressed gladness for Tussy's chance to live "the only free life a woman can live—the artistic one." Eleanor's biographer places the conflict she faced at this time in the context of a continuing opposition "between filial duty and her own independence" that beset Eleanor throughout her life.[68] Yet if she was trying to achieve independence by entering the theater, to do so did not really remove her from the influence of her father. In fact it is from Eleanor that we learn some of the ways in which dramatic fantasy played a continuing part in her father's life. For both of them dramatic fictions were a means of compensating for harsh realities.

In her memoir of Marx published in 1895, Eleanor emphasized that Marx was a "unique, an unrivaled storyteller." Eleanor gave two examples of his talents in this sphere, and her linking of them seems to have had partly conscious and partly unconscious elements. We have met the first one before.

> I have heard my aunts say that as a little boy he was a terrible tyrant to his sisters, whom he would "drive" down the Markusberg at Trier full speed, as his horses, and worse, would insist on their eating the "cakes" he made with dirty dough and dirtier hands. But they stood the "driving" and ate the "cakes" without a murmur, for the sake of the stories Karl would tell them as a reward for their virtue. And so many and many a year later Marx told stories to his children.[69]

Did Eleanor mean that Marx also told stories to his children as payment for their having to take what he called the "crap" and "crud" that his insistence on following his own goal "through thick and thin" brought with it? The story Eleanor recalled most forcefully from her childhood was a kind of allegory of Marx's own situation. It concerned a magical toy maker, Hans Röckle. Marx made up new chapters and episodes in his history month after month. "Though he was a magician, Hans could never meet his obligations either to the devil or to the butcher, and was therefore—much against the grain—constantly obliged to sell his toys to the devil." The adventures of the toys formed the plots for the stories; they ranged from the grim to the comic, and Eleanor remembered being very deeply affected by them. No wonder: Hans Röckle was Marx, transformed by that dramatic and powerful "spirit of generalization" with which he infused every facet of his experience.

Eleanor believed that she, too, possessed this dramatic talent. "I have seen too often—and with such different people—that I can *move* an audience—and that is the chief thing." There is some evidence that she was right, but her greatest success seems to have occurred with a set piece that painfully prophesied her own end. It was "The Bridge of Sighs," by one Thomas Hood, a monologue of a lonely and desperate girl who took her own life. When, later, she took a part in a regular play (by Edward Aveling, with whom she was then living) the result was a disastrous failure, the critic complaining that she could not be heard and did not convincingly represent her character.[70]

Her dramatic enthusiasm may have been based partly on a conviction that she had talent, but equally prominent in it was her ability to see the theater as the mirror of her own life. She became an early and passionate promoter of Ibsen, whom she admired not only for his social and political convictions, or for the sympathy she could feel with his heroines, but also for his sense of life, which was hers. She wrote to George Bernard Shaw:

> How odd it is that people complain that his plays "have no end" but just leave you where you were, that he gives no *solution* to the problem he has set you! As if in life things "ended" off either comfortably or uncomfortably. We play through our little dramas, and comedies, and tragedies, and farces, and then begin it all over again. If we *could* find solutions to the problems of our lives things would be easier in this weary world.[71]

Ibsen might have written the history of Hans Röckle.

By the time Eleanor wrote those passionate and unhappy words she was deeply entangled in the drama from which she would find no escape, her romance with Edward Aveling. She had begun to see Aveling regularly soon after her father's death, and by 1884 found herself ready to tie her life to his. Unfortunately Aveling was already married, and although no longer in any contact with his wife, divorce and marriage to Eleanor were not legally possible for him. Not without uneasiness, but with clear determination, Eleanor decided to "set up" with him. They moved in together and she took his name.

Nearly all those who knew Aveling—Eleanor was one of very few exceptions—agreed that he was a wretched human being, selfish, indulgent, irresponsible, insensitive, and disloyal. He often inspired a strong feeling of dread. Nonetheless, he was attractive to certain women, perhaps because he could radiate a sense of vitality, and because his enthusiasms were animated by genuine intellectual power. He had begun as an advocate of free thought, but by the early 1880s called himself a socialist and a follower of Marx. Engels, who overcame his early dislike for Aveling, believed in his abilities and engaged him to help translate Volume One of *Capital* into English.

Life with Aveling did little to lift Eleanor out of her depression. Only a month after her decision to live with him she wrote to a friend, Dollie Radford: "I am *very* lonely, Dollie, and I never felt lonelier that I do just now. . . . I have been seriously unwell for the last two weeks, and as I was threatened with an absolute breakdown I am just resting." Friends who saw her found her melancholy. When, in 1887, she made an attempt at suicide, Havelock Ellis, who knew her well, believed that "her friends were grieved; they were scarcely surprised."[72]

In spite of her psychic state she achieved a great deal. In addition to her efforts on behalf of Ibsen she translated Flaubert's *Madame Bovary* (another story of suicide) into English, and worked with great energy and effectiveness in the labor movement. In this she was everywhere known as her father's daughter, and her politics were remarkably true to the course Marx had followed in the First International, taking existing movements as they were but seeking to make the final goal the touchstone of policy and organization. Until 1895 Engels' advice helped shape her political activity, but her own understanding and determination were deep and powerful in their own right.

Eleanor brought into the open one element of her father's personality which ambivalence had veiled for him: she felt positively and self-consciously Jewish. Her Jewishness was not a religious faith however, it was—what her father had never denied—a personal identity. "My happiest moments," she told Max Beer, "are when I am in the East End amidst Jewish workpeople." Her friends included Amy Levy, a Jewish novelist, and Israel Zangwill, the more famous writer and dramatist. Zangwill shared Eleanor's enthusiasm for Ibsen, and Amy Levy was the author of *Reuben Sachs*, a novel of Jewish life in London. Much like Arthur Schnitzler's *Der Weg ins Freie* (*The Way Into the Open*) twenty years later, *Reuben Sachs* chronicled the personal distortions that occurred in the lives of Jews who sought to move (as one of the characters said) "from the tribal duck-pond into the wider and deeper waters of society." In the novel a doctor is made to say that the majority of his patients with nervous complaints were Jews, whose mental suffering was their punishment for "too high a civilization." Shortly after finishing the story Amy Levy committed suicide. Eleanor, declaring her sympathy with her friend's "hopeless melancholy," translated the book into German.[73]

That Eleanor followed Amy Levy's example was in good part the fault of Aveling, whose cruelties and infidelities grew as the years went on, and who finally—once his first wife had died—secretly married another woman, twenty years younger. Yet this bleak finale did not occur before Eleanor and Aveling had established a household with eerie echoes of the one in which she had grown up. Of course Aveling was not Marx, either intellectually, morally, or personally. Nonetheless, on the surface he could resemble him, and Eleanor, however closely she matched her father's character, found herself playing a role that recalled her mother's. It is merely curious and ironic that Aveling at one point derived some of his income from a German-language New York paper, the *New Yorker Volkszeitung*, and that he tried to make arrangements to have the $5 per article paid in advance. That attempt, however, was part of a larger pattern of domestic economy in which maintaining a comfortable life style masked continual indebtedness and the threat of financial collapse. Behind the Avelings' economic problems lay a personal relationship, which Eleanor described in familiar terms.

> If you had seen him, for example, to-day, going about like a happy child with never a sorrow or sin in his life, you would have marveled. Yet apart even from all the other troubles, we have mere money troubles enough to worry an ordinary man or woman into the grave. I often don't know where to turn or what to do. It is almost impossible for me now to get work that is even decently paid for, and Edward gets little enough. And while I feel utterly desperate he is perfectly unconcerned.

The result, she said, was that "The *constant* strain of appearing the same when nothing *is* the same, the constant effort not to break down, sometimes become intolerable."[74]

There were many reasons for Eleanor's plight, and one must be careful not to interpret her situation too one-sidedly. Yet it is difficult to gainsay the power that recurrence played in shaping her history. Having escaped from a life in which her independent desires were sacrificed to her parents during her crisis of 1881-82, she unerringly discovered a man with whom love meant crushing her own life in very nearly the same mold that had shaped her own childhood.

It was while she was feeling herself broken by Aveling's disloyalty and indifference that Eleanor discovered the truth about Freddy Demuth. That she learned first from Louise Freyberger was especially painful, for Kautsky's ex-wife was engaged in ingratiating herself with Engels in order to transfer control over Marx's manuscripts from Eleanor to the Austrian socialists. Threatened with losing her father's intellectual legacy she found the moral legacy in jeopardy too. As she wrote to Laura Lafargue a year after discovering the truth: "After all Marx the 'Politiker' and 'Denker' can take his chance, while Marx the Man . . . is less likely to fare as well."[75] Incredulous at first, Eleanor began to draw closer to the man she had long known, but only now recognized as her half-brother. He had his own troubles. His wife had run away sometime in 1892, taking most of his money and belongings; Eleanor had aided him then, and he gave sympathy and comfort now. On January 13, 1898, she wrote:

> Yes, sometimes I have the same feeling as you, Freddy, that nothing will ever come right for us. I mean you and me. Naturally poor Jenny had her share of trouble and grief, and Laura has lost her children. But Jenny was glad to die, and it was so sad for the children, but sometimes I think it was all for the best. I would not have wished for Jenny that she should go through the life I have had to go through. I don't think you and I have been particularly bad people—and yet, dear Freddy, it really seems as though we are being punished.[76]

In her mind Aveling was only the executor of a fate ordained for her from her past. Its origin was in her family.

Ten weeks later she was dead. Apparently she and Aveling had arranged a suicide pact after Eleanor learned of his secret marriage. Her biographer speculates that Eleanor announced her decision to Aveling, and that he—perhaps doubting that she was in earnest—agreed to share it. That would explain why they both participated in procuring the poison from a chemist, using the excuse that it was for a sick dog. But only Eleanor took it. Aveling walked away.

5. Marx in his Family: Need and Rejection

Next to the portraits by children and friends that show Marx as a devoted father and husband must be placed some images that reveal the weariness and estrangement he sometimes felt toward family life. *"Beatus ille der keine Familie hat,"* he groaned to Engels in 1854 ("Happy the man who has no family"). In 1867 while seeing Volume One of *Capital* through the press in Germany he looked to his return to London and the troubles of his domestic life with dread. A year earlier, writing to Paul Lafargue about his determination not to let his daughter's life be wrecked on the same shoals as his wife's had been, he explained: "You know that I have sacrificed my whole wealth to the revolutionary struggle. I do not regret it. On the contrary. If I had to begin my life again I would do the same. Only I would not marry."[77]

Did he mean it? To conceive Marx as a bachelor requires a truly acrobatic imagination, shifting many parts and extensions of his person to other positions, while still leaving the whole upright. But granted that on one level Marx was serious in what he told Lafargue, his statement was made for his family's protection. The implication was that if Lafargue were unable to support his family any better than Marx had done he ought not to marry either. The hypothetical withdrawal of his person from family life was a tactical one; one must say about it, *mutatis mutandis*, what Marx had said years earlier about Adolphe Bartels' withdrawal from politics: it was a way of participating in his family, like many others.

Some of the deeper functions that marriage and family served for Marx appear from a letter he wrote to Jenny while she was in Trier in June of 1856. Deeply passionate, the letter reveals how Marx's feelings for his wife were tied up with his fantasies, his uncertainties, and his overall relationship to the real world. It is long, and intimate, but we must quote it at length.

> Darling of my heart,
>
> I am writing to you again because I am alone, and because it makes me uncomfortable, always to have a dialogue with you in my head, without your knowing or hearing any of it or being able to answer. Bad as your portrait is, it provides me the best of services, and I understand now how even "the black Madonnas," the most disgraceful portraits of the mother of God, can find untiring admirers, and even more admirers than the good portraits. In any case, none of these black madonna pictures is any more kissed, tenderly regarded, and adored than your photograph, which to be sure is not black, but is unpleasant, and thoroughly fails to reflect your dear, sweet, kissable, "dolce" face. But I improve on the sun's rays that have painted falsely, and I find that my eyes, however spoiled by lamplight and tobacco, can still paint, not only in dreams, but also awake. I have you lovingly before me, and I take you by the hands and I kiss you from head to foot, and I fall on my knees before you and I groan: "Madame, I love you." And I love you indeed, more that the Moor of Venice ever loved. The false and corrupt world conceives all characters falsely and corruptly. Who of my many defamers and forked-tongued enemies has ever reproached me with being called to play the first lover's part in a second-class theater? And yet it is true. Had the scoundrels possessed enough wit, they would have painted "the relations of production and exchange" on the one side, and me at your feet on the other. "Look to this picture and to that," they would have written underneath.

It is hard to reconcile this outpouring with the calm declaration to Lafargue that had he begun his life over again "I would not marry." Where are appearance and reality, truth and fantasy, in this letter? Marx thanks a bad likeness for giving him free rein to adore an imaginary Jenny. Could he behave in real life as he did in imagination, in Dean Street, in the midst of the "crud" and in the shadow of Frederick Demuth? Marx went on to answer that question in the negative, and to say more about the relations between the private and the public man.

> Great passions, which in the presence of their object take the form of little habits, grow and take on the size befitting their nature through the magical operation of distance. So is it with my love. You need only to be removed from me by mere space, and I know that the passage of time has only served to make love grow, as sun and rain do the plants. My love for you, as soon as you are away, appears as what it is, a giant, in which all the energy of my spirit and all the character of my heart press together. I feel like a man again, because I feel a great passion; and the complexity in which study and modern culture entangle us, and the scepticism with which we necessarily impugn all subjective and objective impressions are all calculated to make us weak and trembling and undecided. But love, not for a Feuerbachian humanity, not for Moleschottian commerce, not for the proletariat, but love for one's darling, and namely for you, makes the man a man again.[78]

It was a touchingly beautiful letter and, given the family's history, a ringing declaration of faith that essential human relationships could survive the demeaning and sordid conditions within which they must sometimes exist. Yet much of the force behind it was unfulfilled desire transformed into fantasy, and the highly colored view of Marx's feelings it gave was—as he admitted—far from the everyday reality of his habitual life. Jenny had had to confront that contrast between ideal and reality in her relationship with Karl all her life; we saw earlier how she had written him in 1839 or 1840 that she often had to remind him "of external matters, of life and reality, instead of clinging wholly, as you can do so well, to the world of love, to absorption in it and to a higher, dearer, spiritual reality."[79] Now as then, life with Karl brought both idealized love and realized suffering.

Marx's words to Jenny clarify the relations between person, work, and family in his life. However much his outside involvements conflicted with it, Marx was drawn ever back into his family, to counter the feeling of weakness that the attempt to comprehend and transform society bred. Clinging, as Jenny said, to a higher reality in the face of an experience that failed to embody it, Marx recurringly found himself vibrating back and forth between idealization and rejection of the actual world in all its aspects. That double motion in relation to his family matched the alternation between commitment and withdrawal in his political life. The same dialectic shaped Marx's attempts to comprehend the economic foundations of modern society.

Part Three

ECONOMICS: MARX'S FATE

CHAPTER TEN

Value, Revelation, and the Method
of Political Economy

BECAUSE Marx's theory of history and society attributed so much importance to economic relations, his concentration on economic theory in his
last decades may seem to reflect a conscious resolve to make economics his
life work. In fact Marx never made such a decision. He was occupied by
economics for most of his life; his first contract with a publisher for a book
on the subject dated from 1845, and both he and his friends expected him
to produce a "big" book on it during the 1840s. In 1851 he described
himself as bored with economics and happy to be (as he thought) nearing
the end of his work on it. He even began to do research on other matters.
What made economics Marx's chief theoretical concern through so much
of his life was not conscious determination: the subject continued to occupy him only because he could not rid himself of it.

The history of Marx's involvement with economics must be understood
as part of the project he imposed on himself at every stage in his life: replacing his own and other thinkers' abstract and idealist perspectives with
a realistic point of view based on empirical knowledge of the actual world.
That project received fully developed expression in *The German Ideology*'s
determination to abandon philosophy in favor of the empiricism of ordinary men. Philosophy belonged to the past: in the present, with its palpable revolutionary transformations, men's senses needed no philosophic enlightenment to perceive the real conditions of their lives. But this solution
made Marx a hostage to history; if society failed to reveal its underlying
truth on the visible surface of politics, then Marx would have to resume
the role of philosophic critic, privy to secrets other men did not possess.
In the 1850s he did resume that role, as his political writings show. But
the conditions that faced Marx with a revived need for philosophy created
more and deeper problems for his economic theory than for his political
criticism. Marx had first to revise his ideas about economics to take account of the changed situation after 1851, and then to make the requirements of his materialist world view jibe with the implications of a
methodology whose procedures were basically Hegelian. These tasks
would keep him occupied with economic theory long after he expected to
be finished with it.

In tracing the evolution of Marx's views about economics, his developing attitude toward the basic categories of economic analysis—value, labor, competition, profit—must be set next to his changing views of how surface appearance related to underlying reality. The relationship between these two questions helped define Marx's conception of the proper method of political economy—and the role of philosophy within it—at each stage. Three separate phases need to be distinguished: the Paris writings of 1844; the period from *The German Ideology* to Marx's virtual abandonment of economics for several years after the end of 1851; and the new shape Marx gave to economic theory beginning with the so-called *Grundrisse* of 1857-58. Only the last of these stages marked the emergence of Marxian economics in the sense we know it from *Capital*.[1]

1. Value, Empiricism, and Philosophy, 1844-51

When Marx first gave sustained attention to economics while living in Paris during 1844, his general orientation still reflected the Feuerbachian critique of Hegel he had begun a year earlier. Marx's determination to free himself from abstraction was expressed in opposition to Hegel's speculative method, but from Marx's own later perspective this Feuerbachian approach to empirical reality still perceived the world through "philosophic spectacles." The main features of Marx's economic thinking at that time have already been outlined above, in Chapter Five, but we must return to them now long enough to recall the mixture of empiricism and philosophy they contained.

In his essay, "Outlines of a Critique of Political Economy," Engels had rejected the economists' concept of "real value," as a mere abstraction from the actual conditions of commercial exchange. The notion of a real value separate from price and determined by the costs of a commodity's production left out of account the obvious fact that those costs themselves were determined by supply and demand, by competition. The only value any commodity actually possessed was its price, and this value fluctuated "with the fortuitous relationship of supply and demand." The pretense that prices were bound up instead with an underlying value was the economists' way of justifying existing society; without it "the immorality of trade would become too obvious."[2]

Following Engels, Marx in 1844 rejected the theory that value was determined by labor time. The costs of production determined commodity prices only "according to the sporadic chance happenstance correspondence of supply and demand." Since supply and demand never corresponded completely in the real world, "value and costs of production stand in no necessary relationship."[3] This was still Marx's view in *The Holy Family*: "The determination of value is entirely fortuitous and need have no connection either with the costs of production or with social utility."[4] To Marx, the shape of economic relationships could not be com-

prehended by purely economic analysis, but only in the philosophical category of alienation. Whereas the economists could not explain the origin
and development of private property with their abstract notion of value,
the critic who began with alienation—which was a real experience of men
living in the present—could make up for their lack. "Just as we have derived the concept of *private property* from the concept of estranged, alienated labor by *analysis*, so we can develop every *category* of political economy with the help of these two factors; and we shall find again in each
category, e.g., trade, competition, capital, money, only a *definite* and *developed expression* of these first elements."[5]

Marx was concerned to make clear the relationship between appearance
and reality—existence and essence—this analysis presumed. The critic
who understood the role of alienation in economic life could discover
man's essential nature where others would not think to look for it: in economic life. From this viewpoint commerce and the division of labor appeared for the first time as *"perceptibly alienated* expressions of human *activity* and of *essential human power* as a *species* activity and power." Production
and exchange provided evidence for something that only religion, politics, art or literature had seemed to reveal before, namely "the reality of
man's essential powers and *man's species activity*." Grasping alienation allowed men to see the reality of their inner essence displayed in "ordinary
material industry."[6]

Marx regarded his views on political economy in 1844 as marking an
important advance toward a purely empirical study of human nature and
history. As he later explicitly acknowledged, however, this new perspective was only available to "the eyes of the philosopher." In 1844 Marx
depicted men actually engaged in production and exchange as confined in
a world of illusion. "My *social* relationship with you and my labor for your
want is just plain *deception* and our mutual reintegration is *deception* just as
well." The objects men produced did not display their own relationship to
each other, but distorted it. "Each of us actually *does* what the other thinks
he is doing. . . . For you, your own object is only the *sensuous shell* and
concealed form of my object; its production *means* and *expressly* is the acquisi-
tion of my object." Moreover, the projection of human powers and
capacities onto the universal object of alienation, money, turned "an *image*
into *reality* and *reality* into a mere image." Money turned men's "real essential powers" into "tormenting chimeras," while also transforming individual fantasies with no inherent power to realize themselves into "real
powers and faculties." To ordinary experience, therefore, the everyday
world was a place of illusion and inversion. Only under socialism could it
be said that "the senses will become theoreticians," perceiving the human
essence that philosophy alone had understood before. Only then would
"our productions be so many mirrors reflecting our nature."[7]

Hence, in 1844 Marx's rejection of value theory and his attempt to make alienation the central category in economic criticism were tied up with a conviction that philosophy in the present saw through to essential truths which ordinary vision could encompass only in the future. Marx still believed, as he had in the days of the *Rheinische Zeitung*, that philosophy could overcome the blindness of everyday experience. This view of the triangular relationship between economics, philosophy, and real experience would not survive Marx's reorientation of 1845-46, with its program of leaving philosophy aside in order to perceive reality "like an ordinary man."

This program not only recast Marx's view of the relations between history, philosophy, and empirical experience, it also transformed his views of economics. In *The German Ideology* he no longer rejected value theory as an abstraction from real conditions; properly interpreted, it was a realistic description of them. When production costs were considered in conjunction with competition, they did provide a measure of value: "within the framework of competition the price of bread is determined by the costs of production and not by the whim of the bakers." In another place he declared flatly that the value of coin "is determined exclusively by the costs of production, i.e., labor."[8]

Marx made these comments in passing, however, for the settling of accounts with Feuerbach, Stirner, and Bauer gave little occasion for the sustained discussion of economic questions. That occasion arose a year later, in Marx's polemic against Proudhon, *The Poverty of Philosophy*, written in answer to Proudhon's *The Philosophy of Poverty*. Here Marx gave the most extended account of his views on economics in the period before 1848. His acceptance of value theory now became complete: "Ricardo's theory of values is the scientific interpretation of actual economic life." The basic truths of economics started from this point: "Once utility is admitted, labor is the source of value. The measure of labor is time. The relative value of products is determined by the labor time required for their production. Price is the monetary expression of the relative value of a product."[9]

Marx still recognized—as he had in 1844—that the notion of value could be employed in an abstract way that attributed more stability and order to capitalist production relations than they actually possessed. As a subscriber to Ricardo's theory of value he was just as determined to forestall that possibility as he had been while he still rejected it. The value Marx spoke of did not exist apart from the actual exchange relations of society; it was created through the fluctuations of supply and demand. Value was therefore equivalent to price. Proudhon had mistakenly sought a measure of value independent of supply and demand, a stable underlying proportional relation which the prices of commodities necessarily expressed. (His proposal to establish direct relations between producers based on the immediate exchange of equivalent amounts of labor time, and thereby to eliminate money and assure laborers the full value of their products, presupposed the discovery of this proportion.) In Marx's view such an attempt left aside the destabilizing effect of supply and demand, not only on the prices of goods, but on the underlying value of labor itself. Proudhon had "simply forgotten about supply and demand." He did not understand that "the competition among the suppliers and the competition among the demanders form a necessary part of the struggle between buyers and sellers, of which marketable value is the result." If he admitted that labor time determined the value of products, "he should equally admit that it is the fluctuating movement alone that in society founded on individual exchanges makes labor the measure of value. There is no ready-made 'proportional relation,' but only a constituting movement." Capitalist production could never create a stable set of economic relationships: "The moment the labor time necessary for the production of an article ceases to be the expression of its degree of utility, the exchange value of this same article, determined beforehand by the labor time embodied in it, becomes quite unable to regulate the true relation of supply to demand."[10]

What Marx was getting at appears perhaps more clearly in *Wage Labor and Capital*, a pamphlet based on a set of lectures he delivered late in 1847 in Brussels, and published (in an incomplete form) in the *Neue Rheinische Zeitung* during 1849. Here Marx stated, much as he did in *The Poverty of Philosophy*, that exchange values and prices were determined by the cost of production, and that even though "the real price of a commodity . . . is always above or below its cost of production," these rises and falls of prices "reciprocally balance each other." Marx derived this analysis from the economists, but he did not employ it in the way they did.

> This determination of price by cost of production is not to be understood in the sense of the economists. The economists say that the *average price* of commodities is equal to the cost of production; that this is a *law*. The anarchical movement, in which rise is compensated by fall and fall by rise, is regarded by them as chance. With just as much right one could regard the fluctuations as the law and the determination of the cost of production as chance, as has actually been done by other economists.[11]

As Marx put it in the polemic against Proudhon, it was not the stable relationship between one man's labor and another's that regulated commerce under modern conditions, but the "anarchy of production."[12] However much one admitted that values were determined by the costs of production, the reality of modern life could only be understood through observing this anarchy.

It is solely these fluctuations, which, looked at more closely, bring with them the most fearful devastations and, like earthquakes, cause bourgeois society to tremble to its foundations—it is solely in the course of these fluctuations that prices are determined by the cost of production. The total movement of this disorder is its order. In the course of this industrial anarchy, in this movement in a circle, competition compensates, so to speak, for one excess by means of another.[13]

Only through the constantly upsetting force of competition did the determination of value by labor time cease to be an abstraction and enter into the real world of work and commerce. Hence the determination of value by labor time guaranteed that capitalist society would "pass in constant succession through vicissitudes of prosperity, depression, crisis, stagnation, renewed prosperity, and so on."[14]

Interpreting value theory in this way, Marx rejected Proudhon's attempt to use it as the basis for establishing a socialist organization of productive relations. The labor theory of value was "merely the scientific expression of the economic relations of present-day society." It was "inevitably the formula of the present enslavement of the worker, instead of being, as M. Proudhon would have it, the 'revolutionary theory' of the emancipation of the proletariat."[15] What pointed the way to that emancipation, Marx believed, was no theoretical formulation based on categories employed in political economy, but the power of class conflict in modern life. Class conflict determined the evolution of productive relations. "The very moment civilization begins, production begins to be founded on the antagonism of orders, estates, classes, and finally on the antagonism of accumulated labor and actual labor." The relations of supply and demand reflected the class structure of society, for both the means and the needs of every consumer were "determined by his social position, which itself depends on the whole social organization. True, the worker who buys potatoes and the kept woman who buys lace both follow their respective judgments. But the difference in their judgments is explained by the difference in the positions which they occupy in the world, and which themselves are the product of social organization." Why were "cotton, potatoes and spirits the pivots of bourgeois society? . . . Because in a society founded on *poverty* the poorest products have the fatal prerogative of being used by the greatest number." As long as society remained divided into classes "the last word of social science will always be [Marx ended his book with a quotation from George Sand]: "Combat or death; bloody battle or nothing."[16]

Neither philosophy nor alienation could occupy the place in this vision that Marx had attributed to them earlier. The notion of alienation played no identifiable role in *The Poverty of Philosophy*. As for philosophy itself, if the book's title were not evidence enough of what Marx meant to say about its power to reform economics, his criticism of Proudhon's attempt to mix the two disciplines make his views perfectly clear. To improve on economic literature from a philosophical standpoint had been just Proudhon's error: by making use value and exchange value into abstract categories—rather than expressions of real productive relations—Proudhon turned things "upside down like a true philosopher." The "reason" he professed to find operative in human affairs at various historical periods "betrays itself nevertheless, at every moment, as the individual reason of M. Proudhon."[17] The correct method of economics was, like Ricardo's, "historical and descriptive." In Ricardo's account of modern economic life one saw that "the cynicism is in the facts and not in the words that express the facts." Ricardo and his school allowed men "to see economic relations exposed in all their crudity, to see the mysteries of the bourgeoisie unmasked."[18]

These views envisioned quite a different relationship between surface appearance and underlying reality than Marx had posited in 1844. In his Paris writings Marx had still described actual production relations as creating illusions which only the eyes of philosophical criticism could penetrate. In *The Poverty of Philosophy*—as in *The German Ideology*—he believed that the surface appearances of social relations were the direct and undistorted expression of the essential reality that shaped them. The polemic against Proudhon explained Marx's turn from philosophy to ordinary empirical perception even more clearly than the criticism of Stirner and Feuerbach had. The socialists and communists, Marx declared, were the theoreticians of the proletariat, just as the economists were the "scientific representatives" of the bourgeoisie. Under modern conditions, however (as we noted earlier), they could abandon the utopian mentality that led earlier reformers to "improvise systems and go in search of a regenerating science." As the outlines of the proletariat's struggle grew more clear, socialists "no longer need to seek science in their minds; they have only to take note of what is happening before their eyes and to become its mouthpiece."[19] Science became revolutionary by turning from the images in the mind of the thinker to the real conditions increasingly visible in modern life. Its method was empirical and not philosophical.[20]

In other economic writings of the same period Marx also evoked the growing clarity with which social experience revealed its real basis. In a manuscript on "Wages of Labor," written in the second half of 1847, Marx spoke about "The positive side of wages." Here he described the consequences arising from the diffusion of the wage relationship through modern society. "Let us even take wages in the kernel of their objectionableness," Marx proposed, "that my activity becomes a commodity, that I become through and through a saleable item." Still, modern wage labor had a positive side: "*First*: Every patriarchal relationship collapses thereby, in that between employer and worker there is only haggling, buying and selling the only connection, the money relationship the only relationship. *Second*: The halo has fallen generally from all the relationships of the old society, in that they have dissolved into pure money-relationships." The destruction of the halo surrounding certain activities in society meant that the real relations between men now emerged to view: "What great progress it was that the whole regiment of priests, doctors, lawyers etc., thus religion, law etc. is now defined only by its commercial value."[21]

In these comments, as in the *1844 Manuscripts*, Marx saw money as controlling not only the way men related to each other, but also the way they perceived their interrelationships. In 1844, however, money's role had been to conceal or invert those relations; now it revealed them for what they were. Unlike the alienated human essence, class conflict was visible to men who did not wear philosophic spectacles. Like the anarchical movement that constituted the real determination of value by labor time, class conflict grew more visible on the social surface as purely monetary relationships spread out through society. Unaided human vision could now be an organ of theory in the present, not only in the socialist future.

It is difficult to specify how long this configuration, which made value equivalent to price and saw appearance approaching ever more closely to reality, lasted in Marx's mind. Marx first had to reconsider his conviction that class conflict itself was becoming clearer on the surface of society after Bonaparte's successful *coup d'état* at the end of 1851. We witnessed his renewed awareness of the power of illusion, testified to by the contrasts between *The Class Struggles in France* and *The Eighteenth Brumaire*, earlier. Marx did not believe that the veils and masks he wrote about in 1852 would remain in place very long, however. In the first years of the 1850s he continued to expect revelations in British affairs, as his newspaper reports show, only to be disappointed by the survival of ambiguity and archaism in British politics. One would expect Marx's similar economic perspective of the late 1840s to have survived at least until the end of 1851, too, and the evidence, incomplete as it is, indicates that (for the most part at least) it did. However, Marx's only surviving economic writing of the time, a brief comment on Ricardo, is too fragmentary to tell us for sure.

In that manuscript, which Marx set down in the early spring of 1851, he repeated his earlier insistence that economics take account of the real movement of production and not just of the value relations said to lie behind it. "Ricardo abstracts from that which he regards as accidental. It is a different thing to exhibit the *real process*, wherein the two sides—what he calls accidental movement, but which is the constant and real factor, and its *law*, the average relationship—both appear equally essential." Although supply and demand determined the distribution of capital in the various branches of industry, "On the other side both supply and demand are determined by production itself." Included in the notion of production were the class relations on which capitalism was based.[22]

Whether Marx's basic perspective on economics had begun to shift by 1851 or not, that year marked an important stage in his work on economics: it saw the dissolution of his belief that his study was nearing completion and its replacement with five years of virtual withdrawal from the subject. At the beginning of April 1851, Marx told Engels that he was within five weeks of finishing his reading of economic literature, "and that finished, I shall compose the work on economics at home, and throw myself into another discipline in the [British] Museum. This one begins to bore me. At base this science has made no progress since A. Smith and D. Ricardo, however much special—often overly refined—research has been done." When, in August, Marx was asked by Charles Dana to write for the *New York Daily Tribune*, he requested Engels to begin the articles for him so that he could continue to give attention to completing his book.[23]

Yet he did not finish in 1851, and during the following year Marx no longer worked on economics. His literary energy was absorbed by other projects: *The Eighteenth Brumaire*, *Revelations of the Cologne Communist Trial*, and the exposé of the 1848 emigrés that would become *The Great Men of the Emigration*. When next Marx gave his attention to economics, in the early months of 1853, his earlier sense of being nearly ready to write the book had disappeared. The already thick pile of notebooks he had accumulated by 1851 grew still larger while Marx extended his reading, "as if," in the words of one of the most careful Marx scholars, "he still had much to learn."[24] This period of work seems to have ended with the bout of sickness Marx suffered in early March, and for two years afterward his correspondence contains practically nothing about his work on economics. Early in 1855 he began to reread his earlier notes, until inflammation of the eyes made him stop another time.[25]

Only late in 1856 does Marx seem to have taken up the subject again. In October of that year he read about the history of silver currency. The following January he looked into a book by a disciple of Proudhon, Alfred Darimon, whose work on banking and currency reform would provide the jumping-off point for the manuscript that became the *Grundrisse*. It was during the fall and winter of 1857-58 that Marx undertook the enormous effort necessary to put his fundamental notions about economic theory down on paper. In early December he wrote to Engels: "I am working like mad through the nights to put my economic studies together, so that I at least have the basic lines (*Grundrisse*) clear before the deluge." In the middle of the following January Marx told Engels that he had been taken sick from overwork, but that he was happy about his results, and that he had developed a totally new doctrine of profit. By the end of March he had signed a contract for his book, and in April he sent Engels a partial summary of what it would contain.[26]

A number of reasons have been advanced to explain Marx's virtual abandonment of his work on economics during this period. The difficult state of his domestic finances and his need to support his family through journalism certainly had something to do with it; we have seen how much of Marx's time and energy went into the dealing with his family situation in the 1850s. Yet this cannot explain Marx's retreat from economics by itself, for even in the years in Soho he found time for other projects requiring extensive research, notably his *Life of Palmerston* and *Secret Diplomatic History of the Eighteenth Century*. Nor were Marx's domestic troubles in any way finished during the fall and winter of the *Grundrisse*'s composition. 1857-58 were very difficult years for the family's finances, yet Marx was able to do his work then despite the "pressure from without."

A second reason sometimes advanced for Marx's failure to continue his work was the difficulty of getting his book printed in Germany. Early in 1852, the radical Leipzig publisher Otto Wigand told Marx he could not accept the work, apparently out of fear that—given the intensely conservative political atmosphere—it would be confiscated. The following August Marx proposed a book on modern British economic theory to another German publisher, Brockhaus, but this was also refused.[27] Yet these difficulties were more annoyances and irritations than real barriers to Marx's work. In March 1853 Engels still prodded Marx to complete his book on economics, saying that if necessary it could appear in weekly installments "as soon as we have a newspaper"—a situation both Marx and Engels then thought to be close at hand. The following September Marx wrote to Adolph Cluss in America that it was only the lack of a period of undisturbed work that prevented the book's completion, not mentioning the publication problem.[28] At other times Marx dealt with the difficulty of publishing in Germany by having his work printed in German in London, and then taken to the continent. The plan misfired when the book about the Cologne Communist Trial failed to reach the German market, but this did not prevent Marx following the same course with the long (and, as Marx then thought, very important) *Herr Vogt* in 1860.

If the political situation of the 1850s did not pose any fundamental problem for the work on economics Marx had been planning since 1844, the economic situation did. The view of capitalist economic relations Marx put forward during the 1840s depended heavily on the regular recurrence of industrial crises. It was at the moments of crisis—as, in the political sphere, at the moment of revolution—that the truth of bourgeois economic life appeared most clearly on the surface of society. An economic crisis was a palpable demonstration that anarchy was of the essence in capitalist production, that "with just as much right one could regard the fluctuations as the law and the determination by the cost of production as chance." Just as the revolution of 1848 had failed to consummate the union of political appearance and social reality the 1840s seemed to promise, so did the disappearance of economic crisis between 1847 and 1857 cast doubt on the earlier evidence that society's own actions revealed the true nature of its economic relations.

Continually disappointed as they were, Marx's expectations of renewed economic crisis were clearly connected with the sporadic attempts to work on economic theory he made during the 1850s. The bout of reading in economic literature Marx went through in the early months of 1853 was triggered by the conviction—based on earnings reports and interest rates—"that the crisis now will become due." Again, two years later, it was the appearance of signs of economic crisis that led Marx to reread his notebooks on economics, "if not to compose the work, in any case to master the material and have it ready to be worked out." In the fall of 1856, after the Marx family had moved out of Soho, and accompanied by his own and Engels' assurance that the crisis would certainly appear during 1857, Marx studied the history of currency. When, in the fall of 1857, the crisis did finally occur, Marx told Lassalle that it had "spurred me on to give myself seriously to the composition of my basic features of economics."[29]

What Marx said about the economic collapse of 1857, however, shows that he no longer viewed a crisis in the way he had before. In contrast to his earlier descriptions of the recurring crises as evidence that the reality of capitalism was the anarchy of its surface upheavals, Marx now spoke of the crisis as a phenomenon that had emerged from a deeper level, where reality and visibility were not the same. "Take all in all," Marx avowed in February 1858 "the crisis has worked in the earth like a fine old mole."[30] Like revolution in *The Eighteenth Brumaire*, the crisis had gone underground; the reality of economic life was a creature of the depths. The implements necessary to perceive it were ones he had used and then abandoned in earlier life. In mid-November 1857, he exclaimed to Engels: "The delays also explain themselves so rationally now that even Hegel would have rediscovered, to his great satisfaction, the 'Concept' in the 'empirical separation of the world of finite interests.' " A few weeks later Marx spoke of capitalists whose ruin was already determined but who were not themselves aware of it as "implicitly [*an sich*]—as Hegel would say— bankrupt capitalists."[31] No such invocations of Hegel would have been appropriate to Marx's economic writings of the late 1840s (certainly none appeared in them), for discovering the truth of economic relations did not then require the special vision of philosophy. How much philosophy was necessary in the 1850s would appear in the "basic lines" of economic theory Marx now traced, the work that has come to be known as the *Grundrisse*.

2. The *Grundrisse*: Plumbing the Depths of Economic Life

Marx's *Grundrisse* (as the manuscript of 1857-58 is known even in its English translation) makes up a thick book of over 800 pages. The theory it contains is in essence that of *Capital* but, whereas there the material would be carefully arranged and consistently worked out, here it still appeared as a kind of pulsing embryo of thought, certain of its vitality, but not yet sure of its structure or its form. Some questions that appear fully worked out in *Capital* were still in process of formation.

The manuscript begins in a way that hardly promises its subsequent development, namely as a criticism of Proudhon's disciple, Alfred Darimon. Yet this beginning was significant, too. Once before Marx had been impelled to write down his basic views on economics by his reaction to a Proudhonian treatise: in *The Poverty of Philosophy*. Comparing Marx's strictures on Proudhon of 1847 with his criticism of Proudhon's follower ten years later reveals exactly the direction his thought had taken. In 1847 the flaw in Proudhon's method had been the attempt to find the hidden proportional relation underlying commodity exchanges, instead of starting out with the visible, concrete movement of supply and demand. Proudhon had sought to discover value as a mystery, instead of recognizing that it was equivalent to price. In 1857, the reverse: the basic defect of the Proudhonian school was its failure to distinguish the surface appearance of capitalist society from the reality hidden beneath. The beginning of economic wisdom was the distinction between price and value.

Proudhon and his followers thought to assure that workers would receive the full value of their labor by eliminating money and replacing it with "hour-tickets" or "time-chits," certificates that would not represent an abstract value but a concrete amount of time actually worked by individual members of society. Since all exchanges would employ these tickets, everyone would receive the exact value of his labor. In 1847 Marx's objection to this system (which was not yet quite so fully worked out as it would be ten years later) was essentially that it would be swamped by the anarchy of bourgeois production; the only rational way to organize distribution in an industrial society was to do away with individual exchanges altogether. In 1857 Marx still believed this, but he demonstrated it in a new way. He argued that the attempt to exchange equivalent quantities of labor for each other, and for goods whose value would be expressed in similar terms, would soon vanish in the space that necessarily separated value from price in a society based on commodity production.

The relationship in which goods acquired a price, determining the quantity of one that must be given for another, was the relationship of supply and demand. The value of goods, however, arose quite independently of price; what determined it was the labor time necessary for a commodity's production. The system of the Proudhonians might work momentarily, therefore, but eventually supply and demand would operate to give goods a price different from the value expressed in the "hour ticket" or "time-chit" originally attached to them; in the end the new medium of exchange would simply come to function as money.[32]

This argument was based on the same distinction between the concrete reality of price and the abstract nature of value that had shaped Marx's attitude toward value theory in 1844 and again from 1845. In 1844, however, the difference between value and price had led Marx to reject the concept of value; after 1845 he had employed "value," but only in a sense that made it equivalent to price. Now Marx regarded the separation of value from the uncertain movement of prices as the proof that value was a more real and essential quality than price. Labor time now represented "real value," whereas price was only "nominal value." The value determined by labor time was, to be sure, only "average value," and "this average value appears as an external abstraction if it is calculated out as the average figure of an epoch." So had Marx (and Engels) regarded it in 1844. No longer: "But it is very real if it is at the same time recognized as the driving force and the moving principle of the oscillations which commodity prices run through during a given epoch." Now Marx distinguished price from value "not only as the nominal from the real; not only by way of the denomination in gold and silver, but because the latter appears as the law of the motions which the former runs through."[33] Marx had moved 180 degrees away from his assertion in *Wage Labor and Capital*, that "with just as much right one could regard the fluctuations as the law and the determination by the cost of production as chance." Later, in *Capital*, Marx may have been thinking of his own evolution when he wrote: "Exchange value, at first sight, presents itself as . . . a relation constantly changing with time and place. . . . An exchange value that is inseparably connected with, inherent in commodities, seems a contradiction in terms."[34] So had it seemed to Marx himself for many years; but from 1857 it did not.

Out of the fundamental opposition between price and value, all the characteristic phenomena of modern economic life now unfolded. First came money. Since labor time could not be equivalent to price, a different measure of the relative values of commodities was needed. "Because labor time as the measure of value exists as an ideal, it cannot serve as the matter of price comparisons." Price had to acquire "a separate material existence" alongside commodities, and this was money. "Price as distinct from value is necessarily money price. . . . The exchange value of a product creates money alongside the product." The fact that commodities were produced for exchange implied the need for a general medium of exchange, and the power of money in modern life arose from that need. "Money implies the separation between the value of things and their substance. Money is originally the representative of all values; in practice this situation is inverted, and all real products and labors become the representatives of money."[35]

The existence of money as the general representative of wealth gave a new meaning to human industry, for it allowed men to make wealth—as opposed to some particular set of products—the goal of economic activity. "General industriousness is possible only where every act of labor produces general wealth, not a particular form of it; where, therefore, the individual's reward, too, is money." Money was, therefore, "a condition . . . for the development of all forces of production, material and mental." For such a development to take place, however, money had to be the general aim of all individual labor. Hence, labor had to be paid not with goods, but with wages. "Labor must directly produce exchange value, i.e., money. It must therefore be *wage labor*." When labor produced exchange value as such, what it received could only be a money wage.[36]

At the same time, money created a basic contradiction in economic life. If money was the general form of wealth, still it was not wealth itself. Money was not the mass of goods men needed and desired for their existence and well-being, it was only an abstraction from those goods, a ghost of them. "Money in its final, completed character now appears in all directions as a contradiction, a contradiction which dissolves itself, drives towards it own dissolution. As the *general form of wealth*, the whole world of real riches stands opposite it. It is their pure abstraction—hence, fixated as such, a mere conceit. Where wealth as such seems to appear in an entirely material, tangible form, its existence is only in my head, it is a pure fantasy. Midas." That is to say, the wealth that money as a material embodiment seemed to represent could actually be realized only by giving up money, putting it back into circulation, "to disappear in exchange for the singular, particular modes of wealth." When this happened it became lost to the individual who tried to accumulate it, "and this disappearance is the only possible way to secure it as wealth. . . . If I want to cling to it, it evaporates in my hand to become a mere phantom of real wealth. . . . If the other riches do not [also] accumulate, then it loses its value in the measure in which it is accumulated. What appears as its increase is in fact its decrease. Its independence is a mere semblance; its independence of circulation exists only in view of circulation, exists as dependence on it."[37] How then could one bring the dizzying phantom dance to a halt, how could the seeker after wealth get a firm grip on the object of his desire?

The answer was that money had to become capital. As a mere measure of value or medium of circulation money continually lost its character as the embodiment of wealth in general. To retain it while in circulation, money had to be exchanged for some "particular substances of real wealth" which, like it, also represented wealth as such. In this way exchange value would be transformed from the mere result of commodity exchange into its guiding purpose and presupposition. Only one commodity possessed the magic to effect this transformation: labor. Money became capital by making the object of commerce not the goods labor produced, but labor itself. "It must now again posit the point of departure of circulation, which lay outside circulation, was presupposed to it, and for which circulation appeared as an external, penetrating and internally transforming movement; this point was labor." When money purchased any other particular good, its value disappeared into what it bought; when it purchased labor, however, its value was maintained and expanded. Money, from being a rigid, tangible substance, had "become a process," in which the labor that had originally produced exchange value turned back upon itself: "But the nature of the return is this, that the labor objectified in the exchange value posits living labor as a means of reproducing it, whereas, originally, exchange value appeared merely as a product of labor." This process of reproduction and expansion was capital.[38]

When labor was recognized as the power that preserved and expanded value as such, rather than as the source of particular goods—as the producer of wealth in general rather than of clothes or shoes or fountain pens—then its character, too, appeared in a different light. In order to be the opposite pole of capital, labor had to be *value-creating, productive labor.* It was not merely labor "for the satisfaction of immediate needs"; labor in that form had "nothing whatever to do with capital." The worker worked to support his life; he exchanged his labor for money that bought particular goods to sustain himself and his family. The capitalist, however, exchanged his money for labor that would produce exchange value, for labor in general. What the worker sold was not the same as what the capitalist bought, and their values were not the same either. For the worker, "the exchange value of his commodity cannot be determined by the manner in which its buyer uses it, but only by the amount of objectified labor contained in it; hence, here, by the amount of labor required to reproduce the worker himself." But capital bought labor "as the general productive force of wealth; activity which increases wealth." To whatever degree this activity produced more value in a given time than was necessary to sustain the laborer, the difference went to the capitalist.[39]

Put another way, the "use value" that capital sought from labor was "not this or another labor, but *labor pure and simple,* abstract labor." Labor had exchange value for the laborer because a specific amount of labor was required to support and reproduce particular workers under given conditions. But labor had use value to the capitalist because every particular labor constituted a proportion of "the totality of all labors," which together produced society's wealth. The exchange value of labor for workers was a quantity of specific, "concrete" labor; the use value of labor (later Marx would reserve the term "labor-power" for this aspect of labor's substance) for the capitalist was a portion of the total abstract labor operative in society.[40]

In its day-to-day expression, this contrast between concrete labor and abstract labor took the form of the difference between "necessary labor" and "surplus labor." Necessary labor was the amount of work time (under given social conditions) any worker had to toil in order to produce the amount of value required to purchase goods that would sustain him and his family for a given period, say one day. Under particular conditions, he might be able to do this in five hours. The value produced in that time was the exchange value of one day's labor. But if the workers themselves did not control production, they could be made to stay at their tasks for longer. In the nineteenth century the normal working day was often ten, twelve, or even fourteen hours. The difference between the total hours worked and the labor time necessary to sustain the worker was surplus labor.

This distinction explained why labor meant one thing to workers and another to capitalists. To the worker labor was a mere exchange value, "not a power productive of wealth," and it never produced any value greater than the amount required to reproduce it. "The worker cannot become *rich* in this exchange, since, in exchange for his labor capacity as a fixed, available magnitude, he surrenders its *creative power*, like Esau his birthright for a mess of pottage." The bounds that limited the worker's recompense were not totally rigid, "the sphere of his immediate gratifications is capable of a certain contraction or expansion." But however many times a worker exchanged his labor for wages, he was always left with nothing more than "his living, direct labor itself to exchange."[41]

This analysis of the twofold nature of labor under capitalism was the keystone of Marxian economics. The value of the surplus labor that arose from the difference between the concrete labor the worker sold and the abstract labor power the capitalist bought Marx called "surplus value" (*Mehrwert*). Surplus value was the very heart of capitalist production, the source not only of the capitalist's profit but—as Marx would later show—of all capitalist revenues. Marx believed his analysis demonstrated how surplus value arose "out of circulation itself," despite the fact that, in the nature of circulation, "only equivalents are exchanged." In the published version of *Capital* this discovery would be announced with much more fanfare than in the *Grundrisse*. *"Hic Rhodus, hic salta!"* Marx would write. The Latin motto, meaning "Here is Rhodes, jump here," was a traditional challenge to carry out a boast. Hegel had used it in the *Philosophy of Right* to mark the point where philosophy would prove its ability to link the rational core of existence with its phenomenal shell. To Marx, capitalism could not be theoretically comprehended without an understanding of surplus value, since otherwise "a value greater than that originally present could never be created; no greater exchange value, although perhaps a greater use value, which is quite beside the point here."[42]

Marx had understood neither abstract labor nor surplus value in this sense before. In *The Poverty of Philosophy* he had not thought the distinction between abstract and concrete labor pertinent to economic analysis. "Labor is not a 'vague thing,' " he argued against Proudhon, "it is always some definite labor, it is never labor in general that is bought and sold. It is not only labor that is qualitatively defined by the object; but also the object which is determined by the specific quality of labor." Marx had then distinguished between the amount of labor embodied in a given commodity and the value of the wages paid out to produce it; the first measure had a stability the second lacked. But both were quantities of concrete labor. Exchange value was not determined by anything abstract.[43]

Nor had Marx earlier understood how it was possible for the capitalist to make a profit if labor was sold at its real value. In the manuscript on Ricardo Marx set down in the spring of 1851 he was able to explain profit only by assuming that the workers did not receive what their labor was worth. "In order for the value of the profit to rise, there must be a third element, whose value falls," and this was the working class. The capitalist made a profit by spending, say, £30 for raw materials, £20 for machinery and £50 for wages (a total of £100), while selling the resulting product for £110: "if he had had to pay out 60 for wages instead of 50," he would have made no profit.[44] From the point of view of the *Grundrisse*, to argue in this fashion made no sense, for to pay £60 for wages instead of £50 would have been to buy the workers' labor above its value. As soon as Marx understood how surplus value arose from the distinction between abstract and concrete labor, he could point out the logical fallacy in the argument that capitalist profit arose from selling products above their values (or purchasing labor below its worth): if all goods were sold above their values, every trader would lose as buyer what he gained as seller. "It is clear even empirically that if everyone sold for 10 percent too much, this is the same as if they all sold at the cost of production. The surplus value would then be purely nominal, artificial, a convention, an empty phrase." In *Capital* Marx would insist that "The creation of surplus-value, and therefore the conversion of money into capital, can consequently be explained neither on the assumption that commodities are sold above their value, nor that they are bought below their value."[45]

The discovery of surplus value was Marx's greatest innovation in economic theory; only with the appearance of this analysis—and not in any of Marx's earlier economic writings—can one speak of a specifically Marxian economics. That Marx now saw economic theory as the basis for understanding society and history in a way he had not done before is shown by his presentation of the necessary transition from capitalism to socialism in strictly economic terms. Earlier, in *The Poverty of Philosophy*, Marx had denied that economic categories pointed the way from capitalism to socialism. The present was indeed pregnant with the future, but the matrix of the new society had to be found in the development of class antagonisms, not in any strictly economic consequence of value's determination by labor time.[46] Similarly, in 1844 it had been alienation theory rather than any category of economics that showed the limited role private property had to play in human history. Now, however, Marx discovered the basis for society's development beyond capitalism in the nature of capital itself. Capital was *"an essential relation for the development of the social productive forces*. It ceases to exist as such only where the development of these productive forces themselves encounters its barrier in capital itself." Much of the second half of Marx's manuscript was devoted to demonstrating what this barrier was, and how society, in rising above it, would leave capital behind. A full analysis of the concept of capital "must bring out all the contradictions of bourgeois production, as well as the boundary where it drives beyond itself."[47]

The underlying contradictions in capitalist production arose from its basic need as a specific form of economic organization: the continuing expansion of surplus value. To meet this need capitalists had to introduce innovations in technique or organization that would make labor more productive. As labor produced more in each working period, the amount of time necessary to produce what the worker required for his own needs shrank, and the amount the capitalist could appropriate as surplus value increased. Capital drove unceasingly toward an increase in surplus labor and a decrease in necessary labor. "Capital as such creates a specific surplus value because it cannot create an infinite one all at once; but it is the constant movement to create more of the same." Every boundary to the creation of surplus value "has to be a barrier for it."[48]

The first dilemma this need created was that capital profited less from each subsequent innovation than it had from every previous one. If productivity doubled at a time when necessary labor was half a day, then necessary labor would be reduced to one-quarter of a day. Surplus labor increased to three-quarters of the day, and surplus value grew to an amount 50 percent greater than it had been before. But the same increase in productivity under the new conditions would be able to reduce the workers' needs by a smaller proportion of the total day (only by one-half of one-quarter, or one-eighth), and thus would add a smaller increment to the capitalist's surplus value. At each new stage the capitalist would reap less new profit from industrial advance. "The more developed capital already is, . . . the more terribly must it develop the productive force in order to realize itself in only smaller proportion. . . . The self-realization of capital becomes more difficult to the extent that it has already been realized."[49]

What these difficulties expressed was a contradiction in capital's relation to necessary and surplus labor. Capitalist production presupposed the necessity of labor for workers in order to be able to employ them; hence, it could only exist where necessary labor was a reality. But its inner dynamism required the constant decrease of necessary labor in order to increase surplus labor. "Capital must therefore constantly posit necessary labor in order to posit surplus labor," while at the same time "suspend" necessary labor in order to add to the surplus. "Capital, as the positing of surplus labor, is equally and in the same moment the positing and the not-positing of necessary labor; it exists only in so far as necessary labor both exists and does not exist."[50] Capitalism itself, therefore, could not develop productivity beyond a certain point, for its barrier was its need to retain a certain level of necessary labor. From this arose *"a limit, not inherent to production generally, but to production founded on capital."* Capitalism by its nature "posits a *barrier* to labor and value-creation, in contradiction to its tendency to expand them boundlessly. And in as much as it both posits a barrier *specific* to itself, and on the other side equally drives over and beyond *every* barrier, it is the living contradiction."[51]

As Marx continued his examination of these contradictions within capitalist production, he came increasingly to identify the barrier or limit capitalism created for itself with one concrete expression of it: the declining rate of profit. Although previous economists had spoken of a fall in the rate of profit, Marx gave it little attention in his earlier economic writings. In the *Grundrisse* Marx first approached the problem of profits in his comments on the increasing difficulty that raising the level of surplus value presented as capitalist production advanced. But that analysis only suggested a difficulty in raising the level of profit, not in maintaining it. At a certain point, however, Marx recognized that his analysis of how surplus value originated seemed to imply that the rate of profit would actually fall as capitalist development progressed. Capitalism increased productivity by building up ever larger industrial plants, expanding both the size of machinery and the quantity of raw materials employed in production. These factors absorbed an increasing relative share of capital expenditures, while the relative amount devoted to labor declined. But machines and raw materials did not produce surplus value; they merely transferred the value they already contained to the new product. Raw materials contributed a value equal to the quantity of them used up in production; machines added an amount equal to their original value divided by the proportion of their usable life devoted to producing any given quantity of goods. Labor alone provided a surplus above what the capitalist paid for it. As the amount of capital expended on labor declined in proportion to the sum represented by plant and materials, the portion of capital that could contribute to surplus value—and hence to profit—declined too. Assuming that the rate of productivity did not rise faster than the share of labor in production fell, the rate of profit had to decline.

It seems that Marx first came to believe in the correctness of this analysis during the time he wrote the *Grundrisse* manuscript in the winter of 1857-58. In the middle of January he wrote to Engels that in his work he was "finding some pretty developments. For example I have overthrown the whole doctrine of profit as it previously existed."[52] Marx's text gives evidence that the theory of the declining rate of profit was being shaped in Marx's mind as he progressed. After several pages of intricate and—as Marx himself admitted—confusing calculations, Marx wrote: "But, understood differently, is there not after all something correct in these figures? Does not absolute new value decrease despite an increase in the relative [i.e., in productivity], as soon as relatively more material and instrument than labor is introduced into the component parts of capital?" Marx continued to worry the question for a few pages more, growing more confident that he was right. Even if productivity was higher for capitals with a larger investment in plant and materials, profit would still be less. "The profit of the larger capital, working with more machinery, therefore, appears smaller than that of the smaller capital working with relatively or absolutely more living labor, precisely because the *higher profit on living labor* [i.e., higher productivity] appears as smaller, when calculated on the basis of a total capital in which living labor makes up a lesser proportion of the whole, than the *lower profit on living labor* which makes up a larger proportion of the smaller total capital." This conclusion—that it was a problematic one we shall see later—allowed Marx to regard his analysis of profit as superior to Ricardo's. "Nor does Ricardo seem to have understood the matter, for otherwise he would not have tried to explain the periodic decline of profit merely by the rise in wages caused by the rise in grain prices (and hence of rent)."[53]

A few pages more, and Marx began to employ a terminology that would be basic to *Capital*. He now called the capital expended on labor "variable" capital, because its value was expanded by being invested in production. The capital spent on machines and materials was "constant" capital because its value was transferred to the new products unchanged. The new terminology made the source of surplus value, and hence of profit, still more clear.[54]

Marx used these new perspectives to discuss a variety of other questions about capitalist production: the determination of actual price and profit levels; the relations of the various branches of industry to each other and to the whole configuration of society; the development of capitalism out of earlier forms of social organization; and the relation between circulation and the production process. We shall examine some of these matters later on, in connection with *Capital*. Having dealt with them, however, Marx returned again to the question of the barrier capitalism could not overcome, and specifically to the declining rate of profit.

He summarized "the general laws developed previously" by noting the dependence of surplus value on "the relation of surplus labor to necessary labor," and added that the profit derived from surplus value was measured "by the total value of the capital presupposed to the production process."

> Presupposing the same surplus value, *the same surplus labor in proportion to necessary labor*, then, the *rate of profit* depends on the relation between the part of capital exchanged for living labor and the part existing in the form of raw material and means of production. Hence, the smaller the portion exchanged for living labor becomes, the smaller becomes the rate of profit. Thus, in the same proportion as capital takes up a larger place as capital in the production process relative to immediate labor, i.e. the more the relative surplus value grows—the value creating power of capital—the more *does the rate of profit fall*.

The rate of profit could be maintained or rise only if the rate of surplus value increased faster than the proportion of capital spent on living labor fell. Such a presupposition, however, "contradicts the law of the development of capital, and especially of the development of fixed capital." The maintenance of a relatively high proportion of labor to plant and materials was possible only at early stages or in relatively undeveloped branches of production, such as agriculture. To be sure, the total sum of profits might rise as the total invested capital expanded, even though the rate of profit was falling. "However, even this statement is only true for a restricted stage of the development of the productive power of capital or of labor." Marx expected that, as capitalism developed, the profit rate would decline faster than the size of total capital grew; hence, the overall sum of profits would be likely to fall too.[55]

The importance of these conclusions was beyond exaggeration.

> This is in every respect the most important law of modern political economy, and the most essential for understanding the most difficult relations. It is the most important law from the historical standpoint. It is a law which, despite its simplicity, has never before been grasped and, even less, consciously articulated.[56]

"From the historical standpoint" it was the decline in the rate of profit that created the limit beyond which capitalism could no longer serve the development of society's productive forces. The falling rate of profit revealed "that the development of the productive forces brought about by the historical development of capital itself, when it reaches a certain point, suspends the self-realization of capital, instead of positing it. Beyond a certain point, the development of the powers of production becomes a barrier for capital; hence the capital relation a barrier for the development of the productive powers of labor." At this point capital appeared as a barrier to social and economic development, just as had "the guild system, serfdom, slavery, and is necessarily stripped off as a fetter." As capitalism developed, its preservation became inseparable from the self-destructive tendencies revealed in "bitter contradictions, crises, spasms. The violent destruction of capital not by relations external to it, but rather as a condition of its self-preservation, is the most striking form in which advice is given to it to be gone and to give room to a higher state of social production."[57]

Capitalists could and would attempt to check the decline in surplus value and profit. Crises themselves served to retard the fall by destroying some of the constant capital, violently reducing its quantity in relation to labor "to the point where it can go on . . . fully employing its productive powers without committing suicide." So did the "constant devaluation of a part of the existing capital" by removing it from direct production, the reduction of taxes or rents that cut into existing rates of profit, and the "creation of new branches of production in which more direct labor in relation to capital is needed." None of these developments reduced the importance of the profit law or allowed one to speak of profits as ultimately determined by competition, wage levels, or rent, as Adam Smith and Ricardo had done. *"The rate of profit is nothing but the relation of the surplus value to the total value of the capital presupposed to production.* Its proportion falls and rises, hence, in relation with the part of the capital exchanged for living labor relative to the part existing as material and fixed capital."[58]

The falling rate of profit thus led capitalism downward into oblivion. But for mankind this path was also an upward one. Stripping off its capitalist skin, society would emerge stronger and freer. Marx wove his vision of human society's liberated future together with his analysis of capital's limitations at a number of stages in his discussion. Production based on capital led to "the cultivation of all the qualities of the social human being, production of the same in a form as rich as possible in needs, because rich in qualities and relations." The system of production capital fostered was "a system of general utility, utilizing science itself just as much as all the physical and mental qualities."[59] These characteristics of capitalism received clearest expression in the development of machine industry. Production by machines, and especially the "automatic system of machinery" was the culmination of the development that capitalism imposed on labor. Machinery was the realization of capital's tendency toward "the increase of the productive force of labor and the greatest possible negation of necessary labor." The development of automatic machinery was not merely a matter of technical advances, but an unfolding of the inner nature of capitalist production itself. "The development of the means of labor into machinery is not an accidental moment of capital, but is rather the historical reshaping of the traditional, inherited means of labor into a form adequate to capital." Machinery was, therefore, *"the most adequate form of capital* as such."[60]

As this development progressed, the production process was transformed "from the simple labor process into a scientific process, which subjugates the forces of nature and compels them to work in the service of human needs." In comparison with the power this process set in motion, "individual labor as such has ceased altogether to appear as productive." The new situation set aside the very premises on which capitalism had been based.

> To the degree that large industry develops, the creation of real wealth comes to depend less on labor time and on the amount of labor employed than on the power of the agencies set in motion during labor time, whose "powerful effectiveness" is itself in turn out of all proportion to the direct labor time spent on their production, but depends rather on the general state of science and on the progress of technology, or the application of this science to production. . . . Real wealth manifests itself, rather—and large industry reveals this—in the monstrous disproportion between the labor time applied, and its product, as well as in the qualitative imbalance between labor, reduced to a pure abstraction, and the power of the production process it superintends.

The human being was no longer so much a part of the production process as its overseer and regulator. "He steps to the side of the production process instead of being its chief actor."[61]

Capitalism, which presupposed labor as the source of all exchange values, could not survive in the new atmosphere. "The *theft of alien labor time, on which the present wealth is based*, appears a miserable foundation in face of this new one, created by large-scale industry itself. As soon as labor in the direct form has ceased to be the great well-spring of wealth, labor time ceases and must cease to be its measure, and hence exchange value [must cease to be the measure] of use value." Capitalism, which called into being all these previously hidden powers, but which could only survive by using "labor time as the measuring rod for the giant social forces thereby created," was exploded by the forces its own magical formulas had released.[62]

Under conditions of developed machine industry the division of society into those whose only identity was to work, and those for whom leisure gave the opportunity for personal development, would fall away. With capitalism the disposable time created by increased productivity appeared only "as not-labor time, free time for a few." But capitalism created so much surplus labor time that "despite itself" it brought conditions that could "free everyone's time for their own development." Just as future advances in social productivity required "that the mass of workers must themselves appropriate their own labor," so would their doing so guarantee that in the future, *"disposable time* will grow for all." Wealth would then be measured by the free time it created.[63] Both the division of society into capitalists and workers, and the principle that value was measured by labor time, would be set aside.

These two aspects of the *Grundrisse*—the falling rate of profit and the vision of society beyond the value principle—formed the climax of Marx's drama of capital and its role in human history. The manuscript did not end with them, but the remaining pages were taken up with additions to and reconsiderations of matters dealt with before. The profit law and the vision of future society were linked together: both expressed the same growth in productivity, reflected first in the mirror of capitalist social organization, then in the mirror of overall human development. Society was both drawn powerfully forward toward its expanding future, and squeezed willy-nilly out of the increasingly narrow confines of the capitalist present. Capitalism's development of the social productive forces prepared the promised land of human liberation, at the same time that the shrinking profit margins made the old country of bondage uninhabitable.

The basic lines of Marx's economic analysis led—one pointing upward and the other down—through capitalism to socialism. But the *Grundrisse* was not the final form of Marx's economic theory. Written in the white heat of creative discovery, and intended for his eyes alone, Marx's manuscript would have to undergo many changes before he would subject any of it to the cool light of public view. In the process, the inner link between the future vision and the profit law would break. *Capital* would offer a less optimistic prospect. And it would never be finished.

3. Illusion, Alienation, and Method

The relation between surface appearances and underlying reality defined by the economic theory of Marx's *Grundrisse* was clear: because the surface relations of capitalism hid the essential element of surplus value and the distinction between concrete and abstract labor that created it, they were illusory. "In present bourgeois society as a whole, this positing of prices and their circulation etc. appears as the surface process, beneath which, however, in the depths, entirely different processes go on."[64] The *Grund-risse* thus canceled out Marx's premise of the late 1840s, that the reality of social relationships was becoming increasingly visible on the surface of events. That expectation had been overturned before, in *The Eighteenth Brumaire* and in Marx's work on Palmerston and the history of diplomacy. But in 1851 Marx had believed Bonaparte's triumph would be short-lived, and the writings about Palmerston and diplomacy were not close enough to the center of Marx's concerns to mark a reorientation in his general perspective. With the *Grundrisse*, however, the opposition be-tween appearance and reality—so deeply etched in his personal life dur-ing these years—became a basic element in Marx's view of contemporary society.

Marx discovered illusions created by capitalist production relations at every stage in his dissection of them. Money was "a mere phantom of real wealth. . . . Its independence is a mere semblance." Likewise, the circula-tion of commodities "on the surface of bourgeois society" was "pure semblance. *It is the phenomenon of a process taking place behind it*." Later Marx described circulation as "a haze under which yet another whole world con-ceals itself, the world of the interconnections of capital." It was part of capital's nature to produce this "mystification."[65]

Wages, too, participated in the mystery making. The relation between worker and capitalist seemed to be based on equal exchange, because the worker was paid the value of his labor. Thus, the real use to which the capitalist put labor—creating wealth that could go only to capital—was hidden. The semblance of equality "exists, nevertheless, as an illusion on [the worker's] part and to a certain degree on the other side, and thus essentially modifies his relation by comparison to that of workers in other social modes of production." Moreover, as soon as the money the capitalist paid the worker began to derive from wealth accumulated earlier for the capitalist by labor, the appearance of an exchange of equivalents became "only illusory . . . *a mere semblance*." "This exchange of equivalents pro-ceeds; it is only the surface layer of a production which rests on the appro-priation of alien labor *without exchange*, but with the semblance of ex-change." What appeared on the surface was "a mere *illusion*, but a *necessary illusion*." The fact that workers worked only part of each day even for the wages whose value their own labor had originally produced, laboring the rest of the time without receiving an equivalent for the surplus labor ex-pended, was also hidden. Slaves had also worked without pay, but unpaid labor "shows itself in this open way where relations of bondage exist. With capital [it is] covered up by money."[66]

Profit was illusory too, for the form in which it appeared to arise, as a return on capital, hid its true origin in surplus value. "*When capital is pos-ited as profit-creating, as a source of wealth independently of labor, each part of the*

capital is thereby assumed to be equally productive." This led to "a mass of confusion," in which profit was explained from exchange rather than production, or "by ascribing to capital some magic power which makes something out of nothing."[67]

In *Capital*, the theme that reality was consistently hidden by capitalist
production relations would become still more highly developed and
insistent. In the *Grundrisse* the illusions seemed to begin only with money
and circulation, but in *Capital* the phantoms of bourgeois life emerged at
the very first stage in the process, with commodities themselves. To demonstrate this was the task of the famous section on "The Fetishism of
Commodities and its Secret."

Feuerbach had employed the notion of the fetish in his analysis of religion, and Marx had used it as long ago as the *Rheinische Zeitung*. Marx still
used the term fetish in this earlier, quasi-religious sense: although in reality purely human products, commodities "appear as independent beings
endowed with life, and entering into relations both with one another and
the human race." "A commodity appears, at first sight, a very trivial
thing, and easily understood. Its analysis shows that it is, in reality, a very
queer thing, abounding in metaphysical subtleties and theological
niceties." Whereas in appearance what seemed to be exchanged when
commodities circulated was the concrete labor of specific individuals,
what was actually exchanged was their abstract labor, their labor as average members of society. The latter was, therefore, hidden behind the visible circulation of particular goods: "The mutual relations of the producers, within which the social character of their labor affirms itself, take the
form of a social relation between the products." The qualities of commodities as social products were "at the same time perceptible and imperceptible by the senses," because the abstract labor that determined value
was hidden within the concrete labor that produced specific products.
"The existence of the things *qua* commodities, and the value relation between the products of labor which stamps them as commodities, have absolutely no connection with their physical properties and with the material relations arising therefrom. There it is a definite social relation
between men, that assumes, in their eyes, the fantastic form of a relation
between things."[68]

How far this approach to economics departed from Marx's views of the
late 1840s is shown by the way Marx had then mocked Proudhon for his
attempt to find mysteries and revelations behind the surface of economic
relationships. Proudhon had insisted that behind the contrast of use value
and exchange value lurked something deeper than the economists
realized. Against his declaration that "we must show that this alleged
simplicity conceals a profound mystery into which it is our duty to penetrate," Marx had defended the "historical and descriptive" method of the

economists.[69] He denied that there was anything significant in bourgeois production that was not revealed by its surface anarchy. Now it was he who found in the combination of use value and exchange value embodied by commodities "metaphysical subtleties and theological niceties."

A society that produced commodities made it impossible for men to perceive their true relations to each other. Marx, as a critical, scientific, observer saw through to a reality which capitalist society—including its economists—could only conceal. "The recent scientific discovery, that the products of labor, so far as they are values, are but material expressions of the human labor spent in their production, marks, indeed, an epoch in the history of the development of the human race, but by no means dissipates the mist through which the social character of labor appears to us to be an objective character of the products themselves." The semblance that the actual relationships within commodity society were relations between goods rather than relations between men "appears to the producers, notwithstanding the discovery above referred to, to be just as real and final, as the fact, that, after the discovery by science of the component gases of air, the atmosphere itself remained unaltered."[70]

In *Capital*, Marx even came close to making the contrasts with his earlier views of capitalist society explicit. The *Communist Manifesto* had pictured capitalist life as involving the continual revolution of production relations, so that "all fixed, fast-frozen relations, with their train of ancient and venerable prejudices and opinions are swept away. . . . All that is solid melts into air . . . and man is at last compelled to face with sober senses, his real conditions of life and his relations with his kind." Now, however, when the proportions according to which various goods were exchanged for each other "have, by custom, attained a certain stability, they appear to result from the nature of the products." Set against this appearance, the law of the determination of value by labor time had the character of "a secret, hidden under the apparent fluctuations in the relative values of commodities." Although the spread of money relationships throughout society made possible the scientific analysis of the reality underlying commodity relationships and the discovery of the law of value, the same development further veiled this reality from the producers themselves: "It is, however, just this ultimate money form of the world of commodities that actually conceals, instead of disclosing, the social character of private labor, and the social relations between the individual producers."[71]

The reversal of Marx's earlier views appeared more clearly still when Marx went on to contrast capitalist society with other social forms. In the *Communist Manifesto* and other writings of the same period, Marx had described feudal society as hiding the realities of exploitation behind patriarchal relationships and the halos attached to certain occupations; bourgeois society revealed what feudal society had covered over. In *Capital* this was turned around. In feudal society, the dependence of some men on others was openly admitted. Thus, "for the very reason that personal dependence forms the groundwork of society, there is no necessity for labor and its products to assume a fantastic form different from their reality." It was not capitalism that now made the relationship between laity and priesthood a simple monetary relation but feudalism: "The tithe to be rendered to the priest is more matter of fact than his blessing." Whatever else one might say about medieval life, "the social relations between individuals in the performance of their labor appear at all events as their own mutual personal relations, and are not disguised under the shape of social relations between the products of their labor."[72]

In 1891 Engels brought out a new edition of Marx's old pamphlet, *Wage Labor and Capital*. There Marx had written, in the straightforward terms he thought appropriate for economics in the late 1840s: "The capitalist *buys* their [the workers'] labor with money. They *sell* him their labor for money." Revising Marx's words in the light of *Capital*, Engels wrote: "The capitalist, it seems, therefore, *buys* their labor for money. But this is merely the appearance. In reality what they sell to the capitalist for money is their labor *power*." Engels saw clearly that making *Wage Labor and Capital* conform to Marx's later thinking required precisely the introduction of the previously absent distinction between appearance and reality.[73]

Along with this distinction, the Hegelian philosophy Marx had so insistently cast aside in 1846 now returned as an essential element in his method and analysis. In the *Grundrisse*, one thing that marked this return was the reappearance of alienation as a central category. In a minor way, the notion of alienation had remained in Marx's writings of the late 1840s. *The German Ideology* used the term as a description of the situation in which men were placed by the division of labor and private property: "The division of labor offers us the first example for the fact that man's own act becomes an alien power opposed to him and enslaving him instead of being controlled by him—as long as man remains in natural society, as long as a split exists between the particular and the general interest, and as long as the activity is not voluntarily but naturally divided."[74] Even in *Wage Labor and Capital* Marx recalled some of the effects of alienation he had analyzed in 1844.

> But the exercise of labor is the worker's own life-activity, the manifestation of his own life. And this *life-activity* he sells to another person in order to secure the necessary *means of subsistence*. Thus his life-activity is for him only a means to enable him to exist. . . . He does not even reckon labor as part of his life, it is rather a sacrifice of his life. . . . Life begins for him where this activity ceases, at table, in the public house, in bed.[75]

These passages show that Marx had never lost his concern for the dehumanizing effects of life under capitalism. But *The German Ideology* had determinedly and explicitly rejected Marx's own earlier attempt to make alienation the central category for a philosophical analysis of history, and the notion had been entirely absent from *The Poverty of Philosophy*. In the *Grundrisse* it returned in a role very like—though as we shall see in a moment, not quite identical to—the one it had played in 1844.

Just as every aspect of capitalism produced illusion, so did each feature of bourgeois economic relations alienate men from themselves. With exchange value objectified as money, "the social character of activity, as well as the social form of the product, and the share of individuals in production here appear as something alien and objective, confronting the individuals, not as their relation to one another, but as their subordination to relations which subsist independently of them." As in 1844, Marx found alienation also in labor. The worker necessarily impoverished himself while creating wealth for the capitalist because "the creative power of his labor establishes itself as the power of capital, as an *alien power* confronting him. He *divests* himself [*entäussert sich*] of labor as the force productive of wealth." Labor continually added to the size of the power that enslaved it; it "progressively extends and gives an ever wider and fuller existence to the objective world of wealth as a power alien to labor."[76]

Moreover, the alienation that pervaded capitalist society also created the conditions for its own abolition. The same development which created "the alienation of the individual from himself and from others" also brought forth "the universality and the comprehensiveness of his relations and capacities." Hence, the historical process that brought alienation also pointed toward the emergence of "universally developed individuals, whose social relations, as their own communal relations, are hence also subordinated to their own communal control." The "most extreme form of alienation" produced the conditions for its own transcendence; the situation in which each individual confronted the conditions of his activity "as those not of his *own* but of an *alien wealth* and of his own poverty" was "fleeting, and produces the real conditions of its own suspension."[77]

In *Capital*, too, the languages of alienation and the view of human development associated with it would be clearly present. There Marx wrote of "the objectified and estranged character which the capitalist mode of production as a whole gives to the instruments of labor and to the product, as against the workman." The laborer produced wealth only "in the form of capital, of an alien power that dominates and exploits him." Capitalist methods for raising social productivity "transform themselves into means of domination over, and exploitation of, the producers; they mutilate the laborer into a fragment of a man, degrade him to the level of an appendage of a machine, destroy every remnant of charm in his work and turn it into a hated toil; they estrange from him the intellectual potentialities of the labor process in the same proportion as science is incorporated in it as an independent power." At the same time modern industry created the conditions for the overcoming of this situation: "Modern industry, indeed, compels society, under penalty of death, to replace the detail-worker of today, crippled by lifelong repetition of one and the same trivial operations, and thus reduced to the mere fragment of a man, by the fully developed individual, fit for a variety of labors, ready to face any change of production, and to whom the different social functions he performs are but so many modes of giving free scope to his own natural and acquired powers."[78]

Many of these formulations were identical to those Marx had used in 1844; nonetheless, the role alienation played in his thinking now was not quite the one in which he had cast it earlier. In 1844 Marx had tried to develop the notion of alienation in opposition to value theory. Value to him then seemed a mere abstraction, without reality, whereas alienation was a genuine experience of contemporary life. In 1844 Marx's whole analysis of economic relations depended on alienation and unfolded from it. That this was no longer true in the *Grundrisse* and *Capital* should be evident from the fact that we were able to give an account of Marx's specifically economic analysis above without making any reference to alienation. Marx no longer claimed that alienation was prior to private property, or that the other economic categories could be developed out of it.

Marx acknowledged this change in the *Grundrisse* when he wrote that "To develop the concept of capital it is necessary to begin not with labor but with value, and, precisely, with exchange value in an already developed moment of circulation."[79] Marx could no longer picture the labor process as standing at the beginning of historical development in the way he had in 1844. One reason for this was that the distinction between abstract and concrete labor made the notion of alienated labor appear in a different light. In 1844 the worker simply alienated his labor, all of it, transforming it into objects that could be bought and sold. This was not strictly true in Marx's later view. What the worker alienated now was not labor in an unqualified sense, but only labor as the power that capital used for its self-expansion, the abstract labor that produced wealth, as opposed to the concrete labor that sustained life. Capital bought labor "as the general productive force of wealth; activity which produces wealth." The worker alienated his labor "as the force productive of wealth." Labor did not give up the whole of itself; it "appropriated for itself only the subjective conditions of necessary labor—the means of subsistence for actively producing labor capacity."[80] The distinction may seem narrow to us, but it was important in Marx's schema. It explains why he no longer could develop the concept of capital from labor. This kind of alienation only existed when labor confronted capital, that is, once money assumed its ultimate form as capital. Hence, alienated labor could not be said to be the cause of private property, or of any of the relations that followed from it, as Marx had claimed in 1844.

In one regard this meant that Marx's view of the relationship between alienation and history made philosophy less central to the understanding of human development than it had been in 1844. Economic categories were not to be replaced by philosophical ones. Yet in another connection Marx now stood closer to philosophy than he had in the *Paris Manuscripts*. In 1844 Marx had been moving determinedly and self-consciously away from Hegel, and the use of alienation was part of a Feuerbachian method whose purpose was to free thought from Hegelian abstraction. In 1857 the opposite: Marx was no longer fleeing from Hegel, but quite the contrary, finding himself drawn back again into a close and powerful—albeit ambivalent—relationship with him.

Marx made the specific link between his return to Hegel and his work on economics clear in the same letter to Engels that announced he had formulated a new doctrine of profit.

> In the *method* of the treatment it was of great service to me that by mere accident—Freiligrath found a few volumes of Hegel originally belonging to Bakunin and sent them to me as a present—I had paged through Hegel's "Logic" again. If ever the time comes again for such works, I would have great pleasure in making available to ordinary common sense in two or three printer's sheets, what is *rational* in the method Hegel discovered but at the same time mystified.[81]

In fact the *Grundrisse* is permeated with Hegelian language. Marx wrote about money "existing for itself" and for others, about wealth as existing only in opposites, but having potential for development "in the suspension of these opposites," about values condensing themselves "out of the form of unrest . . . into a resting, objective form, in the product," about capital's consumption of labor as a "suspension of the material" that was "the suspension of this suspension and hence the positing of the same."[82] These passages, like a good number of others, referred directly to places in Hegel. The notion of abstract labor itself had appeared in *The Philosophy of Right*. Marx had used it too in 1844, but it had dropped out of his vocabulary in the late 1840s.

When Marx wrote to Engels about delimiting what was rational in Hegel's method, he might have added that he had already discussed that question, insofar as it applied to economics, in an Introduction written for the *Grundrisse*.[83] The Introduction contained the only sustained discussion Marx wrote of "The Method of Political Economy." Here Marx posed the question of how to approach "the material in detail" of economics. Should one start with "the real and concrete aspect of conditions as they are," in particular "with population which is the basis and the author of the entire productive activity of society?" No, Marx explained, population was a mere abstraction considered apart from the classes composing it, and apart from the bases of these classes "such as wage-labor, capital, etc." In its early stages political economy had begun from "the living aggregate" of population, but analysis always led "toward ever more simple concepts," to "a small number of determinant abstract general relations, such as division of labor, money, value, etc." Once these abstract concepts had been discovered, political economy shifted to a second method; it set out from "simple conceptions" such as labor or exchange value, and proceeded from them to consider population, the market, the state, and so on. "The latter is obviously the scientifically correct method," for it alone grasped the concrete world as a rational whole. "The concrete is concrete because it is a combination of many objects with different destinations, i.e., a unity of diverse elements. In our thought, it therefore appears as a process of synthesis, as a result, and not as a starting point, although it is the real starting point and, therefore, also the starting point of observation and conception." Marx's approach to economics, therefore, did not begin with analysis of empirical data but with abstractions evolved by economic theory. The abstractions allowed him to hold up a mirror to the concrete empirical world which reflected its underlying rational structure: "The abstract determinations lead toward a reproduction of the concrete by way of thought."[84]

This method of proceeding from the abstract to the concrete was, as Marx acknowledged, Hegel's method. Although the method had led Hegel into error, Marx did not think it would lead him astray. "In this way Hegel fell into the illusion of conceiving the real as the product of thought concentrating itself, probing its own depths, and unfolding itself out of itself, by itself, whereas the method of rising from the abstract to the concrete is only the way in which thought appropriates the concrete, reproduces it as the concrete in the mind. But this is by no means the process by which the concrete itself comes into being." That is to say, Marx was employing Hegel's logic but not his ontology, his method of thinking but not his view of what reality was and how it came to exist. Neither the world nor the thinker's image of it was "in any way a product of the concept which thinks and generates itself outside or above observation and conception." The world existed independently of thought, and mental images of it reflected its real existence. It was understandable that "the philosophic consciousness" should err as Hegel had, because: "The totality as it appears in the head, as a totality of thought, is a product of a thinking head, which appropriates the world in the only way it can, a way different from the artistic, religious, practical and mental appropriation of this world." The theorist of society had no choice but to proceed from the abstract to the concrete. Therefore, the thinker had to be reminded that "the real subject retains its autonomous existence outside the head just as before," and not confuse the process by which he reproduced it with the process of its own development. By keeping this in mind Marx would not fall into Hegel's error.[85]

Was there, as Hegel believed, any essential connection between the succession of logical categories that led from the abstract to the concrete and the actual development of human society? Marx seemed at first to deny that there was, insisting that "the simplest economic category, say e.g. exchange value . . . can never exist other than as an abstract, one-sided relation within an already given concrete, living whole." But a page later Marx asked the question again: "But do not these simpler categories also have an independent historical or natural existence predating the more concrete ones? That depends." Taking as examples the simple category of possession (used by Hegel) in abstraction from any particular set of legal relationships, or the simple category of money before the appearance of capital or banks, Marx found that these simple forms were in a certain degree both logically and historically prior to the more developed relationships. "The simpler category can express the dominant relations of a less developed whole, or else those subordinate relations of a more developed whole which already had a historic existence before this whole developed in the direction expressed by a more concrete category. To that extent the path of abstract thought, rising from the simple to the combined, would correspond to the real historical process."[86] Marx followed this path in the *Grundrisse* (and in *Capital*), arriving at capital and its fully developed features only by way of the simpler categories of value and money. The progression was a necessary one, for the contradictions of exchange value required the development of money, and the contradictory features of money could only be resolved by its transformation into capital.

Marx stopped well short of any general identification of reason and history. He specifically pointed out that different societies have different patterns of development; complex economic forms (e.g., cooperation, division of labor) had appeared in relatively undeveloped societies (Peru), while very simple economic forms (money) sometimes only made their appearance in quite advanced stages of other societies (ancient Greece and Rome). In fact, Marx went on to explain, the simplest economic categories only attained their full development in the most advanced societies. This was specifically true of the most basic category of all, labor, which classical economic theory had recognized as the source of all wealth. This recognition, while it seemed to proclaim a truth apparent in any society, in fact could only have dawned in the modern world. "When it is economically conceived in this simplicity, 'labor' is as modern a category as are the relations which create this simple abstraction." Before men could recognize the existence of "labor" *tout court*, the social division of labor had to develop to the point where labor as an abstraction could emerge separately from any particular form of agricultural or industrial labor. "As a rule, the most general abstractions arise only in the midst of the richest possible concrete development, where one thing appears as common to many, to all. Then it ceases to be thinkable in a particular form alone."[87]

Marx's ultimate conclusion from this was that "even the most abstract categories," those which could be applied to all historical epochs, were "a product of historic relations, and possess their full validity only for and within these relations." But even in making reason thus dependent on history, Marx gave thought a kind of inverted power over history: "The simplest abstraction, then, which modern economics places at the head of its discussions, and which expresses an immeasurably ancient relation valid in all forms of society, nevertheless achieves practical truth as an abstraction only as a category of the most modern society."[88] As society developed, it gave to abstraction a descriptive power lacking before. This conclusion gave an extra twist to one of Hegel's famous metaphors. The owl of Minerva was a night-bird; only at the end of day could her special eyes see clearly.

These views of the proper method in political economy recalled some features of Marx's attitude toward Hegel in 1844, but they contrasted with it too. In the *Paris Manuscripts* Marx had praised Hegel for developing "the dialectic of negativity as the moving and generating principle," and for being the first thinker to conceive "the self-creation of man as a process." The *Grundrisse*'s formulations about alienation and its overcoming were essentially equivalent to the features of Hegel's thinking Marx had approved in 1844:

> The *real*, active orientation of man to himself as a species being, or his manifestation as a real species being (i.e., as a human being), is only possible by the utilization of all the *powers* he has in himself and which are his as belonging to the *species*—something which in turn is only possible through the cooperative action of all of mankind, as the result of history—is only possible by man's treating these generic powers as objects: and this, to begin with, is again only possible in the form of estrangement.[89]

Yet, in contrast to the *Grundrisse*, Marx in the *Paris Manuscripts* had not proposed to follow Hegel's method of proceeding from the abstract to the concrete. Instead, he had invoked Feuerbach's criticism of Hegel as a justification for "starting out from the positive facts which we know by the senses."[90] His point of departure in economics had been the analysis of "concrete" categories—wages, profit, and rent—the "trinity" that would appear only at the very end of *Capital*, and which he rejected as his starting point in 1857.[91] Feuerbach had written: "The path of speculative philosophy up to now, from the abstract to the concrete, from the ideal to the real, has been an inverted one. Along this way one never arrives at true objective reality but only at the realization of his own abstractions." In 1844 Marx agreed: "It goes without saying that the abstract thinker who has committed himself to direct observation, observes nature abstractly. . . . His observation of nature is only the act of confirming his abstraction from the observation of nature."[92] Marx's methodology in 1857 contradicted his conclusion of 1844, that the thinker who began with abstraction never arrived at the real empirical world. The attempt to reproduce actual experience by reasoning from "simple conceptions" brought Marx closer to Hegel's way of proceeding than he had been at any time since 1843.

In this way Marx's return to Hegel recalled a pattern we observed in his earlier life. Each of the successive positions he had occupied before 1848 had appeared to him as a move from abstraction and idealism to empiricism and realism: Hegelianism, Feuerbachianism, historical materialism. Yet each new position had revealed to Marx that his earlier one contained a residue of abstract thinking he had not perceived when he embraced it. Now, in the conditions of the 1850s, Marx was brought to the recognition that historical materialism also kept alive a powerful underlying link with his idealist past. Ever working to liberate himself from idealism, Marx repeatedly found himself still entangled with it.

The entanglement was more complex now. Marx could neither settle accounts with idealism by considering reality "like an ordinary man," as he had proposed in 1845, nor return to the idealist project of transcending ordinary experience philosophically he had posited as a youth. He was still a realist and a materialist, and this tied him inescapably to the everyday world of exchange relations with all its mystifications: however illusory that world might be, it was still the only realm of real material existence. The realism Marx sought now could no longer be identified so closely with empiricism as in the years before 1851; yet if the formulations of theory were not to remain mere abstractions, they had to find some confirmation in the illusory realm of sense-experience.

The theoretical formulations of *Capital* would thus have to bear a heavy weight. Marx was now looking to capitalist society's underlying economic laws of motion to restore the broken unity of appearance and essence he had expected the transformative power of revolution to effect before. (Revolution itself would still be present in *Capital*, but in a way that made its force depend in large part—as we shall see—on these same economic laws.) If Marx's categories of economic analysis—value theory in general and the profit law in particular—could mediate between the rational core of social production relations and their irrational shell, then he would be safe from the pitfalls of abstraction he had sought to escape all his life. If not, however, Marx would find himself—in economics as in politics— caught between rejecting the ordinary world of experience because it was irrational, and submitting to it because it alone was real. His struggle to rise above that dilemma would trace the shape of his fate.

CHAPTER ELEVEN

Reality, Surface, and Inversion in *Capital*

1. *Capital*: Coherence and Recurrence

ON February 20, 1866, as Marx's work on *Capital* advanced toward the point when he would be able to give Volume One to the publisher, he wrote happily to Engels: "You understand, my dear fellow, that there must be many shortcomings in detail in a work like mine. But the *composition*, the overall structure, is a triumph of German science, something an individual German can avow since it is in no way *his* merit, but belongs much more to the *nation*. All the more happily, since otherwise it is the *silliest nation* under the sun!" Yet, five years later, in a very different mood, Marx informed his Russian friend Danielson that much more time would be required before the work could be continued past the first volume. "I have come to regard a complete reworking of the manuscript as necessary. In addition until this moment I was missing some necessary pieces of evidence, which however will be forthcoming from the United States." To discover what lay between the jubilation expressed in the first letter and the stagnation evidenced by the second we must search both Marx's thought and his life. We begin in this chapter with *Capital* itself. By examining its structure and content, we shall try to understand why Marx regarded it as a triumph, and why that triumph faded away. What that same disappearance meant in Marx's psychic history will occupy us in the final chapter.[1]

The economic theory of *Capital* was that of the *Grundrisse*, but worked out and presented in a more organized and clearly structured way. Marx began with the basic product of capitalist manufacture or industry in all its stages: the commodity, the good produced for exchange. "The wealth of those societies in which the capitalist mode of production prevails, presents itself as 'an immense accumulation of commodities,' its unit being a single commodity. Our investigation must therefore begin with the analysis of a commodity."[2]

The analysis of commodities started from the observation that things produced for exchange had to be both useful in themselves and commensurable with others; they had to combine "use value" and "exchange value." To be useful each article had to satisfy some need, but to be exchangeable each had to be equivalent to some definite quantity of another product. Commodities acquired these two separate capacities in different

ways. They possessed utility either on the basis of inherent natural characteristics (coal could be burned), or because they "contained useful labor,
i.e., productive activity of a definite kind and exercised with a definite
aim" (a table was the product of a carpenter). But these natural features
and specific forms of labor were different and incommensurable. So different were the needs they met that the utility of a ton of coal could not be
measured against that of a particular table, or a fountain pen. If two
commodities of such differing natures were subject to being exchanged for
each other in definite quantities, then they had to contain some common
substance, on the basis of which they could be measured against each
other.[3]

In a society in which men exchanged the products of their effort, this
common substance could only be human labor: not the specific labor of
carpenters or miners or writers, but the general quality common to them
all, "human labor in the abstract." Only because all commodities contained abstract labor in varying amounts (measured by the common de-
nominator of time) was it possible for them to be exchanged for each other
in definite quantities. While the specific utility of any commodity derived
from its inherent qualities or from the particular form of concrete labor
that lay behind it, each commodity's exchange value was determined by
the quantity of abstract labor required to reproduce it under given circumstances, the "socially necessary labor time" it embodied.[4]

Use value and exchange value were opposites: "The [exchange] value of
commodities is the very opposite of the coarse materiality of their substance, not an atom of matter enters into its composition." In capitalist
society, however, these two opposing natures were made to embody and
stand for each other. "Use value becomes the form of manifestation, the
phenomenal form of its opposite, value." From this basic contradiction,
all the characteristic features of capitalist society derived.[5]

Taking commodity exchange as his starting point, Marx went on—
following lines he had traced in the *Grundrisse*—to show how first money
and then capital arose from the contradictions the commodity form of
products contained. Once he had demonstrated that the contradictions
within commodities—their "fetish character"—required the emergence of
money for a solution, and that money created impasses which only capital
could resolve, Marx went on to analyze the origin of surplus value, much
as he had in his manuscript of 1857-58. The same concrete labor that was
an exchange value for the worker contained the abstract labor ("labor
power") that was a use value for the capitalist: it merely supported and
reproduced the worker's conditions of existence, but created wealth for his
employer. The contradiction out of which surplus value arose was the
same opposition between use value and exchange value—the products, respectively, of concrete and abstract labor—that defined the nature of

commodities themselves. In each of the three volumes into which Marx's work came to be divided, the principal theoretical constructions all grew out of this analysis of value and surplus value.

The rest of Volume One was devoted to an exhaustively detailed account of the ways in which surplus value was produced, to the accumulation of capital which it made possible, and to the effects of these processes on the condition of the working class. The unpaid labor of society accumulated as capital; modern industry developed out of earlier forms of manufacture in order to satisfy capital's need to control and exploit ever larger numbers of workers.[6] That the well-being of these workers could never increase to a point that threatened capital's continued ability to extract surplus value from their labor was "the general law of capitalist accumulation."[7]

Volume Two was devoted to the many appearances surplus value took on as it circulated through society in the forms of commodities and capital.[8] Marx analyzed the overall circulation process as a complex interaction between the separate movements of money-capital, commodity-capital, and productive-capital. What all three circuits had in common was "The self-expansion of value as the determining purpose, as the compelling motive." The simultaneous existence of all the forms of capital and the continual transformation of each into the others demonstrated what lay beneath all the surface appearances of capitalism: "Capitalist production exists and can endure only so long as capital-value is made to create surplus-value, that is, so long as it describes its circuit as a value that has gained independence."[9] Marx traced this circuit through the whole economy by means of a *"tableau économique"* that illustrated the relationships—and the possible imbalances—of the industrial sectors devoted to capital goods and consumer goods.[10]

The topics dealt with in Volume Three were the most crucial in showing that Marx's analysis of the underlying structure of capitalism could account for the day-to-day exchange relationships met with "on the surface of society."[11] Here Marx dealt with the source and rate of capitalist profit, with the determination of selling prices, and with the origin of rent. Basic to all these topics was the distinction between the value and the "cost price" of commodities. The value of any capitalist product was equal to the amount the capitalist paid to have it produced, plus the "unpaid labor" or surplus value added to it by the worker. The capitalist's expenses, however, consisted only of production costs. Thus the formula for the value of a commodity (V) was V equals $c + v + s$: constant capital (raw materials, plant) plus variable capital (labor costs) plus surplus value. But the cost of the product to the capitalist was only $c + v$, and this was the cost price. Because $c + v$ was always less then $c + v + s$ (assuming a positive rate of surplus value), the capitalist could sell his product below its real value while still making a profit on it. In other words, the capitalist system of production could function without commodities being sold at their values.[12]

Next to the distinction between cost price and value Marx employed a second notion basic to his analysis: the "organic composition of capital." By this Marx meant the ratio of constant capital to variable capital (c/v) in any enterprise or in society as a whole. Since constant capital represented plant and machines as well as raw material, while variable capital was the value of the labor employed in production, the ratio of c to v would differ from industry to industry depending on the amount of investment and the degree of mechanization in each. The ratio would also increase in society as a whole with the progress of industrial growth and productive technology. Armed with the two concepts of the distinction between cost price and value, and the organic composition of capital, Marx derived the three important conclusions of Volume Three from them: the determination of the selling price of commodities, the law of the declining rate of profit, and the theory of rent.[13]

The need to determine a selling price for commodities different from their values arose because the organic composition of capital differed from industry to industry. Given differing ratios of c/v, but assuming a constant rate of surplus value (s/v), industries or enterprises investing the same amount of capital in their products would actually produce goods embodying different amounts of value. If the £100 of productive capital in example A were divided into $10c$ and $90v$, and the rate of surplus value were 100 percent, then the value of the product would be $10c$ plus $90v$ plus $90s$, or 190. But if example B had an organic composition at the other end of the scale, so that its £100 went for $90c$ and $10v$, its products at the same rate of surplus value would be only $90c$ plus $10v$ plus $10s$, or 110. If the products of these two enterprises were sold at their values the first would produce a profit of 90 percent while the second would yield a gain of only 10 percent.

Such a situation might actually obtain temporarily or by a lucky accident in favor of capitalist A, but it could not remain as a permanent feature of any market society. In the real world, the rate of profit in various industries never differed very much in the long run. Marx, therefore, theorized that competition among the various capitals led to the establishment of an average rate of profit for the whole of society. An enterprise like example A above would attract many investors; competition and the consequent growth in output would then reduce the selling price of its products below their values. The opposite process in the case of example B would lead to a decrease in production and allow a selling price above the actual value of its products. Through this competition of capitals, "one portion of the commodities is sold above its value in the same proportion in which the other is sold below it." Individual capitalists did not obtain the selling price of their products by adding the actual surplus value to their cost of production, but instead by adding in a sum computed by the average rate of profit. The total of cost price plus average profit Marx called the "price of production." It was the basis on which changing conditions operated to establish any article's actual selling price. "So far as profits are concerned, the various capitalists are just so many stockholders in a stock company . . . so that profits differ in the case of the individual capitalists only in accordance with the amount of capital invested by each."[14]

The determination of prices of production and selling prices through the establishment of an average rate of profit was necessary in order to show that value theory could account for the actual exchange relations of capitalist society, but it was less important to Marx's overall purpose than the second important discovery announced in Volume Three, the law of the declining rate of profit. As in the *Grundrisse*, Marx argued that the rate of profit under capitalism was basically an inverted reflection of the organic composition of capital. With a constant rate of surplus value, the rate of profit produced by the value of commodities fell as the proportion of constant capital in an enterprise grew. This growth in constant capital was precisely the long-range tendency of capitalist production, the historical function of which was to accumulate productive capital in the form of machines and industrial plants. If it was assumed that this took place "more or less in all, or at least in the key spheres of production, so that it involves changes in the average organic composition of the total capital of a certain society, then the gradual growth of constant capital in relation to variable capital must necessarily lead to *a gradual fall of the general rate of profit*, so long as the rate of surplus value, or the intensity of exploitation of labour by capital, remain the same."[15]

We shall see in a moment that Marx in *Capital* hedged this conclusion with many more conditions and qualifications than the *Grundrisse* had contained. Its place in the overall logic of his system was still the same, however. The falling rate of profit demonstrated that the eventual demise of capitalism was implicit in the original character of capitalist commodity production from the start. The very attempt to increase the mass of surplus values produced in society by accumulating productive capacity led to a situation where the proportion of labor exploited to capital invested sank, and with it the possibility of capitalist profits.

Finally, the distinction between cost price and value, and the concept of the organic composition of capital, allowed Marx to propose a new theory of rent. According to the classical theory, inherited from Ricardo, rent arose from the difference in productivity between various pieces of land. Because of higher or lower fertility, the same amount of seed, work, and technique applied to two plots of land would yield a different amount of agricultural produce on each. Food produced on better land could be sold more cheaply, or if sold at the same price as food produced on poorer land, would yield more profit.

Ricardo posited that a society would always use the best land first, and would employ only as much of the poorer land as was necessary to feed the total population. The price of food would be set by the conditions of production on the poorest land used, rising as population grew. As poorer land was brought into cultivation, the revenue from farming the better land would rise, following the rise in the price of the product. Better land thus became increasingly valuable as more poorer land was cultivated, and the difference in value yielded rent. The poorest land in cultivation yielded no rent, the next grade higher a small rent and so on to the best land, which yielded the highest rent. Rent arose, therefore, only through the differences in productivity between one piece of land and another. Some land would always be cultivated to yield no rent.

Marx accepted the main lines of this analysis of "differential" rent, although he revised it at various points to make rent more clearly the yield on capital invested in land; to make rent a payment for the value of land was incorrect, since land was not a product and, strictly speaking, had no value. He departed fundamentally from Ricardo, however, by denying that differences in fertility were the only source of rent in capitalist society, and by positing a totally different source for rent, apart from and in addition to differential rent. This rent Marx called "absolute rent."

The source of absolute rent was surplus value. The lower organic composition of capital in farming as compared with other spheres of production meant that agriculture yielded a higher level of surplus value and profit. Since technical progress came first and fastest in industry, the growth of constant capital was most rapid there. By contrast, agriculture had a lower organic composition of capital (c/v) than other spheres of capitalist production. "If the composition of the capital in a given sphere of production is lower than that of the average social capital, i.e., if its variable portion, which is used for wages, is larger in its relation to the constant portion, used for the material conditions of labour, than is the case in the average social capital, then the value of its product must lie above the price of production." Were agriculture simply an ordinary sphere of production like any other, this difference would be leveled down by the competition of capitals and the establishment of the average rate of profit. But this was prevented by the limited availability of land. In landed property, capital met "an alien force which it can but partially, or not at all, overcome, and which limits its investment in certain spheres, admitting it only under conditions which wholly or partly exclude that general equalization of surplus value to an average profit." The result was that part of the surplus value produced in agriculture could be converted into rent. Rent, like every other economic category in capitalist society, thus had its origin in the surplus value produced when labor became a commodity.[16]

Marx's reasons for describing his work as "a triumph of German science" should now be fairly clear. The overall structure had a remarkable coherence and unity. Every principal conclusion (including some we have not examined) was based on the underlying analysis of commodity values with which Marx began; the contradiction between use value and exchange value and the need to produce surplus value for its own sake together created the system of capitalist production.* In Volume Three Marx was able to recall the argument of his whole work as an elaboration of the devotion to commodity production and surplus value which capitalism presupposed.

> Capitalist production is distinguished from the outset by two characteristic features. *First*. It produces its products as commodities. . . . Being a commodity is the dominant and determining characteristic of its products. . . . The characteristic 1) of the product as a commodity and 2) of the commodity as a product of capital, already implies all circulation relations, i.e., a definite social process through which the products must pass . . . ; it likewise implies definite relations of the production agents. . . . But even apart from this, the entire determination of value and the regulation of the total production by value results from the above two characteristics of the product as a commodity, or of the commodity as a capitalistically produced commodity. . . . The *second* distinctive feature of the capitalist mode of production is the production of surplus value as the direct aim and determining motive of production. Capital produces essentially capital, and . . . there reigns complete anarchy within which the social interrelations of production assert themselves only as an overwhelming natural law in relation to individual free will.[17]

In this way Marx was able to fulfill the methodological program he had announced for himself in the Introduction to the *Grundrisse*. Beginning with the simplest categories, commodities and surplus value, Marx's analysis revealed their historical embodiments in capitalist society as logically necessary developments from their basic characteristics. "The abstract determinations lead toward a reproduction of the concrete by way of thought." As Hegel's *Phenomenology* had begun by analyzing the simplest intellectual operations of sense-perception and arrived finally at an account of the concrete forms of art, religion, and philosophy in the

---

* I have refrained from adding an account of Marx's theory of crises; they emerged out of these same contradictions at each stage in the development of capital.

nineteenth century, so Marx's *Capital* began with the simplest forms of commodity value and came at last to profit and rent as they existed under developed capitalism. The social relations of advanced capitalist society were infinitely complex, but they were the projections, on a giant screen, of the basic contradictions of simple commodity production.

Entangled by these contradictions at every level of its existence, capitalism moved forward toward its inescapable collapse. The limits and barriers to its survival appeared at various points in its logic and history, but they were most clearly announced in the falling rate of profit. The profit law occupied a central place in *Capital*, just as it had in the *Grundrisse*. Yet several things about it had changed in the interim, and they indicate some of the difficulties Marx found with his book.

2. The Profit Law: Simplicity and Complexity

In the *Grundrisse* Marx had called his law of the falling rate of profit "in every respect the most important law of political economy." No other economic theorist had understood it, "despite its simplicity." Its effects provided "the most striking form in which advice is given capital to be gone and to give room to a higher state of social production." In *Capital* Marx was somewhat more restrained about his discovery, but he still called it "a mystery whose solution has been the goal of all political economy since Adam Smith." In a letter to Engels outlining the unpublished parts of *Capital* in 1868, Marx referred to the law as "one of the greatest triumphs over the asses' bridge of all previous economics." In his manuscript he said it showed the limitations and "the merely historical, transitory character of the capitalist mode of production." It demonstrated that "The *real barrier* of capitalist production is *capital itself*."[18]

Only a few years separated *Capital* from the *Grundrisse*. But the earlier work had been written in the—to Marx—exhilirating atmosphere of the economic crisis of 1857-58. Marx and Engels had exulted at the approach of the crisis, and the two friends expected the revolutionary politics of the late 1840s to return. These hopes were disappointed. Rereading Engels' 1844 book on English workers in 1863, Marx complained that "the very illusion that the result will leap into the daylight of history tomorrow or the day after gives the whole thing a warmth and vivacious humor compared with which the later 'gray in gray' makes a damned unpleasant contrast."[19] It was during the years 1863 to 1865, in this joyless gray light, that Marx's manuscript of *Capital* took shape. Marx himself revised the portion that became Volume One for publication in 1867; but the version from which Engels worked to edit Volume Three in 1894 (he had published Volume Two in 1885) was still—not counting a few relatively minor reworkings and additions—Marx's draft of the early 1860s. The "gray in gray" cast its shadow on the law of profits.

In its basic form the law still expressed the essential nature of economic development under capitalism. The "progressively higher organic composition of the social capital" was "just another expression for the progressive development of the social productivity of labor, which is demonstrated precisely by the fact that the same number of laborers, in the same time, i.e., with less labor, convert an ever-increasing quantity of raw materials into products." With a capitalist organization of production, this development was reflected in the falling rate of profit. "The progressive tendency of the general rate of profit to fall is, therefore, just *an expression peculiar to the capitalist mode of production* of the progressive development of the social productivity of labor."[20]

However, this expression was now a muted one. Its impact on capitalists themselves was softened first of all by the fact that the falling rate of profit was accompanied by an increase in the total amount of profit as the scale of industry expanded. In the *Grundrisse* Marx had noted such a growth in the "mass" of profit, but he had thought it would be limited to an early stage in capitalist development, following which the total of profits would fall along with the rate. In *Capital* Marx abandoned this expectation. The falling rate of profit, he concluded, would always be accompanied by a growing "absolute mass of profit," because the scale of capitalist accumulation was such as to bring "a growth of the total capital at a pace more rapid than that at which the rate of profit falls." Marx did not explain why this had to be true, but he observed that it would allow capitalists to regard the falling rate of profit with relative unconcern. They would even believe that they were reducing the rate of profit willingly, because with the growth of total profits they did not need to maintain it.[21]

Thus, the law never entered ordinary consciousness. The capitalists' belief that they reduced profits voluntarily was an inversion of the truth: "Just as everything appears reversed in competition, and thus in the consciousness of the agents of production, so also this law, this inner and necessary connection between two seeming contradictions."[22]

Not only was the fall in the rate of profit hidden by the growth in the total sum of profits, the rate itself simply did not behave in practice as Marx's theory would have had it do. In the *Grundrisse* Marx had noted that capitalists could and would attempt to retard the decline in profits in various ways, but he had not presented the delays this might cause as having much significance. In *Capital* Marx treated these counteracting influences and their effects with much more respect.

If we consider the enormous development of the productive forces of social labor in the last 30 years alone as compared with all preceeding periods; if we consider, in particular, the enormous mass of fixed capital, aside from the actual machinery, which goes into the process of social production as a whole, then the difficulty which has hitherto troubled the economist, namely to explain the falling rate of profit, gives place to its opposite, namely to explain why this fall is not greater and more rapid. There must be some counteracting influences at work, which cross and annul the effect of the general law, and which give it merely the characteristic of a tendency, for which reason we have referred to the fall of the general rate of profit as a tendency to fall.[23]

Marx discussed six of the "most general counterbalancing forces." The first was "increasing the intensity of exploitation," through lengthening the working day, speeding up machinery, or (most generally) raising productivity through technical innovations. "This factor does not abolish the general law. But it causes that law to act rather as a tendency, i.e., as a law whose absolute action is checked, retarded, and weakened, by counteracting circumstances." Second, wages might be reduced "below the value of labor power." In his draft Marx did not discuss this phenomenon, but he called it "one of the most important factors checking the tendency of the rate of profit to fall."

Third, although the components of constant capital grew enormously, its value relative to the labor employed did not increase "in the same proportion as its material volume." The reason for this was that increased productivity reduced the value of all commodities (by reducing the labor required to reproduce them), including machines and raw materials. Hence, the value of the capitalist productive plant did not grow as rapidly as its size, and the proportion between constant and variable capital did not alter in value terms as much as the physical changes made it seem. Fourth, the relative overpopulation created by capitalist industry provided a pool of unemployed laborers with no choice but to work for low wages. They could be used in new lines of production that "start out predominantly with living labor" and with little capital investment, and which would therefore have a high rate of profit. By this means the overall average rate of profit in society would be raised; therefore, "the same factor which brings about the tendency in the rate of profit to fall, again produces a counterbalance to this tendency and more or less paralyzes its effects."

The rate of profit could also be raised by foreign trade, because goods would command a higher price in less developed countries not able to produce them as cheaply. Finally, investment in safe securities yielding low rates of return retarded the fall in profits, because it allowed a greater proportion of the total social profit to go to direct industrial investors.[24]

The result of all these counteracting forces could not be gainsaid:

The same influences which produce a tendency in the general rate of profit to fall, also call forth counter-effects, which hamper, retard, and partly paralyse this fall. The latter do not do away with the law, but impair its effect. Otherwise, it would not be the fall of the general rate of profit, but rather its relative slowness, that would be incomprehensible. Thus, the law acts only as a tendency. And it is only under certain circumstances and only after long periods that its effects become strikingly pronounced.[25]

In spite of all the influences working against the law and delaying the appearance of its effects, Marx was certainly not ready to give it up. Exactly what significance he attached to it in *Capital*, and what he meant by calling it a law that "acts only as a tendency," it is not easy to say. But the answers to these questions have been obscured by a fact that has remained unknown to readers of Marx's book until now. The published text of *Capital* in the section devoted to the falling rate of profit is not exactly as Marx left it in his manuscript. Engels, in editing Volume Three after Marx's death, made some significant changes which he did not reveal, and which make Marx's meaning even less clear than it ought to be.

All the printed versions of *Capital* based on the text Engels published in 1894 divide Part III of Volume Three, "The Law of the Tendency of the Rate of Profit to Fall," into three chapters. The first, Chapter 13, has the title "The Law as Such." The second, Chapter 14, is called "Counteracting Influences." The third, Chapter 15, has the heading "Exposition of the Internal Contradictions of the Law." Marx's manuscript, however, which can be consulted in the library of the International Institute for Social History in Amsterdam, does not contain these divisions. In fact, although Marx left titles for the seven major parts into which Volume Three is divided, most of the fifty-two chapter headings were provided by Engels. In the case of Part III, however, Engels did not merely create the chapter divisions and provide the titles. In order to divide the manuscript in the way he did, he shifted some of Marx's pages to a different place in the text. The result was to alter the focus and balance of Marx's argument.[26]

In the published editions there is a break a few pages from the end of Chapter 13, "The Law as Such," indicated by a short line separating two paragraphs in the text. This is the point at which Engels reordered Marx's manuscript. In Marx's version the pages that follow do not come here, before the section (now Chapter 14) on "Counteracting Influences," but after it. These pages contain a reaffirmation of the validity of the profit law. By moving them forward into the chapter "The Law as Such," Engels separated the discussion of "Counteracting Influences" from the recapitulation of the law with which Marx had followed it, thus giving the factors working against the law a more independent place in the argument than Marx had. In this way Engels made Marx's confidence in the actual operation of the profit law seem weaker than Marx's manuscript indicated it to be.[27]

Even if productivity grew—Marx declared in the section Engels transposed—and with it the total amount of profit, the profit to be made on individual commodities would still diminish. "The mass of profit on each individual commodity will shrink considerably with the development of the productiveness of labor, in spite of a growth in the rate of surplus value," because the "absolute mass of labor newly incorporated in individual commodities" decreased "enormously as production develops." The fall in the rate of profit was only delayed by the various factors described as counteracting influences. Except in a few cases, "the rate of profit will fall, in spite of the higher rate of surplus value." To be sure, "The rate of profit could even rise if a rise in the rate of surplus value were accompanied by a substantial reduction in the value of the elements of constant, and particularly of fixed, capital. But in reality, as we have seen, the rate of profit will fall in the long run." Marx repeated his earlier point that the growing total of profits would make it appear as if "the capitalist adds less profit to the price of the individual commodity of his own free will, and makes up for it through the greater number of commodities he produces." But this illusion only arose because "all things appear distorted, namely, reversed, in competition."[28]

Only by moving the pages that contained this recapitulation of Marx's argument from their place following the section (made by Engels into a separate chapter) on "Counteracting Influences" into the earlier chapter called "The Law as Such" could Engels make the title he gave to Chapter 15, "Exposition of the Internal Contradictions of the Law," plausible. Marx never referred to internal contradictions in the profit law. When he spoke of contradictions in this section, they were contradictions within capitalism, not in his law about its fundamental direction. The point of the pages gathered by Engels into Chapter 15 was not to expound internal contradictions in the law, but to reveal the contradictions within capitalist society that its underlying presence created.

The page with which Engels began the chapter on "Internal Contradictions" starts out by observing that the rate of profit was always lower than the rate of surplus value (because the former was computed on the basis of the total capital and the latter on the necessarily smaller, variable portion), and added: "We have just seen that even a rising rate of surplus value has a tendency to express itself in a falling rate of profit." (The "we have just seen" referred to the pages Engels had moved forward, into Chapter 13.) As accumulation accelerated, the rate of profit fell, because of the "higher composition of capital." That this had to do not with an internal contradiction of the law, but with an inner tension in capitalism, was clear in the following paragraphs. Here Marx explained that although more total profit would be produced as capitalism developed, the lower rate of return available on investments "checks the formation of new independent capitals and thus appears as a threat to the development of the capitalist production process. It breeds overproduction, speculation, crises, and surplus-capital alongside surplus population." Bourgeois economists were made so anxious by the observation that returns on capital diminished (attributing it to "nature" in the form of rising rents on land) because it gave them a feeling that capitalist production encountered a barrier "which has nothing to do with the production of wealth as such." In the falling profit margins the industrialists and their spokesmen glimpsed the limits of capitalist production, and the fact that "at a certain stage" capitalism would conflict with the further development of society's productive forces.[29]

Moreover, Marx went on (in the chapter supposed to be about internal contradictions of the law), the greater mass of goods produced as production expanded would bring diminishing benefits to the capitalists who called them forth. To be sure, the "mass of surplus value produced swells to immense dimensions," but in order for that value to be realized those goods had to be sold, and the conditions for their sale were being undermined at the same time that the conditions of production were being strengthened. The "consumer power of society" was determined not by its productive power, but by "antagonistic conditions of distribution, which reduce the consumption of the bulk of society to a minimum varying within more or less narrow limits." Hence, "The more productiveness develops, the more it finds itself at variance with the narrow basis on which the conditions of consumption rest."[30]

The development of capitalism thus led to its own destruction. Until it arrived at that end, capitalism would continue to expand, for as long as any profit could be made at all, capitalists would continue to accumulate new capital. Indeed, they would do so at an increasing rate, because the falling rate of profit meant not that more of the product went to workers—it did not—but that "a larger portion of the annual product of labor is appropriated by the capitalist under the category of capital (as a replacement for consumed capital) and a relatively smaller portion under the category of profit." Such appropriation meant a growth in the size of productive capitals, a concentration and centralization expressed in "the swallowing up of the small capitalists by the big," so that capitalism came to expropriate not only laborers but small capitalists too. "This process would soon bring about the collapse of capitalist production if it were not for counteracting tendencies"—the ones Marx had already indicated—"which have a continuous decentralizing effect alongside the centripetal one."[31]

Only now did Marx come to matters that might fit Engels' description of Chapter 15 as devoted to internal contradictions in the profit law. But these contradictions were exactly the same ones Marx had referred to before under "counteracting influences," and in discussing them again

Marx's purpose was to underline their limits, not their force. The fact that an increase in productivity took place at the same time that the proportion of variable capital fell in relation to constant capital meant that two quite different movements took place, which "affect the rate of profit in opposite ways." Of the two factors that determined the rate of profit, one, "the rate of surplus value, rises, and the other, the number of laborers, falls." But the two movements could not develop in the same degree. "The compensation of the reduced number of laborers by intensifying the degree of exploitation has certain insurmountable limits." If the number of workers fell far enough, no increased rate of exploitation could make up for it: "Two laborers, each working 12 hours daily, cannot produce the same mass of surplus value as 24 who work only 2 hours, even if they could live on air and hence did not have to work for themselves at all." (It is difficult to see what Marx thought the force of this argument was, since by his own account the absolute number of workers was rising, not falling; only relative to the value of raw materials and plant could their number and the value of their labor power be said to fall.) From this Marx concluded that rising productivity might "well check the fall in the rate of profit, but cannot prevent it altogether."[32]

As for the other factors that could act to delay the fall in the rate of profit, their very presence in capitalist society testified to the basic structural fault that would eventually bring about its collapse. Increasing productivity affected the value of constant capital in opposite ways: by reducing the amount of labor necessary to produce new raw materials and machines, the rise in productivity lessened the value of existing capital; but by making possible higher levels of production and accumulation, it caused both the mass and value of capital to grow. These opposing developments did not exist merely "side by side in repose," however (as Ricardo would have had it), but contained a contradiction. They set capitalist development going in opposite directions at once, so that from time to time at least, their antagonism "finds vent in crises." These "violent eruptions" were "momentary and forcible solutions of the existing contradictions" that "for a time restore the disturbed equilibrium."

> The contradiction, to put it in a very general way, consists in that the capitalist mode of production involves a tendency toward absolute development of the productive forces, regardless of the value and surplus value it contains, and regardless of the social conditions under which capitalist production takes place; while, on the other hand, its aim is to preserve the value of the existing capital and promote its self-expansion to the highest limit.

It was on this basis that Marx felt able to state the clearest general implications he saw in the falling rate of profit: "The *real barrier* of capitalist production is *capital itself*."[33]

We will not follow Marx into the detailed examination of the relationship between excess capital and excess population. The conclusion was the same as before: the increase in productivity and in the value of capital "which grow much more rapidly than the population, contradict the basis, which constantly narrows in relation to the expanding wealth, and for which all this immense productiveness works. They also contradict the conditions under which this swelling capital augments its value. Hence the crises."[34]

The nature of Marx's argument should now be clear: the internal contradictions were not in the profit law but in capitalist society. The inner structure of capitalist development called forth both a fall in the rate of profit and a series of checks to that fall, but both the decline in profits and the barriers to their decline expressed the basic contradictions and limitations of capitalism. Both, separately and together, led to crises. The significance of the falling rate of profit was not exhausted by the degree to which actual empirical profits might decline. Even without an actual fall in profit rates the law that predicted their fall remained essential to the analysis of capitalist development because of what it revealed about the basic structure and destiny of capitalism. By calling it both a law and a tendency Marx preserved his own conviction about the eventual confirmation of its empirical predictions, while at the same time pointing to the structural defects in capitalism it reflected, and which hindered capitalist development whether actual profit rates declined or not.

Did Engels therefore misunderstand and distort Marx's meaning when he rearranged the text of this part of *Capital*, and created a chapter with the title "Exposition of the Internal Contradictions of the Law"? He certainly complicated the problem of understanding what Marx meant to say, although not enough to make the argument indecipherable; the pages of *Capital* were still Marx's pages, and some readers have grasped the point without needing to have the text reconstructed.[35] Moreover, it seems probable that Engels did his editorial juggling both because he doubted the value of Marx's profit law himself, and because he believed that Marx was somehow aware of inner contradictions in it too.

What Engels thought about the rate of profit is not hard to discover. Marx had left one chapter of Volume Three unwritten, on "The Effect of Turnover on the Rate of Profit." To fill the gap Engels wrote a chapter on that subject (the only chapter in *Capital* written entirely by him) and published it—frankly acknowledged as his own work—as part of Marx's book.

In this chapter Engels made clear his view that technical improvements in modern industry did not in general lead to a fall in the profit rate, as Marx theorized, but instead to a rise in it. The specific subject of the chapter—the shortening of turnover periods for capital investment—was one reason for this. As means of transportation and communication improved, goods could be sold more quickly and the capital realized from their sale reinvested at shorter intervals. If the rate of profit realized each time a capital was invested remained the same, while the capital was being turned over twice as often as before (say, once every six months rather than once a year), then the effective rate of profit per year on that capital would double. The revolution in transport had created just such a situation in world commerce, so that "the efficacy of the capital involved in it has been more than doubled or trebled. It goes without saying that this has not been without effect on the rate of profit."

This was not all. In stating the general relationship between productivity and the profit rate, Engels very nearly inverted the pattern Marx had found there. Referring to "higher labor productivity, which is commonly called industrial progress," Engels explained: "If this does not involve a simultaneous considerable increase in the outlay of total capital resulting from the installation of expensive machinery, etc., and thus a reduction of the rate of profit, which is calculated on the total capital, this rate must rise. And this is decidedly true in the case of many of the latest improvements in metallurgy and in the chemical industry." New chemical processes allowed dyes to be produced in weeks that formerly took years, "and this by means of already existing coal-tar dye-producing installations." That is to say, Engels pointed to a phenomenon of modern industry Marx had neglected: some technical improvements do not raise the ratio of capital investment ("constant capital") to labor employed, but leave it the same or even reduce it, while still raising productivity. Under these circumstances the mechanism Marx saw at the base of the falling profit rate was simply bypassed.[36]

Whether Marx saw internal contradictions in the profit law or not, therefore, Engels did.* Yet his editing of Marx's manuscript may have

---

*Some readers may wish to reflect on the implications of these differences and changes for the debate that still rages about how close the intellectual perspectives of Marx and Engels really were, and whether Engels gave to Marxism a "positivistic" coloration it did not have in Marx's own hands. Engels was both theoretically less acute and original, and considerably more practical than Marx, as both men recognized, but in general I cannot agree with those writers who attempt to attribute contrasting viewpoints to them in their underlying approach to either theory or practice. The implications of Engels' changes in Volume III go against the usual view that it was Engels, not Marx, who saw Marxism in terms of positivistic or quasi-scientific laws. The profit law was close to Marx's heart, but not to Engels'. That Engels could be much more cautious and sceptical than Marx in his reception of "scientific" laws of social development and organization is also shown by a little-known correspondence between the two friends that took place in the summer and fall of 1866 about the book of P. Trémaux, *Origine et Transformations de l'Homme et des autres Etres* (Paris, 1865). Trémaux believed that national character was shaped by geological formations. Marx regarded Trémaux's work as superior to Darwin for what it purported to show about the influence of physical environment on human nature: "Only here is a natural basis found for certain questions, such as nationality," he declared. (To Engels, Aug.

expressed more than just his own doubts. Engels may have suspected that Marx was more worried about the possibility that his law was vitiated by its contradictions than Marx ever explicitly admitted, for he was able to observe certain features of Marx's manuscripts for *Capital* that those limited to the published version have not known about. At one point in the printed text we find the following phrase: "The law, that the fall in the rate of profit caused by the development of the power of production is accompanied by an increase in the mass of profits. . . ." In Marx's manuscript, however, the word *Profitmasse*, mass of profits, was originally *Profitrate*, rate of profits, so that the sentence would have read: "the fall in the rate of profit . . . is accompanied by an increase in the rate of profit." Sometime after originally writing this Marx corrected it to read as it now does in the printed version.[37] Whether the original error was caused by confusion, inattention, or some underlying worry about inner contradictions in the law that made Marx's slip of the pen say what he feared he meant, there is no way to tell. Engels seems to have agreed more with Marx's slip than with his correction of it.

In another place Marx's language revealed that the pattern of counteracting influences and surviving validity in the profit law was so intricate he himself might get lost in it. In this case Engels corrected the text, for if he had not Marx would certainly have contradicted himself. We have quoted earlier the passage in which, summarizing the counteracting influences, Marx wrote that the countereffects "hamper, retard, and partly paralyze this fall. The latter do not do away with the law, but impair its effect." The word in the German printed text for "hamper" is *hemmen*. This was Engels' word. In Marx's manuscript the word is *aufheben* (cancel out). But this is the same verb Marx used in the next sentence: "Sie heben das Gesetz nicht auf," rendered in the English version, "The latter do not do away with the law." Thus, Marx originally wrote both that the counteracting influences cancel out the law and that they do not cancel it out.[38] To be sure, the German verb *aufheben* has many different senses, ranging from "annul" to "preserve," and including "transcend," which was the sense in which Hegel often used it. But even if Marx meant to use the word in slightly different senses in the two sentences, his language

7,1866, in Karl Marx—Friedrich Engels, *Werke* [Berlin, from 1956, abbreviated here as *MEW*] 31: 248). Engels ridiculed the book as soon as he had a look into it, pointing out that Trémaux understood neither geology nor history. Marx eventually gave up trying to interest Engels and others (Kugelmann, for instance) in the work, but not before he had made a pronouncement on it which may have reflected something of what he thought about the profit law: "In my opinion Trémaux's basic idea about the *influence of geological formations* . . . is an idea that needs only to be *articulated*, in order to win once and for all its right of citizenship within science, quite apart from Trémaux's presentation of it." (To Engels, Oct. 3, 1866, *MEW* 31: 258. See also Engels to Marx, Oct. 2 and 5, 1866, and Marx to Kugelmann, Oct. 9, *MEW* 31: 530.)

came dangerously close to admitting what he was struggling so hard to deny, that the profit law could not survive its inner contradictions.

Moreover, the manuscripts for Volume Three of *Capital* Engels used in preparing his edition of it show that Marx continued to worry the question of the profit rate practically to the end of his life, trying either to satisfy himself about it or to establish more definite formulas for it. In the Marx papers in Amsterdam there are eleven manuscripts in Marx's hand relating to Volume Three of *Capital*. One is the main manuscript containing most of the text as Engels published it, and one is a note on Malthus. The other nine all treat formulas and laws determining the rate of profit. Most of these are very short, and some repeat questions dealt with in others. Several examine the relationship between cost price and profit, which Marx dealt with at the beginning of Volume Three, and Engels used them to patch together that part of Marx's work. None of these manuscripts is explicitly devoted to the falling rate of profit. However, a look into one of them, dating from 1875, suggests how closely Marx's procedures for determining the general rate of profit were related to the crucial question of its fall.[39]

In this manuscript Marx tried to develop algebraic expressions for the relationship between the rate of profit and variations in all the elements that contributed to determining it. Marx tried to exhaust all the possible changes in relations among the factors, *viz.*, increase or decrease in size of total capital, increase or decrease in the rate of surplus value, increase or decrease in constant or variable capital—assuming in each case that the others factors were increasing or decreasing at various rates or remaining stable. In addition, Marx sought to work out variations in the difference between the rate of surplus value and the rate of profit brought about by various combinations of factors. (Engels incorporated Marx's discussion of most of these cases in the earlier chapter of Volume Three devoted to the rate of profit as such.)[40] Because Marx tried to do all this algebraically, without employing more sophisticated mathematical techniques of functional analysis, there were more than two dozen separate cases to consider. (In fact Marx understood much more advanced levels of mathematics and once wrote a sophisticated critique of the philosophical foundations of calculus. But he did not bring calculus to bear on these questions of economics in the way later economists would.)[41]

Engels sent this manuscript for comment to his and Marx's longtime friend Samuel Moore, one of the translators of Volume One of *Capital* and a trained mathematician. After summarizing Marx's various cases for Engels, Moore gave his impression of the whole project: "Although he [Marx], no doubt had a general scheme, which he adhered to in his main outlines, yet in details there appear to be considerable deviations—and there is a great deal which he appears to have written with a view to lighting upon some result that might be of importance."[42] Moore cannot have been far from the truth. Marx's manuscript of 1875 suggests a man sifting painstakingly through a haystack, convinced that a small but priceless nugget lay hidden within it, but unsure both of where it was and of the form in which it would appear. Yet Marx's reason for examining the rate of profit so closely is not a mystery: "The rate of profit is the motive power of capitalist production."[43] Although defining and determining that rate in itself was of independent theoretical interest to Marx, there was only one direction of change in it that passionately concerned him: the fall occasioned by the progressive development of industry. In the main manuscript of *Capital* Marx's discussion of the situations leading to that decline sometimes remained open to question because the relations between the factors affecting it were incompletely determined. Marx simply assumed or asserted that the rise in the rate of surplus value took place more slowly than the proportional increase in constant capital over variable capital, or that the growth in productivity and exploitation of labor encountered limits the organic composition of capital did not have to confront. In working out the mathematical formulas of the 1875 manuscript and in his other manuscript attempts to establish clear connections between all the factors affecting the rate of profit, Marx seems to have been seeking more precise and definite formulations of these relationships.

These differences between the text Engels published for the part of *Capital* devoted to the falling rate of profit and the manuscripts Marx left are complex, but their general significance is clear enough. In his own manuscripts Marx shows himself to be both more committed to the law, and more deeply enmeshed in the problems it created, than Engels' version suggested. Marx did not share Engels' view that the law contained internal contradictions which called its general validity into question. But he knew it could not be verified empirically, and his commitment to it led him into a maze of argumentation so intricate that even he himself might sometimes lose his way in it. Assuring himself that he had indeed taken account of all the factors and relationships determining the rate of profit was a project to which he returned over and over again. The rate of profit was one barrier between Marx and finishing his book.

3. Profit, Value Theory, and History

Marx's belief that as capitalism advanced profits would decline was in part a reflection of the roots his economic theory always retained in classical political economy. One of the reasons he expected an actual fall in the rate of profit to take place—even apart from the explanation he gave for it—was that the greatest of the classical economists, Adam Smith and David Ricardo, had assumed the existence of such a decline too. Smith, however, attributed it to the growing fierceness of competition between capitalists that would develop as the economy expanded. Competition would drive down prices and hence reduce profits. Ricardo's argument was more intricate. It emphasized the growing share of the annual product that would need to be devoted to food production—hence to agricultural wages and rents—as population expansion forced society to employ less fertile land. Because it relied on greater quantities of less productive land, society would have to expend proportionally more on rent and labor. As this evolution went forward, capitalists as a group would receive a smaller share of the total, farm workers and landowners a larger one. Profits would therefore make up a decreasing portion of the overall social product.[44]

Both Smith (who died in 1790) and Ricardo (who lived until 1824) presupposed the conditions of the late eighteenth and early nineteenth centuries, the classic era of the labor theory of value. In these years industrial innovation was just getting under way; only textile production was deeply affected by the new methods.[45] Neither railroad construction nor the transformation of heavy industry was yet an important factor in the European economies. Market conditions and labor costs dictated different forms of industrial organization in England and on the continent. In England the combination of relatively high labor costs with a large and unified domestic and foreign market made technical innovation that reduced labor cost per unit of output while expanding total productivity a good investment. England became the first home of machine industry. On the continent, cheaper labor, made vulnerable to pressure on wages by population growth, combined with the survival of smaller-scale local marketing conditions, made investment in expensive labor-saving techniques producing standardized products less attractive as a response to a demand that increased while remaining fragmented. Hence factories which merely gathered traditional workers together in one place, along with an expansion of the putting-out system, still dominated the continental economy before 1850, despite the beginnings of English methods there.[46]

These two situations were, in general, the ones Marx considered in *Capital*. The English model represented what he called modern industry, the continental pattern corresponded to manufacture in the literal sense. Marx correctly recognized that the source of profits and the direction of innovation in capitalist "manufacture" was the concentration of larger numbers of workers within a single enterprise, and (by late in the eighteenth century) the intensification of exploitation through driving down wages and forcing an increase of output. Similarly, he was right to find the driving force of British industrialization's early stages in the attempt to increase production and reduce costs through the development of labor-saving machinery.

However, by the time Marx came to write *Capital* in the 1860s these were no longer the only effective patterns of capitalist production relations. The new technologies introduced the possibility that productivity and profits could also be increased through innovations that either required no increase in fixed capital investment, or actually saved capital. Engels pointed to such advances in the chapter he wrote for Volume Three, when he mentioned new methods of producing chemical dyes. As one twentieth-century economist has written: "With hindsight it is hard to believe that anyone could ever have doubted that capital-saving improvements are as normal a feature of technical change as labor-saving innovations."[47] In this situation, Marx's belief that capitalist development necessarily led to an increase in the proportion of "constant" to "variable" capital no longer held. The direction of change in the organic composition of capital was indeterminate.[48]

At the same time, European industry in the second half of the nineteenth century benefited from a growth in industrial productivity on a much higher level than Adam Smith or Ricardo had thought possible. Marx, observing the changes in industrial technique in the 1850s, was well aware of the new economic and social conditions this would bring.

When Marx first worked out the profit law in the *Grundrisse*, he had made it part of a two-sided description of the already dawning future of capitalism. The decline in profits was the descending path into the socialist future; it was matched by an ascending road that led to the vision of society beyond the value principle. In that vision, modern science and technology created productive forces whose capacity was "out of all proportion to the direct labor time spent on their production." They brought about a "monstrous disproportion between the labor time applied and its product." In this situation, the basic premise of capitalism would dissolve: "*The theft of alien labor time, on which the present wealth is based*, appears as a miserable foundation in face of this new one, created by large-scale industry itself. As soon as labor in the direct form has ceased to be the great well-spring of wealth, labor time ceases and must cease to be its measure, and hence exchange value [must cease to be the measure] of use value." Once the product of industry became completely disproportionate to the living labor employed to produce it, then commodity values could no longer be compared by measuring the human labor power they contained. The labor theory of value would be set aside.[49]

In *Capital*, by contrast with the *Grundrisse*, the vision of society beyond the value principle did not appear. There were certain echoes of it: in one place Marx wrote that the "social power" of capital "no longer stands in any possible relation to that which the labor of a single individual can create." In another he observed that, under developed conditions, "The actual wealth of society, and the possibility of constantly expanding its reproduction process, do not depend upon the duration of surplus-labor, but upon its productivity and the more or less copious conditions of production under which it is performed." But *Capital* was much more pessimistic than the *Grundrisse*. Nowhere did Marx speak of a condition under which men became the overseers of a production process that drew on their knowledge instead of their sweat. The "realm of freedom" lay "beyond the sphere of material production. Just as the savage must wrestle with Nature to satisfy his wants, to maintain and reproduce life, so must civilized man, and he must do so, in all social formations and under all possible modes of production."[50]

As the profit law and the vision of postcapitalist society were intimately linked in the *Grundrisse's* model of the development from capitalism to socialism, so was the disappearance of the vision tied up with the web of difficulties surrounding the falling rate of profit in *Capital*. Marx could not suggest, as he earlier had, that large-scale industry was already demonstrating how modern technology created a product out of all proportion to the quality of labor it employed if, at the same time, he had to describe the fall in profits as a mere tendency, limited in the present to creating imbalances that could be corrected, and whose real effects might become visible only in some indefinite future. To do so would have been to raise the specter of a capitalist society whose boundaries could not be clearly charted. It would have suggested the possibility that wealth might cease to be measured by labor time before private property and wage labor ceased to be the basis of society.

It cannot be demonstrated here that modern industry was destroying the foundation of the labor theory of value in the second half of the nineteenth century by bringing forth a product out of proportion to the direct human labor used to produce it, or even that it has done so since. However, even economists sympathetic to Marxian theory have concluded that the idea of a value inherent in commodities and independent of market determinations cannot survive under modern conditions of production as described by modern methods of analysis.[51] The fact that Marx in the *Grundrisse* spoke of a dawning era in which value would no longer be determined by labor time, but abandoned any reference to it in *Capital*, reflects the difficulty Marx had in accounting for the actual economic experience of the 1850s and 1860s with a theory and a set of expectations that derived from the period before 1848.

Marx recognized that modern productive development under capitalism would eventually overthrow the technical conditions that capitalist social organization had originally presupposed. What he could not admit was the possibility that capitalism might transcend its original economic basis without transforming itself into a different set of social relationships. Yet, without the effective operation of the profit law, this was the prospect modern industry opened up. History may still prove Marx right in the belief that society will be able to realize the full potentiality of modern productive techniques only under socialism. In the interim, however, the limits of capitalism have not turned out to be the ones he supposed.

4. Revolution in *Capital*: Vision and Reality

The profit law was not the only means by which capitalist society prepared the transition to a higher stage of social organization. *Capital* pictured a second bridge to socialism: revolution. The path to that bridge could be easily described, but demonstrating that society was actually embarked on it was much more difficult. The difficulties Marx's expectations of revolution encountered in the 1860s were linked to the problems of the profit law.

Marx's invocation of the approaching working-class revolution in *Capital* was strong and clear.

> Along with the constantly diminishing number of the magnates of capital, who usurp and monopolize all advantages of this process of transformation, grows the mass of misery, oppression, slavery, degradation, exploitation; but with this too grows the revolt of the working class, a class always increasing in numbers, and disciplined, united, organized by the very mechanism of the process of capitalist production itself. The monopoly of capital becomes a fetter upon the mode of production, which has sprung up and flourished along with, and under it. Centralization of the means of production and socialization of labor at last reach a point where they become incompatible with their capitalist integument. This integument is burst asunder. The knell of capitalist private property sounds. The expropriators are expropriated.[52]

Such an image of the concentration and centralization of production on the one hand, and of the growth in working-class unity created by it on the other, reproduced the picture of revolution Marx had carried with him ever since the late 1840s. It tied *Capital* to the earlier stages of his personal and intellectual development.

It was, however, just this identity of the depiction of revolution in *Capital* with Marx's earlier conception of it that made its relationship to his later experience and understanding of capitalist society problematic. Marx did not place this vision of revolution in Volume Three of *Capital*, where all the underlying tensions and contradictions took on their ultimate shape, and where his own analysis arrived at the forms assumed by capitalist production relations "on the surface of society."[53] Instead it appeared near the end of Volume One, where the logic of Marx's argument still corresponded to that earlier stage in both the conception and the development of capitalism in which commodities were sold at their values, and in which the many complications introduced by the further development of industry did not yet have to be considered.[54]

In fact, the conditions leading to revolution were ones Marx saw emerging at quite an early stage of capitalist society. Concentration and centralization began "as soon as this process of transformation has sufficiently decomposed the old society from top to bottom, as soon as the laborers are turned into proletarians, their means of labor into capital, as soon as the capitalist mode of production stands on its own feet." Moreover, although the rise of capitalism took centuries, once it had assumed these clear outlines the distance to socialism could not be very long. "The transformation of scattered private property, arising from individual labor, into capitalist private property is, naturally a process incomparably more protracted, violent, and difficult, than the transformation of capitalistic private property, already practically resting on socialized production, into socialized property."[55]

Such a view of socialist revolution corresponded with what a younger Marx had believed at an earlier stage in the development of capitalist industry. It did not represent his assessment of the real possibilities history offered in the 1860s. The "gray in gray" which (as we noted earlier) Marx told Engels had replaced the two friends' earlier "illusion that the result will leap into the daylight of history tomorrow or the day after" muddled the question of revolution just as it did the fall in profits. In writing about the Commune, Marx asserted that the working classes understood that their liberation could "only be the progressive work of time," that it necessitated "a long process of development," which would "be again and again relented and impeded by the resistance of vested interests and class antagonisms."[56]

Capital provided an explanation for this slowness in the approach of revolution. The conditions for revolution in the economic sphere arose from the same general tendency of capitalist development that Marx posited as the basis of the falling rate of profit: the growing ratio of "constant" to "variable" capital. The recruits to the revolutionary forces were the members of the "industrial reserve army" that grew as capitalism advanced. Capitalism produced this excess population because as the scale of accumulation expanded, industrial growth resulted in "a more accelerated diminution of its variable, as compared with its constant constitutent." Otherwise, capitalist industry would have been able to employ the larger population of workers in the same proportion that the advance of industry called it forth.[57] As we have seen, however, the actual conditions of industry in the later nineteenth century did not necessarily cause the organic composition of capital to develop in the way Marx presupposed, and in discussing the complexities of the profit rate Marx at least partially recognized this fact. In the same degree that the fall in profits was delayed by the failure of the organic composition to rise in the proportion Marx expected, so was the coming of revolution postponed.

Like the decline in capitalist profits, therefore, the revolutionary transformation that seemed so near in some of Marx's formulations receded into an uncertain future when all the conditions for effecting it were brought to light. Revolution was a potential presence that could be glimpsed beneath the surface of capitalist society. But it could be expected to emerge—as Marx said about the profit law—"only under certain circumstances and only after long periods."[58] In the ordinary present both these underlying potentialities could make themselves felt solely in partial, incomplete, and unsatisfying ways: the profit law in crises from which capitalism recovered; the possibility of revolution in disruptions that stopped short of social transformation. The lines of theory might be clearly drawn, but the lines of reality were gray in gray.

5. Prices and Profits: The Logic of Inversion

In Volume Three of *Capital* the determination of the rate of profit was closely linked with another basic aspect of the form taken by value relations "on the surface of society," the selling prices of commodities. As we saw earlier, Marx was well aware that, under developed conditions of capitalist production, commodities could not exchange in the market at their values. The "price of production" might vary widely from the actual value of a commodity (except for those industries whose organic composition of capital approximated the average for society as a whole), and the actual selling prices were subject to still further deviations from values. The market did not value goods according to the proportion of living labor that went into their production, but in proportion to the total capital expended on them: "Commodities are not exchanged simply as *commodities*, but as *products of capitals*."[59]

The question of how the values of Volume One can be related to the prices of Volume Three, and how the determination of actual prices affects the validity of Marx's analysis of capitalism in terms of value, has become famous as the "transformation problem." The issue was widely discussed even before Engels published Volume Three in 1894, and an enormous literature has grown up around it. It has sometimes been maintained that Marx contradicted himself in offering both the Volume One and the Volume Three analyses. Even if he did not, some economists have asserted, the theory of *Capital* stands or falls on the question of whether the totality of everyday market transactions on a price basis, which constitutes the overall economic relations of a given society, can be explained as the transformation of underlying value relationships. This view was given its classical expression in the critique of Marx by the Austrian economist Eugen von Böhm-Bawerk in 1898.[60]

By now, however, all students recognize that Marx was aware of the need to compute prices and values on a different basis throughout the period of *Capital*, and that he did not contradict himself simply by putting forward both calculations. It cannot be maintained—as some critics once attempted to do—that Marx expected to find a strict proportionality between values and prices while putting together Volume One, only to discover that this expectation would not work in reality as his writing progressed: Marx completed the existing manuscript of Volume Three before he published Volume One, and he referred to the connection between actual prices and the establishment of an average rate of profit even in the *Grundrisse*.[61] Marx nonetheless regarded the Volume One analysis as essential, not only because uncovering the existence of surplus value required it but also because the whole unified conception of capitalist society Marx worked out in his book, leading from the nature of commodities in Volume One to the analysis of profit and rent in Volume Three, unfolded from the basic underlying conception of value.

The question of whether the transformation of values into prices can be accomplished in a way that actually makes sense of the economic relations of a given society is more complicated. It requires a somewhat involved mathematical analysis of relations between various sectors of an economy, and Marx himself did not go very far toward resolving it. At one point he considered the problem in a rather simplistic way, arguing that the redistribution of surplus value among various industries by means of the average rate of profit led directly to the result that "the sum of the prices of production of all commodities produced in society—the totality of all branches of production—is equal to the sum of their values." This conclusion can be made to fit the figures only if one proceeds as Marx did here, by calculating the used-up constant capital, variable capital, and surplus value of a series of capitals all in value terms, then redistributing the total surplus value at an average rate, to arrive at "prices of production," which deviate from individual commodity values but still add up to the total of used-up and newly produced value. In this situation Marx's assertion that total prices equal total values is a matter of simple arithmetical redistribution.[62]

The problem grows more complicated, however, once one remembers that the labor, raw materials, and plant employed in any production process must themselves be bought at market prices and not at their values. When the "inputs" are measured in price terms, then the calculations become more complicated, and it ceases to be immediately clear that total prices must equal total values. Marx was aware of this difficulty, but he never seems to have grasped its real complexity. He asserted that even though the profits of one industry entered into the cost-price of another, still, "if we place the sum of the cost-prices of the commodities of an entire country on one side, and the sum of its surplus values, or profits, on the other, the calculation must evidently be right." However complicated the calculations might become, "This always resolves itself to one commodity receiving too little of the surplus value while another receives too much, so that the deviations from the value which are embodied in the prices of production compensate one another." Marx admitted that these complicating factors put some of his earlier definitions and assumptions in a new light. In particular, they meant that the real cost-price of a commodity could not be calculated in the way Marx originally proposed, as the sum of the used-up constant capital contained in a commodity plus the variable capital employed to produce it, both considered in value terms. Real cost-prices stood above or below these theoretical ones, and since commodities used in the production process had to be bought at "prices of production," all the subsequent calculations would be affected by these variations. But apart from keeping in mind the possible sources of error this opened up, Marx did not pursue the matter very far. "Our present analysis does not necessitate a closer examination of this point."[63]

This closer examination has been carried out by various economists. The classic analysis was made by L. von Bortkiewicz in 1907, and it has been refined by others since. By constructing a series of equations that represent both the production process of various economic sectors, and the interrelationships created when the products of one sector become the means of production of another, the relations between total prices and values, and between total surplus value and total profit can be worked out mathematically. Rather than attempt to reproduce this analysis here (a task for which the writer of this book is ill-equipped), we shall simply report its results: "On any plausible set of assumptions regarding the manner in which the different branches of the economy are interrelated, it will soon be found upon experimenting with various sets of figures that if the values of input as well as those of output are to be transformed into prices of production, it is normally impossible to effect a simultaneous transformation which will make total profit equal to total surplus value and at the same time make total prices of production equal to total values. In all but very exceptional cases we may preserve one of these equalities but not both." The most common case is the one in which total prices come out equal to total values, but in which total profit diverges from total surplus value.[64]

The considerations of the transformation problem, therefore, fail to provide answers to all the questions it raises. They show that the basic operations of an economy that functions on the basis of market prices can be accounted for in value terms; that is to say, the equilibrium between goods produced and consumed, which the market establishes on the basis of prices, can be derived from the assumption that every commodity contains a mix of constant capital, variable capital, and surplus value, defined and related to each other in Marxian fashion. This means that Marx's schema, according to which surplus value is created in each economic sector according to the ratio of labor employed, but distributed to each according to the quantity of capital invested, could apply even under conditions in which the commodities that enter into production exchange at prices rather than at values. But these equivalencies, it must be remembered, are merely formal. Even if no gaps in the demonstrations remained, they would still not serve by themselves to prove that, in an actual system of production, exchange ratios are ultimately regulated by value relations, or that the sole source of capitalist profits is the surplus value extracted from workers.

For our present purpose—studying Marx rather than the economy of capitalism—assessing the results of these calculations is less important than understanding why Marx did not undertake them. Marx did not expect to find any clear and regular relationship between prices and values: the lack of any such link between them was part of the irrational and mystifying character of capitalist production relations. "Under capitalist production, the general law acts as the prevailing tendency only in a very complicated and approximate manner, as a never ascertainable average of ceaseless fluctuations. . . . The transformation of values into prices of production serves to obscure the basis for determining value itself. . . . It is only in such crude and meaningless form that we can glimpse that the value of commodities is determined by the labor contained in them. . . . The price of production is an utterly external and *prima facie* meaningless form of the value of commodities."[65]

Marx's recognition of the wide gap that separated prices from values has recently led a prominent American economist, William J. Baumol, to argue that the problems Marx posed in Volume Three of *Capital* were not crucial to the success of his theoretical project; instead, "The first volume is indeed the important one for Marx and his followers." To be sure, it was the Volume One analysis that revealed the basic relationship between labor, surplus value, and profit. But for Marx the demonstration that profit derived from surplus value was not enough. The destiny of capitalist profits was just as important to Marx in mapping the life history of capitalism as was their source. Professor Baumol is certainly correct in concluding that "Marx was concerned primarily with the relationship between profits and surplus value and only incidentally (as a means to get at the former) with that between prices and values."[66] But that relationship was one in which capitalist profits reflected the expansion of values in a peculiar and characteristic way: the falling rate of profit. Not the conversion of prices into values but the falling rate of profit was the demonstration of the law of value "on the surface of society" which Marx's model required.

Why should Marx have looked for a clear and rational reflection of value relationships in the falling rate of profit but not in the selling prices of commodities? The actual rate of profit would have to be calculated on the basis of prices; if capitalism found ways to hinder and postpone the law's effects, why not admit that its operation on the surface of society was just as "crude and meaningless" an image of the underlying process as prices were? The answer to these questions lies in one of the categories of Hegelian logic that shaped Marx's method in *Capital*, the notion of inversion. Earlier we discussed the role that the concept of inversion played in Hegel's thinking, and we have witnessed the many appearances of it in Marx's writings throughout his life. In Hegel, inversion (*Verkehrung*) was the nodal point where reason and irrationality exchanged places, allowing reason both to comprehend the outside world, which seemed to negate it, and to take up the nonrational energy of the day-to-day world into itself and employ that energy for its own progress and elaboration. Marx saw the necessity for a similar dialectical interchange between reason and irrationality in capitalism: "What Hegel says with reference to certain mathematical formulas applies here: that which seems irrational to ordinary common sense is rational, and that which seems rational to it is itself irrational."[67] The mode by which the capitalist surface reflected its true, underlying relationships in a mystified and distorted form was precisely inversion. In the *Grundrisse* Marx wrote that "Competition, in order to compel capital to obey its inner laws through outer necessity, reverses them all in appearance. It *inverts* [*verkehrt*] them." The point was made often in *Capital*, particularly in Volume Three and in the section on the profit law. "*Everything appears reversed in competition.* . . . All things appear distorted, namely reversed, in competition. . . . It is an enchanted, perverted topsy-turvy world [*verzauberte, verkehrte und auf dem Kopf gestellte Welt*]."[68]

Marx looked to the falling rate of profit for a clear and meaningful expression of value relationships on the otherwise irrational and mystified surface of capitalist society because it was the directly inverted reflection of the fundamental characteristics of capitalism as a stage in the history of human industry: the increasing productivity of labor and the growing accumulation of productive capacity. "The progressively higher organic composition of capital," on which the fall in profits depended, was "just another expression for the progressive development of the social productivity of labor." Accordingly, "The progressive tendency of the general rate of profit to fall is, therefore, just *an expression peculiar to the capitalist mode of production* of the progressive development of the social productivity of labor." This expression could only be an inverted one: "The rate of profit is inversely proportional to the development of capitalist production." From a more general perspective, "The way in which surplus value is transformed into the form of profit by way of the rate of profit" was "a further development of the inversion of subject and object that takes place already in the process of production." The irrationality of price determinations was a "crude and meaningless" translation of value relationships on the social surface, but the irrationality of profit rates was a directly inverted reflection of capitalism as a stage in human history. Even though profits had to be calculated in price terms, therefore, Marx did not regard them as meaningless, and he looked to them for the real confirmation of his theoretical analysis.[69]

One reason Hegel had made the notion of inversion a central element in his thinking was that he regarded it both as a principle of dialectical logic, and as a category of psychology. That Marx was aware of inversion in the latter sense as well as in the former in the period of *Capital* is shown by a letter he wrote to Engels in 1869. In April of that year he discovered that he owned two copies of one of his—and Hegel's—favorite books, Diderot's *Rameau's Nephew*. He sent one to Engels as a gift, accompanying it with a quotation from Hegel's *Phenomenology*, which we considered earlier in our study:

> The honest soul takes each discrete element of experience [*Moment*] to be a permanent and essential aspect of existence, and is in the uncultivated and thoughtless condition of not knowing that by this very procedure it does the reverse [*das Verkehrte*]. The disintegrated soul however [the character of Rameau in Diderot's dialogue] is the consciousness corresponding or belonging to inversion, of absolute inversion. What rules in him is the principle of conceptual thinking, which brings together thoughts that lie far apart for the honest soul, and his discourse is therefore rich with spirit.[70]

The difference between Rameau and the common sense of his day paralleled the constrast between Marx's economic theory and the mere surface understanding of bourgeois economists. Marx saw all the "discrete elements" of economic life—wages, profits, interest, rent—as neither permanent nor essential, but as fleeting forms of a single underlying concept, surplus value. Like Diderot's character, Marx saw through the apparently solid features of everyday existence to a revolutionary truth beneath.

Yet, as both Hegel and Diderot had recognized, the vision of a Rameau was so free of the limits of ordinary practical men precisely because of his social and personal isolation: in rejecting the boundaries of common understanding he approached the borders of madness. In the *Phenomenology*

Hegel depicted the inverted consciousness of the isolated and half-mad Rameau as the sign that humanity was about to exchange its old forms of rational understanding for new ones, and he found that prefiguration fulfilled in the real historical inversion that Enlightenment criticism spawned: the French Revolution. Marx's declaration that in capitalist society "that which seems irrational to ordinary common sense is rational and that which seems rational to it is itself irrational" demanded a similar revolutionary confirmation. Without it, the inversion of ordinary common sense he proposed could not be established as the rationality of a higher stage in the development of society. It might even appear to stem from the "perversity" (*Verkehrtheit*) of Marx's own isolated consciousness. Isolation and inversion were aspects of the intellectual character that Marx had found linked to himself—happily or unhappily—all his life. In the years he worked on *Capital*, some of the specific features he had attached to them came back into view.

6. Economics, Logic, and Psychology: Democritus *Redivivus*

The issues surrounding both the transformation problem and the falling rate of profit in Marxian economics point to an important characteristic of the world of capitalist economic relationships Marx analyzed in Volume Three of *Capital*: it was both real and illusory at the same time.

That the surface of economic life was illusory was a major premise of the restructuring of his economic theory Marx accomplished during the 1850s. The illusions of the surface were analyzed in the *Grundrisse*, and they became more pervasive in Marx's account of capitalist life through the notion of the "fetishism of commodities" we considered earlier. These illusions grew as capitalism progressed: "The further we follow the process of the self-expansion of capital, the more mysterious the relations of capital will become, and the less the secret of its internal organism will be revealed."[71]

So basic was this notion of capitalism as a productive system that mystified its own basis that toward the end of Volume Three Marx could summarize the whole structure of *Capital* in terms of it. Starting with the basic categories of commodities and money, Marx recalled that he had "pointed out the mystifying character that transforms the social relations, for which the material elements of wealth serve as bearers in production, into properties of these things themselves." Any society that produced commodities and used money in any degree had to "take part in this perversion," but under capitalism "this enchanted and perverted world develops still more." The productive powers of labor seemed transferred to capital, which "thus becomes a very mystic being." The circulation of commodities compounded the confusion since "both the restitution of the values advanced in production and, particularly, the surplus value contained in the commodities seem not merely to be realized in the circulation, but actually to arise from it." Circulation was further the realm of competition, ruled by chance, and in which "the inner law, which prevails in these accidents and regulates them . . . remains, therefore, invisible and unintelligible to the individual agents in production." Moreover, when surplus value took the form of profit "this obscures more and more the true nature of surplus value and thus the actual mechanism of capital," until the division of profit into industrial profit and interest completed "the ossification of its form as opposed to its substance, its essence." Finally, landed property appeared alongside capital as a second apparent source of surplus value. "Since here a part of the surplus value seems to be bound up directly with a natural element, the land, rather than with social relations, the form of mutual estrangement and ossification of the various parts of surplus value is completed, the inner connection completely disrupted, and its source entirely buried."[72]

Yet, in Marx's conception, the world of false appearances and phantom specters did not exist merely in the confused heads of those who inhabited it. The world of illusion was the real material world; it was the only world of actual existence. As one commentator on Marx has recently observed about *Capital*, in Marx's world "It is not the subject who deceives himself but *reality* which deceives *him*." The absurdity Marx found in capitalism "is the absurdity not of an illusion, but of reality itself." Thus, in Volume One Marx wrote that, to the producers of commodities, "the relations connecting the labor of one individual with that of the next appear as what they really are, material relations between persons and social relations between things."[73] That the world of false appearances was also the world of real existence came out still more strikingly in some of Marx's language in Volume Three. There he observed at one point: "But in reality (i.e., in the world of phenomena) the matter is reversed." In another place he referred to "the final pattern of economic relations as seen on the surface, in their real existence" as "quite the reverse of their inner but concealed essential pattern and the conception corresponding to it."[74]

The same view of the everyday world as both illusion and reality appeared in Marx's letters. In July 1868 Marx wrote to Kugelmann: "The vulgar economist has not the faintest idea that the actual everyday exchange relations can *not be directly identical* with the magnitudes of value. . . . The vulgar economist thinks he has made a great discovery when, as against the revelation of the inner interconnection, he proudly claims that in appearance things look different. In fact, he boasts that he holds fast to appearance, and takes it for the ultimate. Why, then, have any science at all?" Yet a few months earlier he had written to Engels (while he was correcting the proofs of Volume One): "As for Chapter IV, I sweated plenty ascertaining *the things themselves*, i.e., their interconnection. Then, when that had been done, Blue Books came flying in between one after the other as I was whipping the chapter into *final shape*, and I was delighted to find my theoretical results fully confirmed by the facts."[75] In both these letters Marx referred to the theoretical basis of his results as the "interconnection" or "inner interconnection." But these "things themselves" were at one point declared to be in necessary contrast to the mere surface appearances they produced, while at the other regarded as confirmed by the evidence of "the facts"—the very same surface appearances.

Hence, the conflict between appearance and reality Marx posited in *Capital* contained an additional layer of complexity. The world of false appearances was opposed to the world of inner essential truth, but the former was the world of real existence; the world of inverted phenomena and the world of reality were in fact the same. By contrast, the world of inner essence, of value and its laws, had no material reality, no actual empirical existence. Whether this world of theory formed a unity with the realm of experience, charting its development with invisible lines of force, or whether the two spheres instead remained separate and unreconcilable, was the question Marx's economic theory continually posed, but never finally succeeded in answering.[76]

We have met this peculiar configuration of abstraction and materialism before in Marx's life, many years before. It appeared not in any expression of Marx's own attitude toward the world, however, but in the picture of the Greek philosopher Democritus, which Marx gave in his doctoral dissertation. Democritus embodied the inverted consciousness of Greek speculation in its materialist form, as Epicurus had in its idealist one:

> Democritus, for whom the principal element does not enter appearance and remains without reality and existence, is on the other hand faced with the world of sensible perception as a real and concrete world. This world is, to be sure, subjective illusion, but just because of this it is torn free from the principal element, left in its autonomous reality; at the same time it is the unique, real object and as such has value and importance. . . . The knowledge which he considers true is contentless; the knowledge that gives it content is without truth.[77]

So for Marx the "principal element"—value—never entered the world of appearance, remaining without reality and existence in the everyday world that was the only realm of actual material life. The theoretical understanding of value relations with which Marx began in Volume One was "contentless" unless it could account for the real conditions on the surface of society to which Marx came in Volume Three. But, as long as both revolution and the fall in profit rates were delayed, then knowledge of these conditions neither led back to the truth of value nor offered any empirical confirmation of its role. Hence, the real material world was torn free from the determination of value by labor time, and developed according to a different set of laws.

When Marx had originally penned his sketch of Democritus in 1841, its features had not been his own. Marx was then a Hegelian, convinced that the rational truth of philosophical knowledge and its spiritual content were one. Later, when Marx became a full-fledged materialist, he was still free of the Democritean dilemma: he denied that the procedures of philosophy could yield real knowledge (philosophers "turn the world upside down"), and he abandoned all abstraction in favor of what he regarded as a form of empiricism. In the topsy-turvy world of the 1850s, Marx could not continue to conceive empirical experience as an increasingly direct and accurate reflection of the real truth about society and history. Yet neither could he return to his earlier, idealist conviction that the everyday world was animated by an inner, spiritual core. However strongly he was persuaded that only what he saw in the depths of modern life was true, he had to believe with equal force that only what all men experienced in the actual world was real. As the expected transformation of capitalist society receded into an indefinite future, Marx was caught between his philosophical vision and his materialist conviction. Neither Hegel nor history could shield him from the shade of Democritus.

In Marx's original description of Democritus, these inner oppositions had issued in a tragic denouement. "It could be a fable, but it is a true fable because this anecdote of the ancients describes the contradiction in his being. Democritus is supposed to have blinded himself so that the sensible light in the eye would not darken sharpness of intellect. This is the same man who, according to Cicero, traveled through the whole world. But he did not find what he was seeking."[78] We must now see whether Marx, too, made himself pay any penalty in order to preserve the inner light in his mind.

CHAPTER TWELVE

The Unknown Masterpiece

MARX lived out his last years in the shadow of his great unfinished book. His inability to complete *Capital* was a compound of the theoretical dilemmas outlined above and a set of personal circumstances closely linked to them. Now, as before, not finishing his work was Marx's response to the unresolved conflicts represented by the opposition between "ideal" and "material" determinations of human life.

1. The Part and the Whole

Throughout his life Marx envisioned the books he wrote—published or not—as portions of larger projects that never came to fruition. He announced his dissertation as part of a more general study of late classical philosophy; he described the *1844 Manuscripts* as the first in a series of critiques encompassing all the subjects treated in Hegel's *Philosophy of Right*, which Marx listed as "law, morals, politics, etc."; even *The German Ideology* seems to have been intended as the first volume of a larger project, applying the materialist conception of history to particular subject matters.[1] The study of economics Marx proposed to publish in the 1850s and 1860s fit this pattern too.

The scope Marx foresaw for his work on economics as he was completing the *Grundrisse* manuscript early in 1858 recalled his intentions for the *Paris Manuscripts* of 1844. In February 1858, Marx told Lassalle (who was finding Marx a German publisher) that his principal work on economics would be divided into six "books," each devoted to a separate topic: (1) capital; (2) landed property; (3) wage labor; (4) the state; (5) international trade; (6) the world market. He also planned a second work, a critical history of economic theory and socialism, which would be followed by a third, described as a "brief *historical sketch* of the development of the economic categories, or relationships."[2] What Marx finally prepared in the writings he and his editors eventually published encompassed portions of all three of these planned works, although certain specific topics, in particular the state, were not explicitly touched on anywhere. The three volumes of *Capital* dealt with the other five topics listed in the main project, and included some of the related material originally assigned to the other two. *Theories of Surplus Value*, which Karl Kautsky edited from portions of Marx's manuscripts in 1905, corresponded to the second work.

Marx's plans were never quite so grand as the letter to Lassalle made them sound, for he made clear a few weeks later that only the first three topics of the main work would receive extensive elaboration; he intended to treat the remaining three only in outline. Even so, *Capital* did not follow this organization. The shape Marx's book actually took had its origins in a plan Marx announced on March 11, 1858, to begin publication with the part on capital. This installment would form a "relative whole" that could stand by itself, and would contain "the foundation for the whole development." It would be around 100 pages long (five or six German *Bogen*, or printer's sheets) and was to contain three chapters: (1) value; (2) money; and (3) capital in general. The topics of the third chapter would include production, circulation, and the unity of production and circulation in the form of profit and interest.[3]

The outline of this first installment became the program for the work on economics Marx would struggle to complete for the rest of his life. In 1859 Marx published *A Contribution to the Critique of Political Economy*, which treated the first two topics, value and money. The three volumes into which *Capital* came to be divided corresponded to the topics which the section on "capital in general" was to have contained: production in Volume One (here Marx summarized and revised the material on value and money he had published in 1859); circulation in Volume Two; the actual exchange relationships created by the combination of production and distribution—prices, profit, interest, rent—in Volume Three.

That this would be the ultimate shape of Marx's work only began to emerge as he prepared to send the *Contribution* to the publisher during 1858. Until nearly the end of that year Marx left both Lassalle and Engels with the impression that the work about to appear would treat all the topics he had listed on March 11: value, money, and capital. But on November 12 he wrote to Lassalle that his desire to make the abstract questions of economic theory understandable had led him to expand the discussion of particular questions, so that the section on capital in general would take up two volumes instead of one.[4] By January 1859 Marx had decided to send only the first of these to be printed, dealing with value and money. The topics related to capital as such were thus left to the next installment. During 1860, however, Marx's work on economics was interrupted by his drawn-out quarrel with Carl Vogt (to which we shall come shortly) and no more was published. In the following years Marx eventually abandoned the intention of continuing from where he had left off in 1859. From 1861 onward the existing manuscripts of *Capital* took shape. Marx issued Volume One in 1867, Engels and Kautsky editing the rest after his death.

The history of Marx's work in these years was shaped by two forces pulling him in different directions. In his mind, the book—at any rate the part on capital itself—constituted an integrated whole, and several times he resisted publishing a part of it before he had the total in front of him, at least in a rough form. But the only parts Marx was able to bring to a publisher were those dealing with the early topics in his outline of 1858: value, money, and the first aspect of capital, production. Every time the moment of publication arrived, it was to these topics Marx returned. The subjects of what we know as Volume Three—including the profit law— were the ones he could not bring to light.

To Marx in 1858, publishing his economics meant putting forth the whole of its argument and especially its later parts. Describing his first installment to Lassalle in March, Marx mentioned only one highlight of its contents: the doctrine of profit. And in November, as the sections on value and money grew to take up a separate book of their own, Marx insisted that this not appear without the later part on capital (in which prices, profit, and interest were to be discussed): "This second portion must appear *at the same time*. The inner composition requires it, and the whole effect depends on it." That the retreat from this plan troubled and embarrassed Marx can be seen from the way he told Engels about it in January 1859: "The manuscript is about twelve printer's sheets long and— take a grip on yourself—in spite of its title 'Capital in General,' contains *nothing* on capital."[5]

After publishing the *Contribution* Marx set himself an "extreme limit" of the end of December 1859 for completing the discussion of capital, but he made little progress before the quarrel with Carl Vogt interrupted his work on economics. Only in the spring of 1861 did Marx return to his book. In the following two years he produced a manuscript of nearly 1,500 closely written pages, reflecting his renewed determination to have the whole work on paper before any more was published. Of that total, about 750 pages were devoted to the history and criticism of earlier economic theory; this portion later served as the basis for *Theories of Surplus Value*. Over 500 pages continued the discussion of "capital in general" from the place where Marx had left it in 1859 to approximately the point he would take it in Volume One of *Capital*. The remainder (about 175 pages) dealt with subjects that would later appear as Volume Three. (The topics eventually assigned to Volume Two did not receive independent treatment here, a sign that they were of less immediate concern to Marx than those of the first and third books.)[6]

As in 1858, publication of the whole receded as the material mushroomed far beyond the scale Marx originally intended for it—particularly the topics of Volume One and the critical history of economic theory. In June 1862 Marx told Engels that he was expanding "this volume, since the German dogs value the worth of books by their cubic content." That December he informed Kugelmann that the continuation of his 1859 publication was now "ready, that is for the fair copy and the final polishing before printing." It contained what the English called "the principles of political economy," and constituted (together with his earlier book) "the quintessence" of Marx's theory. The title was now *Capital*, with the description "A Critique of Political Economy" only as subtitle. Marx planned to take the book to Germany in January 1863. Yet in June Marx was still at work, adding "much historical material," according to his wife, because the Germans only believed in "fat" books and could not appreciate conciseness and careful editing. The original estimate of the book's size, twenty to thirty printer's sheets, had now grown to fifty.[7]

Interrupted again during 1863 and 1864 by illness, the death of his mother, and the founding of the First International, Marx returned to concentrated work on his book only late in 1864. The original publisher, Duncker, having withdrawn, Lassalle found Marx another, Otto Meissner. Meissner wished to put out the whole of Marx's book at one time, a preference that fit in well with Marx's own desire. During 1864 and 1865 he seems to have devoted himself mostly to Volume Three, and it was then that the manuscript Engels later used to edit that part of Marx's opus took shape. On July 31, 1865, Marx let Engels know that he had only three chapters left of "the theoretical part (the first three books)," plus the fourth book, "the historical-literary part, which is relatively the easiest for me to write"—*Theories of Surplus Value*. Although the end was in sight, it would all have to be done before any could appear: "I cannot bring myself to send any of it away before the whole lies before me. Whatever shortcomings they may have, the advantage of my writings is that they form an artistic whole, and that is only attainable with my method—not letting anything be printed before *the whole* lies before me." The work was still growing, however. In the early weeks of 1866 Marx added historical material on the length of the working day "which was not in my original plan," because illness made him feel not up to more difficult theoretical material. On February 13 he told Engels, "Although it is finished, the manuscript is monstrous in its present form, not presentable for anyone besides me, not even you."[8]

Engels, who had witnessed Marx's difficulties in completing his book for years, never admitted to doubts about what his friend told him. But he worried about whether Marx would ever in fact finish, and he did not like the plan of waiting to publish the whole at once. After Marx told him about his progress and his desire to make an artistic whole, Engels expressed both satisfaction and anxiety. "It pleases me greatly that the book progresses quickly; from some expressions in your earlier letter I had really formed the worry that you might again have arrived at an unexpected turning point, which could delay the whole thing indefinitely." When, in January 1866, Marx had a serious bout of sickness, Engels used the opportunity to urge that Marx publish what he could as soon as it was ready. "Can't you arrange things so that at least the first volume can be sent to the printer as a beginning, and the second a few months later? That way the publisher and the public will be satisfied, and yet no time will really be lost."[9]

Seriously worried by the illness he had just experienced, Marx now gave in to Engels. "I agree with your view and I will take the first volume to Meissner as soon as it is finished." Having already begun to turn his attention to the theoretically less difficult material of Volume One, Marx spent 1866 preparing it for the printer. The difference concentrating on the first volume made for him appears in the letter he sent Engels on November 10, 1866, with the news that the initial batch of manuscripts would be ready in a week: "This summer and fall it was really not the theory that caused the delay, but my bodily and economic circumstances." By the beginning of 1867 Marx was no longer willing to consider putting off the publication until the whole work was ready. To Meissner's request that they retain the old agreement, Marx replied that it would be "impossible without a long postponement of the whole business."[10]

Thus it occurred that Marx published a book called *Capital*, limited to the topic of production, in 1867. Once Volume One had appeared, Marx never summoned up much optimism about publishing the rest. Only two months after the publication, in October 1867, he wrote to Kugelmann that the completion of the second volume (Volumes Two and Three of *Capital* as we know it; at that time Volume Three was still to be *Theories of Surplus Value*) depended "in large part" on the sale of the first: only if Marx could convince an English publisher to take his book, could his material situation improve enough to give him time to work. And six months later he told the same correspondent flatly that Book II "may well never appear if my situation does not change."[11]

This sour mood colored Marx's other correspondence in that spring following the appearance of Volume One. In April 1868 he wrote to his honeymooning daughter Laura Lafargue about various literary matters, adding: "You'll certainly fancy, my dear child, that I am very fond of books, because I trouble you with them at so unseasonable a time. But you would be quite mistaken. I am a machine, condemned to devour them and then, throw them, in a changed form, on the dunghill of history." When, two weeks later, Marx wrote to Engels outlining the argument of the remaining portion of his economics, he added in the same letter: "In a few days I will be 50. If the Prussian lieutenant could say: Twenty years in service and still a lieutenant, I can say, 'Half a century on my back, and still a pauper. How right my mother was! If only Karl had made some capital, instead etc.!"[12]

Not only was Marx depressed about the possibility of continuing his project, he seems to have begun quite soon to see Volume One as the separate work which it in fact became. On October 7, 1868, Marx advised his Russian friend Danielson not to wait for the appearance of the second volume before arranging for the translation of *Capital* into Russian. Marx still needed six months to revise it, and he could not do the work until certain official enquiries then going on in France, the United States and England, were completed or published. "Moreover," he added, "Volume One forms a separate [*abgeschlossenes*] whole." In December 1869 Marx told Engels about a rich German called Menke, who, he said, had read and annotated "*Das Kapital* from beginning to end," not suggesting that Menke might still have reading to do.[13]

From 1870 Marx devoted much of the time he might have given to finishing his book to revising or reissuing the already published part instead. Explaining the delay in finishing his project to Kugelmann on June 27, 1870, Marx pointed to the need to examine a new series of British government Blue Books on agriculture in Ireland and other countries, but he added: "Finally—entre nous—I wished to do the second edition of Volume One first. If that were to come during the ultimate finishing up of Volume Two, it would only be a disturbance."[14] Marx's efforts on behalf of Volume One went not only into the second edition of it, for which a number of changes and additions were made, but much more into the French translation, which appeared in 1875. The translator was Joseph Roy, from whom Marx seemed at first to expect very good work, since he had successfully rendered Feuerbach in French. Once Marx began to examine Roy's translation, however, he found it too literal to satisfy him. Beginning in the spring of 1872 Marx started to redo whole passages, "in order to make them palatable for the French public." By December he was complaining that the work was taking more of his time and effort "than if I had done it without the translator." In the same month his daughter Jenny told Kugelmann that Marx was working on the translation regularly until two or three in the morning. Five months later, on May 12, 1873, she wrote again: "The second volume of *Das Kapital* does not progress at all, as the French translation, which has to be almost rewritten, takes up the whole of Mohr's time." A whole year later, in May 1874, Marx still wrote that he had more to do on the revision of Roy's work. Exactly how much of Marx's energy all this absorbed is not clear, but Jenny was right that Marx made little progress with the later volumes at the same time.[15]

Two years later Marx found himself sidetracked by a similar detour, the German translation of Lissagaray's *History of the Commune*. In this case as in the earlier one Marx began by attempting to assure himself that the translator chosen was really competent for the job, only to find later on that the work was badly done. The responsibility for improving it rested—he felt—on him. Marx rejected one translator on the grounds that revising his work "would cost me more time than if I did it myself," adding "I cannot go through the painful experience I had with the French translation of *Capital* again." Marx approved the next candidate, Isolde Kurz, but only with reservations, telling her at the start that she would have to take more care than she had with the sample she sent him. Once she began the work, in the early spring of 1877, Marx became more critical, finding fifteen errors in as many pages and telling his friend Wilhelm Bracke that if she did not do better if would be necessary to hire and pay a corrector. Several times Marx himself sent lists of errors to be rectified. Finally the job was taken away from Isolde Kurz, and given instead to Wilhelm Blos. Its costs to Marx were not on the same scale as the French translation of Volume One, but it cut into his time during the winter of 1876 and the spring of 1877.[16]

Was Marx attempting to complete his book or finding ways to avoid confronting it? On April 10, 1879, he sent Danielson the "altogether confidential" report that information received from Germany indicated his book could not be published there under the present circumstances. (In the first year of Bismarck's antisocialist laws this may well have been true, but the long-term barrier it constituted to the appearance of *Capital* was hardly significant.) The report, Marx said, not only did not surprise him, it did not displease him either. His reasons were, first, that "I would under no circumstances have published the second volume before the current industrial crisis in England had reached its culmination." Secondly, however, Marx confided that "The mass of material that I have received not only from Russia but also from the United States fortunately gives me the 'excuse' for continuing my researches 'instead of finally completing them for publication.' " Slightly over a year later Marx wrote similarly to Ferdinand Nieuwenhuis that the impossibility of publishing the second part of *Capital* in Germany at the present time "is completely welcome to me inasmuch as just at this moment certain economic phenomena have arrived at a new stage of development and require new treatment." By then twenty-one years had passed since the *Contribution* and thirteen since Volume One. Marx was sixty-two, and within three years of his death.[17]

2. Dissatisfaction and Abstraction

Marx's son-in-law Paul Lafargue observed in a portrait of Marx that "he was never content with what he wrote, altering it again and again, to feel in the end that the presentation remained inadequate to the idea." The truth of this description cannot be doubted—Marx himself often said as much. In 1846 he explained the delay in sending his work on economics to the publisher Leske (from whom he had received an advance) because he had allowed the "nearly completed" work to await the final revisions for six months while he worked on *The German Ideology*: It therefore required a "material and stylistic" reworking. "It is understandable," he wrote, "that a writer who advances cannot allow a work to be *literally* printed six months later which he wrote six months earlier." Twelve years later he had a similar story to tell Lassalle.

> I want to tell you how I am getting along with my work on economics. The fact is that during the last several months I have been putting on the finishing touches. But the job is making very slow progress because things which one has for many years made the chief object of one's investigations constantly exhibit new aspects and call forth new doubts whenever they are to be put in final shape.

And four years afterward Marx explained his delay to Lassalle in terms even closer to those he had used with Leske, explaining it was his "peculiarity that if I look at something I had finished writing four weeks afterward, I find it insufficient and do the work all over again."[18]

Engels understood this characteristic of his friend's personality. As early as January 1845, as we saw earlier, he wrote to Marx: "See that you get done with your book on political economy, even if you should still be dissatisfied with much. It does not matter. . . . Do what I did [with *The Condition of the Working Class in England*]. Set a time limit on the expiry of which you absolutely *will be finished*, and see that the book is printed at once." Again in 1851, after Marx had announced the impending completion of his work, Engels declared: "I am happy you are finally finished with the economics. The thing has really drawn itself out too long, and as long as you still have one book you consider important unread before you, you won't get down to the writing." Yet Marx was not finished in 1851, and Engels had to continue with his urgings for years. In January 1860, as Marx was about to get sidetracked by his dispute with Carl Vogt, Engels implored him to "be a little less conscientious about your own work. It will be much too good for the lousy public anyway." He added: "I know very well about all the disturbances that get in the way, but I also know that the main delay always lies in your own scruples. In the end however it is better that the thing appear than that such considerations keep it from appearing."[19]

It is impossible to know all the sources of Marx's hesitations. Many writers will recognize their own experience in his description of the "new aspects" and "new doubts" called forth by a long contemplated and much worked-over project. In Marx's case, however, one particular problem arose over and over again. This was the repeated discovery (whose effect on his writings during the 1840s we noted earlier) that the approach he had been employing even in the very recent past appeared from each new present perspective to contain troublesome elements of an abstract and idealist point of view. Marx faced similar worries in the time of *Capital*, for the "settling of accounts" with his earlier devotion to philosophy displayed in *The German Ideology* came up for revision once the transforming power of revolution had receded from view. No sooner had Marx acknowledged his continuing need for a philosophical methodology than he became anxious about its effects.

In the Introduction he wrote for the *Grundrisse*, Marx separated his method of moving "from the abstract to the concrete" from Hegel's with surgical neatness, but in the manuscript itself he worried that the diseased organ of abstract idealism still infected him. At one point he made a note to himself to revise a certain discussion. It would be necessary "to correct the idealist manner of the presentation, which makes it seem as if it were merely a matter of conceptual determinations and of the dialectic of these concepts." Using Hegel's method, in other words, brought Marx closer to philosophical abstraction than he wanted to be, or appear.[20]

One way to lessen the possibility that Marx's method would be too closely likened to Hegel's was to eliminate the discussion that explicitly described Marx's method as a progression "from the abstract to the concrete." When he published *A Contribution to the Critique of Political Economy* in 1859 Marx replaced the introduction of 1857 with quite a different kind of preface. Referring to the earlier general introduction, he said he was leaving it out "because on closer reflection any anticipation of results still to be proved appears to me disturbing." Did that mean that the claim to be able to reproduce real and concrete relationships out of "simple conceptions" had better be proved before it was made? Marx seemed to admit as much when he continued: "The reader who on the whole desires to follow me must be resolved to ascend from the particular to the general." Without actually denying that his method began with abstract conceptions, indicating a path "from the particular to the general" gave the impression that Marx's course lay in a different direction.[21]

In place of the earlier discussion of method, Marx's 1859 preface provided his only essay in autobiography. The pattern Marx described in his life was the familiar straight line: from philosophical journalism through the critique of Hegel to historical materialism and the study of political economy. It was here that Marx gave the famous summary of historical materialism that has been so often quoted since: the material productive forces defined relations of production on which a legal and political superstructure was erected; consciousness was determined by social being; the conflict between new productive forces and established relations of production led to revolution. Marx acknowledged that after 1851 he had begun his economic studies "afresh from the very beginning" in order to make use of the riches of the British Museum and take account of "the new stage of development upon which [bourgeois society] appeared to have entered with the discovery of gold in California and Australia." But he did not admit to any significant shift in his method during the 1850s, and the only mention of Hegel was in reference to his and Engels' pre-1848 criticism of German idealism. There was nothing to suggest the return to Hegel which the *Grundrisse* exhibited so richly. That the publication of the *Grundrisse* has contained so many surprises for the generation of scholars who learned to know Marx before its appearance remains as much his fault as theirs: they did not know of his return to Hegel in 1857 because he veiled it in 1859.[22]

Yet he did drop a hint that there was more to the story he was telling than met the eye: he called the summary of historical materialism the "guiding thread" (*Leitfade*) of his studies. An intensely literate person well read in many fields, Marx knew—even if the awareness was not on the most accessible layer of his consciousness in 1859—that the metaphor of the guiding thread was a widespread one in ancient and modern literature. It carried with it a particular set of associations. These connections were commonly made by the classical German writers on whom Marx had been reared: Goethe, Schiller, and Herder. For these men the figure of the *Leitfade* was bound up with the confining and confusing experiences of life symbolized by its companion image, the labyrinth. Goethe used the complete metaphor in one of his scientific works: "When one has such a schema in view . . . he will use it like a good guiding thread to find his way through the labyrinthine fate of many a human life." Herder wrote once in a way even closer to what Marx had in mind: "I have wandered around in a labyrinth among various prospects; now I take hold of my guiding thread again, and I link it up with my earlier material."[23]

Marx in 1859 did not admit that his guiding thread was necessary to keep him from getting lost in a labyrinth, but we know how confusing and mysterious the world of the 1850s had seemed to him. Napoleon III, Palmerston, Russian history, the disappearance of economic crisis and revolutionary politics—all had demanded that Marx penetrate a web of illusion in order to find his theoretical bearings once again. Like Herder, he had found his way by linking up with a past he had earlier thought to leave behind him. The account of his development Marx gave in 1859 hid as much as it revealed. Historical materialism was only one of the bases on which his economic theory rested; the other, the return to Hegel, was concealed behind the straight-line version of his personal intellectual history Marx provided. By refusing to acknowledge this second guiding thread in his life—the philosophical and abstract as opposed to the materialistic and empirical one—Marx also covered up the labyrinth within which he had taken hold of it.

Marx denied the real nature of his Hegelian discipleship in a similar way later, when he published the second edition of *Capital*, Volume One, in 1873. There he responded to a Russian reviewer of the first edition, who in the course of a highly complimentary and sympathetic discussion of Marx's book had referred to the apparent idealism of Marx's method. This idealism was merely on the surface, the reviewer had emphasized. Only "the external form of the presentation of the subject" made Marx seem to be "the most ideal of ideal philosophers, always in the German, i.e., the bad sense of the word. But in point of fact he is infinitely more realistic than all his forerunners in the work of economic criticism. He can in no sense be called an idealist." Marx quoted extensively from the review, because its account of his method provided a good summary of the dialectic method in general. And he went forward from the Russian reviewer's contrast between Marx and "bad" German idealism to make one of his most famous statements about his relationship to Hegel: Marx's dialectic was the "direct opposite" of Hegel's. With Hegel the real world was merely the external form of the Idea. The dialectic "is standing on its head. It must be turned right-side-up again, if you would discover the rational kernel within the mystical shell."[24]

These comments recalled what Marx had written in 1857, but they made the separation between himself and Hegel much simpler than it had seemed to him then. In making them Marx recognized that the difference between his method and Hegel's might not always be apparent. If the "actual movement" of the subject was properly described, "if the life of the subject-matter is ideally reflected as in a mirror, then it may appear as if we had before us a mere a priori construction." Marx reacted to this possibility not only by contrasting his method with Hegel's but also by giving a well-known and often quoted, but in fact strange and unrealistic, account of their relationship. According to this, what led him to return to Hegel after his own early criticism, was the circumstance that at the time he was working on Volume One, "it was the good pleasure of the peevish, arrogant, mediocre *epigonoi* who now talk large in cultured Germany, to treat Hegel in the same way as the brave Moses Mendelssohn in Lessing's time treated Spinoza, *i.e.*, as a 'dead dog.' I therefore openly avowed myself the pupil of that mighty thinker, and even here and there, in the chapter on the theory of value, coquetted with the modes of expression peculiar to him."[25]

Marx's relationship to Hegel in *Capital* was no mere flirtation. The Hegelian notions of inversion and alienation were, as we have seen, central to his work. The first gave form to Marx's conception of the relationship between profits and productivity and was a chief element in the organization and coherence of the book: The image of correcting Hegel's own method by turning the dialectic to stand on its feet instead of its head was also a species of inversion. Alienation was present in *Capital* too, defining Marx's views of labor and human development in a way that recognized the primacy of value theory, but which still made it an important element in his analysis. The claim that, in *Capital*, Marx had merely "coquetted with the modes of expression peculiar to" Hegel, cannot be taken seriously. His real relationship to the philosophic master of his youth had both a greater degree of spontaneous intimacy and a larger component of self-conscious separation than that formula conveyed.

Marx revealed this tension in ways that directly recalled his earlier anxieties. The fear he expressed in 1873 that, "if the life of the subject-matter is ideally reflected as in a mirror, then it may appear as if we had before us a mere a priori construction" echoed the worry of 1844, that he "would have given the *impression* of arbitrary systematism." In the *Paris Manuscripts* Marx had sought to ward off this impression by declaring that it was "hardly necessary to assure the reader conversant with political economy that my results have been attained by means of a wholly empirical analysis." At the same time, however, he was engaged in demonstrating his own empiricism to himself by voraciously devouring knowledge, plunging himself again and again into what Arnold Ruge called "an endless sea of books."

Similarly, in 1873, Marx distinguished the schematic "method of presentation" be used in his work from his more empirical "method of inquiry." If the former related the material to simple conceptions in a way that seemed to give them a life of their own, still it was based on actual researches, whose task was "to appropriate the material in detail, to analyze its different forms of development, to trace out their inner connection." In the period of *Capital* Marx's devotion to the empirical study of economic conditions literally knew no bounds, extending to one country after another. During 1869 he began a project that would cost him much time, learning Russian, spurred by the receipt of a book on Russian agricultural conditions by N. Flerowski, which Marx suspected might be important in his analysis of rent. In view of the fact that Marx later insisted on the particularly Western European content of his book and denied that the development he described would necessarily apply in Russia, his Russian studies seem to have been inspired by something beyond mere conscientiousness. The same was true of much other research. In 1873 alone Marx filled over fifty good-sized notebooks, almost 3,000 closely written pages, with notes and excerpts from books he added to the already enormous list of what he had consulted for *Capital*. Maximilien Rubel, one of the closest students of Marx's manner of work, comments on this that "The passion for reading, which could already be observed in Marx in his great creative periods, transformed itself in his last years into a regular obsession for reading."[26]

Like the Democritus of his doctoral dissertation, Marx was "driven to empirical observation. Dissatisfied with philosophy, he throws himself into the arms of positive knowledge."[27] The language of compulsion and anxiety he had used in 1841 revealed its roots in his own psyche as Marx struggled to find the vision of his economic theory confirmed in the actual world. The path "from the abstract to the concrete" was not a straight road, as he had sought to convince himself in 1857, but—psychologically at least—a circular one, as he had argued in 1844. Marx walked it all his life.

3. External Conditions

All through his career Marx felt that things outside his control determined his ability to finish his work. In the foreword to his doctoral dissertation he regretted that the work was less scientific and more pedantic than he wished, but said he was "constrained by external reasons to send it to the press in this form." In the correspondence with Ruge and Bauer about his literary projects later in the same year, Marx blamed "all manner of external confusion" and "unpleasant external matters" for his inability to finish on time. In the preface to *A Contribution to the Critique of Political Economy* Marx explained his delay in publishing especially on the ground that "the time at my disposal was curtailed by the imperative necessity of earning my living." As for the future of his book, "The total material lies before me in the form of monographs, which were written at widely separated periods, for self-clarification, not for publication, and whose coherent elaboration according to the plan indicated will be dependent on external circumstances." Later, after Volume One of *Capital* had appeared, Marx wrote to Kugelmann that the second volume "may well never appear if my situation does not change."[28]

The external conditions Marx referred to were real. In the London years supporting his family demanded much time. Disputes among the German leftist exiles in London occupied him for much of the period 1850 to 1852, and the leadership of the First International fell on Marx's shoulders from 1864 to 1872. Nonetheless, neither Marx himself nor his friends thought this was the whole story, and nor should we. When Engels wrote to Marx at the beginning of 1860, "I know very well about all the disturbances that get in the way, but I also know that the main delay always lies in your own scruples," he knew Marx would agree with him.[29] During the five years Marx did no work on economics he found time for other projects, the minor and unread works like *The Great Men of the Emigration*, *Revelations on the Cologne Communist Trial*, and *The Secret Diplomatic History of the Eighteenth Century*. Some of these had a political purpose, and some were done in the hope they would earn money, but Marx saw his work on economics as partially political too, and he also expected to make money on it. Eventually the external pressures on Marx lessened. The inheritances he received in the 1860s improved his finances, and beginning in 1869 his economic position reached stability when Engels provided him with a steady income of £350 per year. It is true that in the same period the First International began to cut into Marx's available work time. But although the IWA disrupted Marx's work seriously during the dispute between him and Bakunin in 1871-72, Marx actually prepared the first volume of *Capital* for publication (1867) during the early years of the IWA's existence after 1864, and he worked on the second edition of Volume One at the height of the Bakunin episode.

We have already looked into one of the major forms these outside interferences took, Marx's family life and his domestic economy, in Chapter Nine. In that sphere, we saw that the control external circumstances exercised over Marx was difficult to separate from his own internal conditioning of them. His relations to his work, his wife, and his major provider, Engels, were deeply rooted in the structure of his general relationship to the outside world. Struggle and submission, egoism and self-sacrifice were the organizing poles of his experience.

The power of Marx's internal conditioning also made itself felt in other sorts of interferences with his work. That this was so appears perhaps most clearly from a rather mysterious incident in Marx's life, his year-long quarrel with Carl Vogt during 1860. The affair has usually puzzled Marx's biographers: David McLellan describes it only as "a striking example both of Marx's ability to expend tremendous labor on essentially trivial matters and also of his talent for vituperation."[30] The Vogt episode had a significant impact on Marx's life, however. It interrupted his work on economics just after the publication of *A Contribution to the Critique of Political Economy* in 1859, leading Marx to abandon the plan which would have made that work the first installment of his work on political economy. Without it Marx would have been expected to follow up the *Contribution* more quickly, and in a form that did not begin again from the starting point, as Marx would with Volume One of *Capital* in 1867. It was thus an important link in the chain of difficulties that kept Marx from finishing his book.

Carl Vogt was a German zoologist who had been active in the democratic camp during 1848, and who subsequently emigrated to Switzerland. What led to the public rift between him and Marx was Vogt's sympathy for Napoleon III at the time of the Italian War of 1859. Marx and Engels were always uncompromisingly anti-Bonapartist, and refused to support the war against Austria even though they favored the movement for Italian unification it served, and with which Napoleon was allied in the person of Cavour. Vogt's support of Bonaparte caused Marx to credit rumors that the Swiss democrat was in the pay of the French emperor (the suggestion was first made to him by Karl Blind); these reports were confirmed later on, by a document discovered during the Paris Commune of 1871.[31]

Marx told his suspicions to Elard Biskamp, the editor of a small German paper in London with which Marx became associated in 1859, *Das Volk*, and Biskamp both printed them and sent Vogt a copy. Vogt replied in a Swiss paper. The matter might have rested there had not Marx's friend Wilhelm Liebknecht discovered an anonymous pamphlet against Vogt, set in type on the press that printed *Das Volk*. Liebknecht sent the pamphlet to the *Augsburg Allgemeine Zeitung*, a leading pro-Austrian and conservative paper in south Germany, for which Liebknecht (who shared the paper's hostility to Prussia) was London correspondent. This was much more embarassing to Vogt than the reports in the miniscule *Das Volk* had been. He sued the Augsburg paper and wrote a book in support of his suit. Since he had identified Marx's circle in London as the source of the accusations against him, Vogt directed his book against Marx.

Vogt's book attracted considerable notice, at a time when Germany was being stirred to renewed political consciousness by the Italian events and by the revival of liberal political activity under the so-called New Era in Prussia. Its first printing of 3,000 copies was reported sold, and excerpts were printed in the Berlin *National-Zeitung*. An account of Vogt's charges against Marx and his circle soon found its way into the London *Daily Telegraph*.

The accusations against Marx (beyond authorship of the pamphlet against Vogt) included extorting money from excommunists by threatening to reveal their past, forging paper money, cooperating with the secret police and with the Austrians, tyrannizing over his own followers, and filling the columns of continental newspapers with unjustified invectives against his political enemies. Vogt's baroque imagination placed Marx at the head of obscure organizations with fantastic names: *Schwefelband*, translated by the *Daily Telegraph* as "fire and brimstone band," and *Bürstenheimer*, an insulting name given to a Swiss workers' club.[32] When Marx first encountered some of these charges in Vogt's answer to *Das Volk*'s original report on him, he shrugged them off, even letting *Das Volk* print Vogt's reply. That was in the summer of 1859. But early in the following year Marx became increasingly worried by what Vogt was saying about him. Late in January Lassalle wrote to tell Marx of the success of Vogt's book and the articles in the *National-Zeitung* based on it. The charges were such, Lassalle believed, that no one who knew Marx would find anything believable in them. But people to whom Marx was unknown, or only a name, might well be affected by them, and Lassalle thought Marx would have to answer.[33]

Lassalle's report galvanized Marx (who had been uncertain how to handle the matter) to a decision. Receiving the letter on January 28, he wrote to Engels on February 3, that he regarded Vogt's charges as the *grand coup* of the bourgeois vulgar-democrats against them, and that he would have to do something big in response. "*I will sue the 'National-Zeitung'*," he declared, underlining his words for emphasis, "I am now determined on it." That was ten days before Marx was actually able to read Vogt's book, and three before the details of the *National-Zeitung* articles were confirmed by an article in the *Daily Telegraph*. [34]

From the time Marx decided to proceed against Vogt until the fall of 1860, the affair was his main occupation. He began legal actions against both the *National-Zeitung* and the *Daily Telegraph*; wrote letters (fifty of them during the first week of February, he said) soliciting support or information from friends, old acquaintances, and other persons he thought able to help him; placed declarations in newspapers; obtained a lawyer in Berlin and wrote him detailed descriptions of the case; procured legal affidavits to prove the truth of his earlier statements; and wrote a book against Vogt that grew to over 200 pages. These activities kept him entirely away from his work on economics just at the time its first installment waited for continuation. In the end Marx's suits failed. His book was praised by Engels for its literary qualities, and it may have convinced a few people of the groundlessness of Vogt's charges, but it sold extremely poorly, passing unread then as it has remained unread since.

What led Marx to devote such extraordinary energy to so unfruitful and disruptive a project? Some of the reasons were political. The confrontation with Vogt pitted European democrats with Bonapartist leanings against Marx and his circle at a time when the political situation seemed to be heating up again, and when the view taken of Marx and his friends by liberal German burghers might be expected to have practical consequences. This was the context within which Lassalle thought Marx needed to answer Vogt.

For the most part, however, Marx's reasons were much more personal. Though he sometimes spoke of the need to defend "the party" against Vogt's charges, it was personal vindication that drove him most forcefully. He specifically rejected Lassalle's view of a need to appeal to middle-class opinion: "In the preface I will explain that, as for me, the *devil* can take the judgment of *your German public*." Yet it was this public whose judgment might have had political importance. He did not require their approval to feel that he had justified his own conduct and set the record straight. What he saw in the actions of Karl Blind, who had first told him the story of Vogt's subsidy by Napoleon III but refused to admit authorship of the charges was "a *conspiracy* against me." To one acquaintance to whom he appealed for help he wrote that Vogt "falsifies my whole past." [35]

Vogt's charges led Marx to a general justification of his past actions not only in public, but toward his friends. He now confessed to Lassalle some of the things that lay behind Marx's growing coolness toward him, namely the charges made against Lassalle some years earlier by a workers' group. When Lassalle replied that Marx's listening to the workers' charges showed him to be mistrustful, Marx wrote that he thought he had been guilty of this "spiritual illness" (*Geisteskrankheit*) only twice in his life, once in printing unfounded accusations against Bakunin in the *Neue Rheinische Zeitung*, once in treating August Willich unfairly at the time of the Cologne Communist Trial. In the latter case, he added, however, even Willich's friend Schapper admitted Marx had been "principally in the right."[36]

Marx made a similar attempt to set straight his relationship with Ferdinand Freiligrath, the poet who had been one of Marx's close associates in 1848 and who had often helped Marx in his financial difficulties. He told Freiligrath that he was interested in the vindication of the "party" not in the sense of the membership of specific organizations—Marx himself had belonged to no organizations since 1852 when the Communist League was dissolved at his instance—but in "the great historical sense." Yet it was particular persons he had in mind when he added: "When one knows the *contemporary* history of all the other parties, when one asks in the end what can be *factually* . . . brought against our whole party, one comes to the conclusion that in this nineteenth century it stands distinguished by its *purity*."[37]

Marx's most extended attempts to explain and justify his whole career were in his letters to the lawyer he chose to conduct his suit in Berlin, Weber. His first three letters to Weber dealt only with Vogt's charges and the events in London that had led to them. But on March 3, 1860, after Weber's first reply to Marx's earlier letters brought his actual agreement to take the case, Marx sent him a long (twelve printed pages) dispatch adding more details about the case, and recounting his whole public life. The latter part included a reference to the personal financial sacrifice Marx had made to publish the *Neue Rheinische Zeitung* in 1848-49, as well as the following report, marked *Confidential*: "In the summer of 1844 I received in Paris, following the bankruptcy of the publisher (Julius Fröbel) of the *Deutsch-Französische Jahrbücher*, a letter (enclosing 1000 Taler) from Dr. Claessen in the name of Camphausen and the other share-holders of the *Rheinische Zeitung*, a letter in which my services were hyperbolically colored and which for that very reason I am *not* enclosing."[38] These letters to Lassalle, Freiligrath and Weber reveal that for Marx the significance of the Vogt affair transcended the political importance of Vogt's charges, and that he saw it as presenting the need and opportunity to explain and justify his personal conduct and morality through most of his adult life.

Engels' attitude toward the whole matter helps to put Marx's in a clearer light. Throughout, Engels was extremely supportive to Marx, both in counseling him about what steps to take, and in helping to assemble documents useful for refuting Vogt's charges. Once Marx finished *Herr Vogt* Engels was pleased with it, even calling it Marx's best polemical writing. It is clear, however, that Engels never desired to see the affair take on the proportions Marx gave it, and that he was troubled by Marx's actions. As early as January 31, 1860, after Marx sent him the letter of Lassalle that led to the decision to sue the *National-Zeitung*, he wrote that in spite of Vogt the real need of the moment was a scientific work that would have a big effect on the public, not a propaganda campaign. "The early appearance of your second installment [i.e. following up on *A Contribution to the Critique of Political Economy*] is far and away the most important thing, and I hope that you won't let the Vogt affair keep you from working further on it." A week later, after Vogt's charges were recounted in the *Daily Telegraph*, Engels declared that "If what is in the *Telegraph* is all there is to the matter, then Itzig [Lassalle] has gotten worked up over a fart. 'To parry the thrust' all you have to do is hold your nose."[39]

Later on, as Marx's work on the pamphlet against Vogt dragged on into the summer, Engels wrote with exasperation to Jenny that not to have found a publisher yet was "madness," given the well-known German slowness in printing, "and we will come *piano ma sano* into the year 1861, and no one will be at fault but Mr. Moor himself with his thoroughness. . . . We always write the most wonderful things but we take care that they never come out at the right time and hence they all fall in the water." Engels' exasperation increased when he learned of Marx's plan to have the book printed in German in England and then sent to the continent, a procedure that had given bad results with earlier projects. (Marx nonetheless followed this course, which not only contributed to the book's failure to attract any attention in Germany, just as Engels predicted it would, but in the end also saddled Marx with an unexpected debt that Engels had to pay.) Nor was Engels pleased when Marx proposed to call his book *Da-Da Vogt*, after a Bonapartist agent in North Africa. "I must say I don't like your title at all," Engels declared. "If you want to give him a nickname, it has to be one that a person can understand without having read the book." All in all, it is clear that Engels regarded Marx's whole project against Vogt as unfolding within a sphere that was private to Marx and from which Engels himself felt estranged.[40]

Marx found all this time and energy for the Vogt affair at a moment when he feared that debts and family troubles would make continuing his economics impossible. On October 2, 1859, Marx had written to Lassalle that he needed to do much revision before the continuation of the *Contribution* would be ready, "and as my circumstances don't let me give much time to it now," he would not be finished for some months. A few days later he confessed to Engels that "I am absolutely incapable of writing further on the thing until in one way or another I have cleared away the worst of the bourgeois crap"—bills, threats from his landlord, and so on. Again on January 11, 1860, Marx told Engels that the complaints made against him by tradesmen were keeping him from being able to work at all. This situation did not alter in any fundamental way that year. Yet Marx was able to find time for his polemic and lawsuit which he could not find for his book.[41] What made him do so?

Of course theory posed problems that polemic did not. In February 1858 Marx had told Engels with reference to Lassalle's attempt to write on economics that "He will learn to his cost that to bring a science by criticism to the point where it can be dialectically presented, is an altogether different thing from applying an abstract ready-made system of logic to mere inklings of such a system."[42] By late in 1859, however, Marx felt another dissatisfaction about his book: it was being ignored.

Early in November Marx told Lassalle that he had not expected praise from German readers, only criticism, but that he had not expected what he got—silence. The previous month he had given voice to a worry that the publisher, Duncker, did not wish to go on with the project. Marx told Lassalle that he did not want Duncker as "publisher malgré lui," and intimated that if the second part continued to be ignored he would publish the rest in English. Around Christmastime Jenny Marx wrote a sad letter to Engels about the general mood of depression that had descended on the Marx household in spite of the holiday season. The festivities would lack many things that year, and the *petites misères* were worse now that the girls were old enough to realize them too. "To which has been added, that the quiet, long-cherished hopes for Karl's book were all spoiled by the Germans' conspiracy of silence, broken only by a couple of miserable belletristic articles in feuilletons, relating only to the preface and not to the content of the book."[43]

Marx thus found himself in a doubly troubling situation at the beginning of 1860. His intellectual work was going unrecognized, while at the same time he faced harsh moral criticism of his character and conduct. The combination might have been burdensome enough just by itself, but for Marx it had a special significance: the juxtaposition of these two problems recalled a conflict in his past. Marx's father had been a man of stern morality. He both doubted his son's moral goodness, and specifically made his recognition of the value of Karl's intellectual talents contingent on proof of it. The younger Marx's failure to keep his parents informed of his life at Bonn made Heinrich write to his son (as we saw before): "This confirms me too much in the opinion I carry with me despite all your good qualities, that egoism prevails in your heart." The threat of rejection this reproach contained was explicit in another of Heinrich's letters: "You know that as highly as I value your intellectual talents, they would be totally without interest to me, without a good heart." If Marx acted from hidden, inner motives in allowing the Vogt affair to assume the dimensions it did, perhaps one reason was that the combination of circumstances in which Marx found himself by the end of 1859 reproduced the dilemma in which his father had also placed him.

Heinrich Marx was in his son's consciousness in early 1860. Writing to his lawyer Weber in Berlin, Marx observed: "Since I am myself the son of a lawyer (the deceased legal counselor Heinrich Marx of Trier, who was for a long time a chief officer of the court there, and who was distinguished both by the purity of his character and by his legal talent), I know how important it is for a conscientious jurist to be completely in the clear about the character of his client."[44] It was this memory of his father—whom he had never quite succeeded in putting in the clear about his own character—that led Marx to give Weber details about personal sacrifices he had made and approval he had won. Establishing his moral uprightness with the respected Berlin lawyer took the place of his earlier attempts to do the same with the lawyer from Trier.

The unconscious forces at work in Marx's decision to devote himself to the Vogt affair seem related to ones described recently by Rollo May.

> The cry for recognition becomes the central cry in the need for self-affirmation. If significance and recognition are granted as a matter of course in the family, the child simply assumes them and turns his attention to other things. But if—as is too often the case in our own disrupted day when parents as well as children are radically confused—self-affirmation is blocked, it becomes a compulsive need which drives the person all his life. . . . When self-affirmation meets resistance we make greater effort, we give power to our stance, making clear what we are and what we believe; we state it now against opposition.[45]

Deprived of recognition for his intellectual talent and achievement in the first installment of his work on economics, Marx in the Vogt affair embarked on a driven and compulsive demonstration that he embodied the moral purity his father's ethic demanded. It was this inner impulse that gave external conditions such power over him in 1860, just as similar deeply rooted personal needs determined his relations to work and family. The self-sacrifice he exhibited in these ways also found expression in the last major barrier to the completion of *Capital*: illness.

4. The Sickly Scholar

In the preface to the first edition of *Capital*, Volume One, Marx explained the "long pause" between the *Contribution* of 1859 and his next publication on economics in 1867 as "due to an illness of many years' duration that again and again interrupted my work." In fact Marx seems to have experienced a number of separate but related ailments during the period he lived in London. The one to which he finally succumbed, tuberculosis or pleurisy, may have lurked within him all his life, for the grounds on which he had been excused from Prussian military service in his teens mentioned weakness in the chest. Until the last years of his life, however, Marx does not seem to have suffered from direct symptoms of this illness. His work was sometimes interrupted by eye troubles: painful and debilitating inflammations, probably due to reading in poor light, erupted in the mid-1850s and again in 1863. Marx was subject to another scholar's complaint, hemorrhoids, which sometimes made sitting extremely uncomfortable. He seems also to have had digestive disorders with some regularity, including fairly serious bouts of vomiting.[46]

These last may have been related to the two complaints that most doggedly pursued Marx in the time of *Capital*. One was a liver ailment whose precise nature is not known, but which may have been hereditary in Marx's family. Marx believed that liver trouble had taken his father's life in 1838, and in the 1850s he feared it might claim his own as well. But the illness that plagued Marx most acutely during the years he worked on *Capital* took the form of recurring attacks of carbuncles or boils. Following the first appearance of this malady in the fall of 1863, Marx suffered a return of it nearly every remaining year of his life.

As he was recovering from one of these attacks in the winter of 1868, Marx wrote to Kugelmann that England was "the land of the carbuncle, which is properly a proletarian disease." Marx was referring to the fact that the infection which produces carbuncles is fostered by general physical debility, to which fatigue and poor nourishment are the major contributors. The importance of these factors in causing—or at least predisposing a person to—carbuncles was understood in the nineteenth century; rest and nourishment were continually prescribed to Marx as cures. But the disease did not go away, and at times it attacked Marx in uncomfortable and threatening ways. The swellings would appear all over his body, not only making work impossible, but even causing lying down or sitting to be extremely painful. When the outbreaks approached the area of his penis, Marx amused himself by sending Engels quotations from sixteenth-century pornography. Marx fought the illness with drugs (arsenic was among those that gave him some relief), trips to the seaside, and in the last decade of his life (since proletarian diseases do not have proletarian cures) visits to expensive European spas, notably Carlsbad and Neuenahr. These trips were also intended to give him relief from the liver troubles that continued alongside the carbuncles.[47]

The physical causes of Marx's liver ailment and his carbuncle attacks may or may not have been connected, but what made him chronically subject to both was his manner of living and working. This was understood by his friends and family for years; testimony on the subject was unanimous. In his memoir of Marx, Liebknecht recounted how, "notwithstanding his extraordinarily robust constitution, Marx began to complain of all sorts of troubles at the end of the fifties." The doctor forbade Marx to work at night and prescribed exercise. "But he hardly felt better when he again gradually fell into his habit of night-work until a crisis came that forced him to adopt a more reasonable mode of life, though only as long as he felt the imperative necessity for it." To Jenny's reproaches about the damage he was doing himself through lack of sleep Marx replied that working through the night was in his nature. Liebknecht concluded: "I am convinced—and the physicians who last treated him were of the same opinion—that had Marx made up his mind to a life in keeping with nature, that is, with the demands of his organism and of hygiene, he would still be alive today [1895]."[48]

Paul Lafargue, who was a trained physician, and who observed Marx closely in the period that Volume One of *Capital* was being readied for the press (the same time Lafargue was becoming engaged to Laura), gave a similar diagnosis.

> Although he invariably went to bed very late, he was always afoot between eight and nine in the morning. Having drunk a cup of black coffee and glanced at the newspapers, he would go to his study and work there till two or three next morning—breaking off only for meals, and (when the weather was fine) for a constitutional on Hampstead Heath. . . . He was a poor trencherman, and sometimes found it necessary to stimulate his flagging appetite with highly seasoned food, such as ham, smoked fish, caviar, and pickles. His stomach had to pay forfeit for the colossal activity of his brain, to which, indeed, all his body was sacrificed.[49]

Whereas Liebknecht was commenting on the time when Marx's liver trouble was his major ailment, the period to which Lafargue referred was the period of the carbuncle attacks that interfered with *Capital*. Both were encouraged or aggravated by Marx's mode of life and work.

The truth of this was an open secret between Marx and Engels. After a particularly severe attack of carbuncles in early 1866, Marx wrote to Engels that his doctors "are quite right, that overdone night-work is the main cause of these relapses. But I cannot explain to the gentlemen—it would be quite pointless—the causes that *compel* me to these extravagances." Engels thought the compulsions less strong than Marx believed, for he replied with a determined admonition that "You really must finally do something rational in order to get out of this carbuncle trouble, even if your book is delayed three months more by it. The thing is really becoming too serious. . . . Leave off the night-work for a time and follow a more regular mode of life."[50]

This remained Engels' view of Marx's health problem. Early in 1870 he told Marx that a "change in your mode of life is necessary, in the interest of your second volume itself. You will never be finished with the eternal recurrence of these interruptions; with more exercise in fresh air, which would keep the carbuncles off your body, you would finish sooner or later." At the beginning of July 1873, Engels wrote in more general terms to Kugelmann about Marx's health, that Marx himself "soon discovered that the more he pushed himself, the less capable of work he became."[51]

Kugelmann, himself a prominent physician, had diagnosed Marx's carbuncle trouble as based on bad nutrition a number of years earlier. Agreeing that Kugelmann's attribution of the illness to "sins of the diet" was correct, Marx wrote in April 1866: "I am too much accustomed to working at night, I study by day and write by night. This, together with all sorts of public and private troubles, and—as long as I am seriously at work—neglect of regular diet, exercise, etc., brings my blood to disorder." When in October 1866 Marx wrote to Kugelmann that he thought all the difficulties of his external life which interfered with finishing his work would disappear "tomorrow, if tomorrow I decided to engage in some practical business," he meant both that such a course would better his economic situation, and that his health would improve. At the time of the publication of Volume One of *Capital* both Marx and Engels declared their conviction that Marx's health would recover once the burden of his work on economics was behind him.[52]

Marx understood that his illness was related not only to the style of life his work seemed to impose on him but also to the state of mind it helped to breed. We saw earlier that Marx attributed the illness of his wife and daughters at various times to the mental pressures created by "bourgeois crap" and the need to "keep up appearances." He was equally aware of the inner connection between his psychic state and his own health. In the summer of 1856 he wrote to his wife in Germany that "Engels is coming next week. What a relief! For three weeks I've been hypochondriac as the devil." He told Lassalle on May 31, 1858: "You can easily form an idea of my mood during this illness if you consider that these liver troubles in themselves incline one toward a hypochondriacal disposition, and in addition all kinds of domestic matters plus the annoyance about the publication combined to make me sick of life." Jenny viewed Marx's condition similarly at the same time, confiding to Engels: "His state is made much worse by mental stress and excitement which, with the signing of the publisher's contract, is naturally increasing, as it is simply impossible for him to bring his work to a finish."[53]

Some years afterward Marx himself spoke in like terms to Engels, doubting whether he had really recovered from a bout of carbuncles. "In spite of everything people said to me about my healthy appearance, I have been feeling something wrong all along, and the great decisiveness I had to call up in order to work out difficult themes also belongs to this feeling of inadequacy." A few years later he attributed his insomnia and general restlessnsss much more explicitly to "psychic grounds." On October 19, 1867, he wrote to Engels, "My illness always comes out of my head." Ten years later he gave a similar report from a German health spa: "My liver shows no more sign of enlargement; my digestive system is somewhat disordered, but the real trouble is of a *psychic nature* [*nervöser Natur*]."[54]

Recognizing as he did the link between his unfinished book and the illness that plagued him so mercilessly, Marx not surprisingly gave vent to anger and hostility toward his work. As early as April 1851 he referred to the subject with which he had not succeeded in coming to terms as "economic shit." In 1859, as he readied *A Contribution to the Critique of Political Economy* for the press, he called it "the unhappy manuscript," and worried about whether he should place a statement reserving translation rights "on the crap." In 1862 he spoke of one subject as "the rent shit." In 1863 it was the "slutty book" (*Saubuch*), and in 1866 the "damned book." Even after Volume One was published Marx described himself—as we saw above—as "condemned to devour" books and "cast them, in a changed form, on the dunghill of history."[55]

Marx's words teach us as well as any psychological theory that this anal imagery was the language of repudiation. Given how much of his time and life he had devoted—his word would have been sacrificed—to the project, to speak of his work in this way was to reject an essential part of himself. The inner counterpart of this language was the depression he often suffered. The "black care" of the years in Soho pursued him still. Early in 1862 he moaned to Engels, "Take all in all, it is really not worth while to lead such a lousy life." Matching his mood to the January weather some years later, Marx growled, "No wonder that suicides are now in full bloom here."[56] Marx's depression, his anal language, and his illness were all expressions of a single emotional current. In his life style Marx gave physical form to the aggression against his own being which his language and his mood expressed in words and feelings.

We saw earlier that the same underlying pattern had been visible in Marx's life from his teens. In 1835 he confessed to an impulse to "mock the rights" of his body in order to give himself unreservedly to his intellectual vocation, fearing at the same time that he would turn his life into "an unfortunate struggle between the intellectual and the physical principle." His father saw where Marx's penchant for ignoring physical needs was leading him. "A sickly scholar is the unhappiest being on earth," Heinrich had warned, "Don't study more than your health can stand." His fears were fulfilled at every stage in Karl's life: in Bonn, in Berlin, in Paris, in Brussels, and in London. There were periods when the whole complex of overwork, ill health, and meditations on their linkages receded from view. The years of revolution beginning in 1848 were one; perhaps it is illuminated by Engels' comment on another, the period of the Franco-Prussian War and the Commune: "In his mode of living Marx is far from being as crazy as people imagine. As long as the excitement that began with the war continues, he doesn't work on difficult theoretical matters, and lives rather reasonably, even exercises fairly often *without* my reminding him . . . drinks no beer for a week at a time, as soon as he notices that it does him harm." As Engels understood, the times when Marx did work on "difficult theoretical matters" were the dangerous ones.[57]

When Marx described his situation in the time of *Capital* many of its origins in his parental family came clear. Writing in 1867 to a German socialist who had emigrated to the United States, Sigrid Mayer, Marx excused himself for neglecting his correspondence in the following terms:

> I therefore [because of his illness] had to use *every* moment in which I was capable of working in order to complete my book, to which I have sacrificed my health, my happiness, and my family. I hope that this explanation requires no further supplement. I laugh at the so-called "practical" men and their wisdom. If one wanted to be an ox, then he could turn his back on the pains of humanity and look out for his own skin. But I would have considered myself really *impractical* if I had kicked the bucket without completely finishing my book, at least in manuscript.[58]

Marx's book was evidence that he had indeed made those daily and recurring sacrifices to the good of others which Heinrich's ethic demanded. His claim to practicality was a response to criticisms his father had often made. But it was his very willingness to sacrifice himself to his book that kept him from completing it. The vicious circle was unbreakable: Marx's struggle to finish was identical with his submission to all the conditions that kept his goal beyond reach. *Hic Rhodus, hic salta*.

5. Conclusion: Ideal and Reality in Marx's Thought and Life

The drama of Marx's life was the confrontation of theory and reality, thought and the world. The struggle was powerful because its stage was the whole of human history, and because each of the two protagonists—intellectual vision and actual experience—was equally clothed with the full intensity of Marx's commitment to it. This double devotion was Marx's dilemma and his glory. His life had all the character and dimensions of tragedy.

In the 1860s Marx found a literary image of his own plight in a story of Balzac. Paul Lafargue wrote:

> One of Balzac's psychological studies, "The Unknown Masterpiece" (pitifully plagiarized by Zola), made a great impression on him because it was in part a description of his own feelings. A talented painter tries again and again to limn the picture which has formed itself in his brain; touches and retouches his canvas incessantly; to produce at last nothing more than a shapeless mass of colors; which nevertheless to his prejudiced eye seems a perfect reproduction of the reality in his own mind.

Lafargue's testimony is the only evidence that Marx regarded Balzac's character as an image of his own dilemma, but Marx recommended the story to Engels as a "masterpiece" in February 1867, just at the time Volume One was going to the printer.[59]

Balzac's painter did sound much like Marx, both in his continually disappointed expectations that his great work would soon be finished, and in his description of the difficulties that kept it incomplete. " 'Show my work!' exclaimed the old man, excitedly. 'No, no! I have still to put some finishing touches to it. Yesterday, toward evening, I thought that it was done. . . . This morning, by daylight, I realized my error.' " Like Marx, Balzac's painter was trying to reproduce for others an inner vision, which to begin with only the mind's eye could see. But by working continually at it he found that all his application and his understanding of painterly technique got him no closer to the desired result. "O Nature, Nature! who has ever followed thee in thy flight? Observe that too much knowledge, like ignorance leads to a negation. I doubt my own work!" His attempt to escape his dilemma led him to search the world for evidence: "I have certainly gone wrong in some details, and my mind will not be at rest until I have cleared away my doubts. I have decided to travel, and visit Turkey, Greece, and Asia in search of models, in order to compare my picture with nature in different forms."

When at last the painter's colleagues, long aware of his genius and prepared by years of expectation to see it embodied in a great work, are admitted to the studio, they first see on his canvas—nothing. Peering at the easel from all angles they finally begin to perceive the remnants of what was once the picture of a woman. But it had been covered over with layers of paint, a "chaos of colors, of tones, of uncertain shades," rendering it invisible.[60]

Some features of Balzac's painter recall Marx's own literary creation, the Democritus of his doctoral dissertation. Driven by the contrast between the light in his mind and the pale reflection of his vision reality offered, Democritus had also traveled the world in search of evidence. "Cicero calls him a *vir eruditus*. He is competent in physics, ethics, mathematics, in the encyclopedic disciplines, in every art."[61] So did Marx become a *vir eruditus*, extending his learning to some of the same disciplines Democritus had cultivated. His notebooks and manuscripts bulged with accumulated knowledge. He did not, like Democritus, travel "through half the world in order to exchange experiences, pieces of knowledge, and observations," but he learned new languages and constantly expanded the scope of his reading. He wrote to friends at various times that *Capital* could not be completed until he had at hand one more piece of information—from Belgium, or Russia, or the United States. Marx's self-induced illnesses were less radical and violent than Democritus' blinding himself, but their self-destructiveness served a similar purpose, preserving the theoretical vision underlying *Capital* from the threatened revelation that the empirical reality of market relations might not correspond to it.

Marx had not forgotten his dissertation in the years he worked on economics. When Lassalle sent Marx his book on Heraclitus in 1858, Marx recalled that he, too, had once written about ancient philosophy, and in distinguishing Epicurus' atomism from that of Democritus he had come to a conclusion to which he still held: "Even with philosophers who give their works a systematic form, for instance Spinoza, the true inner structure of the system is totally different from the form in which the philosopher consciously presents it." It was this unconscious inner structure that Marx had pointed to in 1841, when he wrote: "In the general relationship which the philosopher establishes between the world and thought, he merely makes objective the relation between his particular consciousness and the real world."[62]

We have seen the relation between Marx's consciousness and the external world exhibited in each of the barriers that kept his work from completion: the residue of abstraction, the demands of "external circumstances," and the power of illness. In each sphere Marx began by denying the power of the ordinary everyday world over his person and his work; but by doing so he created the need to submit to external reality as a hostile and alien force. To comprehend the world through abstract reasoning from "simple conceptions" was to presuppose the primacy of an inner, rational core, by which outer, everyday appearances were ultimately shaped: Marx's obsessive devotion to the empirical study of facts that never fully met the needs of his theory was the negation of that supposition. To attempt to live without a regular source of income in the name of loyalty to his theoretical project was to assert that Marx was not subject to the rules of practical life to which everyday men had to submit: Marx's persistent domination by "external conditions" brought him ever back to the power of the outside world, with its practical demands and ordinary morality. Continually to work in a manner that denied the power his own physical limitations exercised over his mental life was to assert the primacy of mind over body: Marx's recurring illness was the living contradiction of that assertion. Philosophical idealism and materialist realism were not only the poles of Marx's thought but also of his life. His conscious attempt to view his own history as a steady progress from the first to the second masked the real movement by which he was constantly driven in both directions.

Our project has been to trace the evolution of these patterns in Marx's life, and thereby to comprehend his history and its outcome as part of a single destiny. In Marx's psychic economy, to exchange idealism and abstraction for a standpoint that harmonized with the concrete reality of the material world was to pay off a major debt imposed on him by his parents. Attempting to meet their demands prepared Marx for the parallel transactions of German philosophy, as represented by both Hegel and Feuerbach. Each of his successive intellectual positions represented Marx's abandonment of an earlier idealism for a new realism. Yet Marx could not remain indebted to Hegelianism for long without feeling himself unbearably impoverished by it, because the post-Hegelian philosophical enterprise was too deeply entangled in the need for reconciliation with the dominant culture of Germany. Although tied to that culture in many ways, Marx would never be fully at home in it. His position as a Jew— and as Heinrich Marx's son—left him with a score to settle against political and social powers that failed to live up to the principles their apologists claimed to find embodied in them. Moreover, some deep need of his personality, rooted perhaps in his mother's intrusive and dominating mode of nurture, gave Marx a hostile and aggressive personal style which also helped shape his stance of defiant opposition against outside political authority. This way of acting "with weakness, yet with strength," had an inner parallel in the aggression against his own body which fed Marx's lifelong penchant for self-induced illness.

That Marx would shape these themes into a mature identity by associating himself with another example of "the strength of the weak," the revolutionary proletariat of the 1840s, reflected social reality as much as his own psychic evolution. Nonetheless, the continuities his vision of the proletariat maintained with his earlier identifications, critical philosophy and journalism, and with his image of the purely "material" Jews, all suggest that Marx's mature identity served some of the same inner needs his more youthful ones had.

Moreover, Marx never freed himself so fully from his original philosophical identity as he thought. Once the failure of the 1848 revolutions made it clear that history, even in the nineteenth century, would not effect the idealization of reality necessary to do away with the need for philosophy, Marx found his vision harmonized much less with actual existence than the conditions of the 1840s had led him to believe. In this situation Marx found himself again experiencing—and taking pleasure in—the isolation he had sought to escape at each of the earlier turning points in his life. In his London isolation Marx abandoned economic theory in favor of his discovery that Palmerston was a secret Russian agent, and his revelations about the history of eighteenth-century diplomacy. The promise of the First International allowed Marx to emerge into political activity once more, but when the gap between the "spirit of generalization" and the particular conditions of working-class politics grew too great, Marx found that, like Hegel's Abraham, he had to choose between exercising an authoritarian domination and allowing alien circumstances to dominate him, and his political commitment was again transformed into withdrawal.

Tangled in the false appearances of his private life, Marx had to recast his economic theory to comprehend the thick layer of illusion with which the ebbing of the revolutionary tide had covered over the social realities he believed had been revealed. As a materialist he had to recognize that the new configuration of the surface, however illusory, was also the shape of reality itself. The tension between a theoretical structure which, although the sole source of scientific comprehension, could be easily mistaken for the empty dialectical play of abstract idealism, and an empirical world which, although uniquely real, was also illusory and irrational, led Marx to impasses he could not circumvent. Marx's expectation that the falling rate of profit would provide a verification for his theory in actual experience despite the overall meaninglessness and irrationality of the surface conditions of capitalist life could be justified in terms of the Hegelian logic of inversion Marx employed. But as reality failed to fulfill Marx's expectations he increasingly displayed what Hegel had called inversion in the psychological sense, the perversity that intensified the self-destructive work habits that had characterized him throughout his life. Betrayed by reality, Marx fulfilled the self-prophecy contained in his early portrait of the tortured materialist philosopher, Democritus.

Have we then comprehended Marx's fate? Perhaps we had best not be too sure. Marx belongs to history, and the final destiny of the theory and practice he inspired is not yet decided. He has been called "a dead dog," as he said of Hegel, often enough, but at critical moments deep-seated personal and social needs have brought him back to life. Those who cannot remember the 1930s may recall the 1960s. The immediate reasons for Marx's revival have differed according to time and circumstance, but no other perspective on modern society has persuaded so many people of its ability to find meaning in the chaos of experience, to link thought with action, to find energizing connections between disparate layers of social and individual life. On these grounds it is premature and pretentious to speak of Marx's fate.

Yet if, as Hegel thought, the destiny of any historical movement repeats in some way the original structure of experience that gave birth to it, then the future heirs of Marx may continue to experience some elements of his history in theirs, as many of his disciples already have. They may find that revolution does not free men so totally from the weight of the past in reality as in the dream of liberation that inspires it; that the "essential relations" uncovered by theory are subject to domination by a thousand and one seemingly peripheral, "surface" factors; that the conditions of action in the real political world either subject the "spirit of generalization" to control by particular and local matters, or else offer those who identify with it the uncomfortable choice between authoritarian control and withdrawal; that the visible remnants and seeming portents of revolution that surround us do not free those who struggle for new conditions of social existence from the need to submit to existing ones.

What any person learns from Marx's life will depend on what he or she brings to it. But in some way we are all his heirs. Revolution still promises to transform our lives, yet threatens to leave them unredeemed. The social oppression and personal neurosis of modern life still confront us. As long as we live in such a present Marx will belong to our most usable past. Let his heroic determination to heal what ails us nurture our efforts to fulfill the needs of inner life by remaking the world outside ourselves.

NOTES

A Note on Sources and Citations

BECAUSE existing and widely available books on Marx already contain comprehensive bibliographies, I have not thought it necessary to include yet another one here. I have given fairly extensive bibliographical references at appropriate points in the notes. The best available bibliography for English readers is in David McLellan, *Karl Marx, His Life and Thought* (London and New York, 1973).

The basic sources for Marx's career are available in two multi-volume German collections. The first is Karl Marx—Friedrich Engels, *Historisch-Kritische Gesamtausgabe*, edited by D. Rjazanov, published in Berlin from 1927, but never completed; and Karl Marx—Friedrich Engels, *Werke*, published by the East German Institute for Marxism-Leninism in thirty-nine volumes plus additional material and index since 1956. The editorial standards for the *Gesamtausgabe* were in some respects higher than those for the *Werke*, but the latter is indispensable for serious students. A new German edition, also to be called *Gesamtausgabe*, has been announced, but no volumes have appeared as yet. English readers should know of the *Collected Works* now in process of publication by Lawrence and Wishart, London, International Publishers, New York, and Progress Publishers, Moscow. It will be in some ways more comprehensive than the *Werke*, and both the editorial standards and the translations are to be praised.

Perhaps this is the place to note that all italics given in quotations are present in the original texts. I have not added italics for emphasis in any quoted material. Although I have usually consulted the German texts of Marx's writings, and sometimes given my own translations, I have tried to make use of existing and widely available English translations wherever possible. I have made use of the following abbreviations in the notes, identifying each abbreviation before using it. This list shows the English edition on which I most commonly rely; in the notes reference is often made both to these translations and to the original texts included in the German source collections. Readers should be aware that the *Gesamtausgabe* (*MEGA*) is divided into parts and volumes, then sometimes into half-volumes; thus I, i, (2), 100 means page 100 of the second half-volume of Volume One, Part One. In accord with what seems to be common usage I have cited the Marx-Engels *Werke* volumes with arabic numbers; thus *MEW* 2: 40 means page 40 of Volume Two.

CM   Karl Marx and Frederick Engels, *Manifesto of the Communist Party* (*Communist Manifesto*), cited from *SW*, 35-63.
CS   Karl Marx, *The Class Struggles in France (1848-1850)* (New York, 1964).
CW   Karl Marx and Frederick Engels, *Collected Works* (New York, London and Moscow, from 1975).

EB   Karl Marx, *The Eighteenth Brumaire of Louis Bonaparte*, cited from *SW*, 97-180.

EPM   Karl Marx, *Economic and Philosophic Manuscripts of 1844*, trans. Martin Milligan, ed. Dirk J. Struik (New York, 1964). Also known as the *Paris Manuscripts* and the *1844 Manuscripts*.

ETW   G.W.F. Hegel, *Early Theological Writings*, trans. T. M. Knox, with Introduction, and fragments trans. Richard Kroner (Chicago, 1948; Philadelphia, 1971).

GI   Karl Marx and Frederick Engels, *The German Ideology*, ed. S. Ryazanskaya (London, 1965; Moscow, 1968).

IISG   International Institute for Social History, Amsterdam.

MEGA   Karl Marx—Friedrich Engels, *Historisch-Kritische Gesamtausgabe*, ed. D. Rjazanov (Berlin, from 1927).

METEC   *Marx and Engels through the Eyes of their Contemporaries* (Moscow, 1972).

MEW   Karl Marx—Friedrich Engels, *Werke* (Berlin, 1956 ff.).

NYDT   *New York Daily Tribune*

NRZ   *Neue Rheinische Zeitung*

PC   Karl Marx and Frederick Engels, *On the Paris Commune* (Moscow, 1971).

PP   Karl Marx, *The Poverty of Philosophy* (New York, 1963).

PR   Hegel's *Philosophy of Right*, trans. with notes by T. M. Knox (Oxford, 1952).

RhZ   *Rheinische Zeitung*

SC   Karl Marx and Frederick Engels, *Selected Correspondence* (Moscow, 1955, 1965).

SDH   *The Secret Diplomatic History of the Eighteenth Century*, ed. Lester Hutchinson (published together with *The Story of the Life of Lord Palmerston*, London, 1969).

SW   Karl Marx and Frederick Engels, *Selected Works*, one volume ed. (New York, 1968); whenever the two volume ed., ed. V. Adoratsky (New York, 1933) is cited, it is specifically noted.

Texte   Karl Marx, *Texte zu Methode und Praxis*, ed. Günther Hillmann, 1 (Reinbeck bei Hamburg, 1966).

WLC   Karl Marx, *Wage Labor and Capital*, cited from *SW*, 72-94.

Introduction

1. Norman N. Holland, *Poems in Persons, An Introduction to the Psychoanalysis of Literature* (New York, 1973, 1975), 142. I also owe to Holland the quotation from Yeats used above. In the same spirit: Cushing Strout, "Ego Psychology and the Historian," *History and Theory* 7 (1968), 281-97.

2. W. W. Meisner, quoted in Holland, 157.

3. Clifford Geertz, "Deep Play: Notes on the Balinese Cockfight," in *The Interpretation of Cultures* (New York, 1973), 453. Geertz's point is broader than the one being made here. He writes: "Societies, like lives, contain their own interpretations." On Freud, see William J. McGrath, "Freud as Hannibal: The Politics of the Brother Band," *Central European History* 7 (1974), 31-57, and Carl E.

Schorske,"Politics and Patricide in Freud's Interpretation of Dreams," *American Historical Review* 78 (1973), 328-47.

4. Sigmund Freud, *The Interpretation of Dreams*, trans. and ed. James Strachey (London and New York, 1967), 311-12.

5. *Ibid.*, 135.

6. H. J. Home, "The Concept of Mind," *International Journal of Psycho-Analysis* 47 (1966), 49.

7. There is now a large literature on family therapy. See the review by Elsa First in *New York Review of Books*, Feb. 20, 1975, for some recent contributions, and for a general discussion of the relationship between the family movement and history, Raimund E. Goerler, "Family, Psychology, and History," *Group for the Use of Psychology in History Newsletter* 4 (Dec. 1975), 31-38. I have been especially influenced by Robert D. Hess and Gerald Handel, "The Family as a Psychosocial Organization," in *The Psychosocial Interior of the Family*, ed. Gerald Handel (Chicago, 1967), as well as by other studies in this volume, and by Nathan Ackerman, *The Psychodynamics of Family Life* (New York, 1958), and *Treating the Troubled Family* (New York, 1966).

8. Erik H. Erikson, *Childhood and Society* (New York, 1950, 1963); *Young Man Luther* (New York, 1958); *Identity: Youth and Crisis* (New York, 1968); *Gandhi's Truth* (New York, 1969).

9. Those who emphasize Marx's move from humanism to science include Louis Althusser, *Pour Marx* (Paris, 1966), trans. Ben Brewster as *For Marx* (London, 1969); Althusser and Etienne Balabar, *Lire le Capital*, two volumes (Paris, 1968, 1970), trans. Ben Brewster as *Reading Capital* (New York, 1970); also Adam Schaff, "Studies of the Young Marx: A Rejoinder," and Daniel Bell, "The Debate on Alienation," both in *Revisionism, Essays on the History of Marxist Ideas*, ed. Leopold Labedz (New York, 1962), 188-214. Notable on the other side are: Erich Fromm, *Marx's Concept of Man* (New York, 1961, 1966); Robert C. Tucker, *Philosophy and Myth in Karl Marx* (Cambridge, 1961, 1965); Iring Fetscher, "The Young and the Old Marx," in *Marx and Marxism* (New York, 1971), 3-25; B. Ollman, *Alienation: Marx's Conception of Man in Capitalist Society* (Cambridge, 1971); and in a modified form, David McLellan, *Karl Marx, His Life and Thought* (New York, 1973). Two recent books take a balanced view that sees both evolution and continuity in Marx's thinking, but without offering quite the view presented here: Lucien Sève, *Marxisme et théorie de la personalité*, 2nd ed. (Paris, 1972), 83-98; and Helmut Fleischer, *Marxism and History*, trans. Eric Mosbacher (New York, 1973). Perhaps I should note that Sève's views on the relationship between Marxism and psychology amount to an attempt to construct a personality theory from Marx's explicit formulations about society and economics; they are far removed from the view of Marx offered here.

Chapter One

1. Recent accounts of Hegel's life and thinking include (in English) Charles Taylor, *Hegel* (Cambridge, 1975); Raymond Plant, *Hegel* (Bloomington, Indiana, 1973); Shlomo Avineri, *Hegel's Theory of the Modern State* (Cambridge, 1972); Walter Kaufmann, *Hegel: A Reinterpretation* (New York, 1965). For the intellectual context, George Armstrong Kelly, *Idealism, Politics and History* (London,

1969). Slightly older but still very helpful are Karl Löwith, *From Hegel to Nietzsche*, trans. David E. Green (New York, 1964, orig. ed. 1941); and Herbert Marcuse, *Reason and Revolution: Hegel and the Rise of Social Theory* (New York, 1941, 1954). Classic and influential are Alexandre Kojève, *Introduction à la lecture de Hegel*, abridged as *Introduction to the Reading of Hegel*, ed. Allan Bloom, and trans. James H. Nichols (New York, 1969); and Jean Hyppolite, *Etudes sur Marx et Hegel* (Paris, 1955), trans. John O'Neill as *Studies on Marx and Hegel* (New York, 1969). Recent German scholarship is represented by Manfred Riedel, *Theorie und Praxis im Denken Hegels* (Stuttgart, 1965), and the same author's collection of essays, *Studien zu Hegels Rechtsphilosophie* (Frankfurt am Main, 1969). See also Lucio Colletti, *Marxism and Hegel*, trans. Lawrence Garner (London, 1973). Three useful collections of articles are *Hegel's Political Philosophy*, ed. Walter Kaufmann (New York, 1970); *Hegel's Political Philosophy, Problems and Perspectives*, ed. Z. A. Pelczynski (Cambridge, Eng., 1971); and *Hegel, A Collection of Critical Essays*, ed. Alasdair MacIntyre (New York, 1972). A comprehensive outline of recent work on Hegel emerges from *The Legacy of Hegel, Proceedings of the Marquette Hegel Symposium, 1970*, ed. J. J. O'Malley *et al*. (The Hague, 1973). The active industry of Hegel scholarship has produced two periodicals devoted especially to him: *Hegel-Studien* (from 1961) and *Hegel-Jahrbuch* (from 1971).

2. See Manfred Riedel, "Der Begriff der 'Bürgerlichen Gesellschaft' und das Problem seines geschichtlichen Ursprungs," in *Studien zu Hegel's Rechtsphilosophie* (Frankfurt am Main, 1969), esp. 138-44. Also, *Hegel's Philosophy of Mind* (Part Three of the *Encyclopaedia of the Philosophical Sciences*, 1830), trans. William Wallace, with the *Zusätze* (Additions) of 1845 trans. A. V. Miller, and with a Foreword by J. N. Findlay (Oxford, 1971), para. 523, p. 256 and para. 537, p. 264 (cited hereafter as *Encyclopaedia*); also Hegel's *Philosophy of Right*, trans. with notes by T. M. Knox (Oxford, 1952), para. 185, p. 123 (this text is cited hereafter as *PR*).

3. *PR*, par. 261, p. 161; cf. T. M. Knox in the Foreword to *PR*, xl.

4. *PR*, para. 260, pp. 160-61.

5. From Hegel's essay on the German Constitution, in *Hegel's Political Writings*, trans. T. M. Knox, with an Introductory Essay by Z. A. Pelczynski (Oxford, 1964), 242.

6. See Immanuel Kant, *Anthropologie in praktischer Hinsicht* (Leipzig, 1912). I have not seen the trans. by Mary J. Gregor (The Hague, 1974).

7. *Encyclopaedia*, para. 408, pp. 131, 123-24; para. 406, pp. 102-03. In these references I shall not attempt to distinguish between the originally published text of the *Encyclopaedia* and the *Zusätze* (Additions). On the origin and importance of these additions see J. N. Findlay's Foreword to *Encyclopaedia*, v-vii. Hegel's conception of madness recalls Kant's description of it as "the loss of the common sense [*Gemeinsinn, sensus communis*] and its replacement by a peculiar private logic [*logische Eigensinn, sensus privatus*]." See Kant, *Anthropologie*, 138. On Kant and the context of his theory of madness see Klaus Dörner, *Bürger und Irre* (Frankfurt am Main, 1969).

8. *Encyclopaedia*, para. 408, p. 128.

9. *Ibid.*, p. 124. Perhaps this is the place to observe that Hegel knew mental illness within his own family. His sister lived in his house following her mental breakdown in 1814. She spent time in an asylum in 1820.

10. *Ibid.*, p. 128. Freud, *Introductory Lectures*, trans. Joan Riviere (London, 1922), 345-46: Neuroses arise from the situation "in which the ego in its capacity of independent individual organism has entered into opposition with itself in its other capacity as a member of a series of generations. Such a dissociation perhaps only exists in man, so that, taken all in all, his superiority over the other animals may come down to his capacity for neurosis."

11. *Encyclopaedia*, para. 402, p.92; para. 408, pp. 124-25. As examples of phenomena akin to madness, Hegel discussed prophecy, water-divining and the contemporary therapy of mesmerism, whose validity he accepted (unlike phrenology, which he ridiculed): paras. 405, 406, 408.

12. *Encyclopaedia*, para. 408, p. 130.

13. *Encyclopaedia*, para. 396, pp. 55-60.

14. *Ibid.*, 55, 61.

15. *Ibid.*, and 62.

16. *Ibid.*, 62.

17. *Ibid.*, 63-64.

18. Hegel to Windischmann, May 27, 1810, printed by Kaufmann in *Hegel*, 328-29.

19. Schelling to Hegel, June 20, 1796, in Kaufmann, *Hegel*, 306.

20. Franz Rosenzweig, *Hegel und der Staat* (Munich and Berlin, 1920, but written before 1914), two volumes, I, Chaps. 2 and 3; also Kaufmann, *Hegel*, 9-15.

21. Quoted by Kaufmann, 32.

22. Hegel to Schelling, April 16, 1795, *Briefe von und an Hegel*, ed. Johannes Hoffmeister (Vols. XXVII-XXX of Hegel's *Sämtliche Werke*, Hamburg, 1952), I, 23-24. (Cited below as *Briefe*.)

23. "Erstes Systemprogramm des Deutschen Idealismus," in *Dokumente zu Hegels Entwicklung*, ed. Johannes Hoffmeister (Stuttgart, 1936), 219-20.

24. *Ibid.*, and Hegel to Schelling, April 16, 1795, *Briefe*, 24.

25. "Eleusis," in *Dokumente zu Hegels Entwicklung*, 380-81. There is a different translation in Kaufmann, *Hegel*, 310.

26. Rosenzweig, *Hegel und der Staat*, 73; trans. differently by Kaufmann, *Hegel*, 312.

27. Kaufmann, *Hegel, passim*, esp. Chap. 1 and 15 ff.

28 Friedrich Schiller, *On the Aesthetic Education of Man, In a Series of Letters*, ed. and trans. Elizabeth M. Wilkinson and L. A. Willoughby (Oxford, 1967); Hegel to Schelling, April 16, 1795, *Briefe*, 25; Kaufmann, *Hegel*, 18 ff.

29. Rosenzweig, *Hegel und der Staat*, 70; Hegel, *Early Theological Writings*, trans. T. M. Knox, with an Intro. and Fragments trans. Richard Kroner (Chicago, 1948; Philadelphia, 1971), 157-58. (Cited hereafter as *ETW*.)

30. *Dokumente zu Hegels Entwicklung*, 221.

31. *ETW*, 100-01.

32. *ETW*, 69; Rosenzweig, *Hegel und der Staat*, 71-72.

33. Gisela Schüler, "Zur Chronologie von Hegels Jugendschriften," *Hegel-Studien* 2 (1963), 130-31.

34. First printed by Karl Rosenkranz, *Hegels Leben* (Berlin, 1844), 88-90. Also in G.W.F. Hegel, *Sämtliche Werke*, ed. G. Lasson, VII: *Schriften zur Politik und Rechtsphilosophie* (Leipzig, 1923), 138-41. The text is discussed by

Rosenzweig, *Hegel und der Staat*, Chap. 6, by T. L. Haering, *Hegel, Sein Wollen und Sein Werk* (Leipzig and Berlin, 1929), 595-96, and by Wilhelm Dilthey, in an essay reprinted in his *Gesammelte Schriften* (Leipzig and Berlin, 1921), IV, 122 ff. It is remarkable that a Marxist writer, Cesare Luporini, finds in the situation Hegel describes in this text the basic necessity, revealed by German idealism, for the discovery of a revolutionary will actually operative in history, the requirement Marx would find fulfilled in the proletariat. For Hegel, however, the point was the opposite: historical evolution made revolution unnecessary at the very moment that philosophy revealed it to be impossible and self-defeating. Luporini's attempt to interpret Hegel in a revolutionary way only reminds us that the conditions Hegel conceived as the basis for reconciliation would appear in Marx's later perspective to require precisely the revolution Hegel had abandoned when he moved out of "youth" and into "maturity." Cesare Luporini, "Un frammento politico giovanile di G. F. Hegel," in *Filosofi Vecchi e nuovi* (Florence, 1947), I, 49-111 (with a translation of the fragment, 51-55). Carlo Ginzburg, who kindly called my attention to Luporini's article, tells me that it has provoked considerable discussion in Italy.

35. Rosenkranz, *Hegels Leben*, 88.

36. *Ibid.*, 88-89.

37. *Ibid.*, 89.

38. *Ibid.*, 89-90.

39. *Ibid.*, 90.

40. *Dokumente zu Hegels Entwicklung*, 273-74; Hoffmeister proposes to date this writing in 1798, but Gisela Schüler, "Zur Chronologie," 133, says it is not datable.

41. Hegel to Schelling, Nov. 2, 1800, *Briefe*, 59-60.

42. Rosenzweig, *Hegel und der Staat*, 101. Hegel to his wife, summer of 1811, in Kaufmann, *Hegel*, 333.

43. Published for the first time in *Hegels theologische Jugendschriften*, ed. Herman Nohl (Tübingen, 1907). Cited from *ETW*, 182-301.

44. *ETW*, 183.

45. *ETW*, 185-86.

46. *ETW*, 187, 199-200.

47. *ETW*, 230-31, 241.

48. *ETW*, 231-32.

49. *ETW*, 247, 255, 265, 206.

50. *ETW*, 269, 205-06.

51. *ETW*, 281.

52. *ETW*, 284.

53. *ETW*, 287-88, 300, 301.

54. *PR*, para. 270, p. 167.

55. *Lectures on the History of Philosophy*, trans. E. S. Haldane (London, 1892), 410.

56. *Phenomenology*, p. 96. Except where noted below, I use the translation by J. B. Baillie (London, 1910; rev. ed. 1931; New York and Evanston, Ill., 1967). Although Baillie has rendered the title as *Phenomenology of Mind* I prefer *Spirit* for *Geist*, since it conveys more levels of the original German meaning.

57. *Phenomenology*, 797, 807.

58. *Phenomenology*, 81, 114.

59. I refer here to the German text of the Lectures, *Vorlesungen über die Geschichte der Philosophie* in Hegel, *Sämtliche Werke*, XVII (Stuttgart, 1928), i, 50.

60. *Ibid.*, 52.

61. *Phenomenology*, 517. On the distinction between alienation and objectification see Louis Dupré, "Hegel's Concept of Alienation and Marx's Reinterpretation of It," *Hegel-Studien* 7 (1972), 217-36; also Richard Schacht, *Alienation*, with an Introductory Essay by Walter Kaufmann (New York, 1970). Schacht distinguishes clearly between alienation "as separation" and "as surrender." Both Dupré and Schacht provide bibliographies.

62. Little attention has been paid to the notion of inversion in the literature on Hegel. Hans Georg Gadamer, "Die verkehrte Welt," in *Materialien zu Hegels Phänomenologie des Geistes*, ed. Hans Friedrich Fulda and Dieter Henrich (Frankfurt am Main, 1973), 106-30 (now in English in Gadamer's *Hegel's Dialectic*, New Haven, 1976), does not go very far. J. N. Findlay, *Hegel, A Reexamination* (London, 1958), 94 (see also 204-05), calls the notion of the inverted world "an extremely queer, arbitrary fantasy," without seeing its relationship to the general phenomenon of inversion.

63. Introduction to the *Critical Journal of Philosophy* (1802), quoted by Kaufmann, *Hegel*, 56.

64. *Phenomenology*, 203.

65. *Phenomenology*, 206-07.

66. *Science of Logic*, trans. W. H. Johnson and L. G. Struthers (London, 1929), II, 135 ff., 139.

67. Diderot, *Rameau's Nephew and Other Works*, in new translations by Jacques Barzun and Ralph H. Bowen (New York, 1956), 8. "He has no greater opposite than himself," Diderot added a few sentences later. Lionel Trilling gives a sensitive discussion of this part of the *Phenomenology* from a different point of view: *Sincerity and Authenticity* (Cambridge, Mass., 1971), 26-47.

68. *Phenomenology*, 543; Marx to Engels, April 15, 1869, Karl Marx— Friedrich Engels, *Werke* (Berlin, from 1956; hereafter *MEW*) 32: 303-04. I have retranslated the first paragraph in order to give a more literal rendering.

69. Richard Schacht is right to argue (*Alienation*, 43) that Goethe and Diderot were not Hegel's only sources for the term, but he seems not to be aware of the connection between the Rameau character in the *Phenomenology* and Hegel's theory of the place of madness in the development of concrete reason. Cf. the comments of Baillie, *Phenomenology*, 508, with which Schacht takes issue.

70. *Encyclopaedia*, para. 406, p. 115.

71. *Phenomenology*, Preface, 105.

72. Kaufmann, *Hegel*, 30. The description of Hegel from Heine's *Confessions* is printed in Kaufmann, *Hegel*, 367.

73. Donald Schon, *Invention and the Evolution of Ideas*, formerly published as *Displacement of Concepts* (London, 1963, 1969), 98.

74. "Differenz des Fichteischen und Schellingschen Systems der Philosophie," *Sämtliche Werke* I (Stuttgart, 1927), 46; *Phenomenology*, 209.

Chapter Two

1. A brief notice about existing lives of Marx should be given here. The most recent up-to-date and scholarly biography is David McLellan, *Karl Marx, His Life and Thought* (London and New York, 1973). McLellan's book is accurate, detailed, fair-minded, and reliable on the facts of Marx's life, but it does not attempt to do more than present a "reasonably balanced picture," and some of McLellan's readings of Marx's works need to be revised. Better in some ways, although much shorter and less detailed, is Werner Blumenberg, *Karl Marx, An Illustrated Biography*, trans. Douglas Scott, with a Foreword by Gareth Stedman Jones (London and New York, 1972; orig. ed. *Karl Marx in Selbstzeugnissen und Bilddokumenten*, Reinbeck bei Hamburg, 1962). Two important recent works are not available to Engish readers. One is the most extensive and detailed life and times of Marx ever undertaken, Auguste Cornu, *Karl Marx et Friedrich Engels; leur vie et leur oeuvre* (Paris, from 1955), which has now reached Volume IV, taking the story up to 1846. Cornu provides much interesting and usually reliable information and interpretation; however, his treatment suffers from the seemingly insuperable obstacle of all Marxist accounts of Marx's life—an unwillingness to question Marx's own view of his development. Much more satisfactory in this respect, and in fact the best account of the stages of Marx's intellectual evolution, is Paul Kaegi, *Genesis des historischen Materialismus* (Vienna, 1965). Like Cornu's work, however, Kaegi's does not take the story past the mid 1840s. Since Kaegi's concerns are different from mine, I have little occasion to refer to his work here, but it deserves to be highly recommended. Recently, Maximilien Rubel and Margaret Manale have attempted to offer a completely factual chronology of Marx's life, *Marx without Myth, A Chronological Study of His Life and Work* (London, 1975, New York, 1976). This draws on Rubel's earlier Chronology prepared for the French edition of Marx's works in the Pléiade series (Paris, 1963), and issued separately in German as *Marx—Chronik, Daten zu Leben und Werk* (Munich, 1968). See also *Karl Marx—Chronik seines Lebens*, compiled by the Marx-Engels-Lenin Institut, Moscow (Moscow, 1934). Many interesting observations about Marx's life appear in a work too recent for me to have used it, Fritz Raddatz, *Karl Marx, eine politische Biographie* (Hamburg, 1975). These books supplant the earlier treatments of Marx's life, the classic one by Franz Mehring, *Karl Marx, The Story of His Life*, trans. Edward Fitzgerald (New York, 1935), and Isaiah Berlin, *Karl Marx, His Life and Environment* (London, 1939), although both Mehring and Berlin deserve to be read for their own intrinsic interest. Mention should be made here of the only attempt to write a full-scale psychological biography of Marx: Arnold Künzli, *Karl Marx, Eine Psychographie* (Vienna, Frankfurt, Zurich, 1966). Künzli's treatment is sensitive to many important issues in Marx's life, including his illness and his failure to finish *Capital*. But Künzli's emphasis on "Jewish self-hate" as a determining element in Marx's psychological make-up seems to me quite unjustified, and his quasi-Jungian evocation of a kind of collective Jewish unconscious borders on the mystical. Künzli's treatment of Marx's thought is abstract and arbitrary, as illustrated by his discussion of "The proletariat as the people of Israel," and he gives little attention to the historical dimensions of Marx's intellectual development. One older life of Marx which retains much value is Boris Nicolaievsky and Otto Maenchen-Helfen, *Karl Marx, Man and Fighter*,

trans. Gwenda David and Eric Mosbacher (London, 1936, rev. ed. 1973). This list is by no means exhaustive, even for worthwhile general accounts of Marx's life. Studies of particular aspects or phases of his work will be referred to at appropriate places later on.

2. Most of the information about Trier drawn on here comes from Heinz Monz, *Karl Marx, Grundlagen der Entwicklung zu Leben und Werk* (Trier, 1973; the expansion and revision of Monz's earlier *Karl Marx und Trier*, 1964).

3. The inscription is on the so-called *Rotes Haus* (Red House), built at the end of the seventeenth century. On Trier politics see Monz, *Karl Marx*, Part Two; on the elections, 207.

4. *Ibid.*, 126 ff., esp. 132-33.

5. The text of Heinrich Marx's speech, Monz, 134, from the *Kölnische Zeitung*, Jan. 23, 1834. For Brixius, *Ibid.*, 135-36.

6. *Ibid.*

7. *Ibid.*, Chap. 12; on Wyttenbach, 161 ff.

8. *Ibid.*, 46-50.

9. *Ibid.*, 51-52.

10. *Ibid.*, 97.

11. Ludwig Gall, *Was Könnte Helfen* (Trier, 1825), 6; quoted in Monz, *Karl Marx*, 105-06. On the *Trierische Zeitung*, Monz, *Karl Marx*, 107-09.

12. The best account of Heinrich's career is also in Monz, *Karl Marx*, Chaps. 20 and 21. See also his article, "Die soziale Lage der älterlichen Familie von Karl Marx," in *Karl Marx, 1818-1968, Neue Studien zu Person und Lehre* (Mainz, 1968), 67-129.

13. Monz, *Karl Marx*, 30-36; Horst Fischer, *Judentum, Staat und Heer in Preussen im frühen 19. Jahrhundert* (Tübingen, 1968).

14. On the Marx family's conversion, see Monz, *Karl Marx*, Chap. 19; Hans Stein, "Der Übertritt der Familie Heinrich Marx zum evangelischen Christentum," in *Jahrbuch der Kölnischen Geschichtsverein* 14 (1932), 126-29; Adolf Kober, "Karl Marx's Vater und das napoleonische Ausnahmegesetz gegen die Juden, 1808," *Ibid.*, 115-25; Karl-Georg Faber, "Zur Biographie von Heinrich und Karl Marx," in *Festschrift Johannes Bärmen* (*Geschictliche Landeskunde* 3, Wiesbaden, 1966-67), I, 161-71. Note the evidence of Heinrich's continuing contacts with Jews in Trier, Monz, *Karl Marx*, 251-53.

15. The essay was published by Kober in "Karl Marx's Vater," see 121,124.

16. *Ibid.*, 120.

17. Monz discusses Marx's school and his essays in *Karl Marx*, Chap. 23. All the essays are available in English in Karl Marx, Frederick Engels, *Collected Works* (cited hereafter as *CW*), I (New York, 1975), the main essay on choosing a vocation, 3-9, the others in the Appendix, 636-42. For the quote in this paragraph, 642.

18. *Ibid.*, 638.

19. The German text is in *MEGA* I, i, (2), 164 ff., and in *Texte zu Methode und Praxis*, ed. Günther Hillman (Hamburg, 1966), I, 7-11 (cited below as *Texte*). In addition to the translation in *CW*, there is one in *Writings of the Young Marx on Philosophy and Society*, trans. and ed. Lloyd D. Easton and Kurt H. Guddat (New York, 1967), 35-39. In general I follow this translation; where the German text is also cited I have revised it to give a more literal rendering.

20. *Writings of the Young Marx*, 39; *Texte*, 10-11. On the influence of Wyttenbach, see Monz, *Karl Marx*, 303-04. Monz has discovered and printed all the essays of Marx's Gymnasium class on this subject: " 'Betrachtung eines Jünglings bei der Wahl eines Berufes'—Der Deutschaufsatz von Karl Marx und seinen Mitschülern in der Reifeprüfung," in *Der unbekannte junge Marx, Neue Studien zur Entwicklung des Marxschen Denkens* (Mainz, 1973), 9-113. My survey of these essays convinces me that the themes in Marx emphasized here were not shared by his fellows. For another influence, see J. G. Fichte, *Vocation of the Scholar*, trans. W. Smith (London, 1889). For a nearly contemporary graduation essay by a man who would later make a very different sort of career in German public life, see Rudolf Virchow, "Ein Leben voll Arbeit und Mühe ist Keine Last, sondern eine Wohltat," Reifeprüfung am Gymnasium zu Köslin, in *Briefe an seine Eltern, 1839 bis 1864*, ed. Marie Rabl (Leipzig, 1906), 6-10.

21. Marx and Engels, *Manifesto of the Communist Party*, in *Selected Works* (one vol. ed., New York, 1968, cited hereafter as *SW*), 53. The Feuerbachian notion of man as a "species-being" is also foreshadowed in these comments.

22. *Writings of the Young Marx*, 35-36.

23. *Ibid.*, 36-37; *Texte*, 8-9.

24. "Speech of Dr. Marx on Protection, Free Trade, and the Working Classes," from *The Northern Star*, Oct. 9, 1847, in *MEGA* I, vi, 429.

25. *Writings of the Young Marx*, 38-39; *Texte*, 10.

26. "Communism and the *Augsburg Allgemeine Zeitung*," from *Rheinische Zeitung*, Oct. 16, 1842; *Writings of the Young Marx*, 135.

27. *Writings of the Young Marx*, 37; *Texte*, 8.

28. See above, note 14.

29. Heinrich Marx's memorandum, printed in A. Kober, "Karl Marx's Vater und das napoleonische Ausnahmegesetz . . . ," 124-25.

30. Monz, *Karl Marx*, 242.

31. Henriette Marx to Karl Marx, in postscripts to Heinrich's letters of November 18, 1835, and early 1836, in *MEGA* I, i, (2), 187-88 and 190. English versions in *CW* I, 648-49 and 651-52. Henriette Marx always spelled her son's name "Carl," as it was on his birth certificate, but I have changed it to Karl here. Heinrich wrote Karl. The "angel mother" phrase is in the letter of Nov. 10-11, 1837, on which see below.

32. On Marx's exemption from military service see the documents in Hubert Schiel, *Die Umwelt des jungen Marx* (Trier, 1954), 23. On getting the exemption, see Heinrich's letter of May or June 1836, in *CW* I, 654.

33. Henriette Marx to Marx, May 29, 1840, *MEGA* I, i, (2), 243. Marx to Ruge, Jan. 25, 1843, *MEGA* I, i, (2), 294. Marx to Engels, April 30, 1868, *MEW* 32: 75.

34. This comment comes from Marx's translation of 1846, "Peuchet: von Selbstmord" (Peuchet on Suicide), in *MEGA* I, iii, 391 ff. A discussion of this essay, ignored by all Marx's biographers, appears in Chapter Six, Section 5. The sentence quoted in the text was added by Marx and seems to have no direct basis in Peuchet's *Mémoires tirés des Archives de la Police de Paris* (Paris, 1838) which Marx was translating for the *Gesellschaftsspiegel* of 1846: *MEGA* I, iii, 396; see Peuchet, 127. Peuchet did speak of family tyranny leading to "crises analogous to those of

revolutions," 123-24, but not of the power that cowardly people attempted to exercise as parents.

35. See her letter in *MEGA* 1, i, (2), 242-44.

36. Eleanor Marx-Aveling, "Karl Marx," quoted from *Marx and Engels through the Eyes of their Contemporaries* (Moscow, 1972), 155.

37. This is the view of aggression recently developed by Anthony Storr, D. W. Winnicott, and (in popular but sensitive and persuasive form) Rollo May. See May, *Power and Innocence, A Search for the Sources of Violence* (New York, 1972), 123 and 150 for the quotes in the text. See also Anthony Storr, *Human Aggression* (New York, 1968). For a different view of the origins of Marx's aggressive traits, based on the relationship between frustration and aggression posited by theorists of abnormal psychology, see Helmut Hirsch, "Marxens Milieu" (a comment on Monz's *Karl Marx und Trier*), in *Etudes de Marxologie* (*Cahiers de l'Institut de Science Economique Appliquée*) 9 (1965), 219-30.

38. Rollo May, *Power and Innocence* 124, 128; Anthony Storr, *Human Aggression*, Chap. 5.

39. Marx-Aveling, "Karl Marx," 154.

40. Engels put the portrait of Heinrich in Marx's coffin with him: Blumenberg, *Karl Marx* (English ed.), 22. On Heinrich's library, Monz, *Karl Marx*, 266 ff.; on Kant, see his letter to Karl of Nov. 18, 1835, *CW* 1, 648, and his memorandum, ed. Kober, "Karl Marx's Vater," 120; "what Newton, Locke and Leibniz believed, everyone can submit to," *CW* 1, 647; on his practicality and "prosaic" nature, *Ibid.*, 651, 654, and the quote in Blumenberg, *Karl Marx* (English ed.), 25; more on this hereafter.

41. Letters of Nov. 1836 to Feb. 1837, *MEGA* 1, i, (2), 186, 195, 196, 200; *CW* 1, 646, 661, 662.

42. Letter of Dec. 28, 1836, *MEGA* 1, i, (2),197; *CW* 1, 664.

43. Letters of Nov. 8 and 18, 1835, *MEGA* 1, i, (2), 184-85; *CW* 1, 645-46.

44. Letter of Dec. 28, 1836, *MEGA* 1, i, (2), 197; *CW* 1, 664.

45. On the von Westphalen family and their relation with the Marxes, see Monz, *Karl Marx*, Chap. 24.

46. Letter of March 2, 1837, *MEGA* 1, i, (2), 202-03; *CW* 1, 670-71.

47. Erik Erikson, *Gandhi's Truth* (New York, 1969), 132.

48. Letter of Aug. 12, 1837, *MEGA* 1, i, (2), 206; *CW* 1, 675.

49. Letters of Nov. 18, 1835, early 1836, Nov. 9, 1836, Dec. 28, 1836, *MEGA* 1, i, (2), 186-87,190, 196, 198; *CW* 1, 647, 649, 651, 662, 664.

50. Letter of Nov. 9, 1836, *MEGA* 1, i, (2),195; *CW* 1, 661.

51. Letter of March 2, 1837, *MEGA* 1, i, (2), 204-05; *CW* 1, 673.

52. For the *idéologues* and their struggles with Napoleon, see Sergio Moravia, *Il Tramonto dell'Illuminismo* (Bari, 1968), 17, 600-01.

53. For these quotations, see *The Oxford English Dictionary*, s.v. "Ideologist" and "Ideology."

54. Letter of Dec. 28, 1836, *MEGA* 1, i, (2), 200; *CW* 1, 665.

55. E.g., letter of March 2, 1837, *CW* 1, 672: "I do not readily allow myself to be completely torn up from the earth, which is my solid basis, and wafted exclusively into airy spheres where I have no firm ground under my feet."

56. Letter of Feb. 3, 1837, *MEGA* 1, i, (2), 200; *CW* 1, 667.

57. Letter of Dec. 9, 1837, *MEGA* I, i, (2), 227; *CW* I, 689 (which gives "the new immoralists" for *der neuen Unholde*).

58. *Ibid.* (*CW* I, 689-90).

59. Translated in Peter Demetz, *Marx, Engels and the Poets* (Chicago, 1966), 52; *CW* I, 576, for a different translation.

60. See the letter in *Texte*, 44-53 (German), and translated in *Writings of the Young Marx*, 40-50; *CW* I, 10-21. I use the translation in *Writings of the Young Marx*, except where noted.

61. *Writings of the Young Marx*, 40-41, 46.

62. *Texte*, 28: "Kant und Fichte gern zum Aether schweifen,/ Suchten dort ein fremdes Land,/ Doch ich such' nur tüchtig zu begreifen,/ Was ich—auf der Strasse fand!" Also *CW* I, 577.

63. *Writings of the Young Marx*, 42.

64. *CW* I, 525-26.

65. *Writings of the Young Marx*, 41-42.

66. *Ibid.*, 42-43, 47.

67. Heinrich's letters in *CW* I, 654, 686. Note also *CW* I, 648: "Do you want to find happiness only in abstract idealizing (somewhat analogous to fanciful reverie)?" Henriette's comment in *CW* I, 649. See also above, note 55.

68. *Writings of the Young Marx*, 48.

69. *Ibid.*, 45-47. Marx may have been recalling a passage in Hölderlin's *Hyperion*, which had also affected Hegel: "What I had learned, what I had done in my life, dissolved like ice, and all the projects of youth died away in me." *Hyperion*, trans. W. R. Trask (New York, 1959, 1965), 168.

70. *Writings of the Young Marx*, 45-46, 40-41.

71. Marx cannot have known the theory in quite the detail we examined it in Chapter One, because some of the illustrations and comments drawn on there were only added to the printed text when the *Zusätze* (Additions) were included in the edition of 1845. (On the editions of the *Encyclopaedia*, see Kaufmann, *Hegel*, 218 ff.) The basic structure of the theory was clearly outlined, albeit very concisely, in the editions of 1827 and 1830, however. Marx may also have had access to lecture notes or lore from some students who had heard Hegel, since he was associating with a number of Young Hegelians in Berlin during 1837.

72. *Writings of the Young Marx*, 47-49.

73. Letter of Feb. 10, 1838, *MEGA* I, i, (2), 228; *CW* I, 692.

Chapter Three

1. German text *MEGA* I, i, (1), including the preparatory materials; reprinted with some omissions in *Texte*. The first English translation was that by Norman D. Livergood, in an appendix to his book *Activity in Marx's Philosophy* (The Hague, 1967). Livergood, however, does not give the preparatory materials, some of which are available in *Writings of the Young Marx*. A complete English translation of the dissertation and the preparatory materials can now be found in *CW* I, but since the present chapter was completed before that text appeared, I have not made much use of it. Discussions of the dissertation include Günther

Hillman, *Marx und Hegel* (Frankfurt am Main, 1966), and Rolf Sannwald, *Marx und die Antike* (Zürich, 1967), but the reading given here is of a different kind.

2. Preface and section 1 of the dissertation, in Livergood, *Activity*, 61, 63.

3. *Ibid.*, 64.

4. I cite this essay from the text in *MEGA* I, i, (1), 100-06.

5. *MEGA* I, i, (1), 101.

6. *Ibid.*, 102-03.

7. *Ibid.*, 103-04.

8. *Ibid.*, 104. For Hegel's related characterization of modern philosophy see, for instance, *The Phenomenology*, 546. Marx expressed a similar view of modern philosophy in one of his articles for the *Rheinische Zeitung* (hereafter cited as *RhZ*) a year or so later: "While the earlier philosophers of state and law derived the state from drives of ambition and gregariousness, or from reason—though not reason in society but rather in the individual—the more ideal and profound view of modern philosophy derives it from the idea of the whole." *Writings of the Young Marx*, 130.

9. Hegel, *Lectures on the History of Philosophy*, trans. E. S. Haldane (London, 1892), I, 393.

10. Dissertation, in Livergood, *Activity*, 79.

11. *Ibid.*, 81.

12. *Ibid.*, 84; also 91.

13. *Ibid.*, 82-83.

14. *Ibid.*, 106-07.

15. *Ibid.*, 107.

16. *MEGA* I, i, (1), 100.

17. Dissertation, in Livergood, *Activity*, 109.

18. *Ibid.*, 68-69.

19. *Ibid.*, 108.

20. *Ibid.*, 72.

21. *Ibid.*, 74-75, 71-72.

22. *Ibid.*, 70.

23. *Ibid.*, 75-76, but with "perversity" for "inversion." Marx also used the notion of alienation in his dissertation, but less extensively; see 97.

24. *Ibid.*, 62.

25. *Texte*, 81; *MEGA* I, i, (1), 107-08.

26. Dissertation, in Livergood, *Activity*, 59.

27. The best work on the Young Hegelians is still available only in German: Horst Stuke, *Philosophie der Tat, Studien zur 'Verwirklichung der Philosophie' bei der Junghegelianer und den Wahren Sozialisten* (Stuttgart, 1963). Two recent and very useful works in English are David McLellan, *The Young Hegelians and Karl Marx* (London, 1969); and William J. Brazill, *The Young Hegelians* (New Haven, 1970). The older work by Sidney Hook, *From Hegel to Marx* (New York, 1936; Ann Arbor, 1962), should also be mentioned. There is much of interest in Karl Löwith, *From Hegel to Nietzsche* (also cited above for Hegel), and in Nicholas Lobkowicz, *Theory and Practice, History of a Concept from Aristotle to Marx* (Notre Dame and London, 1967).

28. Stuke, 64-66; see also Lobkowicz, 193-95.

29. Bauer to Marx, April 5, 1840, *MEGA* I, i, (2), 241.

30. Quoted by David McLellan, *The Young Hegelians and Karl Marx*, 68.

31. On Ruge's activities as attempts to unify the movement, see Brazill, *The Young Hegelians*, Chap. 2.

32. Köppen to Marx, *MEGA* I, i, (2), 255-57; on Bauer's move from right to left see Stuke, *Philosophie der Tat*, Chap. 2.

33. On this episode see Chapter Five, Section 4.

34. See Bauer, *Die gute Sache der Freiheit* (Zurich and Winterthur, 1842), 204, 218-19; on Hess and the language of the deed see Edmund Silberner, *Moses Hess, Geschichte seines Lebens* (Leiden, 1966), 71-73. However, Hess may have abandoned this language under Marx's influence: see his essay "Gegenwärtige Krisis der Deutschen Philosophie" ("The Present Crisis of German Philosophy"), written soon after he met Marx, in *Sozialistische Aufsätze 1841-1847*, ed. Theodor Zlocisti (Berlin, 1921), 8-11. Hess is discussed more extensively in connection with Marx's development in Chapter Five, Section 1. The "philosophy of the deed" was also espoused by the enigmatic Polish writer August Cieskowski: see Stuke, Chap. 1; also Shlomo Avineri, *The Social and Political Thought of Karl Marx* (Cambridge, 1968), 124 ff. and the literature cited, 124-25 n.

35. Article of Nov. 29, 1842, *MEGA* I, i, (1), 309.

36. Engels to Theodor Cuno, March 29, 1883, *MEW* 35: 466.

37. These connections between Marx and Jewishness are all dealt with later on.

38. See Chapter Nine, Section 5.

39. Text in Frederick Schiller, *Romances and Early Dramas* (Boston, 1884), 192.

40. Engels, "Marx and the *Neue Rheinische Zeitung*," *SW*, two vol. ed., I, 300; *MEW* 21: 19.

41. See the letter of Weerth quoted by Werner Blumenberg in "Eduard von Müller-Tellering, Verfasser des ersten antisemitischen Pamphlets gegen Marx," *Bulletin of the International Institute for Social History* 6 (1951), 186. (This *Bulletin* is not the same publication as the Institute's *Review*.)

42. Letter of Dec. 9, 1837, *CW* I, 688.

43. Schiller, *Romances and Early Dramas*, 15-17.

44. German text in Gustav Mayer, *Friedrich Engels, Eine Biographie*, 2nd ed. (Cologne, 1971), I, 85; quoted together with a different translation in Nicolaievsky and Maenchen-Helfen, *Karl Marx* (1973 ed.), 42-43.

45. *Writings of the Young Marx*, 63-64, and 252.

46. Schiller, *Romances and Early Dramas*, 154, 157.

47. *Ibid.*, 164.

48. Marx, *Revelations of the Cologne Communist Trial*, trans. Rodney Livingstone (New York, 1971), 79.

49. On the founding and history of the *Rheinische Zeitung* see Joseph Hansen, *Gustav von Mevissen* (Berlin, 1906), I, 243-82; also Edmund Silberner, *Moses Hess*, Chap. 4. A number of documents about the paper are now available in English in *CW* I, 710-26.

50. Bauer to Marx, March 31, 1841, *MEGA* I, i, (2), 250; Marx to Dagobert Oppenheim, *c.* Aug. 25, 1842, *MEGA* I, i, (2), 280.

51. "Proceedings of the Sixth Rhine Province Assembly. First Article: Debates on Freedom of the Press and Publication of the Assembly Proceedings," *RhZ* No. 125, May 5, and following numbers, in *MEGA* I, i, (1), 201; a different translation in *CW* I, 154.

52. *Ibid.*

53. "On a Proposed Divorce Law," *RhZ* No. 353, Dec. 19, 1842; *Writings of the Young Marx*, 140-41.

54. "Proceedings of the Sixth Rhine Province Assembly. Third Article: Debates on the Law on Thefts of Wood," *RhZ* No. 300, Oct. 27, 1842, *MEGA* I, i, (1), 274-75; *CW* I, 233.

55. *Ibid.*

56. Art. cit., *MEGA* I, i, (1), 281-82.

57. *Ibid.*, 282, 287.

58. "Debates on Freedom of the Press," *MEGA* I, i, (1), 185.

59. *Ibid.*, 195, 198-99.

60. *Ibid.*, 219.

61. "The Supplement to Nos. 335 and 336 of the *Augsburg Allgemeine Zeitung* on the Commissions of Estates in Prussia," *RhZ* No.365, Dec. 31, 1842, *MEGA* I, i, (1), 330 and 333.

62. *MEGA* I, i, (1), 341; Dissertation, in Livergood, *Activity*, 103; "Debates on the Law on Thefts of Wood," *MEGA* I, i, (1), 286.

63. "Debates on Freedom of the Press," *MEGA* I, i, (1), 212. See also the article ". . . on the Commissions of Estates," 321.

64. ". . . on the Commissions of Estates," *MEGA* I, i, (1), 335.

65. "The Leading Article in No. 179 of the *Kölnische Zeitung*," *Writings of the Young Marx*, 125.

66. "Debates on Freedom of the Press," *MEGA* I, i, (1), 183.

67. *Ibid.*, 221-23.

68. "Communism and the *Augsburg Allgemeine Zeitung*," *RhZ* No. 289, Oct. 16, 1842; *Writings of the Young Marx*, 133.

69. *Ibid.*, 134-35.

70. Marx to Ruge, March 5, 1842, *MEGA* I, i, (2), 269; Georg Jung to Ruge, Oct. 18, 1841, *MEGA* I, i, (2), 262; "Debates on Freedom of the Press," *MEGA* I, i, (1), 190.

71. Marx to Dagobert Oppenheim, Aug. 25, 1842, *MEGA* I, i, (2), 280.

72. Marx to Ruge, May 1843, published in the *Deutsch-Französische Jahrbücher* in 1844; *Writings of the Young Marx*, 209.

73. "Justification of the †† Correspondent from the Mosel," *RhZ* No. 15 and ff., Jan. 15, 1842 *et seq.*; *MEGA* I, i, (1), 355 ff. The author of the original reports had probably been a radical lawyer, P. I. Coblenz, although they have often been attributed to Karl Heinzen; see *CW* I, 749, n. 127.

74. "Justification," *MEGA* I, i, (1), 359-60; *Writings of the Young Marx*, 144-45.

75. "Justification," *MEGA* I, i, (1), 368-69.

76. *Ibid.*, 371-72.

77. *Ibid.*, 373-74.

78. Marx to Ruge, Jan. 25, 1843, *MEGA* I, i, (1), 293-94; the later recollection in the autobiographical Preface to A *Contribution to the Critique of Political Economy, SW* 182.

Chapter Four

1. Edgar Quinet, quoted by Stuke, *Philosophie der Tat*, 56. On this general subject, see also Felix Gilbert, "Lorenz von Stein und die Revolution von 1848," *Mitteilungen des Österreichischen Instituts für Geschichtsforschung* 50 (1936), 376; trans. in Gilbert, *History: Choice and Commitment* (Cambridge, Mass. and London, 1977).

2. On their relationship see Monz, *Karl Marx und Trier*, 229.

3. Heinrich Heine, *Religion and Philosophy in Germany*, trans. John Snodgrass (Boston, 1882, reprinted 1959 with an Intro. by Ludwig Marcuse), 77, cf. 24. Also Henri Lichtenberger, *Henri Heine Penseur* (Paris, 1905), 121. The notion of "the rehabilitation of matter" was also upheld by August von Cieskowski, who was likewise in Paris at this time, but I do not know whether he, too, was led to it by the St. Simonians. See Avineri, *The Social and Political Thought of Karl Marx*, 128.

4. *Religion and Philosophy in Germany*, 158-60.

5. See Nigel Reeves, "Heine and the Young Marx," *Oxford German Studies* 7 (1973), 44-97. The quote referred to the waters of the river Spree "which washes the soul and dilutes tea." *Writings of the Young Marx*, 47.

6. Interesting discussions of Feuerbach can be found in Löwith, *From Hegel to Nietzsche*, and in Avineri, *The Social and Political Thought of Karl Marx*, as well as in the literature on the Young Hegelians cited in the previous chapter. On Feuerbach's father, the noted jurist Anselm Feuerbach, and his Kantian opposition to his son's Hegelianism, see Brazill, *The Young Hegelians*, 138; and later on in the same chapter for Feuerbach's view of Hegel as "a second father."

7. The pun appeared in a review of Moleschott's *Lehre der Nahrungsmittel*: Brazill, *The Young Hegelians*, 154. On Feuerbach's development see his own comment in the Foreword to his *Complete Works*, quoted by Melvin Cherno in his Introduction to Feuerbach's *The Essence of Faith According to Luther* (New York, 1967), 14-15.

8. Ludwig Feuerbach, *The Essence of Christianity*, trans. from the 2nd German ed. by Marian Evans (London, 1893), 13.

9. *Ibid.*, 274-75.

10. "Vorläufige Thesen zur Reformation der Philosophie," in *Anekdota zur neuesten deutschen Philosophie und Publicistik*, ed. Arnold Ruge (Zürich and Winterthur, 1843; photographic re-edition, Glashütten in Taunus, 1971), II, 63-64, 67. English versions of Feuerbach's shorter philosophical writings may be found in *The Fiery Brook, Selected Writings of Ludwig Feuerbach*, trans. with an Introduction by Zawar Hanfi (New York, 1972). This is a useful selection, but I have preferred to retain my own translations, which were made before it appeared.

11. "Vorläufige Thesen," 71-72.

12. "Grundsätze der Philosophie der Zukunft," in Ludwig Feuerbach, *Kleine philosophische Schriften (1842-45)*, ed. Max Gustav Lange (Leipzig, 1947, 1950), 109, 144, 153.

13. "Vorläufige Thesen," 70, 75.

14. *Essence of Christianity*, 1-2.

15. "Vorläufige Thesen," 75-76, 80; "Grundsätze," 108.

16. "Grundsätze," 110n.; "Vorläufige Thesen," 81-84.

17. From the comment on his evolution cited above, note 7.

18. *MEGA* I, i, (1), 236; *Writings of the Young Marx*, 115.

19. From the Preface to the 2nd ed. of *Essence of Christianity* (1843), viii.

20. See the exchange of letters in *MEGA* I, i, (2), notably those by Ruge of Feb. 1 and March 8, 1843, and Marx's of March 13.

21. Marx to Ruge, March 13, 1843, *MEGA* I, i, (2), 307.

22. Marx's later comment in his letter to his daughter Jenny Longuet of Dec. 7, 1881, *MEW* 35: 241-42. Henriette Marx to Marx, May 29, 1840, *MEGA* I, i, (2), 242 ff.

23. Jenny's letter to Karl, undated, sometime in 1839 or 1840; published for the first time in *CW* I, 695-97.

24. *Ibid.*, 696.

25. *Ibid.*, 696-97.

26. These matters are discussed in Chapter Nine.

27. *CW* I, 698, 707-09, 730.

28. *CW* I, 707.

29. See Louise Dornemann, *Jenny Marx* (Berlin, 1970), 68.

30. There is a complete and scholarly translation of Marx's work: *Critique of Hegel's 'Philosophy of Right,'* by Karl Marx, trans. Annete Jolin and Joseph O'Malley, ed. with intro. and notes by Joseph O'Malley (Cambridge, 1970). I cite O'Malley's ed. below, as *Critique*; at times, however, I prefer the abridged translation in *Writings of the Young Marx*.

31. *Critique*, 31, 99, 119 (but preferring the translation in *Writings of the Young Marx*, 200, in part), and 121. See Avineri, *The Social and Political Thought of Karl Marx*; Richard N. Hunt, *The Political Ideas of Marx and Engels* (Pittsburgh, 1974); Robert C. Tucker, *The Marxian Revolutionary Idea* (New York, 1969); Joseph O'Malley in the Introduction to *Critique*, lxii-lxiii.

32. *Writings of the Young Marx*, 157. This is not meant to imply that Marx limited his search for the real empirical truth about things to what he found in Hegel; his critique shows the influence of much other reading, especially in historical works. See O'Malley, Introduction to *Critique*, xxxix.

33. *Critique*, 12, 39, 40, 8. Note also 64: "Hegel is not to be blamed for depicting the nature of the modern state as it is, but rather for presenting what is as the essence of the state. The claim that the rational is actual is contradicted precisely by an irrational actuality, which everywhere is the contrary of what it asserts and asserts the contrary of what it is."

34. *Ibid.*, 89, 45, 8.

35. *Ibid.*, 50-51; see also 72.

36. *Ibid.*, 81.

37. *Ibid.*, 77-78; see also 107-08 and 110-11.

38. *Ibid.*, 35, 55, 47.

39. The literature on European industrialization is too vast to begin to list here. Up-to-date treatments with bibliographies can be found in David Landes, *The Unbound Prometheus* (Cambridge, Eng., 1969), and in Vols. III and IV of *The Fontana Economic History of Europe*, ed. Carlo M. Cipolla (London, 1973). See also William L. Langer, *Political and Social Upheaval, 1832-52* (New York, 1969), and Maurice Lévy-Leboyer, "Le processus d'industrialisation: les cas de l'Angleterre et de la France," *Revue Historique* 239 (1968), 281-98.

40. Asa Briggs, "The Language of 'Class' in Early Nineteenth-Century England," in Briggs and John Saville, eds., *Essays in Labour History* (London, 1967), 43-73; Armand Cuvillier, "Les antagonismes de classes dans la littérature sociale française de Saint-Simon à 1848," *International Review of Social History* 1 (1956), 433-63; Werner Conze, "Von 'Pöbel' zum 'Proletariat,' " *Vierteljahrschrift für Sozial- und Wirtschaftsgeschichte* 41 (1954), 333-64, reprinted in *Moderne Deutsche Sozialgeschichte*, ed. Hans-Ulrich Wehler (Cologne, 1966), 11-36; Franz von Baader, "Über das dermalige Missverhältnis der Vermögenslosen oder Proletairs zu dem Vermögen-besitzenden Klassen der Sozietät . . ." in *Schriften zum Gesellschaftsphilosophie*, ed. J. Sauter (Jena, 1925), 319-38. Lorenz von Stein, *Der Sozialismus und Kommunismus des heutigen Frankreichs* (Leipzig, 1842).

41. For a general guide to Marx's writings in these years and indeed the whole of his Hegelian period, see Bert Andreas, "Marx et Engels et la gauche Hégelienne," *Annali* (Istituto Giangiacomo Feltrinelli) 7 (1964-65), 353-512. For the letter to Ruge, see *Writings of the Young Marx*, 211.

42. Although there is a translation of the Introduction in the O'Malley edition of the *Critique*, I prefer to cite the version in *Writings of the Young Marx*; for these passages, 250-51.

43. *Ibid.*, 255-56. For the dissertation notes, see *Writings of the Young Marx*, 63.

44. *Ibid.*, 263-64; the more specifically social and political aspects of this essay are dealt with below.

45. See Chapter Three, Section 4.

46. Bruno Bauer, *Vollständige Geschichte der Partheikämpfe in Deutschland, während der Jahre 1842-1846*, two vols. in one (Charlottenburg, 1847); for the praise of Marx's "Defense," I, 72n.

47. *Ibid.*, II, 80.

48. Arnold Ruge, "Die Presse und die Freiheit," *Anekdota zur neuesten deutschen Philosophie und Publicistik* (Zürich and Winterthur, 1843), I, 111-15.

49. *Ibid.*, 111-12.

50. *Ibid.*, 112. Ruge added a moment later: "It also appears as if the writers in opposition to the censorship were *scientific* proletarians, an opinion which is enthusiastically nourished because one thereby divides the world of writers and scholars into two enemy camps." *Ibid.*

51. Cuvillier, "Les antagonismes de classes," 445.

52. German text in *MEW* 1: 378-91.

53. Introduction, in *Writings of the Young Marx*, 251-52, 261-62.

54. *Ibid.*, 263-64.

55. *Economic and Philosophic Manuscripts of 1844*, trans. Martin Milligan (New York, 1964), 155.

56. "Critical Notes on 'The King of Prussia and Social Reform,' " in *Writings of the Young Marx*, 352-53.

57. Edmund Silberner, "Was Marx an Anti-Semite?" in *Historia Judaica* 11 (1949), 3 ff., answers the question in the affirmative; as noted above Arnold Künzli, in *Karl Marx, Eine Psychographie* (Vienna, Frankfurt, Zürich, 1966), bases his whole view of Marx's personality on his presumed "Jewish self-hate." A much more sensible view is presented by Shlomo Avineri, "Marx and Jewish Emancipation," *Journal of the History of Ideas* 25 (1964), 445-50; see also Arthur Prinz, "New Perspectives on Marx as a Jew," *Leo Baeck Institute Year Book* 15 (1970), 107-24. Also Helmut Hirsch, "Marxiana judaica," *Etudes de Marxologie (Cahiers de l'Institut de science économique appliquée)* 7 (1963), 5-52.

58. See "Lassalle," *Neue Rheinische Zeitung* (cited hereafter as *NRZ*), No. 219, Feb. 11, 1849, *MEW* 6: 267-69 (by Marx); and No. 287, May 2, 1849, *MEW* 6: 454-58 (by Engels). According to one of Marx's associates in the Communist League, Marx recommended and stood up for Lassalle at a time when others, notably workers, already did not trust him. See the comments of P. G. Röser, in Werner Blumenberg, "Zur Geschichte des Bundes der Kommunisten," *International Review of Social History* 9 (1964), 119-20.

59. Marx to Engels, March 10, 1853, *MEW* 28: 224.

60. Marx to Engels, March 5, 1856, *MEW* 29: 27-28.

61. Marx to Kugelmann, June 10, 1867, *MEW* 31: 550.

62. Marx to Engels, July 30, 1862, *MEW* 30: 259.

63. Marx to Paul and Laura Lafargue, March 5, 1870, *MEW* 32: 655-56.

64. Ruge to his mother, Sept. 4, 1843, in Arnold Ruge, *Briefwechsel und Tägeblätter, 1825-1880*, ed. Paul Nerrlich (Berlin, 1886), two vols. in one, I, 332-33; Werner Blumenberg, "Eduard von Müller-Tellering, Verfasser des ersten antisemitischen Pamphlets gegen Marx," *Bulletin of the International Institute for Social History* 6 (1951), 178-97.

65. Marx to Engels, July 13, 1851, *MEW* 27: 278; Marx to Engels, Dec. 7, 1855, *MEW* 28: 461; Marx to Lion Philips, Nov. 29, 1864, *MEW* 31: 432.

66. See Edmund Silberner, *Moses Hess*, 111.

67. *Writings of the Young Marx*, 127.

68. Bruno Bauer, *Die Judenfrage* (Braunschweig, 1843), 56-57.

69. Marx to Dagobert Oppenheim, *c.* Aug. 25, 1842, *MEGA* I, i, (2), 279; Marx to Ruge, Mar. 13, 1843, *ibid.*, 307-08.

70. Bauer, *Die Judenfrage*, 19-20, 35-36; many of these ideas can also be found in Feuerbach, who wrote: "The Jews have maintained their peculiarity to this day. Their principle, their God, is the *most practical* principle in the world— namely, egoism, and moreover egoism is the form of religion." Quoted by Silberner, "Was Marx an anti-Semite?" 29.

71. Bruno Bauer, "Die Fähigkeit der heutigen Juden und Christen, frei zu werden," *Einundzwanzig Bogen aus der Schweiz* (Zürich and Winterthur, 1843), 62-66.

72. "On the Jewish Question," in *Writings of the Young Marx*, 221, 231-32. This aspect of Marx's essay was stressed by Avineri, "Marx and Jewish Emancipation," cited in note 57.

73. *Ibid.*, 236-37, 232.

74. *Ibid.*, 243-45.

75. For anti-Semitism in early nineteenth-century German culture, see Eleanor Sterling, *Judenhass. Die Anfänge des politischen Antisemitismus in Deutschland, 1815-1850* (Frankfurt am Main, 1969), 66 ff. Cf. above, note 70, for Feuerbach on the Jews.

76. On the proletariat, Introduction, *Writings of the Young Marx*, 263; on the Jews, "On the Jewish Question," 243-44, 247.

77. Discussed in Chapter Five, Section 5.

78. "On the Jewish Question," 226, 239, 240.

Chapter Five

1. Preface to *A Contribution to the Critique of Political Economy* (1859) in *SW*, 181-82; cf. Hegel, *Philosophy of Right*, para. 189, p. 126. Marx's reading in the period after he left the *Rheinische Zeitung* was heavily weighted toward political rather than social-economic topics. See the calculation by Richard N. Hunt, *The Political Ideas of Marx and Engels*, 1 (Pittsburgh, 1974), 52-53.

2. Gustav Mayer, *Friedrich Engels, Eine Biographie*, two vols., 2nd ed. (Cologne, 1971); Steven Marcus, *Engels, Manchester, and the Working Class* (New York, 1974, 1975). See Engels' later essay, "Ludwig Feuerbach and the End of Classical German Philosophy," *SW*, 596-632. Considerably more will be said about Engels' early life in Chapter Six, Section 1.

3. I cite Engels' "Outlines of a Critique of Political Economy" in the translation by Martin Milligan appended to Marx's *Economic and Philosophic Manuscripts of 1844*, ed. and with an Introduction by Dirk J. Struik (New York, 1964), 197-226 (cited hereafter as *EPM*).

4. Engels, "Outlines," 197-200, 202-03.

5. *Ibid.*, 204-05.

6. *Ibid.*, 206-07.

7. Edmund Silberner, *Moses Hess, Geschichte seines Lebens* (Leiden, 1960). For the meeting with Engels, 122.

8. A similar view of these relations in Mayer, *Friedrich Engels*, 1, 102.

9. Hess to Auerbach, Sept. 2, 1841, in Moses Hess, *Briefwechsel*, ed. Edmund Silberner with the cooperation of Werner Blumenberg (The Hague, 1959), 79-80.

10. Hess, "Gegenwärtige Krisis der deutschen Philosophie," in *Sozialistische Aufsätze 1841-47*, ed. Theodor Zlocisti (Berlin, 1921), 10.

11. "Über das Geldwesen," originally published in Herman Püttman's *Rheinische Jahrbücher zur Gesellschaftlichen Reform* 1 (1845), 1-34; cited here from *Sozialistische Aufsätze*, 158-87. Although it was not published until 1845, Marx had seen the essay by the end of 1843 or early in 1844.

12. "Über das Geldwesen," 160.

13. *Ibid.*, 165-66.

14. *Ibid.*, 166-67.

15. *Ibid.*, 183-85.

16. I cite *The Economic and Philosophic Manuscripts of 1844*, in the translation by

Martin Milligan, ed. with an Introduction by Dirk J. Struik (New York, 1964). Among works that discuss the *1844 Manuscripts* and their place in Marx's development, in addition to those cited above in note 9 to my Introduction, are: H. Popitz, *Der entfremdete Mensch, Zeitkritik und Geschichtsphilosophie des jungen Marx* (Basel, 1953); Werner Schuffenhauer, *Feuerbach und der junge Marx, Entstehungsgeschichte der marxistische Weltanschauung* (Berlin, 1965); Alfred Schmidt, *Der Begriff der Natur in der Lehre von Marx* (Frankfurt, 1962); Erich Thier, *Das Menschenbild des jungen Marx* (Göttingen, 1957); Karl Löwith, "Man's Self-alienation in the Early Writings of Marx," *Social Research* 21 (1954), 204-30; L. Kolakowski, "Karl Marx and the Classical Definition of Truth," in *Revisionism, Essays on the History of Marxist Ideas*, ed. Leopold Labedz (New York, 1962); L. D. Easton, "Alienation and History in the Early Marx," *Philosophy and Phenomenological Research* 22 (1961-62), 193-205. Two recent books in English are István Mészáros, *Marx's Theory of Alienation* (London, 1970; New York, 1972), which refights many of Marx's battles for him, and Bertell Ollman, *Alienation* (Cambridge, 1971), which sees no development in Marx's thinking.

17. *EPM*, 63-64.

18. "Auszüge aus James Mills Buch 'Elemens d'économie politique' (traduit par J. T. Parisot, Paris, 1823)," in *MEW* Erganzungsband I: 445.

19. *Ibid.*; *EPM*, 70-71.

20. *EPM*, 72, 105, 182.

21. *EPM*, 106.

22. *EPM*, 107, 117.

23. *EPM*, 108-15.

24. *EPM*, 117, 118.

25. *EPM*, 118-19.

26. This reading of Marx's argument corrects the one I gave in *History and Theory* 12 (1973), 331-32.

27. *EPM*, 163, 162.

28. *EPM*, 136, 142, 163.

29. *Communist Manifesto* (cited hereafter as *CM*), in *SW*, 38.

30. *EPM*, 139-40; 167, 169; but I have revised the translation to make Marx's employment of the notion of inversion more visible and clear.

31. *EPM*, 134-35. Marx does not name any individuals here, but it is clear whom he had in mind.

32. *EPM*, 135, 146.

33. *EPM*, 187, 154.

34. *EPM*, 172.

35. *EPM*, 177.

36. *EPM*, 176, 178.

37. *EPM*, 180, 183.

38. *EPM*, 184, 189.

39. *EPM*, 175-76.

40. *EPM*, 190-92, but translating *Anschauung* as "direct observation" rather than as "intuition."

41. *EPM*, 182, 187.

42. *EPM*, 137-38; these comments from earlier in Marx's text seem to me to bear most directly on his view of Hegel and the general problem of the philosophical consciousness.

43. *EPM*, 139-40.

44. See *Writings of the Young Marx*, 259.

45. Bauer to Marx, July 25, 1840, *MEGA* I, i, (2), 244. In the previous year Bauer had often prodded Marx to finish with his degree as well.

46. See the letters of Feb. 10 and March 5 in *MEGA* I, i, (2), 267, 269 (in December 1841 Bauer had spoken of Marx as being at work on "his part" of the *Posaune*); Marx to Ruge, March 20, 1842, *Ibid.*, 270-72.

47. Marx to Ruge, Apr. 27, 1842, *Ibid.*, 273-74.

48. Ruge to Marx, late June 1842, *Ibid.*, 275; Marx to Ruge, July 9, 1842, *Ibid.*, 277; Ruge to Marx, Oct.21, 1842, *Ibid.*, 281.

49. Marx was almost certainly not the author of the two-page article "Luther as Arbiter between Strauss and Feuerbach," although it is still often attributed to him (cf. *Writings of the Young Marx*, 93-95): H. M. Sass, "Feuerbach statt Marx," *International Review of Social History* 12 (1967), 108-19.

50. Arnold Ruge, *Briefwechsel und Tageblätter, 1825-1880*, ed. Paul Nerrlich (Berlin, 1886), 343, 345.

51. Quoted in Louise Dornemann, *Jenny Marx*, 67-68.

52. Engels to Marx, March 17, 1845, *MEW* 27: 25-26.

53. Engels to Marx, Jan. 20, 1845, *MEW* 27: 16.

54. *EPM*, 63.

55. Marx to his father, *Writings of the Young Marx*, 42.

56. *EPM*, 63; *Writings of the Young Marx*, 47; there had also been an earlier bout of note taking, 45-46.

57. See Felix Gilbert's article cited in note 1 to this chapter.

58. Marx to Engels, Apr. 24, 1867, *MEW* 31: 290. Marx had found the book in Kugelmann's library, after not having seen a copy for years.

59 *Die Heilige Familie*, in *MEW* 2: 41, 60-63, 7.

60. *Ibid.*, 33-34; trans. excerpt in *Writings of the Young Marx*, 363.

61. *MEW* 2: 38; *Writings of the Young Marx*, 367-68.

62. *Ibid.*, 368.

63. *MEW* 2: 44, 52.

64. *Writings of the Young Marx*, 381.

65. *Ibid.*, 395.

66. *Allgemeine Literatur-Zeitung-Monatschrift*, ed. Bruno Bauer, 1 (Charlottenburg, 1844), 3 ff. The issue was dated December 1843, but published in 1844.

67. *MEW* 2: 91-93.

68. *EPM*, 171; *MEW* 2: 99-100.

69. Karl Marx and Frederick Engels, *The German Ideology*, trans. Clemens Dutt *et al.*, ed. S. Ryazanskaya (London, 1965; Moscow, 1968), 204 for the first quote, and 57 for the second one, on Feuerbach; the "Theses on Feuerbach" are in *Writings of the Young Marx*, 400-01.

Chapter Six

1. Engels used this phrase in a letter of 1884, quoted by Eleanor Marx-Aveling, "Frederick Engels," in *Marx and Engels Through the Eyes of their Contemporaries* (Moscow, 1972), 167; see also Mayer, *Engels*, I, 177-78.

2. Engels to Ruge, June 15, 1842, *MEW* 27: 404.

3. Engels to Marx, Feb. 13, 1865, *MEW* 31: 69.

4. The picture of Barmen and its middle class given here is taken from Wolfgang Köllmann, *Sozialgeschichte der Stadt Barmen im 19ten Jahrhundert* (Tübingen, 1960). See esp. Chap. 4.

5. Köllmann, *Sozialgeschichte*, and Mayer, *Engels*, I, 4-5.

6. Mayer, *Engels*, 14; Marcus, *Engels*, 70-72.

7. See Köllmann, *Sozialgeschichte*, and Engels to Marx, Feb. 22-26, 1845, *MEW* 27: 20.

8. Mayer, *Engels*, 9-10.

9. Engels to Marx, Dec. 31, 1857, *MEW* 29: 245.

10. The lines on Börne in Demetz, *Marx, Engels, and the Poets*, 22, and in *MEW Erganzungsband* I: 90-91. The comment about Bauer, Schapper, and Moll in "On the History of the Communist League," *SW*, 439.

11. Engels to his mother, Apr. 20, 1859, *MEW* 29: 595. There is a sensitive account of Engels' relations with his father, providing some explanations for this pattern of feeling, in Marcus, *Engels*, 74-75.

12. I cite *The Condition of the Working-Class in England* in the translation issued by the Institute of Marxism-Leninism, Moscow, with an Introduction by Eric Hobsbawn (London, 1969). The other available English version, by W. O. Henderson and W. H. Chaloner (Oxford, 1958), is capricious and inaccurate, and should be avoided.

13. *Condition*, 108, 37.

14. *Condition*, 57-58, 108.

15. *Ibid.*, 38, 158, 52, 154.

16. *Ibid.*, 152, 266, 250-51.

17. *Writings of the Young Marx*, 353.

18. *Condition*, 54, 163. This was in fact not an accurate picture of British working-class politics, most of whose leaders were artisans. E. P. Thompson, *The Making of the English Working Class* (London and New York, 1963).

19. *Condition*, 39, 153.

20. See *SW*, 38.

21. "Ludwig Feuerbach and the End of Classical German Philosophy," in *SW*, 603.

22. *Condition*, 26.

23. *Condition*, 39, 245, 324; Engels to Marx, early Oct. 1844, *MEW* 27: 7.

24. See *MEW* 27: 11 ff.

25. *Ibid.*, 11-12.

26. Stirner is treated in the general works on the Young Hegelians listed in the notes to Chapter Three, Section 2, but the central place of the life cycle theory in his writing has not been recognized, I think. There is a recent book on Stirner,

R.W.K. Paterson, *The Nihilistic Egoist* (London and New York, 1971), and he is discussed in histories of anarchism, such as the books by George Woodcock and James Joll. I cite *The Ego and His Own*, trans. Steven T. Byington, with an Introduction by J. L. Walker (London, 1912). The same translation has been reissued with a different Introduction, and different pagination (New York, 1973).

27. Stirner, 59-60, 40, 454.
28. Stirner, 9-11.
29. Stirner, 12-13.
30. *Ibid.*, 14.
31. Stirner, 16. This echoes Hegel, e.g., *The Phenomenology*, 802.
32. Stirner, 76.
33. *Ibid.*, 162.
34. *Ibid.*, 17.
35. Arnold Ruge, *Zwei Jahre in Paris—Studien und Errinerungen* (Leipzig, 1846), Part Two, Chaps. 13 and 14, esp. 134 for the conclusion; Moses Hess, *Die letzten Philosophen* (Darmstadt, 1845), 6-7 on Stirner; 2 on "the son and the father."
36. I cite *The German Ideology* in its most complete edition up to the time of my writing, trans. Clemens Dutt *et al.* and ed. S. Ryazanskaya (London 1965; Moscow, 1968) and cited hereafter as *GI*. Occasionally I have preferred the translation of Part One in *Writings of the Young Marx*, 403-73. Both versions take account of the discoveries by S. Bahne, first printed in *International Review of Social History* 7 (1962), 93 ff.
37. Preface to *A Contribution to the Critique of Political Economy*, *SW*, 183-84. On the history of the composition of *The German Ideology* and the attempts to have it printed, see Bert Andreas and Wolfgang Mönke, "Neue Daten zur 'Deutschen Ideologie'—mit einem unbekannten Brief von Karl Marx und anderen Dokumenten," *Archiv für Sozialgeschichte* 8 (1968), 5-159.
38. Engels to Marx, Mar. 17, 1845, *MEW* 27: 25-26, and Nov. 19, 1844, *Ibid.*, 12.
39. *GI*, 127. See Chapter Three, note 67.
40. *GI*, 132-33; *Condition of the Working Class*, 263.
41. *GI*, 134-36.
42. See Chapter One, note 7.
43. See for instance Arthur Lehning, "Buonarroti's Ideas on Communism and Dictatorship," *International Review of Social History* 2 (1957), 266-87.
44. *MEW* 27: 11.
45. *GI*, 270-71.
46. *Ibid.*, 272.
47. *GI*, 278.
48. See *Writings of the Young Marx*, 214.
49. *EPM*, 154; cf. earlier, Chapter Five, Section 2.
50. *GI*, 276, and Preface, 23.
51. See the third thesis, printed in *GI*, 660, or in *Writings of the Young Marx*, 401.
52. *GI*, 290-91.
53. *GI*, 55.

54. *Writings of the Young Marx*, 36, cf. Chapter Two, Section 2.

55. See the text in *The Utopian Vision of Charles Fourier*, trans., ed., and with an Introduction by Jonathan Beecher and Richard Bienvenu (Boston, 1971), 277.

56. This selection in Charles Fourier, *Harmonian Man*, ed. with an Introduction by Mark Poster, with new translations by Susan Hanson (New York, 1971), 75-76; see also Beecher and Bienvenu's collection, 303-04.

57. Beecher and Bienvenu, *Utopian Vision*, 275-83; see also Nicholas V. Riasanovsky, *The Teaching of Charles Fourier* (Berkeley and Los Angeles, 1969), 40-42; Fourier, *Harmonian Man*, 187.

58. *Writings of the Young Marx*, 204.

59. *GI*, 281-82.

60. *GI*, 291.

61. *GI*, 31, 46-47, 61.

62. *GI*, 50, 77, 85, 87.

63. *GI*, 38, 58, 259.

64. *The Poverty of Philosophy*, with an Introduction by Frederick Engels, trans. anon. (New York, 1963), 125. This work will be discussed in connection with the evolution of Marx's economic theory in Chapter Ten.

65. *GI*, 57.

66. *GI*, 59, *EPM*, 143-44.

67. *Writings of the Young Marx*, 368; *GI*, 46.

68. *GI*, 86 (but using the translation in *Writings of the Young Marx*, 468; the ordering of the text in the two editions is quite different in this section).

69. *GI*, 49, 93.

70. *GI*, 31-32.

71. *GI*, 32-33.

72. *Writings of the Young Marx*, 262-64.

73. Weitling to Hess, Mar. 31, 1846, in Hess, *Briefwechsel*, 151. Other features of this account will be discussed later.

74. *GI*, 47; *Communist Manifesto*, in *SW*, 62.

75. *GI*, 445; cf. *Writings of the Young Marx*, 208 (reading *verkehrte* as "inverted").

76. *GI*, 145, 206, 260.

77. *GI*, 37.

78. *GI*, 671-72.

79. *GI*, 541.

80. *GI*, 23.

81. *GI*, 63.

82. *Writings of the Young Marx*, 259, 240, 247.

83. *Critique of Hegel's 'Philosophy of Right,'* 8.

84. *The Holy Family, Writings of the Young Marx*, 383; "Theses on Feuerbach," *Ibid.*, 400; *GI*, 57.

85. *GI*, 38, 61-62.

86. Schiller, *Aesthetic Letters*, quoted in M. H. Abrams, *Natural Supernaturalism* (New York, 1971), 211; J. G. Fichte, *Philosophie der Maurerei*, ed. Wilhelm Flitner (Leipzig, 1923), 12-13.

87. MEGA I, i, (1), 225; *CW* I, 687.

88. *GI*, 49, 493, 290.

89. *GI*, 201, 205.

90. *NRZ*, June 28, 1848, and Dec. 24, 1848, *MEW* 5: 134, and 6: 138.

91. *MEGA* 1, i, (1), 224; *CW* 1, 686.

92. Peter Blos, *On Adolescence* (New York, 1962); for Hegel see above.

93. Blos, *On Adolescence*, 134-35. The quote from Inhelder and Piaget, *The Growth of Logical Thinking* (New York, 1958) is also in Blos, 124-25.

94. Given these evidences of reconciliation with ideas and values Marx had first encountered in his family, I do not find the suggestion of Victor Wolfenstein very helpful, that certain people evolve "revolutionary identities as a result of essentially interminable conflicts with parental authority" (*The Revolutionary Personality: Lenin, Trotsky, Gandhi*, Princeton, 1967). Much more enlightening to me seems Kenneth Kenniston's study of *Young Radicals* (New York, 1968), which finds that, for the American antiwar activist of the 1960s, "the process of radicalization did not involve acquiring new values, but rather an arduous effort to make his family's values his own" (113). I hope to extend these observations elsewhere through comparing Marx's arrival at maturity with other figures.

95. Silberner, *Moses Hess*, Chap. 9. Also W. Mönke, "Über die Mitarbeit von Moses Hess an der 'Deutschen Ideologie,' " *Annali* (Istituto Giangiacomo Feltrinelli) 6 (1963), 438-509.

96. Preface to *A Contribution to the Critique of Political Economy*, in *SW*, 184.

97. Weitling to Hess, March 31, 1846, in Hess, *Briefwechsel*, 150 ff.

98. Anthony Storr, *Human Aggression* (New York, 1968), 57.

99. Originally published in Russian during 1880 in *Vestnik Evropy*; cited here from the first German publication, "Eine russische Stimme über Karl Marx," *Die Neue Zeit* 1 (1883), 236 ff.

100. See Chapter Three, Section 3; Engels, "Marx and the *Neue Rheinische Zeitung*," *MEW* 21: 19.

101. Quoted by Golo Mann, *The History of Germany since 1789*, trans. Marian Jackson (New York and Washington, 1968), 83.

102. Henry Mayers Hyndman, *The Record of an Adventurous Life* (London, 1911), 282, cf. also 269. It was Hyndman who told the story of Marx's reply to Hyndman's comment that he grew more tolerant as he grew older: "Do you, *do* you?" (271).

103. "Zirkular gegen Kriege," *MEW* 4: 15.

104. *GI*, 259.

105. Marx's replies to questions in the popular Victorian party game "Confessions," *MEW* 31: 596.

106. See Chapter Two, Section 3. *Writings of the Young Marx*, 47.

107. Marx to Philips, May 6, 1861, *MEW* 30: 599.

108. "Peuchet: vom Selbstmord," in *MEGA* 1, iii, 391-407; originally in *Gesellschaftsspiegel. Organ zur Vertretung der besitzlosen Volksklassen . . .* (Elberfeld, 1845-46, reprinted, Amsterdam, 1971), II,14-26. That Marx was indeed the author of the essay cannot be disputed. Hess and Engels had no reason to publish the work of someone else under his name; in addition, Marx later remarked that Hess owed him money in connection with the *Gesellschaftsspiegel*, Marx to Engels, May 15, 1847, *MEW* 27: 82; the work of Peuchet from which the section

was translated was in Marx's library when Roland Daniels made an inventory of it in 1850: *Ex Libris Karl Marx und Friedrich Engels, Schicksal und Verzeichnis einer Bibliothek*, ed. Institut für Marxismus-Leninismus (Berlin, 1967), 212.

109. There is an entry for Peuchet in *Nouvelle Biographie Generale*, XXXIX, 770-71. It relies largely on the introduction by Alphonse Levasseur to Peuchet's book, *Mémoires tirés des archives de la Police de Paris, pour servir à l'histoire de la morale et de la police, depuis Louis XIV jusqu'à nos jours*, six volumes in two (Paris, 1838). Marx also drew on this introduction in identifying Peuchet.

110. Peuchet, *Mémoires*, 175-76, and the Introduction by A. Levasseur, xvii.

111. *MEGA* I, iii, 391.

112. Peuchet, *Mémoires*, 121-22, 141; *MEGA* I, iii, 394-95, 403. I have not made a complete tabulation of all the changes Marx introduced, nor have I referred here to all the ones I have found.

113. Peuchet, *Mémoires*, 119, 120; *MEGA* I, iii, 393, 394.

114. Peuchet, *Mémoires*, 122; *MEGA* I, iii, 395; *MEGA* I, iii, 396; cf. Peuchet, 127. The underlining of the first passage was not unique; Marx underscored a number of Peuchet's more arresting comments, thus giving the Frenchman's pages some of the quality of Marx's own early essays, in which underscoring for emphasis was common. That the second passage was Marx's addition is not noted in *CW* IV, 605.

115. *Writings of the Young Marx*, 349; *MEGA* I, iii, 393.

116. On working until 3 or 4 in the morning, see the letter of George Julian Harney to Engels, March 30, 1846, in Bert Andreas and Wolfgang Mönke, "Neue Daten zur 'Deutschen Ideologie,' " *Archiv für Sozialgeschichte* 8 (1969), 59-60; for Engels' views of Marx's illness see Chapter Twelve, Section 4, and Engels to Kugelmann, Apr. 28, 1871, *MEW* 33: 218-19; Hess to Marx, July 28, 1846, in Hess, *Briefwechsel*, 164; Marx to Leske, Aug. 1, 1846, *MEW* 27: 449.

117. Erikson, *Young Man Luther*, 247.

118. *GI*, 135, 163, 354, 362. *Philosophy of Right*, para. 198, p. 129; para. 192, p. 127; para. 197, p. 129; *Phenomenology*, 528.

119. *Phenomenology*, 515-17; *GI*, 48, 93.

Chapter Seven

1. Among general narratives of the revolutions of 1848 in English are William L. Langer, *Political and Social Upheaval, 1832-52* (New York, 1969), and Jean Sigmann, *1848, The Romantic and Democratic Revolutions in Europe*, trans. L. F. Edwards (New York, 1973). Recent accounts of events in France are Roger Price, *The French Second Republic* (Ithaca, 1972) and two books by Maurice Agulhon, *1848 ou l'apprentissage de la République, 1848-52*, Nouvelle histoire de la France contemporaine 8 (Paris, 1973), and *Les quarante-huitards* (Paris, 1975). George Duveau, *1848, The Making of a Revolution*, trans. Anne Carter (New York, 1967) is a lively introduction. On Germany see Jacques Droz, *Les révolutions allemandes de 1848* (Paris, 1957) and Rudolph Stadelman, *Soziale und politiische Geschichte der Revolution von 1848* (Munich, 1948), Eng. ed., trans. J. G. Chastain (Athens, Ohio, 1975), as well as T. H. Hamerow, *Restoration, Revolution, Reaction* (Princeton, 1958).

2. On working-class organizations see Philip H. Noyes, *Organization and Revolution* (Princeton, 1966), and Remi Gossez, *Les ouvriers de Paris* (Paris, 1968).

3. *CM*, in *SW*, 35.

4. For these earlier motifs, cf. Chapter Three, Section 4.

5. *CM*, 36.

6. *CM*, 37-38.

7. *CM*, 38. For similar notions in *GI* see 77.

8. *CM*, 44, 46-47.

9. Among the best treatments of Marx's participation in the politics of 1848 is that of Jacques Droz, *Les révolutions allemandes de 1848* (Paris, 1957), 527-46. See also Richard N. Hunt, *The Political Ideas of Marx and Engels* (Pittsburgh, 1974), Chaps. 5-7, but Hunt's general thesis that Marx and Engels were democrats must be taken with some reserve. See my criticisms in *European Labor and Working Class History Newsletter* 7 (May 1975), 30-36. Reliable general accounts can also be found in McLellan, *Karl Marx*, Chap. 4; in A. Cornu, *Karl Marx et la Révolution de 1848* (Paris, 1948); and in the new chronology of Marx's life and works by Maximilien Rubel and Margaret Manale, *Marx Without Myth*, 73 ff. and 93 ff. The older study by Hans Stein, *Der Kölner Arbeiterverein, 1848-49* (Cologne, 1921), needs to be corrected by the more recent accounts. Also E. Czobel, "Der Kölner Arbeiterverein, 1848-49," *Marx-Engels Archiv* 1 (1925), 429-37. An East German contribution is Gerhard Becker, *Karl Marx und Friedrich Engels in Köln, 1848-49* (Berlin, 1963).

10. *NRZ*, June 28, 1848, *MEW* 5: 134. The trans. adopted from *The Class Struggles in France* (New York, 1964), cited hereafter as *CS*, 57-58. The articles of Marx and Engels from the *NRZ* can be found in *MEW*, Vols. 5 and 6, and a selection in English in *The Revolution of 1848-49, Articles from the Neue Rheinische Zeitung* (New York, 1972), where a slightly altered version of this passage appears, 45-46.

11. *NRZ*, Dec. 24, 1848, *MEW* 6: 138; *NRZ*, Feb. 28, 1849, *MEW* 6: 308.

12. *CS*, 33, 40, 44.

13. *CS*, 53-54.

14. *CS*, 56.

15. *CS*, 58.

16. *CS*, 110-11.

17. *The Eighteenth Brumaire of Louis Bonaparte* (cited hereafter as *EB*), in *SW*, 180.

18. *EB*, 97-99. Bruce Mazlish has pointed out that Engels suggested some of Marx's basic imagery in a letter to Marx before the latter employed it in his pamphlet. See "The Tragic Farce of Marx, Hegel, and Engels: A Note," *History and Theory* 11 (1972), 335-37. But Marx had laid the groundwork for the comparison in his earlier pamphlet; see *CS*, 73.

19. *EB*, 99. Compare this with what Marx wrote in the *NRZ* at the end of June, 1848: "The best form of polity is that in which the social contradictions are not blurred, not arbitrarily—that is, merely artificially and therefore seemingly—kept down. The best form of polity is that in which these contradictions reach a stage of open struggle in the course of which they are resolved." *The Revolution of 1848-49*, 49.

20. *EB*, 101, 169.

21. *Ibid.*, 116, 118.

22. *Ibid.*, 102, 149; cf. also 109.

23. Marx to Weydemeyer, March 5, 1852, *MEW* 28: 507-08; *SC*, 69.

24. See Chapter Four, Section 4; cf. Asa Briggs, "The Language of 'Class' in Early Nineteenth-Century England," in *Essays in Labor History*, ed. Briggs and John Saville (London, 1960); reprinted in M. V. Flinn and T. C. Smout, *Essays in Social History* (Oxford, 1974).

25. T. B. Macaulay, *Speeches on Politics and Literature* (London and New York, 1909), 6-7.

26. See Dietrich Gerhard, "Guizot, Augustin Thierry und die Rolle des Tiers Etat in der Französischen Geschichte," *Historische Zeitschrift* 190 (1960), 303-04.

27. *The Doctrine of St. Simon*, trans. Georg G. Iggers (New York, 1958, 1972), 64-67, 84.

28. *GI*, 59.

29. *CM*, 43-44. In *The Poverty of Philosophy* Marx distinguished between two phases in the history of class formation. During the first a social group formed a class only "for others." Later, when its political unity was accomplished, it also formed a class "for itself." See 173.

30. *CS*, 88-89. I have altered the translation of the first of these quotations slightly.

31. *CS*, 89, 102, 105, 110.

32. *CS*, 92-93.

33. *CS*, 106, 126.

34. *CS*, 74, 76.

35. *CS*, 122, 124, 128-29.

36. *CS*, 129-30.

37. *CS*, 135.

38. *CS*, 138, 140.

39. *CS*, 143.

40. *CS*, 143-46.

41. *GI*, 218-19. Marx to Engels, Dec. 9, 1851, *MEW* 27: 384. Marx wrote "quite bewildered" in English.

42. *EB*, 103.

43. *EB*, 120.

44. *EB*, 152, 155-56.

45. *EB*, 132.

46. *EB*, 171.

47. *CS*, 115-16.

48. *EB*, 170.

49. *EB*, 100.

50. "Introduction to the Critique of Hegel's *Philosophy of Right*," in Easton and Guddat, *Writings of the Young Marx*, 261-62.

51. *MEGA* I, i, (1), 143.

52. Marx to Freiligrath, Dec. 27, 1851, *MEW* 27: 596.

53. *CS*, 57, and Chapter Six, Section 4.

54. Marx to Engels, Jan. 29, 1853, *MEW* 28: 210.

Chapter Eight

1. Richard Wagner, *Mein Leben* (Autobiography), quoted by Ernest Newman, *Wagner as Man and Artist* (New York, 1960), 219.

2. For a general account of European affairs in the 1850s and 1860s see Eric Hobsbawm, *The Age of Capital* (New York, 1975). For England these themes have been treated in W. L. Burn, *The Age of Equipoise* (London and New York, 1964), and in Asa Briggs, *Victorian People* (Chicago, 1955).

3. For continental industrial development during this period, see Landes, *The Unbound Prometheus*, 194, where a convenient statistical table summarizes several aspects of industrial growth. On real wages see the information gathered and discussed by Jean Lhomme in *Economie et Histoire* (Geneva, 1967), Chap. 4. On the nature of wages see E. H. Hobsbawm, "Custom, Wages and Work-Load," in *Labouring Men* (New York, 1967), 405-36, and on industry and work in Britain, Hobsbawm's *Industry and Empire* (Baltimore, 1968).

4. A good selection of these articles can be found in Marx and Engels, *Articles on Britain* (Moscow, 1971). The complete critical edition of all Marx's articles for the *New York Daily Tribune* (cited hereafter as *NYDT*), announced for some time, has not yet appeared.

5. "The Elections in England—Tories and Whigs," *NYDT*, Aug. 21, 1852; *On Britain*, 110.

6. *Ibid.*, 113-14.

7. *Ibid.*, 118-19.

8. "Political Consequences of the Commercial Excitement," *NYDT*, Nov. 2, 1852; and untitled article, *NYDT*, Nov. 25, 1852; *On Britain*, 134, 137, 141.

9. "The English Middle Class," *NYDT*, Aug. 1, 1854; *On Britain*, 220.

10. "Lord John Russell," *NYDT*, Aug. 28, 1855; *On Britain*, 251.

11. Untitled article, *NYDT*, June 11, 1858; *On Britain*, 296.

12. "The London *Times* and Lord Palmerston," *NYDT*, Oct. 21, 1861; *On Britain*, 311.

13. "The British Constitution," *Neue Oder-Zeitung*, March 6, 1855; *On Britain*, 224.

14. Marx to Engels, Feb. 4, 1852, *MEW* 28: 21; Engels to Weydemeyer, Feb. 27, 1852, *MEW* 28: 502.

15. Engels to Marx, Apr. 20, 1852, *MEW* 28: 52-53; and Aug. 24, 1852, *MEW* 28: 118.

16. Marx to Engels, Sept. 17, 1853, *MEW* 28: 289-90; and Oct. 12, 1853, *MEW* 28: 302-03; Marx to Cluss, Sept. 15, 1853, *MEW* 28: 592.

17. See Hans Rosenberg, *Die Weltwirtschaftskrisis von 1857-1859* (Berlin, 1934); and T. H. Hamerow, *The Social Foundations of German Unification* (Princeton, 1969), I, 6-13.

18. Engels to Marx, Oct. 20, 1857, *MEW* 29: 198; Marx to Engels, Nov. 13, 1857, *MEW* 29: 207; Engels to Marx, Nov. 15, 1857, *MEW* 29: 212.

19. "Lord John Russell," *Neue Oder-Zeitung*, July 28, 1855; *On Britain*, 246. The theme of masks in British politics was one sounded by other observers at the time. See for instance the cartoon of Disraeli from *Punch*, reproduced in Asa Briggs, *Victorian People*, facing 150. As we shall see, however, the problem of

appearance and reality had a special significance, both theoretically and person-ally, for Marx.

20. "Lord Palmerston," *NYDT*, Oct. 19, 1853; *On Britain*, 204-05.

21. *Ibid.*, 206.

22. Marx to Engels, Nov. 2, 1853, *MEW* 28: 306; Marx to Lassalle, Apr. 6, 1854, *MEW* 28: 604.

23. See for instance Palmerston's most recent biography, Jasper Ridley, *Lord Palmerston* (New York, 1971), 423.

24. Marx to Engels, Feb. 9, 1854, *MEW* 28: 324.

25. For the publication history see Lester Hutchinson's introduction to his edition of *Secret Diplomatic History of the Eighteenth Century and The Story of the Life of Lord Palmerston* (London, 1969), cited hereafter as *SDH*.

26. Marx to Engels, Feb. 12, 1856, *MEW* 29: 11.

27. *SDH*, 88, 91.

28. *SDH*, 108; 121, cf. 114.

29. *SDH*, 111, 112, 116.

30. *SDH*, 118.

31. *SDH*, 120, 126.

32. *SDH*, 112. On Hegel's Abraham, see Chapter One, Section 3.

33. See B. Nicolaevsky, "Toward a History of 'The Communist League' 1847-1852," *International Review of Social History* 1 (1956), 234-52; Werner Blumenberg, "Zur Geschichte des Bundes der Kommunisten, Die Aussagen des Peter Gerhardt Röser," *Ibid.*, 9 (1964), 81-122.

34. Marx to Engels, July 13, 1851, *MEW* 27: 278.

35. The March Circular is printed in Marx and Engels, *SW* (two volume edi-tion, New York, 1933) II, 154-68. I have argued against Richard N. Hunt's attempt to attribute these sentiments to other members of the League in *European Labor and Working-Class History Newsletter* 7 (May 1975), 30-36.

36. See the documents in B. Nicolaevsky's and Werner Blumenberg's articles cited in note 33, above; also McLellan, *Karl Marx*, 252 ff., and the Marx-Engels correspondence.

37. Marx to Engels, Feb. 11, 1851, *MEW* 27: 184-85; Engels to Marx, Feb. 12 and 13, 1851, *MEW* 27: 186, 189-90.

38. Engels to Marx, May 9, 1851, *MEGA* III, i, 198; Marx to Cluss, July 20, 1852, *MEW* 28: 537. There is a discussion of the origins and meaning of "Straubinger" in Grimm's *Wörterbuch*, s.v.

39. Marx to Freiligrath, Feb. 29, 1860, *MEW* 30: 489-90.

40. Marx's article from the *Deutsche Brüsseler Zeitung* of Dec. 19, 1847, is printed in *MEGA* I, vi, 370.

41. The Preface to *A Contribution to a Critique of Political Economy* has often been reprinted separately. See *SW*, 181-82.

42. Marx to Engels, Feb. 13, 1863, *MEW* 30: 324.

43. Marx to Engels, Apr. 9, 1863, *MEW* 30: 343; *SC*, 140-41.

44. André Malraux, *Man's Fate* (*La condition humaine*), trans. Haakon M. Chevalier (New York, Modern Library, 1934), 357-58.

45. On the origins of the First International the best summary accounts are in Henry Collins and Chimen Abramsky, *Karl Marx and the British Labour Movement*

(London, 1965), Part One, and the same authors' article in *La Première Internationale: l'Institution, l'Implantation, le Rayonnement*, Colloque du CNRS (Paris, 1968). See also Julius Braunthals, *History of the International*, trans. Henry Collins and Kenneth Mitchell (New York, 1967), 1, Chap. 9.

46. See Braunthals, Chaps. 10-15.

47. A good account of all this is in Collins and Abramsky, *Karl Marx and the British Labour Movement*, Chap. 3.

48. Marx to Engels, Nov. 4, 1864, *MEW* 31: 16; *SC*, 148-49.

49. The Inaugural Address is printed in English in Marx and Engels, *SW* (two volume edition), 342-49.

50. Most notably by George Lichtheim. See *Marxism, An Historical and Critical Study* (New York, 1961), 104.

51. *CM*, Parts Two and Four, in *SW*, 46-47, 62-63.

52. Marx to Engels, March 5, 1869, *MEW* 32: 273 (I have changed the subjunctive verbs here to indicative ones—Marx was explaining the basis of his reply to Bakunin in this letter); Marx to Kugelmann, Oct. 9, 1866, *MEW* 31: 529; Marx to Schweitzer, Oct.13, 1868, *SC*, 214; Collins and Abramsky, 292; cf. also Marx to Paul and Laura Lafargue, Apr. 19, 1870, *MEW* 32: 676.

53. Collins and Abramsky, *Karl Marx*, 288.

54. *Ibid.*, 123; see also 101-04.

55. Marx to Engels, Sept. 11, 1867, *MEW* 31: 342-43.

56. Marx to Engels, Sept. 26, 1868, *MEW* 32: 168.

57. The account that follows is based on Roger Morgan, *The German Social Democrats and the First International, 1864-72* (Cambridge, Eng., 1965).

58. Becker's role in this was not appreciated before Morgan pointed it out.

59. On Bakunin's life and ideas see E. H. Carr, *Michael Bakunin* (London, 1957); also George Woodcock, *Anarchism* (Baltimore, 1963), Chap. 6; James Joll, *The Anarchists* (Boston, 1963), Chap. 4. Bakunin's role and activity in the nineteenth-century socialist movement are being illuminated by the publication of his papers in the *Archives Bakounine*, ed. Arthur Lehning *et al.* (Leiden, from 1961). See also Lehning's article, "La Lutte des Tendances au Sein de la Première Internationale: Marx et Bakounine," in *La Première Internationale*, Colloque du CNRS (Paris, 1968), 331-43.

60. For the history of socialism in Italy during this period and the spread of Bakunin's influence, see Aldo Romano, *Storia del movimento socialista in Italia*, three vols. (Milan, 1954-56). The account given above draws heavily on Richard Hostetter, *The Italian Socialist Movement* 1: *Origins* (Princeton, 1958). These studies revise the older account by Nello Rosselli, *Mazzini e Bakounine* (Turin, 1927).

61. On these developments see Collins and Abramsky, *Karl Marx*, esp. 257, 268.

62. See Engels' letter to F. A. Sorge, Sept. 12, 1874, printed in Marx and Engels, *On the Paris Commune* (Moscow, 1971, cited hereafter as *PC*), 293. On recent literature about the First International and its demise, see Jacques Rougerie, "Sur l'Historie de la Première Internationale," *Le mouvement social* 51 (1965), 23-45. Rougerie draws on work by M. Molnar, *Le déclin de la Première Internationale* (Geneva, 1963), and in general on the papers published in the sym-

posium *La Première Internationale*, cited above. See esp. Molnar's article in that volume, "Quelques Remarques à propos de la Crise de l'Internationale en 1872," 427-43.

63. Marx to Engels, Aug. 8, 1870, *MEW* 33: 32; Aug. 17, 1870, *MEW* 33: 44.

64. "Second Address of the General Council of the IWA on the Franco-Prussian War," *PC*, 46-47.

65. Marx to Engels, Sept. 6, 1870, *MEW* 33: 54; Marx to De Paepe, Sept. 14, 1870, *MEW* 33: 147.

66. I cannot agree with the interpretation of these documents suggested by Avineri, *The Social and Political Thought of Karl Marx*, 245. Avineri claims that "Marx's doubts . . . were not limited to the war situation only. The structure of French society, and of the French working class, makes the outcome of a possible revolutionary attempt appear unpromising to him." This is directly contradicted by Marx's letter to Kugelmann of Apr. 17, 1871, quoted in the text and cited in note 68 below.

67. The letters to the *Times* and to Kugelmann are quoted in *PC*, 281 and 284.

68. Marx to Kugelmann, Apr. 17, 1871, *PC*, 285.

69. The draft is printed in *PC*, 157.

70. *Ibid.*, 146.

71. *Ibid.*, 288, 289.

72. *Ibid.*, 128.

73. "The Civil War in France," *SW*, 290, 294.

74. The draft in *PC*, 207; "The Civil War" in *SW*, 293, 294.

75. Marx's speech in Amsterdam, reported in the New York *World*, Nov. 15, 1871; cf. Collins and Abramsky, *Karl Marx*, 232-33.

76. Marx to Domela-Nieuwenhuis, *PC*, 293.

77. *PC*, 165; *SW*, 297.

78. Engels to Bernstein, Jan. 1, 1884, *SC*, 366.

79. *SW*, 292, 293.

80. *PC*, 152, 156.

81. Bakunin to Lorenzo, quoted by Lehning, "La Lutte des Tendances," 336-37.

82. Engels to Carlo Terzaghi, Jan. 14-15, 1872, *MEW* 33: 374-75; *PC*, 292.

83. Marx to Engels, Aug. 4, 1868, *MEW* 32: 131; Engels to Marx, Aug. 6, 1868, *MEW* 32: 132.

84. Lehning, "La Lutte des Tendances," 338.

85. Braunthals, *History of the International* I, 183; Carr, *Bakunin*, 444.

86. George Lichtheim, *Marxism in Modern France* (New York, 1966).

87. Collins and Abramsky, *Karl Marx*, 292.

88. Marx to Engels, July 31, 1865, *MEW* 31: 131; the same, Aug. 22, 1865, *MEW* 31: 147; the same, Dec. 26, 1865, *MEW* 31: 162, and Aug. 8, 1865, *MEW* 31: 134.

89. Marx to De Paepe, May 28, 1872, *MEW* 33: 479-80; Marx to Danielson, same date, *MEW* 33: 477.

90. The *locus classicus* for the view of Marx as a supporter of centralized control

and authoritarian politics is Lenin's 1917 pamphlet, *State and Revolution*. Recent attempts to claim him for the other side (not each in the same way) include George Lichtheim, *Marxism: An Historical and Critical Study* (New York and London, 1961); Avineri, *The Social and Political Thought of Karl Marx*; Richard N. Hunt, *The Political Ideas of Marx and Engels* I (Pittsburgh, 1974). For specific commentary on some of these views, see my review of Hunt's book, cited in note 35, above, and the reference to Avineri in note 66, above.

Chapter Nine

1. Jenny's brief autobiography, "A Short Sketch of an Eventful Life," cited here from *The Unknown Karl Marx*, ed. with an Introduction by Robert Payne (New York, 1971), 125. Marx to Engels, March 17, 1851 and March 31, 1851, *MEW* 27: 219, 227; Feb. 27, 1852, *MEW* 28: 30; Jan. 21, 1853, *MEW* 28: 207; June 21, 1854, *MEW* 28: 370-71.

2. Marx to Engels, Apr. 12, 1855, *MEW* 28: 444; Marx to Lassalle, July 28, 1855, *MEW* 28: 617; Marx to Engels, March 30, 1855, *MEW* 28: 442; and "Short Sketch," 129.

3. "Short Sketch," 129; Jenny Marx to Bertha Markheim, Jan. 28, 1863, in Bert Andreas, "Briefe und Dokumente der Familie Marx aus den Jahren 1862-73," *Archiv für Sozialgeschichte* 2 (1962), 177. Marx to Engels, Sept. 26, 1856, *MEW* 29: 75.

4. Marx to Engels, Jan. 20, 1857, *MEW* 29: 97; March 18, 1857, *MEW* 29: 110; July 15, 1858, *MEW* 29: 340-41.

5. Marx to Engels, Sept. 21, 1859, *MEW* 29: 480; Oct. 5, 1859, *MEW* 29: 491; Jan. 11, 1860, *MEW* 30: 6; Jan. 29, 1861, *MEW* 30: 148; Oct. 30, 1861, *MEW* 30: 196; Nov. 18, 1861, *MEW* 30: 200; June 18, 1862, *MEW* 30: 248; Jan. 24, 1863, *MEW* 30: 315.

6. For the figures, Werner Blumenberg, "Ein unbekanntes Kapitel aus Marx' Leben," *International Review of Social History* 1 (1956), 66-67; "Short Sketch," 136.

7. Marx to Engels, July 31, 1865, *MEW* 31: 131; Aug. 8, 1865, *MEW* 31: 134; Aug. 19, 1865, *MEW* 31: 143; Oct. 4, 1867, *MEW* 31: 356; Apr. 30, 1868, *MEW* 32: 75.

8. Engels to Marx, Nov. 29, 1868 and Marx to Engels, Nov. 30, 1868, *MEW* 32: 215-17.

9. Blumenberg,"Ein unbekanntes Kapitel," 62; McLellan, *Karl Marx*, 286-87.

10. Marx to Engels, June 10, 1861, *MEW* 30: 170.

11. Marx to Engels, Sept. 10, 1862, *MEW* 30: 287; to Kugelmann, Dec. 28, 1862, *MEW* 30: 640; McLellan, *Karl Marx*, 413-14.

12. Engels to Marx, Nov. 18, 1852, *MEW* 28: 158.

13. McLellan, *Karl Marx*, 287.

14. On the 1852 visit see Engels' letter to Marx of May 19, 1852, *MEW* 28: 74-75.

15. McLellan, *Karl Marx*, 357, citing an East German collection, *Karl Marx, Dokumente seines Lebens*, which I have not been able to consult.

16. McLellan, *Karl Marx*, 264.

17. The story about Marx's arrest while trying to pawn Jenny's silver is told by H. M. Hyndman, *The Record of an Adventurous Life* (London, 1911), 277 ff.

18. A similar point is made by McLellan, *Karl Marx*, 264 ff. Marx to Kugelmann, March 17, 1868, *MEW* 32: 540.

19. See Marx's accounting to Engels in his letter of July 15, 1858, *MEW* 29: 340-43; Jenny Marx to Louise Weydemeyer, May 20, 1850, in *Marx and Engels through the Eyes of their Contemporaries*, 149; Marx to Engels, July 31, 1865, *MEW* 31: 131.

20. Marx to Engels, Nov. 30, 1868, *MEW* 32: 217.

21. Marx to Engels, July 15, 1858, *MEW* 29: 340 and 342; "Short Sketch," 131 f.

22. Marx to Engels, Sept. 8, 1852, *MEW* 28: 129; July 8, 1853, *MEW* 28: 272; Apr. 24, 1852, *MEW* 28: 54; March 9 and June 6, 1854, *MEW* 28: 327 and 371; and July 28, 1856, *MEW* 29: 65.

23. Marx to Engels, March 10, 1853 and Sept. 13, 1854, *MEW* 28: 222, 391.

24. Marx to Engels, Feb. 2, 1859, *MEW* 29: 385; Apr. 16, 1859, *MEW* 29: 420; Feb. 3, 1860, *MEW* 30: 23; May 7, 1867, *MEW* 31: 296.

25. Marx to Cluss, Sept. 15, 1853, *MEW* 28: 592.

26. On Marx's need to have Engels supply articles, see for instance the letters of the fall of 1854, *MEW* 29: 393 ff.; on giving twice the work for half the price, Marx to Engels, Jan. 16, 1858, *MEW* 29: 260.

27. On Marx as honorary constable see his letter of June 27, 1868, *MEW* 31: 107-08.

28. Marx's comment on Freiligrath may have hinted at some of his own feelings about regular work: "Our Freiligrath is unhappy with his place again, although he very comfortably gets £300 a year there, and has nothing to do worth speaking of. What bothers him is, on the one hand the murmuring and complaining of the shareholders, who let out all their ill-humor on him, and in part the position—equivocal in any case—which piles responsibility on him without allowing him more than the appearance of independence. So at least does he express his feeling himself. What in fact lurks beneath, looks to me like repugnance for responsibility in general. A position as a clerk, like Hood's, would spare him that, and remains his ideal. Then too the collision between his fame as a poet and the rate of exchange torments him." Marx to Engels, Apr. 23, 1857, *MEW* 29: 129-30.

29. Marx to Weydemeyer, Feb. 1, 1859, *MEW* 29: 570; Marx to Lassalle, Nov. 7, 1862, *MEW* 30: 637.

30. I believe there exist three separate versions of Marx's answers to the "Confessions" game: one originally in his daughter Jenny's album, *MEW* 31: 596 (photo, 597); one which I assume to be different, but which I have not seen, said to be from Laura Marx's album, in *Mohr und General* (Berlin, 1864); one dated "Zalt-Bommel, Apr. 1, 1865," done for one of his relatives in Holland, printed by Werner Blumenberg, in the article cited earlier, *International Review of Social History* 1 (1956). There are various slight differences between the first and third version; the first gives no reply to the question about happiness and misery, the third lists "to struggle" and "to submit." Engels' list is in *MEW* 32: 695.

31. Jenny Marx to Kugelmann, Dec. 24, 1868, in Andreas, "Briefe und Dokumente der Familie Marx," 193; Marx's letter to Sigrid Mayer, Apr. 30, 1867, *MEW* 31: 542.

32. Marx to Engels, Jan. 8, 1863, *MEW* 30: 310-11.

33. McLellan, *Karl Marx*, 279-80; Chushici Tsuzuki, *The Life of Eleanor Marx, 1855-1898, A Socialist Tragedy* (Oxford, 1967), 73.

34. Engels to Marx, Jan. 13, 1863; *MEW* 30: 312-13.

35. Marx to Engels, Jan. 24, 1863, *MEW* 30: 313-15.

36. Engels to Marx, Jan. 26, 1863, *MEW* 30: 317-18.

37. *MEW* 30: 315 and 319.

38. Jenny Marx to Weydemeyer, May 20, 1850, in *Marx and Engels through the Eyes of Their Contemporaries* (cited hereafter as *METEC*), 146.

39. Wilhelm Liebknecht, "Reminiscences of Marx," *METEC*, 73-74.

40. Liebknecht, "Reminiscences," *METEC*, 69; Eleanor Marx-Aveling, "Karl Marx," *METEC*, 154 and 157; McLellan, *Karl Marx*, 268.

41. Marx to Engels, July 31, 1851, *MEGA* III, i, 226 (*MEW* 27: 293).

42. Jenny Marx to Marx, cited from the manuscript by Arnold Künzli, *Karl Marx, Eine Psychographie*, 320-21; trans. in McLellan, *Karl Marx*, 273; Marx to Jenny, June 11, 1852, *MEW* 28: 527. (Since the date of Jenny's letter is not known to me, I only conclude from the contents that Marx's letter of June 11 was his reply.)

43. On her requests for money, see, e.g., her letter to Engels of Dec. 23-24, 1859, *MEW* 29: 654; her letter to Weydemeyer cited above in note 38, 146; Marx to Engels, note 32, above; Liebknecht, "Reminiscences," in *METEC*, 61.

44. Jenny Marx to Marx, May 9, 1858, *MEW* 29: 650; on her earlier letter (*CW* I, 696) see above, Chapter Four, Section 2.

45. Jenny von Westphalen to Karl Marx, 1839, *CW* I, 696; to Bertha Markheim, Oct. 12, 1863, in Andreas, "Briefe und Dokumente," 185; to Engels, Dec. 24, 1866, *MEW* 31: 593; to Liebknecht, May 26, 1872, *MEW* 33: 702.

46. Marx to Jenny Marx, June 11, 1852, *MEW* 28: 527; to Engels, Oct. 30, 1868, *MEW* 32: 217.

47. *MEW* 30: 310 and 319, for the letters of Jan. 1863, already cited; Marx to Engels, May 7, 1867, *MEW* 31: 297.

48. Jenny Marx to Bertha Markheim, Jan. 28, 1863, in Andreas, "Briefe und Dokumente," 178-79; "Short Sketch," 131.

49. Marx to Engels, July 15, 1858, *MEW* 29: 343; Jan. 24, 1863, *MEW* 30: 315; July 30, 1862, *MEW* 30: 257; Nov. 8, 1866, *MEW* 31: 262.

50. Liebknecht, "Reminiscences," in *METEC*, 75; Marx to Engels, Sept. 28, 1852, *MEW* 28: 147.

51. On Frederick Demuth, see Werner Blumenberg, *Karl Marx, An Illustrated Biography*, 122-25; Robert Payne, *Marx* (New York, 1968), 265 ff., where the birth certificate is printed for the first time, 267 (but in the context of a discussion that is full of unsupported conjectures, including the unlikely opinion that Lenchen was Marx's regular mistress, and the meaningless assertion that "she was the embodiment of 'the dictatorship of the proletariat' "); and Tsuzuki, *Eleanor Marx, passim*.

52. Engels to Marx, Feb. 23, 1877, *MEW* 34: 31.

53. "Short Sketch," 126; Liebknecht, "Reminiscences," *METEC*, 73.

54. Marx to Engels, March 31, 1851; *MEGA* III, i, 179; *MEW* 27: 227.

55. Recently a German biographer of Marx has presented the mystery as too deep to penetrate, concluding that the question of Frederick Demuth's paternity remains undecided. Fritz Raddatz, *Karl Marx* (Hamburg, 1975), 205-11.

56. Marx to Weydemeyer, Aug. 2, 1851, *MEW* 27: 265; F. A. Sorge, "On Marx," *METEC*, 125-26.

57. Marx's answers to "Confessions," above, note 30; Marx to his daughter Jenny, Dec. 17, 1881, *MEW* 35: 250.

58. Marx to Engels, Jan. 21, 1859, *MEW* 29: 386; Liebknecht, "Reminiscences," *METEC*, 61-62.

59. I take the phrase from the noted psychiatrist and family therapist, Nathan Ackerman.

60. Jenny Marx to Engels, Apr. 27, 1853, *MEW* 28: 645; Jenny Marx (daughter) to Kugelmann, July 17, 1870, in Andreas, "Briefe und Dokumente," 223.

61. Jenny Marx to Weydemeyer, May 20, 1850, *METEC*, 144; Marx to Engels, Dec. 10, 1859, *MEW* 29: 521; Feb. 25, 1862, *MEW* 30: 214; Jenny Marx to Bertha Markheim, June 28, 1863, in Andreas, "Briefe und Dokumente," 178; Marx to Engels, Nov. 30, 1868, *MEW* 32: 217.

62. Marx to Engels, June 7, 1866, *MEW* 31: 222; Nov. 11, 1882, *MEW* 35: 110; Engels to Bernstein, Nov. 2-3, 1882, *MEW* 35: 388; "Now in any case the so-called 'Marxism' in France is a very peculiar sort of product, so much so that Marx said to Lafargue: 'ce qu'il y a de certain c'est que moi, je ne suis pas Marxiste.' " See Marx's letters to Jenny Longuet of May 26, 1882, *MEW* 35: 326, and Marx to Laura Lafargue, Dec. 14, 1882, *MEW* 35: 407.

63. Marx to Lafargue, Aug. 13, 1866, *MEW* 31: 519.

64. On her being "glad to die," see the letter cited in note 76, below; Lafargue to Engels, in Friedrich Engels—Paul et Laura Lafargue *Correspondence*, ed. Emile Bottigelli (Paris, 1956-59), III, 497-98; Engels' letter of Dec. 9, 1871, *MEW* 33: 358. Jenny Longuet to Charles Longuet, Oct. 1, 1880, *MEW* 34: 529. These were old themes in Jenny Marx's life. Liebknecht wrote of her (*METEC*, 70-71): "She sometimes had pythonic transports: 'the spirit came over her,' as over Pythia. Her eyes would begin to shine and blaze and she would start declaiming, often the most astonishing fantasies. She had one of those fits one day on the way home from Hampstead Heath and spoke of life on the stars, her account taking the form of poetry. Mrs. Marx, in her maternal anxiety, several of her children having died young, said: 'Children of her age do not say things like that, her precocity is a sign of bad health.' But Moor scolded her, and I showed her Pythia, who had recovered from her prophetic trance, skipping about and laughing merrily, the very picture of health."

65. Laura Lafargue to Engels, *Correspondence*, III, 332. There is an account of Lafargue's life and the couple's suicide in *Dictionnaire Biographique du Mouvement Ouvrier Français* VI (Paris, 1969), 449-53.

66. Tsuzuki, *The Life of Eleanor Marx*, 63.

67. Marx to Sorge, Aug. 4, 1874, *MEW* 33: 634; to Engels, Aug. 14, 1874, *MEW* 33: 110; to Engels, Sept. 1, 1874, *MEW* 33: 112; to Engels, Aug. 18,

1881, *MEW* 35: 26-27; Jan. 12, 1882, *MEW* 35: 34-35; Tsuzuki, *The Life of Eleanor Marx*, 63.

68. Tsuzuki, *The Life of Eleanor Marx*, 66 and 67 for the exchange of letters; 63 and *passim* for the general theme. I am sorry that the biography of Eleanor Marx by Yvonne Kapp appeared too late for me to make use of it.

69. Marx-Aveling, "Karl Marx," *METEC*, 155.

70. Tsuzuki, *The Life of Eleanor Marx*, 64, 67, 169-70.

71. Letter quoted in *Ibid.*, 165.

72. *Ibid.*, 106, 172.

73. *Ibid.*, 253-54.

74. *Ibid.*, 126.

75. *Ibid.*, 264.

76. The letter is published (together with her other letters to Frederick Demuth) in *The Unknown Karl Marx*, ed. Robert Payne (New York, 1971), 333.

77. Marx to Engels, June 13, 1854, *MEW* 28: 371; Marx to Lafargue, Aug. 13, 1866, *MEW* 31: 518-19.

78. The letter was published for the first time in "Lettres et documents de Karl Marx, 1856-1883," ed. Emile Bottigelli, in *Annali* (Istituto Giangiacomo Feltrinelli) 1 (1958), 153-54. Distance fed Marx's penchant for thinking about an ideal Jenny again some years later, when he was in Trier following his mother's death in 1863. "People ask me every day, right and left, about the former 'prettiest girl in Trier' and the 'queen of the ball,' " he wrote. "It is damned pleasant for a man if his wife lives on in the fantasy of a whole city as an 'enchanted princess.' " Marx to Jenny, Dec. 15, 1863, *MEW* 30: 643.

79. *CW* 1, 696.

Chapter Ten

1. Among the works devoted to the evolution of Marx's economic theory are Ernest Mandel, *La formation de la pensée économique de Karl Marx* (Paris, 1967, 1970); Eng. trans., *The Formation of Marx's Economic Thought* (1971); Roman Rodolsky, *Zur Entstehungsgeschichte des Marxschen 'Kapital'* (Frankfurt and Vienna, 1968), mostly on the *Grundrisse*; Walter Tuchscheerer, *Bevor 'das Kapital' entstand* (Berlin, 1968), the most reliable account from a Marxist point of view. Several writers discuss the history of Marx's economic ideas from the point of view of alienation theory, notably McLellan, *Karl Marx*; Jean-Yves Calvez, *La Pensée de Karl Marx* (Paris, 1965, 1970); and Bertell Ollman, *Alienation* (Cambridge, Eng., 1971). An important discussion of Marx's method is Lucio Colletti, "Marxismo e dialettica," published together with Colletti's *Intervista politico-filosofica* (Bari, 1974), and translated in *New Left Review* 93 (1975). See also A. Gamble and P. Walton, *From Alienation to Surplus Value* (London, 1972). I have used most of these works in various ways for what follows, but the periodization and pattern of Marx's economic ideas presented here does not correspond exactly to any of these earlier accounts. I cannot accept the perspective of Marxists who see the development of Marx's economic theory as a straight-line progress toward "science."

2. Engels, "Outlines of a Critique," in *EPM*, 205-07.

3. "Auszüge aus James Mills Buch 'Elemens d'économie politique,' " *MEW* Erganzungsband I: 445.

4. Easton and Guddat, *Writings of the Young Marx*, 363.

5. *EPM*, 118.

6. *EPM*, 163, 142.

7. From Marx's excerpt-notes of 1844, in Easton and Guddat, *Writings*, 279-81; and *EPM*, 168-69.

8. *GI*, 415, 448.

9. *PP*, 49, 43.

10. *PP*, 37, 42, 64-65, 63-64.

11. "Wage Labor and Capital" (cited hereafter as *WLC*), in *SW*, 78-79. The version of the pamphlet translated here was revised in significant ways by Engels when he republished it in 1891, but the revisions did not affect the sections commented on here. How Engels' changes reflected Marx's intellectual evolution is discussed later in this chapter.

12. *PP*, 68.

13. *WLC*, 79.

14. *PP*, 68; cf. *WLC*, 90.

15. *PP*, 69, 52.

16. *PP*, 61, 41-42, 63, 175.

17. *PP*, 33, 117, 109-10.

18. *PP*, 51.

19. *PP*, 125.

20. Cf. *PP*, 33, 49.

21. "*Arbeitslohn*," in *MEGA* I, vi, 471-72.

22. Marx's brief critique of Ricardo was published as an appendix to the edition of the *Grundrisse* (Berlin, 1953). For the above quotes, 803 and 806. Cf. *PP*, 63-64.

23. Marx to Engels, Apr. 2, 1851, *MEW* 27: 228; Aug. 8, 1851, *MEW* 27: 296.

24. Maximilien Rubel, *Marx-Chronik, Daten zu Leben und Werk* (Munich, 1968), 42.

25. Marx's notebooks, preserved in the library of the International Institute for Social History at Amsterdam (cited hereafter as IISG), tell the story of his movement away from economics and toward other subjects. Notebook LVI (IISG B 51), *c*. Oct. 1851, is devoted to the history of technology; No. LIV (IISG B 53), Aug. to end of 1851, records Marx's reading in literary history (cf. his letter to Freiligrath cited at the end of Chapter Seven on the present as fit to be described in verse); the notebooks from 1852 (Nos. LIX and LX, IISG B 61, B 62) are devoted to the history of culture and morals. Marx returned to economics briefly in 1853 and then in 1856.

26. Marx to Engels, Dec. 8, 1857, *MEW* 29: 225; Jan. 16, 1858, *MEW* 29: 259-60; Apr. 2, 1858, *MEW* 29: 311 ff.

27. Rubel, *Marx-Chronik*, 41.

28. Engels to Marx, March 11, 1853, *MEW* 28: 226; Marx to Cluss, Sept. 15, 1853, *MEW* 28: 592.

29. Marx to Engels, Jan. 29, 1853, *MEW* 28: 209; Jan. 19, 1855, *MEW* 28:

424; Feb. 13, 1855, *MEW* 28: 434; Marx to Lassalle, Dec. 21, 1857, *MEW* 29: 548.

30. Marx to Engels, Feb. 22, 1858, *MEW* 29: 286.

31. Marx to Engels, Nov. 13, 1857, *MEW* 29: 207, and Dec. 8, 1857, *MEW* 29: 224.

32. Marx's *Grundrisse* is cited below both in the Ger. ed. (Berlin, 1953), and in the Eng. trans. by Martin Nicolaus (London, 1973). For the discussion of Proudhonian exchange schemes, see, in the Eng. ed., 115-49.

33. *Grundrisse*, Eng. ed., 137.

34. *Capital*, trans. Samuel Moore and Edward Aveling (New York, 1906), I, 43.

35. *Grundrisse*, Eng. ed., 140, 145.

36. *Ibid.*, 223-24.

37. *Ibid.*, 233-34.

38. *Ibid.*, 263.

39. *Ibid.*, 272, 282, 307.

40. *Ibid.*, 296-97. Marx wrote the word for "potentially" in Greek.

41. *Ibid.*, 305-07; 294.

42. *Ibid.*, 312-15; *Capital* I, 185.

43. *PP*, 58.

44. Marx's note on Ricardo, published in *Grundrisse*, Ger. ed., 829.

45. *Grundrisse*, Eng. ed., 315; *Capital* I, 179.

46. *PP*, 49, 69; cf. also 52.

47. *Grundrisse*, Eng. ed., 325, 331.

48. *Ibid.*, 334.

49. *Ibid.*, 340.

50. *Ibid.*, 399, 401.

51. *Ibid.*, 417, 421.

52. Marx to Engels, Jan. 16, 1858, *MEW* 29: 260.

53. *Grundrisse*, Eng. ed., 380, 384-85. For Ricardo's theory of the falling rate of profit see below, Chapter Eleven, Section 3.

54. *Grundrisse*, Eng. ed., 389, 395.

55. *Ibid.*, 747-48.

56. *Ibid.*, 748.

57. *Ibid.*, 749-50. Marx wrote some of this passage in English, hence the rather stilted "give room to" in the text.

58. *Ibid.*, 750-51, 753; repeated 762-63.

59. *Ibid.*, 409; cf. 325.

60. *Ibid.*, 693-94.

61. *Ibid.*, 700, 705.

62. *Ibid.*

63. *Ibid.*, 708. This was, of course, the vision also of the *Communist Manifesto*: "In place of the old bourgeois society, with its classes and class antagonisms, we shall have an association, in which the free development of each is the condition for the free development of all." *SW*, 53.

64. *Grundrisse*, Eng. ed., 246.

65. *Ibid.*, 225, 234, 240, 255, 640.

66. *Ibid.*, 284, 458, 509, 772.

67. *Ibid.*, 759, 761.

68. *Capital* I, 81-83.

69. See *PP*, 30, 35.

70. *Capital* I, 85-86.

71. *CM*, in *SW*, 38; *Capital* I, 86-87. The interesting attempt by G. A. Cohen, "Karl Marx and the Withering Away of Social Science," *Philosophy and Public Affairs* I (1972), 182-203, to argue that Marx throughout his life regarded the fact that a surplus product is extracted as evident under feudalism and concealed under capitalism, while the utilitarian nature of social relations was concealed under feudalism but evident under capitalism, does not stand up to a fuller reading of the texts. In *Capital* both these things are concealed under capitalism, whereas in the writings of the late 1840s Marx regarded all the essential relationships of capitalist society as increasingly evident with the advance of society. That Marx did not then understand the origin of surplus-value in his later way, is, I think, the source of confusion in Cohen's otherwise careful analysis.

72. *Capital* I, 89; see also III, 792 (discussed later).

73. Compare Engels' text, published in *SW*, 73, with Marx's original in *MEGA* I, vi, 413 ff.

74. *GI*, in Easton and Guddat, *Writings of the Young Marx*, 424.

75. *WLC*, 75.

76. *Grundrisse*, Eng. ed., 157, 197, 307-08, 453-55.

77. *Ibid.*, 161-62, 243, 541-42; cf. 488, 515.

78. *Capital* I, 471 (*MEW* 23: 455); I, 625 (*MEW* 23: 596); I, 708 (*MEW* 23: 674); I, 534 (*MEW* 23: 512). Cf. also *Capital* III, 85, 264. Also *A Contribution to the Critique of Political Economy* (Moscow, 1970), 42-43, 49.

79. *Grundrisse*, Eng. ed., 259.

80. *Ibid.*, 307, 452.

81. Marx to Engels, Jan. 18, 1858, *MEW* 29: 260.

82. *Grundrisse*, Eng. ed., 406, 401, 312, 301.

83. First published in English as an appendix to the 1859 *Contribution to a Critique of Political Economy*, trans. I. Stone (Chicago, 1904), 265-312. In the discussion below I have occasionally preferred this translation to the one by Nicolaus in the edition of the *Grundrisse* otherwise cited here.

84. "Introduction" (Chicago, 1904, ed.), 293, and Nicolaus trans., 101.

85. *Ibid.*

86. *Ibid.*, 101-02.

87. *Ibid.*, 103.

88. *Ibid.*, 105.

89. *EPM*, 177.

90. *Ibid.*, 172.

91. *EPM*, 65, 78, 92; cf. *Grundrisse*, 106, 108. "Nothing seems more natural than to begin with ground rent. . . . But nothing would be more erroneous."

92. Feuerbach, *Vorläufige Thesen*, 71; *EPM*, 191-92 (translating *Anschauung* as "direct observation" rather than as "intuition").

Chapter Eleven

1. Marx to Engels, Feb. 20, 1866, *MEW* 31: 183; Marx to Danielson, June 13, 1871, *MEW* 33: 231.

2. I cite Volume I of *Capital*, trans. from the third German ed. by Samuel Moore and Edward Aveling, ed. Frederick Engels, rev. and amplified according to the fourth German ed. by Ernest Untermann (New York, 1906), 41. Marx was here quoting his own earlier phraseology from *A Contribution to the Critique of Political Economy* (1859). On this work and its relationship to the *Grundrisse* and *Capital*, see below, Chapter Twelve, Section 1. Marx wrote to Engels about it on July 22, 1859, that the main points to be made in regard to it were first, that Proudhon's teaching was destroyed at the root, and that second, "the *specifically* social and in no way *absolute* character of bourgeois production is analyzed already in its simplest form, that of the commodity." *MEW* 29: 463.

3. *Capital* I, 49. Marx tried to obviate some of the misunderstanding of this labor theory of value which have arisen since when he wrote (50): "We see, then, that labor is not the only source of material wealth, of use-values produced by labor. As William Petty puts it, labor is its father and the earth its mother."

4. *Capital* I, 45.

5. *Ibid.*, 55, 65.

6. *Capital* I, Chap. 15.

7. *Ibid.*, Chap. 25.

8. I cite Volumes II and III of *Capital* in the translation published by Progress Publishers, Moscow, and Lawrence and Wishart, London, in 1966 and 1967, which draws on the original English trans. by Charles H. Kerr (Chicago, 1909 and 1919).

9. *Capital* II, 103, 108.

10. *Capital* II, 355 ff.

11. "The various forms of capital, as evolved in this book, thus approach the form which they assume on the surface of society, in the action of different capitals upon one another, in competition, and in the ordinary consciousness of the agents of production themselves." III, 25.

12. III, Chap. 1.

13. Marx had in fact introduced the notion of the "organic composition of capital" in Volume I, but we have not had occasion to refer to it before.

14. *Capital* III, 157-58. This analysis assumed that certain other factors, such as the rate of turnover, were held constant.

15. *Ibid.*, 212.

16. *Ibid.*, 758-62.

17. *Ibid.*, 879-81.

18. *Grundrisse* (Eng. ed.), 748, 750; *Capital* III, 213, 242, 250; Marx to Engels, Apr. 30, 1868, *MEW* 32: 74.

19. Marx to Engels, Nov. 13, 1857, *MEW* 29: 207; and Apr. 9, 1863, *MEW* 30: 343.

20. *Capital* III, 212-13.

21. *Grundrisse* (Eng. ed.), 748 (Ger. ed., 634); *Capital* III, 223.

22. *Capital* III, 225; repeated a few pages later, 230-31.

23. *Ibid.*, 232.

24. For these six factors, *Ibid.*, 235-39. With regard to the second, Marx should have written "labor," not "labor-power."

25. *Ibid.*, 239.

26. The main manuscript for Volume III of *Capital* in the Marx-Engels Archiv at the IISG is numbered A 80. My examination of it was greatly facilitated by my being able to make use of a comparison of this manuscript's pagination with the text in the Dietz, 1956, ed. of Volume III, made some years ago by Siegfried Bahne and P. Nijhoff. Although not published, this set of annotations was made available to me by Dr. Langkau of the IISG. I am extremely grateful to him, and also to Dr. Bahne for a communication on this subject. Although Engels acknowledged many editorial changes in Volume III, he never referred to this one.

27. The pages involved are, in *MEW* 25: 236-41, and in the English ed., III, 225-31. The corresponding pages in the manuscript are A 80, 225-228. The section ending at the bottom of 235 of the *MEW* edition, or toward the bottom of 225 of the English ed., corresponds to 214 of IISG A 80; this page resumes in the printed editions on 242 of *MEW* 25, equivalent to 232 of the English ed. In other words, the manuscript section, 225-28, has been transposed to the middle of manuscript page 214.

28. *Capital* (Eng. ed.) III, 226, 230, 235.

29. *Ibid.*, 241-42.

30. *Ibid.*, 244-45.

31. *Ibid.*, 246.

32. *Ibid.*, 247.

33. *Ibid.*, 248-50.

34. *Ibid.*, 266.

35. For instance, J. Steindl, "Karl Marx and the Accumulation of Capital," in *Marx and Modern Economics*, ed. David Horowitz (New York, 1968), 263.

36. *Capital* III, 71.

37. IISG A 80, 225; Dietz, 1956 ed., 253; *MEW* 25: 236; English ed., III, 225-26.

38. IISG A 80, 219; Dietz, 1956 ed., 267; *MEW* 25: 249; English ed., III, 239.

39. "Mehrwertsrate und Profitrate, matematisch behandelt," IISG A 77. The manuscript contains 135 pages. There is one even longer manuscript, "Formeln über Profitrate," dating from 1880-81, apparently Marx's last attempt to work on *Capital*, which is 199 pages (A 81).

40. See Engels' Preface to Volume III, 3-4, and the text and note, 53-69.

41. On Marx and mathematics, see Dirk J. Struik, "Marx and Mathematics," *Science and Society* 12 (1948), 181-96.

42. Samuel Moore to Engels, March 23, 1888; IISG Q 14, p. 1.

43. *Capital* III, 259.

44. On Smith, see William J. Barber, *A History of Economic Thought* (London and Baltimore, 1967, 1970), 38-42; on Ricardo, in addition to Barber, see Mark Blaug, *Ricardian Economics* (New Haven and London, 1958), 10 ff.

45. It seems that under these conditions profit margins were in fact narrowing in the textile industry. See E. J. Hobsbawm, *Industry and Empire, The Pelican Economic History of Britain* III (London and Baltimore, 1968, 1970), 75-76.

46. Cf. Chapter Four, Section 4, and the literature cited there.

47. Mark Blaug, "Technical Change and Marxian Economics," in *Marx and Modern Economics*, ed. D. Horowitz, 235.

48. Even economists who regard themselves as Marxists have rejected Marx's attempt to demonstrate a tendency for profits to fall as a corollary of rising organic composition of capital. See, most notably, Paul M. Sweezy, *The Theory of Capitalist Development*, 100 ff. More recently a debate has grown up among British Marxists, some of them influenced by the neo-Ricardian theory of Piero Sraffa, between one group that is attempting to discard the profit law and still preserve Marxian economics, and another that is trying to retain it. The debate has been largely carried out in the pages of the *Bulletin of the Conference of Socialist Economists* since 1972, and involves Andrew Glynn, Ian Steedman, David Yaffe, Mario Cogoy, and others. See also Geoff Hodgson, "The Theory of the Falling Rate of Profit," *New Left Review* 84 (1974). The literature on the profit law is immense, but one will find references to most of it in the contributions cited here. Since I am not an economist, I have not attempted to pronounce on the actual tendency of profits under advanced capitalism. Nonetheless, it seems to me obvious that Marx's law does not describe the actual movement of profit rates, even though pressures on profits arising from competition and new techniques are, of course, recurring features of capitalist industry. The recent debate on this issue by William Nordhaus and Martin Feldstein seems to leave the question undecided at the moment.

49. *Grundrisse*, 704 ff., and Chapter Ten, Section 2.

50. *Capital* III, 264, 820.

51. Michio Morishima, *Marx's Economics, A Dual Theory of Value and Growth* (Cambridge, Eng., 1973). Although I do not have enough mathematics to follow Morishima's argument in all its details, I think I have the general point right. See especially the last chapter.

52. *Capital* I, 837.

53. Cf. *Capital* III, 25.

54. The most perceptive discussion of Marx's theory of proletarian revolution in connection with its original bourgeois model, and hence of the problem of revolutionary stages, is, I think, Heinrich A. Winkler, "Zum Verhältnis von bürgerlicher und proletarischer Revolution bei Marx und Engels," in *Sozialgeschichte Heute*, Festschrift für Hans Rosenberg, ed. Hans-Ulrich Wehler (Göttingen, 1974), 326-53.

55. *Capital* I, 836-37.

56. First Outline of *The Civil War in France*, in *On the Paris Commune*, 157; cf. *The Civil War in France*, in *SW*, 294-95.

57. *Capital* I, 691.

58. III, 239.

59. III, 175.

60. Eugen von Böhm-Bawerk, *Karl Marx and the Close of His System*, published with Rudolph Hilferding, *Böhm-Bawerk's Criticism of Marx*, ed. by Paul M. Sweezy (New York, 1949). In my view Böhm-Bawerk did not understand Marx's epistemology and method, and subjected his theory to a positivistic criticism that missed the point from the beginning.

61. *Grundrisse*, English ed., 817.

62. III, 159-60; see the tables on 156-57.

63. III, 160-61, 165.

64. I take this summary from Ronald L. Meek, "Some Notes on the 'Transformation Problem,' " in *Economics and Ideology and Other Essays* (London, 1967), 143-57. In addition to Bortkiewicz, "On the Correction of Marx's Fundamental Theoretical Construction in the Third Volume of *Capital*" (which can be found as an appendix to the Sweezy ed. of Böhm-Bawerk and Hilferding, cited above), Meek especially relies on J. Winternitz, "Values and Prices: A Solution of the So-called Transformation Problem," *The Economic Journal* 58 (1948), 276-80. I have taken the quotation from Meek (152) slightly out of context, since he refers here to Marx's own attempts to resolve the difficulty, not those of later writers. Yet Meek's comments on the solutions of von Bortkiewicz and Winternitz, as well as his own contribution, all leave matters in essentially the same state. His solution preserves the Marxian relationship between profit and surplus value but at the cost of allowing total prices to diverge from total surplus values. See also Sweezy, Chap. 7. For still more recent discussions from a Marxist point of view, see Geoff Hodgson, "Marxian Epistemology and the Transformation Problem," *Economy and Society* 2 (1974), 357 ff. with good bibliography; and D. Laibman, "Values and Prices of Production, The Political Economy of the Transformation Problem," *Science and Society* 37 (1973-74). The most vigorous recent anti-Marxist statement by a distinguished economist is Paul A. Samuelson, "Understanding the Marxian Notion of Exploitation: A Summary of the So-Called Transformation Problem between Marxian Values and Competitive Prices," *Journal of Economic Literature* 9 (1971), 399-431. This article has sparked a spirited debate in the same *Journal*, some of the contributors to which have, I think, understood Marx's thinking more clearly than Professor Samuelson (even if they have not challenged him on the economics of prices and profits); see note 66, below.

65. *Capital* III, 161, 167, 172, 198.

66. William J. Baumol, "The Transformation of Values: What Marx 'Really' Meant (An Interpretation)," *Journal of Economic Literature* 12 (1974), 58, 56.

67. *Capital* III, 779.

68. *Grundrisse*, Ger. ed., 647; *Capital* III, 209, 231, 830; cf. 225.

69. *Capital* III, 212-13; 359, 45.

70. Marx to Engels, Apr. 15, 1869, *MEW* 32: 303-04.

71. *Capital* III, 48.

72. *Ibid.*, 826-30.

73. M. Godelier, "System, Structure and Contradiction in *Capital*," *Socialist Register* (1967), 3, quoted by Norman Geras, "Marx and the Critique of Political Economy," in *Ideology in Social Science*, ed. Robin Blackburn (New York, 1973), 296, and Geras's own comment, 293; *Capital* I, 73, quoted by Geras 292.

74. *Capital* III, 47 and 209.

75. Marx to Kugelmann, July 11, 1868, *SC*, 209-10; Marx to Engels, Aug. 24, 1867, *SC*, 192.

76. I believe that this tension lies behind the contradiction Lucio Colletti has discovered in Marx's use of both an "idealist" and a "materialist" dialectic, i.e., speaking at times of resolvable "logical contradictions" and at others of non-

resolvable "real oppositions." But Colletti does not attempt to understand this as a reflection of the evolution of Marx's thinking and its relationship to the different realities of the pre- and post-1848 period. See "Marxismo e dialettica," published together with *Intervista politico-filosofica* (Bari, 1974), 63-113 (trans. in *New Left Review* 93 [1975]).

77. Dissertation, trans. in Livergood, *Activity in Marx's Philosophy*, 69-70.

78. *Ibid.*, 70.

Chapter Twelve

1. On *GI* in this regard, see the Preface, 23, and Engels, "On the History of the Communist League," *SW*, 442; for the other works, see Chapter Five, Section 4.

2. Marx to Lassalle, Feb. 22, 1858, *MEW* 29: 550-51; cf. the Preface to *A Contribution to the Critique of Political Economy*, in *SW*, 181.

3. Marx to Lassalle, March 11, 1858, *MEW* 29: 554.

4. Marx to Lassalle, Nov. 12, 1858, *MEW* 29: 567.

5. See the two letters to Lassalle just cited, and Marx to Engels, *c*. Jan. 13, 1859, *MEW* 29: 383.

6. For the "extreme limit," Marx to Lassalle, Oct. 2, 1859, *MEW* 29: 613; for the return in 1861, Marx to Engels, June 10, 1861, *MEW* 30: 170; for the contents of the manuscript, see Engels' account of it in his Preface to *Capital* II, 2-3.

7. Marx to Engels, June 18, 1862, *MEW* 30: 248; to Kugelmann, Dec. 28, 1862, *MEW* 30: 639-40; Jenny Marx to Bertha Markheim, July 6, 1863, in Andreas, "Briefe und Dokumente der Familie Marx," *Archiv für Sozialgeschichte* 2 (1968), 181-82.

8. Marx to Engels, July 31, 1865, *MEW* 31: 132; Feb. 13, 1866, *MEW* 31: 178; also Engels' description of the manuscripts (note 6, above), which leads me to give a slightly different account of Marx's work than that provided by Andreas, "Briefe und Dokumente," 182 n.

9. Engels to Marx, Aug. 7, 1865, *MEW* 31: 137; Feb. 10, 1866, *MEW* 31: 176.

10. Marx to Engels, Feb. 13, 1866, *MEW* 31: 179; Nov. 10, 1866, *MEW* 31: 263; Jan. 19, 1867, *MEW* 31: 273 (telling Engels what he had written to Meissner).

11. Marx to Kugelmann, Oct. 11, 1867, *MEW* 31: 562; March 6, 1868, *MEW* 32: 539.

12. Marx to Laura Lafargue, Apr. 11, 1868, published in "Lettres et documents de Karl Marx, 1856-1883, A cura di Emile Bottigelli," *Annali* (Istituto Giangiacomo Feltrinelli) 1 (1958), 167. Marx to Engels, Apr. 30, 1868, *MEW* 32: 75.

13. Marx to Danielson, Oct. 7, 1868, *MEW* 32: 563; to Engels, Dec. 10, 1869, *MEW* 32: 414.

14. Marx to Kugelmann, June 27, 1870, *MEW* 32: 686.

15. Marx to Lafargue, March 21, 1872, *MEW* 33: 437; to Danielson, May 28, 1872, *MEW* 33: 477; Marx to Sorge, Dec. 21, 1872, *MEW* 33: 552; Jenny

Marx (daughter) to Kugelmann, Dec. 23, 1872 and May 12, 1873, in Andreas, "Briefe und Dokumente," 286, 291; Marx to Maurice Lachâtre, May 12, 1874, *MEW* 33: 626; to Kugelmann, May 18, 1874, *MEW* 33: 627. It should be noted that Marx at the same time made the French translation the occasion for many changes and revisions in Volume I, which Engels later incorporated into the third German edition.

16. Marx to W. Bracke, Nov. 6, 1876, *MEW* 34: 223; see also Marx to the same Jan. 21, 1877, *MEW* 34: 242; April 11 and 21, *MEW* 34: 263, 267-69 and May 26, *MEW* 34: 277-78.

17. Marx to Danielson, Apr. 10, 1879, *MEW* 34: 370-72; to F. Nieuwenhuis, June 27, 1880, *MEW* 34: 447.

18. Paul Lafargue, "Reminiscences of Marx," in *Karl Marx: Man, Thinker, and Revolutionist*, ed. D. Ryazanoff (New York, International Publishers, n.d.), 191; Marx to Leske, Aug. 1, 1846, *MEW* 27: 449; Marx to Lassalle, Feb. 22, 1858, *SC*, 103 and *MEW* 29: 550; Apr. 28, 1862, *MEW* 30: 622.

19. Engels to Marx, Apr. 3, 1851, *MEGA* III, i, 184; Jan. 31, 1860, *MEW* 30: 15; the 1845 letter is in *SC*, 25-26.

20. *Grundrisse*, Eng. ed., 151.

21. *SW*, 181.

22. *SW*, 184.

23. On the theme of the *Leitfade*, see Edna Purdie, "Some Word-Associations in the Writings of Hamann and Herder," in *German Studies Presented to L. A. Willoughby* (Oxford, 1952), 154 for the quote from Herder; also the commentary to Schiller's *On the Aesthetic Education of Man*, ed. E. M. Wilkinson and L. A. Willoughby (Oxford, 1967), 258, where Goethe is quoted. The classical source was the legend of Ariadne and Theseus.

24. *Capital* I, 22, 25.

25. *Capital* I, 25. Marx used the same explanation in a letter to Kugelmann of July 26, 1870, *SC*, 240; the idea that this was Marx's reason for using Hegel's language probably dates from around 1870, not 1857.

26. *Capital* I, 24-25; Marx to Vera Sassoulitch, March 8, 1881, *MEW* 35: 166; M. Rubel, *Marx-Chronik, Daten zu Leben und Werk* (Munich, 1968), 132.

27. Dissertation, in Livergood, *Activity in Marx's Philosophy*, 69-70.

28. For the 1841 Correspondence, see Chapter Five, Section 4; Foreword to the dissertation, in Livergood, *Activity*, 61; 1859 Preface, *SW*, 181; Marx to Kugelmann, March 6, 1868, *MEW* 32: 538.

29. Engels to Marx, Jan. 31, 1860, *MEW* 30: 15.

30. McLellan, *Karl Marx*, 311 ff.

31. In the French document the agent who received payment was listed only as "Vogt," not as "Karl Vogt," but Marx was convinced that it could refer to no other Vogt, and so far as I know no modern scholar has contested this, although some doubts were expressed at the time. See Marx to Liebknecht, Apr. 20, 1871, *MEW* 33: 214. Some literature on Vogt's scientific and political work is cited by Charles A. Culotta, "German Biophysics, Objective Knowledge, and Romanticism," *Historical Studies in the Physical Sciences*, Fourth Annual Volume, ed. Russell McCormach (Princeton, 1975).

32. For the charges see "The Journalistic Auxiliaries of Austria," in *The Daily*

Telegraph (London), Monday, Feb. 6, 1860, 5. On the Schwefelband and the Bürstenheimer see Marx's letter to his lawyer Weber of Feb. 24, 1860, *MEW* 30: 476-77.

33. Marx to Engels, June 7, 1859, *MEW* 29: 448, and *Das Volk* (London), No. 6, June 11, 1859, 3, for the pamphlet "Zur Warnung," which contained these accusations. Lassalle to Marx, late Jan. 1860, in Ferdinand Lassalle, *Nachgelassene Briefe und Schriften* (Stuttgart and Berlin, 1922) III, 241.

34. Marx to Engels, Feb. 3, 1860, *MEW* 30: 22.

35. Marx to Lassalle, Jan. 30, 1860, *MEW* 30: 438; Marx to Engels, Feb. 9, 1860, *MEW* 30: 35; to Joachim Lelewel, Feb. 3, 1860, *MEW* 30: 442.

36. Marx to Lassalle, March 3, 1860, *MEW* 30: 498.

37. Marx to Freiligrath, Feb. 29, 1860, *MEW* 30: 492.

38. Marx to Weber, March 3, 1860, *MEW* 30: 509.

39. Engels to Marx, Jan. 31, 1860, *MEW* 30: 15; Feb. 7, 1860, *MEW* 30: 27.

40. Engels to Jenny Marx, Aug. 15, 1860, *MEW* 30: 554; to Marx, Oct. 1, 1860, *MEW* 30: 98.

41. Marx to Lassalle, Oct. 2, 1859, *MEW* 29: 613; to Engels, Oct. 5, 1859, *MEW* 29: 491; to Engels, Jan. 11, 1860, *MEW* 30: 6.

42. Marx to Engels, Feb. 1, 1858, *MEW* 29: 275; *SC*, 102.

43. Jenny Marx to Engels, Dec. 23 or 24, 1859, *MEW* 29: 653; on Marx's relations with Duncker, which recalled those with the publisher Bruno Bauer had introduced him to in 1841, see "Marx' und Engels' Briefwechsel mit Franz Duncker," ed. Werner Blumenberg, *International Review of Social History* 10 (1965), 105-19.

44. Marx to Weber, March 3, 1860, *MEW* 30: 504.

45. Rollo May, *Power and Innocence* (New York, 1972), 40-41.

46. *Capital* I, 11. On Marx's health and illnesses, see Felix Regnault, "Les Maladies de Karl Marx," *Revue Anthropologique* 43 (1933), 293-317, and Arnold Künzli, *Karl Marx, Eine Psychographie*, 422-65; most of the standard biographies give this question some attention too.

47. Marx to Kugelmann, Feb. 11, 1868, *MEW* 32: 533; McLellan, *Karl Marx*, 337 ff. and 425 f. Modern medical literature emphasizes the role of bacterial infection in causing carbuncles or boils, while still recognizing that physical debility may predispose a person to them. See William A. R. Thomson, M.D., *Black's Medical Dictionary* (New York, 1969), s.v. "Boils." I am grateful to Dr. Luke Zander for discussing this question with me.

48. Wilhelm Liebknecht, "Reminiscences of Marx," in *Marx and Engels Through the Eyes of their Contemporaries*, 63.

49. Paul Lafargue, "Reminiscences of Marx," in *Karl Marx*, ed. Ryazanoff, 187.

50. Marx to Engels, Feb. 10, 1866, *MEW* 31: 174; Engels to Marx, Feb. 10 (*sic* in *MEW*), 1866, *MEW* 31: 176.

51. Engels to Marx, Jan. 19, 1870, *MEW* 32: 426; Engels to Kugelmann, July 1, 1873, *MEW* 33: 593-94.

52. Marx to Kugelmann, Apr. 6, 1866, *MEW* 31: 513; Oct. 9, 1866, *MEW*

31: 529; Marx to Engels, Apr. 24, 1867; Engels to Marx, Apr. 27, *MEW* 31: 291 and 292.

53. Marx to Jenny, Aug. 8, 1856, in "Lettres et documents de Karl Marx," ed. Bottigelli, 155; to Lassalle, May 31, 1858, *MEW* 29: 560-61; Jenny to Engels, Apr. 9, 1858, *MEW* 29: 648.

54. Marx to Engels, May 26, 1864, *MEW* 30: 399; Jan. 19, 1867, *MEW* 31: 274; Aug. 17, 1877, *MEW* 34: 71.

55. Marx to Engels, Apr. 2, 1851, *MEW* 27: 228; Jan. 29, 1859, *MEW* 29: 386; June 18, 1862, *MEW* 30: 248; June 22, 1863, *MEW* 30: 359; Feb. 13, 1866, *MEW* 31: 178.

56. Marx to Engels, Feb. 25, 1862, *MEW* 30: 214; Jan. 13, 1869, *MEW* 32: 242.

57. Engels to Kugelmann, Apr. 28, 1871, *MEW* 33: 218-19.

58. Marx to Sigrid Mayer, Apr. 30, 1867, *MEW* 31: 542.

59. Lafargue, "Reminiscences of Marx," in *Karl Marx*, ed. Ryazanoff, 191. This passage has been excised from the version of Lafargue's memoir printed in *METEC*, 30. Marx to Engels, Feb. 25, 1867, *MEW* 31: 278; here Marx mentioned one other Balzac story as well, "Melamoth Reconciled."

60. Honoré de Balzac, "The Unknown Masterpiece," in The *Edition Définitive* of the *Comédie Humaine* XLIII, trans. Burnham Ives (Philadelphia, 1899), 21, 23, 33-34.

61. Dissertation, in Livergood, *Activity in Marx's Philosophy*, 69-70.

62. Marx to Lassalle, May 31, 1858, *MEW* 29: 561; dissertation, in Livergood, *Activity in Marx's Philosophy*, 72.

INDEX

Material in the endnotes is included in this index only if it adds substantively to the text.

Library of Congress Cataloging in Publication Data

Seigel, Jerrold E.
  Marx's fate.

  Includes bibliographical references and index.
    1.   Marx, Karl, 1818-1883.   2.   Communists—
Biography.   3.   Socialism.   I.   Title.
HX39.5.S36   335.4'092'4   [B]   77-85563
ISBN 0-691-05259-X